Structural Racism

This book explains how racial inequality in the United States is produced and perpetuated and what should be done about it. It develops the elusive concept of "structural racism," presenting a precise definition that is clear and comprehensible, and illustrates how it operates methodically and rigorously.

Many other books are long on problems and short on solutions, whereas this book develops the key principles that must ground a structural reform agenda, and then presents a broad-ranging set of interventions organized around ten themes that will reduce racial disparities while expanding opportunity for all.

Unlike most books on race which focus on a particular issue or sector, this book is comprehensive in its scope, encompassing the vital systems that shape racial inequality in contemporary American society: from education and public schools to income and wealth disparities to housing and health care to policing and the criminal justice system. As such, this book is the ideal text for readers seeking to learn more about structural racial inequality in society, how it came to be that way, and what we should do about it, while deepening our understanding and challenging many misguided or simplistic prevailing notions.

In a time of backlash to racial justice and growing doubts about racial equity initiatives, this book is a timely and necessary entry. A must read for advocates, students, policymakers, and researchers alike.

Stephen Menendian is the Assistant Director and Director of Research at the Othering & Belonging Institute at UC Berkeley, where he leads several major initiatives, including projects advising state, local, and federal housing authorities. His research focuses on inequality between social groups, especially in the areas of housing and education, and the design of effective and lawful policy remedies. Stephen is the author of many scholarly publications, journal articles, and other notable books.

"'Structural racism' is a term too easily thrown around nowadays as a substitute for careful thought. If you want to know what it really means, and why understanding its nuances is so important, Stephen Menendian's book is the place to start."

Richard Rothstein, Author, The Color of Law: A Forgotten History of How Our Government Segregated America

"While the term 'structural racism' is widely evoked in the popular political discourse of race, its precise meaning and conceptual underpinnings have remained sketchy and ill-defined. With this book, we finally have a clear, accessible, and compelling explanation of what structural racism is. Drawing upon illustrative stories of racial inequality across a wide range of institutional sites and practices, Menendian maps the enduring and intractable character of structural racism. He effectively demonstrates how opportunity in the United States is racialized and what this means for the remedies to address it."

Michael Omi, *University of California, Berkeley, Co-author,* Racial Formation in the United States

"This book on structural racism is much needed in a field where there is already a great deal written on race and racism. With important and consequential discussions about what it is, where we stand, and what remains to be done, Stephen tackles all these issues and many more. He helps us understand how our imprecise and confusing way of thinking and talking about race has often undermined not just our understanding but produced many incomplete and contradictory policy efforts. He shows us that in talking about race we are not just talking about past harms, but the present and the future. He also forcefully makes that case racism today cannot be understood or addressed at an individual level. In this book Stephen is not content to just define the problem, but presents concrete and realistic solutions. As the country continues, at times reluctantly and at times aggressively, to struggle with race, Stephen's work is and will be a 'must' read. This work is thorough, insightful, and deeply illuminating. We owe a debt of gratitude to Stephen for bringing such light to one of the more important issues in our society."

john a. powell, *Director of the Othering & Belonging Institute at UC Berkeley, Robert D. Haas Chancellor's Chair in Equity & Inclusion, Professor of Law, African-American, & Ethnic Studies, at the University of California at Berkeley*

Structural Racism
The Dynamics of Opportunity and Race in America

Stephen Menendian

NEW YORK AND LONDON

Designed cover image: Shutterstock

First published 2025
by Routledge
605 Third Avenue, New York, NY 10158

and by Routledge
4 Park Square, Milton Park, Abingdon, Oxon, OX14 4RN

Routledge is an imprint of the Taylor & Francis Group, an informa business

© 2025 Stephen Menendian

The right of Stephen Menendian to be identified as author of this work has been asserted in accordance with sections 77 and 78 of the Copyright, Designs and Patents Act 1988.

All rights reserved. No part of this book may be reprinted or reproduced or utilised in any form or by any electronic, mechanical, or other means, now known or hereafter invented, including photocopying and recording, or in any information storage or retrieval system, without permission in writing from the publishers.

Trademark notice: Product or corporate names may be trademarks or registered trademarks, and are used only for identification and explanation without intent to infringe.

Library of Congress Cataloging-in-Publication Data
Names: Menendian, Stephen, author.
Title: Structural racism : the dynamics of opportunity and race in America / Stephen Menendian.
Description: New York, NY : Routledge, 2025. |
Includes bibliographical references and index.
Identifiers: LCCN 2024061005 | ISBN 9781032913520 (hbk) | ISBN 9781032902968 (pbk) | ISBN 9781003562764 (ebk)
Subjects: LCSH: Racism--United States. | Equality--United States. | Opportunity--United States.
Classification: LCC HT1521 .M465 2025 |
DDC 305.800973--dc23/eng/20250212
LC record available at https://lccn.loc.gov/2024061005

ISBN: 978-1-032-91352-0 (hbk)
ISBN: 978-1-032-90296-8 (pbk)
ISBN: 978-1-003-56276-4 (ebk)

DOI: 10.4324/9781003562764

Typeset in Sabon
by KnowledgeWorks Global Ltd.

Contents

List of Figures and Tables	*viii*
Introduction	1
1 The Structure of Opportunity	10

Upward Mobility in America 13
The Structure of Opportunity 16
Place Matters 18
Regional Conditions 19
Municipal Inequality 21
Neighborhood Effects 26
Economic Segregation 29
Social Networks 31
Family Matters 34
Geographic Mobility 39

2 Structural Racial Inequality	59

Race and Economic Mobility 61
Childhood Poverty 64
Concentrated Poverty 67
Durable Poverty 72
Race versus Class 75
Racial Segregation 76
Educational Attainment 83
The Racial Wealth Gap 85
The Spatial Mismatch 89
Racial Networks 91
Mass Incarceration 93
Health and Environment 97
Exclusionary Localism and Jurisdictional Fragmentation 99

3 The Origins of Structural Racism 129

From Jim Crow Segregation to Residential Segregation 132
*The Origins of Racial Residential Segregation in
   the United States 134*
Institutionalizing Segregation 142
Suburbanization 147
Public Housing and Urban Renewal 150
Resistance to Fair Housing 153
White Flight and School Desegregation 157
Deindustrialization 161
Mass Incarceration and the War on Drugs 164
Predatory Lending and the Subprime Mortgage Crisis 167
Municipal Fiscal Distress 173

4 Toward a Structural Agenda 203

The Individual Racism Model 204
Black Lives Matter 208
The Uprisings of the 1960s 209
Systemic versus Structural Racism 213
The Goal of Racial Justice 218
Principles for a Structural Change Agenda 221
Disparate Impact 224
Affirmative Action 225
Reparations 231
The Kerner Report Revisited 232

5 Realizing the American Dream 252

The New Great Migration 253
An Opportunity Agenda 256
1) Embrace Fiscal Regionalism 257
*2) Protect Residents from Displacement and Adopt Smart
   Place-Based Strategies 260*
3) Pursue and Support Mobility Strategies 264
*4) End Snob Zoning and Curtail Exclusionary Land Use
   Policies 270*
*5) Enforce Fair Housing Laws and Pursue Residential
   Integration 275*
6) Expand Public Education 277
7) End Mass Incarceration and the War on Drugs 284
8) Reform the Criminal Justice System 291

9) Limit Occupational Licensing, Non-Compete Clauses, and Other Employment Barriers 299
10) Subsidize Core Capabilities and Critical Access Points 302

Conclusion 341

Acknowledgments 346

Index 348

Figures and Tables

Figures

2.1	Black and White Childhood Poverty Rates, 1974–2020	66
3.1	Black Residential Segregation, 1890–2020	134

Tables

1.1	Geographic Mobility, 1951–2021	39
2.1	Poverty and Race in the United States, 2020	65
2.2	The Racial Composition of Neighborhoods of Concentrated Poverty, 2019	68
2.3	Racial Predominance of Neighborhoods of Concentrated Poverty, 2019	69
2.4	High Poverty and Concentrated Poverty Neighborhoods by Racial Predominance, 2019	70
2.5	Racial Composition of Schools by Level of Poverty, 2019–2020	71
2.6	Percentage of Americans 25 or Older with a Bachelor's Degree by Race, 1959–2020	84
2.7	The Black-White Racial Wealth Gap, 2009–2022	86
2.8	Racial Composition of Incarcerated Persons by Year, 1970–2020	94
3.1	Homeownership by Race in the United States, 1940–2020	172

Introduction

Long an undercurrent in American society, race and racial inequality once again surged to the surface and into mainstream of American public discourse in recent years.[1] Researchers and journalists have long tracked, compiled, and reported large and persistent disparities by race in the United States.[2] But a series of shocking and widely reported killings of Black Americans by police officers precipitated a mass protest movement at the same time that the disturbing racial dimensions of mass incarceration and harmful collateral consequences of the War on Drugs gradually seeped into the popular consciousness.

Considering these tragedies and other events, talk of a "post-racial" society during and after the final term of the nation's first Black president seemed at best quaint.[3] In fact, the contrast of a Black American serving in the nation's highest office with the undeniable racial aspect to so many of these episodes helped engender broader awareness of the more deeply structured nature of racial inequality. With each fresh tragedy, the accumulative evidence made it harder to deny the larger pattern or explain a particular incident in terms of a bad actor or unique circumstances. In surveys, more white Americans registered the reality of persistent racial inequality as a societal problem and recognized its institutional and systemic dimensions.[4]

This recognition, however, has not translated into significant and sustained policy change nor reduced racial inequality along key dimensions. In fact, some attempts to address racial disparities have triggered backlash and organized opposition, resulting in the rollback of "Diversity, Equity, and Inclusion" (DEI) programs and curbs to educational and training initiatives intended to broaden awareness of racial disparities and their causes.[5]

Nor has broader awareness of racial inequality translated into a consensus on causes or produced consistent explanatory framing. Terms like "systemic racism" or "structural racism" are more frequently employed to describe or explain patterns of racial inequality,[6] but these terms and the definitions offered are as likely to mystify as clarify.[7] There is a lack of specificity and precision among many popular definitions or, worse, available definitions are so esoteric or convoluted as to defy easy comprehension.

DOI: 10.4324/9781003562764-1

This book is an attempt to define and clarify, using a simple framework, the meaning of these terms and illustrate how they operate through that framework. If the idea or concept of structural racism seems miasmic or too abstract, this book is the antidote. This book presents a definition of structural racism that is (hopefully) more easily comprehensible than has been developed before, and then illustrates how it operates methodically and rigorously, specifying its key components, mechanisms, dynamics, and effects.[8]

This book is written for a general audience, but is intended to help readers searching for a deeper understanding of the nature and causes of racial inequality in contemporary American society. In particular, it is aimed at open-minded readers who perceive race as a profound cleavage in American society and recognize it as an enduring problem, but are not quite sure how to define that problem in contemporary terms or what to do about it, and who may also be skeptical of DEI practices or wary of conventional forms of racial justice advocacy. It is also aimed at readers well-acquainted with social and racial justice advocacy but who want to strengthen their understanding with rigorous empirical research that supplements, challenges, or broadens their thinking.

At its essence, structural racial inequality is the idea that the forces and arrangements that foster human development, nurture potential, extend opportunity, and facilitate well-being in the United States are racialized, meaning that they generate and reinforce group advantages and disadvantages on the basis of race. It is this reality, rather than racist ideas about group-based inferiority or presumed cultural differences, which explains much of the stark and persistent racial disparities in educational attainment, employment, income, wealth, health, and incarceration. Simply put, unequal opportunity produces unequal outcomes.[9]

Critically, structural racial inequality depends neither on racist individuals nor racist ideas. Race is so deeply structured in our society that even if we curbed acts of racial discrimination and drove out racist ideas, racial disparities would persist on a massive scale. Structural racial inequality is the result of a complex set of relationships and interactions between many institutions, policies, and people over many years, many of which are either well-intended or not colored by racial animus or based on racist ideas. They nonetheless result in significant and persistent racial disparities based upon a structural logic that, once established, requires only indifferent policies preferences and largely self-interested individual and collective action. Structural racism is the persistent indifference and lack of regard to the conditions of structural racial inequality. Left undisturbed in that way, structural racial inequality is a highly adaptive perpetual motion machine that maintains itself indefinitely and operates independently of racist actors or ideas.[10]

That is not to say that racist ideas, race prejudice, and racial discrimination (narrowly understood) are irrelevant, or incidental, but they are secondary to explaining the maintenance of racial inequality in contemporary American society, and yet tend to receive the most attention. By focusing on the mechanisms and forces that are empirically and analytically driving racial outcomes—persistent and observable group-level differences in well-being—this book draws our attention away from symptoms, and toward root causes.

This investigation into structural racism begins with a careful examination of opportunity in America. A powerfully compelling but ambiguous concept, the first chapter distills the essence of this complex and multi-faceted idea into a functional concept. Often expressed through a constellation of different metaphors, this book suggests that opportunity is best understood as the full range of pathways available to individuals during their life course.

This simple metaphor illuminates subtle aspects of how opportunity is created, extended, enlarged, and pursued. In particular, it helps illustrate the interplay of agency and contextual constraints, and of personal liberty and the cultivated development of human capabilities. Some individuals have a clear path, while others have a rough road. Opportunity as a range of pathways is a metaphor that envisions the variety of possible destinations for individuals to choose among, the varying degrees of visibility and accessibility of those options, the supports that facilitate or ease advancement along them, as well as burdens, impediments, and hazards that thwart such advancement. Many critical pathways have barriers that obstruct progress or gatekeepers that block access.

The pathways that can be traversed and the rewarding destinations that can be pursued depend upon the supports and capabilities enjoyed by the traveler, including the technological aids, tools, and resources available to them, not just the removal of barriers and alleviations of burdens to ease passage. In contemporary society, institutions and public goods play a central role in the development of opportunity and its pursuit. These institutions, such as public schools and universities, imbue individuals with essential competencies and skills needed to participate in both civic and economic life.

If opportunity is the range of pathways available to individuals, the *opportunity structure* is the interconnecting lattice of pathway relationships and networks that enhance or impinge individual and group life chances. The opportunity structure defines the range of opportunity pathways as well as the resources or capacities needed to advance along them. The economic development of a society sets a lower bound on the number and quality of pathways available, but investments in people and places ultimately help us reach our full potential, enabling our pursuit of existing destinations and facilitating the formation of new ones.

Decades of social science research investigating "neighborhood effects" demonstrates the powerful influence of place on well-being and individual life outcomes. The latest studies on economic and social mobility help us understand not only the extent of opportunity in the country but identify the most critical layers and forces that operate within the contemporary opportunity structure. Geographically varying rates of economic mobility demonstrate that opportunity is unevenly distributed across space and help pinpoint how different layers of geography shape respective opportunity inputs.

Within the United States, the generation and endowment of opportunity occurs chiefly across three geographic scales: neighborhoods, municipal jurisdictions, and regions. These nested scales are the arterial layers within the opportunity structure. Industries and key markets, such as housing and labor markets, are regional in nature. The level, quality, and mixture of services are determined at the municipal level. Peer social networks, many amenities, environmental hazards, safety and crime are in large part localized to the neighborhood.

The crucial point is that the opportunity structure is a web of influences beyond our control that affect our life chances. It does so directly, by imparting critical skills through the educational system and providing access to quality employment opportunities, transportation, and health care or by depriving us of those resources and capacities. However, it also shapes our chances indirectly by providing certain incentives and imposing constraints, nudging us in one direction or another, as we navigate the opportunity structure. The range and quality of opportunities available to individuals depend upon our location within the opportunity structure, and that local architecture influences our choices in ways that shape access to future opportunities.

In this book's simple formulation, structural racial inequality is a claim that outcomes produced by opportunity structures are visibly racialized, and that it is these structures which are principally responsible for the contemporary production and maintenance of racial inequality. Chapter 2 demonstrates how, in the United States, the opportunity structure generates and reinforces racial group advantages and disadvantages. This chapter reviews the latest research on economic mobility by race, and then explores each of the mechanisms that influence the location of racial groups within the opportunity structure.* Since opportunity structures are geographic in nature, racial segregation sorts racial groups within regions and thereby situates them disadvantageously with respect to opportunity enhancing resources and institutions.

If you are Black, you are far more likely to have been born into a family with significantly less wealth, reside in neighborhoods with more poverty, inhabit communities with underperforming schools, fewer jobs and less job growth, a smaller tax base served by fiscally constrained leadership, and personally have less access to health care, and experience greater entanglement with the criminal justice system, exposure to crime, *and* surveillance and harassment by police than a non-Black person. The forces and layers that

---

* Although this book uses a wide lens to examine racial dynamics, patterns, and disparities encompassing many racial groups in its presentation of data, the narrative focus of this book is principally on Black-white disparities and experiences, largely due to space limitations. To the extent that readers are interested in looking more comprehensively beyond this dynamic, data is presented that should allow readers to glean a more nuanced view of how these forces and structures affect different racial groups. Relatedly, although the focus of this book is the United States, the model, findings, and data presented here is suggestive of how similar dynamics may play out elsewhere due to the similarities of contemporary opportunity structures globally.

structure opportunity tend to shuttle Black Americans along fewer and more constrained pathways, through more disadvantaged environments, and toward less desirable destinations.

Chapter 3 explains how these arrangements arose, how the mechanisms that perpetuate racial advantage and disadvantage were forged and institutionalized. Patterns of racial residential segregation became entrenched long before anti-discrimination norms took effect. Chronologically, housing discrimination was not effectively prohibited nationwide until 1968, long after patterns of residential development and housing segregation had been established in the postwar period. Since housing is the locus opportunity, this fact explains the effects that run through the opportunity structure, from employment to educational opportunities.

The forces of globalization and deindustrialization also played a role in shifting the center of economic activity within major metropolitan regions, making good jobs and employment opportunities less accessible to racially segregated urban residents, especially low-skill workers. Moreover, the efforts to desegregate public schools, and the jurisdictional rules and boundaries that protect and shield affluent homeowners from the threat of desegregation, generated and accelerated white flight.

It is a mistake, however, to assert or presume—as is often done—that structural racism is entirely or even principally the residue or legacy of past discrimination or our nation's sordid racial history. The forces that shape racial destinies today are a product of both historical forces as well as more recent insidious developments.[11] Among the latter are the rise of the carceral state, mass incarceration, disinvestments in public goods, and the reorganization of metropolitan space, pushing millions of people of color into lower opportunity environments. Racial disparities in neighborhood and school poverty are worsening, not leveling. Racial disparities in homeownership are widening, not closing. The absolute racial wealth gap is exploding into a chasm. Municipal fiscal disparities and inequities in public goods and services are becoming more extreme and imbalanced. The structural racism we live under today becomes more evident, pronounced, and severe over time, not less, as we head deeper into the 21st century.[12]

Nor are these developments explained by racial prejudice, animus, resentment, aversion, or even anxiety and discomfort. In many cases, they are a product of self-interest, opportunism, callous indifference, and inadequate foresight. In a sense, structural racism is like the federal tax code: the accretion of generations and product of countless decision makers that has resulted in a sprawling, byzantine complex of practices, rules, institutions, and interactions that were, in at least some cases, designed for the common good but have been exploited or manipulated by the well-heeled, special interests, and well-connected.

Chapter 4 grapples with the challenge of building and advancing racial justice agenda based upon a structural understanding of the production of racial inequality. A structural model is a challenge to the interpersonal conception of racism which locates itself within individual ideas, attitudes and beliefs, and the therapeutic brand of antiracism, organized around guilt, blame, and consciousness-raising it spawns. It is equally skeptical of attempts to reduce more deeply structured forms of racial inequality to individual behaviors and actions. Even while acknowledging the realities of institutional, systemic, and structural racism, too many antiracism advocates exhibit a tendency to reduce these dynamics to the properties of individuals, assuming that a racist actor or intentionality lay behind them or at their root, or to conflate the non-individualistic forms. This chapter resists that conflating tendency, and delineates between conceptions of institutional, systemic, and structural racism, and specifies their relationship.

This book challenges shibboleths held by both opponents of race-conscious policymaking and racial justice advocates alike and strives to provide a more nuanced view than is typical of leading exponents of antiracism. In a period of strengthening backlash to racial justice initiatives, this book is a timely entry by challenging many simplistic or misguided notions ascribed to "wokeness" just as it challenges colorblindness and the untenable status quo. In the process, Chapter 4 examines how a structural analysis fundamentally reconfigures our nation's most contentious racial debates, including affirmative action, reparations, and public policy responsibility.

A structural lens not only reconfigures familiar debates over race, but it suggests a different model for action and remedy. Instead of searching for someone to blame and overcoming the defensiveness that arises from fear of being labeled racist, we can become aggressively solution oriented. When confronted with a racial problem, instead of first looking for the racist perpetrator, we can instead ask "what authority has the power to do something about it, and what should they do?" Instead of first dividing the world into racists and antiracists, we can instead focus on possible solutions and implementation strategies. And instead of judging policies based upon good intentions and laudable motives, we should evaluate them largely on outcomes. We should condemn the ineffective and counterproductive as harshly as the nefarious or malign.

Chapter 4 outlines the contours for reform suggested by a structural model, prefiguring the policy agenda presented in the final chapter by furnishing the principles upon which to set an effective racial justice agenda. In the process, it attempts to resolve perennial debates such as whether such policies should be targeted or more universalistic in form, or whether a structural racism policy change agenda must always push for transformative change or can embody reformist impulses as well. The templates for policy interventions are reconsidered under the light of a structural analysis.

The ultimate goal is not that Americans, especially white Americans, recognize their racial privileges or participate in anti-racism workshops and DEI trainings. As cathartic as that might be, such acknowledgments and hand-wringing, even if accompanied by tangible reforms, are poorly tailored to a structural change agenda. The goal of racial justice, rather, is a society where race no longer significantly shapes access to opportunity and therefore life chances. To accomplish this, we will need to develop an agenda that is race-conscious but is also focused on enlarging and expanding access to opportunity more broadly.

The present system of structural inequality benefits, at least in the short-run, a small few at the expense of the many. Thus, a structural change agenda will demand sacrifices from some, but the benefits of reform reach well beyond racially marginalized peoples, even those most directly impacted by structural racism. By targeting structures rather than people and by focusing on the expansion of opportunity broadly, a race-conscious structural change agenda can be strategically framed and designed in a way that is positive-sum and avoids alienating potential allies who may fear being labeled racist, and therefore blunt the inevitable backlash to a racial justice agenda.

Derived from a structural racism analysis, Chapter 5 calls for a set of interventions to realize the American Dream for all Americans while simultaneously reducing racial disparities along critical dimensions. What we need is a relentless focus on building, extending, and enlarging opportunity matched to a structural perspicacity. This chapter presents a ten-point policy agenda, supported by research and best practices, to expand opportunity, and access to it. Many books on social issues are long on analysis, but short on solutions. This book leans in the opposite direction: Chapter 5 is the longest in the book and provides many actionable policy prescriptions.

Stark inequality of opportunity by place or class, let alone by race, is not inevitable. We have made headway against racial and economic inequality before, and can do so again with the right mix of interventions and policies. The policies and programs that will dismantle structural racism will also promote greater equality of and improved opportunities for all Americans.

Structural racism ultimately harms us all, diminishing our collective potential, not just that of racially marginalized populations. America's founding philosophy promised to unshackle its people from the limitations of patronage or patrimony, from inheritance or circumstance of birth. While that promise yet remains unrealized, it has served as a guiding ideal. Our challenge is to refashion the pathways and revitalize the conditions of opportunity in our time to make that aspiration a reality.

Notes

1 The term "race" is fraught and contested, and there is a wide and varied literature across multiple academic domains attempting to provide analytical and conceptual clarify or specify its contours, and to processes of racialization. As used in this book, "race" refers to certain socially constructed identity categories. The categories used to denote race in this book generally hew to contemporary U.S. government conventions, with the main exception that the Census Bureau currently regards Hispanic as an ethnic, rather than racial, category. See U.S. Census Bureau, "About the Topic of Race," Census.Gov, updated December 20, 2024, https://www.census.gov/topics/population/race/about.html. In this book, the term "Latino" is used as a racial category that generally encompasses groups

that the census denotes as "Hispanic, non-white," and therefore this book classifies "non-Hispanic whites" as simply white, and so on. "The term Hispanic" or "Hispanic, non-white" is retained generally only in direct reference to specific census figures. Although the term "Latino" is gendered, the use of the term here is intended to be gender neutral. Relatedly, the book uses the term "Native American" as a racial category, although tribal membership is not necessarily an indicator of racial identity. The definition or conceptualization of the related term "racism," and related variants, is discussed in chapter 4.

2 Stephen Menendian et al., "Racial Disparities Dashboard," *Othering & Belonging Institute*, https://belonging.berkeley.edu/racial-disparities-dashboard; "Demographic trends and economic well-being," in Pew Research Center, *On Views of Race and Inequality, Blacks and Whites Are Worlds Apart* (2016), https://www.pewresearch.org/social-trends/2016/06/27/1-demographic-trends-and-economic-well-being/; Patrick Sharkey, Keeanga-Yamahtta Taylor, and Yaryna Serkez, "The Gaps between White and Black America, in Charts," *New York Times*, June 19, 2020, https://www.nytimes.com/interactive/2020/06/19/opinion/politics/opportunity-gaps-race-inequality.html; Mabinty Quarshie et al., "12 Charts Show How Racial Disparities Persist across Wealth, Health, Education and Beyond," *USA Today*, June 18, 2020, https://www.usatoday.com/in-depth/news/2020/06/18/12-charts-racial-disparities-persist-across-wealth-health-and-beyond/3201129001/.

3 Daniel Schorr, "A New, 'Post-Racial' Political Era in America," *NPR*, January 28, 2008, https://www.npr.org/2008/01/28/18489466/a-new-post-racial-political-era-in-america.

4 Meredith Conroy and Perry Bacon Jr., "White Democrats are Wary of Big Ideas to Address Racial Inequality," *FiveThirtyEight*, July 14, 2020, https://fivethirtyeight.com/features/white-democrats-are-wary-of-big-ideas-to-address-racial-inequality/; Alexander Agadjanian, "Charting Recent Racial Attitude Change among Democrats," April 4, 2018, *Agadjanian Politics*, https://agadjanianpolitics.wordpress.com/2018/04/06/charting-recent-racial-attitude-change-among-democrats/; "The ANES Guide to Public Opinion and Electoral Behavior," *American National Election Studies*, accessed September 25, 2024, https://electionstudies.org/data-tools/anes-guide/anes-guide.html?chart=racial_resentment_1.

5 Chronicle Staff, "DEI Legislation Tracker," *Chronicle of Higher Education*, updated August 30, 2024, https://www.chronicle.com/article/here-are-the-states-where-lawmakers-are-seeking-to-ban-colleges-dei-efforts; Jessica Bryant and Chloe Appleby, "These States' Anti-DEI Legislation May Impact Higher Education," *BestColleges*, updated May 22, 2024, https://www.bestcolleges.com/news/anti-dei-legislation-tracker/.

6 A widely circulated example: "7 Ways We Know Systemic Racism Is Real," Ben & Jerry's, 2016, http://www.benjerry.com/whats-new/systemic-racism-is-real.

7 And alternatives like "white supremacy" are even more likely to confuse and confound when used to describe these patterns and forces. See, for example, Michael Powell, "'White Supremacy' Once Meant David Duke and the Klan. Now It Refers to Much More," *New York Times*, October 17, 2020, https://www.nytimes.com/2020/10/17/us/white-supremacy.html (explaining how white supremacy is sometimes used to refer to systemic and structural forces). Similarly, the use of the term "equity" has also produced substantial confusion. Stephen Menendian, "Equity vs. Equality: What's the Difference?," *Othering and Belonging Institute*, March 28, 2023, https://belonging.berkeley.edu/equity-vs-equality-whats-difference.

8 This book also differs from prior scholarly efforts in trying to match available empirical evidence with a theoretical model to guide both understanding and solutions. See, for example, Joe R. Feagin, *Systemic Racism: A Theory of Oppression*

(New York: Taylor & Francis Group, 2006) (which provides a theoretical model, but leaves it to future scholars to validate the model empirically).

9 This is not to say that all unequal outcomes are caused by unequal opportunities, but unequal opportunity does cause, and help explain, unequal outcomes.

10 This is not to suggest or imply that structural racism is merely inertial or what scientists call "path-dependent"—the present-day effects of past discriminatory action. In some cases, that is what is occurring. But in many other instances, dynamics within the opportunity structure replicate themselves or adapt themselves in such a way as to "lock-in" racial advantage. For an excellent discussion of how this can occur, see Daria Roithmayr, *Reproducing Racism: How Everyday Choices Lock in White Advantage* (New York: New York University Press, 2014).

11 Some of the more recent features that define or shape structural racism are adaptations or re-inscriptions of past institutional practices, such as the re-segregation of public schools (especially in the south) or the reverse redline. But, even then, it would be a mistake to understand these new developments as inevitable or a direct consequence of the past.

12 This is not to deny the reality of racial progress along many dimensions of well-being, such as high school graduation rates or voting rates. See Menendian et al., "The Racial Disparities Dashboard Project Progress Report Card, 1970–2020," Othering & Belonging Institute (OBI), accessed April 21, 2025, https://belonging.berkeley.edu/racial-disparities-progress-report-card-1970-2020 (showing areas of progress and regress). But even where disparities have shrunk (as with life expectancy), they often remain stubbornly pronounced. And, more importantly, the defining aspects of structural racism are the disparities have gotten worse or remain persistently wide. If structural racism were largely or entirely a product of historical policies and actions, then we would expect either gradual improvement or, at worse, stasis. Instead, we see worsening outcomes across many critical dimensions, suggesting that contemporary policies and actions do more than passively maintain inequality, but actively contribute to it.

1 The Structure of Opportunity

Christopher Marten's formative years were spent in the affluent suburb of Upper Arlington, whose mascot, the Golden Bear, is best known as the sobriquet of its most famous son, the professional golfer and major-championship record holder, Jack Nicklaus.[1] The summer before his first-grade year, Chris Marten's parents loaded their belongings into a Mayflower moving truck and relocated the family less than a mile from their home in northwest Columbus to a neighborhood just within the suburban boundary.[2]

The Marten's new home was strikingly similar in age, appearance, and size to the one they vacated in the city. Both neighborhoods were spacious and tranquil despite the telltale signs of families with young children. Both homes were roughly the same walking distance from a neighborhood school, park, and playground, and both neighborhoods were furnished with sidewalks and well-kept lawns. The Martens built lifelong friendships with their Columbus neighbors and cooled in the summer heat together at the community pool. Why uproot, pay a premium for a new home, and bother with the hassle of moving such a short distance?[3] The Martens were persuaded by family friends that the Upper Arlington school system afforded their children a much better education and safer environment than the Columbus City Schools.

Although the Martens were squarely middle class, Chris ultimately benefited from their robust social ties, excellent community institutions, and a thick envelope of supplemental resources beyond their affordance. Upper Arlington features some of the best schools, public or private, in the entire state of Ohio, and is even nationally ranked.[4] His grandmother provided "free" babysitting services and transportation to and from school while his parents worked, and eventually helped with college tuition as well. His parents leveraged their limited resources to enroll him into a diverse range of enrichment programs and recreational activities.

During the school year, Chris participated in sports leagues and arts programs, from soccer and little league to community theater and drawing classes. In the summers, he attended most of the science programs offered by central Ohio's premiere science museum, COSI, and the world-class Columbus Zoo and Aquarium. He attended summer camps in the forested hills of southern Ohio with friends and neighbors, where he made friends and developed

DOI: 10.4324/9781003562764-2

outdoor skills. Excellent primary and secondary schools, boosted with other inputs, including summer and extracurricular programs, helped buoy him to a professional career, with several stops in publicly supported state institutions of higher education along the way. Chris rode an upward escalator.

America regards herself as "the land of opportunity."[5] It is our credo that if we "work hard and play by the rules," we can make a better life for ourselves and our children. Many Americans hold as a matter of faith to the ideal that our institutions guarantee opportunity for each generation, by giving them the freedom to pursue their dreams without regard to caste, creed, or class.

A range of metaphors are commonly invoked to illustrate this powerful idea. In practice, opportunity in contemporary American society is often thought of as a good school or a well-paying job. In this way, opportunity is conceived as a pathway to a better life. When opportunity "knocks," it is a door to be opened and a threshold to be crossed. When opportunity is a ladder, the rungs must be climbed.[6] Each of these metaphors illuminates different aspects of opportunity. Some opportunities present themselves as with a "knock," and others must be searched out, forged, or discovered. Some opportunities may be within reach, reachable only with great effort, or beyond reach, as when ladder rungs are spaced too far apart.[7]

These metaphors share a mobility element—that available opportunities require some effort or initiative on the part of the individual pursuing them, whether that is walking, searching, reaching, or climbing.[8] Abraham Lincoln, one of the great expositors of American ideals, brilliantly nuanced the pathway metaphor, and connected it to our national purpose, in his first message to Congress. Lincoln declared that our nation's great purpose is "to elevate the condition of men—to lift artificial weights from all shoulders—to clear the paths of laudable pursuit for all—to afford all an unfettered start, and a fair chance, in the race of life."[9]

This book maintains that *opportunity* is best understood as the complete range of pathways available to people, during the life course, to pursue their dreams and aspirations, and to develop and achieve their potential.[10] As Chris Marten's story suggests, whether a pathway is available for pursuit depends not only upon the skills, characteristics, and capacities of the individual traveler, but upon the previous efforts of others.

In his essays on self-reliance, Ralph Waldo Emerson exhorted others to "not go where the path may lead," and instead go "where there is no path and leave a trail."[11] Yet, as his admonition implies, although we may choose among the pathways before us (even those where none have gone), the paths we start upon are trails left by others. Even the most industrious pioneers and adventurous spirits must set forth from the pathways they were placed upon and draw upon the technologies, tools, and resources developed by those before them.

In his book *Outliers*, Malcom Gladwell doubts whether Steve Jobs or Bill Gates would have achieved their full potential in an earlier era, before the personal computer revolution.[12] No matter how well the underlying skills were developed or might translate to other marketable tasks, genius in software programming would have little value in a time before the invention of the transistor semiconductor. Most opportunities today depend upon prior investments, developments, and technologies. Even commonplace jobs such as marketing cell phone contracts for mobile carriers could not exist without communication satellites or rocket propulsion technology to launch those satellites.

An opportunity-oriented society would afford new opportunities for its members by creating new pathways and by clearing obstacles and removing other barriers to open existing pathways to more travelers. By the mid-19th century, Lincoln understood this principle well. As a young man working on flatboats down the Mississippi, "primitive roads, clogged waterways, lack of rail connections, [and] inadequate schools" were "hurdles he worked all his life to overcome in order to earn his ampler share of freedom."[13] Lincoln believed that "improvements" to infrastructure would "enable thousands of families to emerge from the kind of poverty in which the Lincoln family had been trapped, and would permit new cities and towns to flourish."[14] Paving roads, clearing trails, erecting bridges, building canals, and burrowing tunnels can ease travel between two points, and therefore permit access to more distant jobs and new markets.

But it is not just the clearing or creation of pathways that affords opportunities. Whether an opportunity can be seized depends upon more than the mere existence of an open pathway, but the capacity to perceive and ultimately traverse it.[15] Many pathways require training, specialized knowledge, or tools to spot, let alone pass over and through.[16] Our skills, experiences, and endowments as travelers ultimately determine which pathways are accessible to us, and this also depends upon the efforts and investments of others.

Opening or revealing new pathways to individuals and helping individuals advance along them requires investments in what economists denote as *human capital*, the knowledge, skills, and experience that people bring to the market.[17] Better paying jobs generally require more skills and experience, each cumulatively building over time, as greater experience and finely honed skills open more job opportunities. Degree requirements, certificates, and other credentials are generally the formal expression of the achieved skills needed to perform a job. Our institutions, particularly public education and workforce development programs, play a large role in creating and fostering human capital.[18] This is why parents, like Chris Marten's, fret so much over the quality of their children's education.

The pathways that can be traversed depend upon the burdens and capacities of the traveler, not just the removal of barriers or construction of easements to facilitate passage. As Lincoln observed, some people are freighted with artificial weights, impeding their progress or circumscribing desired pursuits. When businesses or firms refuse to hire workers because of their race, gender, sexual orientation or religion, they fence off pathways of opportunity to entire classes of people. In this context, anti-discrimination laws expand opportunity by lifting those "artificial weights."

Drawing on the idea of opportunity as the pathways available to people during their life course, this chapter canvasses the conditions and forces that promote upward mobility by expanding pathways of opportunity and easing access through them, and those which constrict, impinge, and impede them. In the process, this chapter introduces a model of how opportunity is organized, fostered, and distributed, and identifies the core components and critical pathways of opportunity in 21st-century America. It will also explore the relationship between opportunity and the perceived choices available. To accomplish this, we first review the facts of social and economic mobility in America.

Upward Mobility in America

Economic inequality has risen significantly in the United States in recent decades, especially compared to other wealthy countries.[19] The Gini coefficient, a popular measure of economic inequality, increased by nearly 20% from 1980 to 2019.[20] The top 1% of earners in 2021 earned 27.6% of pre-tax income in the United States, levels not seen since the late 1920s.[21] Wealth inequalities may be larger still. According to estimates, the top 10% wealthiest Americans hold around 70% of the nation's wealth in 2022.[22] Widening economic inequality as a troubling social concern has captured broad public attention in the last decade or so.[23]

One assumption underlying these concerns is that enormous income and wealth inequality reflects growing inequality of opportunity.[24] Extreme economic inequality is sometimes defended as fair so long as reasonable equality of opportunity exists.[25] Many in our society seem comfortable with a game that produces big winners and losers as long as everyone has a fair chance at the same prizes.

This is the essence of the American Dream, the ideal that individuals born at the bottom of the economic scale can rise to the top with enough talent, determination, and hard work.[26] Although cynics may deride such notions as fanciful myths, the American Dream is more than a national creed or article of faith, it is also an aspirational goal shared by many Americans which guides public policy and investments in people and places.

Americans in recent years, however, have grown pessimistic about the reality of American Dream. A 2024 Wall Street Journal survey found that many Americans feel that the American Dream is out of reach.[27] A Pew survey taken around the same time found that 41% felt that the American Dream was once possible, but no longer existed.[28] An ABC poll earlier that year found that just 27% of Americans felt that "if you work hard, you get ahead," down from 50% in 2010.[29]

These concerns have focused research interest and directed inquiry into what some scholars denote the "opportunity gap."[30] Because opportunity cannot be directly measured, researchers assess inequality of opportunity in terms of intergenerational social and economic mobility.[31] Utilizing publicly available data sets, survey data, and anonymous tax records, researchers have managed to measure economic mobility over time.[32]

To make sense of this research, imagine that all American households are represented and sorted into a single income scale, with the highest income earners at the top and the lowest income earners at the bottom.* We can measure and assess the extent of economic mobility by tracking children as they become adults, comparing their starting point in the income distribution to where they end up. If upward mobility was merely a matter of talents, determination, and hard work—and if these traits exist among people of all backgrounds—we would expect children born into poor families to have a similar chance of becoming affluent as adults as children from rich families.[33]

More generally, if children of all backgrounds had an equal chance in life, then we would expect that roughly equal proportions of children from households in each income segment would ultimately end up in every other segment (including the one they started in) throughout the income distribution as adults. In a perfectly economically and socially mobile society, children born into poor families would not only have the same chance of becoming rich as the children of the rich, but also the same chance of becoming rich adults as children from rich families would have of becoming poor adults (in terms of annual earned income, at least).

In statistical terms, we can measure the extent of actual economic mobility by examining these chances for people born into every income segment, and we can measure upward mobility in particular by examining the rates of children from the lower-income segments that rise above their starting point. Consider for a moment what percentage of children from low-income households (say, the bottom 20%) you imagine vault to the top income quintile as adults, bearing in mind that in a perfectly equal opportunity society that figure would be 20%. It is probably unsurprising, however sobering, that reality does not reflect the ideal, and is not particularly close.

The best research shows that, on average and nationwide, a child born into the bottom fifth of the income distribution has a 7.5% chance of making it to the top 20% as an adult.[34] In contrast, children born into the top income quintile have a 36.5% chance of remaining there as adults.[35] Children from upper-income families—those earning in the top 20% of the income distribution—are nearly five times more likely to become high-income earning adults as children from poor families.

These differences are enormous in terms of income, not just percentiles. Children born in the 90th-percentile of households are projected to earn

---

* Researchers presenting this data typically organize such distributions into quintiles (20% segments), deciles (10% segments), or percentiles (1% segments). In a society of perfect economic mobility, the probability of landing in any segment should be equal to the size of the segment. For example, the probability that someone born in the second decile of the income distribution (the 11th to 20th percentile) should end up in the ninth decile (the 81st to 90th percentile) should be 10%.

three times more than the children of 10th-percentile earners on average.[36] To mix metaphors, children born with a silver spoon appear to have a leg up. The class advantages of upward mobility in the United States contravene one of our most cherished ideals and our expectations regarding opportunity fairness. This explains why surveys show that Americans consistently overestimate rates of upward mobility.[37]

But perhaps that leap from the bottom to the top, while the ideal, is not representative of American social and economic mobility. Unfortunately, this pattern exists throughout the income distribution. The chances of making it to the top of the income distribution as adults improve for children born into each successive segment of the income distribution, with the best chances for those born at or near the top.

Although "rags to riches" stories are inspiring, perhaps judging American economic mobility by who makes it the top is the wrong lens or benchmark to judge American economic mobility. Perhaps what matters more is not who becomes rich, but how easy it is to escape poverty—how much economic and social mobility exists in the middle or lower portions of the income distribution. Unfortunately, not only do children from poor families have a harder time making it to the top (a steeper climb, if you will), they also have fewer routes out of poverty.

Although the percentage of children leaping from the bottom to the top has not changed much in recent decades, children born into poverty in America today have a much harder time simply climbing into the middle class than a generation or two ago.[38] A child born into poverty today has only a 33% chance of making it into the middle class, compared to 50% after World War II.[39]

More generally, absolute income mobility—the fraction of children who earn more than their parents—has fallen dramatically since the post-war period. More than 90% of children born in 1940 earned more than their parents, even at the highest rungs of the income ladder, compared to just half of children born in the early to mid-1980s.[40] The reality that children are less likely than preceding generations to surpass their parents may also contribute to the perception that the economy is unfair, especially since the notion of progress is an element of the American Dream.[41]

Overall, this data suggests that wealthier parents transmit advantages and provide greater opportunities to their children. It is, alternatively, possible to believe that differences in incomes and earnings reflect innate or hereditary characteristics, such as IQ. That assumption would explain such disparate outcomes without abandoning belief in opportunity fairness. If this were true, however, then the degree to which income and wealth explain upward mobility would be relatively constant over time and across regions. In other words, poor people and rich people, beginning life with different genetic advantages, would have similar rates of mobility everywhere and across generations. However, significant geographic and temporal variability in rates of upward mobility suggests that structural forces explain this variation more than inherited traits.

Upward mobility based on parental income and wealth not only varies over time, but children born in certain parts of the United States have much lower rates of upward mobility than average, and vice versa. For example, the probability that a child born into the bottom income quintile reaches the top falls to 4.4% in Charlotte, North Carolina, far below the national average.[42] On the other hand, children in the bottom quintile in the San Jose metropolitan region of California have a nearly 13% chance of making it to the top. That may not be the perfect ideal, but it is much closer to our intuitions of equal opportunity.

Broadly speaking, regions with the lowest rates of upward mobility in the United States are disproportionately concentrated in the South.[43] Overall, the East and West coasts and the Great Plains states have higher rates of upward mobility than the industrial Midwest or South.[44] The researchers behind these studies, led by the economist Raj Chetty, launched a publicly searchable mapping tool that allows users to compare rates of upward mobility down to the neighborhood level, with often surprising results.[45]

The accumulative research into upward mobility reveals critical facts about the pathways of opportunity. Utilizing the latest population datasets available and anonymous tax records and correlating them with variations in local conditions, researchers have shown that upward mobility is determined largely by contextual factors and resource inputs that accrue before individuals enter into labor markets.[46] The next section of this chapter introduces a model of opportunity that reflects these discoveries.

The Structure of Opportunity

The *opportunity structure* represents the complete range of opportunity pathways and the relationships between those pathways.[47] The pathways of opportunity are formed out of critical institutions, collective investments, and private resources, which are further shaped and distributed by markets, larger systems, new technologies, and policies and laws, including antidiscrimination laws. Collectively, these forces structure opportunity because they so powerfully influence individual life chances, delimiting what is possible and what is not.

In that sense, the opportunity structure is the web of influences beyond our control that enhance and impinge our ability to develop our potential and excel in life. While individual traits and characteristics, such as habits, talents, and choices within the opportunity structure matter, the important point is that these structures shape our life chances regardless of the decisions we make. They do this by enhancing or constraining an individual's options, imparting skills and capabilities, providing certain incentives and disincentives, and by establishing parameters on the range of opportunities reachable in the structure. In other words, the opportunity structure influences and shapes not only a person's achieved socioeconomic status (SES), but also their experiences and life decisions.[48]

The opportunity structure operates directly on individuals, shuttling us forward along one pathway or another, by imparting skills and capabilities through the formal educational system and providing access to employment opportunities, transportation options, quality childcare, and health care, among other provisions. The opportunity structure also operates indirectly by influencing the decisions that people make within the structure.[49] The range and quality of opportunities available or visible depend upon one's location within the structure, which reveal, distort, or conceal future possibilities, destinations, and rewards.

Individuals with limited skills and few economic opportunities confront not simply fewer choices, but fewer incentives and expected benefits from making decisions that may tend to yield better life outcomes, such as refraining from childbearing until marriage or after attaining certain job-related skills. Behaviors that policymakers and social scientists may regard as harmful to future opportunity, such as dropping out of high school, selling drugs, or teenage pregnancy, are not just a cause of limited opportunity and reduced socioeconomic mobility but a consequence of it.[50] Such decisions may be a response to a lack of opportunities or visible career paths.[51] As Trevor Noah wittily noted about growing up in a poor community, "crime offers internship programs and summer jobs and opportunities for advancement."[52] The sociologist William Julius Wilson observed that criminal businesses "actively recruit" teenagers in low-income neighborhoods with keen awareness of their limited prospects.[53]

Consequently, choices made within low-opportunity contexts often feedback to the detriment of individuals located within that space in the form of criminal records, reduced educational attainment, and fewer marketable job skills.[54] If the perceived benefits from making decisions that promote upward mobility and economic opportunity are warped, then the decisions people make within the opportunity structure will be equally distorted.[55] For individuals growing up in hard neighborhoods with failing schools, the idea of pursuing a university education may seem unrealistic and fanciful, even if it were attainable. The opportunity structure does more than distribute access to prizes and punishments; it shapes our behavior and aspirations by positioning us differently relative to those possible outcomes.

Ultimately, the opportunity structure is a complex lattice of nodes and connections shaped by institutions, infrastructure, social networks, markets, and public and private resources. Like an upwelling bringing nutrients toward the ocean surface, a strong and healthy local opportunity structure facilitates upward economic and social mobility for everyone in the ecosystem. In contrast, a weak and anemic opportunity structure hampers upward mobility and dampens everyone's prospects, even the relatively privileged.

The idea of an opportunity structure was first described in the late 1960s by a scholar trying to understand the relationship between individuals completing their education and entering labor markets in search of jobs, and how that transitioned was accomplished.[56] In the 1970s, political scientists adapted the concept to help explain opportunities for social change and political entrepreneurship.[57] By the 1990s, scholars such as George Galster built elaborate statistical models designed to identify and explicate critical relationships within the broader urban opportunity structure, connecting housing and employment markets with educational and criminal justice systems.[58] This work, along with more recent economic research on upward mobility, helps delineate the components of the opportunity structure, many of which can be measured and mapped.

The remainder of this chapter draws upon this research, synthesizing it into a more easily comprehensible theoretical framework. This framework describes the three key geographic layers within the opportunity structure and emphasizes three critical forces operating across it which distribute or deny access to its vital components.

Place Matters

The idea of America as "the land of opportunity" contains a practical truth Americans have long understood: where a person is born or raised matters. Not because there is something intrinsically magical about one place or another but because of the institutions, resources, and conditions that exist in those places.

Where one lives affects one's life chances despite individual talents, work ethic, ambition, drive, or personal life choices. Creative genius and industrious spirit may have free rein or limited outlet depending upon prevailing cultural norms, laws, and available resources. This is why Americans have been willing to pull up roots and relocate in pursuit of a better life.

In the 19th century, this meant moving west in search of inexpensive but fertile land, as with the Homesteaders or Oklahoma Sooners, or mineral wealth, as with the Forty-Niners during the Gold Rush.[59] In the 20th century, millions of Americans moved out of the ruin of the dust bowl or oppression of the rural south to industrial factories of the west and the north. Today, families routinely move for better jobs, good schools, and safe neighborhoods.

Research validates this intuition and explains this impulse.[60] Opportunity has a spatial footprint. Contrary to the presumption of equal opportunity, the opportunity structure is geographically sensitive. As noted earlier, one of the most important findings from recent research on upward mobility is the remarkable degree of geographic variation in the United States. Children born into the bottom income quintile in Charlotte or Atlanta have less than a 5% chance of rising to the top income quintile, whereas children from the same income segment born in San Jose or Salt Lake City have a two or three times better chance to make it to the top.[61]

Could these differences simply reflect differences in aptitudes or prevailing attitudes of the people within these communities? Using records of families with children who moved to and from various communities, researchers have been able to establish the specific causal effects of growing up in certain communities.[62] This research demonstrates, for example, that growing up in Baltimore, Maryland has a causal effect, reducing a child's future earnings by 0.7% per year.

The longer a child resides in Baltimore, the greater the cumulative harm. In contrast, growing up in Dupage, Illinois, increases expected earnings by 16%.[63]

All told, about 70% of the observed variance in upward mobility is attributed to the causal effects of place and community characteristics.[64] The strength of a job market in a region, for example, affects nearly every measure of prosperity, from income and wage growth, to demand for social services and rates of crime. The spatial variation in intergenerational mobility allows researchers to pinpoint factors that correlate with upward mobility.[65] When examining these relationships against a larger body of research, we can begin to understand what these forces are, and how they interact within and across place.

Different opportunity-enhancing inputs and resources tend to exist at different geographic scales. Within the United States, the web of influences that constitute the local opportunity structure vary across three nested and concentric spatial domains: 1) metropolitan regions, 2) municipal jurisdictions, and 3) neighborhoods. This is not to say that other geographies (such as states) are irrelevant, but these three scales play an outsized role in the production of opportunity and human development. This is because the critical geographic layers of the opportunity structure include regional markets, municipal services, and neighborhood conditions.

This is not simply a theoretical observation. Recent research quantified the specific contribution to upward mobility from each geographic scale. Approximately 32% of the variance in upward mobility is attributed to regional conditions, 13.5% to counties, 28% to municipal characteristics, particularly high school catchment zones, and about 27% to census tracts, or neighborhoods.[66] Across and within these geographic scales, there are powerful forces that enhance or impinge access to opportunity.

To briefly summarize, labor markets and transportation systems tend to be regional in scope. The quality of local services and public goods, such as schools, libraries, safe potable drinking water and sewage systems, and recreational offerings, depend more on municipal administration, and vary tremendously within regions. Neighborhood characteristics, including amenities such as parks, financial institutions, and grocery stores, as well as rates of violence or the degree of public safety, can vary tremendously within municipal boundaries. Collectively, these geographic layers structure access to opportunity by organizing these critical inputs.

Regional Conditions

The economic health and vitality of a region broadly shapes the fortunes of everyone in them. To appreciate the influence of regional conditions, consider and compare two regions that have played an outsized role in shaping the U.S. economy, past and present, and are firmly associated in the popular imagination with leading industries: The Detroit metropolitan area and the San Francisco Bay Area.

For nearly a century, the American automotive industry powered the Detroit regional economy. As talent and capital poured into Michigan, American car manufacturing geographically consolidated in a single region, and Detroit became known as "the Motor City," home to Ford, General Motors, Chrysler, and many other global car companies.[67] Detroit grew to become the fifth largest city in the United States by 1950. Countless ancillary businesses emerged, from auto parts suppliers and distributers and marketing firms to glass, chemical, steel, and machine tool production companies that sprawled around Detroit and beyond.[68]

Just as the economy of mass production and industry buoyed Detroit, the wrenching process of de-industrialization had an equally devastating impact. Since 2000, Michigan lost more than 300,000 manufacturing jobs, and real wages fell by $8 an hour.[69] By 2022, the Detroit population fell by two-thirds from its mid-century population peak.[70] The inflation-adjusted value of the city's assessed property values fell 79% from its peak in 1958, and the value of its income tax revenues fell by 76% from its peak in 1972.[71] As the historian Thomas Sugrue pithily observed, "Detroit rose and fell with the automobile industry."[72]

The gradual decline of the automotive industry dragged down the regional economy, culminating in the federal bailouts to Detroit's "big three" car manufacturers in 2008–2009 and the municipal bankruptcy of Detroit itself in 2013.[73] Private businesses shuttered, tax coffers collapsed, and public services shriveled. Despite pockets of wealth in Detroit's affluent suburbs, nothing and no one, from teachers and pensioners to the local art museum, escaped the effects of the decline of regional industry.

The San Francisco Bay Area is a vivid contrast. Home to many of the world's largest technology companies, such as Google, Apple, and Facebook, the Bay Area is the geographic hub for the leading industries of the 21st century, just as Detroit was in the 20th century. A 21st-century gold rush, these companies attract massive amounts of investment capital and have become among the most valuable companies in the world, making fortunes for shareholders, and producing one of the nation's largest concentration of millionaires and billionaires.[74]

As was the case of the "Motor City," the Bay Area's "Silicon Valley" has incubated countless technology start-ups and drawn technology workers from across the globe. The demand for engineering talent has lured hundreds of thousands of workers to the Bay Area, and many more students into computer science or coding camps. Housing prices have skyrocketed and the demands on the regional infrastructure have choked highways with cars. The high cost of living pressures non-tech businesses to keep pace with salaries and cities to raise minimum wages.[75]

As contrasting case studies, Detroit and San Francisco illustrate the regional effects of industry. The economies of both regions were dramatically reorganized by the geographic concentration of a leading growth industry. Both regions created enormous wealth, incubated new businesses, and were engines for the national economy. But they also shaped the fortunes of all their residents, not just unionized autoworkers and high-paid tech workers. The quality and range of services and amenities is shaped by the quality of jobs in a region and the industries that produce those jobs.

Regional industries play a major role in defining large-scale economic conditions within a region, which in turn affects the health and vitality of a region more broadly. This is not only true of labor markets, which determine economic opportunity, wage scales, and competitive salaries. Regional housing markets and transportation infrastructure are additional regional conditions that shape access to opportunity.

Regional housing markets determine where workers and their families can afford to live, and whether they can access employment opportunities that might arise. As we will see, the cost of housing is one of the greatest barriers to opportunity in the Bay Area. Similarly, regional infrastructure enhances or limits the capacities of individuals within the regions.

Well-funded, broad-based levels of public transportation and infrastructure through a region can connect families across that region to the entire economy and economic opportunities or services on offer. Transit options and infrastructure improvements allow breadwinners in one community to pursue job opportunities that would have been beyond commuting distance in previous eras or in regions with inadequate infrastructure. This not only expands the range of opportunities available, but also incentivizes a broader search for those opportunities.

Conversely, poorly funded, haphazard and unreliable public transit and infrastructure can isolate families and communities from the larger economy and job opportunities outside of their community. Government researchers operationalize this insight with the concept of "commuting zones," more than 740 different geographical regions in the country that are regarded as distinct labor markets.[76] Commuting zones are one of the most important layers in the opportunity structure.

The cases of metropolitan Detroit and the San Francisco Bay Area represent polar extremes of economic growth and decline rooted in the health of leading regional industries. Most major metropolitan regions lie somewhere along the spectrum in between. Either way, regions matter. Regional industry, labor markets, housing markets, and transportation infrastructure shape economic opportunity and the capacity of individuals to access those opportunities. Although regions define large-scale conditions and set parameters on the structure of opportunity, in many respects, municipalities more directly shape individual life chances.

Municipal Inequality

Although regional dynamics expand or compress opportunity pathways for the region's residents, local conditions that contribute to upward mobility and afford greater opportunity vary significantly within regions. Many major metropolitan regions within the United States house dozens of municipal governments and school districts. The quality and range of services provided, including primary and secondary educational provision, recreational programs, water and sewer infrastructure, as well as health and safety services—each of which shapes life chances—vary dramatically within metropolitan areas. Although counties provide critical services, especially to unincorporated areas, a large sheaf of these opportunity-shaping services and programs are provided by municipalities. And, as noted above, nearly a third of the differences in observed rates of upward mobility is explained by municipal-level forces, defined as those arising at the high school catchment level.[77]

The quality of municipal services, amenities, and public goods plays an outsized role in generating the developmental opportunities that foster human and social capital, as well as shape ambition, grit, and other character-building traits. Public schools are where most Americans learn not only learn to read, write, and acquire other rudimentary life skills, but also more advanced skills, from algebra to organizational management. Few parents have time or expertise to instruct knowledge and skills that is taught even in middle school curriculum, as many exasperated parents can attest after trying to help their children with befuddling homework assignments.

The range and quality of municipal services, however, depends principally on the resources available to that jurisdiction, particularly the tax revenue drawn by the jurisdiction. The tax base capacity of the municipality, along with state-aid, generally delimit the services that can be offered by local government, regardless of local need, citizen demands, or the policy proclivities or aspirations of municipal leaders.[78] Fiscal realities circumscribe both grandiose plans and urgent provision for basic needs.

The tax base capacity of a jurisdiction, in turn, is largely a function of property values and commercial business activity. Of particular importance to local tax base capacity is revenue from local property taxes on homes and businesses. Sales taxes, income taxes, user fees, and civil and criminal fines also contribute to municipal revenue, but property taxes are the one of the most reliable and stable revenue sources for local government.[79] It is not surprising, then, that local services and the quality of those services vary so widely.

One of the most unfortunate features of the contemporary opportunity structure is that private wealth inequality, which already shapes life chances, manifests inequitable public provision through the structural relationship of tax base capacity and the quality and range of public services. This fundamental relationship generates reinforcing characteristics which compensatory schemes and redistribution formulas are incapable of fully overcoming.

Consider the specific case of public-school funding. In the United States, only a sliver of funding for local schools flows from the federal government. Ninety percent of school funding derives from state and local revenues.[80] In particular, about two-thirds of all property taxes are allocated to school funding.[81] This average figure masks considerable variation. In wealthier jurisdictions, the bulk of funding is generated locally, sometimes 90% or more. In poorer districts, a greater portion—often a majority—of the local school funding is derived from state sources topped with federal compensatory schemes and state redistribution formulas.

Wealth disparities play a large role in generating not only economic inequalities between municipal jurisdictions, but structural disparities in opportunity through the inequitable distribution of public goods and services. Consider, for example, the revealing and powerful relationship between test scores and median home values, a proxy for wealth. A 2019 study found that home values are $205,000 higher on average in the neighborhoods of high-scoring than low-scoring schools.[82] The evidence suggests a relationship between wealth and student performance mediated by the mechanisms for school funding. Research shows that per-pupil funding plays a significant role in the educational performance of a district, with relatively greater funding improving outcomes.[83] This creates a structural condition that affords more opportunity in affluent communities, even if per-pupil funding is formally equalized subsequently.

Affluent communities not only tend to have a greater capacity to provide public services, but they also have more private resources to draw upon. It is not uncommon for the affluent communities to supplement public educational programming by raising substantial private funds. Parents in Los Angeles organize ambitious fund-raising drives, setting targets like $45,000 a drive.[84] In Palo Alto, parents are asked for $1,500 per child, per year.[85] These resources may be put toward extracurricular programming and specialized instruction materials.[86]

Private fund-raising for public schools compounds inequality in public education. The Center for American Progress estimates that PTAs raised $425 million in 2010, with 10% of the funds going to one-tenth of 1% percent of schools.[87] Generating these resources through fund-raising drives and private donations allows exclusive public schools to provide outstanding services while keeping taxes and levies lower. By enhancing the quality of the local school without a corresponding cost to local homeowners, property values may enjoy a corresponding boost, further enhancing the wealth of the local residents.

In contrast, poor districts not only have less capacity for public provision, but fewer private resources to buffer and supplement public provision. Worse still, ample avenues for private contributions to hyperlocal public education may soften public support for state, regional, or district-wide educational funding enhancements, especially when they are perceived as principally benefitting non-local schools.

Communal resources in the form of property wealth and tax base capacity is more than an input into municipal service provision, it is also an output. High-quality public services, especially great public schools, elevate local property values. One study found that parents will pay an additional 2.5%

in housing costs for a 5% increase in local test scores.[88] Another found a 2% premium for each standard deviation increment increase in test scores.[89]

School districts and municipalities with improving test scores and reputationally high-quality schools enjoy correspondingly strong demand for housing within them.[90] As a result, home prices are often bid up in districts with great schools.[91] And in districts with declining test scores, families who can afford a better district may leave or, if they remain, opt out of public schools altogether, enrolling their children in private or charter schools. While these families may be contributing to the tax base, those districts still suffer from the absence of those parents in educational system, in the form of volunteer time, extracurricular involvement, or additional fund-raising support. Families that move out or opt-out of declining districts leave those districts with fewer resources to turn around conditions and often higher-need populations. This leads to another reinforcing dynamic: the stratification and clustering of affluent and poor families across municipal jurisdictions.

Economists have long observed that families buy more than a home when they purchase a house, that people "choose their municipality and school district in the same sense that they choose to purchase property and assume mortgages to finance it."[92] In other words, individuals are not just buying property or a home, they are buying access to a set of services, amenities, and even opportunities paid for in the form of fees and property taxes. This is known as the "Tiebout mechanism," named after the author of an academic paper published in the 1950s that first described this dynamic.[93]

The relationship between tax base capacity, private wealth, and the quality of public provision generates a structural dynamic that sorts people into different communities based upon their ability to pay. To simplify, residents seek the best mix of services, amenities, and taxes, while businesses seek the best mix of customers, workers, and taxes, and municipal leaders strive to maximize property values for their residents while providing the highest-quality services. The net effect of these understandable dynamics is significant municipal stratification and school district inequality.

From the perspective of municipal leadership, the key objective is to attract the most affluent residents and businesses. This will not only shore up the tax base capacity to provide the highest-quality services, but it will minimize tax rates and maximize local property values. The higher the property values and the greater the tax base capacity, the lower are the rates that are needed to generate equivalent revenue for local services. The top 5% of localities can generate more than three times the revenues of the bottom 5% at the same tax rate.[94]

The relationship between the range and quality of municipal services, residential property values, and commercial business activity is also reinforcing. Affluent customers attract businesses, and more commercial business activity means more contribution to the tax base, which reduces the individual and residential tax burden. As a result, affluent municipalities can afford to keep tax rates lower relative to less affluent jurisdictions.

Poorer communities, in contrast, have fewer assets, less valuable property, and fewer commercial businesses to generate revenue for urgent needs. Compounding these problems, lower-income community residents tend to have more needs and are therefore more reliant upon public services. For example, low-income communities disproportionately rely on public transportation, due to lower levels of car ownership, and community health centers or free clinics for health care, due to lower rates health insurance coverage. To meet the needs of poorer residents, municipal governments in distressed communities must levy relatively higher taxes to fund services, prompting more residents and businesses to flee to lower tax jurisdictions.

In order to maintain high-quality services, keep taxes low and business happy, municipalities and local governments have a strong incentive to maintain their exclusivity or position in the hierarchy of communities in their region. Municipal zoning ordinances and related land use policies play a key role in this process. "Exclusionary zoning" refers to a broad array of zoning practices that have the effect of keeping lower-income families priced out.[95] This can include lot size restrictions or density requirements or outright prohibitions on apartments and other multi-family or renter-occupied housing stock. Enacted in the name of local control or community aesthetics, these measures are often designed to maximize the stream of local property taxes and local property values.

Research shows a consistent relationship between restrictive land use policies and home and rental prices. As one economist studying California found, in the vast Los Angeles region, rents are 32% higher and home values 38% higher in jurisdictions with stringent minimum lot size requirements compared to jurisdictions that are relatively lenient.[96] Moreover, he found that the share of land zoned for single-family detached use predicts higher housing home values. The study also found that regulatory mechanisms such as local project approvals were associated with income segregation generally. The study found that municipal review processes, measured by the number of approvals that local governments require for new housing developments, were strongly related to the segregation of low-income households.

Municipalities with high performing school districts maintain or improve their educational quality through exclusionary tactics such as this. These municipalities have strong incentives to attract residents that will contribute to the tax base while keeping out lower-income entrants who might impose demands upon it. The predictable result is that affordable housing in these localities is either scarce or non-existent, and low-income families, over time, are priced out.

Although the problems of widening income and wealth inequality have received significant attention, there has been less focus on the structural problem of growing fiscal inequality and municipal stratification. Municipal competition is currently structured as a zero-sum game, with winners and losers both in terms of cities and the people who reside within them. As a result of this competition, people are increasingly sorted into jurisdictions based upon their ability to afford residence, with consequences for their access to quality municipal services. Thus, the greatest structural inequalities are no longer within cities or school districts, but rather between them.

Buying into a high- or low-opportunity community is like buying a ticket into an amusement park. A high-opportunity amusement park may have a higher entry fee at the gate, but it has a superior rides, a wider range of entertainment options, shorter lines, higher-quality food offerings, better customer service and safety. A low-opportunity amusement park may have a lower entry fee, but there are fewer rides, longer wait times, exorbitant prices for unhealthy food and refreshments, more mechanical malfunctions and delays, and poor customer service.

Much of the inequality in the contemporary opportunity structure is a by-product of municipal inequality. Even within municipal jurisdictions, however, neighborhood conditions play a powerful role in shaping the quality of life and distribution of opportunity. Neighborhoods vary in terms of housing stock, peer influences, safety and amenities, as well as social networks and organizations. The proximity to parks, sidewalks, and safe playgrounds has a direct impact on physical and emotional well-being.[97] At the same time, neighborhoods expose residents to both environmental toxins as well as physical violence.

Neighborhood Effects

Most Americans readily appreciate the importance of growing up in a "good" neighborhood while few deny the lasting harm of growing up in a bad one. Decades of empirical research validate these intuitions, vividly illustrating a series of powerful relationships between residence and an individual's projected life chances. A voluminous body of research under the header "neighborhood effects" helps us understand the specific ways in which neighborhoods shape human development and well-being.

Just as regions shape the markets and economies of municipalities nested within them without determining the level of municipal provision or mixture of services, local governments influence neighborhood conditions and characteristics without entirely determining the neighborhood experience. Regions broadly reflect macroeconomic conditions, and municipalities determine the level, mixture and quality of services provided to a community, but neighborhoods characteristics and conditions also structure opportunity and shape well-being, often more intimately.

Recall that although regions and municipal characteristics independently shape opportunity, nearly 27% of the differences in rates of upward mobility are explained by forces at the census tract, or neighborhood level.[98] Although the precise definition of "neighborhood" varies considerably in the social science literature, neighborhoods are generally smaller than municipal jurisdictions or school districts.[99] The "neighborhood effects" research aims to distinguish the precise effects of neighborhood environments from other forces, and to demonstrate the often profound ways that environment shapes human development and social and economic outcomes.

Experiments moving families from one neighborhood to another are difficult, costly, and ethically dubious, but studies based upon policy interventions or other "natural experiments" allow social scientists to observe the exposure effects of one neighborhood compared to another. The most famous of these studies was the "Moving to Opportunity" (MTO) experiment funded by Congress and administered by the Department of Housing and Urban Development (HUD) in five cities between 1994 and 1998.[100]

The MTO experiment involved more than 4,500 families, who were assigned to one of three groups. The treatment group received a housing voucher that could only be used in a census tract with a poverty rate below 10%. Another group was given a voucher that could be used only in a neighborhood where they were originally offered. And another group was not offered a voucher, but lived in public housing.

The initial results were mixed, if not somewhat disappointing. Girls in the experimental group generally did better. They improved in school, felt safer, and had fewer risky behaviors.[101] Boys, on the other hand, had elevated rate of risky behaviors, and no other measurable positive effects. The effects on parents were also mixed. Although parents in the treatment group reported feeling safer and had notable improvements in mental health and slight improvements in physical health, there were no gains in income or labor market participation.[102]

Some early critics pointed out that the moves required for the treatment group were inadequate. By simply requiring families to move to low-poverty neighborhoods, many of the moves were not far or significant enough to extricate themselves from corrosive social networks, unhealthy environments, or even require them to change school districts.[103] While the families in the treatment group moved to low poverty neighborhoods, many of those communities were on a downward trajectory and not high opportunity.

However, a long-term evaluation of the MTO families conducted many years later revealed more profound and enduring impacts. Children from families assigned to the experimental voucher group under age 13 at the time of the move earned $1,624 more on average per year relative to the control group by their mid-twenties.[104] These children were also more likely to attend college between the ages of 18–20.

By comparing siblings at different ages, researchers were able to establish a causal connection to the effects of moving to lower poverty neighborhoods, and also confirm the theory that neighborhoods "expose" residents to certain conditions, and that the duration of that exposure also matters.[105] A major HUD-funded study of involving the Denver Housing Authority drew very similar findings.[106] Interestingly, researchers found that neighborhood effects measured as cumulative exposure were stronger than those measured at a particular point in time.[107]

Much of our civic and social life is neighborhood-based, not municipal-wide. Neighborhoods are where young children play and make friends, adults casually socialize, many social institutions are rooted, and community is built. Neighborhoods are also places where community members can act collectively to establish and enforce norms, organize events, and pool resources to address local problems ignored by municipal government. For example, they may raise money to sponsor a neighborhood sports team or parade float, undertake beautification projects, or organize festivals and other events.

Neighborhood associations, leagues, clubs, nonprofit organizations, and other community-based organizations tend to be rooted at the neighborhood level. These organizations help shape the connections between people, what social scientists call *social capital*.[108] A few decades ago, Robert Putnam famously argued that a decline in these forms of association diminished American social capital, inspiring the title of his book, *Bowling Alone*.[109] Although there is an unresolved debate about whether social capital is in decline or has simply morphed in the digital age, social capital plays a significant role in facilitating economic and social mobility. For example, the presence of mentors or coaches in a neighborhood has been found to be significant factor in child outcomes, especially for boys.[110]

One of the most important forms of social capital are peer networks. Adolescents in particular spend more time with peers than adults.[111] Peers shape outlook and aspirations, establish social norms, model and behavior and habits, such as use of technology and social media. High-achieving and motivated peers model and instill behaviors that reinforce upward mobility just as disaffected youth model and reinforce dysfunctional behavior in their social networks. Accordingly, studies have consistently demonstrated the effect of peer influence on educational achievement.[112] Although adolescent peer groups are not entirely neighborhood-based, peers in the neighborhood vicinity are likely to have a strong social influence.

The presence of nonprofit organizations, whether they are social clubs for adults, churches, and other religious institutions, or centers for youth recreation and socialization, play a major role in local communities and neighborhoods. These institutions connect people with each other, foster community and establish and reinforce behavioral expectations and norms. The sociologist Robert Sampson claims that collective action is concentrated "ecologically" and explained more by the density of community organizations than individual factors.[113] A more recent study estimates that every ten additional nonprofit organizations focusing on crime and community life in a city with 100,000 residents leads to a 9% reduction in the murder rate, a 6% reduction in the violent crime rate, and a 4% reduction in the property crime rate.[114]

More than any other level of geography, neighborhood characteristics shape safety and physical health. In addition to providing close access to parks and recreational space and activities, neighborhoods largely determine exposure to crime and violence. This is because a relatively small number of neighborhoods, known as "hot spots," concentrate violent crime based upon narrow social networks.[115] Residing in high-crime neighborhoods is a major cause of stress and anxiety, even trauma, with negative effects on physical and mental health.[116] Indeed, three-quarters of the MTO applicants told researchers that "getting away from gangs and drugs" were the first or second more important reason they signed up to participate.[117]

Drawing on the data made available from the Opportunity Atlas, a 2019 study of Chicago neighborhoods found that three factors were particularly important in shaping economic and social mobility: violence, incarceration, and lead exposure, dwarfing all other considerations.[118] These factors are rooted at the neighborhood level. Air and water pollution, particulate matter, smog and other toxins and industrial activity are also unevenly distributed across neighborhoods within the same municipal jurisdictions.

Economic Segregation

Because the opportunity structure is geographically organized, there is perhaps no more important force shaping access to opportunity than economic segregation. We observed how regional markets, municipal services, community wealth, and neighborhood conditions and characteristics enhance or impinge social and economic mobility. Inequalities of opportunity across each geographic layer makes economic segregation functionally equivalent to opportunity segregation, or the segregation of people from opportunity itself. Economic segregation situates people within the opportunity structure, either proximate to or more distantly from critical opportunity pathways.

Unfortunately, the geographic sorting of Americans by class has been intensifying in recent decades. Fifty years ago, most neighborhoods and communities were economically diverse. In 1970, 65% of Americans lived in middle-income neighborhoods, but by 2012, that share had fallen to 41%.[119] Living in either poor or affluent neighborhoods is now the norm.

There is evidence to suggest that this dynamic is driven by growing income inequality, economic polarization, and the decline of the middle class.[120] The middle class has been shrinking in the United States, especially relative to other wealthy countries.[121] For the first time in several generations, by 2015 more Americans were classified as either poor or affluent than middle class.[122] It makes intuitive and mathematical sense that the decline of the middle class would result in fewer middle-income or mixed-income neighborhoods.

But income inequality, by itself, does not produce income segregation. Affluent and poor people could live in the same mixed-income neighborhoods, if they so desired and if housing stock was sufficiently diverse to allow lower-income residents to reside there. Instead, Americans are sorting themselves (or being sorted) into more economically distinctive environments. A research report from 2012 found that economic segregation of upper- and lower-income households rose significantly in 27 of the nation's largest metropolitan regions since 1980. Specifically, the share of upper-income households living in majority upper-income neighborhoods doubled, to 18% in 2010 from 9% in 1980, and the share of low-income households living in poor neighborhoods rose to 28% from 23% in that same period.[123]

If widening income inequality and the decline of the middle class were entirely or mostly driving income segregation, then the share of lower-income and upper-income neighborhoods would likely balloon in size at the same pace and in proportion to the loss of residents from middle-income neighborhoods or decline in those neighborhoods. Instead, income segregation appears to be rising faster than income inequality.[124] According to a measure that controls for changes in income inequality, income segregation increased by about 29% from 1970 to 2009, much greater than the increase in the Gini coefficient in that period.[125]

Although there is evidence that the segregation of the affluent (who are selecting more consistently for upper-income neighborhoods) may be playing a key role in the increase in income segregation, income segregation appears to be occurring across the entire income distribution. Not only are all income segments more segregated from each other, but neighborhoods today are more economically uniform. Rather than income segregation sorting people toward two poles, which we would expect if income inequality and economic polarization were the only culprits, all neighborhoods are becoming more economically homogeneous and elaborately tiered within regions.[126] This is why economic segregation is more than simply polarization; it is neighborhood stratification.

Although income inequality and the shrinking middle class may be troubling developments in their own respects, rising economic segregation more directly undermines upward mobility and impedes access to opportunity.[127] The segregation and concentration of affluence and spatial separation from the poor and lower middle classes means that less-advantaged families are unlikely to benefit from investments made by the more affluent in public goods, including parks, local amenities, public services, and, perhaps most importantly, public schools.

Because most school districts are organized at the municipal level (the main exception being the south, where many districts are organized at the county level), regional economic segregation translates directly into educational inequality. Although some researchers find that spending on extracurricular activities and other educational supplements has held steady among more affluent parents, those parents are spending more of their income and wealth on moving into the "ideal neighborhood."[128]

The incentives for municipal competition reinforce growing stratification of resources and economic inequality between districts. As noted earlier, schools are one of the most important amenities purchased when seeking housing. Housing, properly understood, is a hub or conduit to a set of resources, among which public educational provision is among the most important.

The spatial segregation of the affluent from all other families not only denies those families the spillover benefits of higher-quality amenities and access to terrific public goods, but it also reduces the likelihood of professional, casual, or other informal social connections between them. This relates to the next force flowing across the geographic layers of the opportunity structure.

Social Networks

The adage "it's not what you know, but who you know" reflects the commonsense wisdom of the importance of social connections in accessing economic and social opportunities. But how do we become connected to the people we know, and what advantages do those connections confer? Within the opportunity structure, social networks reveal pathways of opportunity and facilitate movement along them by connecting people with helpful resources, assistance and insight, inspiring mentors and gatekeepers. Social networks are part of the opportunity structure, transmitting information and resources as well as shaping outlook and ambition.

One way to conceptualize the dynamics of social networks is to think in terms of high school cliques. These constellations of connections do more than simply define friendships, interests, and tastes, they establish norms, shape outlook, aspirations, and worldview, and ultimately influence decision-making. Some cliques are organized by an interest in theatre and the arts, as dramatized on the popular television show *Glee*, while others may be organized around athletics (also dramatized on the television program *Friday Night Lights*). Some cliques are large; some are small. Some are tightly woven, while others are loose and open. Some are marginal to school culture or community values, and others are more traditional or conformist. Some may be defined by interests or activities, and others may be defined by circumstance and chance.

Research shows that social networks play, digital and in the real-world, a major role in facilitating social and economic mobility. A landmark study of 21 billion Facebook relationships found that a greater share of friends with higher SES among individuals with low SES "is among the strongest predictors of upward income mobility identified to date."[129] Social networks are hugely influential.

To appreciate the connection between networks and upward mobility, consider the centrality of networks to the pursuit of job opportunities. Research demonstrates that most job opportunities are discovered through networks rather than formal job postings or responses to employment advertisements.[130] Between 70% and 80% of jobs are landed through networks, either by referral or by friends, relatives, and acquaintances informing interested applicants of the opportunity.[131] Employers rely heavily on referrals for many reasons, but in part because of they provide assurances regarding the requisite skills of the candidate.[132]

Henry Ford donated money to churches to foster close relationships between clergy and his recruiters, creating an employment network that functioned so that ministers could "prescreen" potential employees for reliability.[133] Today, alumni associations, social clubs, fraternal organizations, and religious orders disseminate information on employment opportunities to individuals who are members of these networks while also burnishing credentials to potential employers based on that membership.

Alumni associations in particular are organized for the purpose of transmitting such information by institutionalizing these channels.[134] Membership in Greek fraternities and sororities can also be a powerful source of information and opportunity, by drawing on strong social bonds to credential applicants and entice hiring managers.[135] Research shows that membership in fraternities may increase social capital even if it decreases academic performance marginally, with net positive effects on lifetime earnings.[136]

Social networks connect individuals and families with informational resources and expand the options individuals enjoy, but they also shade individual perceptions of opportunity, including the expected benefits of a particular decision. The opinions and views of an individual's local social network of family, neighbors, friends, kin, and formal institutions play an important role in providing information about an opportunity, evaluating the quality and merits of the opportunity, and shaping the perception of that information as it may relate to individual's aspirations and values.[137]

When choosing schools for their children, for example, parents may be influenced by the views of friends and extended family members regarding the quality or general perception of their options, or how commuting time or driving distance might burden members who could be responsible, in an emergency, for dropping off or picking up their children. They may be pressured, for that reason, to select lower-performing schools closer to home. Similarly, low-income individuals or first generation college students who may qualify for admission to elite private or flagship public universities may be dissuaded from applying or enrolling in those institutions, and pressured to remain close to home to help care for family members.[138] In contrast, affluent families often encourage their offspring to move away for college, to facilitate greater independence and self-discovery.

Decisions about fertility, educational attainment, or participation in illicit activities are shaped not simply by the actual opportunities that exist, but by the perceived set of available options and the valuation and weight given to those options. Peers, teachers, parents, coaches, and school counselors in high-opportunity environments may provide more inspiring examples and role models while also providing more encouragement for students to aspire and reach for more and a broader range of opportunities. If young adults, on the other hand, perceive few legitimate options for earning a living or making competitive wages, and readily observe successful illicit ones, they may be more inclined to follow that path.

An individual's perception about the risks and expected benefits of any particular life choice is shaped dramatically by local social networks, which include kin, neighbors, peers and friends, who tend to weigh in with their opinions, offer guidance, or otherwise express their views on such decisions. Because such decisions are consequential in terms of expanding or limited subsequent opportunities, the content of the information that flows through the social network is enormously significant.

Research shows, however, that it is not only the quality or content of the social network that matters, but the shape and architecture of ties within the network as well. The number and quality of linkages, the arrangement of ties, and the overall size, diversity or insularity of the network is also critically important.[139] The pattern of connections or ties among and between people matters as much as the composition of that network and the individuals that constitute it.[140]

In general, a larger and more diverse network is better. By definition, more information is transmitted in networks with more connections and more nodes. A larger network also tends to expose individuals to a wider variety of viewpoints, experiences, and opinions, especially if that larger network is diverse, including people from varying backgrounds, professions, and different walks of life. This can undermine groupthink and provide contrasting perspectives and divergent models of success. Insularity results in fewer known opportunities, but also more conformity regarding the value or potential of those opportunities.

However, larger networks also have disadvantages. In larger networks, more people may ultimately learn about and pursue the same job opportunities.[141] Diseases and social epidemics, such as retaliatory gang violence, may spread more widely in larger networks. But insularity is not protective either. Sexually transmitted diseases may spread faster and infect a greater portion of the network in insular contexts simply because smaller networks and thicker ties facilitate transmission celerity, even if rates of sexual activity are lower.[142]

Insular networks may occlude critical information and reinforce misinformation. High-achieving students from families unfamiliar with the college experience are more likely to assume that they will attend a community college and apply to non-selective colleges, often closer to home, than students from college-educated families. Remarkably, 30,000 first generation college students score in the top 10% on the SAT or ACT every year and yet do not attend selective schools, and nearly a quarter of such students who score in the top 25% never attend any college.[143] Seeking to explain this problem, one study found that first generation college students have only a "negligible probability of meeting a teacher, high school counselor, or schoolmate from an older cohort who herself attended a selective college."[144]

Network connections are also institutional. Universities and colleges cultivate relationships with the most promising pipelines and may overlook schools without a strong tradition of enrollment in their recruitment or scouting efforts. A study of 150 colleges and universities conducted in 2017 shows that they systematically send representatives to communities that are wealthier, and disproportionately visit private schools.[145] In these recruitment visits, the colleges share information to potential applicants about their programs. The study found, for example, that nearly half of such visits occurred in neighborhoods where families earned more than $100,000 per year, although only a third of households earn as much.

Because of network dynamics, many first-generation college students are less likely to know about financial aid packages or the quality or program offering differences between various institutions. Private schools, in particular, may have high sticker prices, but offer an array of discounts and aid packages for students from low-income families that may not be obvious at first glance. Unlike the large public schools or more distant elite private schools, many students from low-income families are unlikely to have heard of many smaller, high-quality private colleges. As a result, students who may qualify for either admissions or financial aid are less much less likely to apply than those who are better informed.[146]

The strength of ties within a network may be as important as its size or composition. Strong network connections can overwhelm differences of opinion. Membership in dense social networks with many reinforcing linkages may inadvertently narrow an individual's ambitions to those opportunities that are valued by the network, and suppress those that are ignored or undervalued by it. The social pressures of strong ties can lead to conformity and poor decision making. For example, dense local social networks with strong ties may pressure young boys join gangs, even as a defensive mechanism, which may foreclose or limit employment opportunities later in life if criminal behavior is detected. Weaker networks can provide the same information, but without the additional social pressure to conform. Social scientists call this the "strength of weak ties."[147]

Subsistence and other social support networks operate similarly. For poor individuals, social networks tend to ensure individual survival more than facilitate upward mobility.[148] These may provide a place to sleep or food in an emergency, with the expectation of reciprocity in the future. Yet, as Douglas Massey points out, such networks also have a leveling effect which undermines advancement, because any surplus material resource is under threat of being called upon from extended networks.[149] This happens when successful musicians or athletes "make it," and networks of acquaintances and extended relations call for loans, help, or other assistance.[150] Such networks provide a floor even if they impose a ceiling. The structure of the networks we inhabit and the behavior of people beyond our reach reverberate throughout our networks and touch our lives in many ways.

Family Matters

No model of human potential, structural or otherwise, would be complete without accounting for the role of the family and recognizing the importance of a nurturing and healthy home environment. The family plays a critical role in developing human potential, modeling success, generating and revealing pathways of opportunity, and encouraging and supporting its members along those pathways.

Until modern times, the extended family and kinship networks have long been a primary source for the generation of human capabilities and skill development. Primary school education was not widely available, free of charge, until the late 19th century.[151] But even parents without advanced formal educational instruction transmit language and culture to their children and instill many fundamental skills, including basic literacy, numeracy, and hygiene. Children may not always learn to read or write at home, but they often learn to recognize symbols (numbers and letters), colors, shapes, and the meaning of words.

Research suggests, nonetheless, that one of the most important predictors of educational performance and college matriculation is the educational attainment of parents, especially mothers.[152] Educated parents impart many important advantages. College-educated parents are more likely to read to their children every night. Before Kindergarten, middle-class children have a vocabulary triple the size of those raised by low-income single parents.[153] But parents with advanced education may be more likely, and successful, in encouraging their children to follow a similar pathway.

The advantage of a college-educated parent is structurally reinforced by university admissions policies that give an edge to the children of alumni. Preferences for legacy applicants and donors to university endowments are legal advantages that the wealthy and college educated may confer on their offspring.[154] Children of alumni may account for as much as 25% of the students at the top 100 universities.[155]

In modern America, where formal educational institutions are charged with developing critical life and marketable skills, the parental role may be less important in terms of direct instruction and development of advanced skills, and more significant in setting expectations and direction, modeling behavior and habits, and providing resources for enrichment. It is especially in the development of non-cognitive skills, such as patience, fortitude, grit, the ability to follow directions, and emotionally self-regulate, that the family plays a critical role.[156] Some research suggests that these skills may be more important to success than cognitive ability or relative intelligence, as traditionally assessed by measures like IQ.[157] Children who grow up chaotic environments or high-poverty neighborhoods are far less likely to develop these skills.

Parents not only form character and shape ambition, but a healthy family life is also critical to cognitive and emotional development. Chronic stress and emotional trauma have a devastating impact on human development. Yet, the opposite extreme can also be harmful to the development of these skills. Some families seek not only to insulate their children from unusual dangers, but to cocoon them from ordinary difficulties and hazards. What used to be described a generation ago as "overprotective parenting" has evolved into an array of disparaging types, such as "snowplow" and "bulldozer" parenting. These are parents who "clear the way for their children to get in to college, while shielding them from any of the difficulty, risk and potential disappointment of the process."[158] In terms of the pathway metaphor for conceptualizing opportunity, these parents do more than provide a wider and superior set of options for their offspring; they go so far as to ease their children along them. Although this looks like privilege in the short run, this can be detrimental if their children fail to develop the fortitude, confidence, or other skills needed to ascend further, beyond the parent's influence and control.

Beyond parenting styles, family wealth plays a critical role in the development of human capital and the pursuit of opportunity. Wealthy parents invest much more in their children than poorer ones.[159] Or, to invoke Richard Reeves memorable metaphor, "upper middle-class families have become greenhouses for the cultivation of human capital."[160] In the early 1970s, affluent families spent an average of $2,500 more per child than poor parents on enrichment activities.[161] By 2005, that gap grew to more than $7,500, and there is evidence that it is much larger today.[162]

Research shows that affluent parents are more likely than middle-income or lower-income parents to enroll their children in organized sports, music, dance, or art lessons.[163] These parents provide for extracurricular enrichment, including weekend and summer programs, including trips to museums, Kumon math tutoring, coding, and robotics camps.[164] These programs play an important role in building contextual knowledge and confidence in academic settings.

According to one estimate, a child born into an affluent family will have heard about 30 million more words by the age of three.[165] Children in affluent families are not only more likely to be read to, and are exposed to more books, but enjoy additional advantages, such as exposure to more varied and stimulating environments, travel, and a broader range of experiences.[166] Children raised under such conditions have a wider frame of reference, less discomfort in novel and unusual settings, and may have greater confidence engaging or questioning authority figures on substantive topics.[167]

Family wealth affords more than enrichment programs and extracurricular activities, but also school tuition fees, from pre-school onward. As of 2019, only 53% of four-year-old children whose families earn below the federal poverty line were enrolled in preschool compared with 76% of their counterparts with a family income at five times the poverty level (about $125,000 for a family of four).[168] An even greater income disparity in preschool enrollment is evident for three-year-olds in the United States.[169]

At the other end of the educational cycle, college is increasingly unaffordable, and young adults need financial support and encouragement to pursue it. Parental assistance with college tuition statistically correlates with college attendance and completion.[170] In 2016, 67% of high school graduates from low-income families immediately transitioned to college, compared with 83% of graduates from high-income families.[171] Of the 46% of millennials who pursued college or post-secondary education, over 60% received helped from their parents.[172]

Individuals are less likely to attend college, and less likely to attend elite universities, if they cannot afford it or would take on greater debt. This explains a growing achievement gap between high-income and low-income families since 1960.[173] College completion for households in the top quarter of the income distribution rose between 1970 and 2013 from 40% to

77%.[174] In contrast, only about 8% of children born in bottom quartile of income bracket graduate college.[175] This is a tenfold disparity, and it persists even when controlling for academic aptitude. Another study found that high-SES students who scored in the bottom quarter of test takers on an 8th grade test were more likely to earn a college degree than low-SES students who scored in the top quarter on the same test.[176]

Using private records, researchers have now calculated the socioeconomic distribution of student bodies with greater precision than ever before. In a sampling of 38 colleges in America, including five in the Ivy League, more students came from the top 1% of the income scale than from the entire bottom 60%.[177]

Family wealth and income play an outsized role in the pursuit of higher education broadly, not just tuition fees and living costs. Affluent parents buy access to the best primary and secondary schools, as well as niche extracurricular activities and expensive elite sports, like polo or sailing, that stand out on a college application. These parents also afford test prep courses, application consultants, and leverage their social networks to generate stand-out letters of recommendations.

In addition to these advantages, SAT scores correlate with greater strength with grandparent wealth than any other identified factor.[178] In fact, one study found that moving up every income decile was associated with a 12 point average increase in SAT performance.[179] A close examination of applicants to the University of California system found that the relationship between family income and standardized test scores was three times as strong as the relationship between family income and high school grade point averages.[180]

The opportunity advantages afforded by family wealth extend well beyond higher education. Affluent parents are not only more likely to help with college tuition, but also help with a down payment on a house or security deposit on an apartment.[181] Forty percent of young adults in their early twenties receive financial assistance from their family for rent.[182] Gifts, loans, and inheritances from family members may also be used to capitalize business enterprises. Donald Trump famously received a $1 million loan from his father, helping jump start his own foray into real estate.[183] Jeff Bezos' parents gifted him more than a quarter of a million dollars to capitalize Amazon in 1995.[184]

Financial support for offspring in early adulthood has risen significantly among the general population since the early 1980s, but even more so among affluent families.[185] Young adults with parents in the top quartile of the income distribution received seven times the amount of financial assistance as young adults whose parents were in the bottom quartile.[186]

As important as the family is as a conduit of resources that inculcate human capital and open access to opportunity for individuals, the family itself is also a structural formation that shapes the distribution of opportunity more broadly. Researchers tracking families since the 1960s have found that family structure affects economic mobility, and that children from two-parent households enjoy higher rates of upward mobility.[187] More recently, large data studies of upward mobility have identified the presence of single-parent households as the single strongest correlate of lower economic mobility.[188] This research, however, is easily misconstrued.

There are undeniable disadvantages to growing up in a single-parent household, including less total parenting time to help with homework and provide emotional support, and higher rates of household poverty.[189] But family structure in relation to economic upward mobility is not, according to the latest research, statistically significant at the individual or family level. The critical factor is not whether a child grows up in a single parent household, but rather the fraction of single-parent households in the *neighborhood*.[190] Children raised in single-parent households residing dual-parent neighborhoods appear to do as well as their neighbors. What matters is the prevailing family structure of the community.

As of 2012, 41% of children in the United States are born to unmarried parents, and nearly a quarter of American children live in single-parent households, a historic high.[191] Some researchers even partly attribute widening economic inequality to the decline in marriage rates and family formation since the 1960s.[192] But the solution is more complicated than simply urging low-income people to get married.

Poverty itself plays a role in discouraging marriage. A major study conducted in 2013 found that low wages and job insecurity were the primary reasons for declining rates of marriage and rise of single-parent households.[193] Rather than the "foundation" of life, many young adults view marriage as the "capstone," which can be achieved only after completing education and finding career and financial stability.[194]

Relatedly, one of the most significant trends for the reproduction of class advantages is "assortative mating."[195] In the United States, people are now more likely to marry people with similar educational attainments. One of the reasons for this appears to be that Americans are marrying later, and therefore more likely to meet their spouses at work. This means that marriage now bears significant network effects. While dating pools have always been shaped by social networks, especially through families, religious institutions, and educational environments, the segregation of people occupationally and economically means that assortative mating by income and education is now more pronounced. Therefore, the advantages of marriage scale for parents with higher incomes, and are fewer for low-income households. In fact, there is evidence that marriage can depress women's earnings.[196] For low-income women, marriage may result in fewer resources for offspring, by diverting resources from children to struggling men.[197]

Geographic Mobility

Having canvassed the contemporary opportunity structure, the critical layers within that structure, and the forces that facilitate flows across those layers, we might expect that a society with a high degree of economic and social mobility would also exhibit high levels of geographic mobility, and a society with low levels of geographic mobility would have lower rates of upward mobility. After all, if opportunity is shaped by regional macroeconomic conditions as well as municipal and neighborhood geographies, then we would expect families like Chris Marten's to make similar moves—across jurisdictional boundaries—just as we would expect individuals to move across state lines in search of opportunity. As the pathway metaphor suggests, opportunity is not only about the existence of opportunities—it is about the freedom to pursue and the capacity to seize them.

Historically, the United States has been one of the most geographically mobile countries in the world.[198] Americans regularly moved to areas and regions where jobs were abundant and wages attractive. During the 20th century, the automotive industry lured hundreds of thousands of migrants to the upper Midwest from rural Appalachia and impoverished regions of the Deep South. The labor mobilization of World War II drew more workers to factories, ports and shipyards. After World War II, labor migration accelerated further as veterans resettled and post-war industries (and air conditioning) drew families to new housing developments in the arid Southwest.

In the 1950s and 1960s, roughly 20% of Americans moved every year. By 1970, a quarter of Americans lived in a different place than where they were born, up from 15% in 1940.[199] Since then, labor mobility and internal migration entered what some economists call a "period of continuous decline."[200] Table 1.1 tells the tale.

By 2001, overall geographic mobility slipped below 15%. Two decades later, the Census Bureau reported that just 8.4% of Americans moved the preceding year, the lowest rate of geography mobility since the Bureau began tracking moves in 1948.[202] Rates of interstate mobility, although smaller than overall migration, follow this pattern as well.[203] The share of Americans moving to a different state or county has fallen by half since 2001 alone, from 2.8% to 1.4%.

One possible explanation for this pattern is longer life expectancies and an aging population. Older people may be less inclined to move, for a variety

Table 1.1 Geographic Mobility, 1951–2021[201]

Year	1951	1961	1971	1981	1991	2001	2011	2021
All moves (% of households per year)	19.1%	20.6%	18.7%	17.2%	17%	14.2%	11.6%	8.4%
Moves: different county, same state	3.6%	3.1%	3.1%	3.4%	3.2%	2.7%	1.9%	1.9%
Moves: different state	3.5%	3.2%	3.4%	2.8%	2.9%	2.8%	1.6%	1.4%

of reasons, including deeper community roots and social and family obligations.[204] Conversely, young adults heading to college, just entering the labor market, or making critical early career decisions may be more inclined or capable of relocating a greater distance. Yet, this theory does not to explain the data. Although young adults have the highest rates of geographic mobility, around 20% as of 2019, they are also far less mobile than young people of previous decades. Since the 1980s alone, mobility among young adults dropped more than 40%.[205]

Rather, this worrisome trend of declining geographic mobility appears to relate to mounting barriers to the pursuit of opportunity. Job prospects encourage geographic mobility. The 2018–2019 Census Population Survey found that the most common reason people move to a different county or state was a job opportunity.[206] In another national survey, 44% of workers said they would move for a job.[207] But only 32% of employers said they would pay to relocate an employee, most likely highly skilled professionals or college graduates.[208] Most workers must pay their own freight. Unsurprisingly, these surveys show that the top impediment to relocating is the higher cost of living in job-rich places.

The places in the United States with the combination of highest wages and most job growth tend to be the most expensive, epitomized by cities like San Francisco, Seattle, Boston, and New York. This pattern of high-cost/high-opportunity communities and low-cost/low-opportunity communities appears to be general, true of neighborhoods within cities, cities within regions, and between states themselves.

Another piece of evidence in support of the view that declining geographic mobility is largely a consequence of the fact that high-opportunity places today are prohibitively expensive is the differential rates of mobility based upon educational attainment. Geographic mobility has slowed at all income levels in recent decades, but people with the lowest levels of education had the lowest rates of interstate mobility while those with a college degree were more than twice as high.[209] Today, only the most highly educated workers have the income prospects to afford the high cost of living in these places.

In California, median rents escalated beyond what most low-income families can afford without subsidy or rent protection, and home prices are about 40% more expensive in California than the 35 lowest-cost states.[210] From 2010 to 2019, 6.2 million people left California for other states. This apparent "exodus," however, masks the fact that California is also one of the highest receiving states of people moving out of other states, about 4.9 million people in the same time frame. This paradox is explained by the fact that California is a magnet for college graduates and high-skilled workers with its booming job market and high pay, but the cost of living has driven many low- and middle-income people out of state.[211] Most of California's emigrants moved to low-cost states.

The economist Tyler Cowan predicted that states like Texas may be the future, not because they hold the nation's leading industries or sectors or serve as engines for upward mobility, but because they have abundant cheap housing

The Structure of Opportunity 41

and lower overall costs of living.²¹² The trade-off is that the lower-cost states have lower wages, worse schools, and fewer public services.²¹³ Texas has no income tax, but it has a lower minimum wage and more affordable housing.

Although it may seem logical if not inevitable in economic terms that places with the most jobs and best wages would have the most housing demand, and therefore the tightest housing markets and highest costs of living, this has not always been the case. Since at least the middle of the 19th century, America consistently drew workers to higher growth places, creating "boom-towns."²¹⁴ Today, communities with the highest economic growth have much slower population growth.²¹⁵

The wage gains associated with relocating need to offset the higher costs of housing. But economists have also observed that wage gains associated with mobility have largely dissipated for low-skilled workers due to a variety of factors, such as standardized wage scales for large employers like Wal-Mart and Amazon.²¹⁶ This also undermines the incentives to relocate to higher-opportunity regions or states.

Even if higher opportunity areas have fewer good paying jobs for low-skilled workers than they did a generation or two ago, such regions may still be much better places to live. They have higher minimum and wage scales, stronger public services, infrastructure and schools, and more attractive amenities, features which don't necessarily appear in wage reports or apartment listings. Moreover, high-growth regions may have more jobs, making it easier to find and remain employed and build work experience or change jobs, in a pinch.

The problem is not just inequality of opportunity; it is that the geographic concentration of opportunity is becoming more intense, and the stratification of place is becoming more fine grain and elaborately tiered. This is happening in a way such that even if public investments were equalized, vastly unequal private resources structure unequal opportunity and outcomes.

The traditional American conception of opportunity as largely the product of individual initiative and hard work is partly a product of the historical experience of a settler society with a frontier mentality, where the key resources to advancement were fertile land and cheap labor. In a skill-based knowledge economy, opportunity is largely a product of investments in human capabilities. Social institutions, networks, and larger economic realities all play an outsized role, and increasingly so. The fact that per couple expenditures on children have risen dramatically and continue to rise is indicative of the kinds of investments that are required not merely to succeed in the modern world, but to stay in the game.

***

The key concept in this chapter is the opportunity structure. Like a Plinko game with pegs, chutes, and valves, the opportunity structure is a complex arrangement of components that constrain or facilitate our ability to reach a desired destination. It defines both the range of possible destinations as well as the pathways that connect us to those destinations. Our starting position or location within that structure may not strictly foreclose a possible destination, but it may render it improbable, channeling us in other directions. This, in turn, shapes our aspirations and ambitions.

Although we may not generally talk or even think about opportunity in this way, many of our most significant life decisions reflect an intuitive appreciation that we each inhabit structures which influence our destinies and shape our life chances. After all, when Americans describe their country as the "land of opportunity," move to a better school district or for a job, or aspire to qualify for admissions at a more selective university, these characterizations, moves, or aspirations are based upon assumptions that different places and institutions afford different opportunities and possible rewards.

The important point is that individual life chances are shaped as much, if not more, by the opportunity structure than innate individual characteristics. This is not because individual decisions, traits, capabilities, or habits don't matter. Rather, they are shaped by our environment and the perceived payoff from critical life choices. In that way, the capacities and talents we develop, the burdens we carry, and the choices we make in life cannot be disentangled from the structures we inhabit. Unfortunately, as we will now see, the opportunity structure also has a startling racial dimension, which dramatically shapes the life chances of people by race, and which is essence of structural racism.

Notes

1. "Our Mascot: The Golden Bear," Upper Arlington Historical Society, accessed September 3, 2024, https://uahistorytrail.upperarlingtonoh.gov/our-mascot-the-golden-bear/.
2. The real names of the individuals presented in the vignettes that open this and other chapters have been changed to protect their privacy.
3. Estimate of 15–20% premium for the same home in the suburbs. Robert McMunn, "School Busing Cited in Home Price Rises," *CD Publications*, December 2, 1980.
4. In 2015, Upper Arlington was ranked the third-best public school district in the entire State of Ohio. "2016 Best Public High Schools in Ohio," Niche, archived May 28, 2016, at the Wayback Machine, https://web.archive.org/web/20160528132422/https://k12.niche.com/rankings/public-high-schools/best-overall/s/ohio/, & 36th-best public high school in the nation "America's Best High Schools: Student Body," Best Colleges, archived July 24, 2015, at the Wayback Machine, https://web.archive.org/web/20150724221912/https://www.bestcolleges.com/features/best-high-schools-in-america/.
5. Isabel V. Sawhill, "Still the Land of Opportunity?," *Brookings*, March 1, 1999, https://www.brookings.edu/articles/still-the-land-of-opportunity/.
6. See, for example, Barack Obama, "Remarks by the President on the Economy in Osawatomie, Kansas," *White House President Barack Obama*, December 6, 2011, https://obamawhitehouse.archives.gov/the-press-office/2011/12/06/remarks-president-economy-osawatomie-kansas ("Over the last few decades, the rungs on the ladder of opportunity have grown farther and farther apart").
7. Raj Chetty et al., "Is the United States Still A Land of Opportunity?: Recent Trends in Intergenerational Mobility," *American Economic Review, American Economic Association* 104, no. 5 (2014): 141–147, https://ideas.repec.org/a/aea/aecrev/v104y2014i5p141-47.html. ("A useful visual analogy … is to envision the income distribution as a ladder, with each percentile representing a different rung. The rungs of the ladder have grown further apart (inequality has

increased), but children's chances of climbing from lower to higher rungs have not changed (rank-based mobility has remained stable)").

8 The prevalence of mobility metaphors is perhaps more than a byproduct of the centrality of economic and social mobility to our deepest national values, but also the fact the "journey" metaphor is a root metaphor in human language and thinking. See George Lakoff and Mark Johnson, *Metaphors We Live By* (Chicago: University of Chicago Press, 2003), 46, 104.

9 Abraham Lincoln, "July 4, 1861: July 4th Message to Congress," *Miller Center of Public Affairs*, July 4, 1861, https://millercenter.org/the-presidency/presidential-speeches/july-4-1861-july-4th-message-congress.

10 Opportunity as a range of pathways is a richly textured metaphor that suggests options available to individuals to choose among, varying accessibility or visibility of those options, as well as the possibility of hazards and challenges associated with movement or advancement along those pathways. For these reasons, the root pathway metaphor has many interesting elaborations in popular parlance and in the opportunity literature. Some people have a clear path, while others have a "rough road." Some follow footsteps, and others are trail blazers. Some avenues are clearly labeled and well kept, and others are harder to see let alone follow. As an illustration of the richness of the metaphor and the insights that can be gleaned from it, see Timothy Smeeding, "Gates, Gaps, and Intergenerational Mobility," in *The Dynamics of Opportunity in America: Evidence and Perspectives*, eds. Henry Braun and Irwin Kirsch (Switzerland: Springer, 2016), 3 (employing a "gates, gaps, and gradients" elaboration on the pathway metaphor. A gradient can be quite steep, which suggests how difficult some pathways are to travel. And "gates" and "gaps" are two quite different types of obstacles or barriers along pathways.)

11 Muriel Strode, "Miscellaneous: Wind-Wafted Wild Flowers," *Open Court, a Quarterly Magazine* 17, no. 567 (1903): 505.

12 Malcolm Gladwell, *Outliers: The Story of Success* (New York: Little, Brown and Company, 2008). This book renders visible many of the invisible forces that shape opportunity, including historical contexts and unique opportunities to develop critical skillsets.

13 Doris Kearns Goodwin, *Team of Rivals: The Political Genius of Abraham Lincoln* (New York: Simon & Schuster, 2005), 90.

14 Goodwin, *Team of Rivals*, 90.

15 This idea is partly captured by the "capabilities approach" to human development pioneered and refined by Amartya Sen and Martha Nussbaum. Amartya K. Sen, "Poor, Relatively Speaking," *Oxford Economic Papers* 35, no. 2 (1983): 153–169; Martha C. Nussbaum, *Creating Capabilities: The Human Development Approach* (Cambridge, MA: Belknap Press of Harvard University Press, 2011). In a very simple sense, a "capability" is a skill, freedom, or developed ability that allows individuals to accomplish some task or pursue some goal.

16 In another sense, the pathways themselves, such as access to a good education, build these human capacities or skills, and thereby open up new pathways, just as an experienced hiker is able to pursue successively difficult trails as a result of those experiences. See Henry Braun, "The Dynamics of Opportunity in America: A Working Framework," in Braun and Kirsch, *Dynamics of Opportunity*, 3 (defining opportunity similarly but more narrowly than this book "as pathways to the development of human and social capital").

17 Theodore W. Schultz, "Investment in Human Capital," *American Economic Review* 51, no. 1 (1961): 1–17, https://www.jstor.org/stable/1818907; Gary Becker, *Human Capital: A Theoretical and Empirical Analysis, with Special Reference to Education* (Chicago: University of Chicago Press, 1964); Claudia Goldin, "Human Capital" in *Handbook of Cliometrics*, eds. Claude Diebolt and Michael Haupert (Heidelberg, Germany: Springer Verlag, 2016), https://scholar.harvard.

edu/files/goldin/files/goldin_human_capital.pdf. Because of its widespread use and easily understood meaning, this book frequently employs this term despite valid concerns that it is reductive and dehumanizing. See, for example, Branko Milanovic, "Junk the Phrase 'Human Capital'," *Al Jazeera America*, February 13, 2015, https://america.aljazeera.com/opinions/2015/2/junk-the-phrase-human-capital.html. The idea of "capabilities," developed by Sen and Nussbaum, covers much of the same conceptual territory.

18 Jencks and Tach distinguish between "equal opportunity" and "equal educational opportunity" or "equal developmental opportunity." See Christopher Jencks and Laura Tach, "Would Equal Opportunity Mean More Mobility?" in *Mobility and Inequality: Frontiers of Research from Sociology and Economics*, eds. Stephen L. Morgan, David B. Grusky, and Gary S. Fields (Stanford, CA: Stanford University Press, 2006). This book uses the term "opportunity" expansively to encompass each of these ideas, but the opportunity structure concept developed in this chapter corresponds most closely to the idea of developmental opportunity.

19 Juliana Menasce Horowitz, Ruth Igielnik, and Rakesh Kochhar, "Trends in income and wealth inequality," (Washington, DC: Pew Research Center, January 2020): https://www.pewresearch.org/social-trends/2020/01/09/trends-in-income-and-wealth-inequality.

20 World Bank, "GINI Index for the United States," *FRED, Federal Reserve Bank of St. Louis*, accessed July 23, 2024, https://fred.stlouisfed.org/series/SIPOVGINIUSA (from 34.7 in 1980 to 41.5 in 2019).

21 Emmanuel Saez, "Striking it Richer: The Evolution of Top Incomes in the United States (Updated with 2022 Estimates)," *Emmanuel Saez*, March 2024, https://eml.berkeley.edu/~saez/saez-UStopincomes-2022.pdf.

22 Ana Hernández Kent and Lowell R. Ricketts, "The State of U.S. Wealth Inequality," *Federal Reserve Bank of St. Louis*, May 3, 2024, https://www.stlouisfed.org/institute-for-economic-equity/the-state-of-us-wealth-inequality; "Top 10% net personal wealth share," World Inequality Database, accessed August 15, 2024, https://wid.world/world/#shweal_p90p100_z/US;FR;DE;CN;ZA;GB;WO/last/eu/k/p/yearly/s/false/38.656/100/curve/false/country (estimating the top 10% share to be 67% and 70.7%, respectively).

23 Notable books on this topic include Thomas Piketty, *Capital in the Twenty-First Century*, trans. Arthur Goldhammer (Cambridge, MA: Belknap Press of Harvard University Press, 2014); Joseph Stiglitz, *The Price of Inequality: How Today's Divided Society Endangers Our Future* (New York: W. W. Norton, 2013); Kate Pickett and Richard Wilkinson, *The Spirit Level: Why Greater Equality Makes Societies Stronger* (New York: Bloomsbury Press, 2009); Tyler Cowan, *Average is Over: Powering America Beyond the Age of the Great Stagnation* (New York: Penguin Group, 2013); Robert B. Reich, *Saving Capitalism: For the Many, Not the Few* (New York: Alfred A. Knopf, 2015); Thomas M. Shapiro, *Toxic Inequality: How America's Wealth Gap Destroys Mobility, Deepens the Racial Divide, and Threatens Our Future* (New York: Basic Books, 2017).

24 And vice versa: "[I]nequality of opportunity may harm economic growth because it hinders human capital accumulation by low-income individuals. Moreover, perceptions of unequal opportunities, which affect individual aspirations, may also reduce investments in human capital." Shekhar Aiyar and Christian Ebeke, "Inequality of Opportunity, Inequality of Income and Economic Growth" (working paper, International Monetary Fund, 2019), 4, https://www.imf.org/en/Publications/WP/Issues/2019/02/15/Inequality-of-Opportunity-Inequality-of-Income-and-Economic-Growth-46566.

25 See, for example, David Brooks, "The Inequality Problem," *New York Times*, January 16, 2015, https://www.nytimes.com/2014/01/17/opinion/brooks-the-inequality-problem.html.

26 The phrase itself is generally attributed to a popular book published in 1931: James Truslow Adams, *The Epic of America* (New York: Routledge, 2017), 404. Adams defined it as "that dream of a land in which life should be better and richer and fuller for everyone, with opportunity for each according to ability or achievement." Jonas Clark, "In Search of the American Dream," *Atlantic*, June 2007, https://www.theatlantic.com/magazine/archive/2007/06/in-search-of-the-american-dream/305921/. From a wider lens, the "American Dream" is a multi-faceted concept with different areas of potential emphasis. See Cal Jillson, *Pursuing the American Dream: Opportunity and Exclusion Over Four Centuries* (Lawrence: University Press of Kansas, 2004), xi–xv.

27 Rachel Wolfe, "The American Dream Feels Out of Reach for Most," *Wall Street Journal*, August 28, 2024, https://www.wsj.com/economy/consumers/american-dream-poll-us-economy-e5ddf640; Aaron Zitner, "Voters See American Dream Slipping Out of Reach, WSJ/NORC Poll Shows," *Wall Street Journal*, November 24, 2023, https://www.wsj.com/us-news/american-dream-out-of-reach-poll-3b774892.

28 Gabriel Borelli, "Americans are split over the state of the American dream," *Pew Research Center*, July 2, 2024, https://www.pewresearch.org/short-reads/2024/07/02/americans-are-split-over-the-state-of-the-american-dream/.

29 Jared Sousa, "American dream far from reality for most people: POLL," *ABC News*, January 15, 2024, https://abcnews.go.com/Politics/american-dream-reality-people-poll/story?id=106339566.

30 See, for example, Prudence L. Carter and Kevin G. Welner, *Closing the Opportunity Gap: What America Must Do to Give Every Child an Even Chance*, eds. Prudence L. Carter and Kevin G. Welner (New York: Oxford University Press, 2013).

31 Jonathan D. Fisher and David S. Johnson, "Inequality and Mobility over the Past Half-Century Using Income, Consumption, and Wealth," in *Measuring Distribution and Mobility of Income and Wealth*, ed. Raj Chetty et al. (Chicago: University of Chicago Press, 2022), 437–455; Tom Hertz, "Understanding Mobility in America," *Center for American Progress*, April 26, 2006, https://cdn.americanprogress.org/wp-content/uploads/issues/2006/04/Hertz_MobilityAnalysis.pdf?_ga=2.261835341.178104652.1614126095-351619165.1614126095.

32 Typically, these measures are divided into two terms: "Absolute" mobility refers to improvements in income earnings for adults compared to their parents at the same age, adjusted for inflation, whereas "relative" mobility compares the income of parents within the income distribution to where their children end up within that distribution as adults, in percentile terms. Sean McElwee, "Absolute and Relative Mobility, A Short Primer," *Demos*, January 23, 2014, https://www.demos.org/blog/1/23/14/absolute-and-relative-mobility-short-primer. To assess the degree of opportunity within a society or the reality of the "American Dream," relative economic mobility is our principal interest. Absolute mobility may be one gauge of a healthy society, but this can exist even if relative economic mobility is low. A growing economy should generate larger per capita incomes over time, such that many children should earn more than their parents, even adjusted for inflation. High relative mobility, on the other hand, can only occur when children from the lower rungs of the income distribution have a good chance of climbing to the upper rungs.

33 The assumption that talents are distributed evenly across the income distribution is a big assumption because "winners" from previous rounds of economic competition may have endowments or traits that they naturally pass to their offspring, not just through human capital investments and structural supports. See Fishkin, Bottlenecks 1C.1, "*The problem of the family*," 48–56 (presenting the "warrior family" thought experiment, a scenario where families readily and advantageously transmit acquired skills to a degree unavailable to others.) If these traits are entirely inherited, however, then the ideals of the American Dream and

upward mobility are fantasy. The best available data does not appear to support either assumption, for reasons explained later in this chapter.

34 Raj Chetty et al., "Where is the Land of Opportunity? The Geography of Intergenerational Mobility in the United States," *Quarterly Journal of Economics* 129, no. 4 (2014): 1553–1623. Notably, this figure lands precisely between two figures generated by two other studies conducted by the Brookings Institution and Pew Charitable Trusts, which pegged this figure at 10% and 4%, respectively. Richard V. Reeves, "Saving Horatio Alger: Equality, Opportunity, and the American Dream," *Brookings*, August 20, 2014, https://csweb.brookings.edu/content/research/essays/2014/saving-horatio-alger.html#; Susan Urahn et al., *Pursuing the American Dream: Economic Mobility Across Generations* (Philadelphia: Pew Charitable Trusts, 2012), https://www.pewtrusts.org/~/media/legacy/uploadedfiles/wwwpewtrustsorg/reports/economic_mobility/pursuingamericandreampdf.pdf. These studies relied upon two different data sources, the Panel Survey of Income Dynamics (PSID) and the U.S. Department of Labor's National Longitudinal Survey (NLS). See *National Longitudinal Surveys* (Washington, DC: National Bureau of Labor Statistics, 2022), https://www.nlsinfo.org/. See also Katherine A. McGonagle et al., "The Panel Study of Income Dynamics: Overview, Recent Innovations, and Potential for Life Course Research," *Longitudinal and Life Course Studies* 3, no. 2 (2012), https://psidonline.isr.umich.edu/. In contrast, Chetty et al. get their data from de-identified tax records, which is more accurate since the data set covers the entire population, not a sample survey like the PSID or NLS.
35 Chetty et al., "Where is the Land," 1577.
36 Joe Pinsker, "America Is Even Less Socially Mobile Than Most Economists Thought," *Atlantic*, July 23, 2015, https://www.theatlantic.com/business/archive/2015/07/america-social-mobility-parents-income/399311/.
37 Shai Davidai and Thomas Gilovich, "Building a More Mobile America—One Income Quintile at a Time," *Perspectives on Psychological Science* 10, no. 1 (2015): 60–71, https://cpb-us-e1.wpmucdn.com/blogs.cornell.edu/dist/b/6819/files/2019/12/Davidai-Gilo-PPS-2015.pdf.
38 Chetty et al., "Still a Land of Opportunity?," 145. ("For instance, the probability of reaching the top quintile conditional on coming from the bottom quintile of parental income is 8.4 percent in 1971 and 9 percent in 1986.")
39 Terence Ball, Richard Dagger, and Daniel I. O'Neill, *Ideals and Ideologies: A Reader*, 9th ed. (London: Routledge, 2016), 128.
40 Raj Chetty, et al., "The Fading American Dream: Trends in Absolute Income Mobility Since 1940" *Science* 356, no. 6336 (2017): 398–406.
41 David Leonhardt, "The American Dream, Quantified at Last," *New York Times*, December 8, 2016, https://www.nytimes.com/2016/12/08/opinion/the-american-dream-quantified-at-last.html; Andrew Ross Sorkin and Megan Thee-Brenan, "Many Feel the American Dream Is Out of Reach, Poll Shows," *New York Times*, December 10, 2014, https://dealbook.nytimes.com/2014/12/10/many-feel-the-american-dream-is-out-of-reach-poll-shows/ (finding that 45% of respondents felt that our economy was unfair).
42 Chetty et al., "Where is the Land," 1554.
43 Chetty et al., 1556. See also Raj Chetty et al., "The Opportunity Atlas: Mapping the Childhood Roots of Social Mobility," (working paper, National Bureau of Economic Research, 2020): 1–58, https://www.nber.org/papers/w25147;
44 "The Best and Worst Places to Grow Up: How Your Area Compares," *Upshot*, May 14, 2015, https://www.nytimes.com/interactive/2015/05/03/upshot/the-best-and-worst-places-to-grow-up-how-your-area-compares.html.
45 Raj Chetty et al., "The Opportunity Atlas," Opportunity Atlas, https://www.opportunityatlas.org/.
46 Chetty et al., "Where is the Land," 1602. See also Raj Chetty, Nathaniel Hendren, and Lawrence F. Katz, "The Effects of Exposure to Better Neighborhoods on

Children: New Evidence from the Moving to Opportunity Experiment," *American Economic Review* 106, no. 4 (2016): 855–902.
47 See Joseph Fishkin, *Bottlenecks: A New Theory of Equal Opportunity* (New York: Oxford University Press, 2014), 2–3, 130 ("The opportunity structure in any real society is vast and complex. It is an intricate lattice of forking and intersecting paths, leading to different educational experiences and credentials, different jobs and professions, different roles in families and communities, and different goods of intrinsic or instrumental value.").
48 See George Galster, *An Econometric Model of the Urban Opportunity Structure: Cumulative Causation Among City Markets, Social Problems, and Underserved Areas* (Washington, DC: Fannie Mae Foundation, 1998), V.
49 Opportunity is both exogenous and constitutive – it influences our behavior as well as shapes our sense of self. See Fishkin, *Bottlenecks*, 182 (describing opportunity structures as a playing field that shapes the player); George Galster, *Making Our Neighborhoods, Making Ourselves* (Chicago: University of Chicago Press, 2019) (arguing that our environments also shape our sense of self and identities). See also Charles M. Blow, "Black Lives and Books of the Dead," *New York Times*, July 9, 2015, https://www.nytimes.com/2015/07/09/opinion/charles-m-blow-black-lives-and-books-of-the-dead.html. ("The more nuanced and sophisticated position is that personal choices are made within a social construct, and that construct is heavily influenced by oppressive forces — interpersonal biases, structural inequities, aversion to otherness.")
50 Some research on fertility suggests that young women in low-opportunity environments, for example, find self-esteem and attention in becoming mothers, even if a decision to have children too young impacts their education or career trajectory. See, for example, Susan B. Crockenberg and Barbara A. Soby, "Self-Esteem and Teenage Pregnancy," in *The Social Importance of Self-Esteem* (Berkeley: University of California Press, 1989) (a classic study on the relationship between teenage pregnancy, limited opportunity, and self-esteem); Lindsey Howald, "Sociology Professor Delves Into Why Poor Women Find Redemption in Having a Baby," *Columbia Daily Tribune*, April 3, 2009, https://www.columbiatribune.com/article/20090403/Lifestyle/304039648.
51 William Julius Wilson describes these behaviors as "cultural responses to constraints and limited opportunities." See William Julius Wilson, *When Work Disappears: The World of the New Urban Poor* (New York: Vintage Books, 1996), xviii. Similarly, Fishkin refers to these as "adaptive preferences" to limited opportunities. Fishkin, *Bottlenecks*, 143.
52 Trevor Noah, *Born a Crime: Stories from a South African Childhood* (New York: One World, 2016), 209.
53 Wilson, *When Work Disappears*, 22.
54 George C. Galster, "Urban Opportunity Structure and Racial/Ethnic Polarization," in *Research on Schools, Neighborhoods, and Communities: Toward Civic Responsibility*, ed. William F. Tate IV (Lanham, MD: Rowman and Littlefield, 2012), 47–66.
55 See Roithmayr, *Reproducing Racism*, 16 (which makes the point that, life choices that may seem counterproductive to an outside observer may in fact be entirely rational in a context of limited opportunities).
56 Ken Roberts, "The Entry into Employment: An Approach Toward A General Theory," *Sociological Review* 16, no. 2 (1968): 165–184.
57 Peter K. Eisinger, "The Conditions of Protest Behavior in American Cities," *American Political Science Review* 67, no. 1 (1973): 11–28, https://doi.org/10.2307/1958525. For a more recent review of how this concept has evolved in that context, see Marco Giugni, "Political Opportunities: From Tilly to

Tilly," *Swiss Political Science Review* 15, no. 2: 361–368 (2009), https://doi.org/10.1002/j.1662-6370.2009.tb00136.x.
58 George C. Galster and Sean P. Killen, "The Geography of Metropolitan Opportunity: A Reconnaissance and Conceptual Framework," *Housing Policy Debate* 6, no. 1 (1995): 7–43. See also George C. Galster, "Polarization, Place, and Race," *North Carolina Law Review* 71, no. 5 (1993): 1421–1422.
59 Timothy Noah, "Stay Put, Young Man," *Washington Monthly*, November 2013, https://washingtonmonthly.com/magazine/novdec-2013/stay-put-young-man/.
60 D'Vera Cohn and Rich Morin, *American Mobility: Who Moves? Who Stays Put? Where's Home?* (Washington, DC: Pew Research Center, Social & Demographic Trends, 2008), https://www.pewresearch.org/wp-content/uploads/sites/3/2010/10/Movers-and-Stayers.pdf.
61 Chetty et al., "Where is the Land," 1557.
62 Raj Chetty and Nathaniel Hendren, "The Impacts of Neighborhoods on Intergenerational Mobility II: County-Level Estimates," *Quarterly Journal of Economics* 133, no. 3 (2018): 1163–1228, https://doi.org/10.1093/qje/qjy006.
63 Chetty and Hendren, "Impacts of Neighborhoods on Intergenerational Mobility II" 1167.
64 Chetty et al., "Opportunity Atlas," 5.
65 See, for example, Chetty et al., "Where is the Land," 1553–1623 (identifying five key factors: racial and economic segregation, income inequality, K-12 quality, social capital, and family structure).
66 Chetty et al., "Opportunity Atlas," 22, Figure III.
67 Brian Palmer, "How Did Detroit Become Motor City?," *Slate*, February 29, 2012, https://slate.com/news-and-politics/2012/02/why-are-all-the-big-american-car-companies-based-in-michigan.html.
68 Thomas J. Sugrue, *The Origins of the Urban Crisis: Race and Inequality in Postwar Detroit* (Princeton, NJ: Princeton University Press, 2014), 13.
69 Mark Binelli, "Inside Trump County, USA," *Rolling Stone*, January 25, 2017, https://www.rollingstone.com/politics/politics-features/inside-trump-county-usa-124726/.
70 *1950 Census of Population: Preliminary Reports* (Washington, DC: U.S. Department of Commerce, 1951), https://www2.census.gov/library/publications/decennial/1950/pc-05/pc-5-17.pdf; "Detroit City, Michigan," QuickFacts, accessed October 10, 2024, https://www.census.gov/quickfacts/detroitcitymichigan.
71 Galster, *Making Our Neighborhoods*, 98.
72 Thomas J. Sugrue, "From Motor City to Motor Metropolis: How the Automobile Industry Reshaped Urban America," *Automobile in American Life and Society*, University of Michigan – Dearborn, 2004, https://www.autolife.umd.umich.edu/Race/R_Overview/R_Overview1.htm.
73 Nathan Bomey, *Detroit Resurrected: To Bankruptcy and Back* (New York: W. W. Norton, 2016), 119.
74 Richard Florida, *The New Urban Crisis: How Our Cities Are Increasing Inequality, Deepening Segregation, and Failing the Middle Class-and What We Can Do About It* (New York: Basic Books, 2017), 39, 42; Katelyn Newman, "San Francisco Is Home to the Highest Density of Billionaires," *U.S. News*, May 10, 2019, https://www.usnews.com/news/cities/articles/2019-05-10/san-francisco-is-home-to-the-worlds-most-billionaires-per-capita.
75 Tomi Kilgore, "Facebook Raising Minimum Wage to $20 Per Hour for Bay Area, New York and D.C.," *MarketWatch*, May 13, 2019, https://www.marketwatch.com/story/facebook-raising-minimum-wage-to-20-per-hour-for-bay-area-new-york-and-dc-2019-05-13.
76 *Commuting Zones and Labor Market Areas*, distributed by U.S. Department of Agriculture Economic Research Service, https://www.ers.usda.gov/data-

products/commuting-zones-and-labor-market-areas/documentation/; Charles M. Tolbert II and Molly Sizer Killian, *Labor Market Areas for the United States* (Washington, DC: Economic Research Service, U.S. Department of Agriculture, 1987).
77 Chetty et al., "Opportunity Atlas," 22. Note that municipal boundaries and school districts do not always correspond but are conflated for simplified presentation in this section.
78 See Myron Orfield, "Appendix A: Tax Capacity Calculations," in *American Metropolitics: The New Suburban Reality* (Washington, DC: Brookings, 2002), 189–194.
79 See Orfield, *American Metropolitics,* 19 ("Since local governments are able to utilize the benefit tax features of the property tax, the property tax has been, and will continue to be, the main source of revenue for local governments in the United States."); Rajul Awasthi, Tuan Minh Le, and Chenli You, "Determinants of Property Tax Revenue: Lessons from Empirical Analysis" (working paper, World Bank Group, 2020): 3, https://openknowledge.worldbank.org/bitstream/handle/10986/34485/Determinants-of-Property-Tax-Revenue-Lessons-from-Empirical-Analysis.pdf?sequence=1.
80 Diana Epstein, *Measuring Inequity in School Funding* (Washington, DC: Center for American Progress, 2011), 1, https://files.eric.ed.gov/fulltext/ED535988.pdf.
81 Kern Alexander, Richard G. Salmon, and F. King Alexander, "Taxation for Public Schools," in *Financing Public Schools: Theory, Policy, and Practice* (New York: Routledge, 2015).
82 Jonathan Rothwell, *Housing Costs, Zoning, and Access to High-Scoring Schools* (Washington, DC: Metropolitan Policy Program at Brookings, 2012), https://www.brookings.edu/wp-content/uploads/2016/06/0419_school_inequality_rothwell.pdf.
83 C. Kirabo Jackson, Rucker C. Johnson, & Claudia Persico, "The Effects of School Spending on Educational and Economic Outcomes: Evidence from School Finance Reforms" (working paper, National Bureau of Economic Research, 2015), 157–218, https://www.nber.org/papers/w20847. Examining data on more than 15,000 children born between 1955 and 1985, this study found that poor children whose schools were estimated to receive a 10% increase in per-pupil spending (adjusted for inflation) before they began public school, and to maintain that increase over their 12 years of school, were 10% points more likely to complete high school than other poor children. They also had 10% higher earnings as adults and were 6% points less likely as adults to be poor. See also Julien Lafortune, Jesse Rothstein, and Diane Whitmore Schanzenbach, "School Finance Reform and the Distribution of Student Achievement," *American Economic Journal: Applied Economics* 10, no. 2 (2018).
84 Kyle Stokes, "Here's How Much Money LA Parents Are Fundraising For Schools, and What It Buys," *LAist,* January 10, 2022, https://laist.com/news/education/los-angeles-unified-parent-fundraising.
85 Mark McBride (@mccv), "A few notes from a Palo Alto resident," Twitter, December 28, 2016, https://twitter.com/mccv/status/814227350955003904?refsrc=email&s=11.
86 Dana Goldstein, "PTA Gift for Someone Else's Child? A Touchy Subject in California," *New York Times,* April 8, 2017, https://www.nytimes.com/2017/04/08/us/california-pta-fund-raising-inequality.html ("Only 9 percent qualified at the second-richest, Public School 87 on Manhattan's Upper West Side, where the PTA's revenue exceeded $1.5 million. The money was used to pay for dance, yoga, chess, and math and literacy coaching").
87 Catherine Brown, Scott Sargrad, and Meg Brenner, *Hidden Money: The Outsized Role of Parent Contributions in School Finance* (Washington, DC: Center

for American Progress, 2017), https://www.americanprogress.org/article/hidden-money/.
88 Sandra Black, "Do Better Schools Matter? Parental Valuation of Elementary Education," *Quarterly Journal of Economics* 114, no. 2 (1999): 577–599.
89 James E. Ryan, *Five Miles Away, A World Apart: One City, Two Schools, and the Story of Educational Opportunity in Modern America* (New York: Oxford University Press USA, 2010).
90 Marsha Ginsberg, "Educated Buyers: Test Scores, School Ratings Drive Decisions as Much as Floor Plans and City Services," *San Francisco Chronicle*, February 15, 2004, https://www.sfgate.com/bayarea/article/Educated-buyers-Test-scores-school-ratings-2796677.php. See also Donald Haurin and David Brasington, "School Quality and Real House Prices: Inter- and Intrametropolitan Effects," *Journal of Housing Economics* 5, no. 4 (1996): 351–368, https://econpapers.repec.org/article/eeejhouse/v_3a5_3ay_3a1996_3ai_3a4_3ap_3a351-368.htm.
91 Michele Lerner, "School Quality Has a Mighty Influence on Neighborhood Choice, Home Values," *Washington Post*, September 3, 2015, https://www.washingtonpost.com/realestate/school-quality-has-a-mighty-influence-on-neighborhood-choice-home-values/2015/09/03/826c289a-46ad-11e5-8ab4-c73967a143d3_story.html?tid=a_inl&utm_term=.e0863a7f4a4c.
92 William A. Fischel, *Zoning Rules! The Economics of Land Use Regulation* (Cambridge, MA: Lincoln Institute of Land Policy, 2015), 116.
93 Charles M. Tiebout, "A Pure Theory of Local Expenditures," *Journal of Political Economy* 64, no. 5 (1956): 416–424, https://www.jstor.org.libproxy.berkeley.edu/stable/1826343.
94 Orfield, *American Metropolitics*, 57.
95 Stephen Menendian, "The Uneven March of Progress: The Past, Present, and Future of Zoning Reform in the United States," *Rutgers Journal of Law & Public Policy* 21, no. 2 (2023): 75, 93.
96 Jonathan Rothwell, *Land Use Politics, Housing Costs, and Segregation in California Cities* (Berkeley: Terner Center, 2019), https://californialanduse.org/download/Land%20Use%20Politics%20Rothwell.pdf.
97 *Backgrounders from the Unnatural Causes Health Equity Database* (San Francisco: California Newsreel, 2008), 2, 13, https://unnaturalcauses.org/assets/uploads/file/primers.pdf.
98 Chetty et al., "Opportunity Atlas," fig. 3.
99 It should be noted that the term "neighborhood" is used variably and imprecisely in the "neighborhood effects" literature, and can refer to studies of larger geographic scales, from cities to commuting zones. Generally, social scientists tend to use census tracts as a proxy for neighborhoods, as it is most reliably available approximation to popular conceptions of neighborhood. Tracts are generally designations that encompass a population between 2,500 to 8,000 people. See Paul A. Jargowsky, *Poverty and Place: Ghettos, Barrios, and the American City* (New York: Russell Sage Foundation, 1997), 8. For a more nuanced construction of what a "neighborhood" constitutes, see George Galster, "The Meaning of Neighborhood," in Galster, *Making Our Neighborhoods*, 20–42.
100 The cities were Baltimore, Boston, Chicago, Los Angeles, and New York. "Moving to Opportunity (MTO) for Fair Housing Demonstration Program," *National Bureau of Economic Research*, https://www2.nber.org/mtopublic/.
101 Jeffrey R. Kling, Jeffrey B. Liebman, and Lawrence F. Katz, "Experimental Analysis of Neighborhood Effects," *Econometrica* 75, no. 1 (2007): 83–119.
102 Kling, Liebman, and Katz, "Neighborhood Effects," 99–102.
103 Kling, Liebman, and Katz, 87; Emily Rosenbaum and Laura Harris, "Low-Income Families in Their New Neighborhoods: The Short-Term Effects of Moving From Chicago's Public Housing," *Journal of Family Issues* 22, no. 1 (2001):

183–210, https://doi.org/10.1177/019251301022002004 (finding that families in Chicago were more likely to maintain close social ties with formerly poverty-stricken neighborhoods even after moving).
104 Chetty, Hendren, and Katz, "Effects of Exposure," 857.
105 Chetty, Hendren, and Katz, 859.
106 "How Neighborhoods Matter for Latino and African-American Children," HUD User, https://www.huduser.gov/portal/pdredge/pdr_edge_research_012615.html
107 Anna Maria Santiago et al., *Opportunity Neighborhoods for Latino and African-American Children* (Washington, DC: U.S. Department of Housing and Urban Development, 2014), xxii, https://www.huduser.gov/portal/Publications/pdf/Opportunity_Neighborhoods.pdf.
108 See, for example, Edward L. Glaeser, David Laibson, and Bruce Sacerdote, "An Economic Approach to Social Capital," *Economic Journal* 112, no. 483 (2002): F438, https://doi.org/10.1111/1468-0297.00078 ("We define individual social capital as a person's social characteristics – including social skills, charisma, and the size of his Rolodex – which enables him to reap market and non-market returns from interactions with others").
109 Robert D. Putnam, *Bowling Alone: The Collapse and Revival of American Community* (New York: Simon & Schuster, 2000), 18–19; Robert Putnam, "Bowling Alone: America's Declining Social Capital," *Journal of Democracy* 6, no. 1 (1995), https://www.canonsociaalwerk.eu/1995_Putnam/1995,%20Putnam,%20bowling%20alone.pdf.
110 Raj Chetty et al., "Race and Economic Opportunity in the United States: An Intergenerational Perspective," *Quarterly Journal of Economics* 135 no. 2 (2020): 768, https://doi.org/10.1093/qje/qjz042.
111 James P. Connell and Bonnie L. Halpern-Felsher, "How Neighborhoods Affect Educational Outcomes in Middle Childhood and Adolescence: Conceptual Issues and an Empirical Example," in *Neighborhood Poverty I: Context and Consequences for Children*, eds. Jeanne Brooks-Gunn, Greg J. Duncan, and J. Lawrence Aber (New York: Russell Sage Foundation Press, 1997).
112 Ron W. Zimmer and Eugenia F. Toma, "Peer Effects in Private and Public Schools Across Countries," *Journal of Policy Analysis and Management* 19, no. 1 (2000): 75–92. See also Jacob Vigdor and Thomas J. Nechyba, "Peer Effects in North Carolina Public Schools," in *Schools and the Equal Opportunities Problem*, eds. Ludger Woessmann and Paul E. Peterson (Cambridge, MA: MIT Press, 2006), 73–101.
113 Robert J. Sampson, *Great American City: Chicago and the Enduring Neighborhood Effect* (Chicago: University of Chicago Press, 2012), 180–181. Jeffrey D. Morenoff, Robert J. Sampson, and Stephen W. Raudenbush, "Neighborhood Inequality, Collective Efficacy, and the Spatial Dynamics of Urban Violence," *Criminology* 39, no. 3 (2007): 180–181, https://scholar.harvard.edu/files/sampson/files/2001_crim.pdf.
114 Patrick Sharkey, Gerard Torrats-Espinosa, and Delaram Takyar, "Community and the Crime Decline: The Causal Effect of Local Nonprofits on Violent Crime," *American Sociological Review* 82, no. 6 (2017): 1215, https://journals.sagepub.com/doi/full/10.1177/0003122417736289.
115 Chase Sackett, "Neighborhoods and Violent Crime," *Evidence Matters: Transforming Knowledge into Housing and Community Development Policy* (2016): 16–24, https://www.huduser.gov/portal/sites/default/files/pdf/EM-Newsletter-summer-2016.pdf.
116 See, for example, David Weisburd et al., "Mean Streets and Mental Health: Depression and Post-Traumatic Stress Disorder at Crime Hot Spots," *American Journal of Community Psychology* 61, no. 3–4 (2018): 285–295; David Weisburd and Clair White, "Hot Spots of Crime Are Not Just Hot Spots of Crime:

Examining Health Outcomes at Street Segments," *Journal of Contemporary Criminal Justice* 35, no. 2 (2019): 142–160.
117 Jens Ludwig, *Moving to Opportunity: The Effects of Concentrated Poverty on the Poor* (Washington, DC: Third Way, 2014), 10, https://www.thirdway.org/report/moving-to-opportunity-the-effects-of-concentrated-poverty-on-the-poor.
118 Robert Manduca and Robert J. Sampson, "Punishing and Toxic Neighborhood Environments Independently Predict the Intergenerational Social Mobility of Black and White Children," *Proceedings of the National Academy of Sciences* 116, no. 16 (2019): 7772–7777, https://www.pnas.org/doi/10.1073/pnas.1820464116.
119 See Sean F. Reardon and Kendra Bischoff, *Growth in the Residential Segregation of Families by Income, 1970-2009* (New York: US2010 Project-Russell Sage Foundation Brown University, 2013), 11, https://web.archive.org/web/20210301144556/https://s4.ad.brown.edu/Projects/Diversity/Data/Report/report111111.pdf; Sean F. Reardon and Kendra Bischoff, *The Continuing Increase in Income Segregation, 2007-2012* (Stanford, CA: Stanford Center for Education Policy Analysis, 2016), 5–7, https://cepa.stanford.edu/content/continuing-increase-income-segregation-2007-2012.
120 Sean F. Reardon and Kendra Bischoff, "Income Inequality and Income Segregation," *American Journal of Sociology* 116, no. 4 (2011): 1092–1153, 1138, https://doi.org/10.1086/657114 (claiming that "increasing income inequality was responsible for 40–80% of the changes in income segregation from 1970–2000").
121 Rakesh Kochhar, "Middle Class Fortunes in Western Europe," *Pew Research Center*, April 24, 2017, https://www.pewglobal.org/2017/04/24/middle-class-fortunes-in-western-europe/.
122 "The American Middle Class Is Losing Ground," *Pew Research Center*, December 9, 2015, https://www.pewresearch.org/social-trends/2015/12/09/the-american-middle-class-is-losing-ground/ (defining middle class as "for a three-person household, the middle-income range was about $42,000 to $126,000 annually in 2014 (in 2014 dollars)."); Alicia Parlapiano, Robert Gebeloff, and Shan Carter, "The Shrinking American Middle Class," *New York Times*, January 26, 2015, https://www.nytimes.com/interactive/2015/01/25/upshot/shrinking-middle-class.html.
123 D'Vera Cohn, "The Middle Class Shrinks and Income Segregation Rises," *Pew Research Center*, August 2, 2012, https://www.pewresearch.org/social-trends/2012/08/02/the-middle-class-shrinks-and-income-segregation-rises/. See also Richard Florida and Charlotta Mellander, *Segregated City: The Geography of Economic Segregation in America's Metros* (Toronto, ON: Martin Prosperity Institute, 2015), 11, https://www-2.rotman.utoronto.ca/mpi/content/segregated-city/.
124 Reardon and Bischoff, *Continuing Increase in Income Segregation*, 11, Table 4.
125 Kendra Bischoff and Sean F. Reardon, "Residential Segregation by Income, 1970–2009," in *Diversity and Disparities: America Enters a New Century*, ed. John Logan (New York: Russell Sage Foundation, 2014), 214, Table 7.1 (from a rank-order information theory index score of 0.115 in 1970 to 0.148 in 2009).
126 Reardon and Bischoff, *Continuing Increase in Income Segregation*, 6–7, Figure 2 & Table 1. The far-right bar chart (2012) in Figure 2 shows that all six income segments are becoming more equal in size.
127 Recall that Chetty et al., "Where is the Land," 1607-11," found that economic segregation was one of the key factors associated with lack of upward mobility. See also Richard Florida and Charlotta Mellander, "The Geography of Economic Segregation," *Social Sciences* 7, no. 8 (2018): 123–140, https://www.mdpi.com/2076-0760/7/8/123/htm (concluding that "policies should specifically focus on reducing segregation in addition to addressing income inequality").

128 Families with children are more economically segregated than families without children. See Ann Owens, "Inequality in Children's Contexts: Income Segregation of Households With and Without Children," *American Sociological Review* 81, no. 3 (2016): 549-574, https://socialinnovation.usc.edu/wp-content/uploads/2017/09/American-Sociological-Review-2016-Owens-1.pdf. See also Ann Owens, "How the rich wanting the best for their kids is segregating our neighborhoods," *USApp – American Politics and Policy Blog*, December 22, 2016, https://eprints.lse.ac.uk/69305/ ("Among childless households, income segregation has been stable, but segregation increased by over 20 percent among families with kids from 1990 to 2010 in large metropolitan areas. Income segregation was nearly twice as high among families with kids as among childless households in 2010").
129 Raj Chetty et al., "Social capital I: measurement and associations with economic mobility," *Nature* 608 (2022): 108–121, https://doi.org/10.1038/s41586-022-04996-4; Raj Chetty et al., "Social capital II: determinants of economic connectedness," *Nature* 608 (2022): 122–134: https://doi.org/10.1038/s41586-022-04997-3.
130 Linda Datcher Loury, "Some Contacts Are More Valuable Than Others: Informal Networks, Job Tenure, and Wages," *Journal of Labor Economics* 24, no. 2 (2006): 299–318; Mark S. Granovetter, *Getting a Job: A Study of Contacts and Careers* (Cambridge, MA: Harvard University Press, 1974).
131 Hannah Morgan, "Don't Believe These 8 Job Search Myths," *U.S. News*, September 17, 2014, https://money.usnews.com/money/blogs/outside-voices-careers/2014/09/17/dont-believe-these-8-job-search-myths.
132 As many as 50% of jobs are filled by referral. Robert L. Nelson, Ellen C. Berrey, and Laura Beth Nielsen, "Divergent Paths: Conflicting Conceptions of Employment Discrimination in Law and the Social Sciences," *Annual Review of Law and Social Science* 4 (2008): 103, 116.
133 Sugrue, *Urban Crisis*, 25–26.
134 Nicholas Christakis and James H. Fowler, *Connected: The Surprising Power of Our Social Networks and How They Shape Our Lives* (New York: Back Bay Books, 2009), 6.
135 Alan D. DeSantis, *Inside Greek U: Fraternities, Sororities, and the Pursuit of Pleasure, Power, and Prestige* (Lexington: University Press of Kentucky, 2007), 201.
136 Jack Mara, Lewis Davis, and Stephen Schmidt, "Social Animal House: The Economic and Academic Consequences of Fraternity Membership," *Contemporary Economic Policy* 36, no. 2 (2018): 265, https://papers.ssrn.com/sol3/papers.cfm?abstract_id=2763720. In other words, the negative consequences of lower grades are more than offset by valuable social connections.
137 Galster and Killen, "Geography of Metropolitan Opportunity," 14.
138 Jeff Guo, "Why Poor Kids Don't Stay in College," *Washington Post*, October 20, 2014, https://www.washingtonpost.com/news/storyline/wp/2014/10/20/why-poor-kids-dont-stay-in-college/. See also Harry J. Holzer, "Improving Opportunity Through Better Human Capital Investments for the Labor Market," *Dynamics of Opportunity*, eds. Braun and Kirsch, 392.
139 Christakis and Fowler, *Connected*, 103.
140 Christakis and Fowler, *Connected*, 9. The example of a bucket brigade fighting a fire illustrates this idea.
141 Antoni Calvó-Armengol, "Job Contact Networks," *Journal of Economic Theory* 115, no. 1 (2004): 191, https://doi.org/10.1016/S0022-0531(03)00250-3.
142 Christakis and Fowler, *Connected*, 102-105.
143 Tina Rosenberg, "Guiding a First Generation to College," *New York Times*, April 26, 2016, https://opinionator.blogs.nytimes.com/2016/04/26/guiding-a-first-generation-to-college/.

144 Caroline M. Hoxby and Christopher Avery, "The Missing "One-Offs": The Hidden Supply of High-Achieving, Low Income Students," *Brookings Papers on Economic Activity* 2013, no. 1 (2013): 1–65, https://muse.jhu.edu/article/524135.

145 Ozan Jaquette and Karina Salazar, "Colleges Recruit at Richer, Whiter High Schools," *New York Times*, April 13, 2018, https://www.nytimes.com/interactive/2018/04/13/opinion/college-recruitment-rich-white.html.

146 Caroline Hoxby and Sarah Turner, "Expanding College Opportunities for High-Achieving, Low Income Students," *SIEPR* Discussion Paper no. 12-014 (2013): 25, https://www8.gsb.columbia.edu/programs/sites/programs/files/finance/Applied%20Microeconomics/Caroline%20Hoxby.pdf.

147 Mark S. Granovetter, "The Strength of Weak Ties," *American Journal of Sociology* 78, no. 6 (1973): 1360–1380.

148 Silvia Domínguez and Celeste Watkins, "Creating Networks for Survival and Mobility: Social Capital Among African-American and Latin-American Low-Income Mothers," *Social Problems* 50, no. 1 (2003): 111–135, https://doi.org/10.1525/sp.2003.50.1.111.

149 Douglass Massey, *Categorically Unequal: The American Stratification System* (New York: Russell Sage Foundation), 203. See also Noah, *Born a Crime*, 218.

150 See, for example, Michael David Smith, "Tavon Austin Says Everybody He Knows is Asking for Money," *NBCSports*, May 12, 2013, https://profootballtalk.nbcsports.com/2013/05/12/tavon-austin-says-everybody-he-knows-is-asking-for-money/.

151 Lawrence A. Cremin, *American Education: The National Experience, 1783-1876* (New York: Harper & Row, 1970).

152 Sandra Tang et al., "Adolescent Pregnancy's Intergenerational Effects: Does an Adolescent Mother's Education Have Consequences for Her Children's Achievement?," *Journal of Research on Adolescence* 26, no. 1 (2016): 180–193, https://doi.org/10.1111/jora.12182.

153 Robert J. Gordon, *The Rise and Fall of American Growth* (Princeton, NJ: Princeton University Press, 2016), 606.

154 Raj Chetty, David J. Demming, and John N. Friedman, "Diversifying Society's Leaders? The Determinants and Causal Effects of Admission to Highly Selective Private Colleges," *National Bureau of Economic Research*, no. w31492 (2023): https://www.nber.org/papers/w31492 (quantifying the effect of legacy on admissions at elite and selective institutions).

155 Harold O. Levy with Peg Tyre, "How to Level the College Playing Field," *New York Times*, April 7, 2018, https://www.nytimes.com/2018/04/07/opinion/sunday/harold-levy-college.html.

156 Paul Tough, *Helping Children Succeed: What Works and Why* (New York: Houghton Mifflin Harcourt, 2016), 9–13.

157 Angela Duckworth, *Grit: The Power of Passion and Perseverance* (New York: Scribner, 2016).

158 Claire Cain Miller and Jonah E. Bromwich, "How Parents Are Robbing Their Children of Adulthood," *New York Times*, March 16, 2019, https://www.nytimes.com/2019/03/16/style/snowplow-parenting-scandal.html.

159 Gary S. Becker et al., "A Theory of Intergenerational Mobility," *Journal of Political Economy* 126, no. 1, 7–25, https://doi.org/10.1086/698759.

160 Richard V. Reeves, *Dream Hoarders* (Washington, DC: Brookings Institution Press, 2017), 38.

161 Greg J. Duncan and Richard Murnane, eds., *Whither Opportunity?: Rising Inequality, Schools, and Children's Life Chances* (New York: Russell Sage Foundation, 2011), 11; Sabino Kornrich and Frank Furstenberg, "Investing in Children: Changes in Parental Spending on Children, 1972–2007," *Demography* 50, no. 1 (2013): 1–23.

162 "Top-quintile spending on children's enrichment (special classes, music, camps, and other experiences) is now almost $8900 per year, three times that of low-income quintile parents, who spend about $1320 on the same goods and services." Smeeding, "Gates, Gaps, and Intergenerational Mobility," 268.

163 *Parenting in America: Outlook, Worries, Aspirations are Strongly Linked to Financial Situation* (Washington, DC, Pew Research Center, 2015), 6, https://www.pewresearch.org/social-trends/2015/12/17/parenting-in-america/. A total of 84% of families earning more than $75K a year said their children participated in sports compared to 59% for low-income families.

164 Elizabeth A. Harris and Kristin Hussey, "In Connecticut, A Wealth Gap Divides Neighboring Schools," *New York Times*, September 11, 2016, https://www.nytimes.com/2016/09/12/nyregion/in-connecticut-a-wealth-gap-divides-neighboring-schools.html ("Fairfield parent associations raise money for field trips, white boards or boxes of school supplies. And then there is what residents spend out of school. "A suburban family can get their kids to museums, they can travel, can get special tutors, they can get enrichment classes," Mr. Dwyer said. "Poverty is a word, but what really separates the two districts is suburban children have more enrichment activities before they even start public school than the typical urban child, and that makes a difference").

165 Betty Hart and Todd R. Risley, "The Early Catastrophe: The 30 Million Word Gap by Age 3," *American Educator* 27, no. 1 (2003), https://www.aft.org/sites/default/files/periodicals/TheEarlyCatastrophe.pdf.

166 Richard Rothstein, "Social Class, Student Achievement, and the Black-White Achievement Gap," in *Class and Schools: Using Social, Economic, and Educational Reform to Close the Black–White Achievement Gap* (Washington, DC: Economic Policy Institute, 2004), 58.

167 Eleni Karagiannaki, "The Effect of Parental Wealth on Children's Outcomes in Early Adulthood," *Journal of Economic Inequality* 15, no. 3 (2017): 217–243, https://doi.org/10.1007/s10888-017-9350-1; *Indicators of Higher Education Equity in the United States* (Washington, DC: Pell Institute for the Study of Opportunity in Higher Education, 2015).

168 Lynn A. Karoly and Jill S. Cannon, "Making Preschool Investments Count Through the American Families Plan," *RAND Blog*, June 3, 2021, https://www.rand.org/blog/2021/06/making-preschool-investments-count-through-the-american.html.

169 Juliana Herman, Sasha Post, and Scott O'Halloran, *The United States Is Far Behind Other Countries on Pre-K* (Washington, DC: Center for American Progress, 2013), https://www.americanprogress.org/article/the-united-states-is-far-behind-other-countries-on-pre-k/.

170 Dalton Conley, "Capital for College: Parental Assets and Postsecondary Schooling," *Sociology of Education* 74, no. 1 (2001): 59–72. (Finding that a doubling of parental assets results in a 8.3% increase in college attendance, and a 5.6% increase in graduation.)

171 *The Condition of Education 2018* (Washington, DC: National Center for Education Statistics, 2018), 152, https://files.eric.ed.gov/fulltext/ED583502.pdf.

172 Aaron Terrazas, "The Doubly Lucky 3 Percent," *Zillow*, June 30, 2015, https://www.zillow.com/research/the-doubly-lucky-3-percent-10061/.

173 Sean F. Reardon, "The Widening Income Achievement Gap," *Educational Leadership* 70, no. 8 (2013): 10–16, https://www.ascd.org/publications/educational-leadership/may13/vol70/num08/The-Widening-Income-Achievement-Gap.aspx.

174 Margaret Cahalan and Laura Perna, *Indicators of Higher Education Equity in the United States* (Washington, DC: Pell Institute for the Study of Opportunity in Higher Education, 2015), 31. See also Fabian T. Pfeffer, "Growing Wealth Gaps

in Education," *Demography* 55, no. 3 (2018): 1033–1068, https://fabianpfeffer.com/wp-content/uploads/Pfeffer2018.pdf.
175 Thomas G. Mortenson, C. Stocker, and N. Brunt, "Family Income and Educational Attainment, 1970 to 2009," *Postsecondary Education Opportunity* 221 (2010): 1–16 ("By one recent estimate, by the age of twenty-four, 82.4% of individuals from families in the top income quartile had completed a bachelor's degree, whereas among students from families in the bottom income quartile, only 8.3% had completed a bachelor's degree").
176 Mary Ann Fox, Brooke A. Connolly, and Thomas D. Snyder, *Youth Indicators 2005 Trends in the Well-Being of American Youth* (Washington, DC, U.S. Department of Education, National Center for Education Statistics, 2005), 50–51, table 21, https://nces.ed.gov/pubs2005/2005050.pdf. 176
177 Raj Chetty et al., "Mobility Report Cards: The Role of Colleges in Intergenerational Mobility" (working paper, National Bureau of Economic Research, July 2017), https://www.nber.org/papers/w23618.
178 Lani Guinier, "The Miner's Canary," *Liberal Education* 91, no. 2 (2005): 30 ("Test scores, in fact, tell us more about your grandparents' wealth than they tell us about your first-year college grades").
179 Catherine Rampell, "SAT Scores and Family Income," *New York Times*, August 27, 2009, https://economix.blogs.nytimes.com/2009/08/27/sat-scores-and-family-income/.
180 Saul Geiser, "Norm-Referenced Tests and Race-Blind Admissions: The Case for Eliminating the SAT and ACT at the University of California," in *The Scandal of Standardized Tests Why We Need to Drop the SAT and ACT*, ed. Joseph A. Soares (New York: Teachers College Press, 2020), 11–43, https://cshe.berkeley.edu/sites/default/files/geiser_chapter_1_final.pdf.
181 Robert F. Schoeni and Karen E. Ross, "Material Assistance from Families during the Transition to Adulthood," in *On the Frontier of Adulthood: Theory, Research, and Public Policy*, eds. Richard A. Settersten Jr., Frank F. Furstenberg, and Rubén G. Rumbaut, 397–407; "Survey of Household Economics and Decisionmaking," *Board of Governors of the Federal Reserve System*, last modified September 18, 2020.
182 *PSID Transition into Adulthood Supplement 2013: User* Guide (Ann Arbor, MI: Institute of Social Research, 2013), https://psidonline.isr.umich.edu/CDS/TAS13_Userguide.pdf.
183 Scott Stump, "Donald Trump: My Dad Gave Me 'A Small Loan' of $1 Million to Get Started," *Today*, October 26, 2015, https://www.today.com/news/donald-trump-my-dad-gave-me-small-loan-1-million-t52166.
184 Zameena Mejia, "Jeff Bezos Got His Parents to Invest Nearly $250,000 in Amazon in 1995 — They Might Be Worth $30 Billion Today," *CNBC*, published August 2, 2019; last modified August 3, 2018, https://www.cnbc.com/2018/08/02/how-jeff-bezos-got-his-parents-to-invest-in-amazon–turning-them-into.html.
185 Patrick Wightman et al., *Historical Trends in Parental Financial Support of Young Adults* (Ann Arbor, MI: Population Studies Center at the University of Michigan, 2013), 8. The class of 2001 is 10–20% points more likely to receive support than the class of 1978.
186 Patrick Wightman, Robert Schoeni, and Keith Robinson, "Familial Financial Assistance to Young Adults" (working paper, National Poverty Center, 2012): 7, https://npc.umich.edu/publications/u/2012-10%20NPC%20Working%20Paper.pdf.
187 Thomas Deleire and Leonard M. Lopoo, *Family Structure and the Economic Mobility of Children* (Washington, DC: The Pew Charitable Trusts, 2010), 15, https://www.pewtrusts.org/en/research-and-analysis/reports/0001/01/01/family-structure-and-the-economic-mobility-of-children.

188 Chetty et al., "Where is the Land," 1618 ("Across all the specifications, the strongest and most robust predictor is the fraction of children with single parents").
189 As of 2017, 41% of children living in single-mother families were poor, compared with 8% of children living in married-couple families. *Children in Poverty* (Bethesda, MD: Child Trends, 2019), https://web.archive.org/web/20210120232042/https://www.childtrends.org/indicators/children-in-poverty.
190 Chetty et al., "Where is the Land," 1558.
191 Brady E. Hamilton et al., "Births: Preliminary Data for 2013," *National Vital Statistics Report* 63, no. 2 (2014): 4, https://www.cdc.gov/nchs/data/nvsr/nvsr63/nvsr63_02.pdf; Stephanie Kramer, "U.S. Has World's Highest Rate of Children Living in Single-Parent Households," *Pew Research Center*, December 12, 2019, https://www.pewresearch.org/fact-tank/2019/12/12/u-s-children-more-likely-than-children-in-other-countries-to-live-with-just-one-parent/.
192 Chetty et al., "Where is the Land," 1618.
193 Sarah M. Corse and Jennifer M. Silva, "Intimate Inequalities: Love and Work in the Postindustrial Landscape," in *Beyond the Cubicle: Job Insecurity, Intimacy, and the Flexible Self*, ed. Allison J. Pugh (New York: Oxford University Press, 2017), 283–304.
194 Kay Hymowitz et al., *Knot Yet: The Benefits and Costs of Delayed Marriage in America* (Charlottesville: National Marriage Project at the University of Virginia, 2013), 4, https://nationalmarriageproject.org/wp-content/uploads/2013/03/KnotYet-FinalForWeb.pdf.
195 Christine R. Schwartz & Robert D. Mare, "Trends in Educational Assortative Marriage from 1940 to 2003," *Demography* 42, no. 4 (2005): 621–646.
196 David S. Loughran and Julie M. Zissimopoulos, "Why Wait? The Effect of Marriage and Childbearing on the Wages of Men and Women," *Journal of Human Resources* 44, no. 2 (2009): 326–349, https://www.ncbi.nlm.nih.gov/pmc/articles/PMC3444509/.
197 Eduardo Porter, "Politicians Push Marriage, But That's Not What Would Help Children," *New York Times*, March 22, 2016, https://www.nytimes.com/2016/03/23/business/for-the-sake-of-the-children-not-marriage-but-help.html; Sara R. Jaffee et al., "Life with (Or without) Father: The Benefits of Living with Two Biological Parents Depend on the Father's Antisocial Behavior," *Child Development* 74, no. 1 (2003): 109–126, https://www.jstor.org/stable/3696345.
198 Joseph P. Ferrie, "History Lessons: The End of American Exceptionalism? Mobility in the United States Since 1850," *Journal of Economic Perspectives* 19, no. 3 (2005): 199–215, https://www.aeaweb.org/articles?id=10.1257/089533005774357824. quoted in Quoctrung Bui, "The States That College Graduates Are Most Likely to Leave," *New York Times*, November 22, 2016, https://www.nytimes.com/2016/11/22/upshot/the-states-that-college-graduates-are-most-likely-to-leave.html (describing several waves of labor mobility). Fischel claims that "before the 1970s, there seem to have been no significant barriers for internal migrants to relocate to centers of opportunity, save those created by slavery and segregation." Fischel, Zoning Rules, 314.
199 Joseph P. Ferrie, "Historical Statistics of the U.S., Millennial Edition: Internal Migration," *Department of Economics Northwestern University and NBER*, 2002, https://faculty.wcas.northwestern.edu/~fe2r/papers/essay.pdf.
200 Raven Molloy, Christopher L. Smith, and Abigail Wozniak, "Internal Migration in the United States," *Journal of Economic Perspectives* 25, no. 3 (2011): 173–196, https://pubs.aeaweb.org/doi/pdfplus/10.1257/jep.25.3.173 (See Figure 1 and Figure 2, representing changes in the rates of geographic mobility from 1900–2010). See also Ferrie, "Historical Statistics," 12 ("Among males age 20-29 in the 1850-60 linked sample, 56% changed county over a decade; in the

Young Men cohort of the National Longitudinal Survey, the rate of inter-county mobility among males age 20-29 was only 49% over the period 1971-81").
201 "Table A-1. Annual Geographic Mobility Rates, By Type of Movement: 1948-2021," *United States Census Bureau*, November 2021, https://www.census.gov/data/tables/time-series/demo/geographic-mobility/historic.html.
202 "2021 CPS-ASEC Geographic Mobility Data Release," *United States Census Bureau*, November 17, 2021, https://www.census.gov/newsroom/press-releases/2021/cps-asec-geographic-mobility.html.
203 Greg Kaplan and Sam Schulhofer-Wohl, "Understanding the Long-Run Decline in Interstate Migration," *International Economic Review* 58, no. 1 (2017): 61–62, https://onlinelibrary.wiley.com/doi/epdf/10.1111/iere.12209.
204 Sabrina Tavernise, "Frozen in Place: Americans Are Moving at the Lowest Rate on Record," *New York Times*, November 20, 2019, https://www.nytimes.com/2019/11/20/us/american-workers-moving-states-.html.
205 William H. Frey, "For the First Time on Record, Fewer Than 10% of Americans Moved in a Year," *Brookings*, November 22, 2019, fig. 4, https://www.brookings.edu/blog/the-avenue/2019/11/22/for-the-first-time-on-record-fewer-than-10-of-americans-moved-in-a-year/.
206 Frey, "Fewer Than 10% of Americans Moved in a Year."
207 Matt Ferguson, "Should You Move for a Job?," *Harvard Business Review*, March 22, 2012, https://hbr.org/2012/03/should-you-move-for-a-job.
208 "Nearly One-Third of Employers Willing to Pay to Relocate Employees in 2012, CareerBuilder Survey Finds," *CareerBuilder*, January 18, 2012, https://press.careerbuilder.com/2012-01-18-Nearly-One-Third-of-Employers-Willing-to-Pay-to-Relocate-Employees-in-2012-CareerBuilder-Survey-Finds.
209 Noah, "Stay Put."
210 Jonathan Lansner, "What exodus? California has serious attraction problems," *East Bay Times*, October 2, 2021, https://www.eastbaytimes.com/2021/10/02/what-exodus-california-has-serious-attraction-problems/.
211 Danny Dougherty et al., "Where Graduates Move after College," *Wall Street Journal*, May 15, 2018, https://www.wsj.com/graphics/where-graduates-move-after-college/?mod=article_inline (showing where graduates from every major university move and that a handful of regions are magnets for high-skill workers). The flip side is Quoctrung Bui, "States That College Graduates Are Most Likely to Leave."
212 Tyler Cowen, "Why Texas Is Our Future," *Time*, October 21, 2013, https://time.com/80005/why-texas-is-our-future/.
213 Richard Florida, "Is Life Better in America's Red States?," *New York Times*, January 3, 2015, https://www.nytimes.com/2015/01/04/opinion/sunday/is-life-better-in-americas-red-states.html.
214 Emily Badger, "What Happened to the American Boomtown," *New York Times*, December 6, 2017, https://www.nytimes.com/2017/12/06/upshot/what-happened-to-the-american-boomtown.html; David Schleicher, "Stuck! The Law and Economics of Residential Stagnation," *Yale Law Journal* 127, no. 1 (2017), https://www.yalelawjournal.org/article/stuck-the-law-and-economics-of-residential-stagnation.
215 See David Schleicher, "City Unplanning," *Yale Law Journal* 122 (2013): 1670–1675, https://heinonline.org/HOL/LandingPage?handle=hein.journals/ylr122&div=45&id=&page= where the author describes slow population growth in rich cities and regions.
216 David H. Autor, "Work of the Past, Work of the Future," *American Economic Association: Papers and Proceedings* 109, no. 5 (2019): 1–32, https://economics.mit.edu/files/16724; Sabrina Tavernise, "Frozen in Place: Americans Are Moving at the Lowest Rate on Record," *New York Times*, November 20, 2019, https://www.nytimes.com/2019/11/20/us/american-workers-moving-states-.html.

2 Structural Racial Inequality

A single-mother of two young girls, Kelley Williams-Bolar wanted the best for her daughters. Rather than send them to the struggling Akron public school system for which they were zoned, she enrolled them in the nearby suburban district where her father lived, a fact which the school district uncovered by hiring a private investigator. The investigator filmed Williams-Bolar dropping her children off at the bus stop, evidence which was presented by the prosecution in her trial. At the time, Williams-Bolar worked as a teaching assistant for children with special needs, and was only a few credits short of completing her teaching degree. For trying to provide her children a better education, a jury convicted Williams-Bolar in 2011 of falsifying documents, a felony sentence that jeopardized her professional aspiration of becoming a schoolteacher.[1]

Although the jury deadlocked on the grand theft charge, based on prosecution's claim that she "stole" $30,000 worth of educational services from the district, some residents complained that by sending her children to their community school, she and other parents like her deprived local students of those funds and resources. The superintendent maintained that his district lost hundreds of thousands of dollars because of children improperly enrolled in its schools, explaining why they hired investigators to ferret out violators.[2]

In certain respects, the story of Kelley Williams-Bolar is a conventional and familiar story about the pursuit of opportunity in contemporary America. Like millions of Americans, Ms. Williams-Bolar sought a better education, and hopefully, a better life for her children, and for herself. Yet, her story also illustrates the common yet obscure ways in which exclusionary controls deny too many people of color access to opportunity. Ms. Williams-Bolar is Black, but her father lived in a predominantly white school district.

In contrast to the explicitly institutionalized racism of Jim Crow, the prosecution of Kelley Williams-Bolar painfully reveals the structural barriers that separate Americans by race and class today, and the lengths to which the privileged will go to guard and protect them. Her case garnered considerable public sympathy, and an organized campaign prompted Ohio Governor John Kasich to commute her sentence and reduce her conviction from a felony to a misdemeanor.[3] Nonetheless, the system she transgressed and the inequities she challenged remains virtually untouched by the episode. If anything, they were reinforced by it.[4]

Racial inequality is a well-documented panoramic feature of American society. By virtually any major indicator of well-being or important life outcomes, Black Americans often fall far behind the rest of the nation. Such disparities may be a relatively minor concern if they were improving. But in many cases, racial disparities in critical areas of life are worsening or widening.[5] In 2020, Black median income was 63.3% that of white households, or $43,674 to $68,943. This disparity has grown larger in absolute terms over the preceding 50 years.[6] Moreover, white households hold six times the net worth of Black households.[7] Similarly, the absolute racial wealth gap is grown enormously in the same period.[8]

These racial inequities may be troubling to many, but such statistics (even when framed directionally over time rather than as a static snapshot) provide insufficient explanatory power or insight, and have failed to motivate a policy agenda capable of remedying them. One reason is that such disparities could plausibly be the product of individual choices, talents, and traits or random circumstances.[9] On the other hand, inequality of opportunity, rather than outcomes, is more troubling and strikes at the heart of our most cherished ideals and beliefs. Americans are tolerant of enormous differences in income and wealth so long as everyone has a fair shot at the same rewards.[10]

The previous chapter examined the dynamics of economic mobility in contemporary American society, and introduced the concept of an "opportunity structure" to explain these dynamics. It traced the pathways of opportunity through the critical layers of the opportunity structure and identified several forces that broadly shape and distribute opportunity, and either facilitate or impede access to it.

This chapter attempts to demonstrate that these structures are "racialized," in the sense that these structures generate and reinforce advantages and disadvantages on the basis of race or with clear and measurable racial effects. In other words, the outcomes produced by opportunity structures are visibly and consistently racialized, meaning that these outcomes predictably vary for different racial groups. Moreover, it is the opportunity structure itself that explains and largely causes these racial disparities.[11] This is the operational meaning of the term "structural racism" employed throughout this book.

Within the opportunity structure, white Americans, despite their many challenges and obstacles, are buoyed by a subtle updraft, whereas Black Americans must strive against immense downward pressure. The data on economic mobility unequivocally illustrates this dynamic. As we will see, upward economic mobility is, to a considerable extent, a white phenomenon. In the other words, the American Dream, as generally conceptualized, is largely denied to Black and brown people. Before we investigate why this might be, consider the facts of both upward and downward mobility by race.

Race and Economic Mobility

The previous chapter surveyed the most recent data on upward mobility in the United States. If equal opportunity were a fact, then we would expect children from families earning anywhere in the income distribution, top, middle, or bottom, to have an equal chance of making it to the top of the income distribution (or landing anywhere) as adults. As we saw, this is more aspiration than reality, with profound differences in outcomes shaped by a variety of circumstances, especially the starting point in the income distribution and zip code. But when we examine the facts of upward mobility by race, however, an even more disturbing portrait emerges.

Less than a third of Black Americans believe that "if you work hard, you'll get ahead," a notably lower percentage than Americans generally.[12] Unfortunately, these views are not without foundation. Studies of race and economic mobility in America consistent show a profound and disturbing relationship. An overwhelming body of research finds that Black Americans have substantially less intergenerational upward mobility, and substantially more downward mobility, than white Americans.[13] Although the details vary depending on the data sets and time periods examined, the overall findings are uniformly directionally consistent and similar in magnitude.

A widely circulated report authored by Richard Reeves and published by the Brookings Institution in 2014, for example, found that 16% of white Americans born into families earning within bottom 20% (quintile) of the income distribution rise to the top quintile as adults, far better than the national average of 7.5% noted last chapter.[14] Yet, the same study indicated that only 3% of Black children born from the bottom income quintile make it to the top as adults. In short, whites achieve the "American Dream" at rates verging on what would be expected in a society enjoying true equality of opportunity, and free social and economic mobility from one generation to the next. Whites vault from the bottom to the top at roughly double the national average, while Black Americans do so at less than half the average, and a quarter the rate of whites.

Of course, such acrobatics within the income distribution are not the only measure of economic mobility. Even if white Americans are much more successful vaulting from the bottom to the top and achieving the American Dream, perhaps Black and white children escape poverty at similar or nearly similar rates. Unfortunately, the disparities between white and Black children in terms of their chances of escaping poverty are far more disturbing, for reasons that will become clearer over the course of this chapter.

A 2005 study found that 83% of white children born in the bottom 10% of the income distribution rise out of that decile as adults, compared to just 58% of Black children.[15] Nearly a decade later, a different study published by the Federal Reserve found that 84% of white children whose parents earned in the bottom 10% of incomes managed to rise out as adults, whereas only 65% of Black children were able to do so.[16] In other words, only about

16–17% of white children, but between 35–42% of Black children, born into the poorest families remain there as adults.

These studies may understate the proportion of Black children born into poverty or near-poverty who remain there as adults. If we broaden our view slightly to the bottom 20% of the income distribution, we see even larger disparities. The same Federal Reserve study found a Black-white gap of 27% for rising out of the bottom 20%. The Reeves' study found that a whopping 51% of Black children born into the bottom quintile remain there as adults, compared to only 23% of white children (a similar 28% disparity).

A study by the Pew Charitable Trusts, utilizing a more recent data source, found that this figure was even greater: 53% of Black (and 33% for white children) remained in the bottom quintile as adults (yielding an even larger 30-point disparity).[17] A similar study by the Urban Institute found that 64% of Black children born into the bottom 20 remain there, compared to just 26% of whites.[18]

Probably the best and most accurate data, however, comes from an Opportunity Insights report, which was based upon tens of millions of confidential tax records. They found that 37.7% of Black children born into the bottom quintile remain there as adults, compared to 29% of white children.[19] Although that disparity is much smaller than other studies, this study was able to disaggregate further by gender, and found that 49% of Black boys remained in the bottom quintile as adults, a figure that approximates the findings of the Pew and Brookings studies.[20]

Consider that if American society were perfectly mobile, only 20% of children would remain in the bottom income quintile. That between 23–29% of white children do suggests that whites experience something approximating true economic and social mobility in their ability to escape poverty. Yet, that so many Black children remain there as adults—between 38–53%—is dystopic by contrast. Not only do precious few Black children born into the lower reaches of the income distribution make it to the top, but an outsized portion are stuck at the bottom.

Unfortunately, the data shows similar disparities in racial economic mobility across the entire income distribution. Overall, white children are far more likely than Black children to earn more than their parents at all income levels in absolute and relative terms. The Pew study found only 66% of Black children raised in the second quintile (21st–40th percentile) surpass their parents' family income compared with 89% of white children.[21] Similarly the Federal Reserve study found that only 15% of whites born into the lower-middle income quintile remain there as adults compared to 26% of Black children.[22] Overall, it found that Black Americans are 25% less likely to leap a quintile or more above their parents income rank than whites.

It is not just the fact that whites experience greater rates of upward mobility than Black Americans. Black children who earn more than their parents do not rise as far as their white counterparts. The most comprehensive and detailed data on upward mobility, the de-identified tax records used by team led by Raj Chetty were not initially racially identifiable.[23] However, in a subsequent study, they disaggregated the results by race.[24] They found that, on average, white children born at the 25th percentile reach the 45th percentile, compared to Black children who only reach the 32.6th percentile on average.[25] From the starting block of the 25th income percentile, white children leap nearly three times as far as Black children.

A cursory review of the studies on intergenerational mobility leaves the misleading impression that white children are highly socially and economically mobile, whereas Black children are largely immobile, or as Patrick Sharkey's book title suggests, *Stuck in Place*. Even this dismal portrait is too sanguine for reality. The truth is that Black children are highly economically mobile—only in the wrong direction.

The relationship between race and downward mobility is so stark that the sociologist Robert Sampson observed that the greatest predictor of downward mobility is being Black.[26] According to a Federal Reserve study, 60% of Black children born to families in the top half of the income distribution fell out of it from the 1950s to the 1980s.[27] Looking more closely at the top, a 2005 study found that 30% of white children born in the top 10% remain there, compared to just 4% of Black children.[28]

A more recent study found that 41% of white children born in the top 20% remain there, compared to just 18% of Black children. That study also found that Black boys born into the top income quintile are more likely to fall all the way to the bottom (not just out of the top) as remain at the top, 21.5% to 17.4%.[29] In plain English, economically advantaged Black boys raised in affluent families are more likely to end up in poverty or near poverty as adults as retain their affluence. In contrast, white children are nearly four to five times as likely to remain there as fall to the bottom. The same study found that white boys, in particular, were 39.3% likely to remain in the top quintile as an adult, with only a 10% chance of falling to the bottom quintile.

But downward mobility is not simply evident among upper-income Black families, where there is more room to fall. Most Black children born to middle-income parents earn less income in rank terms than their parents as adults.[30] In one study, researchers found that 45% of Black children from solidly middle-class families end up falling to the bottom of the income distribution, compared to only 16% of whites.[31] More specifically, 38% of Black men fall out of the middle class compared to just 21% of white men. A different study found only 32% of white children born in the middle quintile fall below than their parents in percentile rank, compared to 56% of Black children born there.[32] Another study part of the same project found 78% of Black children fall from the top three quintiles of the income distribution from one generation to the next, compared to 43% of whites.[33]

White and Black Americans are economically mobile; only in opposite directions. When we focus on the bottom half of the income distribution, whites appear highly mobile, achieving the American Dream at rates approaching perfect economic mobility, while Black children seem stuck, especially in terms of escaping intergenerational poverty, with a majority or large portion born in that class remaining there as adults. But when we focus on the top half of the income distribution, it is whites who seem socially and economically immobile, virtually a mirror image of Black immobility from the bottom. A large portion of white children stick around the top as adults, with a much smaller portion falling to the bottom. Black children, in contrast, are highly mobile—falling out of the middle and upper classes at disturbing rates.

In summary, Black Americans are not only less likely to achieve the American Dream by vaulting from the bottom to the top, but they are less likely to rise out of poverty at all, and when they do, do not rise as far as their white counterparts. In fact, Black children are less likely than other children to rise out of any income segment, and much more likely to fall below their parents' position as adults. From practically every vantage point, Black children have worse economic outcomes, even when sharing the same starting point. This data, then, would seem to establish the reality of inequality of opportunity (not just outcomes) by race, not just class or geography, as was documented last chapter.

A pertinent question that is often raised in debates over racial inequality generally, but especially when discussing economic disparities by race, and is likely to be posed here, is whether the core or root issue is "race or class?" Although the disparities just presented, by comparing cohorts from the same economic classes with similar starting points in the income distribution, would seem to preclude this question, it nonetheless requires a direct answer. After all, the forces canvassed last chapter that compose the opportunity structure and define the myriad pathways of opportunity may seem largely socioeconomic in nature. Perhaps there is a hidden economic variable that explains these racial differences. If so, then perhaps "class" is the root problem, and a racial lens obscures that reality.

The question, "is it race or is it class?," assumes that the answer is reducible to one side of the question or another. That is, either class and socioeconomics explain racial inequality or, if not, racial disparities must be explained by race or race-specific factors. As we will see, the forces canvassed last chapter that distribute and shape access to opportunity have racial dimensions that cannot be reduced entirely to class or economics. But there are, in fact, hidden economic variables that help explain these racial disparities. The problem is that these variables are highly and distinctively racialized. To begin to appreciate this, we must look more closely at poverty. But not just poverty generally; a few particularly insidious forms of poverty.

Childhood Poverty

For decades, a welter of government programs aimed to elevate families out of poverty. In 1964, President Johnson declared a war on poverty and

Table 2.1 Poverty and Race in the United States, 2020[34]

	White	Black	Hispanic	Asian	All Races
Total persons (2020) (in millions)	15.9M	8.5M	10.4M	1.6M	37.2M
Poverty rate (2020)	8.2%	19.5%	17.0%	8.1%	11.40%
Children (2020)	3.53M	3M	4.3M	0.35M	11.6M
Child poverty pate (2020)	9.9%	27.7%	23.1%	8.4%	16.1%

launched a series of initiatives through the Office of Economic Opportunity, including Head Start and food stamps.[35] The impetus was a recognition that, in a nation as wealthy as the United States, children should not suffer from malnutrition, lack of health care, and poverty-related developmental disadvantages. There are unresolved debates about whether, and to what extent, those initiatives helped raise Americans out of poverty, kept others from falling into it, or alleviated the suffering of those in poverty. Without resolving that debate, there is broad agreement that poverty is harmful, and that getting people out of poverty is an worthy policy goal.

In absolute numbers, there are more poor white people living in poverty in the United States than members of any other racial or ethnic group. But this simple fact masks considerable differences in the *rate* of poverty, as shown in Table 2.1. Black people and Hispanics are more than twice as likely as white Americans to live below the federal poverty line (19.5% and 17%, respectively, compared to 8.2%).

The racial disparity in the poverty rate suggests something important about the distribution of opportunity by race in America, both as an input and an outcome, a cause and a consequence. Poverty inhibits human development and reflects the limited opportunities individuals with few capabilities enjoy to begin with.[36] But the overall poverty rate by race obscures an even larger disparity in rates of poverty by race for *children*. Black children are nearly *three* times as likely to live in poverty as white children. More than a quarter of Black children grow up in poverty compared to just one in ten white children.

Remarkably, these facts reflect significant improvement in recent years. From 1974 to 2016, Black youth poverty rates were consistently above 30%, and often well above 40%. In 1982 and 1992, for instance, Black youth poverty was measured at 46.6% and 47.6%, respectively. In simple terms, that means nearly half of Black children were growing up in poverty in the 1980s and 1990s. Figure 2.1 illustrates fluctuating rates of Black and white youth poverty as well as a massive disparity. This is the context in which many Americans now working and parenting have grown up. These are economically distinctive home environments, with implications far beyond the simple figures presented here.

Childhood poverty is particularly damaging from a developmental perspective. It is not just that poverty depletes the resources that can be invested

66 *Structural Racism*

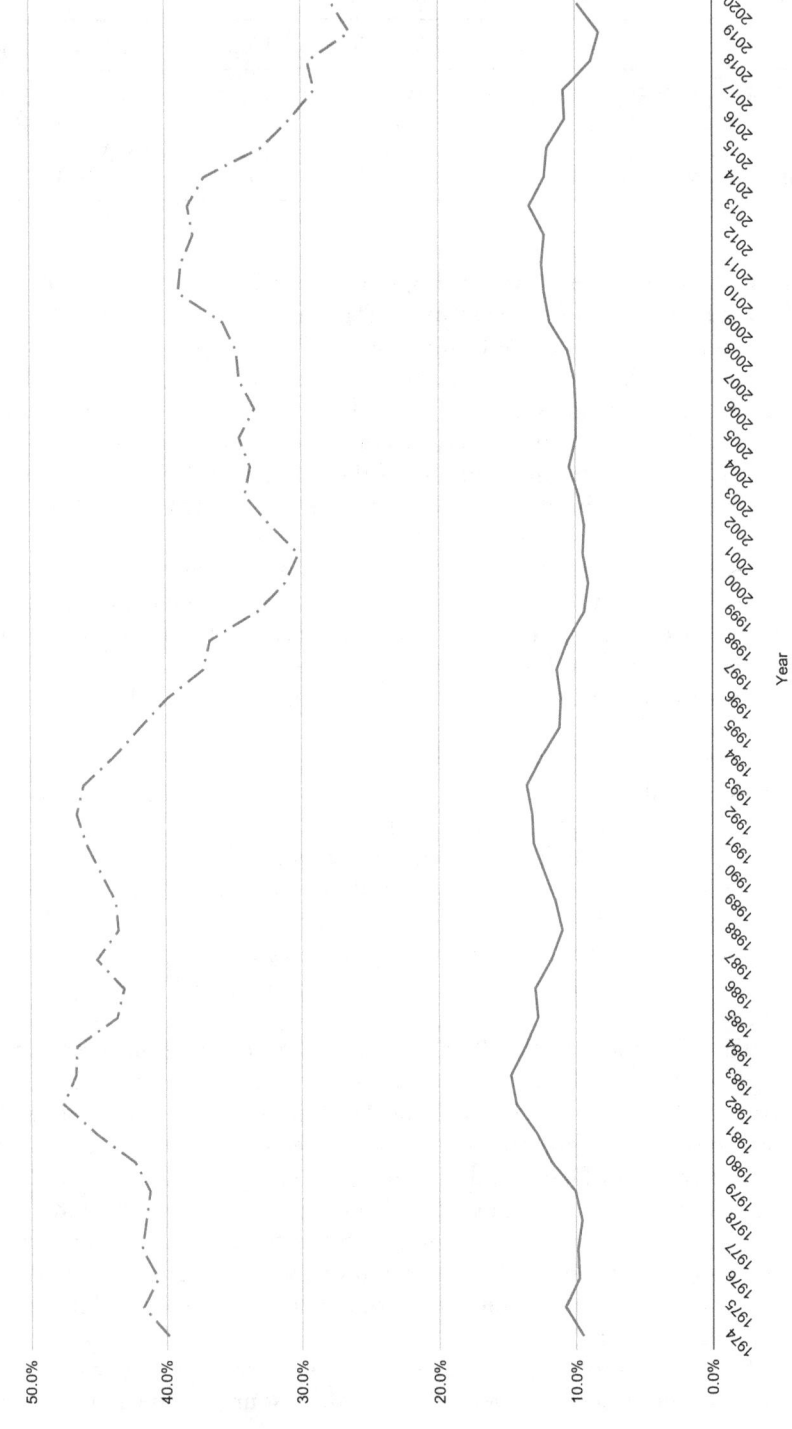

Figure 2.1 Black and White Childhood Poverty Rates, 1974–2020[37]

in skills, capabilities, and an enriching environment, the stress of growing up in poverty may be toxic to the brain and to emotional health and physical well-being.[38] Childhood poverty should be regarded as a particularly pernicious form of poverty, more harmful with more lasting effects than merely earning below the poverty level as an adult.

But before moving on, it is worth looking beyond the simple federal poverty measure. The poverty rate is too restrictive to provide a full sense of economic inequities by race. Perhaps a more revealing fact is that 61% of Black children were raised in the bottom income quintile (which extends above the federal poverty line), compared to just 16% of whites.[39] Given the importance of family resources in shaping child outcomes, these statistics are more alarming than the simple disparities in Black and white rates of poverty. These facts begin to suggest some of the ways in which poverty is racialized in a way that shapes access to opportunity and ultimately life outcomes.

Concentrated Poverty

There are distinctive and peculiarly harmful features to the experience of poverty in the United States for many non-white families beyond the relative rates of poverty or disadvantages of growing up in a poor household. One such feature relates to neighborhoods, the broader environment, and the relative dispersion or concentration of poverty by race.

Poverty matters in shaping life outcomes, especially childhood poverty, but the experience of living in high or concentrated poverty matters more. In the social science literature, high-poverty neighborhoods are generally defined as those where 20–30% or more of the residents earn below the poverty line.[40] Very high, or "concentrated" poverty, is generally defined as a geographic area, typically a neighborhood or census tract, in which 40% of more of the residents earn below the federal poverty line. Social scientific research finds that the effects of neighborhood poverty is negligible until the rate exceeds 20%, whereupon the harmful effects grow rapidly until the rate reaches about 40%.[41] In other words, living in a high poverty neighborhood is harmful, but living in a neighborhood of concentrated poverty is worst of all.

Recall the racial disparities in household income and wealth presented near the beginning of this chapter. In the aggregate, these differential levels of income undeniably contribute to varying neighborhood levels of poverty by race. But when controlling income level, racial disparities in neighborhood poverty rates become more severe, not less. To state the problem briefly, low-income white people tend to be dispersed among a broad middle-class whereas low-income Black and Latino Americans are highly concentrated among each other.

In the last chapter we saw how communities are increasingly stratified by income, and residents are thereby segregated by income. This phenomenon, while general, is not as advanced in predominantly white communities. Although there are more poor whites in absolute numbers than any other group, whites are not concentrated in high-poverty neighborhoods in either the same degree or proportions as non-whites. Only about one in three poor white families live in poor neighborhoods whereas about two in three poor Black and Latino families live in poor neighborhoods.[42] Somehow, lower-income white families manage to escape low-income environments whereas Black and Latino families do not.

A study of neighborhood income by race found, for example, that white families earning just $13,000 per year live in neighborhoods where the median household income is $45,000.[43] Yet, white families earning $50,000 annually were found to reside in neighborhoods where the median income is roughly $53,000. In contrast, Black families earning $50,000 annually live in neighborhoods with a median income of $43,000, less than the typical neighborhood inhabited by poor white people. In terms of neighborhood environments that are generative of opportunity and human capability development, poor whites may be better off than middle-class Black and Latino families.

The deeper problem, however, is that poor Black people on average reside in especially difficult environments, with neighborhood poverty rates of 45% as of 2010.[44] In other words, poor Black families tend to reside in conditions of concentrated poverty. Out of 73,057 census tracts in the United States (excluding those in Puerto Rico and other non-state U.S. territories), only 2,875 tracts (nearly 4%) feature concentrated poverty, where 40% or more of households earn below the federal poverty line.[45] Black households predominate these neighborhoods, as shown in Table 2.2, which compares the racial composition of neighborhoods of concentrated poverty to the general U.S. population.

Black Americans, in particular, are vastly overrepresented in extremely high-poverty neighborhoods. Black Americans are just 12.1% of the general population (according to the 2020 census), but 34.4% of the population of neighborhoods of concentrated poverty. Latinos are just 18.7% of the overall population but 25% of the population residing in such neighborhoods. This cross-sectional view of these neighborhoods, however, may understate just how racialized concentrated poverty is. We can glean a more revealing view of this dynamic if we look at neighborhood racial predominance, not merely overall racial composition.[46]

As shown in Table 2.3, of neighborhoods of concentrated poverty in the United States, by far the largest portion (45%) are predominantly Black, and 21% are predominantly Latino, meaning that nearly two-thirds of these tracts are either predominantly Black or Latino neighborhoods. Only 31%

Table 2.2 The Racial Composition of Neighborhoods of Concentrated Poverty, 2019[47]

Race	Black	Latino	White	Asian	Other
% of the population (2020)	12.1	18.7	57.8	5.9	4.8
% of tracts with 40%+ poverty rates (2019)	34.4	24.9	31.3	4.3	4.9

Table 2.3 Racial Predominance of Neighborhoods of Concentrated Poverty, 2019[48]

Census Tracts	All	Predominantly Black	Predominantly Latino	Predominantly White	Predominantly Asian
Tracts with 40%+ poverty rates	2,875	1,283	599	900	36
% of tracts with 40%+ poverty rates	100	44.6	20.8	31.3	1.3

are predominantly white, and this includes poor regions like Appalachia. More than nine and a half million people live in these neighborhoods, or about 3% of the U.S. population, but these are the places where opportunity is most conspicuously absent and life is most difficult.

With respect to the opportunity structure, growing up in a low-income *household* is not as disadvantageous as growing up in a low-income *neighborhood* or an economically impoverished community. Low-income families residing in wealthy neighborhoods may have fewer resources, but they benefit from their community's affluence, including strong and well-funded schools, well-maintained infrastructure, plentiful amenities, and high-quality municipal services. In contrast, low-income families in concentrated poverty are doubly disadvantaged—they suffer from the lack of resources at home and in their broader environment. Living in poverty means inadequate resources within the home, but living in concentrated poverty means inadequate resources throughout the broader environment.

A monumental study of over 2,000 children over seven years in the Chicago metropolitan area directly measured the impact of living in high-poverty neighborhoods. The study discovered serious negative effects on verbal ability as measured by standardized tests. Specifically, the long-term effect of living in a high-poverty neighborhood affected verbal ability to the equivalent of 4 IQ points, comparable to an entire year of school.[49] Moreover, this is particularly devastating since verbal ability predicts success later in life. This problem is compounded by the fact that children living in concentrated poverty neighborhoods actually have greater learning and behavior disabilities and more special needs.[50]

Concentrated poverty is the anchor weighing down Black families, neighborhoods, and communities. Residents of high-poverty neighborhoods have fewer resources, services and amenities, such as parks, libraries, businesses and health clinics.[51] Not only does growing up in high poverty or concentrated poverty denote fewer resources to draw upon, but it frequently entails exposure to harmful elements. Crime is considered an outgrowth of poverty, but clustering or concentrating poverty exacerbates this problem. Concentrated poverty does more than concentrate crime, it actually increases it.[52] Desperation and living on the margins may fuel petty crime as a form of subsistence and contribute to a perception of disorder. The harmful direct effects of residing in high-poverty neighborhoods are compounded by higher levels of stress, trauma, and anxiety through exposure to violence, crime, and gang activity.

It is not just the fact that neighborhoods of high and concentrated poverty are predominantly Black and mostly non-white that defines structural racism. Although a relatively small portion of the American population reside in such tracts, such tracts constitute a large percentage of predominantly Black neighborhoods, as shown in Table 2.4, and thus the Black community experience, in America. If we delve just a bit deeper, we can see this reality with greater clarity, and its role in shaping local opportunity structures and life experience by race.

Despite their greater absolute numbers, all but a tiny percentage of white people earning below the poverty line escape the most harmful effects of poverty concentration. Conversely, the harmful effects of concentrated poverty are visited upon Black Americans to a uniquely extreme degree. Just 1.7% of predominantly white neighborhoods are neighborhoods of concentrated poverty, compared to 17.1% of predominantly Black neighborhoods. If we just look at high-poverty neighborhoods, we see an even more astounding disparity, where 64.1% of predominantly Black neighborhoods are high poverty, compared to 15% of white neighborhoods (a nearly 50% point disparity), although Hispanic Americans suffer the disadvantages of high-poverty environments at distinctively high rates here as well. A super-majority of

Table 2.4 High Poverty and Concentrated Poverty Neighborhoods by Racial Predominance, 2019[53]

Census Tracts	All	Predominantly Black	Predominantly Latino	Predominantly White	Predominantly Asian
All tracts	73,057	7,490	9,354	53,656	1,443
Predominant race tracts with 20%+ poverty rates	17,749	4,798	4,486	8,041	222
% of predominant race tracts with 20%+ poverty rates	N/A	**64.1**	48.0	15.0	15.4
Predominant race tracts with 40%+ poverty rates	2,875	1283	599	900	36
% of Predominant race tracts with 40%+ poverty rates	N/A	**17.1**	6.4	1.7	2.5

Black communities in America are high-poverty or concentrated poverty neighborhoods, and suffer the harmful effects of that reality. This is the import of structural racism.*

Unsurprisingly, the harmful effects of poverty concentration spill over into educational environments. As noted several times before, the quality of the schools one attends powerfully shapes life chances. Concentrated poverty strongly predicts virtually every dismal educational outcome, from lower graduation rates to lower test scores.[54] The socioeconomic composition of the student body has long been recognized as a leading indicator of student achievement.[55] Schools with greater numbers of children from impoverished backgrounds predictably have greater needs, lower graduation rates, higher dropout rates and teen pregnancy.

Children from poor households are more likely to arrive at school undernourished and less academically prepared than their peers. Low-income families also move more frequently, with disruptive effects on learning and curriculum continuity. Putting disadvantaged students together in the same school is a recipe for failure. Even with additional grants or equity formulas, public schools in low tax capacity districts lack the resources needed to compensate for the lack of private capacities and greater needs of disadvantaged children.

Neighborhood poverty rates understate the scale of the concentration effects problem in schools. Families with children have higher poverty rates than the general population, and therefore poverty tends to be even more concentrated in schools. It is not unusual for a merely high-poverty neighborhood to contain schools where 50% or more of children qualify for free and reduced lunch.

Unfortunately, students of color experience the brunt of the disadvantages that flow from concentrated poverty in the educational context as well. If we examine the racial composition of schools based upon poverty rates, we can see that low-poverty schools are heavily white (more than two-thirds) and high-poverty schools are mostly Black and Latino. As shown in Table 2.5 below, the typical low-poverty school is on average 68% white, 12% Asian, 11% Latino and just 4% Black. In contrast, the typical school with a poverty rate of more than 80% is only 51% Latino, 28% Black but just 14% white and 3% Asian.

Table 2.5 Racial Composition of Schools by Level of Poverty, 2019–2020[56]

% Poverty	% White	% Black	% Latino	% Asian	% of Schools in United States
0–20%	67.6	4.4	10.5	11.9	12.8
20.01–40%	64.0	7.9	16.4	5.8	20.7
40.01–60%	55.4	12.0	22.5	4.0	24.7
60.01–80%	32.7	19.1	38.0	4.2	19.7
80.01–100%	13.7	27.6	51.3	2.9	22.1

* Wilson, When Work Disappears, 22.

If we re-organize this data in the opposite way, to view average school poverty rates based upon racial composition, then the disparities become even more evident. School poverty rates climb almost proportionately with the percentage of students of color. On average, in schools that are more than 60% white, only a third of the student body come from families in poverty, as of 2019–2020.[57] However, in schools that are less than 20% white, a shocking three-quarters of the student body come from families in poverty. In schools that are more than 90% white (13.6% of schools in the United States), the student poverty rate was only 3.6%. But in schools that are 90% or more Black and/or Latino (11.5% of schools in the United States), the student poverty rate is 86.3%. These are reverse negative images of race and poverty in our public schools.

In summary, most extremely high-poverty schools are predominantly Black and brown, and most Black and brown schools are extremely high poverty. And as with neighborhood poverty, family income cannot entirely explain this dynamic. Non-white students of all economic backgrounds are far more likely to attend a high-poverty schools than poor white students.[58] This helps explain why Black and Latino schools are less likely to have advanced mathematics, AP classes, or gifted and talented courses than white schools.[59] It is not just that these schools lack certain amenities, these are often deeply troubled, struggling schools. Very few high-poverty schools—perhaps as little only 1%—succeed.[60]

Many of the most critical harms of poverty arise not from the simple fact of growing up in a low-income household, but the experience of growing up in a low-income neighborhood or attending a high-poverty school. As we have seen, the opportunity structure is constituted by the pooling and concatenation of private and public resources. Concentrated poverty denies individuals the benefits of those pooled resources while exposing them to harms of concentrated disadvantage.

Concentrated poverty is a form of poverty that deserves special attention. People growing up in areas of concentrated poverty not only have fewer collective public and private resources to draw from or benefit them, but they also may have greater needs relative to those resources and pay a premium for an environment they cannot escape. It is concentrated poverty, rather than family poverty, which reverberates through the opportunity structure. Nearly 70% of Black children who grow up in the poorest neighborhoods will remain in them as adults, while only 40% of whites would.[61] This temporal component points toward another form of racialized poverty: Durable and inter-generational poverty.

Durable Poverty

There is another critical distinction between white and non-white poverty in relation to the opportunity structure: that of temporary versus durable poverty. Although the percentage of white people in poverty is similar that

Structural Racial Inequality 73

of all other racial groups in poverty (see Table 2.1), they are more likely to experience intermittent or temporary poverty by comparison to racially marginalized populations. Many adults report low or negative income when they enroll in college or become graduate students, as they plan or start new businesses, or because of periodic unemployment during recessions. Among white families who experience poverty in the United States, two-thirds are poor for only three years or less, whereas only 2% are impoverished for more than ten years.[62] In contrast, 17% of Black Americans are poor for ten or more years. Although only 44% of poor people will be poor for the next four to ten years, for Black people, that figure is 61%.[63]

Although household poverty matters, durable poverty is far more detrimental to opportunity and well-being. The deleterious effects of living in poverty become more pronounced when suffered over time rather than temporarily or intermittently. Much like concentrated poverty, the harms of durable poverty are more than additive or even cumulative, they are multiplicative and compounding. Just as living in a poor household in a poor neighborhood is a compound denial of resources, living in poverty produces greater harm over time.

Lacking health insurance for a few years may be of little consequence for a 25-year-old graduate student, but not having health insurance for ten years may cause minor medical issues, untreated, to develop into major health risks or serious conditions. Similarly, being temporarily unemployed in a recession may not seriously impair one's employability when the economy rebounds, but individuals who are persistently unemployed may become disaffected with traditional forms of employment, fail to develop or maintain skills needed to stay current, including the "soft" skills needed to remain competitive in the labor market, such as how to write a resume or interview for a job, and may be viewed as unreliable or risky by potential employers. Long term, cumulative effects of prolonged poverty translate into inadequate health care and lack of access to and engagement in the mainstream labor market.

Just as being persistently unemployed is more harmful than sporadic unemployment, research on student poverty shows that long-term poverty is qualitatively distinct than merely being merely poor. Students who were eligible for free and reduced lunch every year of primary school since kindergarten were much further behind in terms of grade level and National Assessment of Educational Progress (NAEP) test scores than students who were merely "economically disadvantaged."[64] Merely economically disadvantaged students were roughly two grade levels behind those who were not, but those who were "persistently disadvantaged" were nearly three levels behind.

The most extreme form of durable poverty is intergenerational. Intergenerational poverty is also highly racialized. According to a major study released in 2021, only 5% and 1.2% of white families experienced poverty for two and three consecutive generations, respectively, compared to 21.3% and 33% of Black families.[65] Another study looking at just two generations found that only 10% of whites who never experienced poverty as a child will experience it in their thirties, and only 20% of whites who were poor as children will experience poverty in their thirties.[66] In contrast, that study found that Black children have almost the same chance of falling into poverty as adults at some point whether they were poor as children or not. This is consistent with the findings noted from the studies on race and upward mobility noted earlier this chapter, which covered similar ground.

From a structural perspective, however, the most harmful effects of durable poverty might be environmental rather than personal or at the household level. Intergenerational *neighborhood* poverty is the focus of Patrick Sharkey's book *Stuck in Place*. He finds that, on average, few white families live in a poor neighborhood for a more generation, but that the opposite is true for Black American families. Specifically, Sharkey finds that 48% of Black American families reside in poor neighborhoods over consecutive generations, compared to just 7% of whites.[67] The effects of multi-generational neighborhood poverty from one generation to the next may be as pronounced as durable poverty is on individuals, or have transmission effects that flow through individual households.

To measure those effects, Sharkey cleverly compared the test scores of children raised by parents who grew up in high-poverty and parents who grew up in low-poverty environments. He found that children raised in low-poverty environments, but by parents who also grew up in low-poverty environments, performed better than children similarly raised in low-poverty environments but by parents who grew up in high-poverty neighborhoods.[68] Surprisingly, however, he also found that children who grew up in low-poverty neighborhoods, but whose parents grew up in high-poverty neighborhoods, performed about as well on reading and problem-solving tests as children who grew up in high-poverty neighborhoods, but whose parents grew up in low-poverty neighborhoods. In other words, whether a parent grew up in a high- or low-poverty neighborhood mattered, in the long run, nearly much as whether the child did.

Shading nuance, Sharkey finds that the effects of a parent growing up in a high-poverty neighborhood matter more in some respects and less in others. Despite the influence of neighborhood, his research shows that parents play a significant role in shaping aspirations and establishing expectations about the child's future, especially college matriculation.[69] Sharkey finds that parents who grew up in low-poverty neighborhoods are more likely to expect their children to apply to college, with the result that they are more likely to do so.

But these findings should not be interpreted to suggest that parental influences are more important than environment and structures. Rather, it is a reminder that parental influence itself is a product of structures and environment or previous opportunity cycles. The point of Sharkey's research here is that focusing solely on the child's environment misses the effects of a parent's formative environment. Children who grow up in high-poverty neighborhoods are disadvantaged, but if their parents also grew up in the same environment, those children are even more disadvantaged, and suffer the cumulative harms of intergenerational and durable poverty.

Childhood poverty should be regarded differently than adult poverty, as it instills disadvantages at critical life junctures that may never be overcome. Concentrated poverty is more damaging to human development than growing up in low-income household, and durable poverty is also extraordinarily harmful to long run well-being. All three forms of poverty fall disproportionately on Black and brown people in the United States. Although white people experience poverty in greater absolute numbers than any other group, they tend to avoid experiencing the deleterious effects of durable, childhood and concentrated poverty.

Race versus Class

Returning to the question raised earlier, about the relative influence of race versus class on the sources and extent of racial inequality, the experiences of childhood, concentrated, and durable poverty suggest why the racialization of the opportunity structure is not entirely reducible to class. Poor whites generally do not experience these compounding forms of disadvantage in nearly the same degree.[70] In fact, the magnitude of these economic disparities between racial groups and the unique exposure and particularities of the harm is such that they are a difference in kind, not just degree.[71] Nonetheless, since these experiences remain a form of poverty (and thereby of economics), no matter how uniquely experienced by race, one may nonetheless wonder if class or socioeconomic status could serve as a better lens for understanding these experiences and redressing their harmful effects.

The most obvious objection to that suggestion is that a narrow class lens could obscure, rather than illuminate, these facts. A class-exclusive lens would tend to conceal rather than reveal these particularly harmful experiences of racialized poverty. After all, the vast majority of neighborhoods of concentrated poverty are non-white, and concentrated student poverty is even more strongly correlated with race. The experience and effects generated in these environments is not comparable to the experience or effects of simple family-level poverty, and a race-blind lens would make it difficult to recognize that fact. Only by disaggregating these forms of poverty by race can we observe the stark racial dynamics of poverty and take full cognizance of these distinctive and peculiar expressions. More generally, if these experiences are racialized, and race cannot be reduced to class, then a race lens is necessary to recognize and rectify them.

And yet, these racialized expressions of poverty could have class at the root or trunk of the problem, while race is merely a branch or byproduct. Even if some race effects are unique or distinctive, and even if it would be difficult to perceive the racial differences analytically with a class-only lens, addressing the class problems could, according to this theory of the problem, ultimately address the racial disparities as well. It would follow that a remedial policy agenda designed to address these and perhaps other economic racial disparities should be class-targeted rather than race-specific.

This, then, is the critical test: if a class-based policy agenda could fully address or resolve these racial disparities, then racial inequality could be explained by class or viewed as a byproduct of class dynamics. If, on the other hand, a class-targeted or class-focused policy agenda is incapable of addressing let alone fully closing these racial disparities, then race or some race-based factor must have independent or compounding effects. The weight of evidence and experience, unfortunately, supports the latter position.

Both race and class have profound effects on the structure and distribution of opportunity, but this does not mean that they are easy to disentangle. The education scholar and sociologist Prudence Carter dubbed them "fraternal twins," related forces that share a common DNA.[72] The experiences of concentrated and durable poverty illustrate this by featuring both an integral socioeconomic and a distinctive racial dimension. Many socioeconomic disadvantages are compounded by race just as some forms of class privilege are racialized.

More broadly, the experience of race itself is partly felt in socioeconomic terms, and, in the United States, class positions are racially inflected. The terms "middle-class," "working class," and even "underclass" have racial coding and connotations despite their ostensible class designation.[73] The meaning of both class position and racial identities are informed by each other.

The relationship between race and class might be best understood by analogy to the relationship between nature and nurture. For centuries scientists have sought to isolate the relative influence of each, assuming that they were distinct and independent influences. The science of epigenetics has revealed that nature and nurture interact in complicated ways, such as how certain environmental conditions can trigger genes, turning them on or off.[74] In this regard, neither nature nor nurture can be reduced to the other nor isolated from each other.

Due to their entanglement, there are undoubtedly racial disparities that could be addressed or ameliorated by class-based interventions. On the other hand, a class-exclusive policy agenda or package of interventions is not only incapable of fully addressing racial disparities, but in some cases could exacerbate them.[75] To illustrate why race cannot be entirely reduced to class, and explain why the aforementioned forms of poverty are racialized, we must look beyond poverty or class to the racial mechanisms that underpin these expressions of poverty, and to racial residential segregation in particular.

Racial Segregation

Concentrated poverty would not be a racial mechanism of opportunity inequality if it were not for the fact of residential segregation by race, that poor Black and Latino families disproportionately reside in racially isolated neighborhoods where their own groups predominate. Racial residential segregation is the structural mechanism that concentrates poverty by race in a way that mere economic segregation or higher rates of non-white poverty alone cannot do.[76]

The connection between racial residential segregation and poverty concentration has been well-established. In metropolitan areas with higher levels of racial residential segregation, a greater share of Black families reside in neighborhoods of concentrated poverty: 18% of Black families reside in neighborhoods of concentrated poverty in metro areas with high levels of racial segregation compared to just 8% of Black families in metro areas with moderate levels of segregation.[77] The percentages are higher when looking only at low-income Black families. In moderately segregated metropolitan areas, only 17% of low-income Black people live in neighborhoods of concentrated poverty, compared to 33% of low-income Black people in very highly segregated metros.[78] Contrary to the notion that integration harms lower-income Black communities by allowing their more affluent neighbors to flee,[79] racial integration at the regional level is associated with lower levels of concentrated poverty for lower- and moderate-income Black families.

Racial segregation is not just a mechanism that concentrates poverty by race, and thereby intensifies the racially experienced harms of poverty, it also draws non-poor people of color into more disadvantaged and higher-poverty environments, helping also explain why the typical middle-class Black and middle-class white American live in socioeconomically distinctive neighborhoods. More broadly, racial segregation sorts people into advantaged or disadvantaged environments based upon race, and therefore is the linchpin of structural racial inequality, or structural racism. In short, racial residential segregation is the principal mechanism that separates people from opportunity by race in American society.

"Segregation" has common connotations that can cause confusion when using the term in a more precise way. In the American historical context, the most prominent modes of segregation were in public accommodations and recreational facilities (trains, buses, hotels, theaters, and public swimming pools), occupational settings (restricting jobs or departments based on race), or schools (race-based pupil assignment). Although some of these modes persist (although rarely as a matter of law or formal institutional practice), the prevailing contemporary mode of segregation is in terms of residential patterns (housing).

To be clear on terms, segregation is the separation of one or more groups of people on the basis of their group identity in one or more realm of life. Racial segregation in the separation of people on the basis of their racial identity. Racial *residential* segregation is the separation of people by race in terms of their residential location (where people live), generally in the context of neighborhoods, cities, and metropolitan regions. As will be shown, virtually every expression of systemic racial inequality examined in this book, including education, health, the criminal justice system, employment and wealth, are undergirded, reinforced, or compounded by racial residential segregation.

By convention, in journalistic and scholarly writing, "segregated" neighborhoods or schools tend to refer to predominantly non-white, especially heavily Black or Latino, spaces. But predominantly white schools and neighborhoods are often just as segregated, if not more so. Although the experiences of both were starkly different in terms of resources and quality of provision, it is difficult to understand how Black schools in the Jim Crow south could be described as segregated, but not the all-white schools as well. They were both segregated using the same means and resulting from the same design.

Segregation is sometimes confused with other, related concepts, such as racial composition, racial demographics, or racial diversity. Racial composition maps are commonly presented as illustrations of racial segregation. A *Wired* magazine headline, for example, dubbed a racial dot-map as "The Best Map Ever Made of America's Racial Segregation."[80] Such maps may convey a sense or impression that segregation exists, but it is not, in a precise sense, measuring or denoting a state of segregation, let alone the level of segregation that may exist. Similarly, many books, chapters, and reports feature maps illustrating the percentage of a racial group (often percentage of Black) residing in a particular set of census tracts or the racial change in those tracts over a defined period of time claim to denote or represent racial residential segregation.[81] Although such maps can strongly suggest or imply the existence of racial residential segregation, they do not display or indicate it. The racial composition of a neighborhood, or change in composition over time, cannot tell you the precise level of segregation or integration that exists, and whether the arrangement of people is, or is becoming, integrated or segregated.[82]

Despite the apparent simplicity of the concept, measuring segregation has proven challenging.[83] There are unresolved scholarly debates about exactly what spatial dynamics residential segregation measures are capturing or should be representing.[84] Each measure of segregation appears to reveal a different facet or aspect of the underlying phenomenon, as if answering a different question in each case.[85]

The most well-known and widely used measure of segregation remains the Dissimilarity Index.[86] The Dissimilarity Index measures how evenly various racial groups are spread across neighborhoods within metropolitan areas in relation to each other. By looking at two groups at a time, the Dissimilarity Index score indicates the percentage of either group that would have to move to a different-race or integrated neighborhood to completely integrate that city or region. In that regard, a score of zero indicates that both groups are evenly distributed throughout the metropolitan region ("complete integration"), whereas a score of 100 indicates that every neighborhood is racially defined by a single group ("complete segregation"). A score of 60 indicates that 60% of either group would have to move to a different race or integrated neighborhood for the region to become completely integrated.

The scholarly consensus pegs a dissimilarity score of 30 to 60 as the "moderate" range, and scores above and below it as high and low, respectively.[87] Using the 2020 census data, the average metropolitan region in the United States has a Black-white dissimilarity score of 55, suggesting that 55% of Black or white Americans would need to move to a different race neighborhood to achieve complete integration.[88] White-Hispanic and white-Asian national dissimilarity scores were 45 and 40, respectively.[89] These figures suggest that the United States is and remains a racially segregated society, at least residentially.

This snapshot of national dissimilarity scores in 2020 may understate the degree of residential segregation that persists. First, there are considerable regional differences across the United States in terms of the overall level of segregation.[90] In general, the rust-belt cities of the Midwest, like Cleveland, Indianapolis, Chicago, Milwaukee, and Detroit have the highest levels of racial residential segregation, well above the national average, as do large northern cities such as Boston, Philadelphia, and New York.[91] In contrast, cities in South Atlantic states like Charleston, Columbia, Raleigh, Richmond, and Jacksonville and cities in Southwestern states such as Las Vegas and Phoenix have much lower than average levels of segregation.

Second, a static, snapshot view of segregation masks trend lines. Depending on the region, Black-white dissimilarity scores in the United States peaked somewhere between 1960 and 1970, and have generally been declining ever since.[92] Although this may seem like progress, the most significant declines occurred between 1970 and 1980, and the rate of decline has slowed in recent decades, and may be plateauing.[93] On the other hand, white-Hispanic and white-Asian dissimilarity scores have increased in many regions, such as the Bay Area, especially as Hispanic and Asian populations grow larger in either absolute or relative terms.[94]

Most importantly, progress for some can obscure the persistence of segregation for many or most. Dissimilarity scores improve when a fractional proportion of people move into a different-race neighborhood, even if the average or typical member of a racial group resides in a segregated neighborhood. As a result of fair housing laws, non-trivial numbers of affluent and middle-class Black families have moved into traditionally or nominally white neighborhoods, just as more white families have moved into traditionally non-white neighborhoods in the urban core. The result of these trends is far fewer all white or all Black neighborhoods than there were in 1960 or even 1970, but this tells us little about the overall level of integration or the degree or racial isolation experienced by most Black Americans, or other racially marginalized groups. The integration of a significant but relative few may obscure the degree of segregation experienced by most.

For these reasons, alternative measures of segregation should be considered where possible, especially when trying to gauge the overall level of segregation in a multiracial rather than biracial context. When examining the situation of a particular racial group, and trying to assess how isolated that group may be from other groups, the Isolation Indices may be quite useful. These Indices (known independently as the Isolation Index and the Exposure Index) describe the average or typical neighborhood of a person of a particular race in a region or community.[95] These indices tell us, for example, that as of 2020, the average white resident of a metropolitan area resides in a neighborhood that is 69% white, 9% Black, 12% Hispanic, and 6% Asian.[96] In contrast, a typical Black American resident lives in a neighborhood that is 34% white, 12% Black, 45% Hispanic, and 8% Asian.

Although understated by the Dissimilarity Index, these figures reflect demographically different worlds. In addition, they may provide a better point-to-point historical comparison. As the 2020 figures above suggest, the "exposure" of the average Black American to white neighbors is "34," approximately the same as it was in 1950,[97] a fact which significantly complicates the appearance of progress toward integration suggested by the Dissimilarity Index.[98]

When trying to get a holistic sense of the level of racial segregation in a region or city, or when trying to get a more granular indication of segregation at the neighborhood level, then other indices may be preferred.[99] One such index is the Divergence Index, which calculates the proportions of all racial groups at one level of geography (such as a census tract) and compares those proportions to a larger geography (such as a city or a metropolitan area).[100] The greater the "divergence" in proportions between the two levels, the higher the Divergence Index score. This measure is particularly useful because it provides a single score or value (like the Dissimilarity Index), but for individual neighborhoods (at the census tract level) as well as for larger geographies, such as cities or entire regions (at the Metropolitan Statistical Area (MSA) or Core-Based Statistical Area (CBSA) level).[101]

The United States has always been a multiracial nation, but since 1965, it has experienced a dramatic increase in the Latino and Asian populations.[102] If segregation under the Dissimilarity Index decreases between two groups, but increases between another two, we may miss the overall change in segregation. For a nation as diverse as the United States, and growing ever more so, multi-group measures are needed to provide a more accurate sense of the overall level of segregation. Black-white segregation may have fallen since 1970 due to the extreme conditions that existing before then, but that does not mean that Asian and Latino peoples are integrating. In fact, in many regions, they are becoming more segregated.

In the San Francisco MSA, for example, white-Hispanic dissimilarity scores rose from 1980 to 2000.[103] Similarly, white-Asian dissimilarity scores rose during the same period, and up to 2010 and 2020.[104] Similar patterns—of increasing white-Hispanic and/or white-Asian dissimilarity values—can be seen in cities as disparate as Miami,[105] Raleigh,[106] and Milwaukee.[107] These

Structural Racial Inequality 81

dynamics help explain rising levels of segregation according to some multigroup measures.

Out of every metropolitan region in the United States with more than 200,000 residents, 53.8% had a higher Divergence Index score in 2020 than they did in 1990.[108] In many cases, the increase was negligible, but in some cases, it was quite substantial, and stark differences exist between what the Divergence Index revealed and the Dissimilarity Index indicated even when just focusing on Black and white segregation.[109]

Even assuming that segregation has declined in the manner suggested by the Dissimilarity Index (significantly between 1970 and 1980, and then more gradually since) rather than increased, racial residential segregation remains at a higher overall level than economic segregation and income sorting, which many assume is a key driver of racial segregation.[110] At the individual or household level, especially for Black families, greater income does not produce less segregated neighborhoods.[111] This means that middle-class and affluent Black families are more likely to live in poorer neighborhoods than their white counterparts.[112] For example, Blacks and Latinos with incomes more than $75,000 a year reside in neighborhoods with higher levels of poverty than whites who earn less than $40,000 a year.[113] In fact, 37% of Black families in the United States earning more than a $100,000 a year reside in poor neighborhoods, compared to just 9% of whites.[114]

Racial residential segregation is harmful to upward socioeconomic mobility broadly. The investigation of upward mobility using millions of anonymous tax records found that regions with higher levels of racial segregation have lower rates of upward mobility for all groups, not just people of color.[115] This suggests a structural cause rather than an individual race effect. Since places with more Black people tend to be both more economically and racial segregated, it follows that places with more Black people would have lower rates of economic upward mobility. This is also what these researchers subsequently found: a "place-level race effect," regions with larger Black populations had lower rates of upward mobility for children of *all* races.[116]

We have already seen that Black Americans have much lower rates of upward mobility and higher rates of downward mobility. Now we can appreciate the structural underpinnings to these racial outcomes. Black children growing up in racially and economic segregated neighborhoods have worse outcomes, and too many Black children grow up in such circumstances.[117] Specifically, Black children raised in integrated neighborhoods earn nearly $1,000 more as adults per year, and $4,000 more when raised in white neighborhoods, than those raised in highly segregated communities of color.[118] Similarly, Latino children raised in integrated neighborhoods earn $844 more per year as adults, and $5,000 more when raised in white neighborhoods, than those raised in highly segregated communities of color. By itself, racial segregation has been estimated to explain one-third of the differences between Blacks and whites in income, education, and employment, and other key life outcomes.[119]

Racial residential integration (or segregation) is not an inevitable byproduct of racial diversity, and a lower rate of upward mobility is not an inevitable feature of places with more non-white peoples (as the San Francisco Bay Area reflects). But even seemingly modest differences in the level or degree of segregation appear to be correlated with large differences in life outcomes. For example, the Black-white gap of relative income is two to five times smaller in metropolitan areas with moderate levels of segregation compared to metros with very high levels of segregation.[120] Regions with higher levels of segregation generally produce worse outcomes for Black Americans than those that have relatively less segregation.

Racial residential segregation also translates into segregation by race in schools, since about three-quarters of primary and secondary students in the United States attend neighborhood schools.[121] Because most schools draw students from nearby neighborhoods, the demographics of schools reflect that of neighborhoods. Unless districts proactively integrate schools within their systems by drawing attendance boundaries to overcome and compensate for neighborhood segregation, schools mirror segregation in their communities.[122] White neighborhoods produce white schools, and so on. This is why so many American school districts are racially segregated.

A national study released in 2022 of over 400 metropolitan areas found that America's public schools remain persistently segregated.[123] In general, there was an average 21-point gap in the percentage of white students enrolled at the average white student's school and the percentage of white students at the average non-white student's school.[124] In about 10% of metro areas, that difference was over 50 points for the average Black and average white student. Researchers found that, in large school districts, white-Black segregation has increased 35% from 1991 to 2020.[125]

Schools may actually be *more* segregated than neighborhoods, because of racial differences in the school age population and the general population and other dynamics, like enrollment in charter schools and other private schools, that sift or draw children into different school buildings.[126] According to a federal agency report in 2016, "more than 20 million students of color now attend[...] racially and socioeconomically isolated public schools."[127] Only about 1 in 5 of Black students and 1 in 4 of Latino students attended integrated schools.[128] Conversely, about 40% of Black and Latino students attend "intensely segregated schools," meaning schools in which 90–100% of the students are non-white, nationwide.[129] As of 2021, nearly 20% of public schools in the U.S. were intensely segregated, up from 7.4% in 1988.[130] Perhaps more striking, one in six Black or Latino students attend "hypersegregated schools," school in which the student population is 99–100% of color.[131] Many of these students attend schools that were as starkly segregated as those before *Brown v. Board of Education*. These conditions have powerful consequences for educational opportunity and achievement, another powerful force that helps explains racial inequality across a range of important life outcomes.[132]

Educational Attainment

Few can deny the centrality of formal educational provision in opening, revealing, or expanding pathways of opportunity. Because of the capabilities and skills that are developed in educational settings, improving educational attainment is one of the principal mechanisms for expanding access to opportunity. Given the requisite skills and qualifications demanded by the contemporary economy, educational provision, more than any other single program, has the potential to reset trajectories of inter-generational economic mobility and improve individual life chances for the greater number of people. Accordingly, attaining post-secondary education may be the strongest conduit of upward mobility for young people from low-income families.

The annual earnings income gap between individuals holding a college degree versus high school degree is more than $19,500.[133] The average B.A. holder earns roughly 80% more over a lifetime than a high school graduate.[134] A child born into the lowest economic quintile has only a 14% chance of ascending to the top 40% of income without a college degree, but a 40% chance of making it if she does.[135] Unfortunately, there are stark racial disparities in educational attainment that contribute to the racial opportunity gap.

As of 2010, just under 70% of white high school graduates enrolled in a two- or four-year university, compared to 65% of Black high school graduates.[136] This statistic may understate disparities in collegiate matriculation, as white students remain more likely to graduate from high school in the first place, although that disparity has narrowed significantly since the 1960s.[137]

More importantly, Black students are less likely to graduate from college even after successfully enrolling, and this disparity has gotten worse. For the 2016 cohort, 66% of white students graduated in six years compared to 43% of Black students.[138] In 1980, for every young Black adult who had completed college, seven whites had done so.[139] In 2017, for every young adult Black adult who had completed college, eight whites had done so.

Although a large majority of Americans attend *some* post-secondary education, white Americans are 35% more likely to have a bachelor's degree as of 2020. Specifically, 37.5% of white Americans 25 or older have one as of 2020, compared to only 28% of Black Americans and 21% of Latinos. The relative magnitude of the Black-white disparity has oscillated because all groups have improved college graduation rates, but the absolute gap has remained fairly steady since 1980, as shown in Table 2.6.

Black youth are less likely to attend selective or elite institutions and more likely to enroll in for-profit institutions. The latter account for about 30% of Black and a quarter of Hispanic college credentials, respectively, while making up just 11% of white credentials.[140] At elite or selective universities, Black enrollment is the same as it was in 1980.[141] This matters because graduation rates vary significantly by the type of institution. Specifically, Black graduation rates are more than 70% at selective institutions (compared to 80% for white enrollees), but under 45% at private, non-profit

Table 2.6 Percentage of Americans 25 or Older with a Bachelor's Degree by Race, 1959–2020[142]

Race	1959	1970	1980	1990	2000	2010	2020
All	8.1%	11.0%	16.2%	21.3%	25.6%	29.9%	37.5%
White	8.6%	11.6%	17.8%	22.0%	26.1%	30.3%	37.5%
Black	3.3%	4.5%	7.9%	11.3%	16.5%	19.8%	27.8%
Asian	N/A	N/A	N/A	N/A	N/A	52.4%	61.1%
Latino	N/A	N/A	7.9%	9.2%	10.6%	13.9%	20.8%

colleges, 41% at public colleges and universities, and just 20% at for-profit institutions.[143]

Education may not be the answer to all economic inequality by race, but it can help reduce inequality of opportunity and improve financial stability. Every additional year of educational attainment improves chances for socioeconomic mobility and likelihood of stable employment. For Black Americans aged 25 to 29 with a college degree, the unemployment rate in 2013 was 7.6%. For those without one, it was 17.8%.[144] In terms of mobility, 69% of Black Americans with 14 years of education will rise above the bottom quintile in earnings as adults, compared to 28% with exactly 10 years of education, and with 16 years of schooling the race-mobility gap essentially closes.[145] According to another study, with 17 years of education, the race gap in employment and earnings also disappears.[146]

Unfortunately, educational attainment is determined in large part by the structural components of opportunity already reviewed. In particular, segregation, school district resources, and social and family networks shape academic aspiration and achievement. Inequitable investments and other resource flows shape educational environments and help explain unequal access to educational opportunity by race. A landmark study released in 2020 found significant disparities between predominantly white and non-white school districts in terms of per-pupil spending. In 2016, predominantly white school districts spent $23 billion more in state and local funding than majority non-white districts, although they served about the same number of students.[147] This equated to more than $2,200 per year, per-pupil. Recall that per-pupil funding plays a significant role in the educational performance of a district, with relatively greater funding improving outcomes.

In a study of more than 200 metropolitan regions, racial school segregation reduced Black high school graduation rates by more than 5%.[148] Not only are Black youth in segregated schools more likely to drop out before graduation, but students graduating from these schools perform worse on nation-wide tests. Studies of SAT scores show persistent racial gaps, with Black students disproportionately clustered in the bottom ranges.[149] On the math section, for example, the average scores for Black (428) and Latino (457) students are significantly below those of white (534) and Asians

(598).¹⁵⁰ These scores do not simply indicate the chances of being accepted at a selective institution, but they reflect the quality of primary and secondary education that students receive. A 2006 study estimated that growing up in a segregated city may explain as much as a quarter of the gap in the SAT.¹⁵¹

Educational aspirations are shaped by role models, parental expectations, and adult encouragement. Black youth in high poverty and racially segregated neighborhoods are less likely to have role models or other adults encouraging them to aspire to a college education, and less network familiarity with college application processes, and therefore are less like to apply, enroll, or graduate from college.¹⁵² A nation-wide survey revealed that only 49% of Black children growing up in rural or low-income areas were encouraged to apply to college growing up, compared to 65% in middle income neighborhoods.¹⁵³

At the same time, the costs of higher education and the burdens of student debt are a considerable deterrent to pursuing post-secondary education and ultimately greater educational attainment.¹⁵⁴ Black students pursuing higher education are more reliant on student loans than white students, take on and accumulate more student debt, and are more concerned with loan repayments.¹⁵⁵ Black families hold considerably less wealth, and Black families have far less capacity or wherewithal to provide financial assistance for college tuition and other expenses that would facilitate the pursuit of further educational opportunities and educational attainment. This leads to the next structural component that shapes racially unequal access to opportunity, the enormous racial wealth gap.

The Racial Wealth Gap

The racial wealth gap, one of the most shocking racial disparities in American society, has received scholarly significant attention, although the key facts are highly nuanced and surprisingly subtle. In 2019, the average Black household net worth was $142,500 while white mean household net worth was $983,400, a relative disparity of nearly seven times.¹⁵⁶ Although this disparity is skewed by a handful of extremely high wealth families, when looking at the typical, or median, household, the disparity is even greater. The net worth of the typical white family was pegged at $188,200, eight times greater than that of a typical Black family ($24,100) in 2019.¹⁵⁷ When home equity is excluded, the typical white household held $17,150 in net worth compared to just $930 for Black households.¹⁵⁸

The racial wealth gap is both a cause and effect of structural racism, and one that will be among the most difficult to address. Wealth accumulation is ultimately a product of all of the inputs and resources that are enjoyed by families and individuals over time. Given the systematic disadvantages Black people experience in the opportunity structure, it should not be surprising that Black Americans hold less wealth. After all, racial disparities in income and employment alone can produce unequal wealth accumulations. But the racial wealth gap is more deeply rooted than that.

86 *Structural Racism*

A few hundred wealthy white people hold more wealth than all Black Americans combined. In 2015, the 400 wealthiest whites in the United States possessed a cumulative worth of $2.34 trillion, nearly 1.5 times that of all 16 million African-American households ($1.56 trillion) and 1.3 times that of all 15 million Latinx households ($1.82 trillion).[159] But a focus on the wealthiest Americans is misleading: the poorest quintile of white Americans also hold more wealth than all Black Americans combined.[160] On average, a middle income white family has more wealth than a high income Black family, underscoring the critical difference between income and wealth. Income differences between racial groups are dwarfed by differences in wealth.

One of the more disturbing facts about the racial wealth gap is that it is getting larger. This fact is obscured by the ratio of white to Black wealth. The subprime mortgage crisis, described in the next chapter, wiped out a record amount of Black wealth. In the wake of this crisis, Black wealth was pegged at about $2,200 per typical family compared to $97,900 for the typical white family, as seen in Table 2.7. This is a ratio of nearly 45 times. In the ensuing decade, both Black and white wealth have recovered, such that the disparity ratio is now only about 6 to 1. The problem, however, is that this tremendous reduction in the *ratio* of white to Black wealth masks the continued increase in the overall *absolute* disparity.

As with educational attainment, absolute improvement for both groups, combined with a decline in relative terms, contributes to the impression that the disparity is closing, even though the dollar value disparity is larger than ever, at nearly a quarter of a million dollars, as of 2022. The relative rate of wealth growth, however, is what will ultimately determine whether this disparity will close, and at what point in time. Using Federal Reserve survey data, a 2016 study found that white families grew their wealth by 84% over the preceding 30 years, three times as fast as the rate for Black families.[161] A more recent study found that median Black wealth might even fall to zero in a few decades.[162] This is not so far-fetched in light of the fact that 19% of Black families already have negative net worth, compared to just 9% of white households.[163] Although unlikely, that would have devastating consequences for Black Americans in terms of the contemporary opportunity structure.

Table 2.7 The Black-White Racial Wealth Gap, 2009–2022[164]

Year	2009	2011	2013	2016	2019	2022
Median white wealth	$97,900	$111,146	$142,000	$171,000	$188,200	$285,000
Median Black wealth	$2,200	$7,113	$11,000	$17,150	$24,100	$44,900
Absolute disparity	$95,700	$104,033	$131,000	$153,850	$164,100	$240,100
Disparity ratio	45	16	13	10	8	6

Large and persistent difference in net worth between racial groups may explain a wide range of racial disparities in well-being and life outcomes, but it is especially important in terms of generating opportunity or connecting individuals to opportunity. The previous chapter explained the critical role of wealth in the creation, dissemination, distribution, and even the visibility of opportunity. Family resources and especially family wealth was noted as a factor that shapes opportunity for the next generation. Wealth can purchase access to opportunity enhancing resources earlier in the life cycle than income, by providing a down payment on a house or a security deposit and rent for an apartment in a high-opportunity neighborhood, subsidizing low-paying but skill-building and network-enhancing internships or entry-level opportunities, or paying for university tuition or educational supplements. In particular, housing assistance or other subsidies drawn from family wealth enable young adults to acquire human capital and work experience they would otherwise not be able to afford. Income can purchase many goods and services, but wealth is more important to the generation of opportunity as it provides resources and supplements income at critical junctures when income is limited or non-existent. Wealth expands the avenues of opportunity and reveals others.

Consider, in this regard, the racial wealth gap between young families. The median young Black family has almost no wealth ($600) as of 2019, whereas the median young white family has a wealth of $25,400.[165] Young Latino families fall in between, with $11,200. These resources contribute to uneven developmental resources or opportunities for young children. Most Black children enter the starting gate with a marked disadvantaged, and that disadvantage compounds over time. Families with less wealth have a more difficult time obtaining home purchase loans or securing credit to build businesses, while families with greater wealth have more opportunities to grow it.

According a Federal Reserve survey conducted in 2019, about 17% of white families expect an inheritance, compared to 6% of Black families, 4% of Hispanic families, and 15% of other families.[166] That survey also found that about 30% of white people but only 10% of Black people had ever received a financial assistance in the form of a gift or inheritance. Researchers have long known that gifts and inheritance transfers are a significant contributor to the racial wealth gap.[167] A 2014 study estimated that estimate large gifts and inheritances accounts for 12% of the white-Black racial wealth gap.[168] On average, Black and Latino children are 3.4 and 4 percentage points less likely to report that they received financial assistance from parents as white children, and even less likely than that to receive such supports as young adults.[169]

As tax scholar Dorothy Brown observes, Black college graduates are more likely to provide support *to* their parents, while white college graduates are more likely to receive financial support *from* their parents.[170] White families are more likely to help their children with a house down payment or assist with college tuition. Another Federal Reserve study tracked college-educated households for 20 years, and found that 60% of white households received financial assistance for college from their parents, compared to just 37% of Black households.[171] This assistance undoubtedly contributes to the racial disparity in college graduation rates, and ultimately, educational attainment. A different study found that only 11.2% of Black children complete college without financial assistance, compared to 25% of white children.[172] Family financial assistance matters more to Black youth and young adults.

A similar story exists for housing assistance. One study found that 27% of whites receive home down payment assistance compared to only 7% of Black families.[173] And, among those families who do receive help, white families receive a greater amount of help.[174] As a result, Black children are not only less likely to buy a home, but are likely to wait to buy a home, and lose time building home equity.[175] Indeed, one of the drivers of racial wealth inequality is the appreciation of home values.

Homeowners earn equity on their mortgage payments, compared to renters, and enjoy many favorable tax benefits. Yet, Black homeownership lags whites, and non-whites have fewer opportunities to attain or sustain homeownership. Historical figures are presented next chapter, but as of 2021, 74% of white households owned their own home, compared to 44% and 48% of Black and Latino households, respectively.[176]

The racial wealth gap and the homeownership gap have a reinforcing dynamic. Some researchers claim that eliminating the homeownership gap would reduce the racial wealth gap by more than 30%, because homeownership dramatically improves the return on income.[177] At the same time, some economists estimate that disparate intergenerational transfers resulting from the racial wealth gap may explain 25% of the homeownership gap.[178]

Even for families who own their own home, growth in home equity is racially unequal. White homeowners enjoy higher property values, but more importantly, greater property value appreciation than Black homeowners. In 2022, median home values for white homeowners was $330 thousand, compared to $275 thousand and $250 thousand for Latino and Black homeowners, respectively.[179] Over the course of the 20th century, homes in white neighborhoods appreciated more quickly and rose higher than those in Black or Latino neighborhoods.[180] One study found that from 1970 to 1990, Black homes real appreciation was 5.3% on average compared to white homes average appreciation at 19.7%.[181] Decades later, that equates to hundreds of thousands of dollars in wealth per household. And in the wake of the Great Recession, homes values in white neighborhoods recovered more quickly.[182]

A study conducted in 2001 found that Black homebuyers received 18% less value for their homes than white homebuyers, a penalty the author called a "segregation tax."[183] Indeed, segregation appears to be a key variable. It is not just that homes owned by Black people appreciated more slowly, home appreciation is tied to Black presence. Controlling for other objective features, property values fall as the percentage of Black residents in a neighborhood exceeds 10%, and fall even further as that presence grows.[184] This is a double injury as home equity constitutes a larger share of net worth for Black Americans. For white households, home equity is 43% of net worth, compared to 60% for Black Americans.[185]

Racial disparities in income and earnings play a large role in the racial wealth gap.[186] But another contributory factor to the racial wealth gap is also employment related: Black workers have lower rates of employer-provided health care and pensions.[187] And when they receive pensions, they are more likely to receive less generous "defined contribution" pensions rather than "defined benefit" pensions. Seventy-four percent of white workers receive employer-based health insurance coverage, compared to just 56.6% of Black workers.[188] Similarly, 51% of white workers have a retirement account provided by their union or employer, compared to just 42% of Black workers.[189] This leads to another structural factor that explains differential rates of economic success by race: the so-called "spatial mismatch."

The Spatial Mismatch

Employment opportunities are one of the main arterial pathways in the opportunity structure. Individuals who live far from those jobs effectively have fewer pathways within the opportunity structure, whereas people residing closer to jobs enjoy more routes within the opportunity structure. This helps explain why the research team led by Raj Chetty found that access to jobs, as measured by commuting times and the relationship between residence and place of employment, was one of the strongest predictor of upward mobility.[190]

In other words, access to jobs matter a good deal to the structure of opportunity, and it is here, again, that race plays a critical role. Any review of quarterly government labor data generally indicates significant racial disparities in employment rates. By the third quarter of 2023, unemployment rates for Black Americans were 5.5% compared to 3% for white Americans, and 4.3% for Latinos.[191] Disaggregated by gender and age, these disparities are much larger. Black youth unemployment was nearly 12%, compared to 6.3% for white youth.[192] It is not just that Black unemployment rates are higher, but wages are also lower. Macroeconomic conditions have reduced or widened this gap from decade to decade, but its persistence is notable.[193]

There is ample evidence that racial discrimination in employment may explain some of the racial disparities in employment and earnings. For example, testing studies using identical resumes with different names has shown that the applicants with familiar "white" names are 50% more likely to generate callbacks from employers than Black sounding names.[194] More surprisingly, the sociologist Devah Pager organized a study in Milwaukee which discovered that young Black men with clean records had a more difficult time finding jobs than white men with criminal records.[195] She found that Black applicants in her study who said they had a criminal record had a callback rate of 5% versus a 14% callback rate for those who said they did not. This compared to a 17% and 35% rate, respectively, for white applicants. Racial discrimination in hiring, promotion, and retention all contribute to racial economic inequality. But structural forces are also at work.

In the late 1960s, the economist John Kain hypothesized that segregation and concentration of Black people in central-city neighborhoods limited employment opportunities for these communities because of relatively greater job growth in suburbs and transportation barriers to accessing those jobs.[196] He later dubbed this phenomenon the "spatial mismatch."[197] Evidence of a spatial mismatch between predominantly non-white neighborhoods and job location and job growth is strong. A meta-analysis of 28 studies suggests that at least 21 support this theory that the most job opportunities are in areas with fewer Black and Latino residents.[198] Black neighborhoods have fewer jobs and Black workers have higher average commute time to reach jobs.

Unfortunately, recent research demonstrates that this problem is getting worse, even as more jobs and corporations have returned to the cities. A research report released in 2021 found that the average worker commuting from a high-poverty tract lives in a neighborhood where most residents are Black or Latino but works in a neighborhood where most residents are white.[199] The problem is not simply the mismatch between jobs and affordable housing (although that is a large part of it), it is also the types of jobs that exist. Higher-poverty neighborhoods have lower wages and lower-skilled job options (e.g., retail, car and home repair, beauty and nail salons, and barber shops) compared to the jobs that prevail in lower-poverty, whiter communities (professional services, management, and finance).[200] Black people tend to search for jobs in areas where employment growth is low, whereas whites tend to search in areas where it is high. This, in turn, contributes to disparities in employment and earnings.

Even when Black workers can find and land jobs, they have longer average commute times, and pay more for gas, insurance, car maintenance, or public transit. Research shows a variety of harmful health effects associated with longer commutes, including higher blood pressure, less sleep, and less time to prepare or enjoy healthy meals.[201] The greater the differential in poverty and race between the originating neighborhood and the neighborhood where the job is located, the longer the commute.[202] Low-wage workers are less likely to own or have access to an automobile, and are therefore more reliant on public transit options. Nearly half of all low-skill jobs in white suburbs, however, are inaccessible by public transportation.[203] Even if there are bus routes or other forms of public transit to those areas, they may be circuitous, resulting in multi-hour commutes.[204] These factors discourage low-income workers from seeking employment far from home. At some point the commute is not worth the hassle, time, or expense, even for car owners.[205]

Racial segregation plays a critical role, and may explain as much as 40% of the overall difference in Black-white rates of employment.[206] Research shows that the spatial mismatch between jobs and Black neighborhoods is most pronounced in regions where racial segregation is highest.[207] Furthermore, that research shows that metropolitan areas with greater employment decentralization have a higher spatial mismatch for Black workers.[208] Racial segregation is estimated to increase the share of Black people who are either unemployed or not in school by 6.2%.[209] Or, as Raj Chetty and his colleagues note, the "negative impacts of segregation may operate by making it more difficult to reach jobs or other resources that facilitate upward mobility."[210]

But it is not simply transit dilemmas or distance and location that impedes access to jobs—lack of information and unfamiliarity are also critical factors. Race appears to shape both proximity to employment opportunities as well as the job search process and the networks that share and relay information about job opportunities.

Racial Networks

The importance of social networks to opportunity was carefully reviewed in the previous chapter. These networks encompass our kith and kin, social circles, membership in fraternal and recreational clubs, and affinity groups. Our life choices, and even our income potential, is influenced by the quality and organization of the networks we inhabit. Social networks provide access to gatekeepers, shape aspiration and outlook, and convey knowledge of great opportunities. Information about jobs, internships, special opportunities and more are often transmitted through networks.[211] Darren Walker, the President of the Ford Foundation, admits that he receives "calls and emails from friends seeking help in landing internships for their children."[212]

Unfortunately, race determines the quantity, quality, value, and insularity of social network linkages. In particular, social networks tend to be racially and culturally distinctive, with consequences throughout the opportunity structure. In a major survey asking respondents to identify up to seven people with whom they had important conversations over the past six months, white respondents revealed that 91% of their networks are white.[213] In fact, 75% of whites had no people of color in their social networks at all.[214] Similarly, 83% of an average Black person's closest friends would be Black. The economic consequences are profound. As one sociologist observes, "when whites live around and befriend mostly other whites, their everyday, innocuous decisions about where to move, whom to recommend for a job, and which school to send their children to can have the unintended consequence of maintaining racial inequalities."[215]

The tendency to associate with people "like us," or homophily, may explain some of the racial differences in the composition of social networks. In a world where personal connections and employee referrals convey information and credential or encourage applicants, Black Americans are therefore at a disadvantage—since they have neither as much "social capital" nor are as connected to or enmeshed within networks that can help them find good jobs.[216]

This tendency, however, is structurally reinforced by racial residential segregation and the racial spatial mismatch. Proximity to jobs tends to produce more firsthand knowledge of job openings, and more word-of-mouth in the social networks of those with that knowledge. Because whites and Black people live in separate neighborhoods and move in different social circles (including churches or places of worship, civic organizations, and social clubs), they have differential access to information or employers making hiring decisions.[217] In a study interviewing hundreds of working class and middle-class white people, one researcher found that the lack of network ties or relationships with Black people had profound effects on employment.[218]

Some private institutions that serve as the organizing hubs for strong or influential social networks are, in some cases, legally permitted to discriminate on the basis of race.[219] Fraternities, sororities, and many private social, country, bicycle, or sports clubs are legally permitted to select or exclude applicants on a categorical basis, such as sex, sexual orientation, and religion.[220] Even if unconscious, the tendency to select people "like us" contributes to racially distinctive social networks, with downstream effects that reverberate through the opportunity structure.

The resources transmitted through social networks extend beyond job opportunities. Low-income, isolated communities have fewer connections to elite leaders, weaker ties, and fewer benefits from those relationships.[221] This means that key political leaders may be less responsive to the needs of these communities.[222] Even when community leaders are responsive, those leaders may have less influence or capacity to draw upon state resources or call upon state-level authorities to help their constituents.

In addition to the quality and composition of social networks, race affects the quantity and relative insularity of network ties. Black and Latino job seekers have smaller social networks and fewer linkages per person.[223] In Black and Latino social networks, connections appear to be very tight-knit—meaning that most people in the network tend to know each other. This limits the information flow through them and can undermine opportunity when many job seekers pursue the same opportunities.[224] This is especially important since research suggests that most job seekers in high-poverty neighborhoods were more likely than job seekers in low-poverty neighborhoods to use informal strategies to search for work.[225]

Network insularity may be an adaptation to residency in low-opportunity environments. William Julius Wilson suggests that social isolation is strategic for people who live in dangerous neighborhoods, where perceived gang affiliation or connections can entail risks to safety and heighten exposure to violence.[226] Having a smaller or more limited social network could be an attempt to insulate individuals from the reverberation of social conflict in their communities while paradoxically increasing the perception of possible associations. Police may assume, for example, that all young men of a certain age residing in a particular public housing building or neighborhood are affiliated with a local gang.[227]

Structural Racial Inequality 93

Ultimately, the social networks of Black and Latino Americans undermine economic mobility, individual advancement, and wealth accumulation.[228] Sociologists note that networks among poor people depend on reciprocity for survival—sharing material goods across social networks.[229] While a valuable and community enhancing feature of life in lower-income environments, this means that Black and Latino workers are more likely to stretch their income to support extended family members or neighbors, many of whom have not had the same opportunities or wealth building capacity, rather than make human capital investments that help them and their families get ahead.

Mass Incarceration

An explication of structural racism would be incomplete without specifying the central role of the criminal justice system, and mass incarceration in particular, in producing racial inequality. Black people have been long been heavily policed in America going back to fugitive slave laws in the colonial and antebellum periods, but mass incarceration is a phenomenon that arose midway through the second half of the 20th century and accelerated in the early 21st century. It is a phenomenon that maps to the larger forces of segregation and the spatial mismatch but hardens areas of the opportunity structure into a constricted lattice of warped pipes and corroded circuits.

Mass incarceration refers to the large-scale imprisonment of Americans, but especially Black and brown Americans on a scale that is historically and globally unprecedented. The United States is the world's leading carceral state in absolute terms, with 5.4 million Americans in jail, prison, probation or parole, or 2% of the adult population.[230] That includes 1.9 million people in prison or jail and nearly 4 million on parole or touched by the system.[231] All told, more than seven million Americans are incarcerated per year, and nearly 1 in 3 has some form of criminal record.[232]

To understand how unusual and extreme this is, it is important to put these figures in a global context. Although we have 4% of the world's population, we have 16% of the world's prison population.[233] In 2007, the peak of mass incarceration, 767 out of every 100,000 Americans were locked up.[234] As of 2021, we still have 680 out of every 100,000 people incarcerated.[235] That is compared to about 150 people per 100,000 people in the mid-1970s, figures more in line with other major countries. China, not exactly regarded as the land of personal liberty or lenient justice, has a smaller absolute prison population than the United States despite four times the overall population.[236]

Mass incarceration has produced such shocking racial disparities that even many skeptical observers acknowledge systemic problems. For example, 8% of adults in the United States have a felony record, but over 33% of African-American men do.[237] Black people make up 12% of the U.S. population, but nearly 40% of the prison population (see Table 2.8). In New York state, Black people are 17% of the population, but 49% of the prison population.[238] In

94 *Structural Racism*

Table 2.8 Racial Composition of Incarcerated Persons by Year, 1970–2020[239]

Race	1970 (%)	1980 (%)	1990 (%)	2000 (%)	2010 (%)	2020 (%)
White	60.53	51.50	47.72	37.08	41.61	39.12
Black	39.47	45.71	47.38	45.02	41.75	39.21
Asian	No data	0.26	0.36	0.55	0.64	0.71
Latino	No data	7.68	13.37	15.45	13.63	17.92
Native American	No data	0.92	0.81	1.07	1.35	1.73

"liberal" San Francisco, less than 6% of the city's population is Black, but more than 53% of its incarcerated population is.[240]

In 2023, roughly one in 5 Black and one in 8 Latino men are incarcerated, compared to one in 20 white men.[241] Disparate rates of incarceration have reached such absurd dimensions that in some states African-Americans were statistically eleven times more likely than whites to reside in state prisons.[242] Mass incarceration has a distinctly racial cast(e) that is not reduceable to class or any other socioeconomic indicator. A 2020 study found, for example, that 21% of Black men born to the lowest-income families are incarcerated on a given day, as compared with 6% of such white men.[243]

Educational attainment appears to play a significant role in the odds of incarceration, but in ways that are profoundly racial disparate. A third of all Black male high school drop outs between the ages 20 and 39 were incarcerated, compared to only 13% of white male drop outs.[244] Another study found that, as of 2009, the chances that a young Black man without a high school diploma would eventually be incarcerated at some point in their lives was 68%, compared to 28% for white men.[245] There are more Black American men without a high school diploma behind bars than employed.[246] But even college educated Black men have a 6.6% chance of ending up incarcerated, compared to 1.2% of white men.

Incarceration has a devastating effect on the propagation of opportunity for communities and individuals. As this book maintains, if opportunity is best conceptualized as a set of pathways available to individuals over the course of life, then incarceration blocks off many future possibilities and forecloses the most desirable destinations, with harmful collateral effects on families and communities.

At the individual level, incarceration circumscribes opportunity in at least five interrelated and reinforcing ways. Most obviously, incarceration inhibits the development of human capital. Unless skill training or educational programs are provided during a term of incarceration, there are few pathways for developing or acquiring skills, useful experience, or practical knowledge that might open new pathways after incarceration. As a direct consequence of incarceration, individuals will have fewer pathways available to them over their life course. With fewer pathways and opportunities open to them, we would expect depressed lifetime economic outcomes among the formerly incarcerated. Only 2% of previously incarcerated men who began in the bottom fifth of the earnings distribution ever make it to the top fifth 20 years later, compared to 15% of men who were never incarcerated.[247] By age 48, a former inmate will have earned $179,000 less than a similarly situated man who had never been incarcerated.

It is not simply that individuals enjoy limited opportunities during imprisonment, but incarceration itself may degrade and atrophy the skills and capabilities needed to reveal or pursue future opportunities. This leads to a second way in which incarceration circumscribes opportunity for individuals. The experience of incarceration itself may function similar to that of living in neighborhoods of concentrated poverty. Incarceration may cause trauma and "harden" one's manner and behavior in a way that is difficult to unlearn post-imprisonment.[248] In fact, prison has been found to exacerbate mental illness and other disorders.[249] The behavioral norms and attitudes developed during incarceration may also undermine soft skills and social skills that are vital to labor market success.

Third, incarceration disadvantageously reconfigures the social network of the currently and formerly incarcerated. Just as individuals living in communities with fewer college graduates may have correspondingly fewer role models and reduced expectations of attending college, prison shapes the expectations and outlook of the prisoner. By clustering the most disadvantaged people in society, this outlook is socially reinforced. At the same time, prisoners become enmeshed in the social networks of fellow prisoners while outside connections are severed, due to the limited range of social contacts permitted by incarceration or social distancing by family members, former friends and acquaintances. These networks help explain rates of recidivism by shaping attitudes and aspirations, as well as by the ways in which formerly incarcerated people learn more of criminal labor market opportunities than high-quality job prospects through their networks.

Fourth, the formerly incarcerated are widely discriminated against in labor markets and suffer numerous collateral consequences, foreclosing countless post-incarceration opportunities.[250] The American Bar Association commissioned an inventory of state and federal laws that impose such collateral effects, and identified more than 44,000 of them.[251] Formerly incarcerated persons may be ineligible for certain opportunities, legally barred from receiving certain public benefits, and are more likely to be discriminated against in employment processes. Despite federal Equal Employment Opportunity Commission (EEOC) guidance that prohibits automatic prejudgments, employers are demonstrably reticent to hire formerly incarcerated people.[252] Employers frequently conduct background checks and hire private firms to screen applicants.[253] Employers are less likely to call back applicants or interviewees upon discovering a criminal conviction.[254] This explains why formerly incarcerated persons have reduced wages by approximately 11%, less annual employment by nine weeks, and depressed earnings by 40%.[255] Research shows that 60% of those released from prison in New York were unemployed a year after release.[256] A Pew study found that two-thirds of former inmates with earnings in the bottom fifth income quintile upon release in 1986 remained at or below that level 20 years later.[257]

Finally, the collateral effects of incarceration tend to shunt formerly incarcerated people into low-opportunity environments. Formerly incarcerated individuals are often prohibited from receiving student loans or public housing or other public benefits. Given limited options and fewer viable pathways in the opportunity structure, reentering prisoners have limited living options, and tend to return to the lowest opportunity neighborhoods or fall into homelessness.[258]

The structural harms of incarceration extend beyond individuals. Families are torn apart by mass incarceration and excessively long sentences. Fathers, mothers, siblings, uncles, and cousins are taken—people that serve their family as mentors, parents, breadwinners, babysitters, coaches, teachers, and much more. Fifty-four percent of incarcerated adults are parents of minor children.[259] That's more than 5 million children who have had a parent behind bars at one point, or 7% of American youth.[260] Research documents the devastating effects on children who "share sentences" with parents: behavioral problems, lost sleep and concentration, poor nutrition, and an increased risk of incarceration themselves.[261] These children are more than five times as likely to be expelled or suspended from school as children of free men and women.[262]

More than half of male inmates are the primary source of support for their children.[263] But the harms are perhaps even worse when children lose a mother.[264] Between 60% and 80% of women in jails or prisons have minor children, and most are the primary caretaker.[265] Many of these parents lose custody rights, with tens of thousands of children entering the foster care system, further ramifying the initial harms and suffering of parents and children alike.[266]

Although public safety and social order may be improved by enforcing criminal laws, two-thirds of these parents are incarcerated for non-violent crimes. As a direct consequence, these families have fewer resources and capacities. Family income is 22% lower a year after a father is incarcerated, and 15% lower even when the father is released.[267] Another study found that the incarceration of a family member is associated with a 64% decline in household assets.[268] In fact, struggling families may divert resources to pay fines and legal fees or support the formerly incarcerated upon release.

The race effects are especially pronounced. By 2000 alone, more than 1 million Black children had a father incarcerated.[269] Only 1 in 25 white children have an incarcerated parent, compared to 1 in 4 Black children and 1 in 10 Hispanic.[270] This contributes to disproportionate prevalence of single parent households among African-Americans.[271] Non-marital births in 2012 were highest for Black children at 72.6%, and 54% for Hispanics, and 29% for whites.[272] The families of currently or formerly incarcerated persons are forced to rely more on public services and supports than they would have in many cases.

Health and Environment

Perhaps the most voluminous scholarly literature on race and inequality is in the domain of public health. Racial disparities in health, mortality, morbidity, infection, disease prevalence, treatment, access to health care, and overall well-being are large, persistent and well documented.[273] Studies of maternal mortality, for example, show that both the risk of maternal death and infant mortality rates are much greater for African Americans than white people (41.7 deaths per 100,000 compared to 13.4 for white women).[274] In California, that death rate for recent Black mothers is six times greater than for white mothers.[275]

Twice as many Black Americans rate their health as fair or poor compared to white Americans.[276] Poor health is a serious impediment to opportunity, not just well-being. The Centers for Disease Control and Prevention (CDC) estimates that 12.6% of African-American children have asthma, compared to just 7.7% of white children.[277] Children with asthma have more difficulty sleeping at night and therefore learning in the classroom or concentrating while studying.[278] There are similar effects and correlations for incidence of hunger, poor diet, malnutrition, and post-traumatic stress disorder (PTSD).[279]

The literature on "environmental racism" widens the lens beyond individuals to expose structural conditions that explain many of the racial health disparities collected and reported in the public health literature. This literature documents the tragic but undeniable relationship between low-income communities of color and environmental toxins, from air pollution, unsafe drinking water, particulate matter and exhaust to hazardous waste sites and brownfields to municipal landfills.[280] The city of Houston, for example, deposited most of its trash in Black neighborhoods.[281] Black communities are more likely to have polluting facilities like garbage incinerators or coal or natural gas terminals.[282] One study found that Black Americans live in neighborhoods with concentrations of toxic releases 1.45 times greater than those in white neighborhoods.[283] In general, the health literature has routinely found that non-white neighborhoods have greater exposure to particulate (PM 2.5) air pollution, such as roadway or industrial emissions.[284] Black Americans reside in neighborhoods with far more air pollution white Americans, even after controlling for income.[285]

The most notorious environmental toxin, however, is lead. Lead is a known neurotoxin, and exposure inhibits healthy intellectual development and is known to cause developmental disabilities and delays.[286] A study of school age children in the Detroit Public Schools found that students with significantly elevated blood lead levels were more than twice as likely to perform "less than proficient" as students with low levels.[287] These harms are disproportionately experienced on a racial basis. Neighborhood racial composition predicts elevated exposure and levels of lead.[288]

A study using data collected by the CDC from 1999 to 2010 found that Black children living below the federal poverty level are four times as likely to

98   *Structural Racism*

have elevated levels of lead in their blood as poor white or Hispanic children.[289] A study of Chicago detected clear disparities in blood lead by race and ethnicity in the 1990s, and found that nearly 11% of Black children suffer from lead poisoning, compared with just 2% of white children. In some predominantly Black neighborhoods, more than 90% of tested children had elevated lead levels.[290] Robert Sampson and his colleague were so disturbed by their discoveries in Chicago that they went so far as to speculate that lead toxicity may be a "major environmental pathway through which racial segregation has contributed to the legacy of Black disadvantage in the United States."[291]

Although lead, like asbestos, is found in older buildings, decrepit or decaying infrastructure is also a vector. In particular, urban water infrastructure across much of the United States is at or past it's intended life cycle, disproportionately affecting neighborhood and communities where nonwhite Americans were relegated in the post-war period. Although there are 2 million Americans—disproportionately low-income people in rural areas, people of color and tribal communities—who lack regular access to clean running water at all, many more millions receive water from systems that have been found to violate the Safe Drinking Water Act.[292] The American Society of Civil Engineers found that nearly 21 million Americans live in areas where community water systems fail to meet quality water standards.[293] The Natural Resources Defense Council found that "drinking water systems that constantly violated federal safety standards were 40% more likely to occur in places with higher percentages of residents of color."[294]

More broadly, a robust national literature has identified racial residential segregation as a "determinant" of many racial health inequalities.[295] Racial residential segregation has also been linked to particulates and asthma,[296] cardiovascular disease,[297] hypertension,[298] diabetes,[299] obesity,[300] and many other adverse health conditions.[301] Racial residential segregation shapes access to healthy environments and life enhancing amenities and resources.[302] For example, one finding in the health literature is that access to primary care providers and specialists plays an important role in shaping health outcomes, which health insurance coverage alone cannot solve. Such providers are less prevalent in predominantly non-white segregated communities.[303] Racial segregation has also been significantly linked to the fatality of police encounters.[304]

Given this, it should not be surprising that large gaps in life expectancy have been found between segregated neighborhoods.[305] In New York City, people living in East Harlem live an average of 71.2 years while those living in the Upper East Side, just a few blocks away, live to 89.9 years.[306] A San Francisco Bay Area study found that life expectancy is more than five years greater in white neighborhoods (84 years) than highly segregated Black/Latino neighborhoods (79 years).[307]

The Covid-19 pandemic illustrated not only the direct risk vectors that made non-white communities more vulnerable, but the structural conditions as well.³⁰⁸ During the initial Covid-19 outbreak, African Americans and Hispanics appeared to have much higher rates of infection, hospitalization and death from Covid-19.³⁰⁹ This pattern occurred in places as varied as New Orleans, Minnesota, and New York City.³¹⁰

It wasn't simply that these communities lay in the path of the outbreak. Rather, Black and Latino individuals lived in more crowded housing arrangements, were more likely to work in "essential" roles or in jobs that could not be performed remotely, and faced more economic pressure to clock in to those jobs.³¹¹ Moreover, people in these communities had greater incidence of underlying health conditions, like diabetes, sickle cell anemia, obesity, respiratory disorders, and heart disease, which made the virus more deadly.³¹² The Covid-19 pandemic exposed structural health and economic vulnerabilities in communities of color.

Exclusionary Localism and Jurisdictional Fragmentation

There is another important structural dynamic that fastens racial inequality into the opportunity structure. Both the evolution of the locus of racial segregation from neighborhoods to regions (which will be explored next chapter) and the phenomena of municipal stratification and fiscal inequality (covered last chapter) have been facilitated and accelerated by another set of influential forces, exclusionary localism and municipal fragmentation. These forces reorganize key elements throughout the opportunity structure with negative racial repercussions. In particular, these forces help explain why schools are more racially concentrated and less diverse than the metropolitan regions they are nested within.

Sprawl generally refers to the patterns of development in metropolitan regions that is characterized by ever-outward growth.³¹³ The demand for low-density housing, made possible by widespread use of the automobile and federally funded highways, had an outward, centrifugal momentum during the 20th century.³¹⁴ Families, especially white families, moved out of the urban core to the suburbs, ostensibly for more living and recreational space, and less congestion, noise, and crime. Inner-ring suburbs were surrounded by outer-ring suburbs and new exurbs, as development edged into rural areas. Population growth and suburbanization led to the formation of new municipalities, as communities incorporated or resisted annexation by their neighbors.

Today, there are nearly 91,000 local governments in the United States.³¹⁵ Of those, about 3,000 are county governments, 19,000 are municipal governments, 16,000 are townships, and the rest are special purpose governments, like utility districts or independent school systems.³¹⁶ There has been a gradual increase in the number of local governments since the early 1970s, where the Census counted about 78,000 unique jurisdictions.³¹⁷ Not every new community incorporates into a municipality, township or other local government. Many exurban and rural areas are governed by counties or special districts. And some new jurisdictions and school districts are created out of larger existing ones through organized secession campaigns.

The growth of local governments increases the jurisdictional fragmentation of our regions. Fragmentation refers to the growing number of governments in a region or per capita.[318] The average metropolitan area in the United States has about 40 or so local governments.[319] However, the degree of fragmentation varies significantly across the United States. Midwestern and eastern states tend to be the most jurisdictionally fragmented. The state of Illinois has the most general purpose governments (2,822), but Minnesota has the most per capita, along with Indiana, Ohio, Pennsylvania, Vermont, and Wisconsin.[320] The Pittsburgh metropolitan area is the region with the most local governments per capita, at 463, or one for every 5,000 people in the region.

Given the importance of place, the jurisdictional fragmentation of metropolitan areas and growth of new jurisdictions has profound effects on the distribution of opportunity. The incorporation of new municipalities serves several important functions with respect to the opportunity structure. Incorporation allows communities to exercise greater control over land use, development, and services. By incorporating, communities draw boundaries between themselves and their neighbors, and can determine to whom services shall be provided, and at what level.

While ostensibly more democratic, local control over communal resources and services has exclusionary downsides. When affluent people in a region gather in the same community, and then exercise municipal powers to pool resources for mutual benefit while excluding others, it results in "opportunity hoarding."[321] All of the resources and investments in education and other services and programs are provided on an exclusionary basis, for municipal residents only, or shared with outsiders at a premium.

As described in the last chapter, one of the principal mechanisms for controlling development, excluding lower-income people, and restraining demand for services is land use authority. Many local governmental entities are endowed with zoning power.[322] Land use regulations and zoning restrictions, such as lot size, density minimums, use restrictions and other regulations are direct mechanisms for controlling what can be built and indirectly determines how much new developments will cost on the open market. In this way, municipalities select their residents, rather than the other way around, by screening out high-demand service users and lower-income residents by making housing more expensive. In other words, these controls maximize tax base capacity while minimizing tax burden, with direct effects on the provision of education and other vital services.

The more jurisdictional fragmentation that exists within a region, the greater incentives for opportunity hoarding, and the greater municipal stratification that results. In regions with many jurisdictions, there are more clearly differentiated qualities, amenities, and services between jurisdictions. And depending on the tax base capacity within the jurisdiction and historical wealth, there are different capacities for improvement. It should not be surprising, then, that regions with more jurisdictional fragmentation are more economically and racially segregated.

Research bears this out, showing, for example, that metropolitan regions with greater jurisdictional fragmentation have a greater tendency to sort people by socio-economic characteristics.[323] Another study of the 95 largest cities in the United States finds that metropolitan areas with greater land use controls and regulations are correlated with higher levels of economic and racial segregation.[324] Specifically, the study found that density restrictions, such as minimum lot sizes, were strongly correlated overall municipal fragmentation within regions as well as with segregation and concentration of the affluent.

The last chapter highlighted several studies that connect housing prices with restrictive land use policies. These policies are strongly associated with racial residential segregation as well.[325] In a national study, the economist Jonathan Rothwell concluded, "conservatively," that "somewhere between 25% and 50% of contemporary racial residential segregation is explained by anti-density zoning."[326] Drawing upon a survey of California jurisdictions, Rothwell found that California cities with restrictive zoning policies have more white residents and fewer Black and Latino residents.[327] He also found that citizen opposition to development also predicts the exclusion of Black and Latino residents.

Municipal fragmentation is one of the primary instruments for perpetuating racial segregation by erecting more walls between parts of a region.[328] This is how diverse regions maintain segregated communities. Recall that the most fragmented regions of the country tend to be the older, industrial regions of the Midwest and the mid-Atlantic.[329] These regions are also the most racially and economically segregated.[330] The large national study of school segregation noted earlier found that schools in the Midwest and Northeast not only were more racially and economically segregated than schools in the West and the South, but that "between-district segregation makes up a whopping 76 percent of non-White–White [school] segregation in the Northeast."[331]

As just noted, the more local governments per region, the more tax rates and service quality will vary, facilitating sorting and producing stratification within a region based upon the dynamics of municipal competition. In this regard, greater regional fragmentation of local governments evinces a tendency to increase and intensify competition between jurisdictions both for residents and for taxable resources.[332] In theory, such competition could have positive-sum beneficial effects, as municipalities compete to attract residents with a different mix of services, amenities, and taxes. But decades of experience reveal instead a general pattern of winners and losers. In general, the more jurisdictions that exist within a region, the more elaborately tiered stratification will exist between jurisdictions, and the greater the segregation and economic disparities between populations in the region.[333]

This pattern is both general and racialized. Regions with less municipal fragmentation have higher rates of upward mobility.[334] Opportunity hoarding by jurisdictions and greater stratification between jurisdictions results in greater inequality between the services and human capital development opportunities in those communities. In short, the fragmentation of regions into scores of jurisdictions pursuing their own self-interest "creates a zero-sum state politics in which middle- and upper-class suburbs fare best."[335]

These patterns of municipal fiscal inequality and stratification intersect with race in a particularly disturbing way, as will be shown in vivid detail in the next chapter. For now, it is important to understand that municipal fiscal inequality interacts with racial residential segregation by facilitating the fiscal isolation of people of color from high-quality public goods and infrastructure. Thus, the most fiscally distressed communities are those serving a larger share of people of color, while the municipalities with the strongest tax base are much whiter on average. This dynamic is underappreciated as a major force undergirding structural racism, and helps explain why racial residential segregation produces opportunity segregation.

Political scientists have long observed that social and economic distance between racial groups erodes support for spending on local public goods, based in part upon concerns that such spending would disproportionately flow to members of other racial groups.[336] Jessica Trounstine found that cities with more racially integrated neighborhoods spent about 10% more per capita on services and public goods, such as parks, policing, public welfare, sewers and roads[337] In fact, she finds that the most segregated cities spend about $200 less per capita each year on sewer systems, or an average of about $60,000 less per year.[338] Thus, metro areas with less fragmentation are less likely to view public provision as a zero-sum competition, and therefore more willing to tax themselves to support such investments. This obviously has direct impacts on the opportunity structure and investments in the development of human capital.

Trounstine's argues that white homeowners and their political representatives institutionalized segregation, not because of ignorant race prejudice, but in order to protect their property values, and to secure exclusive access to high-quality public goods and services, generally to the detriment of communities of color. This dynamic interaction between fiscal inequality, segregation, and fragmentation is probably most evident in the context of education.

Recall the disparities noted earlier between white and non-white districts. With the exception of some parts of the south, most school districts are organized and drawn at the municipal level rather than for the broader region.[339] When municipal boundaries and school district boundaries overlap, municipal borders function as a wall that ensures that educational funds generated locally primarily benefit local students by permitting only local students to attend district schools.[340] This is how the segregation of metropolitan regions by race results in inter-district segregation, and helps explains tragic cases like Kelley Williams-Bolar. Nationally, most school segregation (54%) is now inter-district (or between districts) rather than between schools within the same district (as was typical of the Jim Crow south, for instance).[341]

Jurisdictional fragmentation and sprawl produce municipal fiscal inequality, economic and racial segregation, and contribute to educational inequity and the spatial mismatch. In this sense, parochial and exclusionary localism, and its institutional expression in secession and municipal fragmentation, is one of the most critical and underappreciated forces that explain structural racial inequality today.

***

Structural racism is simply a claim that opportunity structures in the United States are deeply racialized, meaning that they *produce* and *reinforce* racial advantages and disadvantages. This chapter explored the mechanisms and forces by which this occurs and teased out the independent role that race plays in each case.

If you are born Black, it is more likely that you are born into a household with lower incomes and less accumulated wealth, residing in a low-income neighborhood nested inside a poor community burdened with fiscal distress or incapacity, suffering from a school system with failing or underperforming schools, exposed to an environment with smoggy air, dirty or unsafe drinking water, and fewer health care providers and healthy amenities. This is what it looks like to say that racial inequality is structural.

If we understand opportunity as the full set of pathways available to us, Black persons in the United States have fewer pathways available to them over the life course and less capacity to perceive or travel across the most potentially rewarding pathways. Instead, Black Americans are channeled into the least desirable and more punishing circuits of the opportunity structure. It is for this reason that we say that the opportunity structures in the United States are racialized. The results are manifest in all the mirrored and panoramic disparities evident throughout American society. This is the full import of structural racism.

It is tempting to reduce structural racism to class and wealth. Wealth especially lubricates movement within the opportunity structure, endowing individuals with greater human and social capital, but it does not define that structure nor determine the range of opportunities accessible for wealthy individuals within it. It is possible to hold great wealth in a region or community with low overall rates of upward mobility and an anemic opportunity structure and suffer the relative deprivations of that fact, just as it's possible to be poor while residing in a high-opportunity neighborhood and attend stellar schools and enjoy world class amenities, as when families who rent cheaply in upper-middle class suburbs enjoy the spillover benefits. It is true that poorer people tend to inhabit weaker local opportunity structures and are disadvantageously positioned within broader opportunity structures, but there is an even more pronounced racial correspondence. Low-income white Americans have real challenges and disadvantages, but they enjoy rates of upward mobility much closer to the ideal.

As we have seen, the forces of opportunity have many socioeconomic elements, but it is racial segregation and other racialized forces that ultimately explain these racial disparities. Although some of the racialized forces can be explained in economic terms, they cannot be reduced to class alone. Only by looking at race can we fully appreciate certain differences in experiences of poverty. Similarly, although educational attainment is also one of those opportunity-enhancing forces, a focus on that factor through a class-only lens would conceal enormous racial disparities in the relationship between educational attainment and incarceration or employment.

Both race and class have profound, sometimes independent and sometimes interacting, effects on the structure and distribution of opportunity, with "place" binding both elements into the opportunity structure. Within this context, the story of Kelley-Williams Bolar acquires deeper meaning, not just as a miscarriage of justice for a young mother.

Since the prosecution and incarceration of Kelley-Williams Bolar garnered national headlines, a cottage industry of investigative services has sprouted to uncover similar "crimes." In a quiet but growing phenomenon, school districts across the country are prosecuting parents for "stealing educational services."[342] But a narrow focus on why these women may have been targeted (i.e., their skin color) for prosecution is less important than the structural location they inhabited in the first place.

In time, Kelley Williams-Bolar's "crime" may be regarded not only with a similar sense of unfairness and injustice as Rosa Parks' prosecution in the 20th century, but perhaps as a rough 21st-century structural racism analog, although the latter was a deliberate challenge to Jim Crow institutional racism. Although the backlash to Kelley Williams-Bolar's prosecution failed to change the system, it provoked broad revulsion at the punitive harshness and elemental unfairness of the structures that continue to circumscribe life chances for too many Americans, and especially people of color.

The mapping of opportunity to race, class, and place is not, properly understood, the result of an nefarious or insidious engineering project or the inevitable byproduct of prior racist policies and structures. It is neither the direct consequence of private prejudice and societal discrimination nor the accumulated disadvantage of prior institutional forms, such as racial slavery or even Jim Crow more recently. Structural racism is an ongoing project as firmly rooted in the late-20th and early 21st centuries as much as the 19th. Now that we have an analytical understanding of the forces and dynamics that racialize opportunity, it is important to understand how they came to be.

Notes

1 Andrea Canning and Leezel Tanglao, "Ohio Mom Kelley Williams-Bolar Jailed for Sending Kids to Better School District," *ABC News*, January 25, 2011, https://abcnews.go.com/US/ohio-mom-jailed-sending-kids-school-district/story?id=12763654. ("It's overwhelming. I'm exhausted," she said. "I did this for them, so there it is. I did this for them.")

2 Michael O'Malley, "Did the punishment fit the crime when Akron mother was jailed for sending her kids to a suburban school?," *Cleveland.com*, February 13, 2011, https://www.cleveland.com/metro/2011/02/did_the_punishment_fit_the_cri.html.
3 Geoff Schotter and Inimai Chettiar, "Ohio Mother Granted Clemency after Being Prosecuted for Sending Her Child to the Wrong School," *ACLU*, September 13, 2011, https://www.aclu.org/news/smart-justice/ohio-mother-granted-clemency-after-being-prosecuted-sending.
4 More districts in more states appear to be prosecuting violators and doing so more aggressively than in previous decades. See Tim DeRoche, Hailly T.N. Korman, and Harold Hinds, When Good Parents Go to Jail: The Criminalization of Address Sharing in Public Education (Available to All, 2023), https://availabletoall.org/report-when-good-parents-go-to-jail/. And, although she was granted some clemency, her father was subsequently ensnared by the episode. Marianna McMurdock, "'It Destroyed Me': Lasting Trauma Years After Districts' Address Crackdowns," *74 Million*, May 21, 2024, https://www.the-74million.org/article/it-destroyed-me-lasting-trauma-years-after-districts-address-crackdowns/.
5 Menendian et al., "Racial Disparities Dashboard Progress Report Card." (showing both areas of progress and areas of regress).
6 Menendian et al., "Racial Disparities Dashboard Progress Report Card." Jacob Tompkins, "Disparities Dashboard," Tableau Public, February 6, 2023, https://public.tableau.com/app/profile/jacob.tompkins/viz/DisparitiesDashboard/MedianHouseholdIncomeDashboard; For a more detailed view of the Black-white income disparity at every income decile, see: Paul F. Campos, "White Economic Privilege Is Alive and Well," *New York Times*, July 29, 2017, https://www.nytimes.com/2017/07/29/opinion/sunday/black-income-white-privilege.html.
7 Aditya Aladangady, Andrew C. Chang, and Jacob Krimmel, "Greater Wealth, Greater Uncertainty: Changes in Racial Inequality in the Survey of Consumer Finances," *FEDS Notes* (2023): https://doi.org/10.17016/2380-7172.3405.
8 Tompkins, "Disparities Dashboard."
9 The conservative social critic Thomas Sowell, for example, has shown how group disparities can arise due to a variety of ordinary and non-discriminatory sources, including initial conditions or random factors in society. See Thomas Sowell, *Discrimination and Disparities* (New York: Basic Books, 2019). See also Fishkin, Bottlenecks 1C.1, "*The problem of the family*," 48-56, describing the problem of the "warrior families," a thought experiment illustrating how a non-discriminatory initial circumstances can engender certain opportunity advantages.
10 The previous chapter documented temporal (generational cohort), class, and geographic disparities in the production and enjoyment of opportunities, but establishing that contemporary opportunity structures also produce and maintain racial inequality matters separately for at least two reasons. First, there may be different levels or degrees of tolerance for inequalities of opportunity on different bases. Even if Americans are, in the main, comfortable with economic inequality so long as there is some degree of opportunity equality, they may also regard class or geographic inequalities in the provision of opportunity with some degree of begrudging ineluctable toleration that is not extended to inequality of opportunity with respect to race or other identities. Second, if inequality of opportunity by race exists as a matter of fact, and is not reducible to other dynamics (such as class or geography), then an opportunity enhancing agenda (either generally or one aimed at the other forms of opportunity inequality) that is race-blind is unlikely to be able to solve or make headway toward solving this problem.
11 This claim is a frequent a source of skepticism and misunderstanding, and there are many nuances that must be drawn out and clarifications that will be made

throughout the remaining chapters. In general, however, the organization of the opportunity structure and the interaction of component elements within it play a significant role in producing these outcomes.

12 Robert P. Jones, Daniel Cox, and Juhem Navarro-Rivera, *Economic Insecurity, Rising Inequality, and Doubts About the Future: Findings from the 2014 American Values Survey* (Washington, DC: Public Religion Research Institute, 2014), 2, https://www.prri.org/research/survey-economic-insecurity-rising-inequality-and-doubts-about-the-future-findings-from-the-2014-american-values-survey/.

13 See, for example, Urahn et al., *Pursuing the American Dream*; William J. Collins and Marianne H. Wanamaker, "African American Intergenerational Economic Mobility Since 1880," *American Economic Journal: Applied Economics* 14, no. 3 (2022): https://www.aeaweb.org/articles?id=10.1257/app.20170656; Bhashkar Mazumder, "Black–White Differences in Intergenerational Economic Mobility in the United States," *Economic Perspectives* 38, no. 1 (2014): 5, https://papers.ssrn.com/sol3/papers.cfm?abstract_id=2434178. Notably, the Urahn et al. study is an exception in that it found identical rates of Black and white mobility from the bottom to top income quintile (at 4% each), despite finding large disparities in almost every other particular.

14 See the table entitled "Social Mobility Matrix: Race," in Reeves, "Saving Horatio." This study appeared to draw upon National Longitudinal Surveys conducted by the U.S. Department of Labor in 1979 and 1997. See *National Longitudinal Surveys* (Washington, DC: National Bureau of Labor Statistics, 2022), https://www.nlsinfo.org/. See also Edward Rodrigue and Richard V. Reeves, "Five Bleak Facts on Black Opportunity," *Brookings*, January 15, 2015, https://www.brookings.edu/blog/social-mobility-memos/2015/01/15/five-bleak-facts-on-black-opportunity/ (providing attribution to the data source).

15 Tom Hertz, "Rags, Riches and Race: The Intergenerational Economic Mobility of Black and White Families in the United States," in *Unequal Chances: Family Background and Economic Success*, ed. Samuel Bowles, Herbert Gintis, and Melissa Osborne (New York: Russell Sage and Princeton University Press, 2005), 165–191

16 Mazumder, "Black–White Differences," 5.

17 Urahn et al., *Pursuing the American Dream*, 20, fig. 15.

18 Gregory Acs, Diana Elliott, and Emma Kalish, *What Would Substantially Increased Mobility from Poverty Look Like?* (Washington, DC: US Partnership on Mobility From Poverty- Urban Institute, 2016), 10, fig. 9, https://www.urban.org/research/publication/what-would-substantially-increased-mobility-poverty-look.

19 Chetty et al., "Race and Economic Opportunity," 730, table 1.

20 Raj Chetty et al., "Online Appendix: Race and Economic Opportunity in the United States: An Intergenerational Perspective," *Quarterly Journal of Economics*, December 2019, table V, https://academic.oup.com/qje/article/135/2/711/5687353#201514694.

21 Urahn et al., *Pursuing the American Dream*, 2.

22 Mazumder, "Black–White Differences," 7.

23 Chetty et al., "Where is the Land," 1605 ("we do not observe race in our data").

24 Chetty et al., "Race and Economic Opportunity," 755.

25 Chetty et al., 714, 732. White children born to parents at the 75th percentile reach the 60 percentile on average. Hispanic children with parents at the 25th and 75th percentiles reach the 43rd and 54th percentiles, respectively. And Asian children with parents at the 25th and 75th percentiles reach the 56th and 64th percentiles, respectively.

26 Sampson, *Great American City*, 302.

27 Mazumder, "Black-White Differences," 5.

28 Hertz, "Rags, Riches, and Race," 179.
29 Chetty et al., "Online Appendix," table V. For an interesting data visualization based upon this data, see Emily Badger et al., "Extensive Data Shows Punishing Reach of Racism for Black Boys," *New York Times*, March 19, 2018, https://www.nytimes.com/interactive/2018/03/19/upshot/race-class-white-and-black-men.html.
30 Julia B. Isaacs, *Economic Mobility of Black and White Families* (Washington, DC: Pew Charitable Trusts, 2007), 2.
31 Acs, Elliot, and Kalish, *Substantially Increased Mobility from Poverty*, 15.
32 Urahn et al., *Pursuing the American Dream*, 20, fig. 15.
33 Patrick Sharkey, *Neighborhoods and the Black-White Mobility Gap* (Washington, DC: Pew Charitable Trusts, 2009), 11, https://www.pewtrusts.org/~/media/legacy/uploadedfiles/wwwpewtrustsorg/reports/economic_mobility/pewsharkeyv12pdf.pdf.
34 Hispanic, here, includes all races, but Black, White and Asian excludes Hispanic. Figures presented here are rounded. Emily A. Shrider et al., *Income and Poverty in the United States: 2020* (United States Census Bureau, 2021), 56, https://www.census.gov/content/dam/Census/library/publications/2021/demo/p60-273.pdf.
35 Lyndon B. Johnson, "Annual Message to the Congress on the State of the Union," *American Presidency Project*, January 8, 1964, https://www.presidency.ucsb.edu/documents/annual-message-the-congress-the-state-the-union-25. For a list of programs, see "Office of Economic Opportunity," Department of Human Services, last modified October 28, 2019, https://mn.gov/dhs/partners-and-providers/program-overviews/economic-supports-cash-food/office-of-economic-opportunity/.
36 Poverty is not simply lack or lowness of income, it is also a lack of capabilities. Amartya K. Sen, *Development as Freedom* (New York: Anchor Books, 1999), 87.
37 See Table B-5 from Shrider et al., *Income and Poverty in the United States*, 62.
38 Gary W. Evans, "Childhood poverty and adult psychological well-being," *PNAS* 113, no. 52 (2016): 14949–14952, https://doi.org/10.1073/pnas.1604756114.
39 Acs, Elliot, and Kalish, *Substantially Increased Mobility from Poverty*, 10, fig. 9.
40 Jargowsky, *Poverty and Place*, 9, discussing the various ways in which social scientists define "high-poverty." The National Equity Atlas, for example, defines high poverty as areas with poverty rates of 30% and higher. See National Equity Atlas, "Neighborhood Poverty: All Neighborhoods Should Be Communities of Opportunity" (Los Angeles: USC Equity Research Institute, 2019), https://nationalequityatlas.org/indicators/Neighborhood_poverty#/?geo=01000000000000000.
41 Galster, *Making Our Neighborhoods*, 137, Figure 6.2.
42 Lincoln Quillian, "Segregation and Poverty Concentration: The Role of Three Segregations," *American Sociological Review* 77, no. 3 (2012): 355, https://www.ncbi.nlm.nih.gov/pmc/articles/PMC3956000/.
43 Sean F. Reardon, Lindsay Fox, and Joseph Townsend, "Neighborhood Income Composition by Race and Income, 1990–2009," *Annals of the American Academy of Political and Social Science* 660, no. 1 (2015): 85, https://ann.sagepub.com/content/660/1/78.full.pdf+html[ann.sagepub.com.
44 Douglas S. Massey and Jonathan Tannen, "Segregation, Race, and the Social Worlds of Rich and Poor," in Braun and Kirsch, *Dynamics of Opportunity*, 19, fig. 2.3.
45 *2019 American Community Survey Summary File 5-year estimates data profiles* (U.S. Census Bureau, 2019), https://www.census.gov/programs-surveys/acs/data/summary-file.2019.html. Note: 2019 ACS data which uses the census tract boundary and names based on the 2010 boundary.

46 Predominance does not necessarily mean a majority, merely that the racial group is proportionally larger than any other particular group.
47 U.S. Census Bureau, "Profile of General Population and Housing Characteristics," Decennial Census, DEC Demographic Profile, Table DP1, 2020, https://data.census.gov/table/DECENNIALDP2020.DP1?g=010XX00US&d=DEC+Demographic+Profile.
48 Original calculation from U.S. Census Bureau, *American Community Survey: 2015–2019*.
49 Robert J. Sampson, Patrick Sharkey, and Stephen W. Raudenbush, "Durable Effects of Concentrated Disadvantage on Verbal Ability Among African-American Children," *Proceedings of the National Academy of Sciences (PNAS)* 105, no 3 (2008): 845–852.
50 Daveen Rae Kurutz and Patrick Varine, "Districts with More Low-Income Families Could Have Higher Special Education Needs," *Pittsburgh Tribune-Review*, June 4, 2014, https://triblive.com/neighborhoods/yourmurrysville/yourmurrysvillemore/6215133-74/education-special-students.
51 See Brett Drake and Mark R. Rank, "The Racial Divide among American Children in Poverty: Reassessing the Importance of Neighborhood," *Children and Youth Services Review* 31, no. 12 (2009): 1264–1271.
52 Gregory D. Squires, *Urban Sprawl: Causes, Consequences, & Policy Responses* (Washington, DC: Urban Institute Press, 2002), 88.
53 U.S. Census Bureau, *American Community Survey: 2015–2019*.
54 Greg J. Duncan and Jeanne Brooks-Gunn, *Consequences of Growing Up Poor* (New York: Russell Sage Foundation, 1997).
55 James Coleman et al., *Equality of Educational Opportunity* (Washington, DC: U.S. Government Printing Office, 1966).
56 National Center for Education Statistics, *The Elementary/Secondary Information System (ElSi): 2019–2020* (United States: 2019–2020), https://nces.ed.gov/ccd/elsi/, but n=82712 (6559 schools were categorized as "No data").
57 *ElSi: 2019–2020*.
58 Gary Orfield, Erica Frankenberg, and Liliana M. Garces, "Statement of American Social Scientists of Research on School Desegregation to the U.S. Supreme Court in Parents v. Seattle School District and Meredith v. Jefferson County," *Urban Review* 40, no. 1 (2008): 96, 106–107.
59 Christina Theokas and Reid Saaris, *Finding America's Missing AP and IB Students* (Washington, DC: Education Trust, 2013), https://edtrust.org/wp-content/uploads/2013/10/Missing-Students-two-pager.pdf.
60 Sheryll Cashin, *Place Not Race: A New Vision of Opportunity in America* (Boston: Beacon Press, 2014), 30.
61 Patrick Sharkey, *Stuck in Place: Urban Neighborhoods and the End of Progress toward Racial Equality* (Chicago: University of Chicago Press, 2013), 38.
62 Rebecca Blank, *It Takes a Nation* (New York: Russell Sage Foundation, 1997), 23.
63 Richard V. Reeves, "The Unbending Arc: America's Race Gap is Stuck," *Brookings*, January 18, 2016, https://www.brookings.edu/blog/social-mobility-memos/2016/01/18/the-unbending-arc-americas-race-gap-is-stuck/.
64 Katherine Michelmore and Susan Dynarski, "The Gap Within the Gap: Using Longitudinal Data to Understand Income Differences in Educational Outcomes," *AERA Open* 3, no. 1 (2017), 11, https://journals.sagepub.com/doi/pdf/10.1177/2332858417692958.
65 See Scott Winship et al., *Long Shadows: The Black-White Gap in Multigenerational Poverty* (Washington, DC: Brookings, 2021), 2, https://www.brookings.

edu/research/long-shadows-the-black-white-gap-in-multigenerational-poverty/ (although they defined "poverty" as families earning in the bottom income quintile, not below the federal poverty line).
66 Acs, Elliot, and Kalish, *Substantially Increased Mobility from Poverty*, 5, fig. 4.
67 Sharkey, *Stuck in Place*, 39, fig. 2.7.
68 Sharkey, 119.
69 Sharkey, 122.
70 Robert Sampson developed a concept called "concentrated disadvantage," which he believes is ecologically distinct from simply high poverty environments. Sampson, *Great American City*, 100. Critically, he finds that "there was not one white community experiencing what is most typical for those residents in segregated black areas...Trying to estimate the effect of concentrated disadvantage on whites is thus tantamount to estimating a phantom reality" (Sampson, 101). See also Robert J. Sampson, "Moving to Inequality: Neighborhood Effects and Experiments Meet Social Structure," *American Journal of Sociology* 114, no. 1 (2008): 221. "The stratification of America's urban landscape by race and class once again reveals that concentrated disadvantage is a different treatment than simple poverty and one experienced almost solely by Chicago's black population." Sampson argues that "race, family structure, and resource deprivation are ecologically knotted at the neighborhood level" (Sampson, 201).
71 The same could be said of other economic racial disparities, including the previously noted differences in neighborhood median income (not just poverty rates) between racial groups, or the racial wealth gap, which will be discussed later this chapter.
72 Prudence L. Carter, "Education's Limitations and its Radical Possibilities," *Contexts* 17, no. 2 (2018): 23, https://journals.sagepub.com/doi/pdf/10.1177/1536504218776956.
73 See john a. powell, "The Race and Class Nexus: An Intersectional Perspective," *Minnesota Journal of Law & Equality* 25, no. 2 (2007): 423, https://scholarship.law.umn.edu/cgi/viewcontent.cgi?article=1126&context=lawineq. (Arguing that race and class meanings and experiences are co-constituted by each other.)
74 See Bob Wienfold, "Epigenetics: The Science of Change," *Environmental Health Perspectives* 114, no. 3 (2006): A164–A167, https://www.ncbi.nlm.nih.gov/pmc/articles/PMC1392256/.
75 The optimal design of policies designed to remediate structural racism is the focus of Chapter 4.
76 This was the thesis of the landmark book by Douglas Massey and Nancy A. Denton, *American Apartheid: Segregation and the Making of the Underclass* (Cambridge, MA: Harvard University Press, 1993), illustrating how a slight difference in poverty or income levels between racial groups combined with segregation can produce stark concentrations of poverty. Massey and Denton, *American Apartheid*, 118. Massey has continued to make this point in the years since. See Massey and Tannen, "Segregation, Race, and Social Worlds," Braun and Kirsch, *Dynamics of Opportunity*, 24 ("geographically concentrated poverty follows directly from two fundamental structural conditions in society: a high rate of minority poverty and a high degree of minority residential segregation, a relation now established both mathematically and empirically); Ford Fessenden and Haeyoun Park, "Chicago's Murder Problem," *New York Times*, May 27, 2016, https://www.nytimes.com/interactive/2016/05/18/us/chicago-murder-problem.html ("what determines concentrated poverty is high levels of black segregation combined with high levels of black poverty").

77 Richard Sander, Yana A. Kucheva, and Jonathan M. Zasloff, *Moving Toward Integration: The Past and Future of Fair Housing* (Cambridge, MA: Harvard University Press, 2018), 4, table 0.2.
78 Massey and Denton, *American Apartheid*, 120–121.
79 As one expression of this idea, see William J. Wilson, *The Truly Disadvantaged* (Chicago: University of Chicago Press, 1990) 136 ("The flight of more affluent families to the suburbs has meant that the central cities are becoming increasingly the domain of the poor and the stable working class").
80 Kyle Vanhemert, "The Best Map Ever Made of America's Racial Segregation," *Wired*, August 26, 2013, https://www.wired.com/2013/08/how-segregated-is-your-city-this-eye-opening-map-shows-you/.
81 See e.g. Jessica Trounstine, *Segregation by Design: Local Politics and Inequality in American Cities* (Cambridge, UK: Cambridge University Press, 2018), 9–10, fig. 1.3; Alex Schafran, *The Road to Resegregation: Northern California and the Failure of Politics* (Oakland: University of California Press, 2018), 9, map 3; Tony Roshan Samara, *Race, Inequality, and the Resegregation of the Bay Area* (Oakland, CA: Urban Habitat, 2016), 11, map 6, https://urbanhabitat.org/resource/race-inequality-and-the-resegregation-of-the-bay-area/.
82 Some presentations of segregation incorrectly assume that a more non-white or more diverse community is a more integrated one. For example, if a city fell from 55% to 45% white between 2000 and 2020, that does not mean that the city has become more integrated. If the growing non-white population moved into mostly non-white neighborhoods, and if the remaining white population was more likely to live in predominantly white neighborhoods, then the measured level of segregation may have increased, even if the city became more technically diverse according to measures like the Diversity Index or Entropy Score. Racial diversity widens the potential for integration or segregation, but whether a place is integrated or not depends upon the residential proximity and degree of spatial separation between people of different races in that place.
83 Social scientists have long debated the best way to measure segregation. See e.g. For more on this, see Christopher D. Lloyd, Ian G. Shuttleworth and David W. Wong, ed., *Social-Spatial Segregation: Concepts, Processes and Outcomes* (Bristol, UK: Policy Press, 2014), 65–72.
84 In their classic work, Douglas Massey and Nancy Denton identified five types of segregation corresponding to different measures: 1) (un)evenness, 2) exposure, 3) concentration, 4) centralization, and 5) clustering. Massey and Denton, *American Apartheid*, 75–76. Subsequent scholarship contends that these types collapse into two dimensions: 1) evenness-clustering and 2) exposure-isolation, where evenness and clustering were extremes on one dimension, and centralization and concentration are subtypes of spatial unevenness. See Sean F. Reardon and David O'Sullivan, "Measures of Spatial Segregation," *Sociological Methodology* 34, no. 1 (2004): 121–162, https://doi.org/10.1111/j.0081-1750.2004.00150.x and Lawrence A. Brown and Su-Yeul Chung, "Spatial Segregation, Segregation Indices and the Geographical Perspective," *Population, Space and Place* 12, no. 2 (2006): 125–143, https://doi.org/10.1002/psp.403.
85 Menendian, Gailes, and Gambhir, *Technical Appendix*, for a description of the formulas, utility and limitations of seven different formulas for measuring racial residential segregation. See also Stephen Menendian and Samir Gambhir, "Comparing and Analyzing Major Measures of Racial Residential Segregation in the United States Over Time," *Othering and Belonging Institute*, https://belonging.berkeley.edu/comparing-and-analyzing-major-measures-racial-residential-segregation-united-states-over-time to see how differently they behave over time and their degree of correlation with each other.

86 Douglas S. Massey and Nancy A. Denton, "The Dimensions of Residential Segregation," *Social Forces* 67, no. 2 (1988): 281–315, https://www.jstor.org/stable/2579183?seq=10#page_scan_tab_contents. This article begins by providing some historical context to the development of various indices and the "index wars" of the 1970s. See also Stephen Gorard and Chris Taylor, "What is Segregation? A Comparison of Measures in Terms of 'Strong' and 'Weak' Compositional Invariance," *Sociology* 36, no. 4 (2002): 875–895, https://doi.org/10.1177/003803850203600405.
87 Massey and Denton, *American Apartheid*, 20 ("A simple rule of thumb in interpreting these indices is that values under 30 are low, those between 30 and 60 are moderate, and that anything above 60 is high").
88 John R. Logan and Brian Stults, *The Persistence of Segregation in the Metropolis: New Findings from the 2020 Census* (Providence, RI: Diversity and Disparities Project, Brown University, 2021), https://s4.ad.brown.edu/Projects/Diversity, 5.
89 Logan and Stults, *Persistence of Segregation*, 8, fig. 4, 10, fig. 6.
90 For a historical perspective (1880–1940) using a different measure of segregation, see: Trevon D. Logan and John M. Parman, "The National Rise in Residential Segregation," *Journal of Economic History* 77, no. 1 (2017): 127–170, https://ideas.repec.org/a/cup/jechis/v77y2017i01p127-170_00.html. For a more contemporary comparison, see Sander, Kucheva and Zasloff, *Moving Toward Integration*, 174–194. (comparing different regions and MSAs to assess why some places integrated more than others after 1970).
91 Menendian, Gambhir, and Hsu, "Most to Least Segregated Metro Regions in 2020, According to 2020 Census Data," in "Roots of Structural Racism, 2020," https://belonging.berkeley.edu/most-least-segregated-metro-regions-2020; Logan and Stults, *Persistence of Segregation*, 3.
92 Massey and Denton, *American Apartheid*, 47, table 2.3.
93 Logan and Stults, *Persistence of Segregation*, 3.
94 Stephen Menendian and Samir Gambhir, *Racial Segregation in the San Francisco Bay Area, Part 3: Measuring Segregation* (Berkeley: Othering & Belonging Institute, 2019), https://belonging.berkeley.edu/racial-segregation-san-francisco-bay-area-part-3.
95 One additional nuance is that the "typical" or "average" calculation of the Isolation/Exposure Indices can differ depending on whether the formula is using mean or median values. See John E. Farley, "Residential Interracial Exposure and Isolation Indices: Mean Versus Median Indices, and the Difference It Makes," *Sociological Quarterly* 46, no. 1 (2005): 19–45.
96 The "Exposure" component measures the percentage of non-white peoples in the White neighborhood, whereas the "Isolation" component measures the percentage of white people in the average white neighborhood. See *Housing Patterns: Appendix B: Measures of Residential Segregation* (United States Census Bureau, 2021), https://www.census.gov/topics/housing/housing-patterns/guidance/appendix-b.html. Logan and Stults, *Persistence of Segregation*, 3.
97 Logan and Stults, *Persistence of Segregation*, 4.
98 At the same time, the Isolation Index values can fall as white people, as suggested by this example, decline in relative terms as a percentage of the population, which has the converse problem of making segregation look worse than it is.
99 One index that is preferred by social scientists for measuring segregation is Theil's Multigroup Entropy Index, known as "Theil's H." John Iceland, "The Multigroup Entropy Index (Also Known as Theil's H or the Information Theory Index)," *U.S. Census Bureau*, December 2004, https://www2.census.gov/programs-surveys/demo/about/housing-patterns/multigroup_entropy.pdf; Sean F. Reardon and Glenn Firebaugh, "Measures of Multigroup Segregation,"

112 Structural Racism

      Sociological Methodology 32, no. 1 (2002): 32–67, https://pure.psu.edu/en/publications/measures-of-multigroup-segregation.
100 Elizabeth Roberto, "The Divergence Index: A Decomposable Measure of Segregation and Inequality," *arXiv*, December 2, 2016, https://arxiv.org/pdf/1508.01167.pdf.
101 It is possible to get this level of granularity with the Dissimilarity Index, but only with privileged access to micro data. See Sander, Kucheva, and Zasloff, *Moving Toward Integration*, xvi–xvii.
102 From 1970 to 2029, the population of Hispanics increased from 9.1 million to 62.1 million, while the population of Asians increased from 1.8 million to 24 million. See U.S. Census Bureau, "Table 1: Persons of Spanish Origin by Sex and Urban and Rural Residence," in *Subject Reports: Persons of Spanish Origin* (Washington, DC: U.S. Department of Commerce, 1970), https://www2.census.gov/library/publications/decennial/1970/pc-2-1c/42043782v2p1a1cch7.pdf; U.S. Census Bureau, *Supplementary Report: Race of the Population of the United States, by States: 1970* (Washington, DC: U.S. Department of Commerce, 1970), Table 60, https://www2.census.gov/library/publications/decennial/1970/pc-s1-supplementary-reports/pc-s1-11.pdf; Nicholas Jones et al., "2020 Census Illuminates Racial and Ethnic Composition of the Country," U.S. Census Bureau, August 12, 2021, https://www.census.gov/library/stories/2021/08/improved-race-ethnicity-measures-reveal-united-states-population-much-more-multiracial.html.
103 *San Francisco-Oakland-Fremont, CA Metropolitan Statistical Area: Data for the Metropolitan Area from Diversity and Disparities* (Providence, RI: Spatial Structures in the Social Science, 2021) https://s4.ad.brown.edu/projects/diversity/segregation2010/msa.aspx?metroid=41860.
104 Menendian and Gambhir, *Racial Segregation Part 3*.
105 "US2020 Segregation Scoring: Cities" (White-Hispanic dissimilarity rising from 40.9 in 1980 to 50.6 in 2020).
106 "Raleigh: Data for the City Area," Diversity and Disparities Project, Brown University, accessed August 10, 2024, https://s4.ad.brown.edu/projects/diversity/segregation2020/city.aspx?cityid=3755000 (White-Hispanic dissimilarity rising from 25.3 in 1980 to 45.1 in 2020, and White-Asian dissimilarity rising from 24.2 to 32 in the same time period).
107 "US2020 Segregation Scoring: Cities" (White-Hispanic dissimilarity rising from 55 to 56 from 1980 to 2020, and Asian-Hispanic dissimilarity rising from 28.5 to 54.4 in the same period).
108 Stephen Menendian, Samir Gambhir, and Chih-Wei Hsu, "Roots of Structural Racism: The 2020 Census Update," *Othering and Belonging Institute*, October 11, 2021, https://belonging.berkeley.edu/roots-structural-racism-2020.
109 Menendian, Gailes, and Gambhir, "Comparing Black-White Segregation Measures," in *Roots of Structural Racism*, https://belonging.berkeley.edu/comparing-black-white-segregation-measures.
110 They are, however, correlated, and regions with more Black people have more of both. Jennifer Hochschild and Shanna Weitz, *Challenging Group-based Segregation and Isolation: Whether and Why* (Cambridge, MA: A Shared Future: Fostering Communities of Inclusion in an Era of Inequality, 2017), 3, https://www.jchs.harvard.edu/sites/jchs.harvard.edu/files/a_shared_future_challenging_group-based_segregation.pdf; Rajini Vaidyanathan, "Why Don't Black and White Americans Live Together?," *BBC News*, January 8, 2016, https://www.bbc.com/news/world-us-canada-35255835.
111 Racial sorting appears to be stronger. See John Logan, *Separate and Unequal in Suburbia* (Providence, RI: Brown University, 2014): https://s4.ad.brown.edu/

Projects/Diversity/data/report/report12012014.pdf, 5–6 ("A standard theory in urban sociology is that a group's isolation—the degree to which group members live in separate racial/ethnic zones—depends on the income level of individual members. Higher income minorities are expected to live in less segregated settings. [...] It turns out that the standard theory applies only to Hispanics. Lower income Hispanics (earning below $45,000) lived on average in suburban neighborhoods that were 43 percent Hispanic. Affluent Hispanics' neighborhoods (those earning above $75,000) were only 35 percent Hispanic. But there was no such relationship for whites, blacks or Asians. For these groups, their isolation was unrelated to their income").

112 Maria Krysan et al., "Does Race Matter in Neighborhood Preferences? Results from a Video Experiment," *American Journal of Sociology* 115, no. 2 (2009): 527–559. See also Quillian, "Segregation," 357.

113 Logan, *Separate and Unequal*, 1–2.

114 john a. powell and Stephen Menendian, "Opportunity Communities: Overcoming the Debate over Mobility versus Place-Based Strategies" in *The Fight for Fair Housing: Causes, Complications and Future Implications for the 1968 Federal Fair Housing Act* (New York: Routledge, 2017).

115 Chetty et al., "Where is the Land," 1557.

116 Chetty et al., "Where is the Land," 1605 ("The correlation between upward mobility and fraction black is -0.580. They called this the "most obvious pattern in the maps...").

117 Chetty et al., "Race and Economic Opportunity," 776.

118 Menendian, Gailes, and Gambhir, table 5.

119 David M. Cutler and Edward L. Glaeser, "Are Ghettos Good or Bad?," *Quarterly Journal of Economics* 112, no. 3 (1997): 827–872, 828, https://www.jstor.org/stable/2951257.

120 Sander, Kucheva, and Zasloff, *Moving Toward Integration*, 2–3.

121 National Center for Education Statistics, *Fast Facts Public School Choice Programs* (Washington, DC: National Center for Education Statistics, U.S. Department of Education, 2016), https://web.archive.org/web/20160303022602/https://nces.ed.gov/fastfacts/display.asp?id=6; Richard D. Kahlenberg, Halley Potter and Kimberly Quick, *A Bold Agenda for School Integration* (New York: Century Foundation, 2019), https://tcf.org/content/report/bold-agenda-school-integration/.

122 See Alvin Chang, "We Can Draw School Zones to Make Classrooms Less Segregated," *Vox*, August 27, 2018, https://www.vox.com/2018/1/8/16822374/school-segregation-gerrymander-map.

123 Halley Potter, "School Segregation in U.S. Metro Areas," *Century* Foundation, May 17, 2022, https://tcf.org/content/report/school-segregation-in-u-s-metro-areas/.

124 This was actually higher than the income segregation gap, using free and reduced lunch status as the divider, which was only a 19-point gap.

125 "New 'Segregation Index' shows American schools remain highly segregated by race, ethnicity and economic status," *Stanford Graduate School of Education*, May 17, 2022, https://ed.stanford.edu/news/new-segregation-index-shows-american-schools-remain-highly-segregated-race-ethnicity-and?print=all. See also "The Segregation Tracking Project," Educational Opportunity Project at Stanford University, accessed February 26, 2025, https://edopportunity.org/segregation/. Although whether it is getting worse or not, depends on the measure used. See Alvin Chang, "The data proves that school segregation is getting worse," *Vox*, March 5, 2018, https://www.vox.com/2018/3/5/17080218/school-segregation-getting-worse-data.

126 Ann Owens, "Racial Residential Segregation of School-Age Children and Adults: The Role of Schooling as a Segregating Force," *Russell Sage Foundation Journal of the Social Sciences* 3, no. 2 (2017): 63–80, https://doi.org/10.7758/RSF.2017.3.2.03. Poverty concentration in schools is also more intense in schools than neighborhoods for the same reasons. For example, gentrifying newcomers are both less likely to have school-age children, are more likely to enroll their children in private schools, especially if the neighborhood or district schools have poor ratings. Matt Barnum, "What Does Gentrification Mean for Local Schools? Fewer Students," *Chalkbeat*, January 23, 2020, https://www.chalkbeat.org/2020/1/23/21121796/what-does-gentrification-mean-for-local-schools-fewer-students; See also Francis A. Pearman II and Walker A. Swain, "School Choice, Gentrification, and the Variable Significance of Racial Stratification in Urban Neighborhoods," *Sociology of Education* 90, no. 3, (2017): 221, https://doi.org/10.1177/0038040717710494. Another factor is that charter schools tend to be more racially segregated than public schools. Ryan Pfleger and Gary Orfield, *Segregated Choices: Magnet and Charter Schools* (Los Angeles: UCLA Civil Rights Project, 2024), https://www.civilrightsproject.ucla.edu/news/press-releases/press-releases-2024/new-new-research-reveals-u.s.-charter-schools-exhibit-higher-racial-segregation-compared-to-magnet-schools-in-same-districts; Erica Frankenberg, Genevieve Siegel-Hawley, and Jia Wang, "Choice without Equity: Charter School Segregation," *Education Policy Analysis Archives* 19, no. 1 (2011): https://doi.org/10.14507/epaa.v19n1.2011.

127 Jacqueline M. Nowicki, *K-12 Education: Better Use of Information Could Help Agencies Identify Disparities and Address Racial Discrimination* (Washington, DC: United States Government Accountability Office, 2016), https://www.gao.gov/assets/680/676745.pdf.

128 Janet M. Ruane and Karen A. Cerulo, *Second Thoughts: Sociology Challenges Conventional Wisdom* (Thousand Oaks, CA: Pine Forge Press, 2012), 130.

129 Anurima Barghava, Erica Frankenberg, and Chinh Q. Le, *Still Looking to the Future: Voluntary K-12 School Integration — A Manual for Parents, Educators, and Advocates* (New York: NAACP Legal Defense and Education Fund; Los Angeles: Civil Rights Project, UCLA, 2008), 11, https://www.naacpldf.org/wp-content/uploads/Still_Looking_to_the_Future_Voluntary_K-12_School_Integration_A_Manual_for_Parents_Educators_and_Advocates_EDUCATION_.pdf.

130 Gary Orfield and Ryan Pfleger, *The Unfinished Battle for Integration in a Multiracial America – from Brown to Now* (Los Angeles: Civil Rights Project, UCLA, 2024), 34, Fig 2, https://www.civilrightsproject.ucla.edu/research/k-12-education/integration-and-diversity/the-unfinished-battle-for-integration-in-a-multiracial-america-2013-from-brown-to-now/National-Segregation-041624-CORRECTED-for.pdf.

131 Bhargava, Frankenberg, and Le, *Still Looking to the Future*, 11.

132 See "The 2009-2019 Educational Opportunity Explorer," Accessed February 25, 2025, Educational Opportunity Project at Stanford University, https://edopportunity.org/opportunity/explorer/. Users can select any school district, county, city or even school in the entire country, and see the demographic breakdown and school performance, including the test scores disaggregated by race, gender, and class.

133 Kim Parker et al., *Is College Worth It? College Presidents, Public Assess Value, Quality and Mission of Higher Education* (Washington, DC: Pew Research Center, 2011).

134 David H. Autor, "Skills, Education, and the Rise of Earnings Inequality Among the 'Other 99 Percent'" *Science* 344, no. 6186 (2014): 844, https://www.science.org/doi/10.1126/science.1251868.

135 Julia B. Isaacs, Isabel V. Sawhill, and Ron Haskins, *Getting Ahead Or Losing Ground: Economic Mobility In America* (Washington, DC: Brookings Institution, 2008), 106, https://www.pewtrusts.org/~/media/legacy/uploadedfiles/pcs_assets/2008/pewempgettingaheadfull2pdf.pdf.
136 Ben Casselman, "Race Gap Narrows in College Enrollment, But Not in Graduation," *FiveThirtyEight*, April 30, 2014, https://fivethirtyeight.com/features/race-gap-narrows-in-college-enrollment-but-not-in-graduation/.
137 "Percentage of Persons 25 to 29 Years Old with Selected Levels of Educational Attainment, by Race/Ethnicity and Sex: Selected Years, 1920 Through 2017," National Center for Education Statistics: Digest of Education Statistics, https://nces.ed.gov/programs/digest/d17/tables/dt17_104.20.asp.
138 "Graduation rates within 150 percent of normal program completion time at Title IV institutions among students who started as full-time, first-time degree/certificate-seeking undergraduate students, by race/ethnicity, level and control of institution, and gender: United States, cohort years 2016 and 2019," *National Center for Education Statistics: Integrated Postsecondary Education Data System (IPEDS)*, Winter 2022–2023, accessed September 16, 2024, https://nces.ed.gov/ipeds/search?query=&query2=&resultType=all&page=1&sortBy=date_desc&overlayTableId=36023.
139 "While the share of young adult African Americans who had completed college grew by 128 percent, the growth for whites was 143 percent (from 17 to 42 percent of young adults)," "Selected Levels of Educational Attainment" National Center for Education Statistics, 2017, quoted in Stephen Menendian and Richard Rothstein, with Nirali Beri, *The Road Not Taken: Housing and Criminal Justice 50 Years After the Kerner Commission Report* (Berkeley, CA: Othering & Belonging Institute, 2020), 8, https://belonging.berkeley.edu/road-not-taken.
140 See data from "Table A-2. Percent of People 25 Years and Over Who Have Completed High School or College, by Race, Hispanic Origin and Sex: Selected Years 1940 to 2021," *CPS Historical Time Series Tables* (Washington, DC: United States Census Bureau, last modified February 24, 2022), https://www.census.gov/data/tables/time-series/demo/educational-attainment/cps-historical-time-series.html.
141 CJ Libassi, *The Neglected College Race Gap: Racial Disparities Among College Completers* (Washington, DC: Center for American Process, 2018), https://www.americanprogress.org/article/neglected-college-race-gap-racial-disparities-among-college-completers/.
142 "Integrated Postsecondary Education System," U.S. Department of Education: National Center for Education Statistics, accessed August 12, 2024, https://nces.ed.gov/ipeds/.
143 Dorothy Brown, *The Whiteness of Wealth: How the Tax System Impoverishes Black Americans—And How We Can Fix It* (New York: Random House, 2021), 100, Table 3.1.
144 Casselman, "Race Gap Narrows."
145 See Mazumder, "Black-White Differences," 10–11.
146 Jonathan M. V. Davis and Bhash Mazumder, "The Decline in Intergenerational Mobility After 1980," rev. ed. (working paper, Federal Reserve Bank of Chicago, 2022), 11, https://www.chicagofed.org/publications/working-papers/2017/wp2017-05.
147 EdBuild, *$23 Billion* (Jersey City, NJ: 2019), https://edbuild.org/content/23-billion.
148 Cutler and Glaeser, "Ghettos," 842, table 3.
149 *2015 College-Bound Seniors Total Group Profile Report* (New York: College Board, 2015), https://secure-media.collegeboard.org/digitalServices/pdf/sat/total-group-2015.pdf.

150 Richard V. Reeves and Dimitrios Halikias, "Race Gaps in SAT Scores Highlight Inequality and Hinder Upward Mobility," *Brookings Institution*, February 1, 2017, https://www.brookings.edu/research/race-gaps-in-sat-scores-highlight-inequality-and-hinder-upward-mobility/ ("But test scores reflect accumulated advantages and disadvantages in each day of life up the one on which the test is taken. Race gaps on the SAT hold up a mirror to racial inequities in society as a whole. Equalizing educational opportunities and human capital acquisition earlier is the only way to ensure fairer outcomes").

151 David Card and Jesse Rothstein, "Racial Segregation and the Black-White Test Score Gap," *Journal of Public Economics* 91, no. 11–12 (2007): 2159.

152 Cutler and Glaeser, "Ghettos," 862–863.

153 *Discrimination in America: Experiences and Views of African Americans* (Washington, DC: National Public Radio, 2017), 16, https://media.npr.org/assets/img/2017/10/23/discriminationpoll-african-americans.pdf.

154 Jason N. Houle and Fenaba R. Addo, *A Dream Defaulted: The Student Loan Crisis Among Black Borrowers* (Cambridge, MA: Harvard Education Press, 2022).

155 Fenaba R. Addo, Jason N. Houle, and Daniel Simon, "Young, Black, and (Still) in the Red: Parental Wealth, Race, and Student Loan Debt," *Race and Social Problems* 8, 64–76, https://doi.org/10.1007/s12552-016-9162-0.

156 Neil Bhutta et al., *Disparities in Wealth by Race and Ethnicity in the 2019 Survey of Consumer Finances* (Washington, DC: Board of Governors of the Federal Reserve System, 2020), https://www.federalreserve.gov/econres/notes/feds-notes/disparities-in-wealth-by-race-and-ethnicity-in-the-2019-survey-of-consumer-finances-20200928.htm.

157 Kristin Mcintosh et al., "Examining the Black-White Wealth Gap," *Brookings*, February 27, 2020, https://www.brookings.edu/blog/up-front/2020/02/27/examining-the-black-white-wealth-gap/.

158 At least, it did in 2016. William Darity, Fenaba R. Addo and Imari Smith, "A Subaltern Middle Class: The Case of the Missing 'Black Bourgeoisie' in America," *Contemporary & Economic Policy*, 39, no. 1 (2020): 5, https://socialequity.duke.edu/wp-content/uploads/2020/05/DarityAddoSmithCEP2020.pdf.

159 Carter, "Education's Limitations," 24.

160 Darity, Addo, and Smith, "Subaltern Middle Class," 5.

161 Board of Governors of the Federal Reserve Board, *2022 Survey of Consumer Finances* (Washington, DC: Board of Governors of the Federal Reserve System, 2023), https://www.federalreserve.gov/econres/scfindex.htm; Darity, Addo, and Smith; Bhutta et al., *Disparities in Wealth by Race and Ethnicity*; *What Resources do Families Have for Financial Emergencies?* (Philadelphia: Pew Charitable Trusts, 2015), https://www.pewtrusts.org/-/media/assets/2015/11/emergencysavingsreportnov2015.pdf; Aladangady, Chang, and Krimmel, "Greater Wealth, Greater Uncertainty."

162 Dedrick Asante-Muhammad et al., *The Ever-Growing Gap: Without Change, African-American and Latino Families Won't Match White Wealth for Centuries* (Washington, DC: Institute for Policy Studies and CFED, 2016), 5, https://ips-dc.org/wp-content/uploads/2016/08/The-Ever-Growing-Gap-CFED_IPS-Final-1.pdf.

163 Dedrick Asante-Muhammad et al., *The Road to Zero Wealth: How the Racial Wealth Divide Is Hollowing Out America's Middle Class* (Washington, DC: Institute for Policy Studies and Prosperity Now, 2017), 5.

164 Shelley Stewart III et al., *The economic state of Black America: What is and what could be* (New York: McKinsey Institute for Black Economic Mobility and the McKinsey Global Institute, 2021), Exhibit E7, 17, https://www.mckinsey.com/featured-insights/diversity-and-inclusion/the-economic-state-of-black-america-what-is-and-what-could-be.

165 Bhutta et al., *Disparities in Wealth by Race and Ethnicity*.

166 Bhutta et al., *Disparities in Wealth by Race and Ethnicity*.
167 Francine D. Blau and John W. Graham, "Black-White Differences in Wealth and Asset Composition," *Quarterly Journal of* Economics 105, no. 2 (1990): 321-339, https://www.jstor.org/stable/2937789; Paul L. Menchik and Nancy Ammon Jianakoplos, "Black-White Wealth Inequality: Is Inheritance the Reason?," *Economic Inquiry* 35, no. 2 (1997): 428-442, https://doi.org/10.1111/j.1465-7295.1997.tb01920.x; Maury Gittleman and Edward N. Wolff, "Racial differences in patterns of wealth accumulation," *Journal of Human Resources* 39, no. 1 (2004): 193-233, https://doi.org/10.2307/3559010.
168 Signe-Mary McKernan, "Do Racial Disparities in Private Transfers Help Explain the Racial Wealth Gap? New Evidence From Longitudinal Data," *Demography* 51, no. 3 (2014): 949-974, https://doi.org/10.1007/s13524-014-0296-7.
169 Patrick D. Wightman et al., *Historical Trends in Parental Financial Support of Young Adults* (Ann Arbor, MI: Population Studies Center, 2013), 14, https://coilink.org/20.500.12592/g23hm3.
170 Brown, *Whiteness of Wealth*, 153.
171 Tatjana Meschede et al., "'Family Achievements?': How a College Degree Accumulates Wealth for Whites and Not for Blacks," *Federal Reserve Bank of St. Louis Review* 99, no. 1 (2017): 124, https://heller.brandeis.edu/iere/pdfs/racial-wealth-equity/racial-wealth-gap/family-achievements.pdf.
172 Richard Fry and Anthony Cilluffo, *A Rising Share of Undergraduates Are From Poor Families, Especially at Less Selective Colleges* (Washington, DC: Pew Research Center, 2019), https://www.pewresearch.org/social-trends/2019/05/22/a-rising-share-of-undergraduates-are-from-poor-families-especially-at-less-selective-colleges/.
173 Kerwin K. Charles and Erik Hurst, "The Transition to Home Ownership and the Black-White Wealth Gap," *Review of Economics and Statistics* 84, no. 2 (2002): 281, 295.
174 Bhutta et al., *Disparities in Wealth by Race and Ethnicity*, table 2.
175 Charles and Hurst, "Transition to Home Ownership," 296.
176 "Housing and Homeownership: Homeownership Rate," FRED Economic Data, Federal Reserve Bank of St. Louis, 2021, https://fred.stlouisfed.org/release/tables?rid=296&eid=784188&od=.
177 Laura Sullivan et al., *The Racial Wealth Gap: Why Policy Matters* (New York: Demos; Waltham, MA: Institute on Assets and Social Policy, Brandeis University, 2015), 2, https://www.demos.org/sites/default/files/publications/RacialWealthGap_2.pdf.
178 Charles and Hurst, "Transition to Home Ownership," 295.
179 Federal Reserve Board, *2022 Survey of Consumer Finances*.
180 Junia Howell and Elizabeth Korver-Glenn, "The Increasing Effect of Neighborhood Racial Composition on Housing Values 1980-2015," *Social Problems* 68, no. 4 (2021): 1062, https://academic.oup.com/socpro/advance-article-abstract/doi/10.1093/socpro/spaa033/5900507?redirectedFrom=fulltext (finding that From 1980 to 2015, homes in white neighborhoods appreciated at twice the rate of those in communities of color).
181 Chenoa Flippen, "Unequal Returns to Housing Investments? A Study of Real Housing Appreciation Among Black, White and Hispanic Households," *Social Forces* 82, no. 4 (2004): 1529, https://www.jstor.org/stable/3598444
182 Michela Zonta, "Racial Disparities in Home Appreciation," *Center for American Progress*, July 15, 2019, https://www.americanprogress.org/issues/economy/reports/2019/07/15/469838/racial-disparities-home-appreciation/.
183 David Rusk, *The "Segregation Tax": The Cost of Racial Segregation to Black Homeowners* (Washington, DC: The Brookings Institution, 2001), 3, https://www.brookings.edu/wp-content/uploads/2016/06/rusk.pdf.

184 David R. Harris, "Property Values Drop When Blacks Move in, Because...': Racial and Socioeconomic Determinants of Neighborhood Desirability," *American Sociological Review* 64, no. 3 (1999): 474, 476, https://www.jstor.org/stable/2657496.

185 Alanna McCargo and Jung Hyun Choi, *Closing the Gaps: Building Black Wealth through Homeownership* (Washington, DC: Urban Institute, 2020), https://www.urban.org/sites/default/files/publication/103267/closing-the-gaps-building-black-wealth-through-homeownership_1.pdf.

186 Dionissi Aliprantis, Daniel R. Carroll, and Eric R. Young, "The Dynamics of the Racial Wealth Gap" (working paper, Federal Reserve Bank of Cleveland, 2022), http://dx.doi.org/10.2139/ssrn.3467718; Blau and Graham, "Black-White Differences."

187 Brown, *Whiteness of Wealth*, 135.

188 Brown, 162.

189 Brown, 149.

190 Chetty et al., "Where is the Land," 1611. The correlation between commute times and upward mobility is 0.6, higher than the univariate correlation with any of the measures. It should be noted, however, that in a subsequent paper Chetty et al. find no correlation between job *growth* and upward mobility. See Chetty et al., "Opportunity Atlas," 3 ("the factors that lead to highly productive labor markets with high rates of job, wage, and productivity growth apparently differ from factors that promote human capital development and result in high levels of upward income mobility across generations"). This counter-intuitive finding is explainable by the framework of this book. Many new jobs are inaccessible to low-skilled workers. High-skilled jobs require skilled workers, and the labor market is not primarily responsible for creating high skilled workers; educational institutions and workforce policies do that. Thus, we would only expect a correlation between *entry*-level job growth or job density and upward mobility.

191 "Table A-2. Employment Status of the Civilian Population by Race, Sex, and Age," *U.S. Bureau of Labor Statistics*, last modified December 8, 2023, https://www.bls.gov/news.release/empsit.t02.htm; "Table A-3. Employment status of the Hispanic or Latino population by sex and age," *U.S. Bureau of Labor Statistics*, last modified December 8, 2023, https://www.bls.gov/news.release/empsit.t03.htm. See also Paul Krugman, "The Good News on Unemployment for Black Americans," *New York Times*, May 23, 2023, https://www.nytimes.com/2023/05/23/opinion/unemployment-black-americans.html.

192 "E-16. Unemployment Rates by Age, Sex, Race, and Hispanic or Latino Ethnicity," *U.S. Bureau of Labor Statistics*, last modified October 6, 2023, https://www.bls.gov/web/empsit/cpsee_e16.htm.

193 Margery Austin Turner, "Residential Segregation and Employment Inequality," in *Segregation: The Rising Costs for America*, ed. James H. Carr and Nandinee K. Kutty (New York: Routledge, 2008), 154.

194 Marianne Bertrand and Sendhil Mullainathan, "Are Emily and Brendan More Employable than Lakisha and Jamal? A Field Experiment on Labor Market Discrimination," *American Economic Review* 94, no. 4 (2004): 991–1013; Devah Pager, Bruce Western, and Bart Bonikowski, "Discrimination in a Low-Wage Labor Market: A Field Experiment," *American Sociological Review* 74, no. 5 (2009): 777–799, https://www.ncbi.nlm.nih.gov/pmc/articles/PMC2915472/.

195 Devah Pager, *Marked: Race, Crime, and Finding Work in an Era of Mass Incarceration* (Chicago: University of Chicago Press, 2007).

196 John F. Kain, "Housing Segregation, Negro Employment, and Metropolitan Decentralization," *Quarterly Journal of Economics* 82, no. 2 (1968): 175–197.

197 John F. Kain, "The Effect of the Ghetto on the Distribution and Level of Nonwhite Employment in Urban Areas" (Proceedings, Annual Meeting of the American Statistical Association, Chicago, December 27–30, 1964), https://www.asasrms.org/Proceedings/y1964/The%20Effect%20Of%20The%20Ghetto%20On%20The%20Distribution%20And%20Level%20Of%20Nonwhite%20Employment%20In%20Urban%20Areas.pdf. See also John F. Kain, "The Spatial Mismatch Hypothesis: Three Decades Later," *Housing Policy Debate* 3, no. 2 (1992): https://doi.org/10.1080/10511482.1992.9521100.
198 Keith R. Ihlanfeldt and David L. Sjoquist, "The Spatial Mismatch Hypothesis: A Review of Recent Studies and Their Implications for Welfare Reform," *Housing Policy Debate* 9, no. 4 (1998): 849–892.
199 Elizabeth Kneebone, "Commuting to Opportunity: Employment Patterns of People Living in High-Poverty Neighborhoods," *Enterprise Community Partners*, June 9 2021, 22, https://www.enterprisecommunity.org/blog/new-research-commuting-opportunity.
200 Kneebone, "Commuting," 7.
201 Thomas J. Christian, "Trade-Offs Between Commuting Time and Health-Related Activities," *Journal of Urban Health* 89, no. 5 (2012): 746–757; Christine M. Hoehner et al., "Commuting Distance, Cardiorespiratory Fitness, and Metabolic Risk," *American Journal of Preventative Medicine* 42, no. 6 (2012): 571–578; Lisa D. Sabin et al., "Characterizing the Range of Children's Air Pollutant Exposure During School Bus Commutes," *Journal of Exposure Science & Environmental Epidemiology* 15, no. 5 (2005): 377–387; Bhashkar Mazumder and Zachary Seeskin, "Breakfast Skipping, Extreme Commutes, and the Sex Composition at Birth," *Biodemography and Social Biology* 61, no. 2 (2015): 187–208.
202 Kneebone, "Commuting," 14. ("The typical commute that both begins and end in a high-poverty neighborhood is almost 6 miles. That distance stretches to more than 10 miles for moderate-poverty destinations and more than doubles for low-poverty places of work (12.5 miles).")
203 Harry J. Holzer, *What Employers Want: Job Prospects for Less Educated Workers* (New York: Russell Sage Foundation, 1996), 166.
204 See e.g. Conor Dougherty and Andrew Burton, "A 2:15 Alarm, 2 Trains and a Bus Get Her to Work by 7 A.M.," *New York Times*, August 17, 2017, https://www.nytimes.com/2017/08/17/business/economy/san-francisco-commute.html.
205 Rucker C. Johnson, "Landing a Job in Urban Space: The Extent and Effects of Spatial Mismatch," *Regional Science and Urban Economics* 36, no. 3 (2006): 331–372, https://gsppi.berkeley.edu/~ruckerj/johnson_SMH_RSUEpub.pdf.
206 Michael A. Stoll and Steven Raphael, "Racial Differences in Spatial Job Search Patterns: Exploring the Causes and Consequences," *Economic Geography* 76, no. 3 (2000): 221, https://doi.org/10.2307/144290.
207 Turner, "Residential Segregation and Employment Inequality," in Carr and Kutty, *Segregation*, 154.
208 Michael A. Stoll, *Job Sprawl and the Spatial Mismatch Between Blacks and Jobs* (Washington, DC: Brookings Institution Metropolitan Policy Program, 2005).
209 Cutler and Glaeser, "Ghettos," 843.
210 Chetty et al., "Where is the Land," 1611.
211 Janell Ross, "Black Unemployment Driven By White America's Favors For Friends," *Huffington Post*, March 29, 2013, https://www.huffingtonpost.com/2013/03/29/black-unemployment-nancy-ditomaso_n_2974805.html. See also Deirdre A. Royster, *Race and the Invisible Hand: How White Networks Exclude Black Men from Blue-Collar Jobs* (Berkeley: University of California Press, 2003).
212 Darren Walker, "Internships Are Not a Privilege," *New York Times*, July 5, 2016, https://www.nytimes.com/2016/07/05/opinion/breaking-a-cycle-that-allows-privilege-to-go-to-privileged.html.

213 Daniel Cox, Juhem Navarro-Rivera, and Robert P. Jones, *Race, Religion, and Political Affiliation of Americans' Core Social Networks* (Washington, DC: Public Religion Research Institute, 2016), https://www.prri.org/research/poll-race-religion-politics-americans-social-networks/.

214 Cox, Navarro-Rivera, and Jones, *Race, Religion, and Political Affiliation*; Robert P. Jones, "Self-Segregation: Why It's So Hard for Whites to Understand Ferguson," *Atlantic*, August 21, 2014, https://www.theatlantic.com/national/archive/2014/08/self-segregation-why-its-hard-for-whites-to-understand-ferguson/378928/.

215 Lauren A. Rivera, "Hiring as Cultural Matching: The Case of Elite Professional Service Firms," *American Sociological Review* 77, no. 6 (2012): https://www.asanet.org/sites/default/files/savvy/journals/ASR/Dec12ASRFeature.pdf.

216 Neil Shah, "Need for Networking Puts Black Job Seekers at Disadvantage," *Wall Street Journal*, March 27, 2013, https://blogs.wsj.com/economics/2013/03/27/need-for-networking-puts-black-job-seekers-at-disadvantage/.

217 See Steven Shulman, "The Causes or Black Poverty: Evidence and Interpretation," *Journal of Economic Issues* 24, no. 4 (1990): 1012.

218 Nancy DiTomaso, *The American Non-Dilemma: Racial Inequality Without Racism* (New York: Russell Sage Foundation, 2013), 46–66.

219 Augusta National, the private club that hosts the annual "Masters" golf tournament, did not admit its first Black member until 1990 and didn't offer membership to women until 2012. Karen Crouse, "At Augusta National, Not Talking About Race Is Tradition," *New York Times*, November 10, 2020, https://www.nytimes.com/2020/11/10/sports/golf/lee-elder-masters-augusta-national.html.

220 Clio Chang, "Separate but Unequal in College Greek Life," *Century Foundation*, August 12, 2014, https://tcf.org/content/commentary/separate-but-unequal-in-college-greek-life/; Brianna Zhou, "Greek life promotes discrimination, exclusivity," *Campanile*, October 18, 2021, https://thecampanile.org/24432/opinion/greek-life-promotes-discrimination-exclusivity/.

221 Sampson, *Great American City*, 17, 342–345.

222 Sheryll Cashin, *The Failures of Integration: How Race and Class Are Undermining the American Dream* (New York: Public Affairs, 2004), 266–275.

223 Loïc J. D. Wacquant and William Julius Wilson, "The Cost of Racial and Class Exclusion in the Inner City," *Annals of the American Academy of Political and Social Science* 501, no. 1 (1989): 8–25.

224 This differential may explain a good deal of the Black-white wage gap. Kenneth J. Arrow and Ron Borzekowski, "Limited Network Connections and the Distribution of Wages" (working paper, Federal Reserve, 2004), https://www.federalreserve.gov/Pubs/FEDS/2004/200441/200441pap.pdf.

225 James R. Elliott, "Social Isolation and Labor Market Insulation: Network and Neighborhood Effects on Less-Educated Urban Workers," *Sociological Quarterly* 40, no. 2: 199–216.

226 William Julius Wilson, *More Than Just Race: Being Black and Poor in the Inner City* (New York: W.W. Norton, 2009).

227 Dena Carson and Natalie Kroovand Hipple, "Comparing Violent and Non-Violent Gang Incidents: An Exploration of Gang-Related Police Incident Reports," *Social Sciences* 9, no. 11 (2020): https://doi.org/10.3390/socsci9110199.

228 Leann M. Tigges, Irene Browne, and Gary P. Green, "Social Isolation of the Urban Poor: Race, Class, and Neighborhood Effects on Social Resources," *Sociological Quarterly* 39, no. 1 (1998): 53–77; Roberto Fernandez and David Harris, "Social Isolation and the Underclass," in *Drugs, Crime, and Social Isolation: Barriers to Urban Opportunity*, ed. Adele Harrell (Washington, DC: Urban Institute Press, 1992), 257–293.

229 Massey, *Categorically Unequal*, 203.

230 Emily D. Buehler and Rich Kluckow, *Correctional Populations in the United States, 2022 – Statistical Tables* (Washington, DC: Bureau of Justice Statistics, 2024), https://bjs.ojp.gov/library/publications/correctional-populations-united-states-2022-statistical-tables.

231 Wendy Sawyer and Peter Wagner, "Mass Incarceration: The Whole Pie 2025," *Prison Policy Institute*, March 11, 2025, https://www.prisonpolicy.org/reports/pie2025.html.

232 Zhen Zeng, *Jails Report Series: Preliminary Data Release (2023)* (Washington, DC: Bureau of Justice Statistics, 2024), https://bjs.ojp.gov/library/publications/jails-report-series-preliminary-data-release-2023; "Criminal Records and Reentry Toolkit," National Conference of State Legislatures, updated March 31, 2023, https://www.ncsl.org/civil-and-criminal-justice/criminal-records-and-reentry-toolkit.

233 Helen Fair and Roy Walmsley, *World Prison Population List*, 14th ed. (London: Institute for Crime & Justice Policy Research, 2024), https://www.prisonstudies.org/sites/default/files/resources/downloads/world_prison_population_list_14th_edition.pdf.

234 Ta-Nehisi Coates, "The Case for Reparations," *Atlantic* (2014): 64, https://www.theatlantic.com/magazine/archive/2014/06/the-case-for-reparations/361631/.

235 Ann Carson and Rich Klucklow, *Correctional Populations in the United States, 2021 – Statistical Tables* (Washington, DC: Bureau of Justice Statistics, 2023), https://bjs.ojp.gov/document/cpus21st.pdf.

236 "Incarceration Rates by Country 2025," World Population Review, accessed April 23, 2025, https://worldpopulationreview.com/country-rankings/incarceration-rates-by-country%23top-10-countries-with-the-most-people-in-prison.

237 Sarah K.S. Shannon et al., "The Growth, Scope, and Spatial Distribution of People With Felony Records in the United States, 1948–2010," *Demography* 54, no. 5 (2017): https://pmc.ncbi.nlm.nih.gov/articles/PMC5996985/.

238 "New York," QuickFacts, accessed November 27, 2024, https://www.census.gov/quickfacts/fact/table/NY/PST045223; Liz Johnson, *Trends in the New York State Prison Population: 2008-2023* (New York: Data Collaborative for Justice, 2023), https://datacollaborativeforjustice.org/wp-content/uploads/2023/07/PrisonPop-1.pdf.

239 Mary Kelly Persyn, "Mass Incarceration and Child Trauma," *Poverty & Race Research Action Council* 26, no. 3 (2017): 10, https://www.prrac.org/newsletters/julaugsep2017.pdf.

240 Patrick A. Langan, *Race of Prisoners Admitted to State and Federal Institutions in the United States, 1926-1986* (Washington, DC: US Department of Justice, 1992), 10, Table 7, https://bjs.ojp.gov/library/publications/race-prisoners-admitted-state-and-federal-institutions-1926-86-0; "National Prisoner Statistics, [United States], 1978-2020," *United States Bureau of Justice Statistics*, December 16, 2021, https://doi.org/10.3886/ICPSR38249.v1.

241 Nazgol Ghandnoosh, *One in Five: Ending Racial Inequity in Incarceration* (Washington, DC: Sentencing Project, 2023), https://www.sentencingproject.org/reports/one-in-five-ending-racial-inequity-in-incarceration/.

242 Black people are held in state prisons at a rate of 5 times whites, and in 11 states, at least 1 in 20 adult Black men is in prison. James Forman Jr., *Locking Up Our Own: Crime and Punishment in Black America* (New York: Farrar, Straus, and Giroux, 2017), 218.

243 Chetty et al., "Race and Economic Opportunity," 716.

244 Coates, "Case for Reparations," 64.

245 Bruce Western and Becky Pettit, "Incarceration & Social Inequality," *Dædalus* 139, no. 3 (2010): 8–19, 11, https://www.amacad.org/publication/daedalus/incarceration-social-inequality.

246 Bruce Western and Becky Pettit, *Collateral Costs: Incarceration's Effect on Economic Mobility* (Philadelphia: Pew Charitable Trusts, 2010), 4, https://www.pewtrusts.org/~/media/legacy/uploadedfiles/pcs_assets/2010/collateralcosts1pdf.pdf.
247 Western and Pettit, *Collateral Costs*, 4.
248 Maria Morrison, "Trauma and Incarceration: A Latent Class Analysis of Lifetime Trauma Exposures for Individuals in Prison," *Journal of Trauma and Dissociation* 25, no. 2 (2024): 168–184, https://doi.org/10.1080/15299732.2023.2289189.
249 Ta-Nehisi Coates, "The Black Family in the Age of Mass Incarceration," *Atlantic*, October, 2015, 69, https://www.theatlantic.com/magazine/archive/2015/10/the-black-family-in-the-age-of-mass-incarceration/403246/.
250 Harry J. Holzer, "Collateral Costs: The Effects of Incarceration on the Employment and Earnings of Young Workers," (Washington, DC: Georgetown Public Policy Institute, 2007), 7, https://ftp.iza.org/dp3118.pdf
251 "Welcome to the NICCC," National Inventory of Collateral Consequences of Criminal Conviction, Accessed March 7, 2025, https://niccc.nationalreentryresourcecenter.org/. The database is searchable by jurisdiction.
252 *Enforcement Guidance on the Consideration of Arrest and Conviction in Employment Decisions Under Title VII of the Civil Rights Act* (Washington, DC: Equal Employment Opportunity Commission, 2012), https://www.eeoc.gov/laws/guidance/enforcement-guidance-consideration-arrest-and-conviction-records-employment-decisions; Justina Victor, Evren Esen, and Mark Schmit, *Background Checking—The Use of Criminal Background Checks in Hiring Decisions* (Alexandria, VA: Society for Human Resource Management, 2012), https://www.shrm.org/hr-today/trends-and-forecasting/research-and-surveys/Pages/criminalbackgroundcheck.aspx.
253 Tina Rosenberg, "Have You Ever Been Arrested? Check Here," *New York Times*, May 24, 2016, https://www.nytimes.com/2016/05/24/opinion/have-you-ever-been-arrested-check-here.html.
254 Pager, Western, and Bonikowsi, "Low-Wage Labor Market."
255 Western and Pettit, *Collateral Costs*, 4.
256 George T. McDonald et al., *Report and Recommendations to New York State on Enhancing Employment Opportunities for Formerly Incarcerated People* (New York: Independent Committee on Reentry and Employment, 2006), 9, https://search.issuelab.org/resource/report-and-recommendations-to-new-york-state-on-enhancing-employment-opportunities-for-formerly-incarcerated-people.html.
257 Western and Pettit, *Collateral Costs*, 4.
258 In Chicago, 34% of prisoners returned to 8% of city neighborhoods. Roithmayr, *Reproducing Racism*, 106.
259 *Americans with Criminal Records* (Washington, DC: Sentencing Project, 2015), 1, https://www.sentencingproject.org/wp-content/uploads/2015/11/Americans-with-Criminal-Records-Poverty-and-Opportunity-Profile.pdf.
260 David Murphey and P. Mae Cooper, *Parents Behind Bars: What Happens to Their Children?* (Bethesda, MD: Child Trends, 2015), 1, https://www.childtrends.org/wp-content/uploads/2015/10/2015-42ParentsBehindBars.pdf.
261 *A Shared Sentence: The Devastating Toll of Parental Incarceration on Kids, Families and Communities* (Baltimore: Annie E. Casey Foundation, 2016), https://www.aecf.org/m/resourcedoc/aecf-asharedsentence-2016.pdf; David Murphey and P. Mae Cooper, *Parents Behind Bars: What Happens to Their Children?* (Bethesda, MD: Child Trends, 2015), 1, https://www.childtrends.org/wp-content/uploads/2015/10/2015-42ParentsBehindBars.pdf; Jesus Chaves, "New UTSA Study Finds Link Between Incarcerated Parents and Their Children's Health," *UTSA Today*, May 11, 2017, https://www.utsa.edu/today/2017/05/prisonstudy.

html; Elizabeth J. Gifford et al., "Association of Parental Incarceration with Psychiatric and Functional Outcomes of Young Adults," *JAMA Network Open* 2, no. 8 (2019): 1–12, https://jamanetwork.com/journals/jamanetworkopen/fullarticle/2748665.
262 Western and Pettit, Collateral Costs, 5.
263 Bruce Western, *Punishment and Inequality in America* (New York: Russell Sage Foundation, 2006); Lauren Glaze and Laura Maruschak, *Parents in Prison and Their Minor Children* (Washington, DC: U.S. Department of Justice, Office of Justice Programs, 2008, revised 2010), https://bjs.ojp.usdoj.gov/content/pub/pdf/pptmc.pdf.
264 A powerful and dramatic example of this is the documentary *The Sentence*, directed by Rudy Valdez (2018).
265 Melissa Sickmund et al., *Easy Access to the Census of Juveniles in Residential Placement (EZACJRP)* (Pittsburgh: National Center for Juvenile Justice, 2017); Susan W. McCampbell, *The Gender-Responsive Strategies Project: Jail Applications* (Washington, DC: U.S. Department of Justice, National Institute of Corrections, 2005), 4.
266 Dan Levin, "As More Mothers Fill Prisons, Children Suffer 'A Primal Wound,'" *New York Times*, December 28, 2019, https://www.nytimes.com/2019/12/28/us/prison-mothers-children.html.
267 Rucker C. Johnson, "Ever-Increasing Levels of Parental Incarceration and the Consequences for Children," in *Do Prisons Make Us Safer? The Benefits and Costs of the Prison Boom*, ed. Steven Raphael and Michael Stoll (New York: Russell Sage Foundation, 2009), 177–206.
268 Bryan L. Sykes and Michelle Maroto, "A Wealth of Inequalities: Mass Incarceration, Employment, and Racial Disparities in U.S. Household Wealth, 1996 to 2011," *RSF: The Russell Sage Foundation Journal of the Social Sciences* 2, no. 6 (2016): 141, https://www.rsfjournal.org/doi/full/10.7758/RSF.2016.2.6.07.
269 And half of those were living in the same household as the child. Coates, "Black Family," 66.
270 Anna R. Haskins, Wade C. Jacobsen, and Joel Mittleman, "Optimism and Obstacles: Racialized Constraints in College Attitudes and Expectations among Teens of the Prison Boom," *Sociology of Education* 96, no. 3 (2023): 211-233, https://doi.org/10.1177/00380407231167412.
271 Sharkey, *Stuck in Place*, 167.
272 Braun, "Dynamics of Opportunity" in *Dynamics of Opportunity*, ed. Kirsch and Braun, 150.
273 Gilbert C. Gee and Chandra L. Ford, "Structural Racism and Health Inequities: Old Issues, New Directions," *Du Bois Review: Social Science Research on Race* 8, no. 1 (2011): 115–132, https://www.ncbi.nlm.nih.gov/pmc/articles/PMC4306458/; Nancy Krieger et al., "50 Year Trends in US Socioeconomic Inequalities in Health: US-Born Black and White Americans, 1959–2008," *International Journal of Epidemiology* 43, no. 4 (2014): 1294–1313.
274 Arghavan Salles, Vineet M. Arora, and Kerry-Ann Mitchell, "Everyone Must Address Anti-Black Racism in Health Care," *JAMA* 326, no. 7 (2021): 601–602 https://jamanetwork.com/journals/jama/fullarticle/2783061?.
275 Paula Krakowiak et al., *California Pregnancy-Related Deaths, 2008–2016* (Sacramento, CA: The California Pregnancy Mortality Surveillance System (CA-PMSS), California Department of Public Health, 2021), 31, https://www.cdph.ca.gov/Programs/CFH/DMCAH/surveillance/CDPH%20Document%20Library/CA-PMSS/CA-PMSS-Surveillance-Report-2008-2016.pdf; Kathleen Ronayne, "Lower Death Rates for Black Moms is Goal of California Bill," *AP News*, September 27, 2021, https://apnews.com/article/business-lifestyle-health-california-race-and-ethnicity-5e61307a3b52fd597bd831f9939da86e.

276 Shiwani Mahajan et al., "Trends in Differences in Health Status and Health Care Access and Affordability by Race and Ethnicity in the United States, 1999–2018," *JAMA* 326, no. 7 (2021): 637–648, https://jamanetwork.com/journals/jama/article-abstract/2783069.

277 Sofia Carratala and Connor Maxwell, *Health Disparities by Race and Ethnicity* (Center for American Progress, 2020), 2, https://www.americanprogress.org/issues/race/reports/2020/05/07/484742/health-disparities-race-ethnicity/.

278 Rothstein, *Class and Schools*, 196–197.

279 Angela M. Odoms Young and Marino A. Bruce, "Examining the Impact of Structural Racism on Food Insecurity: Implications for Addressing Racial/Ethnic Disparities," *Family and Community Health* 41 (2018): S3–S8, https://www.jstor.org/stable/48515833; Nathalie M. Dumornay et al., "Racial Disparities in Adversity During Childhood and the False Appearance of Race-Related Differences in Brain Structure," *American Journal of Psychiatry* 180, no. 2 (2023): 127–138, https://doi.org/10.1176/appi.ajp.21090961.

280 Robert D. Bullard, "The Threat of Environmental Racism," *Natural Resources & Environment* 7, no. 3 (1993): 23–26, 55–56, https://www.jstor.org/stable/40923229?seq=1. See also Robert D. Bullard, *Dumping in Dixie: Race, Class, and Environmental Quality*, 3rd ed. (London: Taylor and Francis, 2018).

281 Brian Roewe, "Racism in Pollution and Policing: A Conversation with Robert Bullard, Father of Environmental Justice," *Earthbeat*, June 19, 2020, https://www.ncronline.org/news/earthbeat/racism-pollution-and-policing-conversation-robert-bullard-father-environmental.

282 A fight in Oakland is the exception that proves the rule. Brentin Mock, "How Oakland Defeated Coal," *Bloomberg CityLab*, July 1, 2016, https://www.bloomberg.com/news/articles/2016-07-01/the-story-behind-how-oakland-banded-together-to-defeat-coal; See also Miranda Wilson, "Gas Projects Reveal FERC's Environmental Justice Conundrum," *E&E News: EnergyWire*, August 3, 2021, https://www.eenews.net/articles/how-fercs-environmental-justice-push-might-backfire/.

283 Liam Downey and Brian Dawkins, "Race Income, and Environmental Inequality in the United States," *Sociological Perspectives* 51, no. 4 (2008): 777.

284 Christopher W. Tessum et al., "PM2.5 polluters disproportionately and systemically affect people of color in the United States," *Science Advance* 7, no. 18, 2021, 3, https://www.science.org/doi/pdf/10.1126/sciadv.abf4491.

285 Downey and Hawkins, "Race, Income, and Environmental Inequality."

286 Talia Sanders et al., "Neurotoxic Effects and Biomarkers of Lead Exposure: A Review," *Reviews on Environmental Health* 24, no. 1 (2009): 16, https://www.ncbi.nlm.nih.gov/pmc/articles/PMC2858639/.

287 Nanhua Zhang et al., "Early Childhood Lead Exposure and Academic Achievement: Evidence From Detroit Public Schools, 2008–2010," *American Journal of Public Health* 103, no. 3 (2013): e72, https://ajph.aphapublications.org/doi/abs/10.2105/AJPH.2012.301164.

288 Bruce P. Lanphear et al., "Environmental Exposures to Lead and Urban Children's Blood Lead Levels," *Environmental Research* 76, no. 2 (1998): 20–30, https://doi.org/10.1006/enrs.1997.3801.

289 Heather A. Moody, Joe T. Darden, and Bruce Wm Pigozzi, "The Relationship of Neighborhood Socioeconomic Differences and Racial Residential Segregation to Childhood Blood Lead Levels in Metropolitan Detroit," *Journal of Urban Health* 93, no. 5 (2016): 820–839, https://pubmed.ncbi.nlm.nih.gov/27538746/.

290 Paul B. Stretesky, "The Distribution of Air Lead Levels Across U.S. Counties: Implications for the Production of Racial Inequality," *Sociological Spectrum* 23, no. 1 (2003): 91–118.

291 Robert J. Sampson and Alix S. Winter, "The Racial Ecology of Lead Poisoning," *Du Bois Review* 13, no. 2 (2016): 261, https://scholar.harvard.edu/files/alixwinter/files/sampson_winter_2016.pdf.

292 Meera Jagannathan, "2 Million Americans Don't Have Access to Running Water and Basic Plumbing," *Market Watch*, November 23, 2019, https://www.marketwatch.com/story/2-million-americans-dont-have-access-to-running-water-and-basic-plumbing-2019-11-20; See also Katie Langin, "Millions of Americans Drink Tap Potentially Unsafe Water. How Does Your County Stack Up?," *Science*, February 12, 2018, https://www.science.org/content/article/millions-americans-drink-potentially-unsafe-tap-water-how-does-your-county-stack.

293 Maura Allaire, Haowei Wu, and Upmanu Lall, "National trends in drinking water quality violations," *PNAS* 115, no. 9 (2018): 2078, https://www.pnas.org/doi/pdf/10.1073/pnas.1719805115.

294 Xander Peters and Stephanie Hanes, "First Flint, then Jackson. Is America ready to fix its water supply?," *Christian Science Monitor*, July 21, 2021, https://www.csmonitor.com/Environment/2021/0721/First-Flint-then-Jackson.-Is-America-ready-to-fix-its-water-supply.

295 Dolores Acevedo Garcia and Theresa L. Osypuk, "Impacts of Housing and Neighborhoods on Health: Pathways, Racial/Ethnic Disparities, and Policy Directions," in Carr and Kutty, *Segregation*, 197–235; David R. Williams and Chiquita Collins, "Racial Residential Segregation: A Fundamental Cause of Racial Disparities in Health," *Public Health Reports* 116, no. 5 (2001): 404–416; David R. Williams, Jourdyn A. Lawrence, and Brigette A. Davis, "Racism and Health: Evidence and Needed Research," *Annual Review of Public Health* 40 (2019): 105–125; Zinzi D. Bailey et al., "Structural Racism and Health Inequities in the USA: Evidence and Interventions," *Lancet* 389, no. 10077 (2017): 1453–1463; Michael R. Kramer and Carol R. Hogue, "Is Segregation Bad for Your Health?," *Epidemiologic Reviews* 31, no. 1 (2009): 178–194; Gee and Ford, "Structural Racism and Health Inequities," 115; Kellee White and Luisa N. Borrell, "Racial/Ethnic Residential Segregation: Framing the Context of Health Risk and Health Disparities," *Health & Place* 17, no. 2 (2011): 438–448.

296 Diane Alexander and Janet Currie, "Is it Who You Are or Where You Live? Residential Segregation and Racial Gaps in Childhood Asthma," *Journal of Health Economics* 55 (2017): 186–200; Tessum et al., "PM2.5 Polluters Disproportionately Affect People of Color," 1–6.

297 Kiarri N. Kershaw et al., "Neighborhood-Level Racial/Ethnic Residential Segregation and Incident Cardiovascular Disease: The Multi-Ethnic Study of Atherosclerosis," *Circulation* 131, no. 2 (2015): 141–148.

298 Kiarri N. Kershaw et al., "Metropolitan-Level Racial Residential Segregation and Black-White Disparities in Hypertension," *American Journal of Epidemiology* 174, no. 5 (2011): 537–545; Sharrelle Barber et al., "Abstract MP58: Racial Residential Segregation is Associated with Worse Cardiovascular Health in African American Adults: The Jackson Heart Study," Supplement, *Circulation* 137, no. S1 (2018).

299 Barber et al., "Worse Cardiovascular Health."

300 Imari Smith et al., *Inequity in Place: Obesity and the Legacy of Residential Segregation and Social Immobility* (Durham, NC: Samuel DuBois Cook Center on Social Equity at Duke University, 2019), 2, https://www.researchgate.net/publication/334746172_Inequity_in_Place_Obesity_Disparities_and_the_Legacy_of_Residential_Segregation_and_Social_Immobility.

301 Kirsten M. Beyer et al., "New Spatially Continuous Indices of Redlining and Racial Bias in Mortgage Lending: Links to Survival After Breast Cancer Diagnosis and Implications for Health Disparities Research," *Health & Place* 40 (2016):

34–43; Rachel Morello-Frosch and Bill M. Jesdale, "Separate and Unequal: Residential Segregation and Estimated Cancer Risks Associated with Ambient Air Toxics In U.S. Metropolitan Areas," *Environmental and Health Perspectives* 114, no. 3 (2006): 386–393; Michelle Precourt Debbink and Michael D. M. Bader, "Racial Residential Segregation and Low Birth Weight in Michigan's Metropolitan Areas," *American Journal of Public Health* 101, no. 9 (2011): 1714–1720; Renee Mehra, Lisa M. Boyd, and Jeannette R. Ickovics, "Racial Residential Segregation and Adverse Birth Outcomes: A Systematic Review and Meta-Analysis," *Social Science & Medicine* 191 (2017): 237–250; Michael McFarland and Cheryl A. Smith, "Segregation, Race, and Infant Well-Being," *Population Research and Policy Review* 30 (2011): 467–493.

302 Jason Richardson et al., *Redlining and Neighborhood Health* (Washington, DC: National Community Reinvestment Coalition, 2020), https://ncrc.org/holc-health/; Ana V. Diez Roux and Christina Mair, "Neighborhoods and Health," *Annals of the New York Academy of Sciences* 1186, no. 1 (2010): 125.

303 Roni Caryn Rabin, "Racial Disparities in Health Care Persist Despite Expanded Insurance," *New York Times*, August 17, 2021, https://www.nytimes.com/2021/08/17/health/racial-disparities-health-care.html.

304 Michael Siegel et al., "The Relationship between Racial Residential Segregation and Black-White Disparities in Fatal Police Shootings at the City Level, 2013–2017," *Journal of the National Medical Association* 111, no. 6 (2019): 580–587, https://pubmed.ncbi.nlm.nih.gov/31256868/.

305 Thomas A. LaVeist, "Racial Segregation and Longevity Among African Americans: An Individual-Level Analysis," *Health Services Research* 38, no. 6p2 (2003): 1719–1734.

306 Marc N. Gourevitch, "Large Life Expectancy Gaps in U.S. Cities Linked to Racial & Ethnic Segregation by Neighborhood," *NYU Langone Health*, June 5, 2019, https://nyulangone.org/news/large-life-expectancy-gaps-us-cities-linked-racial-ethnic-segregation-neighborhood.

307 Stephen Menendian, Samir Gambhir, and Arthur Gailes, *Racial Segregation in the San Francisco Bay Area, Part 4: The Harmful Effects of Segregation* (Berkeley: Othering & Belonging Institute, 2019), https://belonging.berkeley.edu/racial-segregation-san-francisco-bay-area-part-4.

308 Leonard E. Egede and Rebekah J. Walker, "Structural Racism, Social Risk Factors, and Covid-19 — A Dangerous Convergence for Black Americans," *New England Journal of Medicine* 383, no. 12 (2020), https://www.nejm.org/doi/full/10.1056/NEJMp2023616.

309 Black people were dying at 3.6 times the rate of white people, and Latinos at 2.5 times the rate of white people. Tiffany N. Ford, Sarah Reber, and Richard V. Reeves, "Race gaps in COVID-19 deaths are even bigger than they appear," *Brookings*, June 16, 2020, https://www.brookings.edu/articles/race-gaps-in-covid-19-deaths-are-even-bigger-than-they-appear/.

310 Monica Webb Hooper, Anna María Nápoles, Eliseo J. Pérez-Stable, "COVID-19 and Racial/Ethnic Disparities," *JAMA* 323, no. 24 (2020): 2466–2467, https://jamanetwork.com/journals/jama/fullarticle/2766098.

311 Frances Robles et al., "The Virus Is Killing Young Floridians. Race Is a Big Factor," *New York Times*, published August 11, 2020; last modified September 2, 2020, https://www.nytimes.com/2020/08/11/us/virus-young-deaths.html.

312 "People with Certain Medical Conditions," Centers for Disease Control and Prevention Archive, last modified May 11, 2023 https://archive.cdc.gov/#/details?q=%22People%20with%20Certain%20Medical%20Conditions%22&start=0&rows=10&url=https://www.cdc.gov/coronavirus/2019-ncov/need-extra-precautions/people-with-medical-conditions.html; "Health Equity Considerations & Racial & Ethnic Minority Groups," Centers for Disease Control and

Prevention, updated January 25, 2022, archived January 26, 2022, at the Wayback Machine, https://web.archive.org/web/20220126234237/https://www.cdc.gov/coronavirus/2019-ncov/community/health-equity/race-ethnicity.html?CDC_AA_refVal=https%3A%2F%2Fwww.cdc.gov%2Fcoronavirus%2F2019-ncov%2Fneed-extra-precautions%2Fracial-ethnic-minorities.html.
313 Squires, *Urban Sprawl*, 2.
314 Alana Semuels, "The Role of Highways in American Poverty," *Atlantic*, March 18, 2016, https://www.theatlantic.com/business/archive/2016/03/role-of-highways-in-american-poverty/474282/.
315 U.S. Census Bureau, "2022 Census of Governments – Organization," last updated July 27, 2023, Table 1, https://www.census.gov/data/tables/2022/econ/gus/2022-governments.html.
316 U.S. Census Bureau, "2022 Census of Governments," Table 2.
317 U.S. Census Bureau, "2022 Census of Governments," Table 1. However, Cutler and Glaeser argued that the number of jurisdictions per MSA has not significantly grown from 1962 to the 1990s. See Cutler and Glaeser, "Ghettos."
318 See Rebecca Hendrick and Yu Shi, "Macro-Level Determinants of Local Government Interaction: How Metropolitan Regions in the United States Compare," *Urban Affairs Review* 51, no. 3 (2014): 417, https://journals.sagepub.com/doi/abs/10.1177/1078087414530546.
319 Cutler and Glaeser, "Ghettos," 838, 848, stating that the average MSA had 40 governments in 1962 and that this has barely changed (98% correlation to 1987).
320 Michael Maciag, "How Many Local Governments Is Too Many?," *Governing*, May 3, 2019, https://www.governing.com/news/headlines/gov-most-local-governments-census.html.
321 Charles Tilly, *Durable Inequality* (Berkeley: University of California Press, 1998), 10.
322 Between 25,000 to 40,000 local governments have zoning authority in the United States today. J. Barry Cullingworth, *The Political Culture of Planning: American Land Use Planning in Comparative Perspective* (New York: Routledge, 2002), 1; William A. Fischel, *The Homevoter Hypothesis* (Cambridge, MA: Harvard University Press, 2001), 23.
323 Randall W. Eberts and Timothy J. Gronberg, "Jurisdictional homogeneity and the Tiebout hypothesis," *Journal of Urban Economics* 10, no. 2 (1981): 227–239, https://doi.org/10.1016/0094-1190(81)90016-4; Keith Dowding, Peter John, and Stephen Biggs, "Tiebout: A Survey of the Empirical Literature," *Urban Studies* 31, no. 4–5 (1994): 767–797.
324 Michael C. Lens and Paavo Monkkonen, "Do Strict Land Use Regulations Make Metropolitan Areas More Segregated By Income?," *Journal of the American Planning Association* 82, no. 1 (2016): 6–21, https://www.ncbi.nlm.nih.gov/pmc/articles/PMC5800413/.
325 Jessica Trounstine, "The Geography of Inequality: How Land Use Regulation Produces Segregation," *American Political Science Review* 114, no. 2 (2020): 443–455, https://doi.org/10.1017/S0003055419000844.
326 Jonathan Rothwell, "Racial Enclaves and Density Zoning: The Institutionalized Segregation of Racial Minorities in the United States," *American Law and Economic Review* 13, no. 1 (2011): 290–358, https://www.jstor.org/stable/42705595. (Specifically, he found that "one standard deviation change in density zoning explained 25%, 25%, and 35% of a standard deviation change in the dissimilarity scores of Latinos, Asians, and Blacks respectively.") See also Jonathan Rothwell and Douglas S. Massey, "The Effect of Density Zoning on Racial Segregation in U.S. Urban Areas," *Urban Affairs Review* 44, no. 6 (2009): 779–806, https://doi.org/10.1177/1078087409334163.

327 Rothwell, *Land Use Politics*, 16.
328 Cutler and Glaeser, "Ghettos," 838–839, table 1.
329 Hendrick and Shi, "Macro-Level Determinants of Local Government Interaction," 427.
330 Menendian, Gailes, and Gambhir, *Roots of Structural Racism*, Figure 1.
331 Potter, "School Segregation."
332 George A. Boyne, "Competition and Local Government: A Public Choice Perspective," *Urban Studies* 33, no. 4–5: (1996), 703–721; Geoffrey Brennan and James M. Buchanan, *The Power to Tax: Analytical Foundations of a Fiscal Constitution* (Cambridge: Cambridge University Press, 1980); Rebecca J. Campbell, "Leviathan and Fiscal Illusion in Local Government Overlapping Jurisdictions," *Public Choice* 120, no. 3–4 (2004): 301–329.
333 Michael Howell-Moroney, "The Tiebout Hypothesis 50 Years Later: Lessons and Lingering Challenges for Metropolitan Governance in the 21st Century," *Public Administration Review* 68, no. 1 (2008): 97–109; Tiebout, "Pure Theory of Local Expenditures"; Gregory R. Weiher, *The Fractured Metropolis: Political Fragmentation and Metropolitan Segregation* (Albany: State University of New York Press, 1991).
334 Chetty et al., "Where is the Land," 1611.
335 Cashin, *Place not Race*, 27, fn 37.
336 Rodney Hero, Morris Levy, and Brian Yeokwang An, "It's Not Just Welfare: Racial Inequality and the Local Provision of Public Goods in the United States," *Urban Affairs Review* 54, no. 5 (2018): 833–865; Alberto Alesina, Reza Baqir, and William Easterly, "Public Goods and Ethnic Divisions," *Quarterly Journal of Economics* 114, no. 4 (1999): 1243–1284.
337 Jessica Trounstine, "Segregation and Inequality in Public Goods," *American Journal of Political Science* 60, no. 3 (2016): 709–725, https://onlinelibrary.wiley.com/doi/full/10.1111/ajps.12227.
338 Trounstine, *Segregation by Design*, 162.
339 According to the 2022 Census of Governments, there are 12,546 independent school districts in the United States. U.S. Census Bureau, "2022 Census of Governments – Organization, Table 2."
340 Laura Bliss, "How School Districts Seal Their Students Into Poverty," *Bloomberg CityLab*, July 22, 2014, https://www.citylab.com/equity/2015/07/how-school-districts-seal-their-students-into-poverty/399116/.
341 Potter, "School Segregation."
342 Noliwe M Rooks, *Cutting School: Privatization, Segregation, and the End of Public Education* (New York: New Press, 2017), 163.

3 The Origins of Structural Racism

Livonia, Michigan is a leafy mid-sized suburb in northwestern Wayne County. Like many Midwestern suburbs, Livonia is filled with single-family homes on tree-lined streets, but it also features unusually abundant acreage for parks and recreation. In the winter, a blanket of snow covers this residential community, which is fine by locals. Livonians enjoy baseball but live for hockey. Several NHL players retired in Livonia, and the Detroit Red Wings and local clubs are perennial topics of conversation.

The median annual family household income in Livonia is over $92,000, and many executives and middle managers, working in businesses ancillary to the auto industry, make Livonia their home.[1] While Livonia may not be a gilded community, it is not poor. Fewer than 3% of its residents live below the poverty line, well below the national average.

According to the 2000 decennial census, Livonia was the whitest city in America with a population over 100,000 people.[2] At the time, it was 97% white, and less than 1% Black. And yet, Livonia is only about 13 miles from downtown Detroit, the Blackest city in America.[3] Livonia and Detroit are connected by a 25-minute freeway commute and a regional economy powered by the automotive industry, but in a sense, they seem worlds apart.

Brian Bernet fondly recalls growing up outside of Detroit in the 1980s. His family wasn't initially wealthy, but his dad eventually "made it," and his family relocated from middle-class Livonia to the more affluent exurbs, where spacious mansions house the families of auto industry executives. Like Chris Marten's move from Columbus to Upper Arlington, Brian's family re-settled as their income grew, in a step pattern.

This is the American Dream in action, the outward manifestation of upward economic mobility, coinciding with successively safer neighborhoods, stronger schools, better resourced communities, and often more attractive amenities. Like Chris, Brian seamlessly transitioned from there into strong public institutions of higher education, in his case the University of Michigan and Michigan State for college and graduate school, and then into a comfortable professional career. Yet, an important part of both stories has been left out of the presentation.

DOI: 10.4324/9781003562764-4

Chris Marten's parents decision to move from the city of Columbus to the suburb of Upper Arlington wasn't just about better schools, enrichment, and advancement. There was a corollary motive tied to these goals. As was the case in many larger northern cities, a lawsuit in the 1970s resulted in a court-ordered desegregation plan for the Columbus city schools.[4] Large urban school districts like the Columbus Public Schools operate more than a hundred schools for tens of thousands of students. But because of residential segregation and neighborhood assignment policies, Black students attended predominantly Black schools, and white students attended predominately white schools within the same district. Desegregation plans generally had multiple components, but one of the more visible and vilified elements in northern settings were "busing" measures that would transport children from their local neighborhood to more distant schools.[5] These plans faced enormous resistance from fearful white parents, precipitating protests, and even episodes of communal violence.

Perhaps the most notorious flashpoint for northern desegregation was the Boston plan. In 1974, a federal district court ordered the Boston school system to desegregate 200 schools and reassign some 18,000 students.[6] Some schools in the system were 90% Black, and others were entirely white. Although many white parents contended that systemwide segregation reflected parental preferences, Black parents often felt otherwise.[7] The Boston school board defiantly ignored a directive of the state legislature to desegregate up until a federal court intervened.

South Boston High School was the epicenter of opposition. Even before the plan went into effect, hundreds of parents rallied against it. When the school year began, 1,300 Black students were to be assigned to South High, but only 100 showed up. White parents formed a cordon to intimidate the new students, even though police were assigned to guard them.

Despite heavy law enforcement presence and the imposition of curfews, a mob mentality took over. Angry parents hurled rocks at buses, and spit at and harassed the new students. An attorney involved with the case was brutally attacked. Amid the tumult, bused students were stabbed and beaten, and the vitriolic mood and violent resistance to desegregation shook the community. Eventually, the National Guard and state police were called in to tamp down the disorder. The episode is now regarded as a traumatic memory within Boston.[8]

The ultimate result of this upheaval was not integration, but widespread white flight from the Boston public system. Some 30,000 students were pulled from the system and transferred to private and parochial schools or moved out of the district altogether. Three decades later, the district remained 50% white, but the public school system was only 13% white. Boston became a shameful example of a place in which court-ordered desegregation led to more school segregation.

The mere threat of busing turned many district boundaries into *de facto* redlines. Families that could afford to move to the suburbs were able to escape the desegregation mandate. This is because, in 1974, the Supreme Court ruled that desegregation plans could not be ordered across jurisdictional boundaries, absent an extraordinary showing.[9] The ruling was a signal, if not an invitation, to parents like Brian Bernet's and Chris Marten's, that moving, even a short distance, could protect their children from integrative busing.

The decision to shield suburban jurisdictions from inter-district desegregation remedies fueled a dramatic demographic change that reconfigured our nation's metropolitan regions. In 1975, when a federal court placed the district under a desegregation order, the Columbus Public Schools were 68% white.[10] Chris Marten's family left the district in 1985, and by 2000 Columbus schools were just 20% white and significantly poorer, with proportionally more students from low-income families. Recognizing that their child would be one a dwindling number of white students in the city school system, Chris's parents feared that he might be bullied, that the classrooms might become more disordered, and the quality of instruction decline, or worse, that their child might be bused far from their cozy neighborhood to a remote school in the sprawling system.

The demographic transformation of the Columbus City schools is emblematic of a wider pattern that occurred across the country. More broadly, the story of northern school desegregation and white flight begins to show how contemporary opportunity structures became more deeply racialized despite formal anti-discrimination laws and civil rights enforcement.

The previous chapter revealed the racial dimensions of the opportunity structure, explaining how they generate systemic disadvantages for persons of color. To answer the question of how these racialized structures came into being, it is tempting to focus on American slavery or Jim Crow. After all, racial slavery was by definition a system brutal control, domination, and exploitation that circumscribed upward mobility for the enslaved. The laws of slavery completely determined the life pathways available to those suffering under it. As property, slaves were subject to dominion and direction of owners, without recourse or right of refusal.[11] Jim Crow was a broad social order that similarly circumscribed life pathways, defining what Black people could do, and what they couldn't, under color of law and force of social custom.[12]

Given all of this, one might understandably assume that contemporary structural racism can be traced to these institutions, perhaps comprehensible as present-day effects of past policies and practices, as accumulated impacts or some sort of residue of our troubled racial history, or perhaps a re-iteration and re-inscription of previous systems and structures.[13] Indeed, inter-group inequality can linger long after exclusionary barriers have come down, and there are both legacy effects and accumulated impacts from past practices and arrangements. But this is not the entire basis for contemporary structural racial inequality. Many of its crucial features are recent developments, not the legacies (in any direct sense) of racist policies of the past, or inertial after-effects of historical discrimination.

Although racialized structures of opportunity existed in the past, the structural racism we live under today becomes more evident, pronounced, and severe over time, deeper into the 21st century, not less so. If structural racism was merely or even principally vestigial, then we would expect it to be most pronounced in places with the most disturbing racial histories and prominent institutional forms. Yet, recall that most racially segregated neighborhoods and schools in the country are in the Northeast and Midwest, places like Detroit, Chicago, and Milwaukee, not in the south.[14]

Although racial slavery and Jim Crow were brutalizing experiences and formative institutions that shaped and set the development of contemporary opportunity structures,[15] structural racism cannot be reduced to these experiences or even largely explained by them. In fact, attempts to do so will neglect, overlook, and elide the key forces that drive and sustain of structural racism, and fail to apprehend its most important feature and binding element: mid-20th to 21st-century racial residential segregation.

From Jim Crow Segregation to Residential Segregation

The word "segregation" conjures many of the most harrowing and dramatic moments in American history, from the confrontation of the National Guard with Bull Connor's state police in Little Rock to sit-ins at lunch counters, freedom rides, and Thurgood Marshall triumphantly standing on the steps of the Supreme Court.[16] Jim Crow segregation is a story of separate and unequal public schools, accommodations, and transportation. The imagery of state-mandated segregation is "colored only" drinking fountains and "whites only" swimming pools.

In its initial American form, segregation was a series of regulations imposed principally by southern municipal and state governments. Segregation was an expression of racial hierarchy purportedly consistent with the requirement of "equal protection" under law enshrined in the Constitution's Reconstruction Amendments. The Supreme Court's endorsement of the "separate, but equal" legal fiction in *Plessy v. Ferguson* gave way to segregated railway cars, restrooms, court rooms, restaurants, theaters, buses, and schools.[17] Despite the ubiquity of state-based segregation and the myriad of laws and customs that enforced it, it was not principally a scheme for separating housing and residence by race. Rather, segregation generally denoted the separation of the races in public accommodations, occupations, and public institutions, like schools.

If buses, theaters, restaurants, churches, parks, and schools were all racially segregated, why would it be necessary to enforce strict residential segregation? Jim Crow so thoroughly regulated social and economic relations between white and Black southerners that residential segregation was not only unnecessary and redundant, but also counterproductive.

The south was an agricultural region before and during Jim Crow. Just as enslaved people lived on the plantation they coercively served, so Jim Crow tenant farmers and domestic workers lived near the white families for whom they worked.[18] Obviously, the residential proximity of Black and white people in the antebellum south was partly due to slavery, but even free Black people were relatively integrated in terms of residence.[19] This residential pattern continued well past the Reconstruction period into Jim Crow.

That is not to say that Blacks and whites lived in the same streets or even the same homes, but they often lived in the same communities or in adjacent neighborhoods. Streets with large homes for white families sat next to smaller streets where domestic workers lived.[20] Urban slaves typically resided in the "downtown sections behind the big houses of the white elite."[21] The grid patterns of white avenues and Black alleys that defined southern style housing patterns kept residential segregation relatively low.

Although Black families were often forced into inferior housing stock, Black and white families lived in relatively close physical proximity to each other in the late 19th century, in both the north and the south.[22] In northern cities, middle- and upper-class Black people had long resided in neighborhoods with many white neighbors and frequented white businesses. As a result, northern cities tended to be only moderately segregated between 1860 and 1910, even though they had higher levels of racial residential isolation than the south.[23] In 1890, over 93% of Black people in the north lived in predominantly white neighborhoods.[24] And the average Black resident of a northern city lived neighborhood that was close to 90% white.[25]

One of the most racially residentially segregated northern cities was Indianapolis, but even there the average Black person resided in a neighborhood that was only 13% Black in 1890.[26] In 1880, two-thirds of Black households in Chicago had a white neighbor.[27] In Montana, every county in the state had Black settlers by 1890.[28] This helps explain why most studies of the North show that there was little systematic exclusion of Black people from white neighborhoods in this period.[29] The intense form of residential Black isolation that would eventually characterize most northern cities did not yet exist. Histories and ethnographies of 19th-century northern cities reveal frequent interracial contact as well as detailed descriptions of the racial composition of those cities.[30] The locus of racial segregation in the North, to the extent it generally existed, was occupational opportunities rather than place of residence or public accommodations.

The foregoing facts, however, should not lead one to conclude that the North was a racially egalitarian region. Northern Black populations were relatively small in the antebellum period, and only slightly larger during and after Reconstruction. The vast majority of Black Americans in the 19th century resided in the south. Providing separate facilities and accommodations was not only unnecessary to maintain racial social control and white predominance, and unseemly to northern sensibilities, but also a further expense.

According to the Dissimilarity Index, Black-white segregation in southern cities averaged just 29 circa 1860, and rose modestly to 38.3 by 1910.[31] Although substantially below the northern average of 45.7 in 1860, and

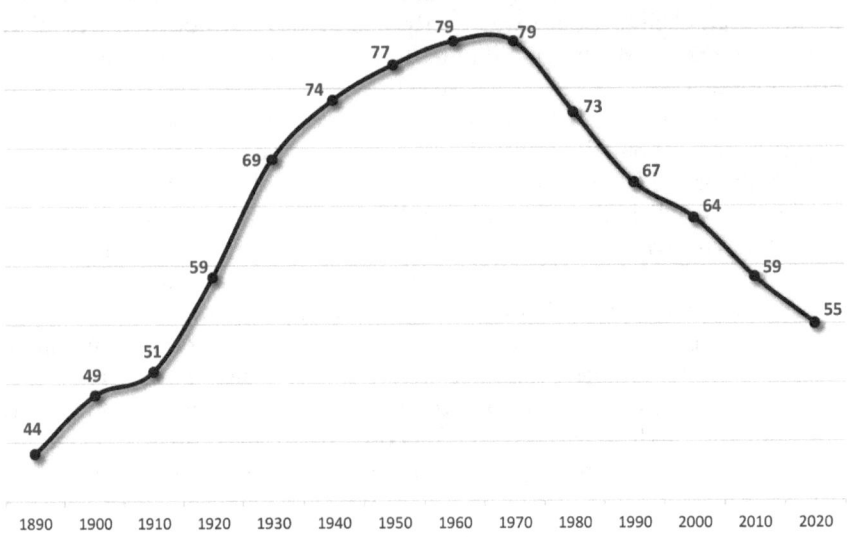

Figure 3.1 Black Residential Segregation, 1890–2020[32]

59.2 in 1910, by comparison these scores were similar to the level of spatial separation of recent immigrant groups, such as the Irish and Germans, from native-born whites in those decades. But by 1940, there was a rapid regional convergence, and cities in both the south and the north had become extraordinarily segregated by race, with many cities reaching dissimilarity scores in the 80s and 90s, levels that are virtually complete residential segregation.

The national dissimilarity score tells the tale. Despite significant regional variation (much lower in the south), national Black-nonBlack dissimilarity scores ranged in the 40s by the turn of the century, and still only around 50 from 1910 to 1920, the height of Jim Crow, and well below contemporary levels. Yet, it rose to nearly 80 by 1970 (see Figure 3.1). The key question is: how and why did this happen?

The Origins of Racial Residential Segregation in the United States

Racial residential segregation in the United States fully emerged and rapidly spread with the onset of the Great Migration. Between 1910 and 1970, more than 6 million African-Americans moved from the south to the north and the west, with the first major wave occurring roughly from 1915 to 1930. Before World War I (WWI), the rate of Black migration north was about 1% per decade.[33] From 1915 on, Black migration north occurred at a rate about ten times the prewar scale. In 1910, 91% of African-Americans lived in the south, and 73% lived outside of cities.[34] By 1966, the number of African-Americans outside of the south had multiplied 11-fold, from just under a million to almost ten million.[35]

Several agricultural disasters in the south, including the arrival of the Mexican boll weevil and subsequent infestation of cotton crops as well as a series of floods, coincided with recruiters from the north offering factory jobs to unskilled laborers in rapidly industrializing northern cities.[36] These businesses offered wages that surpassed what Black workers could get in even the best paid southern industries.[37] As dramatized in Isabel Wilkerson's landmark book, *The Warmth of Other Suns,* Black migrants fled a combination of poverty and oppression.[38]

As a result, Black populations swelled rapidly in the north and the west. In Chicago, the Black population quintupled from 44,000 to 234,000 from 1910 to 1930.[39] New York's Black population tripled.[40] In Detroit, the Black population bounded from 6,000 to 120,000 in a single decade.[41] In Cleveland, the Black population grew from 8,500 to nearly 72,000 in the same period.[42] Similar dynamics occurred throughout the industrial north in this period.

This process accelerated during and after WWII. The entry of the United States into the war prompted a massive war mobilization that spurred further demand for labor in wartime industries across the north and west, drawing more migrants out of the south. For example, the Kaiser Company built four shipyards in the San Francisco Bay Area between 1941 and 1943, and sent recruiters to the south to find workers.[43] In both the earlier wave and wartime periods, established migrants found jobs and housing for friends and relatives, reinforcing the initial flow.[44] For example, Detroit's Black population, which had grown rapidly before the War, doubled between 1940 and 1950.[45]

The large influx of Black workers hardened racial attitudes in the north. Working-class whites regarded Black migrants as labor competition while many middle-class whites were alarmed at the pace of demographic change. In particular, white workers feared the use of Black labor to undermine wages, break strikes, or weaken unions. The American Federation of Labor—the organization that represented skilled and crafts unions—officially kept Black workers out until the 1930s.[46] And the Congress of Industrial Organizations, representing industrial workers, only accepted Black members begrudgingly.[47] Because Black workers were generally excluded from labor unions, union leaders and members feared that the newcomers could be used as scab labor and drive down wages.[48]

Although national unions officially and formally supported antidiscrimination policies in general, resistance from local leaders and rank-and-file members undermined those efforts on the ground.[49] Rather than making unions more inclusive, too often white workers targeted their Black colleagues with threats, violence, and a mob mentality. White racial prejudice and labor competition reinforced each other in the north, driving demands for residential segregation.[50] In 1942, 84% of white Americans polled felt that Black people should live in separate sections of town.[51]

Industrialization and urbanization changed residential and economic life in other ways that would facilitate residential segregation more easily than was possible before. The new, large industrial plants were often clustered together in places that housed thousands of workers. This shifted employment from small shops or business corridors to dense districts. Housing and transportation, in turn, were redesigned for these needs.

Engineering improvements allowed builders to construct taller and more vertical housing, and large tenements and other residential structures were erected to accommodate these numerous workers. Urban areas grew larger and more densely populated. Massive infrastructure investments, subsidized with public coffers, built electric streetcar grids in urban city centers and business districts, conveying passengers to more outlying neighborhoods in most large northern cities.[52] The advent of streetcars on light rail, and later the affordable automobile, made it possible for ordinary workers to commute from distant neighborhoods for the first time.[53] Previously, most ordinary or daily travel was by foot or by horse. As such, there was little geographic differentiation between places of work and residence.

Policy innovations based upon these developments also facilitated and enabled residential segregation. Zoning regulations were partly an outgrowth of these developments since land and space could be reserved for different or specialized purposes more easily. At the same time, heavy industry created new public health hazards through smog, chemical waste, and other refuse. As a prophylaxis and alternative to nuisance law, municipalities around the country turned to zoning to prevent noxious or injurious land uses.[54]

Promoted by progressive reformers, the purpose of zoning was ostensibly to keep these varied uses, such as industrial, agricultural, and residential, separate for the health and benefit of all. Boosters saw zoning as a way to "rationalize" the use of land and bring order to bustling metropolises.[55] For example, one zoning ordinance restricted where laundries in San Francisco could operate.[56] Los Angeles was the first city to implement so-called "use" zoning when the city adopted a provisional zoning plan in 1904,[57] and New York City followed suit with the first comprehensive zoning plan in 1916,[58] motivated by a desire to keep "tenements and garment factories out" of certain neighborhoods.[59]

In 1922, the Hoover administration's Commerce Department issued a primer endorsing "use" zoning, arguing that it would help stabilize property values, not just prevent "malodorous" uses of land in local neighborhoods.[60] Even though they were fiercely opposed by property rights advocates, zoning ordinances proliferated in the inter-war period, and by 1936, 85% of all places had some sort of zoning ordinance.[61]

Some of the earliest forms of zoning, however, explicitly mandated racial segregation. In 1890, San Francisco adopted the "Bingham Ordinance" which sought to exclude Chinese residents from certain areas of the city.[62] In 1911, Baltimore adopted the first comprehensive municipal racial zoning ordinance, which divided the city into racial districts.[63] Many other southern cities, such as Atlanta, Birmingham, Miami, Charleston, Dallas, Louisville, and New Orleans, adopted this type of racial zoning ordinance until they were struck down by the Supreme Court in 1917 in *Buchanan v. Warley*.[64] Critically, these ordinances were not invalidated on account of their racial features or discriminatory effects, but as an unconstitutional restriction on property rights.

Less than a decade later, "use" zoning was upheld by the Supreme Court in the landmark case of *Village of Euclid, Ohio v. Ambler Realty Co.*, involving a Cleveland suburb.[65] In the long run, this form of zoning would play a critical role in maintaining and perpetuating racial residential segregation. Although racial zoning was held unconstitutional, the desire to racially segregate regions had strengthened rather than abated. But in the immediate term through the middle of the century, racial residential segregation was principally erected through three mechanisms: racially restrictive covenants, housing discrimination based on a segregationist ideology promulgated by the nascent real estate industry, and widespread and unregulated violence to deter racial pioneers.

Restrictive covenants are contractual provisions attached to property sales in new developments, and were widely adopted in the first decades of the 20th century. A modern restrictive covenant in a neighborhood development might requires lawn maintenance or prohibit fences above certain heights.[66] The kinds of racially exclusionary restrictive covenants that were devised during this period were contractual agreements among property owners stating, for example, that the "premises shall not at any time be conveyed, mortgaged or leased to any person or persons of Chinese, Japanese, Moorish, Turkish, Negro, Mongolian or African blood or descent."[67] Signing such covenants bound heirs and purchasers, and any violation could be enforced by neighbors.

One of the reasons that restrictive covenants were such effective tools for institutionalizing segregation was that they compelled parties to obey them whether they agreed with them or not. Even today, changing restrictive covenants is extremely difficult, requiring 85% or more of property owners bound to agree in some instances.[68] Thus, white homeowners bound by racially restrictive covenants could not sell to Black homebuyers, regardless of their personal preferences or desires.

Because they require the consent of all or nearly-all property owners, such covenants were more difficult to establish in neighborhoods that had already been built out than in growing suburban areas or in larger new subdivisions.[69] Accordingly, racially restrictive covenants became more widespread in the era of the housing subdivisions and planned developments. Developers recorded such restrictions in initial plats and deeds, preventing non-whites from moving into new communities.

The importance of restrictive covenants was that they functioned to exclude Black people from entire neighborhoods and communities, not simply individual parcels or lots. Like racial zoning, racially restrictive covenants first arose in California in the 1880s, but proliferated after the turn of the century.[70] Although they were initially struck down by state courts, federal courts began upholding them.[71] By 1910 restrictive covenants were being used widely throughout the United States, and they were vigorously enforced.

Precise national estimates are difficult to come by, but recent regional and local documentation projects are providing a glimpse of how widespread such covenants were. An examination of property records in Minneapolis uncovered and geocoded more than 25,000 deeds with racially restrictive language throughout Hennepin County, the first precise visualization of racial covenants for a major American city.[72] A similar project found racial and religious restrictions on 15,000–20,000 properties in King County's Seattle and surrounding suburbs.[73] Another project in Chicago has discovered restrictive covenants across dozens of neighborhoods and hundreds of subdivisions, searchable with aerial images and deed excerpts.[74] Yet another project, studying Washington DC, found more than 7,000 race covenants in property deeds.[75] Even today, more than 1,200 racist restrictive covenants are inscribed in lot deeds in Kansas City.[76]

As many as half of the new subdivisions built in the United States in this era may have contained racially restrictive covenants.[77] It was not until 1948 that the U.S. Supreme Court held that such were unenforceable in *Shelley v. Kraemer*.[78] Despite *Shelley*, many developers continued to insert and record them into property deeds throughout the 1950s and even well into the 1960s even as real estate agents honored them to avoid incurring anger from clients and white homeowners. Similarly, federal agencies dragged their feet implementing the *Shelley* ruling and modifying their policies accordingly.[79]

Like zoning regulations, restrictive covenants are best understood as a late 19th- and early 20th-century legal innovation, not a vestige of antebellum or postbellum racial controls. Prior to 1900, most legal restrictions on the transfer or sale of property took the form of deed restrictions, which were less efficient and systematic.[80] Restrictive covenants were a collective action solution that institutionalized segregation, even above or contrary to the preferences or property interests of buyers and sellers.

Another early 20th-century development was the formative "association" movement intended to organize collective interests, and which resulted in a proliferation of new institutional associations, including the NAACP, the ACLU, the Association of American Law Schools, the Association of American Colleges and Universities, and the National Association of Realtors, among others. A critical product of this movement was the rapid growth in neighborhood improvement and homeowners associations. These associations, along with the emergent organized real estate industry, played a critical role in fostering racial residential segregation.

Local real estate professionals and the nascent real estate industry systematically discriminated against Black homeseekers. Not only did real estate boards routinely promote racially restrictive covenants, but they also established professional standards, backed by threat of sanctions, that institutionalized discrimination. The Washington D.C. Real Estate Board's code flatly stated that "[n]o property in a white section should ever be sold, rented, advertised, or offered to colored people."[81] The Chicago Real Estate Board, in 1920, not only issued a public congratulation to the Kenwood and Hyde Park Property Association for keeping out African-Americans, but also adopted a resolution penalizing any member that sold property to Blacks in a white neighborhood.[82]

Although the local Chicago Board's actions may have been more punitive than usual, they took their cue from the National Association of Real Estate Brokers (NAREB), which in 1924 adopted an article in its code of ethics stating that "a Realtor should never be instrumental in introducing into a neighborhood... members of any race or nationality... whose presence will clearly be detrimental to property values in that neighborhood."[83] Members found violating this rule were expelled, and in 1939, the NAREB issued more explicit guidance, explaining that members should not sell homes in white neighborhoods to "a colored man of means who was giving his children a college education and thought they were entitled to live among whites."[84] NAREB published pamphlets and periodicals warning that racial minorities threatened property values and that neighborhoods should be racially homogenous to maintain their desirability.[85]

The influx of many poor Black families from the south during the Great Migration became the justification for an exclusionary real estate ideology that associated the presence of Black residents with declining property values and neighborhood instability. The real estate industry, its agents and trade associations, justified these practices on the grounds of risk and interest in housing stability. A number of early real estate textbooks stressed the importance of segregation for maintaining neighborhood value and profitable land sales.[86]

The use of racially restrictive covenants helped cement and reinforce racist stereotypes that identified Black living space with deteriorating neighborhoods and dilapidated housing. Housing surveys provided supposedly objective evidence for emerging stereotypes. Thus, early in the 20th century, the young real estate industry, composed of local land developers, realtors, brokers, and homeowners associations, helped nurture a segregationist ideology by fostering an image of the Black ghetto as "a pathological, dangerous and nefarious place."[87] The historian Thomas Sugrue claims that, in Detroit at least, the practices of the real estate industry were more effective at protecting the city's racial boundaries than restrictive covenants.[88]

Neighborhood improvement associations, ostensibly organized to promote neighborhood security and improve conditions, were often formed in response to Black entrants.[89] They lobbied city councils for zoning restrictions, threatened boycotts of real estate agents who sold homes to Black families or business who catered to Black customers, collected money to buy out Black homeowners, and implemented restrictive covenants.[90] In Detroit alone between 1943 and 1965, white communities founded at least 192 such organizations.[91]

Homeowners Associations were made up of private homeowners or apartment owners, and similarly launched campaigns to promote and patrol segregation.[92] They pressured banks and other lenders to deny credit to Black borrowers, and businesses to refrain from hiring Black workers. These associations harassed and coerced Black homebuyers and also persuaded white homeowners to adopt or support racially restrictive covenants.[93] In some cases, they would raise money to purchase property from Black homeowners or buy homes from landlords renting to Black tenants.[94]

Some developers required that residential developments establish homeowners associations to monitor and enforce racial restrictions.[95] The relationship between developers, associations, and the real estate industry was dynamic and reinforcing. Developers created the homeowners associations to enforce restrictive covenants, but neighborhood associations "served as watchdogs," monitoring for violations and gathering complaints, organizing campaigns to keep Black residents out, and pressured real estate boards to create and promote racial segregation while also lobbying city officials for better public services.[96] They not only promoted, enforced, and reinforced segregation, in later years they organized against open housing laws as well.[97]

One example from Upper Arlington, Ohio, a suburb of Columbus described at the outset of the first chapter, illustrates these interlocking dynamics. In 1950, the city of Upper Arlington instituted deed restrictions that not only prohibited Black families from moving into the city, but also forbade owners from selling, leasing or renting "to a person or persons of any race other than Caucasian."[98] A lawsuit brought against the Northwest Arlington Homeowners Association and its trustees in 1971 challenged the restrictions, which resulted in the dissolution of the association. One of the trustees, John Pace, was president of King Thompson Realty, a preeminent real estate brokerage firm in the region, and chairman of the Ohio Real Estate Commission.[99]

The third key mechanism for institutionalizing segregation was violence. Organized violence and intimidation directed at the Black community and to would-be Black migrants, especially racial pioneers into white neighborhoods, was a critical force that helped define race relations in the north in the 20th century and enforced residential segregation. Black migrants to the north needed shelter and relief from overcrowding and poor conditions within established Black neighborhoods, which forced newcomers to search for housing in white neighborhoods.

Just as the Great Migration was underway, outbreaks of racial hostility erupted across the north in an unmistakable and widespread pattern. Between 1917 through the early 1920s, organized violence against Blacks in the north precipitated what the contemporary press reported as "race riots."[100] For example, in 1919, a white mob mobilized to attack Blacks in Washington D.C., and the fighting, which included returning WWI veterans, lasted 5 days. One "riot" that took place in Chicago in July 1919 lasted 13 days and left 38 people dead, 537 injured and 1,000 Black families without homes.[101]

This episode precipitated one of the nation's first "race commissions" to study the problem.[102]

Perhaps the most shocking instance of communal anti-Black violence in this period was the Tulsa massacre in 1921 that destroyed "Black Wall Street," a thriving Black commercial hub that resulted in hundreds of injuries, thousands of arrests, and at least several dozen dead.[103] Although the more notorious instance may have been the St. Louis massacre of 1917, where more than 3,000 whites marched into Black neighborhoods to kill and maim, resulting in more than a hundred deaths and thousands left homeless.[104]

In smaller communities across the north, white residents drove many Black residents out and established the so-called "Sundown towns," which forbid African-Americans from being within city limits after dark not so much by law, but threat of organized violence.[105] There are dozens of confirmed sundown towns across the United States, and perhaps hundreds.[106] This is how Montana went from having a thriving Black community with its own newspaper and small businesses at the turn of the century to almost none a few decades later.[107] The expulsion of Black residents in this period may have contemporary effects, in cementing certain racist attitudes.[108]

By the 1920s, patterns of racial violence morphed from communal conflict to episodes in targeted areas. Solidly Black neighborhoods were generally ignored, while violence aimed at the periphery of the ghetto and at Black residents in white neighborhoods.[109] The intended result was a concentration of the flow of Black residents into specific neighborhoods.

Families of color moving into all-white neighborhoods could expect more than taunts and harassment; they were often victims of vandalism with eggs, bricks, paint, or worse, such as burning crosses and intimating mobs.[110] White vigilante groups targeted Black families and individuals with surgical precision, throwing rocks through windows, firebombing, or even shooting into homes. In Detroit alone, there are over 200 documented such incidents in the post-war period before the adoption of open housing laws.[111] In Cleveland in both 1917 and 1919, white mobs attacked the homes of Black newcomers.[112] Between 1917 and 1921, nearly 60 homes purchased by Black families were firebombed by white arsonists in Chicago.[113]

In most instances, these acts were unpunished or quietly sanctioned. Perpetrators were rarely prosecuted, and police failed to intervene.[114] This kind of violence underscored the relationship between state inaction and community feeling. But the attacks were not simply outbursts of anger; they were "political acts, carefully calculated to intimidate individual Black families."[115] Black people merely caught wandering around white neighborhoods might be viciously attacked, beaten, shot, or lynched.

Following (WWII), racial violence targeting Black movers to white neighborhoods continued. In "Levittown" Pennsylvania, one of several planned suburban tract development built by real estate developer William Levitt & Sons, a white lawyer held off a mob of angry white residents targeting the first Black family to move into the neighborhood in 1957.[116] The family was threatened by phone, by mail and by screaming, spitting protesters. In Chicago, there were reported incidents of such violence, fire-bombs, and 26 arson attacks in the first 10 months of 1947 alone without a single arrest. Similar violence took place in Atlanta, Birmingham, Cincinnati, Cleveland, Dallas, East St. Louis, Indianapolis, Kansas City, Los Angeles, Louisville, Philadelphia, Miami, Tampa, and elsewhere.[117] There were more than 100 recorded incidents of vandalism or move-in bombings in Los Angeles between 1950 and 1965, but only one that led to an arrest and prosecution.[118]

When official announced that a major housing project in a predominantly white area of Detroit, the Sojourner Truth development, would admit Black residents in 1941, white community members staged massive protests, which escalated to violent fighting when Black families tried to move in.[119] In a Chicago suburb in the summer of 1951, a crowd of thousands of whites attacked an apartment building after one Black family had moved into one of its 20 units.[120] Violence and public safety then became an excuse for continuing a policy of racial segregation in public housing projects, or, more passively, to oppose any change to the status quo. As a result, white community groups learned that the threat or fear of violence was an effective tactic to gain leverage in housing debates.

With an ever-growing number of Black people moving to the northern cities but with fewer acceptable housing options, the inevitable result was not just racial segregation, but racial isolation and concentration. Levels of racial isolation rose sharply after 1900 in the north, and by 1930, nearly 50% of Black Americans lived in predominantly Black neighborhoods. Cities in the north and south were fully segregated by the mid-20th century, although it took slightly different forms. As a migrant to the north told his grandson, "you know the difference between the North and South, don't you? In the South, white folks don't care how close you get as long as you don't get too big. In the North, they don't care how big you get as long as you don't get too close."[121]

Institutionalizing Segregation

The nascent forms of racial control that fostered racial residential segregation in the north were soon radically expanded and incorporated into federal policy during the New Deal and post-war period. The New Deal channeled federal resources into housing programs that accommodated the south's racial strictures and nationalized the north's residential preferences. Although the residential color line had been formatively established during the interwar period, the New Deal and the post-war period featured heavy government involvement in expanding and institutionalizing residential segregation. In particular, the role of the federal government in generating and sustaining patterns of residential segregation is central.

From the New Deal onward, the federal government has been an active and an important participant in the American housing market, structuring

The Origins of Structural Racism 143

finance, providing capital and mortgage insurance, incentivizing and subsidizing homeownership, and much more. Throughout the 19th century, and well into the 20th century, housing was primarily viewed as a private matter, and not the concern of state legislatures or city councils, let alone the national Congress. With a brief exception for housing war workers during WWI that produced few developments, government involvement in the housing market, especially federal involvement, was de minimis.[122] That changed with the onset of the Great Depression.

During the Depression, home starts and new construction fell by 95%.[123] Worse, foreclosures mounted as unemployed Americans could no longer afford to pay their mortgages. In 1930, there were 150,000 foreclosures, 200,000 in 1931, and 250,000 in 1932.[124] By 1933, half of all home mortgages in the United States were in default. The incoming Roosevelt administration, supported by overwhelming political majorities, pursued a bold policy agenda known as the "New Deal," a wide-ranging set of recovery programs and relief initiatives aimed at the economic Depression.[125] Since the New Deal, homeownership has been a central goal of federal housing policy. Two key New Deal-era housing policy innovations were the Home Owners Loan Corporation and the Federal Housing Administration, initiatives that would ultimately transform the face of America.

The 1933 Home Owners Loan Corporation (HOLC) declared that it was the policy of the United States to protect homeownership, and was organized to damn the flood of foreclosures. The HOLC issued short-term bonds, using the proceeds to purchase mortgages from lenders.[126] The goal was to refinance mortgages in danger of default and grant low-interest loans to foreclosed homeowners to reacquire their properties.[127] The program refinanced tens of thousands of mortgages deemed at risk of foreclosure.[128] Moreover, through the HOLC, the government subsidized more than a million mortgages between 1933 and 1935, demonstrating the feasibility of longer-term mortgages.[129]

The immediate importance of the HOLC, however, is that it was the first major federal program that introduced, or at least institutionalized and nationalized, a formal and uniform appraisal and risk assessments that would underpin the practice known as "redlining." Appraisal practices for residential real estate were not a new idea, but the systematic approach taken by HOLC was novel. Utilizing detailed questionnaires, HOLC trained appraisers on procedures that could produce similar results by following the same methods. Critically, it was not just the applicant or the property that was appraised, but also the neighborhood and surrounding environment.

The HOLC city survey program sent appraisers across the nation to assess neighborhoods. Every city block was recorded and shaded with the appropriate color on a "Residential Security Map" in the HOLC offices. Using four basic categories to designate risk (A, B, C, and D), neighborhoods were ranked, with the lowest ranked category color-coded red, in more than 200 cities.[130] This is the origin of the term "redlining," a term that is now regularly used to denote a much broader range of housing and credit discrimination.

The problem with the HOLC appraisal system was not mainly the result of HOLC's own assessment decisions (which approved mortgage assistance in all four categories).[131] Rather, the enduring harm of the HOLC's system was how other financial institutions and the broader real estate market adopted the HOLC's race-based appraisal system, and in how that system infiltrated subsequent federal policy, especially mortgage insurance, and spread to other important federal agencies.

The HOLC maps stigmatized Black neighborhoods as risky or unworthy of private investment. Local brokers and lenders relied on the Residential Security Maps and surveys to make lending decisions and determine eligibility. Generally, private loans were only approved for the top two categories, and the highest category included the element "homogenous," referring to the demographic composition of the neighborhood.[132] In this way, homogenous neighborhoods were considered less risky, while integrated neighborhoods were high risk. Redlining was thus a practice of denying credit to residents for homes in low-ranked neighborhoods, especially integrated ones, and to racial minorities in particular.[133]

Even the presence of a few Black residents was regarded as a serious concern, and a major risk for further demographic change.[134] In practice, this meant that new suburban developments outside of the urban core were most likely to be given a higher ranking, which was supposed to indicate "desirable" residential locations. In contrast, the city blocks in the urban core and city center were more likely to be given C or D grades, even in neighborhoods where homes were relatively new and high quality.

The use of race or demographic information for risk and appraisal purposes was not a HOLC innovation but was a common local lending practice.[135] Such practices were developed by the real estate industry but further institutionalized and nationalized through New Deal policy. As such, they were both applied on an unprecedented scale and given the imprimatur of the federal government. HOLC lending mostly wound down by 1936, and shut down entirely by 1951, but the appraisal system it created would live on for decades longer. In particular, this system was adopted throughout the private market, even where it had not already been implicitly present, and, critically, by the Federal Housing Administration.[136]

Despite its limited scope and lifespan, the long-term effects of HOLC designations on development, racial demographics, and neighborhood outcomes has now been thoroughly studied, and the results underscore the role that these policies and practices played in structuring residential patterns decades later. This is true whether we view the HOLC maps as a "cause," extension, or merely a reflection of private housing discrimination. First, there are observable and persistent differences in racial demographics between HOLC designations decades later, with Black residents more likely to live in neighborhoods rated "D" than "C," and so on.[137] Using more direct measures of racial residential segregation, researchers find strong correlations between contemporary levels of residential segregation and HOLC designations.[138]

Consistent with a premise that private investment follows public investment, redlined neighborhoods followed a development pattern starkly different from those in higher-graded areas. By comparing neighborhoods at the borders of HOLC-rated categories, researchers attempted to isolate the causal effects of HOLC designations.[139] They found significant differences in development, homeownership, and home values not simply between "A" and "D" designated areas, but between adjacent designations. For example, by 1970, there is a 27-point home value gap between "C" and "D" neighborhoods, with a corresponding wealth gap.

The other major federal New Deal housing initiative was the National Housing Act of 1934 and the creation of the Federal Housing Administration (FHA), whose purpose was to subsidize the mortgage market by insuring mortgages issued by private lenders.[140] Whereas the HOLC was designed to help families in danger of default, the FHA was intended to help renters purchase homes. The FHA program guaranteed the full value of the collateral for loans made by private banks. By insuring the loans, lenders had less risk and therefore a greater inducement to extend credit. Interest rates on mortgage loans accordingly fell by several points, simply because of the governmental guarantee.

Before the FHA, buying a home was not attainable to most Americans. Prior to this program, the industry practice was that the standard mortgage loan would have a term of 3–5 years and were insured for only two-thirds of the appraised value of a home, so that buyers generally needed at least a 33–50% down payment.[141] Subsequently, young couples could buy a home with only 10% saved up as down payment and could afford lower monthly payment amortized over 25–30 years, and thereby accumulate equity more quickly. As a result of this policy and the standard 30-year mortgage, buying a home became cheaper than renting on a monthly basis. The FHA program not only made it easier to buy a home and build wealth, but by insuring private loans, the FHA encouraged strapped banks to begin lending again, and greatly expanded the market for family homes by making them more affordable to potential homeowners.

The results of this policy were astounding. Until 1972, the FHA helped nearly 11 million American families own their own home, and double that number improve their properties.[142] Between 1934 and 1969, the national homeownership rate rose from 44% of 63%.[143] According to Sheryl Cashin, "[the FHA] gave birth to the dream of home ownership for the masses when it made possible low-interest long-term financing for purchasing a home."[144] From 1938 through the end of the 1950s, the FHA insured mortgages on nearly one-third of all new housing produced annually in the United States.[145] Since 1934, the FHA and HUD have insured over 34 million home mortgages. Even today, roughly 40% of new mortgages are insured by the FHA.[146]

Unfortunately, the FHA's policies and underwriting standards institutionalized segregation in several ways. First, it encouraged the use of racially restrictive covenants.[147] More generally, the FHA virtually refused to underwrite loans that would engender residential integration. In particular, it adopted the neighborhood risk-assessment methods developed by HOLC, and heavily weighted "economic stability" and "protection from adverse influence."[148] The FHA provided agents with an Underwriting Manual in 1935, which defined "adverse influences" to include "the infiltration of inharmonious racial or nationality groups."[149] The 1939 *Underwriting Manual* further instructed personnel not to insure mortgages on homes unless they were in "racially homogenous" neighborhoods.[150]

In short, the FHA institutionalized the presumption that segregation was a condition of neighborhood stability. The FHA refused to lend money to or to underwrite loans for people moving into different-race neighborhoods. Lenders were encouraged to consider these factors if they wished to receive FHA insurance. Whites who actually *wanted* to live in integrated neighborhoods could not get government-insured mortgages, but the main effect was to sharply circumscribe where people of color could live and their access to home mortgage loans.[151] Understandably, private lenders adopted policies conforming to these guidelines, and this system became part of the "free" market.

Even where appraisal standards were not applied in an explicitly racist way, or in conjunction with racist policies, the criteria itself had a clear bias against older, industrial neighborhoods within cities and in favor of new, low-density suburban developments. In this way, predominantly Black neighborhoods were considered higher risk and disinvested, while predominately white suburban developments were subsidized by tens of billions of dollars in federal mortgage insurance in the 1950s and 1960s.

It is sometimes mistakenly assumed or asserted that these redlining practices entirely excluded Black homeseekers from federal mortgage insurance. Although the FHA unquestionably frowned upon racial integration, tens of thousands of Black families ultimately received FHA loans.[152] The problem, however, was that it was on a discriminatory, segregative, and disparate basis, with long-term consequences. Ultimately, African-Americans received less than 1% of FHA loans between 1930 and 1960, and less than 2% between the mid-1940s and late 1950s.[153] Between 1934 and 1962, 98% of the loans the FHA insured went to white borrowers.[154] These were the formative years of suburban growth, propelled by the largesse of FHA and Veteran's Administration subsidies.

By the 1950s, the Federal Housing Administration and the Veterans administration (VA) were insuring half of the mortgages in the United States, but only in "racially homogenous" neighborhoods.[155] The cumulative effect of these policies was to draw whites out of central cities, deny mortgages to Black families trying to integrate, and make it harder for Black families in older urban neighborhoods to get a mortgage or loan for home improvements while channeling capital into suburban housing construction.

In the south, an array of segregated institutions controlled the pathways of the opportunity structure by race. Law and custom separated virtually every facet of daily life except residence. In a sense, the north was the opposite. Integrated living patterns gave way under a massive, initially uncoordinated, but ultimately reinforcing federal, state, and local push for racially segregated housing. Institutionalized discrimination in housing markets ensured that schools, neighborhoods, and other public spaces, were all, in effect, segregated, but without the sordid unseemliness of Jim Crow.

Although the FHA removed explicitly racist language from its manuals in the 1950s, private appraisal associations, real estate agents and firms, and banks continued to use such language into the 1970s.[156] The FHA established national standards in valuation and appraisal criteria that actors throughout the housing market adopted and applied to reinforce and institutionalize racial housing segregation on a national scale. Had these policies been adopted at a different period in American history, they might not have had such a lasting impact. But the post-war period not only had a baby boom, but also an unprecedented housing construction boom.

Suburbanization

The Depression and war effort severely limited housing construction and constrained new household formation. Not only were millions of Americans drafted into military service but building materials, capital, and other manpower was directed overseas. Economic insecurity and war rationing compelled many families to postpone marriage and plans for children. Birth rates rose sharply after the war, with a 20% increase in babies born from 1945 to 1946, and increases every year thereafter peaking around 4 million births per year from 1952 to 1964.[157] Demographers characterized this as America's "baby boom," and the generational cohort of children born during these years are known (sometimes derisively) as "boomers."

By 1960, America's population was evenly divided between cities, suburbs, and rural areas.[158] This was a demographic revolution historically and globally. Never before had urban, rural and suburban living been so evenly balanced. This transformation was accomplished within a generation. But this proved to be merely a waystation toward a different, but equally novel arrangement. In 1940, only one-third of metropolitan residents in the United States lived in suburbs, but by 1990, a majority did.[159] Between 1950 and 1970, the suburban population doubled while nearly three-quarters of the nation's largest cities suffered population decline in absolute terms over the same period.[160]

Over 16 million Americans served in WWII. Returning servicemen and women needed places to live, and new families sought larger homes than were presently available in many densely populated cities. These demands were most easily met by constructing new, more spacious homes on cheap land outside of the central cities. Recognizing the scale of demand, developers drew up plans for affordable tract housing, sought FHA approval for entire subdivisions, and then used that approval to convince banks to issue loans to finance construction. FHA approval and insurance reduced risk to lenders, and allowed builders to pass on those savings to home-buyers.

The Servicemen's Readjustment Act of 1944, also known as the GI Bill, established the VA, whose provisions mimicked the FHA loan program but for returning veterans. By following the practices of the FHA, the VA program subsidized home ownership for millions of returning veterans, and as a result, magnified demand for homes after the war. In the years immediately after WWII, veteran's mortgages accounted for 40% of all home loans.[161] As a result, millions of Americans moved from cities and farms to the suburbs.

In addition to adopting the same discriminatory practices of HOLC, the FHA and VA programs favored the construction of single-family homes over multi-family buildings.[162] The standards for lot size, separation from existing buildings, and other requirements imposed by these programs were more difficult to satisfy in dense urban areas. FHA loans for remodeling were also more expensive relative to new construction. According to some estimates, nearly half of all housing in suburbia in these decades received FHA or VA backing.[163] These criteria nudged families into the suburbs.

The widespread adoption and increased affordability of the automobile, especially in the post-war period, eased commuting and spurred demand for suburban housing. Although automobile production slowed during the war effort, sales surged in the post-war period. This put more drivers on state and local roads, and led to demands by for massive federal investment in highway construction to enable more rapid transit to and from central cities by car.[164]

In 1956, President Eisenhower signed the Interstate Highway Act, a measure that also facilitated residential expansion and sprawl.[165] The Act provided federal funds to erect interstate highways that would ease the transport of freight and people across the country, and provide faster routes for workers to commute from home to work. With $25 billion initially allocated for 41,000 miles of construction, it was the largest public works project in American history.[166] The Act underwrote 90% of the cost of constructing new arterial freeways across the nation.[167]

Ordinary commuters fought heavy traffic on narrow local roads. By more easily connecting suburban residents with jobs in the city, highways reinforced the process of suburbanization. According to one estimate, every new highway built through a central city reduced its population by about 18%.[168] In addition, they also contributed to the decline of public transportation in urban areas by reducing demand and use. Gradually, public transportation systems were decommissioned or abandoned. Urban streetcars and trolleys were ripped out to make room for more automobile drivers.[169]

This new infrastructure changed social and economic life as well. As previously noted, factories and manufacturing plants were often densely built into city districts, where goods could be loaded onto rail or ship. The construction of the highways made it possible to transport more goods and workers by truck and car, and this contributed to the decline of manufacturing in city centers. It was no longer necessary to build factories in the heart of urban environments or near navigable waterways.

The developers of these new suburban subdivisions enjoyed the spoils of federal largesse. Federal policies subsidized their developments and the finances of their customers, but the developers refused to sell to Black families. William Levitt, one of the most famous such developers, was a pioneer of mass tract suburban housing, having created seven "Levittowns" in the United States, the most famous of which were the three in suburban New York and Philadelphia.[170] The first Levittown spanned thousands of housing units in Long Island built between 1947 and 1951, but excluded Blacks families.[171] Even if William Levitt had wanted to, his reliance on FHA and VA loans made it impossible to allow Black residents, as the government would have refused to subsidize the development.[172] Levittowns epitomize the shared segregationist assumptions held by government, developers, real estate brokers, and bankers.

Within a generation, suburban life had become the norm for white Americans, with more and more identifying as middle class. But as record numbers of Americans became homeowners, Black families were kept out of this advancement by a combination of government policy and private discrimination. In fact, large majorities of white Americans in the 1960s believed they had a right to keep Blacks out of their neighborhoods.[173] After several decades of policies institutionalizing segregation, white homeowners absorbed the realtor ideology that segregation led to stability, increased property values, and that they had a general right to keep Black people, and other racial, ethnic, or religious minorities, out of their neighborhoods and communities.[174]

The construction of the interstate highways not only made it easier for suburbanites to commute to jobs in the city, but opened up more land to residential development and led to greater demand for housing in suburban areas, and, ultimately, white flight from the cities. White flight became a substitute for white fight.[175] Violence played a critical role in policing the boundaries of white neighborhoods in the pre- and inter-war periods, but subsided in significance, if not frequency, as a mechanism for perpetuating segregation, in the post-war period.

By the 1970s and 1980s, a nationwide pattern of predominantly Black urban neighborhoods surrounded by white suburbs was evident. By 1980, suburbs were nearly 90% white.[176] Musicians and social scientists referred to this dynamic as the "Chocolate city, Vanilla Suburb."[177] Segregation was no longer just between neighborhoods, but was regionally entrenched.

The system created by the FHA not only subsidized white flight, but also subsidized white wealth. Homeownership in the new suburbs generated enormous equity for the tens of millions of American families who could enjoy the benefits of federal policy. Private money followed public money. The federal funds that subsidized suburbia preceded private investment in new businesses, services, and amenities. The enormous growth of suburbia resulted directly and indirectly in the decline of urban neighborhoods. Retail businesses followed residential developments, as new business sprung into existence to serve these communities with restaurants, offices, and the shopping mall, the ultimate symbol of suburban life.[178]

The growth of the suburbs and appreciation of property in white neighborhoods contributed to a coincident decline and stagnation of Black neighborhoods. The construction boom was so affordable and attractive in the suburbs that demand for urban housing in the inner-city market fell dramatically. This led to declining or stagnating property values, relative to the tremendous appreciation in values in the suburbs. Families trapped by decades of discriminatory and exclusionary policies had a harder time selling their homes, and did not enjoy the home equity appreciation and wealth accumulation of their white counterparts in the suburbs. This led to a cycle of disrepair, deterioration, and disinvestment in non-white neighborhoods, even middle-class Black neighborhoods. This decay and decline became yet another reinforcing feedback loop in the dynamics of segregation. As middle-class whites left, the poor became geographically concentrated. This spurred demand for city services to address social problems. As a result, local governments were compelled to raise taxes and further accelerate white flight, in a vicious cycle.[179]

Public Housing and Urban Renewal

The HOLC, FHA and VA policies subsidizing and insuring the mass production of suburban development and homeownership in every metropolitan area while denying access for Black families helped cement, deepen, and extend segregative residential patterns that originated in local communities and private discrimination. Racially unfair and discriminatory labor policies from the New Deal on ensured that most Black workers, also denied fair and affordable credit, could not afford to move into white neighborhoods, even as housing policies subsidized white neighborhoods.[180] However, federal policies in the post-war period exacerbated these inequities with disastrous public housing and urban renewal programs.

Although millions fled cities during the immediate post-war period, many whites remained, and many businesses and commercial interests were locked in. Even though businesses eventually found footing in the suburbs, many critical institutions were physically tied to the central city. For example, many factories and plants, department stores, theaters, and other establishments could not easily relocate. This was a problem that would be worked through over many years, and accommodations ultimately made, but in the post-war period it prompted politicians and prominent civic leaders to lobby the federal government to address the emerging problems confronting cities due to the flight of affluent white families.

As suburbanization exploded in the post-war period, in no small part due to government largesse, the federal government saw a need to revitalize inner cities. Urban renewal, launched with the Housing Act of 1949, allocated subsidies for slum clearance, housing construction, and economic development.[181] Institutionalized segregation limited the housing options for many Black workers during the post-war period, resulting in crowded and even unsafe living conditions. Workers and family members packed into tenements, well beyond capacity. Urban renewal was, in part, an effort to deal with these problems.

The effect of these policies (and what some perceived as the ulterior motive) was to remove Black residents from commercial and business districts in central cities where white commuters and shoppers worked and traveled. In razing "slums" the program had the effect of dispersing and destroying many Black neighborhoods into even more racially concentrated and isolated areas. For example, in Detroit, the most densely populated sections of the Black community were targeted for highway construction, resulting in the destruction of many Black businesses and institutions.[182] In Baltimore, nearly 9,000 families were displaced in the 1960s, 75% of whom were people of color.[183] James Baldwin famously dubbed Urban Renewal programs as "Negro Removal."[184]

Public housing policies fared little better. The first federal effort to construct housing for the poor was Public Works Administration (PWA), created by the National Industrial Recovery Act, one of the first legislative enactments of the New Deal.[185] Designed to revive the economy and provide temporary housing for the poor, the PWA's housing division was authorized to lend money for slum clearance and to acquire and dispose of property for new housing projects.[186] Very few loans were made to redeveloping slums, partly because no local or state governments had authorizing legislation for such efforts, but the division managed to subsidize 21,000 units of low-income housing construction and nearly 50 projects in the mid-1930s.

Although hampered by litigation and inadequate funding, this initiative received a boost with the 1937 Housing Act, known as the Wagner-Steagall Housing Act.[187] This Act created a permanent housing authority to work with local housing agencies to develop housing projects by providing most of the capital costs and subsidizing construction and maintenance costs. Within a few years, most states had passed legislation that would permit localities to create housing agencies, and by 1938, 221 such authorities were formed.[188] Thus began a national program of public housing construction. Unfortunately, these projects reinforced, by design, federal policies that had institutionalized residential segregation.

Secretary of the Interior, Harold Ickes, established a "neighborhood composition rule" that required federal housing projects to reflect the racial composition of the neighborhood they were sited within.[189] In other words, projects in white areas could only have white tenants. Thus, public housing projects were segregated by rule. As a result, public housing projects built in this period segregated public housing residents by race and reinforced existing neighborhood segregation.

Even where there were previously integrated communities, the Ickes rule, implemented by the PWA, designated such neighborhoods as either white or Black, and then used that designation to make it so.[190] In the process, displaced residents relocated to more segregated neighborhoods than before. It is not just that these policies promoted and reinforced segregation; they unraveled pockets of integration.

The structure of the program, relying on local cooperation and authorization, had reinforcing effects as well.[191] Whereas the PWA offered direct federal funding and construction, the 1937 Act required localities to establish their own agencies to draw upon federal subsidies. Any city or municipality that opposed public housing could simply refuse to create a local agency, despite the federal incentivizes. Hundreds of suburbs refused to create housing agencies or apply for federal aid, even though land may have been vacant or less expensive in their jurisdictions. In addition, local municipalities and housing agencies enjoyed discretion on location and site selection. Predictably, local control and discretion resulted in further residential segregation.

The public housing program was expanded in 1949 to meet the post-war housing needs for returning veterans, and authorized loans and subsidies to construct another 800,000 units.[192] Republicans in Congress opposed this effort, and, as a poison pill, proposed language to integrate the program to scuttle the plan. In order to rescue it, public housing advocates reluctantly accepted a segregated program.[193] Thus, the 1949 Housing Act permitted authorities to continue to design and develop segregated housing projects, and empowered local control toward the same end.

The local control and discretion elements ensured accommodation with racial segregation by deferring to "Not In My Back Yard" (NIMBY) sentiment. This tended to ensure that public housing would be concentrated in poor neighborhoods in inner cities lacking the political clout to stop such developments. Even at the inception of the program, local communities and politicians vigorously opposed siting of projects in their neighborhoods. Over 70 communities made the issue a referenda before the electorate. In Chicago and Detroit, local elected fought vigorously against public housing, and were able to reduce the number of units or redirected local sites.[194] As Detroit Mayor Cobo promised in 1949, "I will not approve federal housing projects in ... single home areas," although federal funds were available to do so.[195] Projects near white communities that were open to Black families were the target of organized opposition and protests.[196] Californians went so far as to adopt a constitutional amendment through ballot referenda in 1950 that required local approval of public housing projects.[197]

By 1963, the program had given shelter to more than two million people in nearly half a million units.[198] The results are now notorious. Funds from this act were used to construct high-rise public housing projects such as the Pruitt-Igoe in St. Louis, the Robert Taylor homes and Cabrini-Green in Chicago, and the Marcy Houses and Holmes Towers in New York City.[199]

Although these large, dense, high-rise projects were the exception rather than the norm, they powerfully influenced public perception of public housing.[200] Public housing was racially segregated, and increasingly concentrated in Black inner-city neighborhoods. Although racial residential segregation had been established and rising since the inter-war period, federal public housing policy reinforced it by further institutionalizing it and accommodating itself to local preferences. By the end of this period, many major metropolitan areas were virtually entirely segregated. Something had to be done about it, even if it the hour was late.

Resistance to Fair Housing

Following the lead of nearly half of the states and dozens of municipalities, the federal government enacted a fair housing law in 1968.[201] The Fair Housing Act not only prohibited racial discrimination in housing, but it also required that the federal government "affirmatively further" fair housing.[202] Unfortunately, the Act relied too heavily on private enforcement and was riddled with ambiguities, weak enforcement architecture, and loopholes.[203] In spite of the mandate that the government "affirmatively further" fair housing, the Act failed to specify what it this meant in practice, leaving it to the federal enforcement agency, the Department of Housing and Urban Development (HUD), to define and enforce.[204] This may not have been a problem were it not for the political backlash to civil rights and the Nixon administration's ambivalence on fair housing.

President Nixon appointed George Romney, the former Michigan Governor to head HUD. Romney wanted to use HUD's administrative authority under the Fair Housing Act to compel suburbs to integrate, by threatening denial of federal funds for infrastructure and housing.[205] For example, Romney instituted an order to reject applications for infrastructure projects from jurisdictions with segregated housing.[206] Dubbed the "open communities" initiative, the Nixon White House intervened, and quashed the initiative. Tensions within the White House escalated as Romney's policies for integration were thwarted, and he was pushed out of the administration in 1973 shortly after Nixon's reelection.

Between 1969 and 1974, the Nixon administration evinced little appetite for coercing localities to integrate or support public housing by threatening federal funds. Since Romney's tenure, only two instances of applications for federal grants from HUD were rejected for fair housing reasons.[207] It is little wonder that, decades later, the situation remains relatively the same. Most of the administrations that followed Nixon emulated his approach, and refused to take a more vigorous stance to enforce fair housing.[208]

Communities, neighborhoods, and municipalities devised new ways to maintain segregation in spite of fair housing laws. At first, voters and interest groups pushed measures designed to thwart or prevent the adoption of fair housing ordinances. They gathered support for ballot initiatives designed to circumscribe the power of local authorities to promote fair housing or required public approval of any non-discrimination ordinance. For example, in a special election with nearly 82% turnout, Berkeley voters overturned a freshly adopted municipal fair housing ordinance in 1963.[209] More proactively, voters in Ohio pushed for a charter amendment to the Akron city charter to prohibit the city council from enacting a fair housing ordinance without a public referendum, a transparent attempt to stymie fair housing.[210] After gathering local momentum, opponents of fair housing pushed for similar measures at the state level. California adopted a referendum amending the state constitution, and which repealed the state fair housing act.[211] Not incidentally, the California Real Estate Association sponsored the ballot initiative.

With the passage of the federal Fair Housing Act, these efforts were moot, but new tactics were employed toward similar ends. Zoning laws and other land-use policies had long been used to restrict access to certain neighborhoods not only to keep out noxious industry, but poor people and "unacceptable classes."[212] This was accomplished in many ways, but primarily by keeping out apartments, public housing, denser and more affordable housing developments. Berkeley pioneered this form of zoning by adopting a municipal ordinance with a zone exclusively for single-family homes in 1916.[213] This approach would become widely emulated in the post-war period. In this way, municipalities could maintain exclusivity for the affluent.

More commonly, however, zoning codes evolved not simply to keep out denser housing options, but to control the forms and dimensions of residential use. For example, zoning in the post-war era, but especially by the 1970s, was used to control property lines, lot and yard size, setbacks, and the like. Thus, "use" zoning, as contrasted from the earlier version of racial zoning, gave way to "fiscal zoning," the application of zoning power to control development and delimit the features of real property, not simply the use of it. Lower density or larger minimum lot sizes, for example, drive up the cost of housing, and thereby limit the income range of potential entrants.[214] The power to enact such laws and shape and determine local land use became a powerful driver of suburbanization. Localities that had resisted incorporation suddenly incorporated to wield this power.

Across the country, homeowners sought restrictiveness not only in terms of use, but development generally. Ostensibly reacting to the untrammeled growth, demolition and redevelopment of the 1950s and 1960s, by the early 1970s, some cities across the country began systematically "downzoning," or rezoning neighborhoods for less density.[215] Berkeley enacted the first Neighborhood Preservation Ordinance in 1973, and then a Landmarks Preservation Ordinance a year later.[216] Many other cities followed suit with similar policies.[217]

In the years after the Fair Housing Act, zoning transformed from a mechanism to order community life in a rational way (the "good housekeeping" model of zoning) into a tool that restricts development and land use much more broadly. Federal housing policy, explicitly promoting homeownership, transformed the nation into a homeowner society, and families predictably supported efforts to protect and enhance their valuable asset. Research shows that communities or neighborhoods with greater proportions of homeowners are more likely to have anti-growth policies and more restrictive land-use regulations.[218]

In that context, zoning laws can be applied to freeze the status quo, and with the predictable effect of excluding poor people of color from more affluent suburban areas. For example, in 1973, the city of Alameda, California, which was 90% white in 1970, adopted a ballot initiative, Measure A, which amended the city charter to prohibit the development of multi-family housing, including apartment buildings.[219]

Exclusionary zoning perpetuates racial and economic segregation. As noted last chapter, studies have found that density restrictions, such as minimum lot sizes, are strongly correlated with overall municipal fragmentation within regions as well as with segregation and concentration of the affluent.[220] Researchers have consistently found a correlation between low-density or restrictive zoning and racial residential segregation as well.

Following the success of fair housing laws at the state level and the eventual passage of the federal Fair Housing Act, restrictive zoning ordinances proliferated into a general pattern of exclusion, rather than one based explicitly on race. As many communities had already discovered, restrictions on architectural standards, lot size, and occupancy could achieve the same objectives without the stigma of explicit racial animus. After the passage of the Fair Housing Act, these ordinances were challenged, but through a series of cases during the 1970s were systematically upheld. The politics of housing changed, and the law along with it.

In *James v. Valtierra*, the U.S. Supreme Court ruled that municipalities could block housing for the poor.[221] The plaintiffs, low-income women of color, were unable to find affordable housing, and struggled to get from their jobs to a residence. California law allowed referendums to defeat any proposed affordable housing development. When a proposed development was predictably defeated, the plaintiffs sued to appeal San Jose's decision. The Supreme Court narrowly decided that the California constitutional amendment requiring a local referendum did not violate the equal protection clause.

In *Village of Belle Terre v. Boraas*, the Supreme Court reviewed an ordinance on Long Island that zoned single-family homes for families and relatives only, ruling against college students who sought to move into a house near Stony Brook.[222] Although restrictive zoning had long been deemed legal, this was one of the first instances that the Court approved a zoning measure that excluded certain people. Although college students were the losers, the implications of this case were already clear.

With the authority to exclude individuals from certain neighborhoods on the basis of non-racial characteristics established, municipalities began to push the envelope even further. A year later, the Supreme Court reviewed another zoning case, *Warth v. Seldin*.[223] In this case, the Court upheld a zoning ordinance in a Rochester, New York suburb that maintained almost all of its housing as single-family, detached residences. Fair housing advocates argued that the zoning ordinance excluded low-income families (who happened to be minorities) from being able to live in the suburb. The Court ruled that non-residents lacked standing to sue, and that their inability to find housing was a result of the housing market rather than wrongdoing by the city. In this way, the Court insulated exclusionary zoning practices from direct attack under the law.

A critical blow to fair housing was *Village of Arlington Heights v. Metropolitan Housing Development Corp.*, a case heard in the 1977 term.[224] In that case, the Supreme Court upheld a refusal to grant a variance to a developer who wished to build multi-family housing in an area zoned for single-family residences. Evidence was introduced regarding both economic (class) and racial impacts of the restrictive zoning ordinance. The Court acknowledged these effects, but nonetheless sided with the city on the grounds that socioeconomic impacts do not trigger constitutional liability, and there was insufficient evidence of racially discriminatory intent. In other words, the Court affirmed the power of localities, under the constitution, to use zoning power to exclude the poor, even if there were clear racial effects.

These decisions sanctioned, if not invited, "snob zoning," where municipalities behave as "super-neighborhood associations" and enact whatever ordinances maximize property values without regard to or concern for the exclusionary effects by class or otherwise.[225] These exclusionary controls were attacked, but, as long as the impact is only detectable by class, then it is likely they will be upheld under the constitution, and making a statutory fair housing case is not much easier. Even if clear statistical evidence of a racially disparate impact is established (an expensive and difficult effort), municipalities have considerable leeway to defend their policies.[226]

The 1988 amendments ultimately strengthened the Fair Housing Act, closing loopholes, expanding its range of application, and strengthening enforcement authority, but it came too late to prevent the sedimentation of segregation across regions.[227] Nor did it resolve lingering doubts or ambiguities over the federal authority and scope of power to "affirmatively further fair housing."[228]

Although racial residential segregation declined (from a very high peak) between 1970 and 1980 according to the Dissimilarity Index, the federal Fair Housing Act was both too weak and too late to disrupt, let alone reverse, widespread entrenchment of racial residential segregation, and the subsequent development and widespread adoption of socioeconomic exclusions led to even greater concentrations of Black poor. These developments have made it more difficult to build affordable housing in exclusionary communities, and empowered neighborhoods and municipal leaders to justify their policies on non-racial grounds. This has resulted in greater and more intense opportunity hoarding within regions.

White Flight and School Desegregation

Although racial and economic housing segregation persisted after the passage of the Fair Housing Act, the nation embarked upon a large-scale experiment in school desegregation in the 1960s and 1970s. The NAACP Legal Defense Fund, under the leadership of Thurgood Marshall and Charles Hamilton Houston, developed a brilliant legal strategy to spur federal courts to dismantle racial segregation in public schools.[229] School districts around the country segregated pupils into different schools based upon their race. In the Jim Crow south, state laws generally mandated the assignment of students to same-race schools. Elsewhere, the same result was generally accomplished through less direct, but equally effective means, such as discretionary assignments, feeder and alternative enrollment plans, and other administrative and regulatory maneuvers by local school authorities.[230]

Beginning with the landmark decisions (five consolidated cases) in *Brown v. Board of Education*, federal courts placed local school districts under federal orders to revise their assignment policies and take other measures to disestablish segregation.[231] These court orders provoked what historians euphemistically regard as a period of "massive resistance," particularly in the south.[232] Dramatized by the ordeal of the Little Rock Nine, desegregation in the south began in fits and starts, as school boards and local authorities searched for ways to slow or stymie federal orders.

Brown itself was part of the problem, as it ultimately demanded integration with "all deliberate speed," subtly inviting intransigence and foot dragging by school authorities.[233] In fact, there was virtually no meaningful progress toward implementing the *Brown* mandate and desegregating public schools in the south between 1954 and 1964.[234] By 1965, only 2% of Black children in the Deep South attended integrated schools.[235]

When courts eventually insisted that local school boards take meaningful action toward desegregation, the general and widespread response was so-called "freedom of choice" plans.[236] Freed from segregation mandates, southern school districts and local authorities maintained that the law merely required them to get out of the business of race-based student assignment altogether. Thus, instead of undertaking extensive remedial measures to accomplish integration, including race-based pupil assignments to ensure it, many districts reverted to policies that were ostensibly integrative, but implemented in a way that maintained the status quo. Freedom of choice plans, or free transfer plans, for example, were supposed to allow parents to select their children's schools, but in practice the requests of Black parents were denied if they were integrative.[237]

In some cases, southern districts closed their public schools entirely rather than integrate, and white parents, if they could afford it, placed their children into private schools.[238] In Dothan, Alabama for example, local leaders, even real estate agents, bankers and pastors encouraged white families to enroll their children in a private academy just outside of town operating with tax exempt status.[239]

By the late 1960s, federal courts began to lose their patience, and were increasingly skeptical of foot-dragging and clever work-arounds. In 1968, the Supreme Court stepped in again, ruled that freedom of choice plans were inadequate, and required that districts dismantle segregation "root and branch."[240] Ultimately, racial integration in American public schools was most effectively pursued between 1968 and 1988, when federal courts enforced desegregation mandates with supervised court orders and close monitoring, with the most vigorous enforcement phase occurring between 1968 and 1972.[241] In 1968, the percentage of Black students attending hyper-segregated schools was nearly 78%. By 1972, that number fell to just under 25%.[242] In the south, school integration in the peaked in the mid-1980s, with around 44% of Black students attending integrated schools in 1988.[243]

Although there was remarkable progress in the effort to desegregate schools, America never realized *Brown's* vision of integrated schools. The most significant progress was realized in the south, and to a lesser extent in the west. The north was a different story, and gains everywhere have been gradually reversed. Even as courts were pushing for southern desegregation, northern schools actually became more segregated. Between 1968 and 1972, Black students became more segregated in the Northeast by a significant margin, and we have already noted that this region has among the highest rates of school segregation today.[244] Over 70 years since the *Brown* decision, our nation's public schools have experienced what some scholars characterize as "re-segregation."[245] Researchers have found, for example, that school segregation between white and Black students has increased by 64 percent since 1988 in the 100 largest districts.[246]

There are several reasons school desegregation was never realized in much of the country, and that schools have since resegregated. First, Federal courts were hampered by facts on the ground. White families were already moving to suburbs in unprecedented numbers, but desegregation mandates accelerated this process.[247] One analysis found that between 1940 and 1970, for every Black arrival, two whites left the central city.[248] By 1980, 72% of Blacks lived in central cities compared to just 32% of whites in metropolitan regions. Suburbanization and sprawl were used to catch and capture urban outgrowth, which undermined district-based desegregation plans.

Recall Chris Marten's parents' decision to move out of a cozy neighborhood in the city of Columbus to an outwardly similar neighborhood in the suburb of Upper Arlington in the mid-1980s. Not only were they motivated by the quality of the Upper Arlington school system and a fear of busing, but they also recognized that Upper Arlington homes were a better bet for property value appreciation. Looking at 100 border neighborhoods across the country in the 1960s and 1970s, one economist found a clear housing price premium rise for suburban homes that were, by all outward appearances, otherwise indistinguishable from their urban district neighbors.[249]

Desegregation fueled the intertwined phenomenon of white flight and suburban property appreciation.

Fateful court decisions, however, made these trends worse. Foremost among them was a case from Detroit that the Supreme Court heard in 1974, noted near the beginning of this chapter, *Milliken v. Bradley*. Parents of minority children argued that, since Detroit was so segregated, meaningful integration could not be practically achieved without involving the surrounding suburban districts.[250] The Supreme Court held that the surrounding school districts did not cause the segregation within Detroit, and were therefore not responsible or liable for the segregation within the Detroit public schools. As a consequence, the ruling in this case prohibited student assignment across district lines unless proof of complicity or coordinated intentional segregation could be established. As of 1980, the Detroit metropolitan region contained 86 municipalities, 45 townships, and 89 school districts.[251] Without a regional approach, it would be nearly impossible to integrate schools in the region.

The Supreme Court's decision in *Milliken* effectively sanctioned white flight, signaling to parents of white children nationwide that they could flee into surrounding municipalities without fear that their children would be bused into a different district or that children from other districts would be bused into their district. Even for white families who harbored no racial prejudice and were unfazed with growing proportions of non-white neighbors in central cities, they understood that suburban districts, offering higher-quality educational services and faster property appreciation, was a better deal.

Suburbanization had already set a path toward greater inter-district segregation relative to intra-district segregation, but the *Milliken* decision buttressed the invisible walls between districts, fueling inter-district residential and educational segregation. We have already noted that most school segregation today is now between districts rather than within them.[252] This is the corollary to inter-municipal residential segregation, driven in part by the response to school desegregation. In 1960, 68% of overall Black segregation from other groups was between neighborhoods (census tracts) within places.[253] By 1980, that portion had fallen to 51%, and to just 40% by 2000.[254] In other words, after 1980 more Black segregation was regional, between central cities and suburbs, and between suburbs than within those places. In fact, there was a 134% increase in segregation between (rather than within) places from 1960 to 2000, the heyday of school desegregation.[255]

Since the Supreme Court held that students couldn't be assigned across district boundaries as a remedy to local segregation, then perhaps resources could be distributed more equitably across districts. Here, too, the Supreme Court made matters worse. In 1973, the Court decided a case arising out of Texas, *San Antonio v. Rodriguez*, which challenged unequal funding for education.[256] The plaintiffs, representing poor school districts, argued that education was a fundamental constitutional right, and that states had a constitutional duty to provide it, where they chose to do so, on an equal basis. The state of Texas relied heavily on local property taxation to fund the operation of schools, a system which produced substantial inter-district disparities in per-pupil expenditures, resulting primarily from differences in the value of assessable property. This system yielded more resources for whiter and more affluent communities.

The Supreme Court rejected both arguments. It held that education was not a fundamental right, and that the equal protection clause of the constitution did not require states to fund schools equally, and that a system of provision which encourages local control was a legitimate state interest. As a result, the *San Antonio* decision stymied more equitable efforts to distribute educational dollars. Whereas *Millikin* insulated affluent white school districts from threat of integration, *San Antonio* insulated them from the federal threat of redistribution. Together, they reinforced the relationship between educational opportunity and race and turbo-charged opportunity hoarding.

When *Brown* was decided, educational segregation was initially regarded as a southern problem. But as *Brown* moved north, public support for desegregated plummeted.[257] Opposition to the intrusions of federal courts was channeled into the Nixon administration's resistance toward "forced busing" and through new Supreme Court appointments which put the brakes on desegregation.[258] Collectively, these decisions undermined *Brown*, obedient to its letter, while hallowing out its animating spirit.

By 1990, three-quarters of whites lived in suburban and rural areas, but a majority of Blacks and Latinos lived in urban areas.[259] This helps explain why federal courts in the 1990s began systematically lifting desegregation orders, declaring many heavily segregated school districts to be "unitary."[260] There was simply nothing more district authorities or federal courts could do to integrate schools within districts that had been depleted of resources and white students. Thus, courts began winding down the project *Brown* started, and the number of non-white students attending non-white schools began increasing again.[261]

Freed from federal oversight, many districts reverted to administrative measures that have the effect of maintaining segregation, such as closing integrated schools or tracking students into separate programs. At the same time, budget cuts and transportation costs have forced more districts to rely on neighborhood schools, which generally mean more segregated schools.[262] The more closely a school resembles the racial demographics of local neighborhoods, the more likely it is to be segregated.[263] Only by bending school composition away from neighborhood demographics can school integration occur.

Many larger districts that experienced court-ordered desegregation initially found the experience painful, but salutary in the end. For example, community leaders in Louisville, Kentucky discovered that educational quality improved when white parents in the district regarded all of the schools in the county district as serving their children.[264] Not only that, but housing segregation declined when school assignments did not depend entirely on where students lived.[265] As a result, even when freed from court orders in the 1990s and 2000s, many districts sought to maintain these benefits through so-called "voluntary integration plans" that resembled the plans they had previously been required to undertake. Adding insult to injury, the Supreme Court struck down two of these plans in 2007, one in Louisville and the other in Seattle, and made it much more difficult to design and maintain such efforts.[266] This is yet another reason that our schools have continued to slide back toward segregation.

Although our national experiment in desegregation is reputationally mixed, with many older Black Americans painfully recalling the trauma that sometimes accompanied desegregation and loss of Black teachers, mentors, and role models in more segregated institutional settings, the empirical record is less equivocal.[267] The most comprehensive research studying the long-term effects of desegregation found improved Black student performance and adult outcomes along a wide range of measures: graduation rates, income, health, and incarcerated.[268] One of the most immediate effects of desegregation was increased levels of per-pupil spending provided by state funds (with insignificant increases in local or federal funds).[269] States provided additional funding to desegregating school districts rather than reduce funding to white schools to the level of what segregated schools had received previously. So, for example, average per-pupil spending was 22.5% greater for desegregated schools than experienced by Black cohorts that preceded the desegregation experience or districts that were not under such mandates.[270] This enhanced investment in education contributed to greater family income (25% greater), declines in adult poverty, and reduced probability of incarceration.[271]

Although the Supreme Court rejected a federal constitutional challenge to inequitable educational funding, advocates had more success at the state level, pressing claims based upon state constitutional provisions. So-called "adequacy suits," which argue that prevailing funding formulas failed to satisfy baseline requirements under state law, have resulted at least 25 successful challenges since 1971, and has resulted in far more resources for disadvantaged districts.[272] Researchers studying these suits found a consistent pattern: in the long run, over comparable time frames, states that send additional money to their lowest-income school districts see more academic improvement in those districts than states that don't.[273]

More recent research on school performance after the period of desegregation tells a similar story.[274] In a study of all public school districts in the United States from the 2008–2009 through the 2015–2016 school years, researchers found that more segregated schools systems have larger racial achievement gaps, and that, on average, those gaps grow faster during elementary and middle school than in less segregated districts.[275] Now that schools have resegregated, albeit for different reasons than before, they are once again separate and unequal.

Deindustrialization

In 1966, Black unemployment was already twice that of white unemployment.[276] But Black unemployment and under-employment crept up during the 1970s and 1980s as a result of macroeconomic changes.[277] As vividly illustrated by William Julius Wilson in *When Work Disappears*, structural changes to the economy during these decades visibly reduced the number and quality of decently paying low-skilled jobs in the American economy. In 1950, factories and farms employed 36% of the American workforce. By 2014, they employed just 10%. The American economy shed millions of industrial jobs, with devastating long-term consequences for these workers, but the pain was especially felt in Black communities and families. Black workers in manufacturing earn $5,000 more per year (17.9% more) than in nonmanufacturing industries while Hispanic workers earn $4,800 more per year.[278] The number of Black men between the ages of 20 and 29 working in manufacturing fell from 3 in 8 to 1 in 5 between 1973 and 1987. Up to half of the decline in employment by low-skilled Black workers was explained by the decline of industrial work.[279]

Although factory employment had been declining as a proportion of the workforce since 1943, factory jobs peaked in absolute terms in the United States in 1979.[280] Starting in the mid-1950s, rust belt cities lost hundreds of thousands of manufacturing jobs. Between 1967 and 1987, Philadelphia, Chicago, New York City, and Detroit lost over half of their manufacturing jobs.[281] Gradually at first, but rapidly over time, industry left the cities for suburban and semi-rural areas as well as for new states and regions. The opening up of the country through expressways and highways in the 1950s, new industries such as aerospace, advances in technology such as air conditioning, weaker labor unions, and government investments during the Cold War redirected business activity toward the south and the Sunbelt.[282]

Globalization and trade deals also allowed large American companies to shift manufacturing jobs and supply chains reliant on lower-skilled workers overseas. Global labor competition pressed wages down for low-skilled workers, while also making higher-skilled workers more valuable, since those were jobs that could not be outsourced as easily. Perhaps most importantly, technological improvements and greater automation meant that fewer workers were needed for the same jobs.

Most occupations in the American economy enjoyed wage growth between 1962 and 1973.[283] Between 1973 and 1987, however, wages began to stagnate. Real wages for men without four-year college degrees have declined 10–20% since their peak in 1980.[284] The sectors that experienced the greatest job and wage growth since were those that required the most advanced skills and formal education, such as technology, software development, pharmaceuticals, and engineering.[285] The result is a bifurcating job market, with high-skilled and high-income jobs on one side, and low-skilled and low-income jobs on the other.[286] the economic restructuring of the economy as a result of globalization transformed cities from industrial and manufacturing centers to "centers of innovation and creatively led by knowledge based sectors."[287]

At the other end of the labor market, non-college educated workers have been pushed into lower paying sectors. Higher-wage, low-skilled jobs, such as blue-collar factory, transportation, and construction jobs, have also gradually disappeared. According to one estimate, the United States created 27 clerical, sales and service jobs per 1,000 workers during the 1980s, but lost 16 production, transportation, or laborer jobs in that same period.[288]

Deindustrialization shifted middle-income occupations from traditionally male production industries to service sector positions. By the end of the 1980s, more than 70% of workers were employed in services, which tended to be lower paying compared to traditional blue-collar work.[289] Workers who shifted from blue-collar to service jobs made 25–30% less.[290] Even where low-skilled workers found employment, they had fewer opportunities for job advancement and lower real wages comparable to earlier decades. Trades and traditional manufacturing jobs were more likely to be unionized, and the decline of blue-collar work coincided with lower rates of unionization, which had a reinforcing feedback effect on wages.[291] Men have had to either acquire more skills to maintain a middle-class income, move into "pink collar" occupations, or settle for work below middle-class pay.

The processes of suburbanization interacted with deindustrialization and joblessness in urban areas, heightening the so-called spatial mismatch. Many of the new jobs moved to the suburbs. In Chicago, for example, the areas of greatest job growth were the northwest suburbs where Black people were less than 2% of the population.[292] Segregation, discrimination, and urban policy prevented many racially isolated workers from moving or transporting closer to jobs. Black neighborhoods have fewer employment opportunities, and deindustrialization put jobs even further out of reach. The historian Thomas Sugrue regarded this process as the "exclusion of a generation of young men from the work force."[293]

For neighborhoods where jobs disappeared, crime, violence, concentrated poverty, and an underground economy grew in their wake, and joblessness itself contributed to the decline of marriage and out-of-wedlock births. The greatest increase in Black neighborhood poverty occurred between 1970 and 1980 in cities where deindustrialization was most powerfully felt—the industrial cities of the Midwest and Northeast. The decline in employment left little formal economic opportunity.

The problem was not simply that deindustrialization led to greater concentrations of poverty as a result of unemployment and declining wages, but that it left these communities have fewer resources to solve the ensuing problems. In addition to fiscal distress, services are more costly to maintain or operate at scale with fewer users and declining population. Schools with fewer children in the neighborhood cost more per pupil. Trash collection is more expensive on a household basis. In addition, these communities are left with less social capital and fewer anchoring institutions, including churches, civic associations, and businesses. These are the coping mechanisms that help communities' weather crises.

Government policy played a role that compounded these harmful consequences. Deindustrialization occurred at the same time as a gradual reduction

164 *Structural Racism*

in federal government support for urban programs to address poverty and support social services. During the Reagan administration, direct aid to cities was cut, including general revenue sharing, public service jobs, block grants, and much more.[294] By consolidating and terminating various programs, more than $130 billion in multiyear funding was cut out of domestic initiatives.[295] In 1980, the federal contribution to city budgets was 18%; by 1990, it had fallen to 6.4%.[296]

This was more than simply cutbacks; it was a shift of power and influence. Mature suburbanization meant that national politicians were less focused on the problems of cities and the need to provide federal aid. The needs of deprived urban dwellers, disproportionately poor people of color, were ignored. The rising influence of the suburban electoral coalition reached an inflection point in 1992, when suburbia represented a majority of voters for the first time.[297] An urban policy agenda that might respond to this crisis was shelved, indefinitely.

Mass Incarceration and the War on Drugs

Like the re-segregation of public schools and deindustrialization, the advent of mass incarceration illustrates the point that structural racism is not simply the legacy, consequence, or even residue of earlier racial structures, but is better understood as products of contemporary policy developments, originating primarily in the north and in the 20th century, but expanding nationally and accelerating into the 21st century. Despite comprehensive systems of racial control in parts of the country, rates of incarceration were relatively stable over decades, if not centuries, in the United States until the 1970s.[298]

The origins of mass incarceration are multiple and varied, and include sentencing policies such as three strikes laws, mandatory minimums, a shift away from rehabilitation, greater prosecutorial zealousness, and, of course, the War on Drugs. Drug offenses account for nearly two-thirds of the rise in the population of federal inmates between 1985 and 2000,[299] and 50% of the federal prison population by 2015.[300]

The origins of the War on Drugs are murky, but some historians trace the phrase to a press conference given by President Nixon in 1971, in which he declared illicit drug use "public enemy No. 1."[301] Others point to a Reagan administration declaration in 1982 which also used the phrase, and appeared to inaugurate a series of initiatives to combat drug use.[302] What is clear, however, is that the policies that undergirded this "war" were developed in critical stages, and not necessarily in direct or proportional response to rates of crime, drug consumption, or levels of public concern.[303]

A key step was the Comprehensive Crime Control Act of 1984, the first major comprehensive revision to federal criminal laws since the early 20th century, and a law that imposed mandatory minimum sentences for various violent and non-violent crimes.[304] Mandatory minimums received bipartisan support. Conservatives sought to reduce judicial discretion, and liberals thought it would curb excessive sentences by prejudiced jurists or prosecutors. In fact, after this reform, prisoners served longer sentences.[305] A study by economists found that this law significantly increased rates of incarceration in the following decade.[306]

Another step in the escalation of the War on Drugs was the 1984 amendments to the Comprehensive Drug Abuse Prevention and Control Act of 1970.[307] These amendments created a perverse and powerful incentive by allowing law enforcement agencies to retain the proceeds of seized assets, known as asset forfeiture.[308] Cash, vehicles, jewelry, or any other valuable assets seized during or as a consequence a drug bust could fill the coffers of law enforcement, creating a perverse cycle in which local law enforcement profited off of drug enforcement. According to one report, between 1988 and 1992, law enforcement seized over $1 billion in assets in this way.[309] Critics speculate that this law may have undermined the efficacy of law enforcement, by shifting the focus from crime control to forfeiture extraction.[310]

In 1986, Congress passed the Anti-Drug Abuse Act, which expanded the established mandatory minimum penalties for drug infractions, specifically possession, based on the drug's classification (or schedule) and pumped $2 billion dollars into international and domestic enforcement.[311] The Anti-Drug Abuse Act of 1988 created new penalties and punishments, including collateral consequences such as denying public housing or student loans to individuals convicted of drug offenses.[312] More importantly, it also ratcheted up mandatory minimums. Simple possession of crack cocaine, even absent intent to sell, resulted in an automatic five-year sentence.

Although these bills collectively expanded funding and increased penalties for drug enforcement, the 1994 federal crime bill is perhaps the most infamous federal law associated with the War on Drugs.[313] A bipartisan law signed by President Clinton, the law was one of the largest spending bills in American history on criminal law enforcement. It allocated $30 billion to the effort, which included over $16 billion for the construction of new prisons and for state and local police forces and funds for hiring 100,000 new officers.

As part of the "tough on crime" mentality that formed in the vortex of the War on Drugs, a number of states adopted notorious "three strikes" laws that impose minimum sentences much greater than the underlying criminal penalty would typically trigger. The 1994 federal crime bill adopted "three strikes" into federal law, which made a third drug offense an automatic 25-year sentence.[314] Criminal defendants could be sentenced to jail for 25 years for offenses that, in the early 1980s, would receive less than a single year sentence.

Although the War on Drugs directly increased federal rates of incarceration, the drug war's policy innovations contributed to mass incarceration beyond the penalization and punishment of drug use and distribution. California was among the first to enact a "three strikes" law after the widely publicized murder of a young woman named Kimber Reynolds in 1992 by two men outside of a roadside restaurant in Fresno.[315] One of the men involved had been recently released on parole. Almost immediately, 'three strikes' laws increased the number of non-violent offenders being jailed for far longer sentences on account of their third strike than would be otherwise be imposed. Convictions or pleas for minor offenses have resulted in absurd sentences. Criminal defendants have been sentenced to 25 to life, under the law, for stealing a pair of tube socks, a car radio or pizzas.[316] The U.S. Supreme Court refused to find such laws unconstitutional in violation of the 8th amendment's prohibition on "cruel and unusual punishment," but the Court did find that overcrowded conditions in the state's prisons, a direct consequence of the law, was unconstitutional.[317]

Rather than a well-intended policy response to a national crisis, Michelle Alexander persuasively characterizes the War on Drugs as the continuation of a political project that sought to tap into white racial resentment and the backlash against civil rights. As she observes, by the late 1960s, "conservative politicians found they could mobilize" white voters by vowing to "crack down on crime."[318] The results are as lamentable as they are predictable.

In 1970, more than 60% of the American prison population was white (see Table 2.8). Today that proportion is inverted. There is a basis for the view that the War on Drugs has been a war on communities of color. Communities of color have been disproportionately targeted by police despite drug usage rates that are comparable across racial groups.[319] Police target high-poverty neighborhoods under the auspices of the War on Drugs, and these are segregated neighborhoods. Black people are far more likely to be arrested for drug offenses.[320] The offenses and sentencing disparities exacerbate these racial consequences, and the incentive structures impel law enforcement to target the poor and marginalized communities.

As a result of these policies, poor Black and brown men are systematically harassed and their rights are abused or violated, even outside of these communities. Racial profiling casts a veneer of criminal suspicion on the innocent, and becomes a justification for abuse. Policies such as "Stop and Frisk" merely represent the formalized and institutionalized practices of daily harassment.[321] In New York City, more than 80% of people stopped were Black and Latino.[322]

Unfortunately, these dynamics extend into schools, through the so-called "school to prison pipeline."[323] Zero tolerance policies enacted to maintain "order" and enforce discipline have led to suspensions and expulsions, even for minor offenses, that disproportionately affect Black and brown youth.[324] Black and brown youth are seven times as likely to be suspended or expelled for the same offenses as their white counterparts. A GAO report found that, in the 2012–13 school year, Black students were 39% of all suspensions despite constituting 15.5% of all school children.[325]

Not only does mass incarceration illustrate the concept of structural racism as more than the residue or legacy of previous systems of racial control, but it also illustrates its complicated origins. Although politicians such as Richard Nixon and Ronald Reagan stoked public racial fears and perceived grievances, the punitive policies that ultimately brought us to the present moment were largely supported by Black politicians and community leaders.[326] As the legal scholar James Forman Jr. keenly observes, "mass incarceration is the result of small, distinct steps, each of whose significance becomes more apparent over time, and only when considered in the light of later events."[327] In other words, numerous, unconnected policy decisions, accumulate over time with much larger, often unintended, effects.[328] As is true of so many features of structural racism, the resulting system is not necessarily the product of discriminatory intent nor a grand nefarious design, but rather the sum of countless collective decisions, large and small, well-intended and not.

Predatory Lending and the Subprime Mortgage Crisis

The global financial crisis of 2007–2008 is one of the seminal events of the 21st century. Racial inequality is baked deep into the crisis, both as a hidden cause and an enduring effect. At the heart of the crisis and resulting "Great Recession" was the collapse of the U.S. housing market. Much ink has been spilled on the forces that caused this event, and many divergent narratives spun out of it.[329]

An early and prominent narrative was that borrowers took out loans that they knew, or should have known, they could not afford. Following a massive federal bailout of failing banks and other businesses in late 2008 by the Bush administration, the new Obama administration crafted a relatively narrow effort to protect homeowners who were either underwater or at risk of foreclosure in 2009.[330] Infuriated that the government would "subsidize the losers' mortgages," Rick Santelli, a financial news anchor on CNBC, called for a tax revolt that precipitated the Tea Party movement.[331]

In the years since, an alternative narrative gradually emerged that illuminated the systemic risk to the economy introduced by Wall Street's use of complex financial instruments, perhaps most famously dramatized by Michael Lewis in *The Big Short*.[332] In the decades leading up to the crisis, the housing finance market gradually transformed from the traditional model of bank to lender finance (although subsidized by the government in various ways) into a far more complex multi-party system involving the secondary mortgage market.[333]

Across the country, home loan mortgages were pooled by investment banks and packaged into securitized bond instruments, called Collateralized Debt Obligations, or CDOs, which were sold to pension funds, hedge funds, banks, and other institutional investors. By 2006, almost 80% of so-called subprime loans were securitized.[334] Subprime loans were loans ostensibly awarded to borrowers with imperfect credit, and the higher cost was supposed to reflect higher risk.

The popularity of these instruments and the return on them fueled a voracious appetite among investment banks, which led brokers and lenders to cut corners, commit fraud, falsify financial information, and more, to keep the conveyor belt of securitized products moving off the assembly line. As the crisis approached, almost 20% of all mortgage originations were subprime.[335]

Higher returns were offered on the assumption of higher risk and higher costs to borrowers, but investors and investment banks believed that the pooled securities would prove safe because of the diversification of risk throughout the pool. Rather than reducing risk, securitization introduced systemic risk to the stability of the financial system.

This scheme worked so long as housing values continued to rise and interest rates were relatively low. Borrowers in subprime products earned equity on account of escalating property values through the teaser periods, and credit rating agencies and risk assessors assumed borrowers could refinance before the rates reset but with tens of thousands of dollars of accumulated home equity.

Because of the growth of the secondary mortgage market, the usual link between a sustainable loan and risk had been severed. Originating banks immediately sold the loans to investment banks, who packaged and sold them to investors. The originating bank no longer assumed the risk of a bad or even fraudulent loan.

The securitized instruments, sold to the secondary market, were filled with so-called "toxic mortgages," which included subprime and other predatory loans. Although the originating banks sold these instruments to the secondary market and ratings agencies stamped them with top line grades, they were ticking time bombs. Eventually, they exploded, leaving communities and the economy in shambles. Gross Domestic Product fell $650 billion, household net worth lost $11.5 trillion in value, and more than 8 million jobs evaporated.[336]

Beneath the story of Wall Street investment banks, deregulation, and systemic greed is another story about how predatory finance targeted communities of color and set off a financial bomb that blew up the global economy. After decades of white flight, redlining, and disinvestment, neighborhoods and communities starved of credit for generations were suddenly awash in subprime loans following deregulations of the 1980s and 1990s.[337] The subprime mortgage market was a crevasse of racial disparities. Low-income nonwhite communities were targeted with subprime loans and other predatory credit instruments.

Although more white borrowers received subprime loans, much larger proportions of Black and Latino borrowers received high-cost loans.[338] More than half of Black families and 40% of Latino families who obtained home loans in the years leading up the crisis did so in the subprime market.[339] This wasn't a simple function of borrower risk. Subprime loans were sold to people in "high-risk" neighborhoods who qualified for prime loans.

Analysis of mortgage data revealed that high-income Black and Latino borrowers were more than three times likely to receive subprime loans as high-income whites, and twice as likely to receive such loans as low-income whites.[340] Another study found that lenders were twice as likely to give Black and Hispanics borrowers subprime loans as white borrowers with the same incomes.[341] Even after controlling credit risk factors, borrowers of color were more than 30% likely to receive a higher rate loan than white borrowers.[342] One analysis of the pre-boom peak found that Black borrowers earning more than $200,000 a year were more likely to get a subprime mortgage than white families earning less than $30,000.³⁴³

Perhaps the most astonishing fact was that *most* of the borrowers who received subprime loans qualified for prime credit.³⁴⁴ Mortgage brokers earned fees and kickbacks by getting borrowers into subprime products, servicing companies earned fees from defaults or late payments, and the originating bank had long since sold the loan—along with the risk—to the secondary market. As noted, even investors felt they were relatively well insulated, since the CDO was packaged with other mortgages.

The problem was not just that individual borrowers of color were more likely to receive subprime loans. The structural problem was that non-white neighborhoods were awash in subprime credit, just as they were denied credit in earlier decades.³⁴⁵ In a meaningful historical resonance, the same neighborhoods were targeted for subprime credit products as they had been disadvantaged decades before. Local mortgage brokers, often friendly or familiar faces, were paid to go door to door, pushing their product on their neighbors. Brokers played a key role in selling loans to residents, and may have taken advantage of their trust by selling higher-priced loans.³⁴⁶ In addition, they may have received kickbacks from the banks for delivering higher-priced loans to otherwise prime-qualified borrowers.³⁴⁷ Too many borrowers assumed that they were given a competitive and fair loan product, but were ultimately taken advantage of and preyed upon.

Even controlling for income, race has long appeared to play a role in the success rate in securing a mortgage. In general, research shows that, even after controlling for credit worthy variables, non-white loan applicants were far more likely than whites to be denied loans well before the emergence of the subprime market. For example, a 1992 Federal Reserve of Boston study found that they were 60% more likely to be turned down than comparably qualified whites.³⁴⁸ A more recent study published in 2018 studying 31 million Home Mortgage Disclosure Act records in 61 metropolitan areas found significant racial disparities in lending approvals even after controlling for nine factors, including income, loan amounts, and neighborhoods.³⁴⁹ Black mortgage applicants were turned down at significantly higher rates than whites in 48 of those metro areas.

Having been historically starved of credit, these new financial products, including subprime mortgages, filled a need for under-served communities. To this day, many historically marginalized communities lack traditional financial services.³⁵⁰ An recent federal survey showed that change to 34% of Black families and 31% of Latino were either unbanked (not serviced by a traditional bank) or underbanked.³⁵¹ The survey shows that more than 5 times as many Black households are unbanked as white ones.³⁵² In Philadelphia, banks placed three-quarters of their branch banks in white neighborhoods.³⁵³

Because traditional banks and conventional lenders had long ignored these communities, subprime lenders were more proactive in reaching out to minority borrowers—soliciting in predominantly Black neighborhoods, and exploiting their need for credit. They hired minority brokers or local residents to sell these loans to their neighbors to gain their trust.[354] Excluded from the mainstream financial institutions and credit markets, many Black families were forced to rely on predatory options that extracted their wealth and resources.

Subprime loans were merely the most recent predatory credit product for communities and neighborhoods without traditional financial services and starved for credit. Although there are many examples, one of the more notorious versions of this were contract-for-deed arrangements, in which buyers put down a large down payment for a home and made monthly installments at high interest rates, but never gained ownership until the contract was paid in full and all conditions were met.[355] These contracts were common in places like Chicago, where as many as 75% and 95% of homes sold to Black families during the 1950s and 1960s made under this type of arrangement.[356] The resulting loss of wealth is difficult to estimate, but one study found that African-Americans who bought on contract paid, on average, an additional $587 (in current dollars) more a month than if they had a conventional mortgage, and lost between $3 billion and $4 billion in total wealth as a consequence.[357]

In more recent years, predatory finance is visible in the form of check-cashing, payday lending kiosks, pawn shops, and rent-to-own services.[358] Payday loans—a short-term loan that advances money based upon future paychecks—grew massively in the 2000s. One estimate shows that the number of storefronts offering this service grew by nearly 50% between 2001 and 2005, with more than 22,000 estimated locations as of 2005 in 37 states.[359] Un- and underbanked customers used these services to secure short term credit, but at much higher costs. One study found that an ordinary $100 payday check entails a $18 fee for the privilege.[360]

Structured inequality has been woven into our society, but the story of the mortgage meltdown and the subprime crisis illustrates the complex ways in which the past interacts with the present. It suggests how contemporary features of structural racism are more than the product of path-dependency or inertia, as either present-day effects or cumulative harms of past policies and practices, but a contingent byproduct of new and novel developments and insidious adaptations to prior and existing arrangements. In this way, the historical redline became a "reverse redline," where communities long-denied traditional credit institutions were flooded with toxic loans.[361] But the voracious appetite for these products was fueled by financial innovations and the secondary market. And, in that way, the episode is a powerful illustration of how many of the sources of structural racial inequality are better understood as a product of greed and opportunism, exploiting the vulnerable for financial gain, rather than racial hostility, bigotry, or even aversion and fear. No matter how wickedly some may regard the group of actors who caused the crisis that the journalist Aaron Glantz characterized as "Wall Street Kingpins, Hedge Fund Magnates, Crooked Banks, and Vulture Capitalists," there has never been a prevailing or strong viewpoint that the financial wizards who devised subprime mortgages nor their adjutants, bosses, and enablers were motivated principally or even in significant measure by racial antipathy.[362]

The proliferation of subprime loans resulted in widespread foreclosures and a tremendous loss of wealth. Between 2007 and 2009, foreclosure rates soared to the highest level seen in 50 years with more than 2.5 million households in foreclosure.[363] This hit non-white families and communities hardest. Although more whites were in foreclosure, Black borrowers higher rates and were 70% more likely to lose their home. In Atlanta, middle-income Black borrowers were 35% more likely to foreclose than white middle-income borrowers. By 2011, there were more than 90 foreclosures per square mile in Detroit.[364]

Neighbors and communities felt the collateral damage of foreclosure. Research shows that foreclosures reduced home values within a mile by as much as 3% of the total value.[365] Neighbors saw their property values plummet. Property value declines also resulted in reduced revenue and tax base capacity. When foreclosures were concentrated, as they were in minority neighborhoods, this has a double injury—reducing overall wealth while also forcing service cuts and tipping municipalities toward bankruptcy.

The municipal costs of foreclosure go beyond lost tax revenue and service cuts. Abandoned properties require more fire service, policing, and upkeep. They are also more likely to become an arson risk or blighted. A lawsuit filed brought by the city of Baltimore against Wells Fargo claimed that each foreclosure cost the city more than $30,000 in damages, including lost tax revenue, and the cost of city services, including police and fire protection.[366] The Baltimore suit resulted in a $175 million settlement.[367] Another, more expansive lawsuit alleged that Morgan Stanley discriminated in the secondary mortgage market, as well as defrauded investors.[368] The complaint details the hunger for these loans by the investment banks and the manner in which minority neighborhoods were targeted.[369]

The housing crash harmed everyone, but the impact hit Black and Latino Americans the hardest, causing housing instability, wiping out a quarter trillion in Black wealth, and reversing decades of progress in reducing the Black-white wealth gap.[370] Median wealth fell about 30% for all groups during the Great Recession, but Black and Latinos lost 52% and 66% of their collective wealth, respectively, compared to just 16% lost for whites.[371] In the wake of the Great Recession, median Black household wealth was just $2,200 (see Table 2.7).

One reason for the greater impact is that Black Americans had a greater portion of their wealth stored in their homes compared to whites. Housing equity makes up nearly 60% of total net worth for Black homeowners, compared with 43% of total net worth for white homeowners.[372]

For better or worse, homes are more than shelter; they are also investment vehicles. Home equity constitutes more than a third of the non-pension wealth in the United States.[373] The post-war housing expansion was one of the most important—and government subsidized—wealth creation endeavors in American history.[374] Adjusted for inflation, home values have more than quadrupled in the United States since 1940, and have risen at an annual rate of 4.6% from 1975 to 2022 alone, despite recessions.[375] But, as already noted, the cluster of policies that facilitated this development largely kept Black Americans from the one of the most valuable and fastest appreciating assets, depressed their

Table 3.1 Homeownership by Race in the United States, 1940–2020[376]

	1940	1950	1960	1970	1980	1990	2000	2010	2020
Total	44%	55%	62%	63%	64%	64%	66%	67%	66%
White	46%	57%	64%	67%	69%	69%	72%	71%	75%
Black	23%	35%	38%	43%	43%	42%	46%	45%	44%
Latino				44%	45%	44%	45%	48%	49%
Asian	16%	30%	44%	49%	52%	52%	54%	59%	60%

appreciation, or subjected them to predatory financial instruments. Table 3.1 displays rates of homeownership by race from 1940 to 2020.

In 1940, only 44% of Americans owned their own home. By 1955, that figure had already risen to 55%, evidence of the effectiveness of post-war policy. Today, roughly two-thirds of all households own their own home. But this figure masks considerable and persistent racial disparities. About three-quarters of white Americans are homeowners—an approximate historical record—while fewer than half of Black and Latino heads of household in the United States are homeowners.

More disturbingly, the Black-white disparity in homeownership has never been larger in documented absolute terms. Although the white-Black homeownership ratio was two-to-one in 1940 (46% to 23%), the absolute gap was only 23%. Even in an era when housing discrimination on the basis of race was legal, the absolute disparity was just 22% in 1950 and 24% in 1960, well below the 31% gap today. As is typical of many facets of structural racism, actual progress masks the persistence of inequality. As Table 3.1 indicates, both Black and white rates of homeownership increased substantially since 1940, but, once again, white progress has outstripped Black progress, leading to ever-larger disparities.

Black homeownership has fluctuated around the mid-40s for much of the last few decades, but peaked at nearly 50% between 2004 and 2006, just before the subprime mortgage crisis.[377] In the wake of that crisis, nearly a quarter of a million Black homeowners lost their homes. The rate of Black homeownership declined gradually in the years that followed, ultimately bottoming out in 2016 at about 41%.[378] Proportionally fewer Black Americans owned their home in the final year of the Obama administration than did in 1970, just after the adoption of the Fair Housing Act.[379]

As noted in the last chapter, even when Black Americans become homeowners, they do not enjoy the same home values or annual appreciation as white Americans. Studies on racial disparities in home appraisals show that, even after the adoption of ostensibly non-discriminatory appraisal standards, there are persistent and widening disparities between appraisals in neighborhoods that are majority-white and those that are predominantly Black and Latino.[380] A city-by-city examination shows that homes in Black neighborhoods are consistently devalued, especially in highly segregated cities.[381]

Initial disinvestments in Black neighborhoods coupled with limited wealth means that Black homebuyers continue to be more likely to buy homes in neighborhoods in non-white neighborhoods or neighborhoods with lower property value appreciation potential.[382] Nonetheless, lower rates of homeownership clearly contribute to the racial wealth gap, and may be the single largest factor.[383] The housing crash of 2008 not only wiped out decades of homeownership gains in absolute terms for non-white Americans but most of their wealth as well.

But it is not just Black families that lost wealth. The targeting of Black neighborhoods for subprime products, predatory credit, and finance instruments has a larger effect: the stripping of community wealth, corroding the tax base and capacity to provide services. These communities were left worse off than when they began, making them a tragic expression of structural racism.

Municipal Fiscal Distress

On January 16, 2016, President Barack Obama signed an order declaring a state of emergency in Flint, Michigan.[384] The crisis that precipitated this order was not a severe storm, tornado, flooding, or landslides, as was the case in South Carolina and Mississippi a few weeks before, or any other natural disaster.[385] The crisis that sent shudders through the nation was the poisoning of a city by government malfeasance.

In a cost-cutting measure justified by ongoing municipal fiscal distress, in April 2014 the city of Flint decided to switch water suppliers. Instead of piping water in from Lake Huron, a supply serviced by Detroit, Flint officials agreed to receive water from a new state and regional water system, but it had not yet come online.[386] In the meantime, the city decided to pump water to the public from the Flint River. After residents begin complaining about the taste and coloration of tap water, positive tests for *Escherichia coli* bacteria prompted officials to add more chlorine into the water supply.[387] The solution proved worse than the problem. The additional chlorine, without additional treatment, corroded the pipes and allowed lead to leach into the drinking water.

Residents reported hair loss, skin rashes, and many other physiological problems, all signs of lead poisoning, a neurotoxin that causes brain damage and developmental and behavioral problems. Dr. Mona Hanna-Attisha, director of the Hurley Medical Center's pediatric residency program in Flint, discovered that the number of children with elevated lead levels had doubled since the water supply switch.[388] Particularly for children under five years old, lead poisoning can lead to long-term health issues such as kidney dysfunction, high blood pressure, and hearing loss. Furious and horrified parents were warned that their children might lose IQ points.

In a financial emergency, which Flint experienced following the financial crisis, state law allowed the Governor to place the city under state receivership and appoint a city manager. In 2011, Republican Governor Rick Snyder exercised his authority to take over Flint's municipal management.[389] The emergency city manager was given temporary, but complete authority over the business of the city, and a mandate to cut costs. The decision to draw tap water from the Flint River and join the new regional water system was projected to save more than $8 million over the next few years.[390] This was in addition to a number of other cost-cutting measures pursued by the emergency manager, including reducing the city's workforce by 25%.[391]

When the Flint city council voted, in early 2015, to switch its supply back to Detroit, the emergency city manager refused to do so, and state authorities continued to insist on the safety of the local water supply despite mounting evidence to the contrary. For six months, the state not only contested the emerging findings, but fought efforts to correct the problem, going so far as to ask a judge to deny a request for an injunction to switch the water supply back to Detroit.[392]

It was not until October 2015, nearly two years after the crisis began, that the Governor convened a task force to investigate the issue.[393] A few months later, the Governor acknowledged the truth, that the water supply had been contaminated and caused a public health crisis, and requested federal assistance. President Obama's declaration of emergency freed up nearly $5 million federal funds to help Flint cope with the crisis, providing water, filters, test kits, and other resources for 90 days.

The poisoning of Flint is more than just an egregious example of governmental malfeasance or a byproduct of fiscal distress. It is a harrowing expression of structural racism. Virtually all the hallmarks of contemporary structured racial inequality are present in Flint's history, demographics, economic and fiscal distress, concentrated poverty, and low levels of social and economic mobility.

Flint is a poor city hit hard by deindustrialization compounded by the financial crisis of 2007–2009 in a region that suffered the same fortunes. In fact, according to the U.S. Census Bureau in 2015, Flint was the second poorest city in the nation (behind Youngstown, Ohio), with more than 40% of its residents earning below the federal poverty line, far below the state average or 16.2% at the time.[394] Median income in the city is half that of the state.

Flint is not only impoverished, but it is predominantly Black. The particular kind of impoverishment that Flint residents suffer partly defines and epitomizes structural racism, as noted in Chapter 2. Only 4% of the U.S. population lives in neighborhoods of concentrated poverty, where 40% or more of the residents live below the poverty line, yet two-thirds these neighborhoods are predominantly non-white. Flint is one of a few cities in the entire country with city-wide levels of concentrated poverty.

Poor communities have less tax base capacity to fund local government and support public services and schools. Retail businesses and local banks flee high-poverty neighborhoods or avoid them in the first place. Due to the difficulty of finding fresh produce and healthy food, many of these places have been described as "food deserts."[395] Flint, according to some reports, does not even have a single traditional grocery store.[396] And what replace them are often predatory businesses that profit off poor customers, such as check-cashing services or pawn shops.

As described in Chapter 2, concentrated poverty is not only a deprivation of community resources, public and private, but it also clusters people with the greatest needs. Whereas poor residents in middle-class neighborhoods benefit from their neighbors wherewithal at the neighborhood and community level, residents in high-poverty neighborhoods compound their shared disadvantage.

For residents trapped in these neighborhoods, it is more than a denial of resources; living in concentrated poverty exacts a tax on residents who suffer it. While this is true generally across the nation, the tragedy of Flint, Michigan illustrates it only too vividly. For a city in desperate need of more services and investment, the austerity measures enacted by the state inflicted grievous injury.

In addition to the harms to the health and well-being of the people in Flint, the damage to the water infrastructure required replacement or a costly retrofit and upgrade. Part of the harm of structural racism is not simply the greater needs, but the incapacity to meet those needs. Wealthier, predominantly white communities have more resources and greater capacity to update and maintain their infrastructure, replace older infrastructure, and command the attention of elected leaders. In the case of Flint, the state simply ignored their needs.

Even as residents protested and the city council voted to switch water suppliers, the state insisted on the safety of local water, ignoring the emerging evidence and attacking the credibility of researchers questioning the state's claims. Local control and community health was sacrificed to save money. Rather than invest in the city and help revive its fortunes, state authorities imposed austerity, poisoning the city in the process.

Although the tragic mismanagement of the water supply by the state may shock our conscience, the problems run deeper than water. The health effects of the water contamination may be expected to compound the disadvantages of the Flint community, but did not create them. Flint's distress preceded the water crises. There are hundreds of fiscally distressed cities across America, from Stockton to Ferguson, grappling with crumbling infrastructure and legacies of disinvestment.

The 2007–2008 financial crisis exposed our nation's municipal fiscal instability as well as deepened it. The loss of tax revenue meant billions of dollars in state budget cuts, which, in turn, meant cuts to localities and municipalities and institutions of higher education who relied on state budget funds to support schools and infrastructure and provide services.[397] Municipal revenues crashed even as state contributions were slashed.

In the years following the crisis, the United States experienced a wave of municipal bankruptcies, trigged by the collapse of local revenue and cutbacks in state-aid resulting from the same.[398] A disproportionate number of these bankruptcies were predominantly non-white communities, from Detroit, Michigan to Stockton, California. Between 2007 and 2013, 27 urban municipalities declared bankruptcy or were taken into state receivership to manage their financial insolvency.[399]

These extreme cases only hint at the depth of the problem. Even politically powerful and more affluent suburbs have been caught in the vice grip of fiscal instability, unable to sustain their strategy of providing high-quality service at low cost by attracting and retaining affluent residents. For example, the suburb of Upper Arlington was forced, in 2014, to pass an income tax increase to generate needed revenue.[400] Newer, outer-ring suburbs can generate new revenue through development projects that draw new residents, and have fewer costs associated with infrastructure maintenance. Older, built-out suburbs, however, must rehabilitate or replace aging infrastructure to maintain their competitive position.

Much of the nation's water infrastructure, in particular, is reaching the end of its life cycle and is failing.[401] The American Society of Civil Engineers grades the nation's wastewater infrastructure as D-plus.[402] Tens of millions of Americans live in areas with water quality below federal standards. One study found that New York State will need to spend $36 billion over to maintain its wastewater system in coming years.[403] Even where the water supply is safe, the piping and infrastructure may not be. In the predominantly Black community of Mount Vernon, New York, more than a thousand families have human waste flow back out of toilets and gush out of sinks and bathtubs on account of century-old piping.[404]

Dozens of cities in the United States may be exposing children to lead poisoning.[405] Fourteen percent of children tested in Cleveland, for example, detected lead in the bloodstream.[406] In 2017, 22% of samples taken from Newark's water supply exceeded federal thresholds for lead.[407] The problem is worse in schools and childcare centers.[408]

In 2018, 56 out of 86 schools tested in Detroit had elevated lead and/or copper.[409] Dozens of schools in Maryland still have elevated levels of lead in the water.[410] A quarter of all childcare facilities in California have elevated lead in the water, with more than 60 such facilities found in Fresno County alone.[411] The CDC estimates that as many as 7.7% of all Black children in the United States may have elevated blood lead levels.[412] These facts help explain and overlay the findings on race and lead poisoning described in last chapter.

No emergency manager could fix these problems, and it is little wonder that they have failed. Whether the case is New Jersey taking over Camden or Michigan taking over Detroit, the problem is lack of resources to begin with, not mere mismanagement.[413] These cities have deferred maintenance and raised taxes. In Jackson, Mississippi, another heavily Black city, the estimated cost of repairing the city's dilapidated water infrastructure is $2 billion, according to the mayor in 2014.[414] Jackson adopted a 1 cent sales tax increase, but that only produces $14 million a year.[415] Even with federal contributions, the costs to repair these legacy systems far outstrip available funds. As a result, these communities suffer.[416]

It's difficult to imagine that the catastrophe in Flint would have occurred in a wealthier and predominantly white suburb of Detroit. Not because of better management, but because a regime of fiscal austerity would never have been imposed in the first place.[417] These communities can afford to repair and upgrade infrastructure or enjoy the political clout to command those resources. The use of the emergency manager has the effect of circumventing local democracy, especially for too many communities of color.[418] In the

The Origins of Structural Racism 177

wake of the disaster, the Michigan state legislatures' relative intransigence in allocating significant funding for Flint, and the parallel gridlock in Congress, reflect the lack of political influence these communities enjoy, no matter how dire their plight or compelling their story.[419]

The relationship between race and infrastructure is hardly new. In 2007, a federal court found a city in Ohio guilty of denying clean water to Black residents.[420] A more recent study found that minority areas were over four times as likely to suffer from an energy blackout than white-majority areas.[421] But these findings point toward a relationship that extends beyond water, sewer, or power systems and are broadly generalizable. From a structural perspective, patterns of residential life and government organization intersect to determine the resources available to different communities.

Perhaps no single incident more painfully illustrates the interlocking dynamics of structural racism and constrained opportunity in the 21st century more than the tragic poisoning of Flint, Michigan. As bad as conditions are in many of these fiscally distressed cities and neighborhoods, there is nowhere else to go. As Flint residents reported, they felt trapped.[422] Too many Black Americans, who had suffered for decades through employment and housing discrimination, the criminal justice system, and other predatory institutions, lack the resources to escape their circumstances.

***

This chapter explored the origins of contemporary structural racism as an ongoing and continuously evolving project, etched into opportunity structures at critical moments of the early 20th century through to the present. The arc of history may bend toward justice, but structural racism evinces a tendency to grow more entrenched and, often, pernicious over time.

This chapter reviewed the major fabrication points in the construction of the contemporary racial opportunity structure, but, due to space constraints, could not be comprehensive. Some critical policies and components were only glancingly touched on, including federal labor policy during the New Deal and after, or federal, state, and local tax policies. What was emphasized, however, is how new and disturbing developments generate and reinscribed racial inequality in contemporary opportunity structures.

Rather than a southern phenomenon that infiltrated or corrupted the rest of the country, structural racism is better understood as northern phenomenon that spread to the rest. The critical developments were more often piloted and initially implemented outside of the south, including northern and post-Jim Crow style residential segregation, the exercise of state authority to take over localities under the pretense of emergencies that were generally precipitated by disinvestment and fiscal austerity, novel forms of predatory lending such as subprime mortgages packaged into CDOs, and punitive sentencing laws such as mandatory minimums and three strikes laws. Rather than a product of Jim Crow or southern racial folkways, these were developments that were pioneered in states like California, Michigan, Illinois, New York, and New Jersey.

The critical point is that the structural racism we live with and under today is better understood as a product of contingency, novel adaptations, and policy choices made at critical moments of our more recent past than as a direct legacy of our nation's more distant past, an ineluctable update of white supremacy and inevitable extension of racial inequality from racial slavery and Jim Crow.

The past shapes the present and the future, but history is not destiny. Previous systems of racial domination and control have been successfully overturned. What replaced them was not inevitable but the product of choices and the outcome of contestation and negotiation, such as the failure to sustain Reconstruction in the wake of the Civil War.[423] There has been progress and regress, but the areas where regress is most evident and disparities most entrenched are those that define contemporary structural racial inequality.

To view contemporary structural racism as inevitable ignores not just the reality of progress but underestimates the power of resistance. American public schools, particularly in the south, were meaningfully desegregated for a generation, a stupendous accomplishment. The resegregation of our public schools was not inevitable, but a byproduct of powerful counter-adaptations and specific policy choices, including pivotal Supreme Court decisions.

Perhaps no episode illustrates this principle better than the subprime mortgage crisis, which shattered the global economy by targeting communities of color and stripping them of their wealth and wherewithal. The redline created the conditions for the reverse redline, but it was rapacious investment banks and their partners that exploited those conditions, aided by untimely deregulation.

This episode also illustrates how new developments may contribute to, extend, or amplify existing inequities and disparities, as they build upon, modify, or repurpose existing institutions, rules, and relationships in novel and unpredictable ways, such as how the HOLC's model city survey program was ultimately adopted by institutions that did not even exist at the time, as well as by the private market. Although many of these developments were racially inflected and produced tremendous racial harm, we misunderstand the etiology of these developments if we reduce them to racial antipathy, animosity, prejudice, or even anxiety, discomfort, or resentment. Such misunderstandings help explain why the typical prescriptions based on them have failed to solve the structural problem or reduce disparities maintained by these structures.

With a clearer understanding of the nature and origins of contemporary structural racism, the next chapter will prefigure a remedial corrective and curative policy agenda by delineating the principles upon which such a reparative agenda should be founded. A structural model for understanding the production of racial inequality radically transforms the terms of many familiar and seemingly settled policy positions and calls for a corresponding reassessment.

Notes

1. "Livonia city, Michigan," *U.S. Census Bureau*, accessed August 31, 2024, https://data.census.gov/profile/Livonia_city,_Michigan?g=160XX00US2649000.
2. "Demographics: Livonia, MI," Livonia, accessed October 13, 2024, https://livonia.gov/403/Demographics.
3. Proportionally, not by absolute numbers. https://belonging.berkeley.edu/city-snapshot-detroit.
4. Penick v. Columbus Bd. of Ed., 429 F. Supp. 229 (S.D. Ohio 1977). For a local history of desegregation in Columbus, see Gregory S. Jacobs, *Getting Around Brown: Desegregation, Development, and the Columbus Public Schools* (Columbus: Ohio State University Press, 1998).
5. As an example of how deep and intense such opposition was, see, Brett Gadsden, "Here's How Deep Biden's Busing Problem Runs," *Politico*, May 5, 2019, https://www.politico.com/magazine/story/2019/05/05/joe-biden-busing-problem-226791/.
6. Bruce Gellerman, "'It Was Like a War Zone': Busing In Boston," *WBUR*, September 5, 2014, https://www.wbur.org/news/2014/09/05/boston-busing-anniversary; Morgan v. Hennigan, 379 F. Supp. 410 (D. Mass. 1974).
7. J. Anthony Lukas, *Common Ground: A Turbulent Decade in the Lives of Three American Families* (New York: Vintage Books, 1986) (dramatizing the desegregation crisis from the perspective of three different families).
8. Bruce Gellerman, "How The Boston Busing Decision Still Affects City Schools 40 Years Later," *WBUR*, published June 20, 2014; last modified December 19, 2014, https://www.wbur.org/news/2014/06/20/boston-busing-ruling-anniversary.
9. Milliken v. Bradley, 418 U.S. 717 (1974); Michelle Adams, "How a Supreme Court Decision Kept School Segregation Alive," *Washington Post*, August 1, 2024, https://www.washingtonpost.com/opinions/2024/08/01/school-segregation-detroit-milliken-supreme-court-anniversary/.
10. Columbus Board of Education v. Penick, 443 U.S. 449 (1979). Bill Bush, "60 Years After Brown v. Board, Charter Schools Add to Segregation," *Columbus Dispatch*, May 17, 2014, https://www.dispatch.com/content/stories/local/2014/05/17/charters-add-to-segregation.html.
11. K-Sue Park, "The History Wars and Property Law: Conquest and Slavery as Foundational to the Field," *Yale Law Journal* 131, no. 4 (2022): 1062–1153, https://www.yalelawjournal.org/article/the-history-wars-and-property-law-conquest-and-slavery-as-foundational-to-the-field
12. C. Vann Woodward, *The Strange Career of Jim Crow* (New York: Oxford University Press, 2002), 7–9.
13. The "legacy" or "cumulative effects" theories of racial disadvantage are prominent in structural presentations or structural conceptions of racial inequality. See, for example, Devah Pager and Hana Shepherd, "The Sociology of Discrimination: Racial Discrimination in Employment, Housing, Credit, and Consumer Markets," *Annual Review of Sociology* 34 (2008): 181–209, https://doi.org/10.1146/annurev.soc.33.040406.131740 (describing these as two of three "structural" conceptions). See also Thomas A. DiPrete and Gregory M. Eirich, "Cumulative Advantage as a Mechanism for Inequality: A Review of Theoretical and Empirical Developments," *Annual Review of Sociology* 32 (2006): 271–297, https://doi.org/10.1146/annurev.soc.32.061604.123127. They are not only well theorized, but they are among some of the earliest deep scholarship on racial inequality, going back to Gunnar Myrdal's landmark *An American Dilemma*, where he introduced the idea of "cumulative causation." Gunnar Myrdal, *An American Dilemma* (New York: Harper & Row, 1944; New Brunswick, NK: Transaction Publishers, 1996), 1065.

14 Logan and Stults, *Persistence of Segregation*, 5. See also Menendian, Gambhir, and Hsu, "Most to Least Segregated Cities," in "Roots of Structural Racism, 2020," https://belonging.berkeley.edu/most-least-segregated-cities-in-2020.
15 For an insightful and revealing view of how this history affected American political and policy development, see Alberto Alesina, Edward Glaeser, and Bruce Sacerdote, "Why Doesn't the US Have a European-Style Welfare State?," *Harvard Institute of Economic Research* (2001), https://scholar.harvard.edu/files/glaeser/files/why_doesnt_the_u.s._have_a_european-style_welfare_state.pdf.
16 Equal Justice Initiative, *Segregation in America* (Montgomery, AL: Equal Justice Initiative, 2018), https://segregationinamerica.eji.org/report/.
17 john a. powell, "The Law and Significance of Plessy," *RSF: The Russell Sage Foundation Journal of the Social Science* 7, no. 1 (2021): 20–31, https://www.rsfjournal.org/content/7/1/20.
18 Sander, Kucheva, and Zasloff, *Moving Toward Integration*, 23.
19 Richard C. Wade, "Residential Segregation in the Antebellum South," in *The Rise of the Ghetto,* ed. John H. Brace, Jr., August Meier, and Elliot Rudwick (Belmont, CA: Wadsworth, 1971), 10–14.
20 Nicholas J. Demerath and Harlan W. Gilmore, "The Ecology of Southern Cities," in *The Urban South*, ed. Rupert B. Vance and Nicholas J. Demerath (Chapel Hill: University of North Carolina Press, 1954), 120–125.
21 Jackson, *Crabgrass Frontier*, 18.
22 Although not necessarily as neighbors. See Logan and Parman, "National Rise in Residential Segregation," arguing that Black people had few white neighbors in the south although they lived closer to whites than communities in the north.
23 Although this is the consensus view, there are several studies arguing that the North was more residentially segregated than is generally appreciated in this period. See John R. Logan and Benjamin Bellman, "Before The Philadelphia Negro: Residential Segregation in a Nineteenth-Century Northern City," *Social Science History* 40, no. 4 (2016): 683–706, https://www.cambridge.org/core/journals/social-science-history/article/before-the-philadelphia-negro-residential-segregation-in-a-nineteenthcentury-northern-city/104BF8472868BF3705F6E7929BEB00DD; Angelina Grigoryeva and Martin Ruef, "The Historical Demography of Racial Segregation," *American Sociological Review* 80, no. 4 (2015): 814–842, https://journals.sagepub.com/doi/pdf/10.1177/0003122415589170.
24 Massey and Denton, *American Apartheid*, 24, table 2.2.
25 Massey and Denton, 23.
26 Massey and Denton, 24, table 2.2.
27 Logan and Parman, "National Rise in Residential Segregation," 159.
28 Richard Rothstein, *The Color of Law, A Forgotten History of How Our Government Segregated America* (London: Liveright Publishing Corporation 2017), 41. Yet, by 1930, only 11 of the state's 56 counties had Black residents.
29 Douglas S. Massey, "Origins of Economic Disparities: The Historical Role of Housing Segregation," in Carr and Kutty, *Segregation*, 41.
30 W.E.B. Du Bois, *The Philadelphia Negro: A Social Study* (Philadelphia: University of Philadelphia Press, 1899), 23.
31 Massey and Denton, *American Apartheid*, 21, table 2.1.
32 john a. powell, Samuel L. Myers, and Susan T. Gooden, "Introduction to the Issue," *Russell Sage Foundation Journal of the Social Sciences* 7, no. 1 (2021): 1–17, https://doi.org/10.7758/RSF.2021.7.1.01; John R. Logan and Brian J. Stults, *Metropolitan Segregation: No Breakthrough in Sight* (Providence, RI: Brown University, Diversity and Disparities Project, 2021), https://s4.ad.brown.edu/Projects/Diversity/Data/Report/report08122021.pdf.
33 Sander, Kucheva, and Zasloff, *Moving Toward Integration*, 43–44.

34 *Report of the National Advisory Commission on Civil Disorders* (hereafter cited as Kerner Report) (Washington, DC: Kerner Commission, 1968), 6, https://belonging.berkeley.edu/sites/default/files/kerner_commission_full_report.pdf?file=1&force=1. For details, see Dan Kopf, "The Great Migration: The African American Exodus from the South," *Priceonomics*, January 28, 2016, https://priceonomics.com/the-great-migration-the-african-american-exodus/.
35 *Kerner Report*, viii, 12.
36 James R. Grossman, *Land of Hope: Chicago, Black Southerners, and the Great Migration* (Chicago: University of Chicago Press, 1989).
37 Sugrue, *Urban Crisis*, 26.
38 Isabel Wilkerson, *The Warmth of Other Suns: The Epic Story of America's Great Migration* (New York: Random House, 2010); Isabel Wilkerson, "Emmett Till and Tamir Rice, Sons of the Great Migration," *New York Times*, February 12, 2016, https://www.nytimes.com/2016/02/14/opinion/sunday/emmett-till-and-tamir-rice-sons-of-the-great-migration.html.
39 Kevin Fox Gotham, "Urban Space, Restrictive Covenants and the Origins of Racial Residential Segregation in a US City, 1900–50," *International Journal of Urban and Regional Research* 24, no. 3 (2000): 620, https://doi.org/10.1111/1468-2427.00268.
40 Sugrue, *Urban Crisis*, 26.
41 Gotham, "Urban Space," 620.
42 Gotham, 620.
43 Rothstein, *Color of Law*, 159.
44 Grossman, *Land of Hope*.
45 Sugrue, *Urban Crisis*, 33.
46 James Gilbert Cassedy, "African Americans and the American Labor Movement," *Federal Records and African American History* 29, no. 2 (1997), https://www.archives.gov/publications/prologue/1997/summer/american-labor-movement.html.
47 Michael Goldfield, "Race and the CIO: The Possibilities for Racial Egalitarianism during the 1930s and 1940s," *International Labor and Working-Class History* no. 44 (Fall 1993): 1–32.
48 David E. Bernstein, *Only One Place of Redress: African Americans, Labor Regulations, and the Courts from Reconstruction to the New Deal* (Durham, NC: Duke University Press, 2001), 47, 53.
49 Sugrue, *Urban Crisis*, 156–157.
50 Gilbert Osofsky, *Harlem: The Making of a Ghetto: Negro New York 1890–1930* (New York: Harper and Row, 1963); Kusmer, *A Ghetto Takes Shape*.
51 Gordon W. Allport, *The Nature of Prejudice* (Garden City, NY: Doubleday Anchor, 1958), 74 cited in Massey and Denton, American Apartheid, 49.
52 Jonathan English, "Why Did America Give Up on Mass Transit? (Don't Blame Cars.)," *Bloomberg CityLab*, August 31, 2018, https://www.bloomberg.com/news/features/2018-08-31/why-is-american-mass-transit-so-bad-it-s-a-long-story.
53 Fischel, *Zoning Rules*, 134, 172.
54 Maureen E. Brady, "Turning Neighbors Into Nuisances," *Harvard Law Review* 134, no. 5 (2021): 1609, https://harvardlawreview.org/2021/03/turning-neighbors-into-nuisances/.
55 Menendian, "Uneven March," 81.
56 Yick Wo v. Hopkins, 118 US 356 (1886).
57 "Los Angeles Zoning Rules," Los Angeles City Planning, accessed April 15, 2025, https://planning.lacity.gov/zoning/local-zoning-rules.
58 Jerry Frug, "The Geography of Community," *Stanford Law Review* 48, no. 5 (1996): 1081, https://doi.org/10.2307/1229380.

59 James Burling, "America's Sordid History of Exclusionary Zoning," *Real Estate Issues* 44, no. 21 (2020): 2, https://www.cre.org/real-estate-issues/americas-sordid-history-of-exclusionary-zoning/.
60 Edward M. Bassett et al., *A Zoning Primer* (Washington, DC: Washington Government Printing Office, 1922), 2, https://www.govinfo.gov/content/pkg/GOVPUB-C13-cf208d8ed0dda43ed677acd6cad8be81/pdf/GOVPUB-C13-cf208d8ed0dda43ed677acd6cad8be81.pdf.
61 Kenneth T. Jackson, *Crabgrass Frontier: The Suburbanization of the United States* (New York: Oxford University Press, 1985), 242.
62 Nicole Montojo, Eli Moore, and Nicole Mauri, *Roots, Race, Place: A History of Racially Exclusionary Housing in the San Francisco Bay Area* (Berkeley, CA: Othering and Belonging Institute, 2019), https://belonging.berkeley.edu/rootsraceplace.
63 Garrett Power, "Apartheid Baltimore Style: the Residential Segregation Ordinances of 1910-1913," *Maryland Law Review* 42, no. 2 (1983): 289–328, https://digitalcommons.law.umaryland.edu/mlr/vol42/iss2/4.
64 Buchanan v. Warley, 245 U.S. 60 (1917). For the cities that adopted them, *see* Rothstein, *Color of Law*, 44.
65 *Village of Euclid, Ohio v. Ambler Realty Co.*, 272 U.S. 365 (1926). This case is the origin of the phrase "Euclidian" zoning. Euclid refers to the city whose ordinance was challenged in this case, and that term is now a synonym for function or "use" zoning.
66 Belle Lettre, "Restrictive Covenants in the 'Modern' Era," *Law and Letters*, May 18, 2021, https://lawandletters.blogspot.com/2006/05/restrictive-covenants-in-modern-era.html.
67 Kirsten Delegard and Kevin Ehrman-Solberg, "'Playground of the People'? Mapping Racial Covenants in Twentieth-Century Minneapolis," *Open Rivers: Rethinking The Mississippi*, no. 6 (2017): 74, https://editions.lib.umn.edu/openrivers/article/mapping-racial-covenants-in-twentieth-century-minneapolis/.
68 This is one reason it is difficult to remove such language from property records. See Greg Latshaw, "Racism Shadows Property Covenants," *USA Today*, August 3, 2010, https://www.pressreader.com/usa/usa-today-us-edition/20100803/282729108188112; see also Catherine Silva, *Racial Restrictive Covenants History: Enforcing Neighborhood Segregation in Seattle* (Seattle: The Seattle Civil Rights and Labor History Project: 2009), https://depts.washington.edu/civilr/covenants_report.htm
69 Rothstein, *Color of Law*, 79.
70 Michael Jones-Correa, "The Origins and Diffusion of Racial Restrictive Covenants," *Political Science Quarterly* 115, no. 4 (2000): 551.
71 See Gene Slater, "Defending Racial Covenants," chap. 8 in *Freedom to Discriminate: How Realtors Conspired to Segregate Housing and Divide America* (Berkeley, CA: Heyday, 2021) for a summary discussion of these cases.
72 *Mapping Prejudice: Visualizing the Hidden Histories of Race and Privilege in the Built Environment* (Minneapolis: University of Minnesota, 2020), https://mappingprejudice.umn.edu/.
73 "Racial Restrictive Covenants," Seattle Civil Rights & Labor History Project, https://depts.washington.edu/civilr/covenants.htm.
74 "Racial Restriction and Housing Discrimination in the Chicagoland Area," Digital Chicago - Lake Forest College, https://digitalchicagohistory.org/exhibits/show/restricted-chicago/restrictive_covenants.
75 Sarah Shoenfeld and Mara Cherkasky, "Mapping Segregation in Washington, D.C.," *Preservation Leadership Forum*, June 22, 2015, https://forum.savingplaces.org/blogs/special-contributor/2015/06/22/mapping-segregation-in-washington-dc; Sarah Shoenfeld and Mara Cherkasky, "The Legacy of Racial

Covenants 1940-2010" *Mapping Segregation DC, 2021,* https://www.mappingsegregationdc.org/

76 Judy L. Thomas, "'Curse of Covenant' Persists — Restrictive Rules, While Unenforceable, Have Lingering Legacy," *Kansas City Star,* July 27, 2016, https://web.archive.org/web/20200926032949/https://www.kansascity.com/news/local/article92156112.html.

77 Massey and Denton, "The Construction of the Ghetto," in *American Apartheid,* 36–38; Gotham, "Urban Space," 616, 618.

78 *Shelley v. Kraemer,* 334 U.S. 1 (1948).

79 Although JFK issued an executive order in 1962 prohibiting the use of federal funds for racial discrimination in financing, it was not until nearly a year and half later that the US Solicitor General allowed that the FHA would no longer insure mortgages with restrictive covenants. Rothstein, *Color of Law,* 87. Despite this, the FHA board announced that it would ignore the rule. Other scholars, contrarily, claim that the *Shelley* ruling was more swiftly implemented and produced significant desegregation. See Sander, Kucheva, and Zasloff, *Moving Toward Integration,* 62–82.

80 Andrew H. Whittemore, "Origins of Deed Restrictions in the United States: The Case of Early-Nineteenth Century Boston," *Journal of Planning History* 23, no. 3 (2024): 214–233.

81 Robert C. Weaver, *The Negro Ghetto* (New York: Russel & Russel, 1948), 216.

82 Clair St. Drake and Horace R. Cayton, *Black Metropolis: A Study of Negro Life in a Northern City* (New York: Harper and Row: 1945, 1962).

83 Weaver, *Negro Ghetto,* 217.

84 Rothstein, *Color of Law,* 228.

85 Gotham, "Urban Space," 621, citing Marc Weiss, *The Rise of Community Builders: The American Real Estate Industry and Urban Land Planning* (New York: Columbia University Press, 1987), 149, and Pearl Janet Davies, *Real Estate in American History* (Washington, DC: Public Affairs Press, 1958), 547–548.

86 Slater, *Freedom to Discriminate,* 85.

87 Gotham, "Urban Space," 618.

88 Sugrue, *Urban Crisis,* 46.

89 Jonathan Rothwell, *A Republic of Equals: A Manifesto for a Just Society* (Princeton: Princeton University Press, 2019), 200–202; Gotham, "Urban Space," 618.

90 Massey, "Economic Disparities," 55.

91 Sugrue, *Urban Crisis,* 211.

92 Kevin Fox Gotham attributes additional significance to these campaigns in fostering an "ideology" of segregation and circulating negative stereotypes. Gotham, "Urban Space," 617.

93 For background on homeowners' associations, see Roithmayr, *Reproducing Racism* 35 (describing them as akin to a "paramilitary cartel"), 38–39, 44–45.

94 Gotham, "Urban Space," 627.

95 Such as J.C. Nichols. Gotham, "Urban Space," 626.

96 Sugrue, *Urban Crisis,* 212; Rothstein, *Color of Law,* 79; Gotham, "Urban Space," 628.

97 Sugrue, 226–227. See e.g., Slater, *Freedom to Discriminate,* 15.

98 Joel Oliphint, "Redlining, race covenants: The roots of Columbus' ongoing color divide," *Columbus Monthly,* June 27, 2018, updated February 16, 2023, https://www.columbusmonthly.com/story/entertainment/human-interest/2018/06/28/cover-roots-columbus-ongoing-color/11644783007/.

99 Diane Kelly Runyon and Kim Shoemaker Starr, *Secrets Under the Parking Lot: The True Story of Upper Arlington, Ohio, and the History of Perry Township in the Nineteenth Century* (CreateSpace Independent Publishing Platform, 2019).

100 David F. Krugler, "Introduction," in *1919, The Year of Racial Violence: How African Americans Fought Back* (Cambridge: Cambridge University Press, 2014), 3.
101 History.com Editors, "The Great Migration: Life for Migrants in the City," *History*, June 28, 2021, https://www.history.com/topics/black-history/great-migration#section_3.
102 The Chicago Commission on Race Relations, *The Negro in Chicago: A Study of Race Relations and a Race Riot* (Chicago: University of Chicago Press, 1922), https://moses.law.umn.edu/darrow/documents/The_Negro_in_Chicago_1922.pdf.
103 Scott Ellsworth and John Hope Franklin, "Race Riot," in *Death in a Promised Land: The Tulsa Race Riot of 1921* (Baton Rouge: Louisiana State University Press, 1992), 66. The official government report on this was released in January of 2025. US Department of Justice Civil Rights Division, *A.C. Jackson–Review and Evaluation* (Washington, DC: US Department of Justice, 2025), https://www.justice.gov/crt/case/ac-jackson. For a visualization, see Yuliya Parshina-Kottas et al., "What the Tulsa Race Massacre Destroyed," *New York Times*, May 24, 2021, https://www.nytimes.com/interactive/2021/05/24/us/tulsa-race-massacre.html.
104 "On July 3, 1917: White Mobs Terrorize Black Residents in East St. Louis," *Equal Justice Initiative*, accessed October 11, 2024, https://calendar.eji.org/racial-injustice/jul/03.
105 James W. Loewen, *Sundown Towns: A Hidden Dimension of American Racism* (New York: New Press, 2005).
106 Matt Cheney, "Historical Database of Sundown Towns," *History and Social Justice*, accessed February 27, 2025, https://justice.tougaloo.edu/sundown-towns/using-the-sundown-towns-database/state-map/.
107 Richard Rothstein, "Furor Over Montana Judge Presents Opportunity to Confront the Origins of Our Racial Divide," *Economic Policy Institute*, March 7, 2012, https://www.epi.org/publication/furor-montana-judge-misses-opportunity-confront/.
108 Keith Oppenheim, "Texas City Haunted by 'No Blacks After Dark' Part," *CNN*, December 13, 2006, https://www.cnn.com/2006/US/12/08/oppenheim.sundown.town/; Shira Li Bartov, "Black Truck Driver Tells Horrifying Story of His Night in a 'Sundown Town,'" *Newsweek*, May 12, 2022, https://www.newsweek.com/black-truck-driver-tells-horrifying-story-night-sundown-town-texas-viral-tiktok-1706156.
109 Massey and Denton, *American Apartheid*, 34.
110 Sugrue, *Urban Crisis*, 232.
111 Sugrue, 233–234.
112 Sheryll Cashin, *White Space, Black Hood: Opportunity Hoarding and Segregation in the Age of Inequality* (Boston: Beacon Press, 2021), 45.
113 Cashin, *White Space, Black Hood*, 50.
114 *See* the story of Mr. and Mrs. Myers, in Rothstein, *Color of Law*, 141–143.
115 Sugrue, *Urban Crisis*, 249.
116 Associated Press, "Samuel Snipes, 99, Dies; Lawyer for First Black Family in Levittown, Pa.," *New York Times*, January 10, 2019, https://www.nytimes.com/2019/01/10/obituaries/samuel-snipes-dead.html.
117 Leonard S. Rubinowitz and Imani Perry, "Crimes Without Punishment: White Neighbors' Resistance to Black Entry," *Journal of Criminal Law & Criminology* 92, no. 2 (2001): 335–428. "Map of 73 Years of Lynchings," *New York Times*, February 9, 2015, https://www.nytimes.com/interactive/2015/02/10/us/map-of-73-years-of-lynching.html using data from Equal Justice Initiative, *Lynching in America: Confronting the Legacy of Racial Terror* (Montgomery, AL: Equal Justice Initiative, 2017), https://eji.org/wp-content/uploads/2005/11/lynching-in-america-3d-ed-110121.pdf.

118 Rothstein, *Color of Law*, 147.
119 Sugrue, *Urban Crisis*, 73–74.
120 Arnold Hirsch, "An Era of Hidden Violence," in *Making the Second Ghetto: Race and Housing in Chicago 1940-1960* (Chicago: Chicago University Press, 1998), 53.
121 Oliphint, "Redlining, race covenants."
122 Jackson, *Crabgrass Frontier*, 197, fn 25 (explaining that one of the reasons for this was that an amendment to the 1863 National bank Act prohibited nationally charted banks from "making direct loans for real-estate transactions").
123 Alexander James Field, "Uncontrolled Land Development and the Duration of the Depression in the United States," *Journal of Economic History* 52, no. 4 (1992): 785–805, https://www.jstor.org/stable/2123227.
124 Jackson, *Crabgrass Frontier*, 193.
125 Lizabeth Cohen, "The Lessons of the Great Depression," *Atlantic*, May 17, 2020, https://www.theatlantic.com/ideas/archive/2020/05/how-rebuild-nation/611704/ ("The New Deal ... funded relief, jobs, and infrastructure. In the longer term, it established a new normal that included a national retirement system, unemployment insurance, disability benefits, minimum wages and maximum hours, public housing, mortgage protection, electrification of rural America, and the right of industrial labor to bargain collectively through unions").
126 Carr and Kutty, "The New Imperative for Equality," in *Segregation*, 7.
127 Massey, "Economic Disparities," 69.
128 Todd M. Michney and LaDale Winling, "New Perspectives on New Deal Housing Policy: Explicating and Mapping HOLC Loans to African Americans," *Journal of Urban History* 46, no. 1 (2019): 151, https://journals.sagepub.com/doi/abs/10.1177/0096144218819429.
129 Charles Courtemanche and Kenneth Snowden, "Repairing a Mortgage Crisis: HOLC Lending and Its Impact on Local Housing Markets," *Journal of Economic History* 71, no. 2 (2011): 307–337, https://www.jstor.org/stable/23018301. More recent estimates place the figure even higher, maintaining that the HOLC approved 2.3 million mortgages in 1934. See also Sander, Kucheva, and Zasloff, *Moving Toward Integration*, 95, citing *Historical Statistics of the United States: Millennial Edition*, vol. 4 (New York: Cambridge University Press, 2000), 540.
130 Jackson, *Crabgrass Frontier,* 199. For a detailed examination and series of examples, see Ryan Best and Elena Mejia, "The Lasting Legacy of Redlining," *FiveThirtyEight*, February 9, 2022, https://projects.fivethirtyeight.com/redlining/. All available HOLC maps have been digitized by the Mapping Inequality project: Robert K. Nelson et al., "Mapping Inequality: Redlining in The New Deal America," *American Panorama: An Atlas of United States History* (Richmond, VA: Digital Scholarship Lab, University of Richmond, 2022), https://dsl.richmond.edu/panorama/redlining/. Apparently, no one knows how many maps were created or used in total, but over 200 have been found and digitized.
131 Jackson, *Crabgrass Frontier*, 199, Figure 11-1.
132 Massey and Denton, *American Apartheid*, 69.
133 There is an unresolved scholarly debate about the extent to which loans were denied to African-Americans in racially *segregated* neighborhoods. See Sander, Kucheva, and Zasloff, *Moving Toward Integration*, 253–255. See also Menendian and Rothstein, "Putting Integration on the Agenda," 164.
134 Jackson, *Crabgrass Frontier*, 201.
135 Jackson, 198. Jackson explains that appraisal literature in the 1930s advised wariness of neighborhoods with increasing populations of certain ethnic groups, while "experts" at the time emphasized correlations between declining property values and increases in Black residents.

136 Price V. Fishback, et al., "The HOLC Maps How Race and Poverty Influenced Real Estate Professionals' Evaluation of Lending Risk in the 1930s" (working paper, National Bureau of Economic Research, 2020, revised 2021), 10, https://www.nber.org/papers/w28146. Although HOLC maps, as noted above, have been digitized and are publicly accessible, most of the FHA redlining maps, however, were apparently destroyed and lost (Fishback et al., 3).
137 Daniel Aaronson, Daniel Hartley, and Bhashkar Mazumder, "The Effects of the 1930s HOLC 'Redlining' Maps," *Federal Reserve Bank of Chicago*, WP 2017-12 (revised 2020): 4, https://www.chicagofed.org/publications/working-papers/2017/wp2017-12. To see another visualization of this, see: Emily Badger, "How Redlining's Racist Effects Lasted for Decades," *New York Times*, August 24, 2017, https://www.nytimes.com/2017/08/24/upshot/how-redlinings-racist-effects-lasted-for-decades.html
138 Bruce Mitchell and Juan Franco, *HOLC "Redlining" Maps: The Persistent Structure of Segregation and Economic Inequality* (Washington, DC: National Community Reinvestment Coalition, 2018): 18, https://ncrc.org/wp-content/uploads/dlm_uploads/2018/02/NCRC-Research-HOLC-10.pdf.
139 See Aaronson, Hartley, and Mazumder, "Effects of Redlining Maps."
140 The National Housing Act of 1934, H.R. 9620, Pub. L. 73–479, 48 Stat. 1246 (1934).
141 Ira Katznelson, *When Affirmative Action Was White: An Untold Story of Racial Inequality in Twentieth-Century America* (New York: W. W. Norton, 2005), 115.
142 Jackson, *Crabgrass Frontier*, 205.
143 See Table 3.1. Fischel, however, attributes at least a quarter of this growth to the rise in middle-class income after WWII. Fischel, *Zoning Rules*, 353.
144 Cashin, *Failures of Integration*, 110–111.
145 Gotham, "Urban Space," 616, 625.
146 John Griffith, *The Federal Housing Administration Saved the Housing Market* (Center for American Progress, 2012), https://www.americanprogress.org/article/the-federal-housing-administration-saved-the-housing-market/.
147 Massey, "Economic Disparities," 72, and only changed its recommendations two years after the Supreme Court ruled them unenforceable.
148 Rothstein, *Color of Law*, 65.
149 Rothstein, 65.
150 Gotham, "Urban Space," 625–626.
151 For example, white families who wanted to move to East Palo Alto could not. Rothstein, *Color of Law*, 11–13.
152 The FHA financed roughly 70,000 loans for Black home purchases between 1935 and 1950. Sander, Kucheva, and Zasloff, *Moving Toward Integration*, 99.
153 Charles M. Lamb and Adam W. Nye, "Do Presidents Control Bureaucracy? The Federal Housing Administration through the Truman-Eisenhower Era," *Political Science Quarterly* 127, no. 3 (2012): 446, 454, https://www.jstor.org/stable/23563185?seq=1#metadata_info_tab_contents.
154 Nikole Hannah-Jones, "Living Apart: How the Government Betrayed a Landmark Civil Rights Law," *ProPublica*, June 25, 2015, https://www.propublica.org/article/living-apart-how-the-government-betrayed-a-landmark-civil-rights-law.
155 David Rusk, *Inside Game/Outside Game: Winning Strategies for Saving Urban America* (New York: Century Foundation Books, 1999), 86–88. Even after the Supreme Court's 1954 *Brown* decision, the Eisenhower administration asserted that the opinion did not apply to housing. Rothstein, *Color of Law*, 33.
156 Gotham, "Urban Space," 626.
157 Sylvia F. Porter, "Babies Equal Boom," condensed from *New York Post, Readers' Digest* (August 1951): 5-6 (for first use of term); Sandra L. Colby and Jennifer M. Ortman, "The Baby Boom Cohort in the United States 2012-2060," *Population*

Estimates and Projections (U.S. Department of Commerce: Economics and Statistics Administration, U.S. Census Bureau, 2014): 2, https://www.census.gov/content/dam/Census/library/publications/2014/demo/p25-1141.pdf.
158 Wilson, *When Work Disappears*, 185.
159 Massey, "Economic Disparities," 63.
160 Jackson, *Crabgrass Frontier*, 283–284, Table 16-1.
161 Matthew Desmond, "How Homeownership Became the Engine of American Inequality," *New York Times*, May 9, 2017, https://www.nytimes.com/2017/05/09/magazine/how-homeownership-became-the-engine-of-american-inequality.html.
162 Massey, "Economic Disparities," 71.
163 Jackson, *Crabgrass Frontier*, 215.
164 Massey and Denton, *American Apartheid*, 63.
165 Richard F. Weingroff, "Federal-Aid Highway Act of 1956: Creating The Interstate System," *Public Roads* 60, no. 1 (1996), https://highways.dot.gov/public-roads/summer-1996/federal-aid-highway-act-1956-creating-interstate-system.
166 Jackson, *Crabgrass Frontier*, 250.
167 Semuels, "Role of Highways."
168 Nathaniel Baum-Snow, "Did Highways Cause Suburbanization?," *Quarterly Journal of Economics* 122, no. 2 (2007): 775.
169 Joseph Stromberg, "The Real Story Behind the Demise of America's Once-Mighty Streetcars," *Vox*, May 7, 2015, https://www.vox.com/2015/5/7/8562007/streetcar-history-demise.
170 Julie Lasky, "Levittown, N.Y.: The Original Starter Community," *New York Times,* December 19, 2018, https://www.nytimes.com/2018/12/19/realestate/levittown-ny-the-original-starter-community.html.
171 Jackson, *Crabgrass Frontier*, 241.
172 Sander, Kucheva, and Zasloff, *Moving Toward Integration*, 106–107.
173 Howard Schuman et al., *Racial Attitudes in America: Trends and Interpretations* (Cambridge: Harvard University Press, 1998).
174 Slater, *Freedom to Discriminate*.
175 Clarence J. Wurdock, "Neighborhood Racial Transition: A Study of the Role of White Flight," *Urban Affairs Review* 17, no. 1 (1981): 75–89, https://doi.org/10.1177/004208168101700105.
176 Logan, *Separate and Unequal*, 1.
177 Parliament, "Chocolate City," track 1 on *Chocolate City*, Casablanca, 1975, compact disc; Reynolds Farley et al., "'Chocolate City, Vanilla Suburbs:' Will the Trend toward Racially Separate Communities Continue?," *Social Science Research* 7, no. 4 (1978): 320.
178 For a summary of this development, Jackson, *Crabgrass Frontier*, 257–261.
179 Massey and Denton, *American Apartheid*, 55.
180 Two prominent examples are the the National Labor Relations Act of 1935, which facilitated union organizing, and the 1938 Fair Labor Standards Act, which mandated a 40-hour workweek and a minimum wage, exempted agricultural and domestic workers, sectors that disproportionately employed Black southerners, in particular. Ira Katznelson, *When Affirmative Action Was White*, 57; Ira Katznelson, *Fear Itself: The New Deal and The Origins of Our Time*, (New York: Liveright Publishing Corporation, 2013), 260–70; Ira Katznelson, "Making Affirmative Action White Again," *New York Times*, August 12, 2017, https://www.nytimes.com/2017/08/12/opinion/sunday/making-affirmative-action-white-again.html
181 Housing Act of 1949, 42 U.S.C. § 1471 (2024).
182 Sugrue, *Urban Crisis*, 47.
183 Cashin, *White Space, Black Hood*, 17.

188 *Structural Racism*

184 James Baldwin, interview by Dr. Kenneth Clark, *Perspectives: Negro and the American Promise*, interviewed by Kenneth Clark, May 24, 1963, https://www.youtube.com/watch?v=T8Abhj17kYU.
185 National Industrial Recovery Act, 15 U.S.C. § 703 (1933).
186 Jackson, *Crabgrass Frontier*, 221.
187 United States Housing Act of 1937, Pub. L. 75-412, 50 Stat. 888 (1937).
188 Jackson, *Crabgrass Frontier*, 224.
189 Rothstein, *Color of Law*, 20.
190 Rothstein, 21.
191 See Katznelson, *When Affirmative Action Was White*, 127, 163, noting that many New Deal era programs had a structure of federal funds administered or controlled by local authorities, as was the case here, and the results tended to be discriminatory in their effects.
192 Alex Kotlowitz, *There Are No Children Here: The Story of Two Boys Growing Up in the Other America* (New York: Doubleday, 1991), 21.
193 See Jackson, *Crabgrass Frontier*, 226, describing where Senator Paul Douglas exhorted his colleagues to "set aside their principles" to pass the law.
194 Kotlowitz, *No Children Here*, 21.
195 Sugrue, *Urban Crisis*, 84.
196 The Oakwood and Sojourner Truth projects were two notable examples. Sugrue, *Urban Crisis*, 249.
197 See Cal. Const. art. XXXIV, § 1, "Public Housing Project Law," https://leginfo.legislature.ca.gov/faces/codes_displayText.xhtml?lawCode=CONS&division=&title=&part=&chapter=&article=XXXIV. See also Liam Dillon, "A dark side to the California dream: How the state Constitution makes affordable housing hard to build," *Los Angeles Times*, February 3, 2019, https://www.latimes.com/politics/la-pol-ca-affordable-housing-constitution-20190203-story.html.
198 Jackson, *Crabgrass Frontier*, 224.
199 Lee DeGraw, "10 Infamous US Housing Projects," *ListVerse*, February 27, 2016, https://listverse.com/2016/02/27/10-infamous-us-housing-projects/; St. Louis Public Radio, "New documentary sheds light on the story of Pruitt-Igoe," *St. Louis Public Radio*, April 4, 2011, https://news.stlpublicradio.org/arts/2011-04-04/new-documentary-sheds-light-on-the-story-of-pruitt-igoe.
200 The Public Housing Authority anticipated this. In Detroit, the City Plan Commission argued that "locating small projects in various areas rather than large ones in one general area" would offer "better means of integration with neighborhoods…and less evidence and feeling of institutionalism." Sugrue, *Urban Crisis*, 86, citing City Plan Commission Minutes, no. 16 (1950), 241; "Speech by Hugo Schwartz to the Eastern Detroit Exchange Club" (speech, Detroit, April 12, 1950), *Detroit Times*.
201 Fair Housing Act, 42 U.S.C. § 3601 (1968). For a list of fair housing ordinances, see Menendian, "Uneven March," 117, Table 2.
202 Stephen Menendian, "Affirmatively Furthering Fair Housing: A Reckoning with Government-Sponsored Segregation in the 21st Century," *National Civic Review* 106, no. 3 (2017), 20, https://www.jstor.org/stable/10.1002/naticivirevi.106.3.0020.
203 john a. powell, "View of Reflections on the Past, Looking to the Future: The Fair Housing Act at 40," *Indiana Law Review* 41, no. 3 (2008): 606, https://journals.iupui.edu/index.php/inlawrev/article/view/3949.
204 "HUD Announces New Proposed "Affirmatively Furthering Fair Housing" Rule, Taking a Major Step Towards Rooting Out Longstanding Inequities in Housing and Fostering Inclusive Communities," *U.S. Department of Housing and Urban Development*, January 19, 2023, https://www.hud.gov/press/press_releases_media_advisories/HUD_No_23_013.

205 Charles M. Lamb, "George Romney's Blueprint for Suburban Integration," in *Housing Segregation in Suburban America since 1960: Presidential and Judicial Politics* (Cambridge, MA: Cambridge University Press, 2005), 56–107.
206 Hannah-Jones, "Living Apart."
207 Hannah-Jones.
208 Although Sander, Kucheva and Zasloff claim that the Department of Justice has been a vigorous enforcer of "pattern or practice" claims. See *Moving Toward Integration*, 144.
209 Douglas Henry Daniels, "Berkeley Apartheid: Unfair Housing in a University Town," *History Research* 3, no. 5 (2013): 323, https://newspack-berkeleyside-cityside.s3.amazonaws.com/wp-content/uploads/2016/02/Apartheid-in-a-University-Town.pdf; Jesse Barber, "Redlining: The history of Berkeley's segregated neighborhoods," *Berkeleyside*, September 20, 2018, https://www.berkeleyside.org/2018/09/20/redlining-the-history-of-berkeleys-segregated-neighborhoods?jr=on.
210 Hunter v. Erickson, 393 U.S. 385 (1969).
211 Raymond E. Wolfinger and Fred I. Greenstein, "The Repeal of Fair Housing in California: An Analysis of Referendum Voting," *American Political Science Review* 62, no. 3 (1968): 753–769.
212 Fischel, *Zoning Rules*, 81.
213 Sonia Hirt and Lou Robinson, *Zoned in the USA: The Origins and Implications of American Land-Use Regulation* (Ithaca, NY: Cornell University Press, 2014), 165.
214 Joseph Gyourko & Sean McCulloch, "Minimum Lot Size Restrictions: Impacts on Urban Form and House Price at the Border," (working paper, National Bureau of Economic Research, 2023) https://www.nber.org/papers/w31710; Maurice Dalton and Jeffrey Zabel, "The Impact of Minimum Lot Size Regulations On Housing Prices in East Massachusetts," *Regional Science and Urban Economics* 41, no. 6 (2011), https://www.sciencedirect.com/science/article/abs/pii/S016604621100072X.
215 Anton Schieffer, "Naturally Occurring Housing Shortage Rooted in Downzoning of 1970s," *streets mn*, June 30, 2017, https://streets.mn/2017/06/30/naturally-occurring-affordable-housing-shortage-rooted-in-downzoning-of-1970s/.
216 Department of Planning and Development, "Urban Design and Preservation Element," *City of Berkeley*, accessed July 1, 2022, https://web.archive.org/web/20150412195700/https://www.cityofberkeley.info/Planning_and_Development/Home/General_Plan_-_Urban_Design_and_Preservation_Element.aspx.
217 Los Angeles is another notorious case of downzoning during this period. See Dario Rodman-Alvarez, Rudi Mattheis-Brown, and Luis Ricardo de la Rosa, *Downzoning is the New Redlining; 1958 Zoning and the Reduction of Housing Capacity in Los Angeles* (Los Angeles, CA: Pacific Urbanism, 2020), https://www.pacificurbanism.com/s/20-0902-1958-Venice-Zoning.pdf.
218 Fischel, *Homevoter Hypothesis*; Vicki Been, Josiah Madar, and Simon McDonnell, "Urban Land-Use Regulation: Are Homevoters Overtaking the Growth Machine?" *Journal of Empirical Legal Studies* 11, no. 2 (2014): 257–258, https://dx.doi.org/10.1111/jels.12040; Schleicher, "City Unplanning."
219 Rasheed Shabazz, "Another History of Measure A (1973)," *Alameda Sun*, January 7, 2020, https://alamedasun.com/news/another-history-measure-1973.
220 Lens and Monkkonen, "Strict Land Use Regulations."
221 402 U.S. 137 (1971). See also Aaron Cavin, "A Right to Housing in the Suburbs: *James v. Valtierra* and the Campaign Against Economic Discrimination," *Journal of Urban History* 45, no. 3 (2017): 427, https://journals.sagepub.com/doi/10.1177/0096144217712928 and Note, "The Equal Protection Clause and Exclusionary Zoning After *Valtierra* and *Dandridge*," *Yale Law Journal* 87 (1971): 61, https://doi.org/10.2307/795184.
222 416 U.S. 1 (1974).

223 422 U.S. 490 (1977).
224 Arlington Heights v. Metropolitan Housing Development Corporation, 429 U.S. 252 (1977).
225 Cashin, *Failures of Integration*, 83–126; Sugrue, *Urban Crisis*, xxi.
226 Specifically, they can defend the policies as necessary to achieve a substantial, legitimate, and nondiscriminatory interest. Department of Housing and Urban Development, "Implementation of the Fair Housing Act's Discriminatory Effects Standard," *Federal Register* 78, no. 32 (2013): 11460–11482, https://www.federalregister.gov/d/2013-03375.
227 For a comprehensive discussion of the 1988 Amendments, see Leland B. Ware, "New Weapons for an Old Battle: The Enforcement Provisions of the 1988 Amendments to the Fair Housing Act," *Administrative Law Journal* 5, no. 59 (1993): 80–96, https://www.acus.gov/sites/default/files/documents/1992-03%20Enforcement%20Procedures%20Under%20the%20Fair%20Housing%20Act.pdf.
228 Florence Wagman Roisman, "Affirmatively Furthering Fair Housing in Regional Housing Markets: The Baltimore Public Housing Desegregation Litigation," *Wake Forest Law Review* 42, no. 2 (2007): 333–392, https://www.wakeforestlawreview.com/wp-content/uploads/2014/10/Roisman_LawReview_04.07.pdf.
229 Rawn James, *Root and Branch: Charles Hamilton Houston, Thurgood Marshall, and the Struggle to End Segregation* (New York: Bloomsbury Press, 2010).
230 Jacobs, *Getting Around Brown*, 27.
231 Brown v. Board of Education of Topeka, 347 U.S. 483 (1954).
232 Civil Rights Movement in Virginia," *Virginia Museum of History & Culture*, accessed April 18, 2025, https://virginiahistory.org/learn/civil-rights-movement-virginia/massive-resistance; Candace Epps-Robertson, "The Race to Erase Brown v. Board of Education: The Virginia Way and the Rhetoric of Massive Resistance," *Rhetoric Review* 35, no. 2 (2016): 108, https://doi.org/10.1080/07350198.2016.1142812.
233 Brown v. Board of Education of Topeka *(aka Brown II)*, 349 U.S. 294 (1955).
234 Rucker C. Johnson, "Long-run Impacts of School Desegregation & School Quality on Adult Attainments," (working paper, National Bureau of Economic Research, 2011), 19, https://www.nber.org/papers/w16664.
235 See Appendix B from Johnson, "Long-Run Impacts of School Desegregation: Online Appendix," 2, https://data-nber-org.libproxy.berkeley.edu/data-appendix/w16664/johnson_desegregation_NBERworkingpaperAppendix_12-10.pdf.
236 Green v. County School Board of New Kent County, 391 U.S. 430 (1968).
237 Adam Cohen, "THE COURTS; The Supreme Struggle," *New York Times*, January 18, 2004, https://www.nytimes.com/2004/01/18/education/the-courts-the-supreme-struggle.html.
238 "The Closing of Prince Edward County's Schools," *Virginia Museum of History and Culture*, accessed September 17, 2024, https://virginiahistory.org/learn/civil-rights-movement-virginia/.
239 Amy Chozick, "How Hillary Clinton Went Undercover to Examine Race in Education," *New York Times*, December 27, 2015, https://www.nytimes.com/2015/12/28/us/politics/how-hillary-clinton-went-undercover-to-examine-race-in-education.html.
240 Green v. County School Board of New Kent County, 391 U.S. 430, 438 (1968).
241 Johnson, "Long-Run Impacts: Online Appendix," 16.
242 Carl Kaestle, "Federalism and Inequality in Education: What Can History Tell Us?," in Braun and Kirsch, *Dynamics of Opportunity*, 44.
243 Cashin, *Place, Not Race*, 21. See also figure 10 from Erica Frankenberg, Chungmei Lee, and Gary Orfield, *A Multiracial Society with Segregated Schools: Are We Losing the Dream?* (Boston: Harvard University, The Civil Rights Project, 2003), 37.

244 Potter, "School Segregation." See also table 3.1 in Kaestle, "Federalism and Inequality," 48, in Braun and Kirsch, *Dynamics of Opportunity*. See also Myron Orfield, "Milliken, Meredith, and Metropolitan Segregation," *UCLA Law Review* 62, no. 2 (2015): 452.
245 See, for example, Orfield and Pfleger, *Unfinished* Battle, Fig. 1.
246 Carrie Spector, "70 years after Brown v. Board of Education, New Research Shows Rise in School Segregation," *Stanford Institute for Economic Policy* Research, May 7, 2024, https://siepr.stanford.edu/news/70-years-after-brown-v-board-education-new-research-shows-rise-school-segregation.
247 Leah Boustan, "Was Postwar Suburbanization 'White Flight'? Evidence from the Black Migration," *Quarterly Journal of Economics* 125, no. 1 (2010): 419, https://www.jstor.org/stable/40506285. Boustan's model concludes that white flight was a product of "distaste for diversity," or, in layperson's terms, avoidance of Black neighbors. She finds that if other factors were the primary motivation, the degree of white movement from the cities to the suburbs would be much less.
248 Boustan, "White Flight," 440.
249 Leah Boustan, "The Culprits Behind White Flight," *New York Times*, May 15, 2017, https://www.nytimes.com/2017/05/15/opinion/white-flight.html; Leah Boustan, "School Desegregation and Urban Change: Evidence from City Boundaries," *American Economic Journal: Applied Economics* 4, no. 1 (2012): 85–108, https://www.aeaweb.org/articles?id=10.1257/app.4.1.85.
250 For a more comprehensive presentation of the dynamics in Detroit leading up to and following this decision, see Michelle Adams, *The Containment: Detroit, the Supreme Court, and the Battle for Racial Justice in the North* (New York: Farrar, Straus and Giroux, 2025).
251 Sugrue, *Urban Crisis*, 266.
252 Potter, "School Segregation."
253 See Appendix Table A1 in Claude S. Fischer, et al. "Distinguishing the Geographic Levels and Social Dimensions of U.S. Metropolitan Segregation, 1960-2000" *Demography* 41, no. 1 (2004): 55, https://link.springer.com/article/10.1353/dem.2004.0002.
254 Fischer et al., "U.S. Metropolitan Segregation," 55.
255 Fischer et al., 46 (A multi-group entropy index, or H score, of .035 to .082).
256 San Antonio Indep. Sch. Dist. v. Rodriguez, 411 U.S. 1 (1973).
257 Jacobs, *Getting Around Brown*.
258 "Nixon, The Supreme Court, and Busing," *Richard Nixon Foundation*, April 2, 2015, https://www.nixonfoundation.org/2015/04/nixon-the-supreme-court-and-busing/.
259 Wilson, *When Work Disappears*, 185.
260 Sean F. Reardon et al., "Brown Fades: The End of Court-Ordered School Desegregation and the Resegregation of American Public Schools," *Journal of Policy Analysis and Management* 31, no. 4 (2012): 876–904, https://doi.org/10.1002/pam.21649.
261 Deborah L. McKoy and Jeffrey M. Vincent, "Housing and Education: The Inextricable Link," Chapter 4 in Carr and Kutty, *Segregation*, 127. See also Gary Orfield et al., "The Growth of Segregation in American Schools: Changing Patterns of Separation and Poverty Since 1968," *Equity and Excellence in Education* 27, no. 1 (1994): 7, https://www.tandfonline.com/doi/abs/10.1080/1066568940270102.
262 "These Are Not 'Neighborhood Schools.' They Are Segregated Schools," *Nation*, performed by Jesse Williams et al., October 7, 2016, https://www.thenation.com/article/these-are-not-neighborhood-schools-theyre-segregated-schools/.
263 Chang, "We Can Draw School Zones."

264 Brief for the Louisville Area Chamber of Commerce and Louisville Metro Mayor Jerry E. Abramson as *Amici Curiae* Supporting Respondents, Meredith v. Jefferson County Board of Education, 551 U.S. 701 (2007), https://blackfreedom.proquest.com/wp-content/uploads/2020/09/meredith12.pdf.

265 Genevieve Siegel-Hawley, "City Lines, County Lines, Color Lines: The Relationship between School and Housing Segregation in Four Southern Metro Areas," *Teachers College Record* 115, no. 6 (2013): 1–45, https://doi.org/10.1177/016146811311500601.

266 Parents Involved in Community Schools v. Seattle School Dist. No. 1, 551 U.S. 701 (2007).

267 Mosi Secret, "The Way to Survive It Was to Make A's," *New York Times*, September 7, 2017, https://www.nytimes.com/2017/09/07/magazine/the-way-to-survive-it-was-to-make-as.html.

268 Johnson, "Long-Run Impacts" (examining the socioeconomic and physical health long-term outcomes resulting from court-mandated school desegregation efforts. While no impact (harm or benefit) was detected for whites, Johnson found significant increases in educational, economic, social and physical benefits, as well as reduced incarceration rates for the Black sample. Johnson's research suggests that mechanisms leading to better outcomes for Black adults included access to better educational resources such as smaller class sizes, and increased spending per-pupil). See also Garrett Anstreicher, Jason Fletcher, and Owen Thompson, "The Long Run Impacts of Court-Ordered Desegregation," (working paper, National Bureau of Economic Research, 2022), https://www.nber.org/papers/w29926 (finding large human capital gains and economic improvements for Black adults with no corresponding harms to whites).

269 Johnson, "Long-Run Impacts," 17. Rather than leveling down, a common critique of contemporary equity policies, Johnson describes this as schools being "leveled up."

270 Johnson, 17.

271 Johnson, 21–22.

272 R. Craig Wood and Bruce D. Baker, "An Examination and Analysis of the Equity and Adequacy Concepts of Constitutional Challenges to State Education Finance Distribution Formulas," *University of Arkansas at Little Rock Law Review* 27, no. 1 (2004): 161, https://lawrepository.ualr.edu/cgi/viewcontent.cgi?article=1211&context=lawreview; "Overview of Litigation History," in SchoolFunding.Info (New York: Center for Educational Equity at Teachers' College, Columbia University, 2022), archived March 30, 2023, at the Wayback Machine, https://web.archive.org/web/20230330091422/https://www.schoolfunding.info/litigation-map/.

273 Julien Lafortune, Jesse Rothstein, and Diane Whitmore Schanzenbach, "School Finance Reform and the Distribution of Student Achievement," *American Economic Journal: Applied Economics* 10, no. 2 (2018).

274 Stephen B. Billings, David J. Deming, and Jonah E. Rockoff, "School Segregation, Educational Attainment and Crime: Evidence From the End of Busing in Charlotte-Mecklenburg" (working paper, National Bureau of Economic Research, 2012): https://www.nber.org/papers/w18487.

275 Sean F. Reardon et al., *Is Separate Still Unequal? New Evidence on School Segregation and Racial Academic Gaps* (Palo Alto, CA: Stanford Center for Education Policy Analysis), 32–33, https://cepa.stanford.edu/sites/default/files/wp19-06-v092021.pdf; Sean F. Reardon et al., "Why School Desegregation Still Matters (a Lot)," *ASCD Educational Leadership* 80, no. 4 (2022): https://www.ascd.org/el/articles/why-school-desegregation-still-matters-a-lot.

276 See Drew DeSilver, "Black Unemployment Rate is Consistently Twice that of Whites," *Pew Research Center*, August 21, 2013, https://www.pewresearch.org/

fact-tank/2013/08/21/through-good-times-and-bad-black-unemployment-is-consistently-double-that-of-whites/. See also *Kerner Report*, 123–127.
277 Algernon Austin, "For African Americans, 50 Years of High Unemployment," *Economic Policy Institute*, February 22, 2022, https://www.epi.org/publication/african-americans-50-years-high-unemployment/.
278 Robert E. Scott et al., *Botched Policy Responses to Globalization Have Decimated Manufacturing Employment with Often Overlooked Costs for Black, Brown, and Other Workers of Color* (Washington, DC: Economic Policy Institute, 2022), https://www.epi.org/publication/botched-policy-responses-to-globalization/.
279 John Bound and Harry Holzer, "Industrial Shifts, Skill Levels, and the Labor Market for White and Black Men," *Review of Economics and Statistics* 75, no. 3 (1993): 395, https://www.jstor.org/stable/2109452.
280 U.S. Bureau of Labor Statistics, "All Employees, Manufacturing (MANENMP)," *FRED Economic Data*, accessed March 5, 2025, https://fred.stlouisfed.org/series/MANEMP.
281 Wilson, *When Work Disappears*, 26.
282 Sugrue, *Urban Crisis*, 127.
283 Autor, "Work of the Past," 2, figure 1. From the 1980s and on, however, wages fanned out depending on the skills required to perform the task.
284 David H. Autor, David Mindell, and Elisabeth Reynolds, *The Work of the Future: Building Better Jobs in an Age of Intelligent Machines* (Cambridge: Massachusetts Institute of Technology, 2020): 16, at the Wayback Machine, https://web.archive.org/web/20201118172025/https://workofthefuture.mit.edu/wp-content/uploads/2020/11/2020-Final-Report.pdf.
285 Enrico Moretti, *The New Geography of Jobs* (Boston: Houghton Mifflin Harcourt, 2012): 225–231.
286 Michael R. Smith, "Income Inequality and Economic Growth in Rich Countries: A Reconsideration of the Evidence," *Current Sociology* 50, no. 4 (2002): 572–593.
287 Malo André Hutson, *The Urban Struggle for Economic, Environmental, and Social Justice: Deepening Their Roots* (Oxfordshire, UK: Routledge, 2015), 24.
288 Wilson, *When Work Disappears*, 27, citing Bill Lewis et al., *Employment Performance* (Washington, DC: McKinsey Global Institute, 1994), https://www.mckinsey.com/featured-insights/employment-and-growth/employment-performance.
289 W. Michael Cox and Richard Alm, *Myths of Rich and Poor: Why We're Better Off Than We Think* (New York: Basic Books, 1999), 141.
290 Andrew Sum and Neal Fogg, "The Changing Economic Fortunes of Young Black Men in America," *Journal of Black Studies and Research* 21, no. 1 (1990), 52, https://www.jstor.org/stable/41067673?seq=1#metadata_info_tab_contents.
291 Rebecca Blank, "Outlook for the U.S. Labor Market and Prospects for Low-Wage Entry Level Jobs," (working paper, Center for Urban Affairs, Northwestern University, Evanston, IL, 1994), 17.
292 Patrick Reardon, "Study Links City Jobless, Suburban Housing," *Chicago Tribune*, May 1, 1991, https://www-proquest-com.libproxy.berkeley.edu/newspapers/study-links-city-jobless-suburban-housing/docview/283071136/se-2?accountid=14496.
293 Sugrue, *Urban Crisis*, 147
294 Andrew W. Kahrl, *The Black Tax: 150 Years of Theft, Exploitation, and Dispossession in America* (Chicago: University of Chicago Press, 2024), 280.
295 Cashin, *White Space, Black Hood*, 81.
296 Wilson, *When Work Disappears*, 49. Also: "Reagan cut urban spending from 12% to 3% of the federal budget." Sugrue, *Urban Crisis*, xviii.
297 William Schneider, "The Suburban Century Begins," *Atlantic*, July 1992, https://www.theatlantic.com/past/docs/politics/ecbig/schnsub.htm.

298 That is, overall rates and rates by race. Franklin E. Zimring, "The Scale of Imprisonment in the United States: Twentieth Century Patterns and Twenty-First Century Prospects," *Journal of Criminal Law and Criminology* 100, no. 3 (2010): 1226. See also Jeremy Travis, Bruce Western and F. Stevens Redburn, *The Growth of Incarceration in the United States: Exploring Causes and Consequences* (Washington, DC: National Academies Press, 2014), https://www.nap.edu/catalog/18613/the-growth-of-incarceration-in-the-united-states-exploring-causes.

299 Marc Mauer, *Race to Incarcerate* (New York: New Press, 2006), 33.

300 E. Ann Carson and Elizabeth Anderson, *Prisoners in 2015* (Washington, DC: U.S. Department of Corrections, 2016), 1-2, https://bjs.ojp.gov/content/pub/pdf/p15.pdf. See also Table A-6 from Warren, et al., *One in 100*, 34, https://www.pewtrusts.org/en/research-and-analysis/reports/2008/02/28/one-in-100-behind-bars-in-america-2008.

301 Brian Mann, "After 50 Years of The War On Drugs, 'What Good Is It Doing for Us?'," *NPR*, June 17, 2021, https://www.npr.org/2021/06/17/1006495476/after-50-years-of-the-war-on-drugs-what-good-is-it-doing-for-us.

302 Andrew Glass, "Reagan Declares 'War on Drugs,' October 14, 1982," *Politico*, October 10, 2010, https://www.politico.com/story/2010/10/reagan-declares-war-on-drugs-october-14-1982-043552.

303 As Michelle Alexander points out, Reagon's declaration was years before the crack cocaine epidemic. Michelle Alexander, *The New Jim Crow: Mass Incarceration in the Age of Colorblindness* (New York: New Press, 2010), 5–6. Alexander also observes that only 2% of Americans thought drugs were the most important issue. Alexander, *New Jim Crow*, 49 citing Katherine Beckett, *Making Crime Pay: Law and Order in Contemporary American Politics* (New York: Oxford University Press, 1999), 56.

304 Comprehensive Crime Control Act of 1984, 98 Stat. 1762 (1984); Russell Crandall, *Drugs and Thugs: The History and Future of America's War on Drugs* (New Haven, CT: Yale University Press 2020), 141.

305 Coates, "Black Family," 73.

306 Economists "estimate that between 1989 and 1992, drug arrests increased by approximately 37% in the treated states." See Shawn Kantor, Carl T. Kitchens, and Steven Pawlowski, "Civil Asset Forfeiture, Crime, and Police Incentives: Evidence From the Comprehensive Crime Control Act of 1984," *Economic Inquiry* 59, no. 1 (2020): 240, https://doi.org/10.1111/ecin.12952.

307 Controlled Substances Penalties Amendments Act of 1984, Pub. L. No. 98-305, 98 Stat. 2068 (1984).

308 State and local could keep up to 80%. Federal 100%. Alexander, *New Jim Crow*, 77.

309 Alexander, *New Jim Crow*, 78.

310 See Alexander, 80–81 for the 2000 reforms and the difference between criminal and civil forfeiture standards.

311 Anti-Drug Abuse Act of 1986, H.R. 5484, 99th Cong. (1986); Harry Hogan et al., "Drug Control: Highlights of P.L. 99-570, Anti Drug Abuse Act of 1986," *National Criminal Justice Reference Service*, October 31, 1986, https://www.ojp.gov/ncjrs/virtual-library/abstracts/drug-control-highlights-pl-99-570-anti-drug-abuse-act-1986.

312 Anti-Drug Abuse Act of 1988, H.R. 5210, 100th Cong. (1988).

313 Violent Crime Control and Law Enforcement Act of 1994, H.R. 3355, Pub. L. 103–322.

314 Michelle Alexander, "Why Hillary Clinton Doesn't Deserve the Black Vote," *Nation*, February 10, 2016, https://www.thenation.com/article/archive/hillary-clinton-does-not-deserve-black-peoples-votes/.

315 Kimber Reynolds, "Retro Report: The Making of 'Three Strikes' Laws," *Takeaway*, December 2, 2013, https://www.wnycstudios.org/podcasts/takeaway/segments/retro-report-looks-back-legacy-three-strikes.
316 Matt Taibbi, "Cruel and Unusual Punishment: The Shame of Three Strikes Laws," *Rolling Stone*, March 27, 2013, https://www.rollingstone.com/politics/news/cruel-and-unusual-punishment-the-shame-of-three-strikes-laws-20130327.
317 Brown v. Plata, 563 U.S. 493 (2011).
318 Alexander, *New Jim Crow*, 54.
319 Alana Rosenberg, Allison K Groves, and Kim M Blankenship, "Comparing Black and White Drug Offenders: Implications for Racial Disparities in Criminal Justice and Reentry Policy and Programming," *Journal of Drug Issues* 47, no 1 (2017): 132–142, https://pmc.ncbi.nlm.nih.gov/articles/PMC5614457/.
320 Geman Lopez, "Black and white Americans use drugs at similar rates. One group is punished more for it," *Vox*, March 17, 2015, https://www.vox.com/2015/3/17/8227569/war-on-drugs-racism.
321 Matt Taibbi, "Frisk and Stop," in *The Divide: American Injustice in the Age of the Wealth Gap* (New York: Spiegel & Grau, 2014), 53–73.
322 Taahira Thompson, "NYPD's Infamous Stop-and-Frisk Policy Found Unconstitutional," *Leadership Conference Education Fund*, August 21, 2013, https://civilrights.org/edfund/resource/nypds-infamous-stop-and-frisk-policy-found-unconstitutional/.
323 Catherine Y. Kim, Daniel J. Losen and Damon T. Hewitt, *The School-to-Prison Pipeline: Structuring Legal Reform* (New York: New York University Press, 2010), 9.
324 Kim, Losen, and Hewitt, *School-to-Prison Pipeline*, 78–79; Jim Freeman, *Test, Punish, and Push Out: How "Zero Tolerance" and High-Stakes Testing Funnel Youth into the School-to-Prison Pipeline* (Advancement Project, 2010): 13–24, https://www.justice4all.org/wp-content/uploads/2016/04/Test-Punish-Push-Out.pdf. See generally Joshua Rovner, *Disproportionate Minority Contact in the Juvenile Justice System* (Washington, DC: Sentencing Project, 2014), https://www.sentencingproject.org/app/uploads/2022/10/Disproportionate-Minority-Contact-in-the-Juvenile-Justice-System.pdf [https://perma.cc/S8LP-28KL]; Zabrina Aleguire et al., *Breaking the Chains* (Oakland: Equal Justice Society, 2016), https://equaljusticesociety.org/breakingthechains/.
325 Erica L. Green, "Government Watchdog Finds Racial Bias in School Discipline," *New York Times*, April 4, 2018, https://www.nytimes.com/2018/04/04/us/politics/racial-bias-school-discipline-policies.html; *K-12 Education: Discipline Disparities for Black Students, Boys, and Students with Disabilities* (Washington, DC: U.S. Government Accountability Office, 2018), https://www.gao.gov/products/gao-18-258.
326 Forman, *Locking Up Our Own*, 156, 47–76 (Forman notes that many of the most aggressive advocates of more punitive "tough-on-crime" policies were black political leaders).
327 Forman, 44–45.
328 Chris Hayes characterizes the dynamic effectively: Christopher Hayes, *A Colony in a Nation* (New York: W. W. Norton, 2017), 114 ("American criminal law is constructed, maintained, patrolled, and enforced through a highly distributed, at times byzantine and chaotic set of overlapping jurisdictions, interacting awkwardly with one another. No one takes orders from any unified entity. No single actor or group of actors created mass incarceration, and no single group of actors can undo it. We have no single switch to flip. The Colony is an emergent phenomenon.") Much the same could be said about structural racism writ large.
329 Adam J. Levitin and Susan M. Wachter, *The Great American Housing Bubble: What Went Wrong and How We Can Protect Ourselves in the Future*

(Cambridge, MA: Harvard University Press, 2020) (examining six basic thesis on the cause of the Great Recession); Robert J. Shiller, "How to Navigate the Coronavirus Real Estate Market," *New York Times*, July 31, 2020, https://www.nytimes.com/2020/07/31/business/housing-market-prices-risk.html; Ben S. Bernanke, Timothy F. Geithner, and Henry M. Paulson, Jr., *Firefighting: The Financial Crisis and Its Lessons* (New York: Penguin Books, 2019); Joy Crane, "The Best Books for Making Sense of the Financial Crash, 10 Years Later," *New York Magazine*, August 20, 2019, https://nymag.com/strategist/article/best-books-about-the-financial-crash.html.

330 The bailout is TARP, and the latter is HARP and HAMP programs. See Julia Kagan, Lea D. Uradu, and Jiwon Ma, "Home Affordable Modification Program," *Investopedia*, updated June 5, 2022, https://www.investopedia.com/terms/h/home-affordable-modification-program.asp.

331 Rick Santelli, interview by Joe Kernen et al, *Squawk Box*, February 19, 2009, https://www.youtube.com/watch?v=zp-Jw-5Kx8k.

332 Michael Lewis, *The Big Short: Inside the Doomsday Machine* (New York: W. W. Norton, 2010).

333 See Christopher L. Peterson, "Subprime Lending, Foreclosure, and Race: An Introduction to the Securitization in Residential Mortgage Finance," Chapter 3 in *Where Credit is Due: Bringing Equity to Credit and Housing After the Mortgage Meltdown,* ed. Christy Rogers and john a. powell (Lanham, MD: University of America Press, 2013): 61–83.

334 Randall L. Wray, "Lessons from the Subprime Meltdown" (working paper, Levy Economics Institute of Bard College, Annandale-on-Hudson, NY, 2007): 30, Table 1, https://www.levyinstitute.org/pubs/wp_522.pdf.

335 Ben Bernanke, "Fostering Sustainable Homeownership," speech, National Community Reinvestment Coalition Annual Meeting, Board of Governors of the Federal Reserve System, March 14, 2008, Washington, DC, https://www.federalreserve.gov/newsevents/speech/bernanke20080314a.htm.

336 "Real Gross Domestic Product," FRED Economic Data, last updated December 21, 2023, https://fred.stlouisfed.org/series/GDPC1; "Households and Nonprofit Organizations; Net Worth, Level," FRED Economic Data, last updated December 7, 2023, https://fred.stlouisfed.org/series/TNWBSHNO; "All Employees, Total Nonfarm," FRED Economic Data, last updated December 8, 2023, https://fred.stlouisfed.org/series/PAYEMS.

337 Some scholars claim that laws such as the Commodity Futures Modernization Act of 2000 and the repeal of Glass-Steagall with the Financial Services Modernization Act of 1999 were two examples of laws that enabled the crisis. Lynn A. Stout, "How Deregulating Derivatives Led to Disaster, and Why Re-Regulating Them Can Prevent Another," *Cornell Law Faculty Publications* 723 (2009), https://scholarship.law.cornell.edu/facpub/723.

338 Justin P. Steil et al., "The social structure of mortgage discrimination," *Housing Studies* 33, no. 5 (2017): 760, https://doi.org/10.1080/02673037.2017.1390076 ("Numerous quantitative studies have found that Black and Latino borrowers over the last decade were frequently charged more for mortgage loans than similarly situated white borrowers").

339 Ellen Schloemer et al., *Losing Ground: Foreclosures in the Subprime Market and Their Cost to Homeowners* (Durham, NC: Center for Responsible Lending, 2002), https://www.responsiblelending.org/sites/default/files/nodes/files/research-publication/foreclosure-paper-report-2-17.pdf, and *Preserving the American Dream: Predatory Lending Practices and Homes Foreclosures, Hearing before the U.S. Senate Committee on Banking, Housing and Urban Affairs*, 110th Cong. (2007) (statement of Martin Eakes, CEO of the Center for Responsible Lending).

340 Sharkey, *Stuck in Place*, 196. See also Federal Reserve studies in 2004, 2005, and 2006 as referenced in Christy Rogers, "Overview," in Rogers and powell, *Where Credit is Due*, 7. See also Jacob S. Rugh and Douglas S. Massey, "Racial Segregation and the American Foreclosure Crisis," *American Sociological Review* 75, no. 5 (2010): 629-651, https://doi.org/10.1177/0003122410380868.
341 Engel and McCoy, "From Credit Denial to Predatory Lending," 92.
342 Debbie Gruenstein Bocian, Keith S. Ernst, and Wei Li, "Unfair Lending: The Effect of Race and Ethnicity on the Price of Subprime Mortgages" (Durham, NC: Center for Responsible Lending, 2006), https://www.responsiblelending.org/sites/default/files/nodes/files/research-publication/rr011-Unfair_Lending-0506.pdf.
343 Jacob W. Faber, "Racial Dynamics of Subprime Mortgage Lending at the Peak," *Housing Policy Debate* 23, no. 2 (2013): 328–349, https://doi.org/10.1080/10511482.2013.771788.
344 Surveys in 2005 and 2006 revealed that 55% and 61% had credit scores high enough to qualify for prime loans. Gary A. Dymski, "Understanding the Subprime Crisis: An Introduction to the Role of Securitization in Residential Mortgage Finance" in Rogers and powell, *Where Credit is Due*, citing Rick Brooks and Ruth Simon, "As Housing Boomed, Industry Pushed Loans to a Broader Market," *Wall Street Journal*, December 3, 2007, https://www.wsj.com/articles/SB119662974358911035.
345 Elvin K. Wyly et al., "Subprime Mortgage Segmentation in the American Urban System," *Tijdschrift voor Economische en Sociale Geografe* 99, no. 1 (2008): 3–23, https://doi.org/10.1111/j.1467-9663.2007.00436.x.
346 See Steil et al., "The social structure of mortgage discrimination," 771 (describing how social networks played a role in persuading these communities to buy higher-risk loans).
347 Engel and McCoy, "From Credit Denial to Predatory Lending," 102.
348 Engel and McCoy, 87.
349 Aaron Glantz and Emmanuel Martinez, "For people of color, banks are shutting the door to homeownership," *Reveal*, February 15, 2018, https://revealnews.org/article/for-people-of-color-banks-are-shutting-the-door-to-homeownership/.
350 "California Reinvestment Coalition and Fair Housing Advocates of Northern California File Fair Housing Complaint, Urging Immediate HUD Investigation Into CIT Groups's OneWest Bank," California Reinvestment Coalition, November 17, 2016, https://calreinvest.org/press-release/cit-group-accused-of-redlining-and-violating-fair-housing-act/ (see the graphic); David BondGraham, "One of Donald Trump's Rumored Cabinet Picks Accused of Financial Discrimination Blighting East Oakland," *East Bay Express*, November 22, 2016, https://eastbayexpress.com/one-of-donald-trumps-rumored-cabinet-picks-accused-of-financial-discrimination-blighting-east-oakland-2-1/.
351 Federal Deposit Insurance Corporation (FDIC), 2023 FDIC *National Survey of Unbanked and Underbanked Households* (Washington, DC: FDIC, 2024), 66, table 7.1, https://www.fdic.gov/household-survey/2023-fdic-national-survey-unbanked-and-underbanked-households-report.
352 *2023 FDIC National Survey*, 2, figure ES.2.
353 Glantz and Martinez, "For people of color."
354 Black and Latino households report higher levels of distrust of conventional financial institutions. See Samantha Masunaga and Jackeline Luna, "Big banks want communities of color to trust them. But it's not so simple," *Los Angeles Times*, June 6, 2019, https://www.latimes.com/business/story/2021-06-19/big-banks-banks-community-people-of-color-trust.

355 Natalie Moore, "Contract Buying Robbed Black Families in Chicago of Billions," *NPR*, May 30, 2019, https://www.npr.org/local/309/2019/05/30/728122642/contract-buying-robbed-black-families-in-chicago-of-billions.

356 Beryl Satter, *Family Properties: How the Struggle Over Race and Real Estate Transformed Chicago and Urban America* (New York: Picador, 2010).

357 Samuel George et al., *The Plunder of Black Wealth in Chicago: New Findings on the Lasting Toll of Predatory Housing Contracts* (Durham, NC: Samuel DuBois Cook Center on Social Equity, 2019), iii, https://socialequity.duke.edu/wp-content/uploads/2019/10/Plunder-of-Black-Wealth-in-Chicago.pdf.

358 These services are predatory in many respects because of the high rates of interest, and because they take advantage of people's desperation and immediate need, such as due rent or utility payments. For a summary definition of "predatory," see Dymski, "Understanding the Subprime Crisis," 34.

359 Sheila Bair, *Low-Cost Payday Loans: Opportunities and Obstacles* (Amherst, MA: Isenberg School of Management, 2005), https://folio.iupui.edu/bitstream/handle/10244/101/FEs3622H334.pdf?sequence=1.

360 "The Victims of Payday Lending," Center for Responsible Lending, accessed September 17, 2024, https://www.responsiblelending.org/issues/victims-payday.

361 "Federal Court Class Action Challenges Predatory 'Rent-to-Own' Housing Scheme Targeted at Minority Communities in Indianapolis," Relman Colfax, May 30, 2017, https://www.relmanlaw.com/news-RainbowRenToOwn (discussing Fair Housing Center of Central Indiana v. Rainbow Realty Group, Inc., No. 1:17-cv-1782 (S.D. Ind.)).

362 Aaron Glantz, *Homewreckers: How a Gang of Wall Street Kingpins, Hedge Fund Magnates, Crooked Banks, and Vulture Capitalists Suckered Millions Out of Their Homes and Demolished the American Dream* (New York: Harper Collins, 2019).

363 Renae Merle, "Minorities hit harder by foreclosure crisis," *Washington Post*, June 19, 2010, https://www.washingtonpost.com/wp-dyn/content/article/2010/06/18/AR2010061802885.html.

364 Sugrue, *Urban Crisis*, xv.

365 Dan Immergluck & Geoff Smith, "The external costs of foreclosure: The impact of single-family mortgage foreclosures on property values," *Housing Policy Debate* 17, no. 1 (2010), https://doi.org/10.1080/10511482.2006.9521561; Jenny Schuetz, Vicki Been, and Ingrid Gould Ellen, "Neighborhood effects of concentrated mortgage foreclosures," *Journal of Housing Economics* 17, no. 4 (2008): 306–319, https://doi.org/10.1016/j.jhe.2008.09.004.

366 Complaint for Declaratory and Injunctive Relief and Damages, Mayor & City Council of Balt. v. Wells Fargo Bank, N.A., No. L08CV 062 (D. Md. January 8, 2008), 2008 WL117894

367 City of Baltimore v. Wells Fargo, 1:08-cv-00062 (D. Md. 2010); "Baltimore Settles Landmark Fair Lending Case Against Wells Fargo," *Relman Colfax*, July 12, 2021, https://www.relmanlaw.com/news-baltimore-settles

368 Adkins v. Morgan Stanley, 656 F. App'x 555 (2d. Cir. 2016).

369 Class Action Complaint, Adkins v. Morgan Stanley, 12-CV-7667 (S.D.N.Y. 2012), https://www.aclu.org/legal-document/adkins-et-al-vs-morgan-stanley-complaint.

370 La June Montgomery Tabron, "Closing the Wealth Gap for Families of Color," *Stanford Social Innovation Review*, February 23, 2016, https://ssir.org/articles/entry/closing_the_wealth_gap_for_families_of_color; Rakesh Kochhar and Richard Fry, "Wealth inequality has widened along racial ethnic lines since end of Great Recession," *Pew Research Center*, December 12, 2014, https://www.pewresearch.org/fact-tank/2014/12/12/racial-wealth-gaps-great-recession/.

371 Peter Dreier et al., *Underwater America: How the So-Called Housing "Recovery" is Bypassing Many American Communities* (Berkeley, CA: Haas Institute

for a Fair and Inclusive Society, 2014), 5, https://belonging.berkeley.edu/sites/default/files/haasinsitute_underwateramerica_publish_0.pdf.
372 McCargo and Choi, *Closing the Gaps*.
373 Erik Hurst, Ming Ching Luoh, and Frank P. Stafford, "The Wealth Dynamics of American Families, 1984-94," *Brookings Papers on Economic Activity* 29, no. 1 (1998): 267–338; Rakesh Kochhar and Mohamad Moslimani, "The assets households own and the debts they carry," in *Wealth Surged in the Pandemic, but Debt Endures for Poorer Black and Hispanic Families* (Pew Research Center, 2023), https://www.pewresearch.org/2023/12/04/the-assets-households-own-and-the-debts-they-carry/ (finding that home equity accounted for a median of 45% of US homeowner's net worth in 2021).
374 Arguably the best since the Homestead Acts of the 19th century, according to Shapiro, *Toxic Inequality*, 35.
375 Emmie Martin, "Here's How Much Housing Prices Have Sky-Rocketed Over the Last 50 Years," *CNBC make it*, June 23, 2017, https://www.cnbc.com/2017/06/23/how-much-housing-prices-have-risen-since-1940.html; Jonathan Lansner, "Is buying a California home really worth it?," *OC Register*, June 11, 2022, https://www.ocregister.com/2022/06/11/is-buying-a-california-home-really-worth-it/.
376 Dedrick Asante-Muhammad, Jamie Buell, Joshua Devine, "60% Black Homeownership: A Radical Goal for Black Wealth Development," *National Community Reinvestment Coalition*, March 2, 2021, https://ncrc.org/60-black-homeownership-a-radical-goal-for-black-wealth-development/. Federal Reserve Bank of St. Louis, "Housing and Homeownership," Q4 2020.
377 Asante-Muhammad, Buell, Devine, "60% Black Homeownership".
378 "Housing and Homeownership: Homeownership Rate: Q3 2016" *FRED Economic Research*, *Federal Reserve Bank of St. Louis*, accessed December 6, 2022, https://fred.stlouisfed.org/release/tables?rid=296&eid=784188&od=2016-07-01.
379 Lauri Goodman, Jun Zhu, and Rolf Pendall, "Are gains in black homeownership history?" *Urban Wire*, February 14, 2017, https://www.urban.org/urban-wire/are-gains-black-homeownership-history.
380 Junia Howell and Elizabeth Korver-Glenn, *Appraised: The Consistent Evaluation of White Neighborhoods as More Valuable Than Communities of Color* (eruka, 2022), https://www.eruka.org/appraised.
381 Rashawn Ray, et al., *Homeownership, Racial Segregation, and Policy Solutions Racial Wealth Equity* (Metropolitan Policy Program at Brookings, 2021), https://www.brookings.edu/essay/homeownership-racial-segregation-and-policies-for-racial-wealth-equity/; Andre Perry, Jonathan Rothwell, David Harshbarger, *The Devaluation of Black Assets in Black Neighborhoods: The Case of Residential Property* (Metropolitan Policy Program at Brookings, 2018), https://www.brookings.edu/wp-content/uploads/2018/11/2018.11_Brookings-Metro_Devaluation-Assets-Black-Neighborhoods_final.pdf.
382 Michela Zonta, *Racial Disparities in Home Appreciation* (Washington, DC: Center for American Progress, 2019), https://cdn.americanprogress.org/content/uploads/2019/06/27074704/BorrowersOfColor-report.pdf.
383 Thomas Shapiro, Tatjana Meschede, and Sam Osoro, "The roots of the widening racial wealth gap: Explaining the Black-White economic divide," *Research and Policy Brief* (2013), https://doi.org/10.13016/pvyx-ebny.
384 The White House, Office of the Press Secretary, "President Obama Signs Michigan Emergency Declaration," January 26, 2016, https://obamawhitehouse.archives.gov/the-press-office/2016/01/16/president-obama-signs-michigan-emergency-declaration.
385 "Mississippi Severe Storms and Flooding," *FEMA*, updated September 28, 2020, accessed November 16, 2022, https://www.fema.gov/disaster/4268.
386 Anna Maria Barry-Jester, "What Went Wrong in Flint," *FiveThirtyEight*, January 26, 2016, https://fivethirtyeight.com/features/what-went-wrong-in-flint-water-crisis-

200 *Structural Racism*

      michigan/; Sara Ganim and Linh Tran, "How tap water became toxic in Flint, Michigan," *CNN*, January 13, 2016, https://www.cnn.com/2016/01/11/health/toxic-tap-water-flint-michigan/; Alana Semuels, "Aging Pipes are Poisoning America's Tap Water," *Atlantic*, July 9, 2015, https://www.theatlantic.com/business/archive/2015/07/dont-drink-the-water/399803/.
387 Lindsey Scullen, "TIMELINE: Here's how the Flint water crisis unfolded," *Michigan Radio*, December 21, 2015, https://www.michiganradio.org/politics-government/2015-12-21/timeline-heres-how-the-flint-water-crisis-unfolded; Jeremy C. F. Lin, "The Reach of Lead in Flint's Water Supply," *New York Times*, January 15, 2016, https://www.nytimes.com/interactive/2016/01/15/us/flint-lead-water-michigan.html.
388 Mona Hanna-Attisha et al., "Elevated Blood Lead Levels in Children Associated With the Flint Drinking Water Crisis: A Spatial Analysis of Risk and Public Health Response," *American Journal of Public Health* 106, no. 2 (2016), https://doi.org/10.2105/AJPH.2015.303003; Erin Schumaker, "Why Pediatricians Are So Alarmed by the Lead in Flint's Water," *Huffington Post*, last modified January 16, 2017, https://www.huffpost.com/entry/flint-lead-poisoning-effects-children_n_56709a0de4b0688701db78d0.
389 Janell Ross, "In Flint, bad tap water runs politically deep," *Washington Post*, January 14, 2016, https://www.washingtonpost.com/news/the-fix/wp/2016/01/14/in-flint-bad-tap-water-runs-politically-deep/.
390 Ross, "Bad tap water runs politically deep."
391 Dominic Adams, "Flint emergency manager Michael Brown says it was 'tough decision' to walk away," *MLive*, September 11, 2013, https://www.mlive.com/news/flint/2013/09/flint_emergency_manager_michae_25.html.
392 Michael Carmody, "Federal judge won't force Flint back to Detroit water system," *Michigan Radio*, June 23, 2015, https://www.michiganradio.org/law/2015-06-23/federal-judge-wont-force-flint-back-to-detroit-water-system. See Coalition for Clean Water v. Flint, No. 2:2015cv12084 (E. D. Mich 2015).
393 Ron Fonger, "Gov. Snyder names task force to review actions in Flint water crisis," *MLive*, October 21, 2015, https://www.mlive.com/news/flint/2015/10/gov_snyder_names_task_force_to.html.
394 Jiquanda Johnson, "Flint, Detroit among nation's poorest cities, new Census data show," *MLive*, September 17, 2015, https://www.mlive.com/news/flint/2015/09/flint_detroit_among_nations_po.html.
395 Renee Walker, Christopher Kane, and Jessica Burke, "Disparities and Access to Healthy Food in the United States: A Review of Food Deserts Literature," *Health & Place* 16, no. 5 (2010): 876–884, https://doi.org/10.1016/j.healthplace.2010.04.013; Kelly M. Bower et al., "The Intersection of Neighborhood Racial Segregation, Poverty, and Urbanicity and Its Impact on Food Store Availability in the United States," *Preventive Medicine* 58, no. 33–39 (2014): https://www.ncbi.nlm.nih.gov/pmc/articles/PMC3970577/.
396 Marlene Cimons, "Flint's 'food apartheid' is impeding recovery from water crisis," *ThinkProgress*, April 23, 2019, https://archive.thinkprogress.org/flint-lead-recovery-food-access-17b75455a9d9/?web=1&wdLOR=c2FE75CA8-6AE2-0E4D-A53D-A5E4C57086B3. "'Flint is a community that suffers under food apartheid," he added. "Over the last decade, all the major grocery stores have pulled out of flint…Now many people in Flint only have access to convenience stores that sell alcohol and processed foods high in salt and sugar."
397 Jason Reece et al., *ARRA and the Economic Crisis: One Year Later* (Columbus, OH: Kirwan Institute for the Study of Race and Ethnicity, 2010), 1, 8, https://www.reimaginerpe.org/files/arraequityoneyearanniv_kirwan_institute_feb2010.pdf.
398 Mike Maciag, "Bankrupt Cities, Municipalities List and Map," *Governing*, March 23, 2012, https://www.governing.com/archive/municipal-cities-counties-bankruptcies-and-defaults.html.

399 Michelle Wilde Anderson, "The New Minimal Cities," *Yale Law Journal* 123, no. 5 (2014): 1118, https://www.yalelawjournal.org/pdf/1118.Anderson.1227_uhkqugsb.pdf; Mike Maciag, "Bankrupt Cities, Municipalities List and Map," *Governing*, March 23, 2012, https://www.governing.com/archive/municipal-cities-counties-bankruptcies-and-defaults.html.

400 Glennon Sweeney and Bernadette Hanlon, "From old suburb to post-suburb: The politics of retrofit in the inner suburb of Upper Arlington, Ohio," *Journal of Urban Affairs* 39, no. 2 (2017): 241–259, 250, https://doi.org/10.1111/juaf.12313.

401 Clean Water for All, "Water, Health, and Equity: The Infrastructure Crisis Facing Low-Income Communities & Communities of Color—and How to Solve It," accessed September 20, 2021, https://www.policylink.org/resources-tools/water-health-equity.

402 *Wastewater* (Reston, VA: American Society of Civil Engineers, 2021), https://infrastructurereportcard.org/wp-content/uploads/2020/12/Wastewater-2021.pdf.

403 *Report Card for New York's Infrastructure* (New York: American Society of Civil Engineers New York State Council, 2015), 77, https://www.infrastructurereportcard.org/wp-content/uploads/2017/01/NY_ReportCard_FullReport_9.29.15_FINAL.pdf.

404 Catherine Flowers and Mitchell Bernard, "When Environmental Racism Causes a Hygienic Hell," *New York Times*, August 25, 2021, https://www.nytimes.com/2021/08/25/opinion/environmental-racism-wastewater-broken.html.

405 Michael Wines, Patrick McGeehan, and John Schwartz, "Schools Nationwide Still Grapple with Lead in Water," *New York Times*, March 26, 2016, https://www.nytimes.com/2016/03/27/us/schools-nationwide-still-grapple-with-lead-in-water.html.

406 Michael Wines, "Flint Is in the News, but Lead Poisoning Is Even Worse in Cleveland," *New York Times*, March 3, 2016, https://www.nytimes.com/2016/03/04/us/lead-paint-contamination-persists-in-many-cities-as-cleanup-falters.html.

407 Liz Leyden, "In Echo of Flint, Mich., Water Crisis Now Hits Newark," *New York Times*, October 30, 2018, https://www.nytimes.com/2018/10/30/nyregion/newark-lead-water-pipes.html.

408 Patrick McGeehan, "Drinking Water in Newark Schools Known to Have Lead Problem at least 6 Years Ago," *New York Times*, April 8, 2016, https://www.nytimes.com/2016/04/09/nyregion/drinking-water-in-newark-schools-known-to-have-lead-problem-at-least-6-years-ago.html.

409 Lori Higgins, "33 more Detroit schools have high lead, copper in drinking water," *Detroit Free Press*, September 9, 2018, https://www.freep.com/story/news/education/2018/09/19/detroit-schools-water-lead/1359606002/.

410 Tolly Taylor, "I-Team exclusive: Data shows many school districts haven't fixed elevated levels of lead in water," *WBALTV*, Updated May 11, 2023, https://www.wbaltv.com/article/lead-levels-school-water-maryland-data-i-team/43797067.

411 Dorany Pineda, "Drinking water at 1 in 4 California child-care centers tests dangerously high for lead," *Los Angeles Times*, May 18, 2023, https://www.latimes.com/california/story/2023-05-18/drinking-water-at-1-in-4-california-child-care-centers-tests-dangerously-high-for-lead; Julianna Morano, "Dangerous levels of metal found in water at dozens of childcare centers in Fresno County," *Fresno Bee*, Updated May 16, 2023, https://www.fresnobee.com/news/local/education-lab/article275431671.html; Ellen Lee, "Does California Have a Lead in Drinking Water Problem?," *Natural Resources Defense Council*, February 16, 2023, https://www.nrdc.org/bio/ellen-lee/does-california-have-lead-drinking-water-problem.

412 Jaime Raymond, Will Wheeler, and Mary Jean Brown, "Lead Screening and Prevalence of Blood Lead Levels in Children Aged 1-2 Years—Child Blood Lead Surveillance System, United States, 2002-2010 and National Health and Nutrition Examination Survey, United States, 1999-2010," *Centers for Disease*

Control and Prevention Morbidity and Mortality Weekly Report 63, no. 2: 38, https://www.cdc.gov/mmwr/pdf/other/su6302.pdf.
413 Matt Taibbi, "Apocalypse, New Jersey: A Dispatch from America's Most Desperate Town," *Rolling Stone*, December 11, 2013, https://www.rollingstone.com/culture/culture-news/apocalypse-new-jersey-a-dispatch-from-americas-most-desperate-town-56174/ (connecting the city's fiscal straits to its racial history); Bomey, *Detroit Resurrected*, (for a nuanced narrative that describes the various fiscal pressures that culminated in the city's bankruptcy).
414 Kayode Crown, "Jackson's Water Problem Affects Business Development, City Official Says," *Jackson Free Press*, March 22, 2021, https://www.jacksonfreepress.com/news/2021/mar/22/jacksons-water-problem-affects-business-developmen/
415 Li Zhou, "Millions of Americans don't have drinkable water. Can the infrastructure bill fix that?" *Vox*, September 4, 2021, https://www.vox.com/22620076/jackson-mississippi-water-infrastructure-bill.
416 The problem exists also in rural Black communities. *See* Alexis Okeowo, "The Heavy Toll of the Black Belt's Wastewater Crisis," *New Yorker*, November 23, 2020, https://www.newyorker.com/magazine/2020/11/30/the-heavy-toll-of-the-black-belts-wastewater-crisis.
417 Kahrl, *Black Tax*, 345.
418 Black-led or predominate cities may be more vulnerable to state takeovers. See Anna Clark, " Michigan Still Allows Emergency Takeovers of Local Governments. Is It Finally Time to Reconsider This Drastic Measure?," Propublica, July 11, 2023, https://www.propublica.org/article/michigan-emergency-takeovers-flint-detroit; Julie Bosman and Monica Davey, "Anger in Michigan Over Appointing Emergency Managers," *New York Times*, January 22, 2016, https://www.nytimes.com/2016/01/23/us/anger-in-michigan-over-appointing-emergency-managers.html ("They also say emergency management gives influence to what is now a mostly white, Republican leadership in Lansing, the state capital").
419 Amy Harder and Kristina Peterson, "Senate Can't Agree on Aid for Flint, Stalling Energy Bill," *Wall Street Journal*, February 4, 2016, https://www.wsj.com/articles/senate-cant-agree-on-aid-for-flint-stalling-energy-bill-1454614755.
420 James Dao, "Ohio Town's Water at Last Runs Past a Color Line," *New York Times*, February 17, 2004, https://www.nytimes.com/2004/02/17/us/ohio-town-s-water-at-last-runs-past-a-color-line.html (Describing Zanesville, Ohio's denial of water to an African-American community for more than 50 years, even though the community existed less than one mile from public water lines and the city provided water to surrounding neighborhoods); see Kennedy v. City of Zanesville, 505 F. Supp 2d 456 (S.D. Ohio 2007), in which a jury awarded nearly $11 million to members of the community who successfully sued for unlawful discrimination under the FHA; Eric Lyttle, "Zanesville's black residents' fight for clean water, bittersweet," *Columbus Dispatch*, February 16, 2014, https://web.archive.org/web/20160314023339/https://www.dispatch.com/content/stories/local/2014/02/16/bittersweet-water.html.
421 JP Carballo et al., "Frozen Out in Texas: Blackouts and Inequity," *Rockefeller Foundation*, April 14, 2021, https://www.rockefellerfoundation.org/case-study/frozen-out-in-texas-blackouts-and-inequity/.
422 Julie Bosman, "Many Flint Residents are Desperate to Leave, but See No Escape," *New York Times,* February 4, 2016, https://www.nytimes.com/2016/02/05/us/many-flint-residents-are-desperate-to-leave-but-see-no-escape.html.
423 W.E.B. Du Bois, *Black Reconstruction* (New York: Harcourt, Brace and Company, 1935).

4 Toward a Structural Agenda

In late August 2005, a tropical storm began to form in the Bahamas and rapidly swelled in strength as it crossed into the Gulf of Mexico. The hurricane, officially designated Katrina, barreled toward the Gulf Coast, with New Orleans in the crosshairs. By the time Katrina made landfall, it subsided to a level 3 storm, and only grazed the historic city. Although New Orleans was spared the devastation of a category 5 hurricane direct hit, it proved nevertheless the most destructive storm in U.S. history. Fifty-three levees breached, homes and businesses were destroyed, power outages were widespread, and large swaths of the city flooded with water.

The damage was estimated at as much as $100 billion and hundreds of thousands of families in the Gulf were forced from their homes.[1] Images of evacuees and displaced families crowding the Superdome, or stranded on rooftops holding makeshift signs pleading for help, seared public consciousness. The unfolding tableau was as shocking as it was tragic. Television viewers could hardly believe this was happening in America. At the same time, the overwhelming number Black faces shown in the coverage made race an inescapable subtext to the disaster.

Five days after the storm flooded the city, leaving city streets under several stories of water, a Red Cross telethon implored viewers to donate money for relief aid. In one indelible segment, the actor and comedian Mike Myers and the entertainer and hip-hop artist Kanye West were paired as co-hosts, tasked with alternating commentary. Reading from a teleprompter, Myers lamented not only the physical destruction to the city, but the damage to the spirit of the community and the will to remain and rebuild. West, on the other hand, veered off script, and began by noting the sharply discrepant media captions of white survivors as "looking for food" while characterizing Black survivors as "looting." [2]

His voice shaking with emotion, West condemned our materialist and consumerist tendencies in times of urgent need, confessing that he had gone shopping before personally donating to relief efforts. He then complained that, although the Red Cross was doing everything it could, the federal response was inexcusably slow, especially for the less well-off, and complained those who might have helped were fighting wars overseas. Building toward

DOI: 10.4324/9781003562764-5

an emotional crescendo, West claimed that responders were even given permission to shoot the storm victims.

West paused as Myers read more script from the teleprompter, but the pause did little to abate West's impassioned state of mind. When cued, West firmly blurted out "George Bush doesn't care about Black people." A slack-jawed Myers did a double take at West in stunned bewilderment just before the network quickly cut away to Chris Tucker, also visibly startled.

Kanye West's outburst sparked a firestorm of commentary on the question of whether President Bush was a racist. Many pundits and commentators swiftly dismissed the accusation, concluding that he was not.[3] After all, no federal workers were instructed to treat Black residents differently or withhold aid. No willful act of discrimination or malign neglect was orchestrated during the rescue operation.

The inescapable and obvious racial dimensions of a major American tragedy were caught within an ill-fitting frame. Within this frame, race was merely a coincidental or background element to the story unless someone was culpably racist. In his brief remarks, West incisively noted a litany of structural elements—the inadequacy of the evacuation plans, the ploddingly slow federal response, the juxtaposition of local disinvestment and poverty with massive spending on foreign wars, callously contrasting media coverage, and the lethal authority given to "rescuers." Although it was undeniable that race had something to do with the disaster, West ultimately framed his assessment in stark interpersonal terms. The resulting cognitive dissonance is a consequence of the inadequacy of our prevailing ways of talking about and understanding race, even when we purport to regard it as something institutional or systemic. A structural analysis provides a way out of this dilemma.

The Individual Racism Model

As Kanye West's outburst reflects, the prevailing model and understanding of racism remains individual and interpersonal. Within this paradigm, racism is said to exist only to the extent that a racist perperator can be found. A racist, in this view, is a prejudiced or racially bigoted individual. A racist person, accordingly, may harbor race hatred, prejudice, or animosity, but whatever their attitudes, they are tend to regard one racial group as inferior or superior to another, and prefer a social order that reflects that hierarchical positioning.[4] As one of the men who murdered Emmitt Till later confessed, he liked Black people—and would never hurt them—as long as they remained "in their place."[5]

This conception of racism, rooted in the beliefs and attitudes of individuals, is at once familiar, with many well-known depictions in popular culture. It conjures a continuum of characters, from good-hearted but ignorant bigots like Archie Bunker from *All in the Family* or Tony Lip from *The Green Book* to the frothing Hollywood villain, like the Ewells in *To Kill a Mockingbird* or their real life counterparts such as Alabama's public safety commissioner Eugene "Bull" Connor ordering police to sic dogs or aim fire hoses at peaceful protestors, Ku Klux Klan member Thomas Edwin Blanton Jr. planting bombs that killed four little girls in Sunday school, or white nationalists like Dylan Roof shooting Black congregants worshipping in church.[6]

The harm of racism, in this model, usually takes the form of discrimination or violence. Operationally, racial discrimination is the behavioral manifestation of racist beliefs or racist ideas through an individual's actions.[7] In denying a Black person or other person of color a job opportunity or a promotion, the racist individual is behaving in accordance with their racist beliefs or internalized stereotypes. In short, the racist individual's behavior harms innocent people through their actions, denying or foreclosing an opportunity.

Within this model, racial disparities are principally a byproduct of prejudicial beliefs and discriminatory actions. For example, the historian Ibram X. Kendi repeatedly asserts in his award-winning survey of the history of racist ideas, *Stamped from the Beginning*, that discrimination is the source of racial disparities, writing that "racial discrimination was stamped from the beginning of America, and explains why racial disparities have existed and persisted."[8] In fact, Kendi defines an "anti-racist," a term he helped bring into popular parlance, as someone who explains racial disparities as a result of discrimination.[9]

The individual racism model is spring-loaded in our collective consciousness, triggered by any racial incident. It structures our assessment of the situation, commences a search for a perpetrator assigns culpability, and prescribes the range of commensurate remedies. If no evidence of racist intentions, beliefs, or ideas can be found, and if suspicions of such covert beliefs or private ideas can be dispelled, then many will reject a claim of racism, as they did when Kanye West appeared to accuse President Bush.

Even scholars and advocates who appreciate or claim to understand the reality of systemic and institutional racism nonetheless exhibit a tendency to explain these phenomena in individualistic terms. After all, they note, *someone* designed these policies or runs these institutions, and it is generally assumed that, given the racialized outcomes and disparities, that person or people must be racist.[10] There is a deep suspicion that a racist actor lurks somewhere within or behind these institutions and policies, and therefore a corresponding desire to expend energy to uncover them and root them out. If there is a web, they assume there must be a spider.[11] Rather than resist methodological individualism, some advocates double down on it: the more pervasive the racial injury or apparent oppression, the more deeply concealed or embedded the perpetrator(s) must be.

Relatedly some scholars emphasize the persistence of racist ideas—or ideation—at the core of these dynamics. Robin DiAngelo is emblematic, when she asserts "all white people have absorbed racist ideology, and it shapes the way we see the world and the way we see ourselves in the world, and it comes out in the policies and practices that we make and that we set up."[12] But this is just as reductive: it explains the policies, practices and institutional behavior as a product of racist ideology manifested, consciously or unconsciously, through individuals, as beliefs or behaviors.

While not universal, the individual racism model remains the model in which most Americans continue to perceive or understand racism. It remains the common sense understanding of "racism": a discriminatory act by a racist actor. In fact, the greater part of our civil rights law is predicated on this model. Claims brought under the Civil Rights Act of 1964, to take but one prominent example, generally require proof of intent or at least indicia of intent.[13] In that sense, plaintiffs bringing discrimination lawsuits not only accuse defendants of racism, but must produce evidence of racial animus, stereotypes, or prejudice.[14]

Racial discrimination claims brought under the auspices of the equal protection clause of the U.S. Constitution have been held by the Supreme Court to require proof of discriminatory intent or purpose, and that this intention was a "motivating factor" in a government official, body, or agency's decision-making process, not merely a contributing or incidental factor.[15] This requirement reveals the presumption that racism, at bottom, resides in the mind, as a belief, a stereotype, or an attitude.

By operating from a model that requires evidence of intentional discrimination, the law generally embodies the individual racism model. Critically, this is true even in cases in which the alleged bad actor is an institution or governmental entity, such as a corporation, municipality, or public university. Accordingly, courts generally require that race-specific remedial state action be narrowly tailored to addressing the effects of proven past intentional discrimination, and sweep no further. In fact, the Supreme Court has explicitly rejected remedial race-conscious policies aimed at "societal discrimination" as too "amorphous" a basis to justify such action.[16]

In the late 1960s, advocates such as Stokely Carmichael (later Kwame Ture) and Charles V. Hamilton formulated an alternative to the individual racism model, denoted "institutional racism."[17] This concept was based on the realization that racially "neutral" policies and practices could nonetheless operate to the disadvantage of non-whites. In other words, policies that made no reference to race, drew no racial distinctions, or seemed free of racial animus could nonetheless contribute to or sustain racial inequality. Many policies instituted in the wake of civil rights legislation seemed designed to maintain the status quo ante, and were therefore thought by reviewing courts to reflect covert racism. For example, on the very day that the Civil Rights Act of 1964 went into effect, one southern power company instituted aptitude tests and high school graduation requirements for new employees to replace the racial hiring guidelines it had previously used.[18]

The concept of institutional racism helped demonstrate that simply scrubbing overtly racist or facially discriminatory language from corporate or public policy was often insufficient to the task at hand. If a company replaces an overtly racist policy with a race-neutral alternative designed to achieve the same effect, then the purpose of the law has been thwarted. In this way, the institutional racism theory helped provide a basis for so-called "disparate impact" claims, in which the courts have permitted suits to proceed even in the absence of evidence of discriminatory intent, provided solid statistical evidence of a disproportionate racial impact can be established.[19]

After more than half a century since the adoption of such civil rights laws, the precise current legal foundation and rationale for disparate impact claims is unsettled and ambiguous, and they sit uncomfortably with the prevailing individual racism model. As such they are routinely attacked by pundits, jurists, and officials alike.[20] Not only are the statutory textual bases authorizing disparate impact claims often fiercely disputed, but some leading jurists suggest that disparate impact claims exist, at least in part, to expose covert intentional discrimination. As Supreme Court Justice Anthony Kennedy explained in 2015, "disparate impact liability under the [Fair Housing Act] plays a role in uncovering discriminatory intent: It permits plaintiffs to counteract unconscious prejudices and disguised animus that escape easy classification as disparate treatment."[21] Although the reference to unconscious prejudice was novel and perhaps significant, Kennedy's opinion nonetheless appears to reflect the view that disparate impact claims are designed to smoke out covert discrimination by racist or prejudiced actors.

Ultimately many courts remain skeptical of disparate impact claims, and have made it difficult for such claims to proceed, by erecting substantial evidentiary barriers and other prerequisites.[22] And, even where such suits are permitted to proceed, courts provide defendants substantial leeway to justify their policies and generally require that remedies be carefully drawn. Disparate impact claims, while alive within our jurisprudence, are marginal within workaday civil rights jurisprudence. The intentional discrimination framework is the dominant paradigm.

By now the limits of the individual racism frame should be apparent. Supposing that Kayne West was correct, that George W. Bush did not care about Black people, and his lack of regard delayed the federal response, what difference would that have made? It probably would have saved some lives, but it would not have changed the fact that African-Americans were disproportionately vulnerable to the natural disaster in the first place nor prevented the flooding of the Lower Ninth Ward, which was 98% Black.[23] The most severe damage occurred in the city's poorest and most segregated neighborhoods.[24]

Before Katrina, little attention was given to the ways in which residential segregation had disproportionately exposed Black residents to a foreseeable natural disaster. Nor was the evacuation plan, predicated on people leaving in their own vehicles, scrutinized against the fact that many of the most vulnerable Black residents in the city did not own cars. The relief effort itself—who was helped and how much, as well as the ensuing fights over reconstruction and the right of return—replicated these inequities.[25] But these were structural and institutional dynamics, not entirely comprehensible through the narrow lens of individual animus or prejudice.

If West was correct, then the solution is simple: replace the president, and the problem of race in the aftermath of Katrina disappears. A series of high-profile police encounters during the Obama administration illustrates the fallacy of this view, and helped usher in a new one.

Black Lives Matter

On August 9, 2014, municipal police officer Darren Wilson confronted 18-year-old Michael Brown in the suburb of Ferguson, Missouri, just outside of St. Louis, on the suspicion of having stolen trifling items from a local convenience store. Eyewitness reports are contradictory, but what is known is that the confrontation escalated, and Darren Wilson shot and killed Michael Brown.[26] Wilson claimed that Michael Brown charged toward him and that he feared for his life. Other witnesses claimed that Michael Brown's hands were up or that he was running away. What is undisputed is that Michael Brown was unarmed and died in the street after being shot by officer Wilson.

Only a few weeks earlier, a middle-aged Black man, Eric Garner, was confronted in Staten Island by NYPD officers on suspicion of having sold cigarettes unlawfully.[27] During the confrontation, Eric Garner was held in a chokehold by the officers, and despite gasping that that he "can't breathe" repeatedly, the officers continued to restrain Mr. Garner, ultimately killing him. Again, some details were murky, but what is clear is that another unarmed Black man was killed by the police after a confrontation based on a suspicion of violating a minor law.

A wave of street protests erupted in the aftermath of these and other police killings.[28] The protestors expressed anger at not only the killings themselves, but the lack of accountability for those killings, with the local prosecutor perceived to have sabotaged the grand jury investigation against Darren Wilson, and ultimately declining to bring charges.[29] A New York Grand Jury also declined to indict officers who killed Eric Garner.[30] In 2019, the Department of Justice also announced it would not bring charges in that case.[31]

The protestors were also angered by the countless incidents of excessive force, abuse, and disrespect that followed, from the use of tear gas on protestors, unconstitutional arrests of journalists, and even racial epithets hurled by police.[32] One notable outrage was a police officer allowing a dog to urinate on the makeshift memorial to Michael Brown.

Nationally organized protests using the social media hashtag #Blacklivesmatter spread across the United States in the months that followed.[33] The hashtag became an organizing tool and a statement of purpose. Each new police killing under similarly disputed, suspicious, or trivial circumstances broadened the national movement as protests amplified the message. Critically, many of these encounters were recorded on cell phone video for all Americans to see, shocking white America's complacency and bursting certain assumptions, just as many northerners were shocked to see police dogs attacking civil rights protesters in the Jim Crow south.[34] The pattern was too widespread and endemic to explain away on the basis of a few bad apples. The impunity and behavior of the police appeared to be institutional and cultural.

The incongruence of the Obama presidency and the galvanizing movement stirring from the deaths of Michael Brown, and so many others, helped drew attention to conditions beyond the interpersonal model of racial inequality and racism. Indeed, the Black Lives Matter movement intensified and spread after the death of Freddie Gray in Baltimore, a deeply segregated city beset by the problems that flow therefrom, yet in which the city's entire leadership structure was staffed by Black officials. Baltimore most starkly highlighted the incongruity: a Black mayor, police chief, district attorney, and city council, yet 1 in 4 poverty rate, and 37% young Black male unemployment.[35] Three trials have been held for police officers involved in Freddie Gray's "rough ride" that resulted in his death in a police vehicle, yet they resulted in two acquittals and a deadlocked jury.[36] This, during the nation's first Black presidency and with a Black attorney general leading the Department of Justice for much of this period.

The protest movement re-emerged on larger scale in the Spring of 2020, in the midst of the coronavirus pandemic, after a series of shocking racial incidents culminating in the murder of George Floyd. On May 25, a former Minneapolis police officer, Derek Chauvin, responded to a 911 call at a local convenience reporting that Mr. Floyd had used a fake $20 bill to buy cigarettes.[37] Chauvin confronted and pinned George Floyd to the ground during an arrest. Even after Mr. Floyd complained that he couldn't breathe and pedestrians urged officers to listen, officer Chauvin refused to move his knee. As seen in a video shot by a bystander, three other officers stood by as Mr. Floyd went unconscious, and died of asphyxiation.[38] It wasn't until May 28, three days later, that the Minneapolis police department fired the officers involved, and another day for the county authorities to charge Derek Chauvin with murder and arrest him.[39]

Protests erupted immediately in Minneapolis, and quickly spread over the world.[40] Some claim that the 2020 Black Lives Matter movement were the largest mass protests in U.S. history.[41] Nearly 40% of counties in the United States had a protest, including heavily white communities, and public opinion swung in support of the movement to a degree not seen before.[42] Conceptions of "systemic racism" gained wider public salience, and dictionary authorities moved to expand or revise definitions of racism.[43] Not only were questions around police training, protocol, use of force, and accountability foregrounded, but broader questions about public safety and life chances were being raised, with calls to shift or allocate more funding to social services, public health, housing, jobs and education.[44]

The Uprisings of the 1960s

The Black Lives Matter movement is not the only mass racial justice protest movement triggered by police violence, but the latest expression of a long continuum of racial justice protest in American history. One of the more renowned examples was when Alabama police viciously attacked protestors on the Edmund Pettis Bridge in Selma, Alabama, in 1963, one of the seminal moments in the Civil Rights Movement.[45] The death struggle of Jim Crow induced other disturbances and violence, but by the mid-1960s these incidents formed a more widespread pattern of civil unrest, most often outside of the south.

In 1964, a white off duty police officer in Harlem shot and killed a 15-year-old African-American boy.[46] Establishing a pattern for such incidents, eyewitness accounts sharply diverged. The officer claimed that the boy attacked him with a knife, although other witnesses claimed the boy was unarmed. During the ensuing protest, police apparently barricaded the precinct station, and a "scuffle broke out" that resulted in six nights of violence.[47] In the end, there were over 500 arrests, 141 injured, and one death.

Perhaps the most notorious incident of the period was the 1965 Watts uprising. A Los Angeles highway patrolman stopped a young Black driver for speeding, and then arrested the driver for intoxication.[48] Although accounts are fuzzy, a backup patrolman reportedly assaulted someone in growing crowd, and the police and crowd exchanged blows, triggering a spasm of violence that spread outward toward passing motorists and nearby property. Although matters calmed temporarily, 30 hours after the original incident, approximately 35,000 people amassed in downtown Watts, drawing families from five nearby housing projects, resulting in six days of intense protest. The National Guard was activated to quell the uprising, and thousands of officers were deployed, arresting protestors in mass for violating curfew and later for public violence. The end result was over $35 million in property damage, 4,000 injuries, and 34 deaths.[49]

The race upheavals of the 1960s, however, reached a fever pitch in the "long, hot summer" of 1967, when police encounters with unarmed Black Americans and other inciting events precipitated major protests in more than a hundred cities, resulting in more than $100 million dollars in property damage, more than 80 deaths, and several thousand injuries.[50] Although at least 41 of these "urban disorders" were later described as "major," the largest and most significant occurred in Detroit, where there was five days of unrest which left 43 people dead and more than 1100 injured, and in Newark, where 26 people died and more than 700 injured.[51]

Following these uprisings, President Johnson appointed a special commission, The National Advisory Commission on Civil Disorders, better known as the Kerner Commission, to study the causes of these events.[52] Helmed by Democratic Governor Otto Kerner of Illinois and Republican New York City Mayer John Lindsey, the Commission was tasked with answering three simple questions: "What happened? Why did it happen? What can be done to prevent it from happening again?"

The Commission itself was bipartisan and composed of politically mainstream and well-regarded establishment figures, including congressmen, local officials, a businessman, a chief of police, and a labor leader.[53] Supported by a team of eminent social scientists, researchers, and field investigators, this

Commission issued a shocking, unanimously signed, 17 chapter final report, better known as "Riot Report," on February 29, 1968.[54] The report was crafted to satisfy and receive the endorsement of a cross-section of moderate politicians, which ultimately underscores the gravity of the findings. It remains one of the most insightful and revealing government documents ever crafted.

In its report, the Commission constructed detailed profiles of 10 of the 23 cities it investigated, which including demographic conditions, interview testimony, and social scientific analysis.[55] The Commission concluded that each of these urban disorders was a product of multiple forces, some many years in the making, but in many cases the spark was a particular encounter, usually involving police, which the Commission termed an "precipitating incident," that galvanized affected communities.

In Tampa, for example, following reports of a robbery from a local camera store, a white police officer shot and killed 19-year-old Martin Chambers in the back after a foot chase.[56] The spark for the Detroit uprising was a police raid of an unlicensed, Prohibition-era liquor establishment.[57] Unbeknownst to the police, the club was hosting a homecoming party for two Black Vietnam servicemen, but more than 80 Black patrons were arrested.[58] Another precipitating event occurred in the Hunter's Point neighborhood of San Fransico when a white police shot and killed 16-year old Matthew "Peanut" Johnson.[59]

The Commission's Report presented details concerning the specific incidents and the more general conditions that fueled a combustible environment. Although the Commission noted, "[a]lmost invariably, the incident that ignites disorder arises from police action," it explained that the

> [d]isorder did not typically erupt without preexisting causes[...] Instead, it developed out of an increasingly disturbed social atmosphere, in which typically a series of tension-heightening incidents over a period of weeks or months became linked in the minds of many in the Negro community with a shared reservoir of underlying grievances.[60]

In New Brunswick, for example, the Commission noted the closing of a local coffee house for teenagers although there was no community swimming pool or other recreational facility.[61] In Atlanta, residents complained about the lack of a swimming pool in a Black neighborhood, and that the nearby public park could not be accessed by Black residents because of the lack of a public road or easement.[62] In Cincinnati, the two swimming pools available to Black youth could only accommodate a small portion of demand and much of the available housing stock was deteriorating or dilapidated.[63]

The Commission found that in almost every city investigated, there was an accumulation of legitimate grievances in the Black community, including discrimination, substandard housing and schools, lack of accessible recreational facilities, unresponsive government, and police abuse and harassment, which it painfully documented. The police encounter or other inciting incidents then became the trigger, "culminating in the eruption of disorder at the hands of youthful, politically-aware activists."[64] One of the sources of pent-up anger in Detroit was the killing of Vietnam veteran Danny Thomas by a white gang, and the lack of an arrest by the police for his murder, in the months before the raid on the unlicensed liquor establishment. Rather than quell the violence, police actions often inflamed it.

The Kerner Commission reported that "Negroes firmly believe that police brutality and harassment occur repeatedly in Negro neighborhoods."[65] It is this belief, the Commission concluded, that was one of the primary reasons for the resentment of police in those neighborhoods. The Commission was careful to note that the complaints it documented were not "the crude acts of an earlier time," referring to explicitly racist police behavior. However, it specifically identified police misconduct—whether described as brutality, harassment, or merely verbal abuse and discourtesy—as intolerable and a critical element of the conditions that contributed to the civil disorders of 1967.

Critically the Commission concluded that the underlying causes of these disturbances, which activists described as rebellions, were these longstanding grievances.[66] Based on more than 1,200 interviews and surveys of the cities by field teams where riots occurred, the Commission concluded that the number one grievance was police practices. Police practices included verbal abuse and harassment, general lack of respect, inadequate mechanisms for civilian complaints and review, and physical abuse. The Commission summarized the grievances into three tiers of intensity: (1) police practices, unemployment and underemployment, inadequate housing; (2) inadequate education, poor recreational facilities and programs, ineffectiveness of the political structure and grievance mechanisms; and (3) disrespectful white attitudes, discriminatory administration of justice, inadequacy of federal programs, inadequacy of municipal services, discriminatory consumer and credit practices, and inadequate welfare programs.[67]

The Kerner Commission report concluded that white society had denied opportunity to Black Americans living in poor urban neighborhoods. In its most famous line, the commission warned that "Our Nation is moving toward two societies, one Black, one white – separate and unequal." Furthermore, it asserted that "What white Americans have never fully understood – but what the Negro can never forget – is that white society is deeply implicated in the ghetto. White institutions created it, white institutions maintain it, and white society condones it."[68]

The Commission not only investigated the immediate disturbances and delved into the root causes, but produced a comprehensive and wide-ranging set of more than 100 policy recommendations.[69] Topics included employment and large-scale job training and creation; education reform, including integrating schools; promoting residential integration by increasing the supply of housing subsidies for poor families; and diversifying local police forces. Many of the recommendations remain sadly relevant today, including calling for hundreds of thousands of affordable housing units, ending "stop and frisk" policing, universal Pre-K education programs, and the development of a universal basic income.

Despite selling millions of copies and becoming one of the best-selling books of the year, few of the Commission's recommendations were ever implemented.[70] The ambitious plan for action ran headlong into the currents of reactionary backlash as well as the political divisions engendered by the wars in Southeast Asia.[71] Johnson also hoped that the Commission would commend his policy initiatives already underway in the form of the War on Poverty. To his dismay, the Commission's report highlighted the inadequacy of existing federal efforts, and called for a much broader and more vigorous set of investments and programs. Sapped of his political capital and strained by war budget, along with massive losses in the congressional elections of 1966, none of the Commission's recommendations for major federal investments were politically viable. President Johnson left the Kerner Commission's recommendations largely untouched during his final months in office.

Despite the Kerner Report's prescient warnings, further uprisings would occur in short order. In the aftermath of the assassination of Martin Luther King Jr., little more than a month after the release of the Kerner Report, the pattern repeated itself, with more than 137 separate incidents, resulting in more than 3,500 people injured, at least 43 deaths, and millions in property damage.[72] The historian Elizabeth Hinton has further documented another nearly 2,000 further separate uprisings arising out of segregated Black communities, predominantly in smaller and mid-sized cities, between May 1968 and December 1972.[73]

Rather than undertake the reforms that might address the root causes of these so-called "disorders," national policy veered in the opposite direction. Richard Nixon, as well as other conservative leaders, charged that the Commission condoned the breakdown of law and order, which they argued was the source of the civil unrest, not institutional or white racism.[74] Richard Nixon and to an even greater extent, George Wallace, organized their presidential campaigns in reaction to the disorders, especially the heightened anxiety and fearful mood, rejecting the recommendations of the Commission as "rewarding the rioters." In a sense, Nixon ran *against* the Kerner Commission's recommendations as much as Johnson was hamstrung in doing anything to advance them.

Systemic versus Structural Racism

Although it did not use this terminology, the Kerner Commission report presented a structural analysis and identified structural conditions and institutional dynamics, including disadvantaged conditions, inadequate opportunity, and unequal public provision, as the foundation of racial inequality in American society.[75] It also went further and identified police impunity and a sense of callous indifference and deliberate disregard by white society as fuel for uprisings and Black anger. Although the details have changed, and many conditions have improved, there remain too many disturbing present-day parallels and contemporaneously relevant recommendations.

A structural lens for understanding the production of racial inequality is necessary to address racial inequality in contemporary American society. While non-structural forces contribute to racial inequality, structural forces play an outsized and less visible role. These forces generate racialized inequities in ways that are so deeply embedded that they operate beyond the awareness of even many well-meaning decision makers and tend to be harder to legislate away or regulate. The key is not intent—it is how the system is organized, meaning how the elements connect and interact, and what outcomes it is producing.

The idea that racial inequalities can arise or persist in the absence of malicious acts or purposeful behavior, planning or guidance toward that end is not an original insight, but not all such realizations are based on a structural analysis.[76] The political philosopher Iris Marion Young was one of the first and most prominent figures to observe that oppression can be a "structural concept," meaning that it does not necessarily result from a "few people's choices or policies" but can arise instead from "everyday practices of a well-intentioned liberal society."[77] Years later, she further elaborated a conception of "structural injustice," which explained how disparities and inequality would persist, due to ordinary and facially neutral "rules, norms, and practices of many institutions."[78] She observed that "[e]ven when overt discriminatory practices are illegal and widely condemned, racialized structures are produced and reproduced in many everyday interactions in civil society and workplaces."[79] She seemed to characterize these observations, however, as an "account of the structural inequalities of institutional racism."[80]

Twenty-five years ago, a public health scholar published an influential article entitled "The Gardner's Tale."[81] This brief article delineated three "levels" of racism: "institutional, personally mediated, and internalized." This was an important effort to distinguish between multiple forms of racism, and used a metaphor that is broadly consonant with the framework presented in this book, emphasizing the role of environment and nurturing conditions in human development. Notably, her article presented a definition of "institutional" racism that moved well beyond the formulations of the 1960s and 1970s and landed closer to the framework here: as "differential access to the goods, services, and opportunities of society by race... and often manifests as inherited disadvantage." This essay used the term "structural" to describe conditions and factors that were often critical in producing these outcomes, but were invisible because they often lacked a perpetrator.[82] Importantly the essay emphasized the role of omission as much as commission and how neglect can be as harmful as hate.

There is ample evidence that racial discrimination continues to occur in many domains of life, and that it is often covert or unconscious.[83] And, there is no doubt that past and present discrimination has significant and present-day effects, and those effects are easy to overlook or underestimate. An exclusionary denial or discriminatory act many years ago not only shapes the opportunities of the individual denied, but reverberate horizontally across society and vertically over a lifetime and even generations.[84]

But a structural model reminds that racial disparities and inter-group inequality can arise and persist even in the absence of intentional discrimination entirely. More than a generation ago, economists modeled how racial income inequality can continue indefinitely given a set of initial conditions.[85] Similarly, simple modeling shows that racial residential segregation can easily be maintained without discrimination.[86] Even if we could eliminate hundreds of thousands of instances of intentional housing discrimination per year, it would not likely change measured levels of racial residential segregation significantly.[87] If we could magically snap our fingers or wave a wand, and scrub the hearts and minds of every American of racial prejudice or stereotypes, what, practically speaking, would change? Would patterns of segregation, achievement gaps, health disparities, and income and wealth inequalities suddenly evaporate or even gradually disappear?

Many (although not all) of the policies, structures, and forces that perpetuate contemporary racial inequality arose for reasons other than racial antipathy or other prejudicial motives. They are a product of the complex interaction of many decisions and policies motivated by many reasons by diverse actors over many years. Like the federal tax code, structural racism is the accretion of generations of layered, disparate policies, many of which were intended for the common good, or on behalf of particular non-racial interest groups (like the elderly, parents, or a business lobby), but which have ultimately produced a byzantine structure with loopholes and unexpected access points that are too easily exploited by the well-heeled and the experts they employ.

More broadly, contemporary structural racial inequality is broadly maintained by the self-interested behavior of tens of millions of Americans on a daily basis. The decisions parents make about where to send their kids to school, buy in a home, or invest their retirement savings are structured by rules and institutional arrangements that tend to reinforce structural racial inequality if made "rationally," with a narrow focus on maximizing returns or appreciation.[88] Support for exclusionary municipal policies, and opposition to taxes for public goods have a larger impact on extant racial disparities by default rather than design.

To the extent that a malign consciousness or intentionality (beyond selfishness) is at work, it would be more accurate to characterize it as profound indifference or extreme neglect rather than prejudice or animosity. As Elie Wiesel wrote, "The opposite of love is not hate, it's indifference."[89] Both Kanye West's remark and the anger in communities of color documented by the Kerner Commission point to a lack of concern and insufficient regard. To the victims of such oppression, actions (or, more often, inactions) based on callousness indifference tend to seem as if they are based on hatred or antipathy. After all, they wonder, why would the rest of America let things get so bad? But to assume it is animus or antipathy misdiagnoses the problem.

Not only does intentional discrimination and the interpersonal racism model fail to explain the ongoing production of racial inequality, it undermines the larger project of racial justice and equality by seducing us into believing that combating prejudice and racist ideas will lead to equitable racial outcomes. This was one of the critiques of the "feel-good" Oscar winner, *The Green Book*, which portrays "racism as the result of the individual ignorances of underexposed white Americans, rather than a systematic structure of purposeful inequity," and thus perpetuates a facile message of racial harmony.[90] This therapeutic model of anti-racism is also embodied in many prominent treatises on race, which emphasize awareness, often in the form of Diversity, Equity, and Inclusion (DEI) trainings or workshops, as the solution to racial inequality. Structural problems require structural solutions.

Nonetheless, some race scholars argue that modifiers like "structural" before "racism" are redundant, and that a clear-eyed anti-racism agenda should suffice to address all racial inequality.[91] Given the prevalent misunderstandings and prevailing narratives on race in America, a generic anti-racism analysis tends to mask the structural features of racial inequality that need to be excavated and centered in our public and policy discourse.[92] Perhaps worse, the absence of a modifier engenders the very conflation, confusion and misunderstandings that the systemic and structural analysis is designed to overcome.[93]

A structural racism analysis helps push back against a model of racial inequality based in interpersonal behaviors and individual attitudes, as well as the cultural pathology frame and other meanings that became attached to some racialized identities.[94] Even well-informed experts and advocates easily slip back onto an assumption that these institutional and structural features must be traceable back to some prejudiced actor or bigoted agent harboring racist ideas. The interpersonal racism model is both tenacious and seductive, deluding us with the illusionary promise of simple explanations and solutions.

Only a structural analysis is capable of actually explaining, and therefore addressing, racial inequality as it exists today. Applying it allows us to reform the ways we talk about race in more productive and effective directions. Under a structural lens, some matters or points of contention that seemed quite important recede to the background, while others acquire new significance. On many important issues, a structural lens changes the dynamics of the conversation. It also changes the prescriptions of what we should do, and how to go about devising a solution. It provides clarity in terms of both analysis and objectives, as described in the remainder of this chapter. This is why structural racism should be named as such.

This book offers a specific definition of structural racism that centers on the articulation and examination of structures of opportunity, the structural lattice of opportunity pathway networks, relationships and forces that inculcate human and social capital, and support social and economic advancement and well-being. These structures are racialized in the United States, propagating racial advantages and disadvantages based largely on people's location within them. That is what is meant by the term structural racism, a term that has been critiqued as "vague and ill-defined" or too "mushy and malleable."[95]

This is not for a lack of effort. In a review of the relevant literature, there are many definitions proffered. For example, two law professors define structural racism as "the processes, procedures, policies, historical conventions, assumptions, and beliefs regarding operational functioning that occur within, between, and among the social institutions that make up a society's infrastructure."[96] Yet another more widely used definition developed by a consortium of foundations proposed: "A system in which public policies, institutional practices, cultural representations, and other norms work in various, often reinforcing ways to perpetuate racial group inequity."[97] Each definition appears to miss a critical element or fails the test of specificity.[98]

As noted earlier, in the wake of the uprising following the murder of George Floyd, the term "systemic racism" gained broader public purchase and wider salience as a shorthand for racism that is broader and more deeply embedded than traditional forms of interpersonal racism. Many speakers either have in mind something approximating structural racism when speaking of "systemic" racism,[99] or are using the term in an inchoate way, referring to the general production of racial inequality. When used in this broader way or with a more precise intention, the adjective "structural" is preferable over "systemic" as a descriptor of more deeply embedded forms of racism and the production of racial inequality.

There is a rich literature on "systems thinking" arising out of various fields, including cybernetics, computer science, organizational management and ecology.[100] Within this literature, a system is an interdependent group of agents working together as a whole, or a set of elements that interact (like a solar system).[101] Systems have certain properties and behaviors. This literature has useful insights on the production of racial inequality, which is one reason why the term "systemic" racism has found such purchase.[102]

Systemic racism helps us understand how the interaction of elements within a system produce and maintain racialized outcomes and other disparities even in the absence of racist actors. The initial conditions of the system, the system design, and the organization or the interaction of elements can generate unexpected, undesirable or unwanted outcomes, sometimes called "emergent properties" or "metaeffects."[103] Discrimination or random initial inequalities in one part of a system can generate feedback loops that spread to other sectors or mount through the system with much greater magnitudes over time.[104] Many systemic effects are unintentional but significant. A systemic lens draws our attention to the interaction and organization of system elements as a causal force.

While offering important insights, the systemic racism frame also has limitations. In general, systems refer to the interaction of elements (institutions and actors) confined within them or specific to a particular system, like the criminal justice system or educational system. Systemic racism is appropriately precise and descriptively accurate when denoting dynamics within a particular system and the systemic effects of those dynamics, which cannot be traced to a singular individual component. Structural racism, in contrast, denotes a larger canvass and broader scope: the interaction of multiple systems, institutions, policies, norms, individuals, and markets. The term "systemic racism," denoting racial inequality within or emanating from systems, ironically understates the extent of problem, which goes beyond particular systems.

Just as systemic racism extends beyond a single institution, structural racism looks beyond a particular system or set of systems and their interrelationships. Structural racism is the broadest view on the propagation of racial inequality. As one definition presented in the Lancet, a world-renowned medical journal, suggests, structural racism is "the totality of the ways in which societies foster [racial] discrimination, via mutually reinforcing [inequitable] systems (e.g. in housing, education, employment, earnings, benefits, credit, media, health care, criminal justice, etc.)"[105]

It is not surprising that the term "structural racism" is perhaps most widely employed and early adopted in the fields of medicine, public health, and epidemiology.[106] These fields take a rigorous and empirical view of the production of racial inequality in their respective domains. They recognize that the role environment plays on individual and communal wellbeing, view health outcomes in terms of "social determinants," a framework that emphasizes the conditions people are born, live, learn, work, play and worship within, and not just the choices they make, but how those choices are structured.[107]

The Goal of Racial Justice

Racial justice advocacy is occasionally stymied by ambiguous or conflicting objectives. On many complex and nuanced issues, you can find racial justice or equity advocates on each side. A proposal for bail reform in California split advocates, who opposed cash bail, but feared algorithmic bias.[108] Tenant's rights and anti-gentrification advocates may oppose light rail, new housing, beautification projects, or infrastructure investments ostensibly designed to help or improve marginalized communities for fear of stimulating property values, rents, and displacement.[109] Some advocates worry that commitment to DEI programs give corporations and other powerful institutions cover—and perhaps mute criticism—in labor disputes.[110]

Too often, symbolic victories are mistaken for or conflated with achievements that change structural conditions or improve people's lives. If a "victory" is achieved, but no lives improve and no disparity meliorated, then such victories must be considered suspect, no matter how significant the effort or unexpected the achievement.

In addition, racial justice advocacy bleeds naturally into the fight against other forms of inequality and "othering."[111] Given the intersectional reality of race, class, gender, disability, and other marginalized identities, it is not uncommon to encounter arguments that "true liberation" and social justice cannot occur without taking on other causes as well.[112] While that may well be true, it is nonetheless important to try to envision a racial justice goal that can then serve as the basis for a racial justice policy agenda. Without clarity of objectives, tactics may be unfocused and poorly tailored.

One possible goal is to drive out racist ideas. Given the prevalence of the interpersonal racism model, the fight against racist ideas and ideologies can loom large among racist justice advocates. Yet, from a structural perspective, real-world effects—outcomes—matter much more than intentions, attitudes, or beliefs. Thus, a racial bigot who nonetheless supports effective racially egalitarian policies would be preferable to a person who opposes ameliorative policy positions, yet holds no racial animus in their heart, or a well-meaning person who supports ineffective or counterproductive racial equity policies.[113]

From a structural racism perspective, an antiracist is someone who supports or advances effective policies to reduce racially disparate outcomes regardless of their beliefs or personal prejudices. This definition perhaps changes our assessment of historical and contemporary figures. The first Justice John Harlan was more racially progressive in his jurisprudence than perhaps any Supreme Court Justice since.[114] Yet, in his famous *Plessy* dissent, he also outed himself as a white supremacist:

> The white race deems itself to be the dominant race in this country. And so it is, in prestige, in achievements, in education, in wealth, and in power. So, I doubt not, it will continue to be for all time, if it remains true to its great heritage and holds fast to the principles of constitutional liberty.[115]

A structural racism perspective is more concerned with his jurisprudence than his personal prejudices. Conversely, a local mayor who is known for fair dealing, personal integrity and a lack of personal prejudice may be justly criticized for their opposition to fair housing initiatives. In the end, would it really matter if George Bush was personally prejudiced, if his administration had done an excellent job helping Katrina victims?

Another possible goal of racial justice is to eliminate, or at least reduce, average group-based racial disparities. To this end, Ibram X. Kendi proposed a set of elaborate policy mechanisms to eliminate entrenched racial disparities.[116] This approach may seem consistent with the theme of this book. After all, racial disparities—statistically significant differences in group outcomes along any particular indicator—are often the result of underlying structural forces or discrimination.

Nonetheless, a narrow focus on disparities has several critical limitations. One of the most obvious is that disparities can be closed by reducing the standing or advantages enjoyed by the more advantaged group without in any way benefiting the marginalized group. For example, by reducing life expectancy or income for whites without any corresponding improvement in Black life expectancy, we can close a disparity gap. That is not the goal of racial justice. Rather, the goal should be to accomplish this only through absolute improvements in well-being.

More simply, it can be difficult to assess whether a disparity is closing or widening. A disparity can appear to be growing larger in an absolute sense, even as it is shrinking in a relative sense. For example, the absolute disparity in the value of home values for Black and white Americans has increased by about $15,000 between 1970 and 2020, but the relative size of that disparity has shrunk considerably because home values have grown faster than the disparity.[117]

Another problem with a myopic focus on disparities is that it takes what the more advantaged group has as the baseline, norm, or goal, even when there are enormous disparities within that group, such as between low-income and wealthy whites, or a decline in the performance of that group as a whole. If the absolute well-being of whites has declined,[118] then reducing the disparity between whites and non-whites may be the wrong goal.

A broader problem is that eliminating all racial disparities so that racial proportionality exists in every significant sphere of American society may not be a desirable goal in a practical sense. Even rejecting the idea of biological or genetic racial difference in intelligence or other endowments, and further granting the argument of this book that structural forces explain much of the panoply of existing racial disparities, they likely do not explain them all or their full extent. Even if structural forces in turn shape preferences and decisions about educational, procreative, and career choices, it is nonetheless possible that situational, cultural, religious and other differences and contingencies may shape interests, behaviors, and preference sets. And not all initial advantages may be unfair, or if unfair, were randomly distributed in a way that was largely unavoidable and unpreventable.

And some disparities may also be incurable, in practical reality. Engineering perfect racial proportionality would not only be coercive to racially advantaged groups, but it could also feel oppressive to racially disadvantaged groups. While it could make sense in certain cases, like critical institutions of higher education, boards of major companies or legislatures, mandating perfect racial proportionality in, say, dental offices, laundromats, or basketball teams seems unreasonable.

The most serious problem with a narrow disparity focus, however, is that they can be reduced—even zeroed out—with redistribution or compensatory schemes that leave underlying structural conditions and relationships intact. In theory, for example, a policy aimed at eliminating a particular health disparity may achieve this narrow equity objective without addressing the conditions or factors that cause this disparity, and which would instantly recur if the policy were discontinued. Similarly, such policies could be achieved without significantly affecting educational attainment, housing stability, income, employment, or wealth disparities.

For these reasons, however, a better approach is to use the presence of glaring racial disparities as a diagnostic tool to draw attention to underlying structural conditions, and to remedy those conditions, rather than to aim at the strict elimination of all racial disparities. Extreme group-based inequality should be generally intolerable, especially in vital areas of human well-being, but a strict elimination of all disparities is not only a more difficult goal than seeking their amelioration, it is not the optimal equity objective. We could theoretically eliminate all group-based disparities and yet fail to achieve a vision of a just and healthy society, one where people are thriving and free. We need a baseline that is independent of what a more advantaged or favored group enjoys, and is based, instead, on normative collective aspirations.

Based upon the framework of this book, the better racial justice goal is a society where the most important opportunity pathways would be largely open and accessible on a roughly equal racial basis. In a racially just society, race would no longer significantly shape life chances.[119] This does not mean that there would be no racial disparities, but many (statistically significant) group-level racial disparities would disappear or significantly decline. Such disparities, to the extent that they persist, would be a product of aggregate individual choices, random factors, and non-structurally influenced cultural preferences rather than discrimination or determined structural forces beyond our control.[120] If this were accomplished, then structural racism would, by definition, cease to exist.

The pursuit of this goal in relation to a structural racism remedial agenda prompts a reassessment of many familiar racial debates, and suggests a different model for assessment and action. Instead of looking for someone to blame, we should analyze the structural conditions.[121] When confronted with a racial problem, instead of first searching for a racist perpetrator we should instead ask which policymaker or authority has the power to do something about it. And instead of judging policies based upon good intentions, we should evaluate them largely on outcomes, and condemn the ineffective and counterproductive as much as the nefarious or malign.

Principles for a Structural Change Agenda

One of the most obvious ways that the policies suggested by a structural analysis differ from traditional racial equity debates is that only some of policy recommendations that flow therefrom seek race-specific answers to structural problems. It may seem paradoxical that a book about structural racism would advance recommendations for racial equity that are not uniformly race-specific. As the journalist Nikole Hannah-Jones asserted, "You can't use race-neutral policies to fix race-specific harms."[122]

Yet, this conclusion depends heavily on what is meant by "neutral" and "specific." Broad structural conditions that propagate racial disparities are certainly not "neutral" with respect to race, nor are universalistic interventions that reduce racial disparities. This is why, as far back as W.E.B. DuBois, racial justice advocates call for a mixture of race-specific and merely race-conscious policies.[123] Moreover, any policy that seeks to achieve racial equity goals is by definition race-conscious, even if the means is not always race-targeted or race-specific.[124]

As a purely racial equity matter, targeted interventions aimed at specific racial groups or members of particular groups appear logical. They confront, in a direct manner, a barrier to opportunity. From a structural perspective, however, they are not always preferable.

Just as members of different racial groups may have different structural positions, many members of the same racial group are differently situated. The child of an African or Caribbean immigrant doctor is unlikely to suffer exactly the same structural disadvantages as the great-grandchild of an American slave (and, in fact, is likely to have some that the latter does not have). A race-specific policy that is blind to their situational differences is unlikely to fully address the disadvantages of both cases.

Conversely, a policy that aims just to help members of a particular racial group, and extend no further, is far less likely to transform or address a structural problem than a policy that aims wider than a particular race-target. That is because structural conditions that undergird disadvantage are rarely confined to affecting members of a single racial group. Structural reforms often have a wider set of beneficiaries, even if they tend to have disproportionate effects.[125]

From a structural perspective, race-targeted policies are likely to be over-inclusive or under-inclusive. They are likely either insufficiently granular to help the most disadvantaged or to address particular forms of disadvantage on the one hand, or they are too narrowly focused to address or transform the structural condition on the other hand.

Race-specificity, in the sense of specifying the beneficiaries of a policy by race, is not the acid test of an effective racial justice policy. Whether it works in terms of reducing disparities and improving outcomes, not its form, is what ultimately matters. Although the expressive or symbolic component of targeted approaches is meaningful, a structural analysis must guide policymakers toward structural solutions. This will require transforming structures or the relationships between structural elements to produce more equitable outcomes, in both racial terms and more generally.

In this way, some targeted policies leave existing structural arrangements largely intact but create a special alternative pathway or accommodation for the disadvantaged group to address the disparity for that group. From a structural perspective, a better solution would be to restructure the system.[126] Thus, instead of a university affirmative action policy that targets and boosts disadvantaged applicants, we might prefer strategies that dramatically improve the quality of their K-12 education or other initiatives that prepare students for competition in admissions decisions.

As a general principle, policies derived from a structural analysis tend to target structures and systems rather than people, especially individuals. Policies that target people can have improve outcomes and even affect structural forces, but they are generally not systemic leverage points, places in a system where the structural trajectory can be reset by isolating and reforming a critical node or entry point that can spur positive feedback loops for greater change.[127]

This does not mean that the policy interventions suggested by a structural analysis are colorblind. Colorblindness may be an understandable formulation as an aspiration but is deeply problematic as a practice. It is the presence of persistent disparities that signals unequal structural conditions. Certain expressions of colorblindness, like French universalism, which bars the collection, let alone, the analysis of race statistics, makes it virtually impossible to assess diagnostically the degree to which structural inequities exist.[128] If there is no data, then can be no way to measure disparities or investigate their causes.

In addition to eliding the bedeviling question of whether someone is a racist, a structural racism reform agenda has the salutary political advantage over more directly targeted race policies like affirmative action: structural interventions tend to be positive-sum, serving a broader range of beneficiaries than traditional race-based remedies. If well designed, such policies would improve outcomes for the most disadvantaged but would improve conditions for the benefit of others as well.[129]

This is one of the advantages of structural reforms. Described as the "curb-cut effect," structural changes to accommodate people with disabilities has eased life and travel for able-bodied people, just as bathroom accommodations for transgender people have improved standards for bathroom privacy for everyone.[130] Similarly, a structural racism repair agenda that targets structures and expands access to opportunity is one that will produce positive effects beyond the intended beneficiaries, even though it is race-conscious.

This is not insignificant. In addition to being analytically correct (in terms of matching solutions to the problem), a structural focus is also more politically achievable and sustainable. Targeted policies are often viewed as unfairly benefiting one group over another, even if the underlying basis for the policy is well-founded. The perception that a situation is zero-sum is a tremendous and persistent challenge for racial equity initiatives, historically and contemporarily.[131] But by targeting structures over people, even a race-conscious structural intervention or reform is more readily framed in a way that is positive-sum. There is compelling research that targeted approaches tend to be less durable over time.[132] Policies that benefit more people are harder to stigmatize and roll back.

This is not to suggest, however, that broader benefits are a litmus test for the quality of the intervention from a structural perspective. Some keen social observers have come to the conclusion that universal policies (or broader class-based policies) that reduce racial disadvantages are the optimal policy sweet spot. But to think that every racial equity intervention must always help racially advantaged groups would be to fall into "interest-convergence" dilemma that Derrick Bell observed decades ago.[133] Bell claimed that outcomes for Black Americans only improved when it served the interests of white Americans. The test of a quality structural intervention is not the breadth or number of beneficiaries, but whether it reshapes structural conditions or dynamics, especially whether it expands opportunity broadly or eases access to it structurally, as when widening a bottleneck or facilitating flows through one.

Thus, a structural racism analysis upends the "targeted versus universal" debate by preferring interventions that target structures of inequality with potential benefits that extend broadly.[134] In almost all cases, the focus is on structures and structural elements, and rarely on creating pathways around current barriers for specific groups to travel through. In this respect, what is unique is the focus on the structure and the emphasis on opportunity. A structural racism analysis calls for a different way of seeing the world, a structural perceptiveness that we too often lack.

Finally it is important to emphasize that the measure of success, although not the goal, must be whether an effort has a directional tendency to reduce or ameliorate racial inequality over time. Any effort or initiative that fails to do this must be regarded as suspect. But by the same token, no single or even set of efforts can close out all racial disparities. Thus, the bar must be set above superficial change, but not so high that any given effort capable of producing tangible improvements but not dramatic change is viewed unworthy.

Disparate Impact

Like the idea of institutional racism, a structural perspective recognizes that facially neutral rules and systems distribute benefits and burdens in uneven ways, and that we must attend to these impacts even in the absence of discriminatory intent or racial motivation. For this reason, a structural analysis provides a much firmer basis for disparate impact liability. Instead of grounding disparate impact liability on the search for covert discrimination or animus, disparate impact claims can be understood as an effort to sensitize policymakers to the potential impacts of their decisions.

Disparate impact liability already exists across the range of civil rights law and other anti-discrimination statutes, as noted earlier. It could theoretically be extended more broadly to apply to other spheres of life, not just housing, employment, and transportation. By holding municipal, state, or federal policymakers potentially liable for causing a racially disparate impact, disparate impact liability asks that policymakers carefully consider the possible consequences of their actions.

Some commentators have suggested that such a regulatory regime is "totalitarian."[135] Such rhetoric and fears are overblown, and misunderstands how it would be operationalized. It is not requiring too much to demand that policymakers and government officials assess the possible impacts of their decisions before proceeding. In fact, this idea already exists in law and policy. Federal policy requires government actors to consider the impact of their actions on religious exercise and freedoms.[136] Environmental law requires this in relation to sensitive waterways and endangered species, and sometimes allows parties to challenge developments based upon possible impacts on traffic or pollution.[137] And myriad federal and state policies already require or provide fiscal and budgetary impacts of possible ballot initiatives or proposed legislation.[138] Given the history of race in our country, the additional burden of asking policymakers to take consideration of possible racial impact seems well justified and reasonable.

Even if a policymaker finds a possible disparate impact arising from a contemplated action, that does not mean they are forbidden from proceeding. Rather, they must weigh the benefits of their desired course against the possible costs in term of racial impact. In that way, remedies for racial inequality need not turn on the presence of a discriminatory motive, but rather should be re-evaluated in terms of cost/benefit. All well-considered decisions should account for costs and benefits, and a disparate impact regulatory regime merely brings such considerations to the forefront, whereas they may otherwise be neglected.

Moreover, if many actions and decisions that contribute to and sustain racial inequality structurally are based on neglect and indifference rather than animus, then a policy that requires conscious consideration of such impacts could gradually improve these outcomes by alerting policymakers to the possible effects of their decisions.[139] Moreover, as noted before, much of our civil rights jurisprudence requires proof that actions or decisions were motivated by race. Actions or inactions resulting from racial indifference will, by definition, never be motivated by race., and therefore generally fall outside the regulation of such laws. Only a policy that aims at such indifference, and attempts to set the gaze of leading officials and other policymakers, can correct for it.

By framing claims in terms of whether they advance or hinder racial disparities, we also remove much of the stigma of being held liable. Defendants will fight vigorously against discrimination claims when losing entails the reputational damage of being labeled a "racist." But if disparate impact liability follows a good faith policy initiative that resulted in an unintended outcome, then policymakers may be more willing to engage on race, less fearful of being accused of racism, and more open to consider the consequences of their actions.

Affirmative Action

Of all of the debates regarding racial inequality, and attempts to remedy them, perhaps the most contentious over the last 50 years has been affirmative action. Although the mechanics are often complicated, the basic idea of affirmative action is to consider the race of a candidate or applicant in making a hiring or admissions decision, giving a slight to moderate advantage to members of under-represented social groups.[140] The justification for such policies is that, without affirmative action, such groups would continue to be excluded or severely underrepresented in critical institutions.

Affirmative action in employment, contracting, and especially higher education, has been heavily litigated and widely debated for decades now. Affirmative action is strongly opposed by many whites (and increasingly Asians), who feel it is fundamentally unfair, and opposition is regarded by social scientists as a source of racial resentment.[141] This has occurred even though tiny numbers of applicants or contractors typically benefit from affirmative action policies, especially in elite institutions, relative to the perceived disadvantages suffered by whites as a result of such policies.

Affirmative action was first formulated in an executive order issued by JFK in 1961 for federal employers and agencies to take "affirmative action" in government contracting to promote diversity and remedy past discrimination.[142] It was understood by policy makers and jurists that simply ending discrimination was not sufficient to remedy past discrimination, but that additional, "affirmative" efforts were needed. Thus began decades of court battles over the constitutionality of such efforts.

Although broadly conceived as a race-based remedy for past intentional discrimination, affirmative action is not a specific remedy to a particular or specific instance of discrimination. When universities adopted affirmative action goals, although they were conscious of their own historical role in excluding women and students of color, race-conscious admissions policies were not devised as recompense for individuals who had, decades earlier, been denied admission (that would be impossible in many cases). This is why debates over affirmative action are so fraught—it cannot be justified or even fully understood within an individual racism model. By moving beyond individual discrimination, affirmative action is a remedy for institutionalized and structural racism. Affirmative action policies may be responsive to decades of exclusion in an industry or any other arena.

A cross-national example perhaps best illustrates the principle. Shortly after independence from Britain, India created affirmative action measures for special groups, including Dalits, a low Hindu caste regarded as "untouchables," with quota targets for admissions and hiring. In 1950, India launched a complex "reservation" system that set aside seats in various legislatures, government jobs, and spots in institutions higher educational institutions for Dalits and other marginalized or disadvantaged castes.[143] As a group, Dalits endured millennia of discrimination on cultural and religious bases. Because of widespread private and public discrimination, which is culturally embedded and privately reinforced, affirmative action programs were developed as a structural remedy.

In the 1960s and 1970s, many American institutions employed affirmative action in a similar manner until the Supreme Court began imposing limits.[144]

Although the Supreme Court has upheld the use of race-based remedies in response to past proven intentional discrimination, demonstrating the linkage between past discrimination and contemporary disadvantage is not easy or simple. A structural analysis paradoxically strengthens and undermines the case for race-based affirmative action. It specifies the manner in which past and contemporary discrimination restricted the opportunities that affirmative action now seeks to remedy. It articulates in specific terms, the ways in which practices and discrimination in other domains creates a bottleneck for members of racially marginalized groups.[145]

In light of this structural reality, a race-specific affirmative action policy is justified as a direct and logical solution to these bottlenecks, admitting underrepresented students, for example, who otherwise would probably not qualify for admissions using more traditional academic criteria, such as GPA or test scores.[146] Indeed, the record shows that virtually everywhere affirmative action policies have been thrown out by reviewing courts or otherwise abandoned (often by ballot referenda), there have often been precipitous declines in enrollment among many of those groups as a result, at least in the short-run.[147]

At the same time, a structural perspective also illustrates the limitations of affirmative action policies as a solution to structural inequality. First, affirmative action in higher education mostly affected admissions in a relatively few institutions, often the most elite and selective colleges and universities. The vast majority of post-secondary students attend non-selective or less selective institutions, who do not need tiebreakers to decide who to admit.[148] Consequently, affirmative action policies make little difference for most students of color, where other policies could make a bigger difference.

Second, universities that, until recently, employed affirmative action measures recognized the disparities and inequities in the provision of K-12 education opportunity and early childhood environments that prepare and qualify students for admissions to competitive institutions. Race-conscious admissions policies may help compensate and correct for structural disadvantage, but it does not address the underlying forces that produce them.[149] It is a jerry-rigged solution that corrects racial underrepresentation in selective institutions of higher education, but does nothing to fundamentally transform pathways to or through institutions of higher education. Not only has affirmative action failed to address or make headway towards solving the problem of educational inequality by race at the primary and secondary level, but it operates to preserve, rather than challenge, conceptions of merit and meritocracy and other dynamics of higher education,[150] such as competition over prestige and rankings that have the effect of constricting opportunity.[151] In fact, it may fortify the underlying structural arrangement by providing an escape hatch which renders that arrangement tolerable and less urgently needful of reform.

An affirmative action alternative, the Texas Ten Percent Plan, illustrates this vividly. When the courts struck down the University of Texas (UT)' affirmative action plan, the state legislature devised an alternative program which automatically admits the top 10% of all Texas high school graduates to UT.[152] This program has the effect of fostering greater racial diversity for UT's freshmen class, but did so by drawing on patterns of extreme racial segregation throughout the state.[153] The Texas Ten Percent plan generates student body diversity, but relies on inter-district segregation to achieve that result. It not only reduces the urgency of addressing the underlying structural problem of inter-district segregation, but it actually creates an incentive to leave it undisturbed. The efficacy, if not the entire functionality, of the plan relies upon racial residential segregation.

A structural perspective illustrates the mismatch between the problem and solution. You can solve the upstream problems that constrict access and create bottlenecks for some people, expand the bottleneck to let more in, or you can create an alternative pathway around the bottleneck.[154] Workarounds such as affirmative action may be an expedient stop-gap or short-term answer, but are rarely the optimal long-term solutions from a structural perspective. They address the immediate barrier to the target opportunity, but do little to transform, directly at least, the underlying structural inequity that renders this opportunity inaccessible in the first place.

Not only do affirmative action policies leave the underlying structure intact, but it is both under- and over-inclusive. Such measures never reach everyone disadvantaged by racist opportunity structures, and will sometimes benefit those who may not be disadvantaged. This is the basis for an incisive critique of race-based affirmative action by the civil rights scholar Sheryll Cashin.[155] Race is strongly correlated with structural disadvantage,[156] but structural conditions that explain racial disparities are rarely perfectly coterminous with racial identity. Although affirmative action may serve to ensure that members of racial groups are represented in many critical institutions, particularly elite ones, students admitted through such policies may not be—and in fact are unlikely to be—among the most structurally disadvantaged. Cashin points out how the disproportionate beneficiaries of affirmative action are children of African or Caribbean immigrants rather than descendants of American slaves.[157] A study of law school students found that "Black" students are disproportionately composed of such students.[158] If the goal is to reach members of groups with the greatest structural disadvantage, then a simple race factor may prove insufficient to achieve that result.

On the other hand, there are meaningful benefits to improved racial representation at the institutional level. The presence of members of such groups improves classroom discourse, increases the exchange of diverse viewpoints, and reduces stereotyping.[159] Ironically, in that defense, affirmative action redounds to the benefit of white students whose academic experience is improved, but it may do comparatively little to improve the status of the most structurally disadvantaged members of marginalized groups.

This is no longer a theoretical debate. In 2023, the Supreme Court signaled the end of affirmative action, and overturned a pair of carefully designed affirmative action plans at Harvard College and the University of North Carolina, despite upholding similar plans several times in the preceding decades.[160] In the immediate aftermath, Black enrollment has fallen at three-quarters of surveyed institutions.[161] Institutions of higher education (as well as private companies, state agencies and local governments) must now grapple with ways to preserve or expand that diversity and other hard-won gains without using race as a selection criterion to do it.

A structurally informed approach to reforming university and collegiate admissions would be race-conscious, but would be more nuanced in the selection process than those that used race as a blunt selection criterion. Given the data on educational attainment in relation to opportunity, we are assured that university admissions processes form a critical portal to economic and social mobility. Although university admissions committees cannot solve inequities in the opportunity structure that occur before students apply to their institutions, they could try to ensure that admissions considerations less obviously advantage the wealthy and privileged. The most obvious way to do this is to curtail "legacy" admissions.

A 2018 survey found that 42% of admissions directors at private colleges and universities included legacy status as a factor in admissions.[162] As of this writing, the only notable selective American private liberal arts university that independently decided to eliminate legacy consideration was Amherst in late 2021.[163] Several state legislatures, however, have weighed in and have banned legacy admissions considerations in the context of public universities and colleges, beginning with Colorado in 2021 up through California in 2024.[164]

More directly, however, selective universities could do a better job of helping students from disadvantaged backgrounds gain admittance. Simple reforms include allowing applicants to use a common or uniform application, waiving application fees for low-income applicants, and reconsidering the use or degree of reliance upon admissions exams. Class-based affirmative action is probably insufficient to the task. Modeling shows that class alone generates surprisingly weak racial diversity.[165] More complicated mechanisms might include percentage plans like UT's, adversity scores that try to measure relative disadvantage, or the creation of adjacent secondary pipelines academies.[166]

There is a nuanced and unresolved debate regarding the validity of standardized admissions tests such as the SAT and ACT. Standardized admissions tests are supposed to help identify high-potential students from disadvantaged environments (and they sometimes do), but research also shows strong and persistent racial disparities among these tests, undermining their potential to promote racial diversity.[167] Black test-takers, for example, score approximately 80–90 points lower than white students on both the verbal test and the math test (roughly, 480 versus 560 on verbal, and 460 versus 550 on math).[168] Latino mean score is the lowest of the racial and ethnic groups, at 1120, compared to a white mean score of 1338, as of 2019.[169] As noted in Chapter 1, one of the strongest predictors of performance on such tests is grandparent wealth, which suggests that performance on such tests is a form of inherited privilege.

Nonetheless, there is also evidence that such standardized admissions tests do predict grades and student performance.[170] What supporters tend to overlook, however, is the lack of a good predictive indicator. Such exams have fairly weak correlations with performance, even if they do perform marginally better than other available indicators.[171]

In light of the disparate racial impact that such tests seem to produce, many universities and college elected to no longer require them in wake of the Covid-19 pandemic, although some have since reinstated them.[172] This approach, or an approach that dramatically expands access to higher education by admitting significantly more students, could reduce racial disparities in access to higher education or elite institutions.[173]

In 2019, the College Board announced that they would append the SAT with an "adversity score."[174] This score would include at least 31 data points and 15 different factors describing school and neighborhood characteristics relating to the applicant.[175] Although the measure was piloted in a number of universities, and the designers of the ACT announced a similar plan, the College Board ultimately shelved the idea. Although the score was merely meant to provide admissions officers with additional context, anxious parents and educators lashed out, worried that the score might harm their children's chances of admission.[176] Although ultimately abandoned, the attempt to balance SAT results with contextual information is a nuanced approach supported by a structural analysis. Preliminary results showed that use of the adversity score improved admissions chances for low-income students, and possibly students of color as well.[177]

A structural analysis complicates the way in which we understand and look at issues like affirmative action in terms of policy design and in terms of the problems they are trying to solve. A structural analysis reveals the inequity in opportunities that justify affirmative action policies as a workaround or pathway around a bottleneck, but it also highlights the limitations of remedies, like affirmative action, that fail to transform the bottleneck or the causes of the bottleneck. The problem with affirmative action from a structural perspective described here is generalizable.

It is of course true that particular institutions can only address bottlenecks within their power,[178] but they should also be conscious of how their decisions impact other elements of the opportunity structure. A university admissions policy that considers race, but depends on residential segregation, may complicate efforts to correct the root problem.[179] Race-based affirmative action policies help ensure access to critical institutions (especially elite ones) for underrepresented and disadvantaged racial groups, but they are not a substitute for larger structural change.

Reparations

Reparations for American slavery has recently become an increasingly serious policy debate, not just among congresspersons, pundits, or scholars, but among the leading contenders for the highest political office.[180] There are sophisticated and persuasive arguments for reparations and how such a policy might be implemented, and a variety of reparations implementation possibilities.[181]

Much of what has just been said about affirmative action or the relationship between historical and contemporary policies and practices is directly applicable to the debate over reparations. Like affirmative action, a structural analysis both strengthens and undermines the case for reparations. By explaining how past policies, including past discrimination, is structured into the fabric of society, a structural racism analysis provides the remedial justification for a reparations policy. On the other hand, it is unlikely that a reparations policy would fully solve contemporary structural racism.

First, if racialized structures of inequality are not merely the legacy of past discrimination and entailment of historical structures, but a product of contemporary policies as well, then a reparations policy, no matter how robust, is insufficient as a solution for contemporary racial inequality. By design, a reparations policy is backward looking rather than forward looking. In his study of intergenerational racial mobility, Raj Chetty and his colleagues concluded that racial inequality of opportunity appeared to fall into a steady state condition or a kind of equilibrium.[182] They warned that "[t]ransitory interventions, such as temporary cash transfers targeted by race, will have limited long-run effects unless they change the process of intergenerational mobility."[183]

Even if reparations benefits were more broadly extended beyond the descendants of slaves to those who experienced more recent forms of structural inequality described in Chapter 3, such as redlining and Jim Crow, reparations policies are unlikely to fundamentally change many structural elements that produce and sustain contemporary structural racial inequality. Although reparations could (and in fact may be one of the only ways to) meaningfully reduce the racial wealth gap, a powerfully structural force with many downstream effects,[184] its long-term effects on patterns racial residential segregation, social network shape or isolation, mass incarceration, perceptions of Black neighborhoods as harmful to property value appreciation, or the spatial mismatch are less clear. A paper by research economists at the Federal Reserve Bank of Cleveland concluded that "[o]ne-time wealth transfers have only transitory effects unless they address the racial earnings gap."[185] The key to a successful reparations policy for addressing structural racial inequality would be to calibrate it toward greater educational attainment and higher earnings.

Wealth redistribution without changing levels of human capital acquisition or structures that produce and distribute wealth is unlikely to solve contemporary structural racial inequality. Nonetheless, there is a powerful moral basis for reparations, to repair the harm of racial slavery. This harm, however, is distinct (however related) from the argument for a policy agenda aimed at addressing contemporary structural racism. A structural policy change agenda would likely go beyond a reparations regime, even more expansive versions.

Although a reparations policy should not be regarded as a specific remedy for solving contemporary structural racial inequality, like affirmative action, reparations would help attenuate and ameliorate some of its effects. One of the significant byproducts of a vigorous development of a reparations policy is that it would bolster the case for interventions aimed at structural racism by educating the public and political leaders on the nature of structural racism in addition to historical injustice. The first step in the bills proposed in Congress on reparations would be a commission or study group to investigate the issue, as was established in California.[186] The debate over the scope of a reparations policy, the components of such a policy, and how to implement such a policy, would do a tremendous service toward addressing structural racism itself by educating the public on the contemporary effects of past practice.

Both policies aimed at past harm and policies aimed at contemporary structures should be pursued. But a reparations policy should not necessarily be construed or sold as a solution to structural racism. The policies discussed in the next chapter are more specifically tailored to the problem of contemporary structural racism rather than simply remedying historical injustices on the basis of race, as profoundly important as that may be.

The Kerner Report Revisited

In 1968, the Kerner Commission announced its most startling warning that America was "moving toward two societies, one Black, one white – separate and unequal."[187] The comprehensive and wide-ranging report went onto to describe this trend as a "division of our country into two societies, one, largely Negro and poor, located in the central cities; the other, predominantly white and affluent, located in the suburbs."[188] Many Americans rejected this description as overly pessimistic, and, even today, may regard it as wrong.[189] Other observers wonder if the Commission's warnings haven't come true.[190]

Mark Twain is reported to have remarked that "history does not repeat itself, but it rhymes." Anyone reading the Kerner Commission report, its description of police encounters, grievance, and outrage, cannot avoid seeing contemporary parallels to the events, causes and contexts of the 1960s. In the executive summary, the Commission included a quote from one of its more eminent witnesses, Dr. Kenneth Clark, which serves as an epitaph as haunting as when it was originally published:

> I read the report... of the 1919 riot in Chicago, and it is as if I were reading the report of the investigating committee on the Harlem riot of '35, the report of the investigating committee of the Harlem riot of

'43, the report of the McCone Commission on the Watts riot. I must again in candor say to you members of this Commission – it is a kind of Alice in Wonderland – with the same moving picture re-shown over and over again, the same analysis, the same recommendations, and the same inaction.[191]

To that, we might add the Ferguson Commission of 2015,[192] the Department of Justice Baltimore Report of 2016,[193] or the Chicago Report of 2017,[194] among many others.

Cumulatively, these episodes and the ensuing parade of blue-ribbon commissions followed by inaction and/or backlash indicate a larger cycle of events, sequenced in six basic stages: (1) racially inequitable background conditions, often inflamed by recent grievances; (2) an inciting event, often a violent police encounter; (3) a lack of swift accountability, implying impunity; (4) public protests and civil revolt, aroused further by a forceful, often violent, police response; (5) political promises for change; (6) followed by retrenchment, backlash, and inaction. And thus, the cycle begins again.

The Commission recognized this pattern, and the report was as prescient as it was exhaustive. The Commission warned that America faced three choices: 1) do nothing, which would risk a repeat of the same violence; 2) enact policies aimed to "enrich the ghetto," without a commitment to integration, which they argued would "create a permanently divided country," or 3) a mixture of "short-term policies to strengthen the ghetto with longer term policies to promote integration."[195]

Unfortunately, many racial equity advocates subscribe to some form of the second option, believing that separation coupled with investment, enrichment, and reparation, can suffice, and help achieve the goal of racial justice. But even if it were capable of advancing toward that goal, it would fail to reach it, for the reasons already developed throughout this book: in a segregated society, equalizing tangible resources does not equalize the intangible. It cannot reconfigure social networks or alumni connections or endow a university with the same prestige. This is why the Supreme Court rejected the claim that a female-only separate institution could provide an equal educational experience to the prestigious Virginia Military Institute.[196]

Even if we could achieve the goal of racial justice through the enrichment choice, of reconstructing opportunity on a more racially equitable basis such that race no longer significantly shapes life chances, and where many racial inequalities and disparities in measures of well-being disappeared, the most that that option could achieve is to realize *Plessy's* infamous legal fiction, a society that is "separate, but equal." Such an extremely unlikely outcome might narrowly satisfy the requisites of racial justice, but fail the conditions for democracy, of constructing a single nation and a cohesive political community in a larger social fabric.

Only the third option, a mixture of short-term investments coupled with a long-term aim at integration, the Kerner Commission warned, would produce a "single society in which every citizen will be free to live and work according to his capabilities and desires."[197] The authors of the Kerner Commission report proposed more than a hundred policies and interventions that may well have set the United States upon a different trajectory.[198] Rather than heed its warnings and implement its recommendations, we largely ignored it. We face that choice still.

* * *

This chapter considered how a structural understanding of the production of racial inequality profoundly changes the nature of our racial discourse, with implications for policy reform. The individual racism model, and the quasi-therapeutic model for solving it, is incapable of addressing racial inequality. Race-sensitivity training provides a feeling of effort without requiring structural change. Similarly, it may feel good to rally against a symbolic target, like confederate statues or buildings named after bigots, but such efforts tend to divert energy and distract focus from the structural forces at work.

Perhaps no greater symbol of the limits of the interpersonal racism model exists than the fall of its heroic avatar, Atticus Finch. The Pulitzer Prize winning novel by Harper Lee, *To Kill a Mockingbird*, narrates the courage of a small town Alabama lawyer, Atticus Finch, in his ardent defense of a Black man falsely accused of raping a young white woman. During the course of the novel, Finch's interpersonal empathy is on full display, epitomized by an admonition for his impressionable daughter: "You never really understand a person until you consider things from his point of view….Until you climb into his skin and walk around in it."[199] For a white southerner, this empathetic assertion is tantamount to a complete rejection of race prejudice.

In 2009, the journalist and popular author Malcolm Gladwell published a provocative essay for the *New Yorker* magazine, contending that Atticus Finch fit the profile of a southern racial moderate, and would likely not have been a likely supporter of the civil rights movement.[200] In fact, the publication of a long-lost sequel (although written before *To Kill a Mockingbird*) in 2015 confirmed Gladwell's conjecture.

In *Go Set a Watchman*, we learn that Atticus Finch personally opposes the Supreme Court's integration mandate in the *Brown* decision, viewing it as unprincipled judicial overreach. Moreover, although he was disdainful of the Klan, and believed forthrightly in the dignity of all people, he privately harbored beliefs about the backwardness of his fellow Black citizens. In this profile, Finch is emblematic of the limits of interpersonal racial egalitarianism as a solution to entrenched racial inequality.

Segregation, both historical and contemporary, illustrates a structural dimension to racial inequality that cannot be corrected simply by treating people well or fairly. Through Finch's impassioned defense of Tom Robinson, the reader is seduced into believing that the way to solve injustice is to fill the courts with people like Atticus Finch rather than transform structures of racial oppression. It is this illusion that that *Go Set a Watchman* unintentionally dispelled for a public that long regarded Atticus Finch as a paragon of moral and civic virtue.

The critical question from a structural racism framework is whether policies and practices tend to maintain, exacerbate, or ameliorate racial inequality, not whether individuals hold prejudiced views or racist ideas. As in the case of the subprime mortgage crisis, greed, opportunism, and self-interest may be larger factors than bigotry and animus. This is not to deny the possibly that these motives can be conjoined, as they often were in the past.[201] But to regard contemporary racial inequalities as principally or consistently a product of intent and design underestimates the effects that systems and structures can produce absent such intent, and therefore fails to recognize the many ways in which racial inequality is created and maintained in the contemporary Untied States. By obviating an insistence on identifying discriminatory intentions, a structural paradigm is aggressively solution oriented. Instead of affixing blame, it assigns responsibility to anyone with the power and authority to solve it.

Ultimately a structural racism analysis is a guide and call to action. The long-called for "national conversation" on race must not be a precondition, let alone substitute, for action.[202] Undoubtedly, a structural change agenda along the lines outlined in this book requires sacrifices from people who currently benefit from structural arrangements, but it is less likely to alienate for fear of being labeled a racist. The ultimate goal is not that Americans, especially white Americans, recognize their racial privileges, historical wrongs, or attend an antiracism workshop. As cathartic as that might be, the goal, rather, is a society where opportunity is fairly open to all, and race no longer shapes life chances. The next chapter proposes a policy agenda that is responsive to a structural racism analysis without requiring a revolution in consciousness.

Notes

1. Jennifer Bayot, "First Estimate Puts Storm's Economic Toll at $100 Billion," *New York Times*, September 3, 2005, https://www.nytimes.com/2005/09/03/business/first-estimate-puts-storms-economic-toll-at-100-billion.html.
2. Kanye West, "Kanye West: George Bush doesn't care about Black people," MSNBC, Concert for Hurricane Relief, September 2, 2005, uploaded September 21, 2007, YouTube video, 1:39, https://www.youtube.com/watch?v=UJUNTcOGeSw.
3. Maxwell Strachan, "The Definitive History of 'George Bush Doesn't Care about Black People," *Huffington Post*, updated September 9, 2015, https://www.huffpost.com/entry/kanye-west-george-bush-black-people_n_55d67c12e4b020c386de2f5e.
4. Herbert Blumer, "Race Prejudice as a Sense of Group Position," *Pacific Sociological Review* 1, no. 1 (Spring 1958): https://doi.org/10.2307/1388607.
5. William Bradford Huie, "The Shocking Story of Approved Killing in Mississippi," *Look Magazine*, January 1956, https://www.pbs.org/wgbh/americanexperience/features/till-killers-confession/.

6 Jeremy Gray, "Bull Connor Used Fire Hoses, Police Dogs on Protestors (May 3, 1963)," *al.com*, May 3, 2013, https://www.al.com/birmingham-news-stories/2013/05/bull_connor_used_fire_hoses_po.html; DeNeen L. Brown, "Thomas Blanton's Role in the 1963 Church Bombing That Killed Four Black Girls," *Washington Post*, June 26, 2020, https://www.washingtonpost.com/history/2020/06/26/thomas-blantons-role-1963-church-bombing-that-killed-four-black-girls/; Jason Horowitz, Nick Corasaniti, and Ashley Southall, "Nine Killed in Shooting at Black Church in Charleston," *New York Times*, June 17, 2015, https://www.nytimes.com/2015/06/18/us/church-attacked-in-charleston-south-carolina.html.

7 There is a large and complex literature variously characterizing the concept of what the law regards as "disparate treatment" or "invidious" discrimination. See Linda Krieger, "The Content of Our Categories: A Cognitive Bias Approach to Discrimination and Equal Employment Opportunity," *Stanford Law Review* 47, no. 6 (1995): https://doi.org/10.2307/1229191 for an excellent breakdown of how the law conceives and operationalizes these ideas. Thomas Sowell distinguishes this type of discrimination (which he calls "Discrimination II") from the more ordinary and benign type of discrimination, of distinguishing between different things, which is not invidious or motivated by racist or other prejudiced ideas or beliefs. Oddly, however, he classifies stereotypes rooted in some statistical reality as Type I. Sowell, *Discrimination and Disparities*, 30–31. See also Pager and Shepherd, "Sociology of Discrimination," for an excellent overview of the social scientific perspective of this idea and methods of measuring and identifying it. This is not to say, however, that all commentators conceive discrimination as narrowly inter-personal. As these sources suggest, the term "discrimination" in the race context is sometimes extended to include institutional or structural dynamics. See e.g. National Research Council, *Measuring Racial Discrimination* (Washington, DC: National Academies Press, 2004), https://nap.nationalacademies.org/catalog/10887/measuring-racial-discrimination; and Mario L. Small and Devah Pager, "Sociological Perspectives on Racial Discrimination," *Journal of Economic Perspectives* 34, no. 2 (2022): 49–67. In law, this broader understanding is operationalized as "discriminatory effects" or "disparate impact." Department of Housing and Urban Development (HUD), "Reinstatement of HUD's Discriminatory Effects Standard," *Federal Register*, May 1, 2023, https://www.federalregister.gov/d/2023-05836.

8 Ibram X. Kendi, *Stamped from the Beginning: The Definitive History of Racist Ideas in America* (New York: Nation Books, 2016), 4. Kendi repeatedly asserts that discrimination is the source of racial disparities. See Kendi, 2, 9, 11. ("When you truly believe that all racial groups are equal, then you must also believe that racial disparities must be the result of racial discrimination"). He even goes so far to say that "protesting racist policies can never be a long-term solution to eradicating racial discrimination – and thus racist ideas – in America," Kendi, 508. Kendi's subsequent writings and public statements clarify or perhaps reflect an evolving view that he understands the production of racial inequality to extend to policies and practices. See, for example, Lonnae O'Neal, "Ibram Kendi, one of the nation's leading scholars of racism, says education and love are not the answer," *Andscape*, September 20, 2017, https://andscape.com/features/ibram-kendi-leading-scholar-of-racism-says-education-and-love-are-not-the-answer/. In contrast to Kendi, conservative critics such as Thomas Sowell argue emphatically that racial and other inter-group disparities can often be caused by many non-discriminatory and random factors and circumstances. See Sowell, *Discrimination and Disparities*, 1-28.

9 Kendi, *Stamped from the Beginning*, 2. Strangely, however, he defines "segregationists," not specifically as people who desire the separation of racial

groups in space or specific institutions, but as people who explain racial disparities in terms of racial differences.

10 Reggie Ugwu, "'Empire City' Investigates the Forgotten Origins of the N.Y.P.D.," *New York Times*, September 9, 2024, https://www.nytimes.com/2024/09/09/arts/nypd-empire-city-podcast.html ("When the N.Y.P.D. does something oppressive, a lot of people on my side of the political spectrum will say it's working as designed," Kumanyika said. "But I think that's actually letting power off the hook. It doesn't acknowledge all the ways it has had to innovate and adapt in response to pushback").

11 Nancy Krieger, "Epidemiology and the Web of Causation: Has Anyone Seen the Spider?," *Social Science & Medicine* 39, no. 7 (1994): 887–903, https://doi.org/10.1016/0277-9536(94)90202-X.

12 Isaac Chotiner, "Robin DiAngelo Wants White Progressives to Look Inward," *New Yorker*, July 14, 2021, https://www.newyorker.com/news/q-and-a/robin-diangelo-wants-white-progressives-to-look-inward.

13 See Title VII of the Civil Rights Act of 1964, 78 Stat. 235, as amended, 42. U.S.C. § 20003-2 ("Except as otherwise provided in this title, an unlawful employment practice is established when the complaining party demonstrates that race, color, religion, sex, or national origin was a motivating factor for any employment practice, even though other factors also motivated the practice").

14 For an classic deconstruction of the flaws in legal doctrine, especially the "motivational" requirement, see Krieger, "Content of Our Categories." Even within that motivational framework, however, discriminatory actions and aversive behavior may also be motivated by discomfort or anxiety or even rational self-interest rather than bigotry or hostility and still be considered race-based.

15 Washington v. Davis, 426 U.S. 229 (1976), 235; *Arlington Heights*, 429 U.S. at 253; Personnel Administrator of Massachusetts v. Feeney, 442 U.S. 256 (1979), 258.

16 See Wygant v. Jackson Board of Education, 476 U.S. 267, 276 (1986). "Societal discrimination, without more, is too amorphous a basis for imposing a racially classified remedy.. . . But as the basis for imposing discriminatory *legal* remedies that work against innocent people, societal discrimination is insufficient and over expansive. In the absence of particularized findings, a court could uphold remedies that are ageless in their reach into the past, and timeless in their ability to affect the future" (Justice Powell). See also Regents of the University of California v. Bakke, 438 U.S. 265, 307 (1978).

17 Stokely Carmichael and Charles V. Hamilton, *Black Power: The Politics of Liberation* (New York: Random House, 1967), 4.

18 Griggs v. Duke Power Company, 401 U.S. 424 (1971).

19 Although the Court first recognized such claims in *Griggs*, courts have subsequently interpreted other civil rights statutes, and legislatures have subsequently drafted or amended such statutes, to permit disparate impact claims. Such claims are permitted under many civil rights laws, including Title VI of the Civil Rights Act of 1964, 42 U.S.C. §2000d, Title VII, 42 U.S.C. §2000e-2, Title VIII (the Fair Housing Act), 42 U.S.C. §§ 3601–3631 (1968), and the Age Discrimination in Employment Act, 29 U.S.C. § 623 (1967).

20 Michael Barone, "HUD's 'Disparate Impact' War on Suburban America," *Washington Examiner*, July 20, 2016, https://www.washingtonexaminer.com/huds-disparate-impact-war-on-suburban-america; See also Justice Scalia in *Ricci v. DeStefano* describing "war between disparate impact and equal protection," Ricci v. DeStefano, 557 U.S. 557, 595 (2009); Christopher F. Rufo, "Counterrevolution Blueprint," *City Journal*, Winter 2025, https://www.city-journal.org/article/counterrevolution-blueprint ("The sixth objective is to eliminate affirmative action and disparate-impact doctrine from federal policymaking").

21 Texas Dept of Housing and Community Affairs v Inclusive Communities Project, Inc., 576 U.S. at 521.
22 See, for example, National Low Income Housing Commission, "Preliminary Analysis of HUD's Final Disparate Impact Rule," September 14, 2020, https://nlihc.org/resource/preliminary-analysis-huds-final-disparate-impact-rule (describing how the Trump administration's 2019 revision to the Disparate Impact regulation makes it more difficult for plaintiffs to bring and prevail on disparate impact claims).
23 john a. powell et al., "Towards a Transformative View of Race: The Crisis and Opportunity of Katrina" in *There is No Such Thing as a Natural Disaster: Race, Class, and Katrina*, eds. Chester Hartman and Gregory D. Squires (New York: Routledge, 2006), 59, 64.
24 Sharkey, *Stuck in Place*, 136.
25 James R. Elliott and Jeremy Pais, "Race, Class, and Hurricane Katrina: Social Differences in Human Responses to Disaster," *Social Science Research* 35, no. 2 (2006): 295–321, https://doi.org/10.1016/j.ssresearch.2006.02.003.
26 *Department of Justice Report Regarding the Criminal Investigation into the Shooting Death of Michael Brown by Ferguson, Missouri Police Officer Darren Wilson* (Washington, DC: U.S. Department of Justice, 2015), 7, https://www.justice.gov/sites/default/files/opa/press-releases/attachments/2015/03/04/doj_report_on_shooting_of_michael_brown_1.pdf.
27 Al Baker, J. David Goodman, and Benjamin Mueller, "Beyond the Chokehold: The Path to Eric Garner's Death," *New York Times*, June 13, 2015, https://www.nytimes.com/2015/06/14/nyregion/eric-garner-police-chokehold-staten-island.html.
28 Mara Gay, "Thousands Protest in Staten Island Over Eric Garner's Death," *Wall Street Journal*, August 23, 2014, https://www.wsj.com/articles/protesters-head-to-staten-island-for-al-sharptons-eric-garner-rally-1408807227.
29 Dana Milbank, "Bob McCulloch's Pathetic Prosecution of Darren Wilson," *Washington Post*, November 25, 2014, https://www.washingtonpost.com/opinions/dana-milbank-bob-mccullochs-pathetic-prosecution-of-darren-wilson/2014/11/25/a8459e16-74d5-11e4-a755-e32227229e7b_story.html.
30 J. David Goodman and Al Baker, "Wave of Protests after Grand Jury Doesn't Indict Officer in Eric Garner Chokehold Case," *New York Times*, December 3, 2014, https://www.nytimes.com/2014/12/04/nyregion/grand-jury-said-to-bring-no-charges-in-staten-island-chokehold-death-of-eric-garner.html.
31 Katie Benner, "Eric Garner's Death Will Not Lead to Federal Charges for N.Y.P.D. Officer," *New York Times*, July 16, 2019, https://www.nytimes.com/2014/12/04/nyregion/grand-jury-said-to-bring-no-charges-in-staten-island-chokehold-death-of-eric-garner.html.
32 Amanda Terkel, "Police Officer Caught on Video Calling Michael Brown Protestors 'F***ing Animals,'" *Huffington Post*, August 13, 2014, https://www.huffpost.com/entry/michael-brown-protests_n_5672163.
33 Shannon Luibrand, "How a Death in Ferguson Sparked a Movement in America," *CBS*, August 7, 2015, https://www.cbsnews.com/news/how-the-black-lives-matter-movement-changed-america-one-year-later/.
34 Joshua Clark Davis, "Birmingham's Use of Police Dogs on Civil Rights Protesters Shocked Liberal Onlookers. But the Backstory Was All-American," *Slate*, May 16, 2023, https://slate.com/news-and-politics/2023/05/birmingham-civil-rights-march-history-dog-photo.html; Elliott C. McLaughlin, "How George Floyd's Death Ignited a Racial Reckoning That Shows No Signs of Slowing Down," *CNN*, August 9, 2020, https://www.cnn.com/2020/08/09/us/george-floyd-protests-different-why/index.html.

35 Ben Casselman, "How Baltimore's Young Black Men Are Boxed In," *FiveThirtyEight*, April 28, 2015, https://fivethirtyeight.com/features/how-baltimores-young-black-men-are-boxed-in/.

36 Kevin Rector, "Charges Dropped, Freddie Gray Case Concludes with Zero Convictions against Officers," *Baltimore Sun*, July 27, 2016, https://www.baltimoresun.com/news/crime/bs-md-ci-miller-pretrial-motions-20160727-story.html.

37 Nicholas Bogel-Burroughs and Will Wright, "Little has been said about the $20 bill that brought officers to the scene," *New York Times*, April 19, 2021, https://www.nytimes.com/2021/04/19/us/george-floyd-bill-counterfeit.html.

38 Lorenzo Reyes, Trevor Hughes, and Mark Emmert, "Medical Examiner and Family-Commissioned Autopsy Agree: George Floyd's Was a Homicide," *USA Today*, June 1, 2020, https://www.usatoday.com/story/news/nation/2020/06/01/george-floyd-independent-autopsy-findings-released-monday/5307185002/.

39 Doha Madani, David K. Li, and Tom Winter, "Ex-Minneapolis Police Officer Derek Chauvin Charged with Murder in George Floyd Case," *NBC News*, May 29, 2020, https://www.nbcnews.com/news/us-news/minneapolis-police-officers-derek-chauvin-arrested-george-floyd-case-n1216011.

40 Audra D.S. Burch et al., "How Black Lives Matter Reached Every Corner of America," *New York Times*, June 13, 2020, https://www.nytimes.com/interactive/2020/06/13/us/george-floyd-protests-cities-photos.html; Zamira Rahim and Rob Picheta, "Thousands Around the World Protest George Floyd's Death Global Display of Solidarity," *CNN*, June 1, 2020, https://www.cnn.com/2020/06/01/world/george-floyd-global-protests-intl/index.html.

41 Larry Buchanan, Quoctrung Bui, and Jugal K. Patel, "Black Lives Matter May Be the Largest Movement in U.S. History," *New York Times*, July 3, 2020, https://www.nytimes.com/interactive/2020/07/03/us/george-floyd-protests-crowd-size.html.

42 Kim Parker, Juliana Menasce Horowitz, and Monica Anderson, "Amid Protests, Majorities Across Racial and Ethnic Groups Express Support for the Black Lives Matter Movement," *Pew Research Center*, June 12, 2020, https://www.pewsocialtrends.org/2020/06/12/amid-protests-majorities-across-racial-and-ethnic-groups-express-support-for-the-black-lives-matter-movement/.

43 Christine Hauser, "Merriam-Webster Revises 'Racism' Entry after Missouri Woman Asks for Changes," *New York Times*, June 10, 2020, https://www.nytimes.com/2020/06/10/us/merriam-webster-racism-definition.html.

44 Scottie Andrew, "There's a Growing Call to Defund the Police. Here's What It Means," *CNN*, June 17, 2020, https://www.cnn.com/2020/06/06/us/what-is-defund-police-trnd/index.html.

45 Christopher Klein, "How Selma's 'Bloody Sunday' Became a Turning Point in the Civil Rights Movement," *History*, March 6, 2015, https://www.history.com/news/selma-bloody-sunday-attack-civil-rights-movement.

46 John Matthew Smith, "'It's Not Really My Country': Lew Alcindor and the Revolt of the Black Athlete," *Journal of Sport History* 36, no. 2 (2009): 229–230, https://www.jstor.org/stable/26405188?seq=1.

47 Smith, "It's Not Really My Country," 230.

48 See generally Jerry Cohen and William S. Murphy, *Burn, Baby, Burn!: The Los Angeles Race Riots of August 1965* (New York: E.P. Dutton, 1966). See also Darrell Dawsey, "To CHP Officer Who Sparked Riots, It Was Just Another Arrest," *Los Angeles Times*, August 19, 1990, https://www.latimes.com/archives/la-xpm-1990-08-19-me-2790-story.html.

49 *Kerner Report*, 38.

50 The exact accounting varies, but the Kerner Commission noted "between 51 and 217 disorders" in the first nine months of the year, ultimately settling on 164 disorders occurring in 128 cities. *Kerner Report*, 112–113.
51 Rick Rojas and Khorri Atkinson, "Five Days of Unrest That Shaped, and Haunted, Newark," *New York Times*, July 11, 2017, https://www.nytimes.com/2017/07/11/nyregion/newark-riots-50-years.html; Bernadette Atuahene, "Don't Let Detroit's Revival Rest on an Injustice," *New York Times*, July 22, 2017, https://www.nytimes.com/2017/07/22/opinion/sunday/dont-let-detroits-revival-rest-on-an-injustice.html.
52 Lyndon B. Johnson, "Executive Order 11365—Establishing a National Advisory Commission on Civil Disorders," *American Presidency Project*, July 29, 1967, https://www.presidency.ucsb.edu/documents/executive-order-11365-establishing-national-advisory-commission-civil-disorders.
53 Steven Gillon, *Separate and Unequal: The Kerner Commission and the Unraveling of American Liberalism* (New York: Basic Books, 2018), iv.
54 *Kerner Report*; Jill Lepore, "The History of the 'Riot' Report," *New Yorker*, June 15, 2020, https://www.newyorker.com/magazine/2020/06/22/the-history-of-the-riot-report; *The Riot Report: A Presidential Commission Defied Expectations by Telling a Hard Truth*, directed by Michelle Ferrari, aired May 21, 2024, https://www.pbs.org/wgbh/americanexperience/films/riot-report/.
55 "Chapter 1: Profiles of Disorder," *in Kerner Report*, 19–61.
56 Paul Guzzo, "Fifty-Two Years Ago Today, a Police Officer Shot a Black Teen in the Back. Then Tampa Erupted," *Tampa Bay Times*, June 11, 2019, https://www.tampabay.com/florida/2019/06/11/fifty-two-years-ago-today-a-police-officer-shot-a-black-teen-in-the-back-then-tampa-erupted/.
57 *Kerner Report*, 47.
58 See Bill McGray, "In a City Already on Edge, Detroit Police Raid on Blind Pig Ignites 1967 Riot," *Detroit Free Press*, December 25, 2016, https://www.freep.com/story/news/local/michigan/detroit/2016/12/25/city-already-edge-detroit-police-raid-blind-pig-ignites-1967-riot/95608776/.
59 Nirali Beri, "The 1966 Hunters Point Uprising in 'the San Francisco America pretends does not exist,'" *Othering & Belonging Institute*, May 29, 2019, https://belonging.berkeley.edu/blog-1966-hunters-point-uprising-san-francisco-america-pretends-does-not-exist.
60 *Kerner Report*, 111.
61 *Kerner Report*, 82.
62 *Kerner Report*, 54.
63 *Kerner Report*, 26.
64 *Kerner Report*, 65.
65 *Kerner Report*, 158.
66 Bayard Rustin, "The Watts," *Commentary Magazine*, March 1, 1966, https://www.commentary.org/articles/bayard-rustin-2/the-watts/.
67 *Kerner Report*, 143–144.
68 *Kerner Report*, 1.
69 For a complete enumeration, see *Key Kerner Commission Recommendations*, Othering & Belonging Institute, https://belonging.berkeley.edu/key-kerner-commission-recommendations.
70 Menendian and Rothstein with Beri, *Road Not Taken* (a detailed review of the criminal justice and housing policy recommendations and where America stands in terms of these recommendations as of 2018).
71 Johnson was attacked from the left because of the war. On the right, conservatives refused to appropriate more money for any social programs. Julian E. Zelizer, "Introduction to the 2016 Edition," in *The Kerner Report* (Princeton, NJ: Princeton University Press, 2016), xiii.

72. Lorraine Boissoneault, "Martin Luther King Jr.'s Assassination Sparked Uprisings in Cities Across America," *Smithsonian Magazine*, April 4, 2018, https://www.smithsonianmag.com/history/martin-luther-king-jrs-assassination-sparked-uprisings-cities-across-america-180968665/.
73. Elizabeth Hinton, *America on Fire: The Untold History of Police Violence and Black Rebellion Since the 1960s* (New York: Liveright, 2019), 10 (resulting in more than 10,000 people injured and 220 deaths).
74. "General Editor's Introduction," *Kerner Report* (2016 edition), x.
75. Nor was it the first. Gunnar Myrdal's landmark report was an even earlier structural analysis of the production of racial inequality. Gunnar Myrdal, *An American Dilemma: The Negro Problem and Modern Democracy* (1944; repr., New Brunswick, NJ: Transaction Publishers, 2009). But the Kerner Report is notable in being an official government document endorsed by a broad panel of officials.
76. See, for example, Edward Bonilla-Silva, *Racism without Racists: Color-Blind Racism and the Persistence of Racial Inequality in America* (2003; repr., Lanham, MD: Rowman & Littlefield, 2018).
77. Iris Marion Young, *Justice and the Politics of Difference* (Princeton, NJ: Princeton University Press, 1990), 40-41.
78. Iris Marion Young, "Structural injustice and the politics of difference," chapter 2 in *Multiculturalism and Political Theory*, ed. Anthony Simon Laden and David Owen (New York: Cambridge University Press, 2007), 60–88. This essay was originally presented as a lecture in 2004, and has been reprinted several times since in other edited volumes.
79. Young, 86.
80. Young, 84.
81. Camara Phyllis Jones, "Levels of Racism: A Theoretic Framework and a Gardener's Tale," *American Journal of Public Health* 90, no. 8 (2000): 1212–1215, https://www.ncbi.nlm.nih.gov/pmc/articles/PMC1446334/pdf/10936998.pdf.
82. "The Gardener's Tale, Dr. Camara Jones," interview by Jesse Richardson Hood, 2002, video, 19:27, May 7, 2014, https://www.youtube.com/watch?v=1QFCcChCSMU.
83. Margery Austin Turner et al., *Housing Discrimination Against Racial and Ethnic Minorities 2012* (Washington, DC: U.S. Department of Housing and Urban Development, 2013), https://www.huduser.gov/portal/Publications/pdf/HUD-514_HDS2012.pdf; Ann Choi et al., "Long Island Divided," *Newsday*, November 17, 2019, https://projects.newsday.com/long-island/real-estate-agents-investigation/; Anthony G. Greenwald and Linda Hamilton Krieger, "Implicit Bias: Scientific Foundations," *California Law Review* 94, no. 4 (2006): 945–967, 961, https://doi.org/10.2307/20439056.
84. Rebecca M. Blank, "Tracing the Economic Impact of Cumulative Discrimination," *American Economic Review* 95, no. 2 (2005): 99–103, https://www.jstor.org/stable/4132798. See also discussion of "cumulative disadvantage" in note 13, page 131.
85. See Roithmayr, *Reproducing Racism*, 56 citing Shelley J. Lundberg and Richard Startz, "Inequality and Race: Models and Policy," in *Meritocracy and Economic Inequality*, eds. Kenneth J. Arrow, Samuel Bowles, and Steven A. Durlauf (Princeton, NJ: Princeton University Press, 2000), 269–295.
86. See Vi Hart and Nicki Case, Parable of the Polygons: A Playable Post on the Shape of Society (website), accessed September 30, 2022, https://ncase.me/polygons/.
87. Richard H. Sander, "Housing Segregation and Housing Integration: The Diverging Paths of Urban America," *University of Miami Law Review* 52, no. 4 (1998): 1010, https://repository.law.miami.edu/cgi/viewcontent.cgi?article=1684&

context=umlr. For a summary of this debate and empirical evidence, see Stephen L. Ross, "Understanding Racial Segregation: What Is Known About the Effect of Housing Discrimination?" in *Neighborhood and Life Chances: How Place Matters in Modern America*, ed. Harriet B. Newburger, Eugenie L. Birch, and Susan M. Wachter (Philadelphia: University of Pennsylvania Press, 2011) https://www.degruyter.com/document/doi/10.9783/9780812200089.288/html.

88 Elie Wiesel, "One Must Not Forget," interview by Alvin P. Sanoff, *US News & World Report*, October 27, 1986.

89 The political scientist Ryan Enos calls this a "classic social dilemma," "where a person's individual incentives, which may be things like the quality of their children's school or the price of their home, don't align with the larger social benefits that take individual actions to achieve — in this case, that action is a willingness to stay in an integrating neighborhood." Thomas B. Edsall, "Who's Afraid of Integration? A Lot of People, Actually," *New York Times*, April 5, 2023, https://www.nytimes.com/2023/04/05/opinion/school-integration-segregation.html.

90 Gabriella Bruney, "The Problems with *Green Book* Start with Its Title, and Don't Stop Coming," *Esquire*, February 23, 2019, https://www.esquire.com/entertainment/movies/a26486233/green-book-true-story-explained/.

91 Ibram X. Kendi, *How to Be an Antiracist* (New York: One World, 2019), 18.

92 Just as Iris Marion Young noted that identity-blindness is incapable of solving certain group-based inequalities, identity-conscious or race-specific policies that focus on discrimination or ideas will be an inadequate remedy for structural injustice. Young, "Structural Injustice," 81.

93 See, for example, John McWhorter, "'Racism' Has Too Many Definitions. We Need Another Term," *New York Times*, May 17, 2022, https://www.nytimes.com/2022/05/17/opinion/buffalo-racism.html; John McWhorter, "When 'Racism' Is Not Really Racism," *New York Times*, November 15, 2022, https://www.nytimes.com/2022/11/15/opinion/racism-systemic-structural.html. On the one hand, McWhorter recognizes the differences between what he calls "racism 1.0" and "racism 2.0," but on the other hand, he dislikes the modifiers used to distinguish between them. The modifiers are what clarifies and differentiates their intended meaning. He proposes an alternative, oddly numerical, lexicon instead.

94 Cultural explanations for racial inequality can be traced at least back to Oscar Lewis, whose "culture of poverty" thesis asserted that maladaptive behaviors explained economic immobility and unemployment. Oscar Lewis, *La Vida: A Puerto Rican Family in the Culture of Poverty—San Juan and New York* (New York: Random House, 1965). A relatively modern version of it can be found, for example, in John McWhorter's book *Winning the Race*, where he blamed low achievement and poor life outcomes on "Black culture" and "Black attitudes." John McWhorter, *Winning the Race: Beyond the Crisis in Black America* (New York: Gotham, 2005). See also John H. McWhorter, "What's Holding Blacks Black?" *City Journal*, Winter 2001, https://www.city-journal.org/html/what%E2%80%99s-holding-blacks-back-12025.html.

95 Rothstein, *Color of Law*, 172; Loïc Waquant, *Racial Domination* (Cambridge: Polity Press, 2024), 38.

96 William M. Wiececk and Judy L. Hamilton, "Beyond the Civil Rights Act of 1964: Confronting Structural Racism in the Workplace," *Louisiana Law Review* 74, no. 4 (2014): 1106, https://digitalcommons.law.lsu.edu/lalrev/vol74/iss4/5/.

97 Institute Staff, "11 Terms You Should Know to Better Understand Structural Racism," *Aspen Institute*, July 11, 2016, https://www.aspeninstitute.org/blog-posts/structural-racism-definition/.

98 For a more extended discussion on the flaws in the operational use or proffered definitions in the literature, see Waquant, *Racial Domination*, 174–188.
99 Aspen Institute, "11 Terms You Should Know." The authors describe the terms as "synonymous."
100 See, for example, Erik Luna, "System Failure," *American Criminal Law Review* 42, no. 4 (2005): 1201, 1203 (noting the application of systems theory to biology, ecology, astrophysics); Jill Steiner Sanko, "Systems Thinking—the new American idea," *The Hill*, April 8, 2020, https://thehill.com/opinion/healthcare/491740-systems-thinking-the-new-american-idea/; Ezra Klein and Zeynep Tufecki, "To Understand This Era, You Need to Think in Systems," February 2, 2021, in *The Ezra Klein Show*, podcast, https://www.nytimes.com/2021/02/02/opinion/ezra-klein-podcast-zeynep-tufecki.html.
101 Donella Meadows, *Thinking in Systems: a Primer* (Hartford, VT: Chelsea Green Publishing, 2008).
102 See, for example, Mahzarin R. Banaji, Susan T. Fiske, and Douglas S. Massey, "Systemic Racism: Individuals and Interactions, Institutions and Society," *Cognitive Research: Principles and Implications* 6, no. 82 (2021): https://doi.org/10.1186/s41235-021-00349-3; Toluse Olorunnipa and Griff Witte, "How Systemic Racism Shaped Floyd's Life and Hobbled His Ambition." *Washington Post*, October 8, 2020, https://www.washingtonpost.com/graphics/2020/national/george-floyd-america/systemic-racism/.
103 Stephen Menendian and Caitlin Watt, *Systems Thinking and Race* (Columbus: Kirwan Institute for the Study of Race and Ethnicity, Ohio State University, 2008), 3, https://web.archive.org/web/20131221051647/https://kirwaninstitute.osu.edu/my-product/systems-thinking-and-race/; Tricia Rose, *Metaracism: How Systemic Racism Devastates Black Lives—and How We Break Free* (New York: Basic Books, 2024), 32.
104 Barbara Reskin, "The Race Discrimination System," *Annual Review of Sociology* 38, (2012): 17–35, https://doi.org/10.1146/annurev-soc-071811-145508, citing Menendian and Watt, *Systems Thinking and Race*, and Stephen Menendian et al., *Structural Racism in the United States* (United Nations Committee for the Elimination of Racial Discrimination, 2008), https://drum.lib.umd.edu/handle/1903/22941.
105 Bailey et al., "Structural Racism and Health Inequities in the USA," 1453. In addition to over-emphasizing discrimination, another possible problem with this definition is that it renders structural racism a "system of systems" lens, rather than also including elements that fall outside of systems and other non-normative behavior that nonetheless contribute to inequitable outcomes.
106 Noor Chadha et al., *Toward the Abolition of Biological Race in Medicine: Transforming Clinical Education, Research, and Practice* (Berkeley: Othering & Belonging Institute, 2020), 9, https://belonging.berkeley.edu/toward-abolition-biological-race-medicine-8 (describing structural racism as "the nomenclature we have been taught in public health and medicine"). See, for example, Theresa L. Osypuk and Dolores Acevedo-Garcia, "Beyond Individual Neighborhoods: A Geography of Opportunity Perspective for Understanding Racial/Ethnic Health Disparities," *Health & Place* 16, no. 6 (2010): 1113–1123, https://doi.org/10.1016/j.healthplace.2010.07.002. And the debate about what these words precisely mean is most advanced. See e.g. Jonathan C. Heller et al., "Keeping It Political and Powerful: Defining the Structural Determinants of Health," *Milbank Quarterly* 102, no. 2 (2024): https://doi.org/10.1111/1468-0009.12695.
107 "Social Determinants of Health," Office of Disease Prevention and Health Promotion, accessed April 8, 2022, https://www.healthypeople.gov/2020/topics-objectives/topic/social-determinants-of-health.

108 California Proposition 25: Referendum on Law that Replaced Money Bail with System Based on Public Safety and Flight Risk, 2020, https://repository.uchastings.edu/ca_ballot_props/1388/.
109 See, for example, Public Advocates' campaign against a BART connector: "Bart/Oakland Airport Connector (OAC)," Public Advocates, accessed April 8, 2022, https://www.publicadvocates.org/our-work/transportation-justice-issues/bartoakland-airport-connector-oac/.
110 Noam Scheiber, "As Trump Attacks D.E.I., Some on the Left Approve," *New York Times*, February 6, 2025, https://www.nytimes.com/2025/02/06/business/economy/trump-dei-democrats-left-unions.html.
111 john a. powell and Stephen Menendian, *Belonging Without Othering: How We Save Ourselves and the World* (Stanford, CA: Stanford University Press, 2024).
112 See e.g. Kendi, *How to Be an Antiracist*, 151, 181, 193. It is not uncommon to encounter broad critiques of capitalism, or market-based economics, in the racial justice literature. The problem with this often-under-specified critique is that racial inequality exists in both capitalist and non-capitalist societies, and that capitalism exists in a remarkable diversity of institutional forms, with varying degrees of inequality. What is required is empirical specification of the particular mechanisms, not broad systems or theoretical processes, by which racial inequality is actively created and maintained. This book aims to do that.
113 As some DEI programs are known to be. Frank Dobbin and Alexandra Kalev, "Why Diversity Programs Fail," *Harvard Business Review*, July 2016, https://hbr.org/2016/07/why-diversity-programs-fail. Poorly designed and ineffective policies may be worse than doing nothing, because it creates the perception of progress or engenders cynicism upon failure. As Milton Friedman, ironically, wisely observed: "One of the great mistakes is to judge policies and programs by their intentions rather than their results." Milton Friedman, "Living Within Our Means," interview by Richard D. Heffner, *Open Mind*, December 7, 1975, https://www.thirteen.org/openmind-archive/public-affairs/living-within-our-means/. This does not mean that evaluating outcomes is easy. In some cases, the situation may not have improved, but the policy or program preventing matters from getting worse. In such a case, the outcome should be considered positive.
114 Goodwin Liu, "The First Justice Harlan," *California Law Review* 96, no. 5 (2008): 1383–1393, https://www.jstor.org/stable/20441050; Stephen Menendian, "The Shadow Constitution: Rescuing Our Inheritance from Neglect and Disuse," *University of Pennsylvania Journal of Constitutional Law* 26, no. 2 (2024): 357–358, https://doi.org/10.58112/jcl.26-2.2; powell, "Law and Significance."
115 Plessy v. Ferguson, 163 U.S. 537 (1896) at 559.
116 Andrew Sullivan, "A Glimpse at the Intersectional Left's Political Endgame," *New York Magazine*, November 15, 2019, https://nymag.com/intelligencer/2019/11/andrew-sullivan-the-intersectional-lefts-political-endgame.html.
117 Menendian, "Racial Disparities Dashboard Progress Report Card."
118 In fact, this has occurred in some contexts. See Anne Case and Angus Deaton, *Deaths of Despair and the Future of Capitalism* (Princeton, NJ: Princeton University Press, 2020).
119 Which is not to say that this is the same goal as economic justice or social justice, more broadly conceived. Racial justice can be achieved in a world that is grossly unfair on any number of other identity or status bases. For example, equality between racial groups could be achieved, in theory, in a society in which gender or class disparities are significant and persistent. Achieving racial justice does not necessarily result in justice and equality for other groups.
120 This could happen, for example, if a racial group demonstrated a strong cultural preference for a career in a low-paying but highly valued or honorable

profession, such as teaching or clergy, such that average incomes between groups were affected.

121 Not only is what Eduardo Porter calls "the accountability debate" a shift from where our focus should lie, which is "how to build fair and just structures of opportunity in the present," but it exacerbates and compounds what are already the enormous political challenges of trying to address the core problem. Eduardo Porter, *American Poison: How Racial Hostility Destroyed Our Promise* (New York: Alfred A. Knopf, 2020), 168, quoting Danielle Allen, "Toward a Connected Society," in *Our Compelling Interests: The Value of Diversity for Democracy and a Prosperous Society*, ed. Earl Lewis and Nancy Cantor (Princeton, NJ: Princeton University Press and Andrew W. Mellon Foundation, 2016), 80 and Porter, *American Poison*, 161–171.

122 Louis Proyect, "Smearing Black Lives Matter...From the Left," *CounterPunch*, July 3, 2020, https://www.counterpunch.org/2020/07/03/smearing-black-lives-matter-from-the-left/ (referring to Hannah-Jones' now-deleted tweet).

123 See, for example, "Vision for Black Lives: 2020 Policy Platform," Movement for Black Lives, accessed April 14, 2022, https://m4bl.org/policy-platforms/.

124 Stephen Menendian, "The Structural Racism Remedies Project," *Othering & Belonging Institute*, February 16, 2022, https://belonging.berkeley.edu/structural-racism-remedies-project.

125 Fishkin discusses the *Griggs* case as an example of how a structural reform, which loosens or eliminates a bottleneck, can benefit substantial numbers of persons outside of the plaintiff's class. Fishkin, *Bottlenecks*, 246–248. This is a feature, not a bug of structural reforms. The "anti-bottleneck" principle, which is an excellent expression of a structural lens, would give priority to "universal alterations of the opportunity structure that would remove or loosen bottlenecks for all rather than only for members of certain groups." Stephen M. Rich, "Equal Opportunity, Diversity, and Other Fables in Antidiscrimination Law," *Texas Law Review* 93, no. 2 (2014): 437–485, 455.

126 Or, as Fishkin puts it, we have "to do more than simply increase the number of people who pass [through a bottleneck]. We have to alter the opportunity structure itself [so that the bottleneck is not as important]." Fishkin, *Bottlenecks*, 170.

127 Menendian and Watt, *Systems Thinking and Race*, 11–12.

128 Norimitsu Onishi, "A Racial Awakening in France, Where Race Is a Taboo Topic," *New York Times*, July 14, 2020, https://www.nytimes.com/2020/07/14/world/europe/france-racism-universalism.html.

129 Fishkin, *Bottlenecks*, 257 ("When we find ways to restructure opportunities so that not everyone needs to push their way through the same bottlenecks, or so that those who cannot make it through have other potential paths open to them, the effect need not be zero-sum, but can be positive-sum").

130 Angela Glover Blackwell, "The Curb-Cut Effect," *Stanford Social Innovation Review* 15, no. 1 (2016): 28–33, https://doi.org/10.48558/YVMS-CC96.

131 See Heather McGhee, *The Sum of Us: What Racism Costs Everyone* (New York: One World, 2022). Although true zero-sum situations are surprisingly rare, there are psychological reasons people tend to perceive them. Damien Cave, "Welcome to the Zero Sum Era. Now How Do We Get Out?," *New York Times*, March 1, 2025, https://www.nytimes.com/2025/03/01/world/asia/trump-zero-sum-world.html, citing Andrews Fearon, Patricia Götz, and Friedrich M, "The zero-sum mindset," *Journal of Personality and Social Psychology* 127, no. 4 (2024): 758–795, https://doi.org/10.1037/pspa0000404.

132 Samuel R. Bagenstos, "Universalism and Civil Rights (with Notes on Voting Rights after *Shelby*)," *Yale Law Journal* 123, no. 8 (2014): 2856, https://www.yalelawjournal.org/pdf/2838.Bagenstos.2876_c5kmzww2.pdf.

133 Derrick A. Bell Jr., "Brown v. Board of Education and the Interest-Convergence Dilemma," *Harvard Law Review* 93, no. 3 (1980): 518–533, https://www.jstor.org/stable/1340546.
134 For another approach that is consistent with this idea, see john a. powell, Stephen Menendian, and Wendy Ake, *Targeted Universalism: Policy and Practice* (Berkeley: Othering and Belonging Institute, May 2019), https://belonging.berkeley.edu/sites/default/files/targeted_universalism_primer.pdf?file=1&force=1.
135 Sullivan, "Political Endgame"; Coleman Hughes, "How to Be an Anti-Intellectual," *City Journal*, October 27, 2019, https://www.city-journal.org/how-to-be-an-antiracist.
136 The Religious Freedom Restoration Act of 1993, Pub. L. No. 103–141, 107 Stat. 1488 (1993).
137 Jennifer Hernandez, David Friedman, and Stephanie DeHerrera, *In the Name of the Environment: Litigation Abuse Under CEQA* (San Francisco: Holland & Knight, 2015), https://www.hklaw.com/en/insights/publications/2015/08/in-the-name-of-the-environment-litigation-abuse-un; Jennifer Hernandez, "In the Name of the Environment Part III: CEQA, Housing, and the Rule of Law," *Chapman Law Review* 26, no. 1 (2022): 57–158, https://digitalcommons.chapman.edu/chapman-law-review/vol26/iss1/2/.
138 See, for example, CA Elec Code § 9005 (2024), https://leginfo.legislature.ca.gov/faces/codes_displaySection.xhtml?sectionNum=9005.&lawCode=ELEC section d.
139 A proposed legal standard that straddles a middle ground between requiring that racism be motivational and the law of disparate impact is the idea of "deliberate indifference." See Derek Black, "The Contradiction between Equal Protection's Meaning and Its Legal Substance: How Deliberate Indifference Can Cure It," *WIlliam & Mary Bill of Rights Journal* 15, no. 2 (2006): 533–586, https://scholarship.law.wm.edu/cgi/viewcontent.cgi?article=1124&context=wmborj&httpsredir=1&referer=.
140 Erwin Chemerinsky, "Making Sense of the Affirmative Action Debate," *Ohio Northern University Law Review* 22, no. 4 (1996): 1159–1176, https://scholarship.law.duke.edu/cgi/viewcontent.cgi?referer=&httpsredir=1&article=2135&;amp;context=faculty_scholarship.
141 John Gramlich, "Americans and Affirmative Action: How the Public Sees the Consideration of Race in College Admissions, Hiring," *Pew Research Center*, June 16, 2023, https://www.pewresearch.org/short-reads/2023/06/16/americans-and-affirmative-action-how-the-public-sees-the-consideration-of-race-in-college-admissions-hiring/.
142 "Establishing the President's Committee on Equal Employment Opportunity," Exec. Order. No. 10925, 26 Fed. Reg. 1977 (March 8, 1961). The order became effective on April 5, 1961.
143 *Human Development Report 2016* (New York: United Nations Development Programme, 2016), 119.
144 *Bakke*, 438 U.S. 265.
145 Fishkin repeatedly asserts that certain identities (such as race, sex, and class) can function directly as a bottleneck, not just that these statuses are affected by practices that constrict opportunities. See, for example, Fishkin, *Bottlenecks*, 174 ("To the degree that membership in some favored racial group enables a person to pursue many paths, for *any* of these reasons, race is functioning as a bottleneck"). In his review of Fishkin's book, Stephen Rich proposes "an alternative—and I believe better—formulation": "to think of race as a feature of a substance passing through a bottleneck that makes the bottleneck either more or less effective at constraining an individual's opportunities." Stephen Rich, "Equal Opportunity, Diversity, and Other Fables in Antidiscrimination Law,"

review of Fishkin, *Bottlenecks*, *Texas Law Review* 93, no. 2 (2014): 469. In either case, the presence of the bottleneck and the way it affects members of the group justifies the targeted intervention.

146 Especially at elite academic institutions with the most stringent admissions criteria. Thomas J. Kane, "Racial and Ethnic Preferences in College Admissions," *Ohio State Law Journal* 59, no. 3 (1998): 988, https://citeseerx.ist.psu.edu/viewdoc/download?doi=10.1.1.828.5851&rep=rep1&type=pdf. An alternative set of admissions criteria capable of promoting racial diversity would undoubtedly be more complicated (involving more factors) and administratively expensive. See john a. powell and Stephen Menendian, "Fisher v. Texas: The Limits of Exhaustion and the Future of Race-Conscious University Admissions," *University of Michigan Journal of Law Reform* 47, no. 4 (2014): 899–933, https://repository.law.umich.edu/cgi/viewcontent.cgi?article=1114&context=mjlr (describing the administrative complexity of more nuanced race-conscious admissions processes).

147 Brief of Social and Organizational Psychologists as *Amici Curiae* Supporting Respondents, Fisher v. University of Texas, 579 U.S. 365 (2016), Table 4, https://belonging.berkeley.edu/sites/default/files/amicus_brief_fisher_v_texas_social_and_organizational_psychologists_0.pdf; Saul Geiser, "Back to the Future: Freshman Admissions at the University of California, 1994 to the Present and Beyond," *Center for Studies in Higher Education Research & Occasional Paper Series: CHSE 4.14* (2014): 2, https://cshe.berkeley.edu/sites/default/files/publications/rops.cshe_.4.14.geiser.backtothefuture.4.24.2014-1.pdf; University of California Academic Council, *Report of the UC Academic Council Standardized Testing Task Force (STTF)* (Oakland: University of California Academic Senate, 2020), 10, https://senate.universityofcalifornia.edu/_files/underreview/sttf-report.pdf.

148 Richard Arum and Mitchell L. Stevens, "For Most College Students, Affirmative Action Was Never Enough," *New York Times*, July 3, 2023, https://www.nytimes.com/interactive/2023/07/03/opinion/for-most-college-students-affirmative-action-was-not-enough.html (describing the relative representation of racial groups across the range of selective to non-selective institutions of higher education).

149 Fishkin asserts that affirmative action is an ameliorative strategy that leaves the production of racial inequality in place. See Fishkin, *Bottlenecks*, 173.

150 Ezekiel Kweku, "On Its 10th Anniversary, 'Hamilton' Looks Heartbreakingly Different," *New York Times*, January 18, 2025, https://www.nytimes.com/2025/01/18/opinion/hamilton-musical-history.html ("programs like D.E.I. and affirmative action are not foes of meritocracy, but rather its servants — intended to correct for biases and inequities that obstruct the proper flow of talent"). Although there have been efforts to refashion or defend affirmative action in terms of new conceptions of merit. See Lani Guinier, "Admissions Rituals as Political Acts: Guardians At the Gates of Our Democratic Ideals," *Harvard Law Review* 117, no. 1 (2003): 113–224; Lani Guiner, *The Tyranny of the Meritocracy: Democratizing Higher Education in America* (Boston: Beacon Press, 2015).

151 Rather than restrict admission to increase prestige, Malcolm Gladwell has long argued that institutions of higher education should expand enrollment to meet demand. Alex Slen and Tanisha Agrawal, "Bestselling author Malcolm Gladwell talks college admissions, sports, and journalism with the DP," *Daily Pennsylvanian*, October 30, 2024, https://www.thedp.com/article/2024/10/interview-malcolm-gladwell-penn-museum-event ("'My biggest problem with Ivy League colleges is you're not big enough [...] If you have a lot of money, tens of billions of dollars in the bank, you should educate more than 10,000 students.' He pointed to his alma mater, the University of Toronto, which has nearly 70,000 students.

'If they [Ivy League schools] truly are elite, they should want to educate as many people as they can'").

152 See generally Angela M. Hough, "All Deliberate Ambiguity: The Question of Diversity, College Admissions, and The Future of the Texas Top-Ten-Percent Plan," *Texas Tech Law Review* 39, no. 1 (2006): 211–217.

153 Brief of Social and Organizational Psychologists, Fisher v. University of Texas, 579 U.S. 365, 10. See Figure 2. "National patterns of segregation and racial isolation are visible across Texas. Despite the fact that Texas has no racial or ethnic majority (non-Hispanic Whites constitute 44% of the population), only 13% of the 1,024 school districts in the state have no racial majority. Nearly 40% of those districts have a racial/ethnic supermajority…The TTTP relies on this fact to generate some degree of student body diversity by channeling these student populations into the freshman class."

154 Fishkin, *Bottlenecks*, 171.

155 Cashin, *Place, Not Race*, xv ("I prefer place, rather than race, as the focus of affirmative action for the pragmatic reason that it will foster more social cohesion and a better politics. More importantly, it will help those actually disadvantaged by segregation.. . . . As I will show in subsequent chapters, race does not, by definition, capture those who suffer the structural disadvantages of segregated schools and neighborhoods. Race is also over-inclusive in that it can capture people with dark skin who are exceedingly advantaged").

156 Sampson, *Great American City*, 99.

157 Cashin, *Place, Not Race*, 50.

158 Kevin D. Brown and Kenneth G. Dau-Schmidt, "Racial and Ethnic Ancestry of the Nation's Black Law Students: An Analysis of Data from the LSSSE Survey," *Berkeley Journal of African-American Law & Policy* 22, no. 1 (2022): 23, Table 2, https://doi.org/10.15779/Z38CN6Z10J.

159 Brief of Social and Organizational Psychologists as *Amici Curiae* Supporting Respondents, Fisher v. University of Texas, 570 U.S. 297 (2013), https://www.scotusblog.com/wp-content/uploads/2016/08/11-345-respondent-amicus-SOP.pdf; Brief of Social and Organizational Psychologists, Fisher v. University of Texas, 579 U.S. 365.

160 Students for Fair Admissions, Inc. v. President and Fellows of Harvard College, 600 U.S. ___ (2023).

161 James Murphy, "Tracking the Impact of the SFFA Decision on College Admissions," *Education Reform Now*, September 9, 2024, https://edreformnow.org/2024/09/09/tracking-the-impact-of-the-sffa-decision-on-college-admissions/; Anemona Hartocollis and Stephanie Saul, "Affirmative Action Was Banned. What Happened Next Was Confusing," *New York Times*, September 13, 2024, https://www.nytimes.com/2024/09/13/us/affirmative-action-ban-campus-diversity.html.

162 Scott Jaschik, "The 2018 Surveys of Admissions Leaders: The Pressure Grows," *Inside Higher Ed*, September 24, 2018, https://www.insidehighered.com/news/survey/2018-surveys-admissions-leaders-pressure-grows.

163 Jacey Fortin, "Amherst College Ends Legacy Admissions Favoring Children of Alumni," *New York Times*, October 20, 2021, https://www.nytimes.com/2021/10/20/us/amherst-college-legacy-admissions.html. Although some universities have banned it for decades. Jessica Bryant, "These Schools Have Banned Legacy Admissions," *BestColleges*, updated May 6, 2024, https://www.bestcolleges.com/research/legacy-admissions-bans/; Nick Anderson, "Pressure mounts on colleges to ditch 'legacy' admissions factor," *Washington Post*, July 16, 2023, https://www.washingtonpost.com/education/2023/07/16/legacy-college-admissions-affirmative-action/.

164 Patty Nieberg, "Colorado ends 'legacy admissions' for higher education," *Associated Press*, May 25, 2021, https://apnews.com/article/co-state-wire-colorado-race-and-ethnicity-higher-education-government-and-politics-edbc95b683b007e34a2ea214b3e19adb; Laura Spitalniak, "A Look at 5 States Weighing Legacy Admissions Bans," *Higher Ed Dive*, March 28, 2024, https://www.highereddive.com/news/5-states-weigh-legacy-admissions-bans/711428/; Shawn Hubler, Soumya Karlamangla, and Stephanie Saul, "California Bans Legacy Preferences at Private Universities," *New York Times*, September 30, 2024, https://www.nytimes.com/2024/09/30/us/california-bans-legacy-preferences-private-universities.html.

165 Aatish Bhatia and Emily Badger, "Can You Create a Diverse College Class Without Affirmative Action?," *New York Times*, March 9, 2024, https://www.nytimes.com/interactive/2024/03/09/upshot/affirmative-action-alternatives.html.

166 There are many examples of the latter, but one is the Metro School in Columbus, Ohio, and attached to the Ohio State University. "2021 College Admissions Profile," Metro Schools, accessed April 14, 2022, https://www.themetroschool.org/page/school-profile.

167 Reeves and Haliakas, "Race gaps in SAT scores." For the case that these tests are racially biased, see Scott Jaschick, "New Evidence of Racial Bias on SAT," *Inside Higher Ed*, June 21, 2010, https://www.insidehighered.com/news/2010/06/21/new-evidence-racial-bias-sat.

168 *SAT Suite of Assessments Annual Report: Total Group* (New York: College Board, 2021), 3, https://reports.collegeboard.org/pdf/2021-total-group-sat-suite-assessments-annual-report.pdf.

169 *Report of the UC Academic Council STTF*, 42, Figure 3C-3.

170 *Report of the UC Academic Council STTF*, 19–20.

171 *Report of the UC Academic Council STTF*, 21, Table 3A-1. The R^2 for GPA was 0.16 (quite bad), but for SAT it was only marginally better: 0.21, a relatively weak correlation.

172 Neil Vigdor and Johnny Diaz, "More Colleges Are Waiving SAT and ACT Requirements," *New York Times*, May 21, 2020, https://www.nytimes.com/article/sat-act-test-optional-colleges-coronavirus.html; "List of Colleges Dropping & Reinstating ACT/SAT Requirements," *Horizon Education*, May 3, 2024, https://horizoneducation.com/blog/colleges-dropping-reinstating-act-sat-requirements.

173 As long as the alternative is well-designed and does not simply replicate advantages and disadvantages. See Jay Caspian Kang, "The Case against 'Excellence' at Universities," *New York Times*, September 13, 2021, https://www.nytimes.com/2021/09/13/opinion/SAT-universities-admissions.html.

174 Douglas Belkin, "SAT to Give Students 'Adversity Score' to Capture Social and Economic Background," *Wall Street Journal*, May 16, 2019, https://www.wsj.com/articles/sat-to-give-students-adversity-score-to-capture-social-and-economic-background-11557999000.

175 Dana Goldstein, "Your Questions about the New Adversity Score on the SAT, Answered," *New York Times*, May 17, 2019, https://www.nytimes.com/2019/05/17/us/sat-adversity-score-explained.html.

176 Anemona Hartocollis, "SAT 'Adversity Score' Is Abandoned in Wake of Criticism," *New York Times*, August 27, 2019, https://www.nytimes.com/2019/08/27/us/sat-adversity-score-college-board.html.

177 Michael N. Bastedo et al., "Admitting Students in Context: Field Experiments on Information Dashboards in College Admissions," *Journal of Higher Education* 93, no. 3 (2021): 342–343, https://doi.org/10.1080/00221546.2021.1971488.

178 Which is why some advocates call for wealthy institutions of higher education to do more at the primary and secondary level, such as setting up special pipeline institutions. See, for example, Tomiko Brown-Nagin et al., "How to Fix College Admissions Now," *New York Times*, July 5, 2023, https://www.nytimes.com/interactive/2023/07/05/opinion/affirmative-action-college-admissions.html#affirmative-action-high-schools.
179 See, for example, Julie Berry Cullen, Mark C. Long, and Randall Reback," Jockeying for Position: Strategic High School Choice under Texas' Top Ten Percent Plan," *Journal of Public Economics, Elsevier* 97(C) (2013): 32–48.
180 Astead Herndon, "2020 Democrats Embrace Race-Conscious Policies, Including Reparations," *New York Times*, February 21, 2019, https://www.nytimes.com/2019/02/21/us/politics/2020-democrats-race-policy.html
181 See, for example, William A. Darity Jr. and A. Kirsten Mullen, *From Here to Equality: Reparations for Black Americans in the Twenty-First Century* (Chapel Hill: University of North Carolina Press, 2020).
182 Chetty et al., "Race and Economic Opportunity," 715.
183 Chetty et al., 723.
184 Darity, Addo, and Smith, "Subaltern Middle Class," 7, table 6.
185 Aliprantis, Carroll, and Young, "Dynamics of the Racial Wealth Gap."
186 Steven Bradford et al., *California Task Force to Study and Develop Reparation Proposals for African Americans Final Report* (California Department of Justice, 2023), https://oag.ca.gov/ab3121/report.
187 *Kerner Report*, 1.
188 *Kerner Report*, 1.
189 Theresa Riley, "America 'Is Moving towards Two Societies, One White, One Black—Separate and Unequal'," *Moyers*, December 7, 2014, https://billmoyers.com/2014/12/07/america-moving-towards-two-societies-one-white-one-black-separate-unequal.
190 Jelani Cobb, "A Warning Ignored," *New York Review of Books*, August 19, 2021, https://www.nybooks.com/articles/2021/08/19/kerner-commission-warning-ignored/.
191 *Kerner Report*, 29.
192 *Forward through Ferguson: A Path toward Racial Equity* (Ferguson, MO: The Ferguson Commission, 2015), 94, https://s3.documentcloud.org/documents/2413166/fergusoncommissionreport-091415.pdf; *Investigation of the Ferguson Police Department* (Washington, DC: United States Department of Justice Civil Rights Division, 2015), https://www.justice.gov/sites/default/files/opa/press-releases/attachments/2015/03/04/ferguson_police_department_report.pdf. See also Matt Apuzzo and John Eligon, "Ferguson Police Tainted by Bias, Justice Department Says," *New York Times*, March 4, 2015, https://www.nytimes.com/2015/03/05/us/us-calls-on-ferguson-to-overhaul-criminal-justice-system.html.
193 *Investigation of the Baltimore City Police Department* (Washington, DC: U.S. Department of Justice Civil Rights Division, 2016), https://www.justice.gov/crt/file/883296/download; Sheryl Gay Stolberg, "Findings of Police Bias in Baltimore Validate What Many Have Long Felt," *New York Times*, August 10, 2016, https://www.nytimes.com/2016/08/11/us/baltimore-police-bias-report.html; Richard A. Oppel Jr., Sheryl Gay Stolberg, and Matt Apuzzo, "Justice Department to Release Blistering Report of Racial Bias by Baltimore Police," *New York Times*, August 9, 2016, https://www.nytimes.com/2016/08/10/us/justice-department-to-release-blistering-report-of-racial-bias-by-baltimore-police.html.
194 *Investigation of the Chicago Police Department* (Washington, DC and Chicago: U.S. Department of Justice Civil Rights Division and United States Attorney's Office Northern District of Illinois, 2017), https://www.justice.gov/opa/file/925846/download; Julie Bosman and Mitch Smith, "Chicago Police Routinely Trampled on Civil Rights, Justice Dept. Says," *New York Times*, January 13, 2017, https://www.nytimes.com/2017/01/13/us/chicago-police-justice-department-report.html.

Toward a Structural Agenda 251

195 The Future of the Cities," Chapter 16 in *Kerner Report*, 221–225.
196 United States v. Virginia, 518 U.S. 515 (1996).
197 *Kerner Report*, 11.
198 As late as the 1970s, Rep. John Conyers was calling for a "Marshall Plan" for Urban America, asking the federal government to "rebuild America's ghettos" just as George Marshall helped rebuild Europe. Forman, *Locking Up Our Own*, 310.
199 Harper Lee, *To Kill a Mockingbird* (New York: Harper Collins, 1960), 39.
200 Malcolm Gladwell, "The Courthouse Ring," *New Yorker*, August 3, 2009, https://www.newyorker.com/magazine/2009/08/10/the-courthouse-ring.
201 See e.g. Adeel Hassan, "An Enduring Race Tax," *New York Times*, April 26, 2024, https://www.nytimes.com/2024/04/26/us/black-americans-homeownership.html ("The people who bid on tax delinquent properties at county tax auctions were not the hooded nightriders or white mobs that we often associate with Black land dispossession in this era. They were often lawyers and land speculators who were seeking to take advantage of others' misfortunes, financial hardships and vulnerabilities for gain").
202 Peter Baker, "Clinton Sounds Call for Dialogue on Race," *Washington Post*, June 15, 1997, https://www.washingtonpost.com/archive/politics/1997/06/15/clinton-sounds-call-for-dialogue-on-race/3ee6706c-5206-46c1-9289-5659d4c5a679/?utm_term=.2adfa1738459.

5 Realizing the American Dream

Kaiser Permanente is the largest health care consortium in the United States, unbeknownst to most Americans because it only operates in eight states.[1] To many West Coast residents, Kaiser facilities are recognizably imposing, rising out of urban landscapes like modern ziggurats. The company's founder, Henry Kaiser, built an industrial empire out of shipbuilding during World War II. At peak capacity, his company supplied the war effort by launching a battleship into the San Francisco Bay every day.[2] After the war, Kaiser turned his company's health care plan and network of physicians and nurses into Kaiser Permanente, one of the largest employers in the Bay Area today.

One of their nurses, Mercedes Garcia, lived in the Mission neighborhood of San Francisco for over ten years. Wedged into the heart of the city, the Mission district is a notable cultural hotspot featured in travel guides and tourist maps. Historically a Latino neighborhood, the community is known for delicious food, nightlife, and vibrant murals that decorate local businesses and buildings.[3]

Whereas Detroit was once the urban hub of the industrial economy and the automotive industry, San Francisco has become a leading urban center of the knowledge economy, and an anchor for Silicon Valley start-ups and titans alike. As this sector became a vanguard in the American economy, jobs, capital, and wealth followed suit. In the wake of the Great Recession, San Francisco alone added more private sector jobs than 47 of the 50 states.[4] By 2015, San Francisco had the highest average income of any major city in the United States, and almost 50% higher than the national median.[5]

Where did these tens of thousands of new workers, often highly paid, live? Those wishing to avoid soul-crushing commutes and astronomical rents moved into traditionally working class, but centrally located, amenity-rich neighborhoods with cultural cache like the Mission. The Mission features a popular destination park (Dolores) with postcard views of the skyline, culinary diversity, two stops on the region's high-speed rail system (Bay Area Rapid Transit (BART)), and convenient walkability. As demand for apartments and housing in the Mission District grew, driven by the creation of high-wage private sector jobs, rents skyrocketed and bidding-wars became notorious. The Mission became the epicenter of gentrification battles that

DOI: 10.4324/9781003562764-6

rattled San Francisco in the previous decade, when numerous ethnic and cultural restaurants and retail establishments closed as rents climbed and locals were pushed out.[6] A one-bedroom apartment in the Mission in 2011 rented around $1,900 a month, but nearly doubled to $3,600 by 2015.[7] That would be a bargain today.

In the fall of 2015, Mercedes Garcia received a notice from her landlord that her rent was tripling. She enlisted a local legal aid attorney for help, but to no avail. Her apartment was not rent protected, and she was evicted a few months later. First, she moved back in with her mother, but then ultimately found a new apartment in Pinole after an exhausting search. Although it was only 20 miles away, in the hellish daily commute across the Bay, it was an additional two hours of time, by car, bus, or rail.

The New Great Migration

Mercedes' experience is all-too common. A 2021 survey found that 92% of region's residents felt that the cost of housing was a serious problem, and 56% said that they would move out of the Bay Area in the next few years.[8] Specialty firms, such as "Leaving the Bay Area," sprouted to offer services facilitating such moves.[9]

Most of the people being pushed out of the region are middle and lower income.[10] This represents the downside of a more hopeful demographic and economic trend. After decades of decay and job loss, urban areas boomed in the first two decades of this century. As prophesied most famously by Richard Florida in *The Rise of the Creative Class*, urban economies were transformed by "knowledge workers, techies, and artists and other cultural creatives."[11] The "creative" economy flourished under the close proximity of researchers, technologists, professionals, and urban amenities compared to the stifling isolation of suburban corporate campuses.[12]

In the San Francisco Bay Area, many tech start-ups relocated from Silicon Valley, the sprawling suburbs south of San Francisco, into the city, where leadership teams cross paths with other entrepreneurs, tech wizards, marketing gurus, and potential investors. Start-ups, especially, are attracted to dense urban environments because it is easier to find highly skilled workers. But even older, large blue-chip corporations relocated back to the cities in this period, partly in search of talent.[13]

Companies benefit from proximity to skilled workers, but workers also benefit from thick networks that relay new job opportunities, circulate ideas, and strengthen social capital. Workers are also more cognizant of the twisting career arc. Rather than climb a ladder within a single company, workers today are more likely to change jobs and companies over their career. Proximate density offers more than a greater number of job opportunities and chance encounters; it also offers a greater range of career path options. These places have lots of high-paying jobs, and you are more likely to learn about trends and opportunities—and pursue them—by living and working in such areas. Career advancement, not just job security, is a reward for residing in heavily networked urban spaces.

This explains why, after decades of decline, so many Americans, especially high-skilled workers and young professionals, flocked back into the urban environments they previously fled.[14] In 1980, Houston was the only American metropolis with most of its residents in the central city.[15] Today, New York leads the pack.[16] By the end of the last decade, the demand for urban residential housing by millennials and young professionals accelerated cultural and demographic change in many of our major segregated metropolises. The patterns of urban change that defined the 20th century, the movement from urban centers to the suburban and exurban periphery—middle-out—began reversing and contracting in the first two decades of the 21st century.[17]

This seemingly hopeful story has a disturbing downside. Across the nation, many long-time residents have been displaced from traditionally ethnic neighborhoods and working-class communities.[18] In the largest cities in America, Black populations declined in relative and absolute terms. From 2000 to 2010, 13 of the 20 cities with the largest Black communities experienced a decrease in Black population.[19] New York City lost nearly 5% of its Black population between 2010 and 2020, with even steeper declines in two Black cultural centers, Harlem and Brooklyn.[20] Chicago's Black population fell by more than 350,000 from 1980 to 2016.[21] Washington DC grew for the first time in half a century from 2000 to 2010, and from 2010 to 2020, but lost Black population, falling from 50% to 41% Black.[22] Similarly, Atlanta lost more than 20,000 Black residents in the same period, even as it gained more than 61,000 white residents, losing its outright Black majority in that time.[23] San Francisco, once a Black cultural hub with renowned jazz lounges and home to icons like Willie Mays, experienced a precipitous decline in its Black population, which is now reportedly small enough to fill the baseball stadium.[24] Oakland lost almost 50,000 African-American residents between 1980 and 2010, while white, Latino, and Asian populations have grown steadily.[25]

The legacies of redlining, disinvestment, and *de facto* racial segregation artificially depressed the value of real estate and rents in many neighborhoods with the shortest commutes to new economy jobs in central cities and urban corridors.[26] Young professionals searching for inexpensive housing discovered the best deals in these neighborhoods, as well as cultural cache. With enough new arrivals, a tipping point is reached, signaling to other young professionals that the neighborhood is "safe" and a good investment. As property values improve, high-quality amenities follow, enticing more arrivals, pushing up rents and ultimately displacing long-time residents. Community embedded institutions such as ethnic grocery stores or churches lose the critical mass of customers or members needed to sustain themselves, and the neighborhood begins a more dramatic transformation, symbolized by high-end restaurants, art galleries, and boutique shops.

Industrialization, two world wars, and suburbanization transformed American residential and economic life in the 20th century. As part of the Great Migration, millions of Black Americans moved to the North and West, and millions more white Americans took advantage of the new opportunities made possible by federal housing subsidies and the new highway system to build or buy a home in the suburbs. After white-flight ran its course, the "vanilla suburb, chocolate city" characterization aptly described most major American metropolises.

By the early 2000s, a growing number of Black and Latino families followed the path of their white predecessors, and moved into the suburbs in search of safe neighborhoods, more spacious homes, and better schools.[27] In 1980, just 6 million African-Americans lived in the suburbs, but by 2010, that number had risen to 16 million.[28] By 2010, the suburbs were as racially and ethnically diverse as central cities were in 1980.[29]

This triggered additional white flight, as more affluent whites returned to the cities or moved further outward, leaving rising levels of poverty detected in the suburbs, especially inner-ring suburbs.[30] Between 2000 and 2014 alone, poverty ballooned by 65% in the suburbs.[31] Even metropolitan regions with the most advanced sector economies exhibited increases in suburban poverty. As a result, hopeful Black and Hispanic families that had moved to the suburbs were once again residing in communities with limited public services, older housing and infrastructure, and poor-performing schools.[32]

Ferguson, Missouri is a paradigmatic example of a decaying inner-ring suburb. In 1990, Ferguson was 75% white, but by 2010, it was two-thirds Black, with poverty rising from 7% to 22% in the same period.[33] Of the ten neighborhoods within Ferguson, three feature concentrated levels of poverty.[34] More broadly, St. Louis' entire inner-ring is among the most racially segregated in the nation.[35] Only Newark, Miami, and Cleveland suburbs were worse in that respect as of 2010.

This dynamic would not have been so disturbing if it had followed the previous trajectory of upward mobility for these families of color moving to the suburbs, or if the return to the city served and boosted the fortunes of long-time residents. But what once appeared an escape route had become a trap for millions, pinched between exclusive, affluent suburbs and expensive cities. And for the long-time urban residents being pushed to the far-flung periphery, the dangers are even greater.

The American Dream will become a nightmare if wealth, income, amenities, services and the best jobs are concentrated in urban centers or high-opportunity suburbs while the poor are displaced to the farthest peripheries of our regions or trapped in declining suburbs. In the 20th century, at least the urban poor could enjoy proximity to city and county services. In the 21st century, the poor may be isolated not only from jobs in booming regions but everything else, from healthy food to reliable public transit.

Unfortunately, we already know places that look like this, and the corrosive effects this pattern yields, evident in places like Paris, France. The poor and recent immigrants are shunted into the periphery, marginalized communities disconnected from the vitality of the economic, political, and cultural life of the metropolis.[36] In these places, discontentment foments and rage swells. This trend must be disrupted, not only if we are to achieve a vision of racially inclusive and equitable society, but one where opportunity is available to all Americans.

An Opportunity Agenda

Although it would not be possible here to offer a comprehensive list of policies that might be implemented to expand opportunity or redress structural racism,[37] this chapter outlines ten broad policy interventions that have the best chance to enlarge and expand access to opportunity, to revitalize, rewire or dismantle the most problematic features of contemporary opportunity structures, and to reduce extreme racial disparities.

The policies advanced here are presented without grand or overarching ideological commitments beyond a focus on expanding access to opportunity while reducing structural racial inequality. The goal of reducing inequality of opportunity (by race or otherwise) is complementary to the goal of enlarging opportunity generally and a broader vision of human flourishing.

Although appealing to the ideal of equality of opportunity, the ultimate goal must reach beyond that. It is possible to equalize, move closer to equalizing, or expand access to opportunity in a society with limited or little overall opportunity.[38] That is why the goal of expanding access to opportunity includes both a reduction in inequality of opportunity (in large part by widening opportunity pathways so that more people can traverse them) as well as an enlargement in opportunity itself, meaning an expansion in the range of opportunity pathways and desirable destinations, not just an expansion of existing pathways towards current ends.

A true opportunity society would do more than expand access to those destinations. It would multiply the number, range, and capacity of desirable destinations. There should be more destinations, not just more people able to pursue those destinations.[39] If you expand access to those destinations without enlarging the carrying capacity of those destinations or number of desirable destinations, you may achieve structural fairness without expanding opportunity directly or access to it broadly. It remains a zero-sum competition in which more people are chasing the same limited rewards, reducing the general chances of reaching them.

To appreciate this difference, reconsider the Plinko game metaphor from Chapter 1. Expanding *access* to opportunity is rearranging the pins and valves so that balls dropped at any starting point, but especially those that were previously obstructed, are subsequently capable of reaching any existing destination, or otherwise improving the odds that they can reach the more desirable destinations. Equalizing opportunity is an arrangement that gives equal probability to landing anywhere from any starting point. In contrast, expanding opportunity is enlarging those destinations so that more chips can land in them before reaching capacity or adding more desirable and rewarding destinations to the game. We must do both.

The intertwined goals of enlarging and expanding access to opportunity, however, are not the only imaginable ones that might inform a broad policy agenda to address structural racial inequality. Some advocates contend that policymakers should focus on helping people achieve financial security or escape poverty.[40] A traditional redistribution agenda featuring social safety net provisions—as the metaphor suggests—are intended to help families and individuals get by or subsist, whereas an opportunity agenda aims to help families can get ahead. Some social and economic policies may relieve material hardship without building human capital, facilitating its development, or removing other barriers to opportunity.[41]

Nor is the policy agenda developed here qualified by political reality or practical feasibility. The degree or type of mobilization and broad public education that would be required to build sufficient collective will to adopt or sustain it is beyond the scope of this presentation. The policy agenda advanced here is perhaps myopic, but it has the merit of being well-tailored to its goals. The ideas presented in this chapter are aimed at leverage points in the opportunity structure—places where policymakers and community leaders can make the most significant impact despite limited resources or influence.

1) Embrace Fiscal Regionalism

The organization and governance of our metropolitan regions is perhaps the most fundamental issue shaping the distribution of opportunity. As described in Chapter 1, many critical layers of the opportunity structure are constituted at a regional level. Economic opportunities are shaped by regional industries, not just local businesses. Housing markets and labor markets may have local features but are regionally defined. Yet our governing structures are not.

Recall from Chapter 2 that American metropolitan regions are deeply fragmented into dozens of local governments. Local governments are a structural form for channeling and controlling resources and services, providing them to some people while denying them to others. It is simply impossible to build an equal opportunity society when the most well-resourced and opportunity-rich communities erect gates, figurative or otherwise, to restrict access.

The antidote to exclusionary or defensive localism is greater regionalism. Regionalism is a governing philosophy based on a recognition that all residents are affected, in some degree, by the health of the region. Accordingly, regionalist governance should be aimed at matters that concern the entire region (like transit) and at ensuring a more equitable distribution of tax dollars within a region. In particular, the imperative of expanding access to opportunity requires that fiscal structures ensure the health of the region over the selfish preferences of local interests. One of the mechanisms for realizing this are regional tax sharing agreements.

The proof of concept is a seven-county tax sharing agreement for Minneapolis region, an extraordinary bargain struck in the aftermath of an intense fight between two of the region's municipalities to annex an area with a power plant. Passed in 1971, this law finally took effect in 1975 after surviving a battery of legal challenges.[42] The measure pools 40% of annual revenue growth in commercial and industrial taxes for more equitable distribution. This clever formula—capturing future revenue—imposed no immediate loss on any particular jurisdiction but ensured that uneven employment and business growth would ultimately benefit all.

Over time, the positive effects of the Minneapolis regional tax sharing policy became clear. By the mid-1980s, researchers found that the program reduced the rate of fiscal inequality within the region to less than one-fifth of what it would have been without it.[43] A 2011 analysis of the law's long-term impact discovered that twice as many municipalities benefited under the law as those that were net losers.[44] The Minneapolis regional tax sharing law was a prescient policy arrangement that disrupted the usual pattern, and scaffolded a more equitable future for the entire region.

More broadly, economists have found that intergovernmental revenue sharing is negatively correlated with both racial and income segregation.[45] Political scientists have found that segregation negatively affects the willingness of white residents to support taxes to provide additional revenue.[46] Fiscal regionalism encourages residents to take a less parochial and narrowly self-interested view of public goods. Regional school systems ensure that all parents are invested in the success of the entire system, as county school districts like Jefferson County, Kentucky, discovered, as described in Chapter 3, rather than just the schools that their children attend.

Such policies, although salutary, compensate for structural problems rather than fix them. State laws that enable or permit defensive localism and opportunity hoarding should be disabled or modified.[47] Prevailing modes of fiscal governance, which rely heavily on local property taxes and state-based compensatory formulas, tend to incentivize further fragmentation, especially among the most fiscally secure and affluent communities. For example, the affluent and white Buckhead community in Atlanta has been organizing to secede from Atlanta, and if they eventually succeed, they will extract more than 100 million from budget of the city of Atlanta and nearly 200 million from the Atlanta public schools.[48] In 2013, a largely white town of Gardendale, Alabama voted to form a new school district out of the larger county-wide district of Jefferson County, which is 50% Black.[49] The presiding judge in the suit challenging the effort ultimately concluded that permitting Gardendale to secede would not only resegregate the school system, but that race was a motivating factor in the decision.[50]

From 2000 to 2017, at least 47 communities broke off from a larger district to form their own out of more than 128 attempts.[51] Organized efforts to carve out new school districts out of existing ones appears to be most common in the south, which has traditionally featured larger and more inclusive districts. The result is that the new districts tend to be whiter and more affluent than the ones they leave behind.[52]

In a few contexts, the imperative of fiscal regionalism is not only recognized, but operationalized. Many utilities, waste disposal services, and public transportation networks tend to be regionally organized and funded. After all, if every municipality and township had its own bus line, individuals might be required to change buses a dozen times just to travel a few miles. This explains why many public transportation systems, from the BART to the Central Ohio Transit Authority, are regional systems.

The necessity of greater fiscal regionalism should not be limited to simple tax sharing mechanisms or utilities and transit systems but may need to extend to infrastructure, emergency services, and even housing and education. Although economists have long argued that reducing government fragmentation would improve economic efficiency, and thereby save tax dollars, excessive jurisdictional fragmentation has proven unsustainable in an era of fiscal austerity and endemic municipal distress.[53]

The inequities of government fragmentation dovetail with the economic inefficiencies. A devastating report by the Justice Department revealed the predatory and parasitic character of Ferguson, Missouri's practices of fining or ticketing poor residents to fund government operations.[54] The inefficacies of jurisdictional fragmentation reinforce the poverty traps of cities like Ferguson, due to fiscal demands in which localities are forced to resort to tickets and fines to fund basic government services, often at the expense—and ire— of their own residents.[55] In 2015, the state of Missouri capped how much municipal revenue could be generated from traffic fines.[56] A subsequent lawsuit alleged that cities began skirting this reform by issuing tickets for building code violations and other minor infractions to make up the revenue shortfall.[57] The core problem, as recognized by Governor Jay Nixon, was that there are too many municipalities, with too little tax base capacity, to support courts, municipal government, and independent police departments.[58] A research group found that there were more than 60 separate police agencies, some extremely small, in St. Louis County.[59]

Like tax sharing, collaborative regional planning also has the potential to overcome many of the more exclusionary features of localism. Regional allocations for affordable housing or other regional contribution agreements are expressions of inclusive regionalism. It can also be institutionalized through the establishment of metropolitan federations or planning organizations ("MPOs") to coordinate land use policies and economic development in large urban areas.

Although local control may appear to be a deeply rooted American political tradition, the historical record belies that presumption. Between 1870 and 1930, most of America's largest cities rapidly expanded their boundaries through consolidation, annexation, and merger.[60] Some did so through a series of small additions, like many Midwestern cities, and others did so through major annexations, like New York, Chicago, and Philadelphia.[61]

Electrification, public schooling, and widespread formation of municipal emergency services, such as police and fire, taxed the finances of small towns and suburbs, spurring municipal consolidation. For example, Fairview, a suburb of Detroit, needed a sewer system that the villagers could not afford, and thus precipitated annexation with Detroit.[62] Although many residents opposed such mergers, the prevailing 19th century sentiment was that local politics should not impede progress and the development of the metropolitan region.[63]

Business and political leaders, in particular, were boosters for consolidation based upon a recognition of the efficiencies, economies of scale, and other benefits that would accrue.[64] For example, the Philadelphia police department was able to reduce its staff from 850 to 650 men after consolidation.[65] Regional service provision facilitated the elimination of wasteful duplication and reduced administrative overhead. Businesses also preferred to operate under uniform codes.

Motives for annexation and consolidation went beyond economic efficiency. One late-19th-century resident of Cincinnati noted that regionalism "kept the wealthy, highly educated, and sophisticated residents of the Hilltop suburban fringe firmly engaged in the city's affairs."[66] Similarly, Bostonians recognized that regional governance drew the middle class into municipal affairs, and ominously predicted that if the middle class had fled, the city would have "shared the fate of ancient Rome."[67] Annexation, consolidation, and regionalism were not only ways to maintain economic integration in a region; they were mechanisms to ensure that everyone had a stake in regional conditions. The general pattern of municipal annexation and consolidation slowed after 1910, and faltered more dramatically by the 1920s.[68]

Neither consolidation nor fragmentation were historically inevitable or natural, but contingent policy choices made in response to evolving needs and changing priorities. Although a repeat of the annexation movement today is unlikely, the arguments for greater fiscal regionalism are compelling, especially in an era of ongoing municipal fiscal distress. Today, regionalism needs to be a more animating force in our governance. The essence of fiscal regionalism is ensuring that the health of the entire region is prioritized, and not the health of a part at the expense of the greater whole.

2) Protect Residents from Displacement and Adopt Smart Place-Based Strategies

In the urban studies and development economics literature, "place-based" strategies take many names: neighborhood revitalization, comprehensive community development, regional economic development, and so forth.[69] And they come in many forms: assisted or affordable housing, workforce training, infrastructure and transit-oriented development, and much more.[70] Fundamentally, place-based strategies are designed to enhance or generate opportunity for lower-income communities and alleviate the problem of concentrated poverty. The principal vehicle for such strategies is directing public investments, subsidies, or tax credits to lure employers and private capital or spur economic activity to that same goal.

This is no easy task. As we have seen, opportunity structures are complex interweavings of public and private activity. Government can direct capital and resources to places to incentivize private sector development and investment, provide critical support services, or even create public sector jobs, but it cannot fabricate opportunity structures from whole cloth. Ambitious experiments in the United States leveraging government dollars along these lines have been judged costly failures.[71] At best, it can foster connections between structural nodes or subsidize and spur private sector activity to create new nodes. Even if government policy played a central role in the corrosive conditions that exist in low-opportunity places, government *alone* cannot repair the damage. Where past policy has led to white flight and disinvestment, government cannot easily replace the businesses, jobs, and services that fled. And it certainly cannot recreate the social networks that frayed or resynthesize the social capital that has been destroyed or lost.

This explains why there is a long and dispiriting catalog of place-based urban anti-poverty programs. In the 1990s there were Renewal Communities, Empowerment Zones, Enterprise Communities, and HOPE VI.[72] The Obama administration launched programs such as the Sustainable Communities Initiative and Promise Neighborhoods.[73] And the Trump administration touted its Opportunity Zone initiative, among many others over the years.[74] These place-based programs may have produced positive tangible benefits, but they have not come close to achieving the aspirations of their proponents.

Supporters and critics of place-based approaches point to Geoffrey Canada's Harlem Children's Zone (HCZ) program, which provides wrap-around services in a defined geographic area combined with large subsidies and charter schools.[75] The goal of the program is to transform the community within the zone by flooding the zone with resources and services. Although evaluation of the HCZ shows that it has improved the lives of those attending the charter schools, it does not appear to have fundamentally changed the lives of neighborhood residents nor has student performance in traditional schools within the zone improved.[76] Although assessment of the program is ongoing, the results thus far have proved mixed and many pertinent questions remain unanswered.[77]

Even where apparently successful, evaluations of place-based programs have raised doubts about their scalability, and efforts to replicate them have generally failed.[78] Success in some cases, for example, may be attributed to unique circumstances, such as a particularly dynamic or visionary administrator or committed parent cohort, rather than program design. Like the HCZ, research shows that most of the placed-based investments and programs benefited the direct recipients or participants, but there is little evidence of broader community benefit.[79] This is consistent with the insight such efforts may enhance individual skillsets or benefit families, but do not revitalize the broader opportunity structure.

Some supporters of place-based strategies argue that place-based initiatives fail because they were not grand enough to overcome a legacy of cumulative resource deprivation. In other words, turning around disadvantaged communities requires a level of investment commensurate with the scale of disinvestment. Although there is an appealing moral and mathematical logic to this claim, it is not congruent with the structural model of opportunity.

Investments, no matter how generous, that are not sensitive to the structure of opportunities which exist in resource disadvantaged environments are unlikely to foster opportunities for local residents nor turn around communities. For example, low-skilled or non-union workers in high-poverty neighborhoods are less likely to benefit from infrastructure investments than unionized workers from nearby communities. Similarly, investments in new plants or manufacturing facilities without training opportunities will create jobs that ultimately flow to highly skilled workers from other communities. And job training programs that are not well-tailored to the needs of local employers won't lead to gainful employment. This is why many "revitalization" plans have failed; they aren't tailored to the needs of the existing community.

The track record shows that poorly designed place-based investments are easily siphoned by the well-off rather than reach intended beneficiaries. For example, the Opportunity Zones program provides significant tax breaks to investors in exchange for "economic development."[80] Instead of producing housing with affordable units, these federal tax breaks are subsidizing luxury developments. Many of these investments are in high-end apartment buildings and hotels, or facilities that employ only a few workers. Not only are the intended residents not benefiting, but they may be at greater risk of displacement as a result.[81] Such developments not only reduce the stock of affordable housing, but they can boost the value of real estate in nearby parcels and draw high-end amenities that lead to a general escalation of rents.

Even in low-opportunity communities, there invariably exist a range of well-resourced, community embedded institutions, known as anchor institutions.[82] Anchor institutions, such as hospitals, universities, libraries, museums, zoos, stadiums, and other major institutions, are often primary employers and receive investments and resources from all levels of government and private sources. These institutions have the potential to enhance and promote opportunity for local residents, so long as local leaders can persuade them to take tangible steps to align that mission to the needs of residents.[83]

Anchor institutions each have their own mission and needs. It is possible, however, to align the interests of the institution with the community.[84] For example, hospital or airport expansions may set local hiring goals, and seek to minimize the negative impacts of construction on local businesses or housing costs. Anchor institutions should and can focus on providing livable wages for low-skilled positions.[85] Similarly, universities, schools, libraries and museums can provide or subsidize programming and training for local residents or provide human capital–enhancing training or educational services. Local governments can set the gaze of such institutions by enforcing community benefits agreements or community workforce agreements.[86]

The strongest record of success for place-based policies is government investment in infrastructure. From urban to rural electrification, to the construction of roads, bridges, and ports, infrastructure development not only reshapes the built environment, but reconfigures the possibilities for people within the local opportunity structure as well. Recall how Lincoln lamented—from personal experience—the lack of such "improvements," and how these "improvements" would help families out of poverty by making it easier to transport goods or access markets. The transcontinental railroad and the interstate highway system are two enormously successful infrastructure policies that opened vast regions to agriculture and housing and created new industries, from steel and retail to commercial trucking.

Strategic infrastructure investments not only have the potential to stimulate economic activity and spur private-sector investments, but they open up new pathways for people. New transit hubs, light rail, bus lines, or other transit infrastructure connect more people with more opportunities. After a certain threshold scale is reached, roads and highways become less effective at connecting residents to labor markets because of congestion and traffic. But investments in mass transit, in contrast, can increase the number of people, especially less advantaged, who can access jobs and amenities. Income-subsidized high-speed rail, in particular, can link people even further away. Unfortunately, there remains tremendous unevenness in the quality of transit infrastructure in the United States,[87] and in the wake of the Great Recession, 70% of public transit agencies either raised fares or cut service.[88] Similar disinvestments in the wake of the Covid-19 pandemic are inimical to an opportunity agenda.[89]

In the wake of the Covid-19 pandemic, many of the nation's largest corporations instituted flexible working arrangement policies for their employees.[90] Such policies may have reduced demand for public transit, but deeper investment in nationwide broadband high-speed internet, especially in a time of rapidly expanding remote working arrangements, can connect workers to a much larger range of job opportunities.

It is not just that poorly designed place-based investments may be wasteful or fail to achieve their intended purpose, they can inflict harm and aggravate underlying problems. As some of the prior examples suggest, place-based investments—whether it is in plant and facilities, transit and roads, or even parks and foliage—may have unintended consequences, and can accelerate gentrification and displacement, putting opportunity further out of reach.

Regions with strong economies produce red-hot housing markets, and these markets tend to shrivel the stock of affordable housing. What this means, paradoxically, is that instead of improving access to opportunity for the most marginalized peoples and lowest income workers, strong economies can result in displacement, especially if jobs are out of reach to these workers, either on account of proximity or skill and credential requirements.[91] Gains made by greater employment opportunities and higher wages are too often overwhelmed by other living costs, principally housing.[92]

When community conditions are improving and opportunity is growing, historically disadvantaged environments are easily overwhelmed with new investments, amenities and jobs. In such cases, long-time residents must be able to remain in place long enough to reap the benefits. In those circumstances, place-based strategies that prevent displacement are the key to unlocking opportunity. A fully realized policy for connecting families to opportunity must not only account for people who live in high-poverty, low-opportunity environments, but for those whose neighborhoods are on the upswing, where job growth and community conditions are improving.

This is where investments in affordable housing, subsidized low-income housing, and other place-based strategies that allow local residents to remain can make a tremendous difference. Even in communities that can produce substantial amounts of housing (what economists denote as a high elasticity of supply), the lower end of the market may simply fail to produce enough housing for extremely low-income people. Subsidies and other protections could be used to keep families housed in improving neighborhoods, just the same as they can be used to help families relocate to better ones, as discussed in the next section. Instead of using tax breaks to create luxury developments, such subsidies could be used to purchase and preserve affordable housing or to construct mixed-income housing in gentrifying communities. The affordable units in these developments could be reserved for local residents at risk of displacement. We must do more to support these families by identifying them and protecting them from displacement.

Although not a place-based strategy in the traditional sense, rent-control policies can help achieve a similar effect in gentrifying communities as investments in affordable housing. Rent control refers to policies which impose restrictions on landlord from increasing rent on qualifying units.[93] They not only prevent displacement of residents to lower-opportunity communities, but they can also be used to preserve integration in either integrated or integrating neighborhoods.

Although rent control may be a clumsy tool, a narrowly tailored rent-control ordinance can make a tremendous difference. For example, a rent-control ordinance with a sunset provision can protect residents in the short-term, allowing them to benefit from improving conditions in the neighborhood, while other subsidy programs are applied to ensure that residents can afford to remain in the long run. Alternatively, an ordinance can carefully target some neighborhoods while excluding others based upon certain underlying criteria, and thereby minimize the disincentives for the construction of new housing in the overall housing market. A rent-control ordinance that only covered certain census tracts based upon prevailing conditions could better balance the need to incentivize new construction against the need to prevent displacement in improving neighborhoods. In any case, a smarter and more strategic place-based investment should ensure that individuals at risk of displacement like Mercedes Garcia are able to remain in neighborhoods of expanding opportunity.

3) Pursue and Support Mobility Strategies

As much as human beings develop a connection to, and feel a certain fondness for, home and community, a healthy free and open society would exhibit a robust degree of geographic mobility as a matter of course, allowing young adults the freedom to find and seize the best job offers elsewhere and follow their dreams wherever it may take them. In this regard, geographic mobility is a corollary to social and economic mobility and a byproduct of the pursuit of opportunity. Unfortunately, geographic mobility has ebbed to historic lows in the United States (see Table 1.1), an ominous development explained by the prohibitive costs of living in high-opportunity places and the declining wage gains of relocation for low-skilled workers. Therefore, a top-line policy objective for expanding access to opportunity must be to ease geographic mobility, and specifically to support and subsidize noncompulsory moves to higher-opportunity areas.

In some ways, this trend of declining geographic mobility understates the true problem. Not all relocation decisions are opportunity enhancing. While many millions make relocation decisions every year for college or based upon job prospects, millions of other Americans are forcibly displaced by escalating rents or general cost of living. The patterns of displacement described at the outset of this chapter are opportunity diminishing, separating people from better jobs, social capital, public services, and amenities.

Within regions and between states, too many low-income people are being displaced from high-growth and high-income regions to low-growth and low-income places, with likely worse life outcomes in the long run as a consequence.[94] Imagine if, instead of encouraging labor mobility, the city and industrial leaders in places like Chicago and Detroit had enacted policies that made it impossible for southern sharecroppers suffering under Jim Crow to relocate there. Yet, that is essentially the effect of our housing policies in places like San Francisco today. Easing geographic mobility should be a policy priority.

Specifically, we need policies that encourage, incentivize, and support voluntary geographic mobility from low-opportunity areas to high-opportunity areas, especially for low-income people. Unlike place-based interventions, which must overcome a range of presently existing deficits, mobility strategies are inherently sensitive to opportunity structures as they are. High-opportunity places do not need to be rebuilt or re-engineered. Simply plugging people into them provides newcomers with access to higher-paying jobs, amenities, great schools, and high-quality public services. It is harder to rebuild opportunity where it is lacking than to simply move people to better positions within the opportunity structure.[95] This is why mobility strategies have such a strong track record.

The inspiring model for many mobility strategies is the judicial remedy ordered in the landmark Supreme Court case of *Hills v. Gautreaux*.[96] In the late 1960s, Dorothy Gautreaux, an African-American community organizer and activist, sued the Chicago Housing Authority, claiming that its procedures discriminated against public housing residents on the basis of race. The expansive settlement her suit achieved created a remarkable mobility experiment. The settlement offered thousands of families a subsidy to move out of neighborhoods of racially concentrated poverty and into higher opportunity, more racial integrated neighborhoods. The families who participated in the settlement were assigned to apartments in low poverty and predominantly white neighborhoods. They did not select or choose these locations, but simply signed up for the program, where they were assigned to a suburb or a unit within the Chicago city limits.

Social scientists have studied the results of the *Gautreaux* settlement for decades now, and available evidence on the long-term effects on families who relocated compared with those who did not. Researchers tracking families who moved found increased employment, higher wages, less welfare enrollment, higher high school completion rates, and increased college attendance.[97] Only 5% of the children in families assigned to the suburbs dropped out of school compared to 20% of the children in families assigned to apartments within Chicago. Moreover, more than half attended college, compared to 21% who stayed in Chicago.[98]

Although some critics claim that the remedy was not sufficiently controlled from a social scientific perspective to draw firm conclusions,[99] the results of the *Gautreaux* inspired a long line of mobility interventions, most notably the Moving To Opportunity (MTO) experiment, funded by the Congress in 1993. As noted in Chapter 1, the experiment involved more than 4,500 families, who were assigned to one of three groups. The experimental group received a restricted voucher that could only be used in a census tract with a poverty rate less than 10%. Another group was given a housing voucher that could be used only in a neighborhood where they were originally residing. And another group was not offered a voucher, but lived in public housing.

The MTO experiment has been subject to extensive scholarship and analysis.[100] Initial empirical results were disappointing or underwhelming. Despite improvements within the experimental group along several key dimensions, including perceived safety and mental health, other anticipated outcomes were either not found or marginal.[101] A subsequent review and analysis revealed flaws in the experimental design. In particular, by focusing only on poverty as the sole and exclusive indicator for "opportunity" neighborhoods, some of the receiving neighborhoods barely met the poverty threshold or were in the midst of racial and economic transition or declining. Many families in the experimental group moved to neighborhoods similar in critical ways to the ones they left, despite having somewhat lower rates of poverty.[102] In other cases, MTO movers in some cities moved into neighborhoods nearby or adjacent to their old neighborhood, such that they inhabited the same social milieu or their children attended the same schools.

Although there were restrictions on usage and more scientific controls, the MTO experiment was not nearly as comprehensive as the *Gautreaux* settlement. Consequently, the relocations in *Gautreaux* were more dramatic and pulled families out of the orbit and social networks of their former neighborhoods, and provided a more comprehensive set of supports to facilitate that transition.

Another criticism of the program, leveled even before its implementation, was that the experiment was insufficiently race-sensitive. By focusing only on neighborhood poverty, the experiment ignored patterns of racial settlement and segregation that may have better stabilized neighborhoods or indicated tipping. The initial report found that 60% of the experimental group families moved into "heavily minority areas," and that three quarters of all moving families were in census tracts that were more than 80% minority.[103] Racial integration this was not.

Decades later, however, scholars re-evaluated the effects of MTO by examining the longitudinal impact of moving on children, who are now adults, using de-identified tax records, as discussed in Chapter 1.[104] Their findings dispelled many doubts regarding the value of these moves. Seen from a long-term perspective, the MTO moves had profoundly positive effects. But the earlier the move, the more pronounced the effects. For example, children who moved before the age of 13 earned 31% more average annual income by their mid-twenties than the control group.

Today, there is a good deal of empirical evidence in support of mobility strategies beyond *Gautreaux* and the MTO experiment. There are a number of "natural" experiments that have been studied with similar results.[105] In 1995, Chicago, like many other major cities, began the process of dismantling large-scale high-rise public housing, the most infamous of which was the Cabrini-Green complex. A recent study found substantially positive effects on the families who moved out of public housing. Children from these families were 9% more likely to be employed, and had 16% higher annual earnings.[106]

In 2014, another major study was published that tracked 1,500 families in scattered-site, single-family units in the Denver metropolitan area.[107] The study was a "natural" experiment because, after 1987, the applicants were offered vacant units randomly anywhere in the entire county of Denver. Unlike voucher recipients, who must search for housing largely on their own, these units were operated by Denver housing authority and families were automatically assigned a unit. Because they were scattered site, the homes blended into the surrounding communities. In some respects, this experiment had advantages over MTO. The average residence duration was almost twice as long, giving researchers more time to understand the effects of the move. Unsurprisingly, researchers found that neighborhood conditions correlated with, if not caused, a wide range of positive outcomes.[108]

The evidence is substantial and growing that mobility strategies enhance upward economic mobility and improve life outcomes. One of the impediments to scaling up a mobility program is cost. Given the magnitude of the problem, it may not be possible to move all residents residing in low-opportunity areas to higher ones.[109] This is compounded by the fact that high-opportunity areas have more expensive housing. The value of the subsidy will constrain the possibilities for relocation.

This problem plagues existing mobility housing programs. In the 1970s, the Housing Choice Voucher program, known as Section 8, was created to give subsidized housing residents more choice.[110] Not only does this program suffer from long wait lists, up to five years in many cases, but the value of the subsidy is limited by the fair market rent of the region.[111] This means that voucher holders are effectively locked out of many high-opportunity neighborhoods. One study of the program found that about half of Black and Hispanic voucher holders end up in low-opportunity areas with high levels of neighborhood poverty.[112] Another study found that just 5% of families using vouchers live in high-opportunity neighborhoods even though those areas account for 18% of all affordable rentals.[113]

To address this problem, in 2012, HUD devised a pilot program, known as the Small Area Fair Market Rent Program (SAFMR), which boosts the subsidy for higher-cost neighborhoods.[114] Instead of pegging housing voucher subsidies to some portion of the metropolitan average, the SAFMR program pegged to the zip code. While this opened up new neighborhoods to lower-income residents and increased housing options in higher-opportunity neighborhoods, HUD's limited resources undermined its potential. The success of this demonstration, however, spurred HUD officials to announce a plan to expand this program to 41 additional metropolitan areas.[115]

Even where voucher subsidies are sufficient to secure housing in higher-opportunity neighborhoods, landlords routinely screen applicants or otherwise discriminate against voucher holders. So-called "source of income" discrimination should be prohibited, not only because it is unfair and defeats policy goals, but because it is often used as a pretext for racial discrimination or discrimination against families with children, both of which are federally prohibited.[116] Only about 20 states and a few dozen municipal jurisdictions prohibit source of income discrimination for housing voucher holders.[117] Since federal law does not prohibit discrimination against voucher-holders, HUD won't investigate complaints against landlords who refuse vouchers.

Lack of portability of Section 8 housing (choice vouchers) across jurisdictions as well as the regulatory and bureaucratic barriers has undermined its potential as much as insufficient funding. Allowing voucher holders to use vouchers in different jurisdictions, prohibiting source of income discrimination, and increasing the subsidy so that voucher holders could move into higher-opportunity neighborhoods, would provide more choice and enhance mobility.

Even where funding is available to provide housing in high-opportunity areas, political resistance to low-income neighbors is intense. This helps explain why the nation's largest subsidized affordable housing program ($8 billion annually), the Low Income Housing Tax Credit (LIHTC), disproportionately results in developments in segregated and higher-poverty neighborhoods.[118] Nationally, only about 21% of these projects are built in high-opportunity neighborhoods.[119] In many places, it is much worse than that. The state of Texas placed 156 of Dallas' 162 LIHTC housing projects in Black- or Latino-majority neighborhoods.[120]

In addition to mechanisms that overcome or remove barriers to access housing in high-opportunity areas, additional supports may be needed. Among them, counseling and other forms of assistance in the search process appear to make a significant difference.[121] In 2019, another mobility experiment conducted in Seattle, the Creating Moves to Opportunity (CMTO) program, provided customized assistance to voucher holders, and the fraction of families that moved to higher-opportunity neighborhoods increased from 14% to 54%.[122] In addition, voucher holders reported much higher levels of satisfaction.

Similarly, another program created in the wake of a landmark lawsuit against HUD's administration of housing choice vouchers, the Baltimore Regional Housing Partnership emphasizes in-house counseling for voucher holders as a critical component of stable and successful moves.[123] Initiated in 2012, the average neighborhood poverty rate of its participant families is just 10% compared to a national neighborhood poverty rate of 24% for national housing voucher holders.

The problem is not that low-income residents prefer to stay in lower-opportunity neighborhoods or the absence of affordable housing in higher-opportunity communities (what the *Opportunity Insights* team calls "opportunity bargains").[124] These homeseekers may not know much about them or the amenities in them. Metropolitan residents of different races have starkly different local information about, and perceptions of, the communities they may consider or rule out at the outset of the housing search process. Segregated social networks and different background knowledge infiltrate our "consideration set" of neighborhoods in the "pre-search stage."[125]

Sociologists studying this problem found that Black residents may rule out far-flung white communities that they know very little about or that have a reputation as unwelcoming to people of color or are unaffordable, even if the community might have much to offer, match their budget, or fit their demographic profile preference.[126] Similarly, white residents may rule out large swaths of communities on the basis of reputation or racial profile without any fact-based assessment or consideration of the communities' amenities or housing options. As a result, residents tend to select housing in communities that are significantly more segregated than their "ideal" community in the abstract. In this way, residential moves are structured by race in ways that reproduce existing residential patterns.

The CMTO experiment provided customized search assistance, landlord engagement, and additional short-term financial assistance for security deposits and other costs, to help families move to higher-opportunity areas.[127] The results suggested that price or affordability was not necessarily the main barrier to higher-opportunity areas, but that more structural or psychological constraints inhibited such moves. Counseling not only helps families make more informed decisions, but also provided much needed emotional support. Many low-income families reported anxiety and stress, and that the counselors increased confidence and reduced demand on families' time and cognitive bandwidth. Similarly, the Baltimore Partnership helps voucher holders set personal and emotional goals while also preparing families for their move. Post-move counseling can reduce the chance that families may leave their new neighborhoods or return to where they started. In short, counseling plays a critical role in supporting both racially integrative and anti-poverty mobility strategies.

Government should connect people to jobs and opportunity by providing subsidies that facilitate mobility by expanding choice, including portable housing choice vouchers for lower-income households, relocation grants and other supports.[128] If people cannot afford to move (even with a subsidy) or remain, then other policy levers should be explored. This includes enhancing public transit systems to connect individuals more effectively and efficiently from low-opportunity neighborhoods to jobs or areas of job growth. As will be discussed in more detail below, strategically designed bus lines or redeployment of existing fleets can connect users and job centers can do a better job than all-purpose bus networks. In addition to proactively connecting people to opportunity, we must also find ways to remove barriers.

4) End Snob Zoning and Curtail Exclusionary Land Use Policies

In a country with stalled mobility and widening inequality, municipal land use policy, especially excessively restrictive zoning, is increasingly recognized as an underlying structural problem. In recent years, a remarkably broad and diverse chorus of voices in academia and policy circles have advanced a vigorous case for zoning liberalization in the United States. Major newspapers routinely editorialize on this once recondite subject.[129] Even conservative pundits and analysts are pressing for reform to local zoning regulations, often on grounds of expanding property rights or individual liberty.[130] Curtailing exclusionary and restrictive land use and zoning policies is a vital part of an opportunity agenda, let alone one seeking to ameliorate racial inequality.

Land use controls regulate the range and type of housing that can be developed, and the uses for which property can be built. Exclusionary or restrictive land-use policies are those that tend to restrict development and make housing more expensive or simply make it more difficult to develop affordable housing (which generally requires greater density to scale). Typical municipal land use controls include zoning regulations, use and density restrictions on developments, parking minimums, height limits, floor area ratios, occupancy limits, lot size minimums, building setbacks, discretionary reviews that slow development, and other restrictions.[131] Above all, the tell-tale sign of exclusionary land use policies are those that restrict, impede, or enable opposition to multi-family housing developments and affordable housing options.

The best available research examining the effects of restrictive land use policy consistently finds, and the evidence is growing, that it impedes mobility, sustains racial and economic segregation, and exacerbates the crisis of inadequate affordable housing and homelessness.[132] Subsidies of the sort recommended in the previous section are limited unless the drivers of exclusionary housings costs and other barriers are addressed. To produce more

Realizing the American Dream 271

affordable housing, reduce escalating home price-pressures in "hot markets" with strong job growth, reduce displacement, expand access to opportunity, and promote racial and economic integration, we need a concerted policy agenda addressing the problem of excessively restrictive land use policy.

To begin, localities must roll back excessive zoning regulations and other restrictive land use policies in their own communities. In recognition of the harms of exclusionary, restrictive zoning to the broader public, the city of Minneapolis voted in 2018 to abolish single-family zoning, and to allow upward of 3 dwelling units in every neighborhood.[133] Seventy percent of the residential land in Minneapolis, and 53% of all land, was zoned for single-family housing only, in essence, banning apartments and other dense forms of housing in those areas.[134] The city also abolished parking minimums for all new construction, and reduced density restrictions near transit.[135] The city's goal was to make it easier for developers to build affordable housing. Other cities have followed suit, such as Sacramento, Berkeley, and Charlottesville, Virginia, while many others have or are considering similar proposals.[136]

Even if organizing efforts are powerful and persuasive enough to convince some municipalities to loosen land use regulations, this will not be sufficient to dramatically change the overall pattern of land use, especially in regions with several dozen, if not hundreds, of municipalities. The greater Los Angeles region, for example, has 191 incorporated municipalities.[137] These are regional problems and require solutions commensurate to the problem.

The most obvious focal point for comprehensive reform is at the state level. Since local governments are creatures of the state, one logical possibility for reform would be to repeal or amend underlying state enabling legislation, returning such authority back to the state level. Even so-called "home rule" states could return land use powers to the state level.

Another possibility is for states to pass legislation abrogating excessively restrictive local zoning or overriding certain features of local zoning and other land use ordinances. The first state to adopt such legislation was Oregon, which, in 2019, prohibited single-family zoning in cities of 10,000 or more people.[138] Several other states have adopted significant reforms, such as Montana, Washington State, and Vermont, although reforms have also been defeated in New York, Colorado, and Texas, among other states.[139] There may also be a federal role in spurring land-use reforms through a variety of sticks and carrots.[140]

Some of the highest profile battles over zoning reform have occurred in California. The California legislature entertained several bills that would have overridden local zoning near transit and "high-resource" communities to permit duplexes and fourplexes, but neither bill made it out of committee.[141] These proposals ran into staunch opposition from an unusual alliance of affluent suburbs and tenants' rights activists who feared that upzoning (loosening restrictions on zoned density) in urban areas would land like a "gentrification bomb."[142] Ultimately, however, California legislators took a narrower approach in 2021 which allows homeowners in some areas to divide their property into two lots or build a duplex.[143] A preliminary analysis found that only 5% of residential parcels would qualify, and the actual impact so far has fairly underwhelming, despite (or perhaps because of) enormous local opposition.[144]

It should be emphasized that the problem is excessively restrictive land use regulations broadly, not zoning specifically. Zoning regulations are simply the most visible and among the most widely abused of those regulations. Houston, Texas is the only major city in the United States that has refused to adopt a municipal zoning regime, and it has been comprehensively studied for that reason. The main insight from this research is that Houston has much more development and affordable housing than cities with zoning, although it has about the same level of racial residential segregation as other major cities due to other land use regulations and controls.[145]

As important as the goal of land use reform is, permitting denser housing, by itself, does not make affordable housing developments pencil out or integration spontaneously occur.[146] The goals of integration, affordable housing, and inclusion may require subsidies, incentives or other mandates, not simply zoning reform. While curbing restrictive land use policies is imperative, more proactive measures are necessary to make longstanding communities accept newcomers, let alone allow affordable housing to emerge. In addition to subsidies, another direct response to long-standing patterns of exclusionary zoning may be properly calibrated inclusionary zoning (IZ) policies or fair share mandates.

IZ ordinances describe a range of municipal policies that require developers to set aside some percentage of new units for low-income or middle-income residents.[147] For example, a typical IZ ordinance might require that 15% of units in any new development with at least 10 units be set for below-market prices, at varying levels of affordability. Estimates vary, but there are hundreds of municipal IZ ordinances in operation within the United States.[148] A disproportionate share of these policies is found in California and New Jersey.[149] These ordinances generally require between 10% and 20% affordability, depending on the jurisdiction, with tremendous variation in compliance measures.[150] Some IZ ordinances are mandatory with penalties or fines for violating them, while others are voluntary, providing incentives or bonuses for compliance. Some IZ ordinances permit in-lieu payments or off-site compliance, while others prohibit such escape hatches.

The Montgomery County, Maryland ordinance is perhaps a leading example of how a strong IZ law has made a real-world difference for residents. The longstanding ordinance has ensured that all new housing developments in the County have 12–15% affordable units, allowing one third of these units to be purchased by the local housing authority, which uses a random lottery for assignment. Since 1976, this has resulted in more than 12,000 affordable housing units.[151]

Consequently, the Montgomery County IZ ordinance has permitted poor public housing residents of color to move into middle class neighborhoods and attend middle class schools.[152] The jurisdiction is a county district, so it is less vulnerable to local fragmentation and segregation and more geographically comprehensive than most such ordinances. Random assignment prevents "creaming" and self-selection. And it ensures that low-income students are not concentrated in a single or few schools within the district. Unsurprisingly, children reassigned as a result performed much better than children that attended high-poverty schools, even those which were given additional resource investments. The Montgomery County case study is an ideal example of how to coordinate housing and educational assignment policies.

Research on the efficacy of IZ ordinances is ongoing, and experts seem uncertain whether the benefits outweigh the additional costs to development.[153] Such ordinances appear most effective during a period of strong economic growth and demand for new housing, where existing developments can be leveraged into increasing the supply of affordable housing. Even in the case of strong ordinances, however, they may be insufficient to produce such housing at scale given their limited geographic reach, or may be a drag on housing production.

Perhaps the best proactive solution are so-called "fair share" policies. Whereas IZ ordinances apply to development projects at the municipal level, fair share laws are state laws that require jurisdictions to assume their "fair share" of affordable housing. In short, where IZ ordinances require that a particular project have its share of affordable units, fair share schemes require that cities have their allocated share. The most famous and first instance of a fair share law arises out of the famous case of *Mount Laurel*.[154]

In the 1970s, the NAACP brought a lawsuit against the township of Mount Laurel, arguing that their exclusionary zoning practices violated the New Jersey Constitution.[155] A group of lower-income, predominantly nonwhite residents organized the suit on account of their inability to find affordable housing in their own city. After partnering with a developer who proposed an affordable housing project, the city of Mount Laurel switched course and claimed that the development violated the city's zoning and land use regulations.

Although zoning controls that excluded low-income residents or had a disparate racial impact had been upheld in federal court under color of federal law, the New Jersey Supreme Court held that these zoning laws were subject to the New Jersey state constitution's general welfare clause. Not only were all municipalities required to permit the construction of affordable housing; they were also required to provide their "fair share" of low-income housing. Importantly, the Court took extraordinary measures to see that its ruling was implemented, including the creation of a specialized lower court to hear claims against communities, endowed with the authority to order violating communities to rezone. Suffice to say, these decisions engendered fierce resistance and decades of litigation.

Ultimately, the "fair share" scheme was codified by the New Jersey legislature with the Fair Share Act of 1985, partly as a way of taking control over the compliance procedure.[156] This law created a council that would coordinate and assess needs and provision throughout the state, as well as require set-asides for affordable housing in new developments. Critically, any municipality or region that fails to meet its quota or portion of affordable housing under New Jersey's Fair Share scheme is subject to a "builder's remedy." This remedy allows builders not only to override exclusionary controls but meet the needs of people and respond to the demands of the market.

In 2008, another major loophole was closed, which allowed wealthier districts to pay poor districts to accept their share through regional contribution agreements.[157] Governor Chris Christie made ending the Fair Share Act a plank of his gubernatorial campaign, demanding courts get out of the business of deciding which cities have enough of their share.[158] However, his efforts were unsuccessful, and the New Jersey Supreme Court subsequently clarified that recalcitrant jurisdictions were responsible for their backlog of unmet affordable housing.[159]

A few other states have adopted similar schemes. In 1969, the Massachusetts state legislature passed the "Massachusetts Comprehensive Permit Act" (known as 40B) that similarly abrogates municipal and local zoning by requiring communities that have less than 10% of their housing stock designated as "affordable" by regional income and housing price measures to require zoning changes to permit more affordable housing.[160] In 2010, voters rejected a state ballot initiative that would have repealed this law. Although the repeal effort failed with 58% opposition, an analysis of the 42 of the states 351 jurisdictions that supported repeal found the core of support in affluent outer-ring suburbs of Boston.[161]

Connecticut adopted a similar policy into state law in 1990, known as 8-30g.[162] That law requires that every community ensure that 10% of its domiciles are affordable to a family earning below the state median. The law has been subject of continuous challenge ever since its enactment but has similarly resulted in significant production of affordable housing.[163]

A less effective but more ambitious approach is California's Regional Housing Needs Allocation (RHNA) policy and housing element laws.[164] RHNA requires that every jurisdiction in the state plan for housing at five different income levels, "very-low," "low," "moderate," "above-moderate," and "high." Working with MPOs, jurisdictions are required to zone for local needs, but in practice, jurisdictions do not meet their RHNA requirements.[165] By delineating more nuanced income levels and quantifiable guidelines, RHNA is a superior framework in many ways. It simply lacks rigorous enforcement, despite more recent amendments to give RHNA "teeth."[166]

As impactful as many of these policies have been, despite overcoming vigorous and sustained opposition, they are far from perfect. In particular, the production of affordable housing under these "fair share" laws has not necessarily translated into economic and racial integration.[167] Indeed, initial data from Mount Laurel showed that most of the applicants were white.[168] Evidence was adduced that towns "cherry-picked" their poor, selectively marketing their quotas to the elderly, divorced moms, and college students.[169]

These problems are yet another reminder that affordable housing policies should have a degree of race-consciousness in their design and implementation. They need not go so far as to have racial quotas or require racial group representation, but cities and regions considering affordable housing developments should consider whether their policies engender racial residential integration or sustain segregation. That is the heart of fair housing concerns, the next area of recommendation.

5) Enforce Fair Housing Laws and Pursue Residential Integration

Any agenda for remediating structural racism should include efforts to strengthen existing fair housing laws, bolster their enforcement infrastructure, and develop initiatives to facilitate residential economic and racial integration. On paper, the United States has robust national anti-discrimination housing laws. These laws, however, have suffered from inconsistent and inadequate enforcement and ambiguities in key terms.

Chapter 3 covered the resistance to fair housing laws, including the federal Fair Housing Act of 1968, as well as various attempts to thwart or work around its key provisions. In its initial form, the Fair Housing Act contained many loopholes, including the so-called "Mrs. Murphy" exemption that permitted live-in landlords to discriminate freely.[170] The 1988 amendments closed some loopholes, clarified the statute's meaning, strengthened the enforcement mechanisms, and expanded HUD's enforcement role, including its power to issue administrative regulations interpreting key provisions and terms.[171]

HUD's enforcement authority proved critically important given that key terms were undefined by the law itself. In addition, the Fair Housing Act's overall orientation, of permitting suits to challenge discrimination on a case-by-case basis, has proven inadequate to reverse long-established patterns of government-perpetuated segregation let alone disrupt structural forces that generate unequal housing opportunities. Although the Department of Justice brought dozens of cases each year,[172] the law generally relied upon private plaintiffs to challenge and prove discrimination, a difficult and expensive process. Furthermore, the Fair Housing Act limited actual and punitive damages and made it difficult to recover attorneys' fees.

A related limitation is the Act's emphasis on discrimination. There is little doubt that racial discrimination in housing availability still occurs, although are intense disagreements about how frequent or pervasive such discrimination may be, and, perhaps even more importantly, the extent to which discrimination today undergirds or sustains racial residential segregation.[173]

The important point is that, since the widespread enactment of fair housing laws, racial residential segregation is sustained by forces beyond discrimination, narrowly understood, but to differences in wealth between racial groups, compositional preferences, and even differences in contextual knowledge in the housing search process. Fortunately, the reach of the Fair Housing Act ultimately extends beyond simple acts of discrimination. The

Act not only prohibits intentional discrimination, but it also prohibits policies or practices that have a "disparate impact."[174] Consequently, barriers to housing—including structural barriers—that have statistically provable racial effects may be illegal. Similarly, improvement or redevelopment schemes that displace people may also be violative of the act, even in the absence of evidence of intent.

This is not a speculative legal theory. The Supreme Court affirmed this interpretation in a landmark 2015 decision, something nearly all circuit courts of appeal had also found.[175] Nonetheless, developing disparate impact claims is costly and time-intensive. Despite guidance and administrative rule codification from HUD specifying the standard and other elements of law relating to such claims,[176] bringing a disparate impact suit that is capable of surviving the initial pleading stage requires technical expertise in multiple areas, including statistical analysis.

Neither a disparate impact framework nor an anti-discrimination policy is sufficient to achieve the kind of integrated and balanced living patterns that the authors of the Fair Housing Act envisaged. As with zoning, more proactive measures are required to disestablished decades of public and private policy that have brought us to the present moment. Yet, fair housing law provides yet another mechanism to advance us toward this goal. The federal Fair Housing Act contained two provisions requiring that HUD and all executive departments and agencies shall "affirmatively further" the purposes of the act.[177] Additionally, the Housing and Community Development Act of 1974 empowers the Secretary of HUD to condition the disbursement of community development block grants, such as those routinely awarded to municipalities for infrastructure, roads, sewers and housing and the like, on the furtherance of fair housing.[178] As of 2021, this amounted to about $5.5 billion in annual grants.[179]

Yet, exactly what was meant by "affirmatively furthering fair housing" (AFFH) was left, in the first instance, to the courts to interpret.[180] It was not until 2015 that HUD finally issued a rule interpreting this phrase as "taking meaningful actions that, taken together, address significant disparities in housing needs and in access to opportunity, replacing segregated living patterns with truly integrated and balanced living patterns, transforming racially and ethnically concentrated areas of poverty into areas of opportunity, and fostering and maintaining compliance with civil rights and fair housing laws."[181] This compound definition weaves together a number of critical elements that are themes of this book.

The duty to "affirmatively further fair housing" is more than a rhetorical exhortation. HUD's 2015 AFFH rule described above did more than clarify the meaning of this ambiguous term, it also created a *process* for enforcement. In particular, it required municipal governments to "perform an assessment of land use decisions and zoning to evaluate their possible impact on fair housing choice."[182] Jurisdictions were asked to identify and examine "fair housing issues" and the underlying "contributing factors" that impede fair housing in their communities. The assessment process required that local municipalities report to HUD on their progress and identify barriers to integration and submit their assessment for review.

As part of this "assessment of fair housing," Community Development Block Grant recipients were required to certify that they are affirmatively furthering fair housing.[183] Millions of dollars of federal money flow every year through block grants to local housing authorities and municipalities. An investigation by ProPublica in 2015 found that, since 1998, HUD secretaries had only invoked that provision twice to deny block grants.[184] Attempts to meaningfully enforce the provisions of the Act by threatening to deny federal funds have met with explosive political resistance and vitriolic defiance.[185]

Opposition to the new rule was swift, with critics decrying it as a "federal takeover" and a "war on suburbia."[186] Although an unsuccessful bill was introduced in Congress that would nullify the AFFH rule and prohibit the collection of demographic data to assess fair housing, the 2015 AFFH rule was ultimately undone by the Trump administration, which issued a replacement rule that denuded the idea of AFFH and purged all references to segregation, integration, and racial composition.[187]

In 2023, however, HUD issued a proposed rule that restores much of the original framework from the 2015 rule, but simplified the definition and promises to ease the burden on jurisdictions with the technicalities of compliance while also rebranding the impediment analysis.[188] That rule was never finalized before the returning Trump administration scuttled it.[189] Nor can we be assured that the courts will continue to uphold disparate impact claims under the Fair Housing Act. But only a vigorous enforcement apparatus paired with a proactive administration of the duty to "affirmatively further fair housing" has the power to reverse longstanding patterns of exclusion and racial residential segregation. These policies are essential to dismantling structural racism.

6) Expand Public Education

Acquired or developed skill sets, both formal and informal, generally determine the range of occupational options and career paths available to individuals. Accordingly, any policy agenda aimed at expanding access to opportunity and reducing racial disparities in the opportunity structure must focus a portion of its attention on public education. Public education is the broadest and most basic form of collective investment in human capital, and it is the most direct route by which we may enlarge opportunity for all.

To achieve these twin goals, we should boost investments in public education, reduce funding gaps between school districts, allocate additional resources to higher-needs schools and school districts, vigorously pursue racial and economic integration of public schools, universalize pre-K programs, reinvest in and expand access to higher education, including community colleges and universities, reduce and cancel student debt, and expand vocational training programs and apprenticeships.

In their influential book, *The Race between Education and Technology*, Claudia Goldin and Lawrence Katz argued that the universalization of high school was a major driver of economic growth in the United States. "The 20th century was the American century," they wrote, "because it was the human-capital century."[190] Between 1910 and 1940, the high school graduation rate for American 18-year-olds leaped from 9% to 50%, and continued to climb in the post-war period.[191]

Although the United States remains in the top 5 of OECD countries in terms of educational spending, at about $15,000 per student, this figure masks significant inequities and disparities between states, districts, and schools, previously noted in this book.[192] As also noted in Chapter 1, hundreds of millions of dollars are raised every year from parents and private sources to supplement public educational provision, with most of these dollars flowing to a tiny fraction of schools. Ultimately, a third of education spending in the United States is now drawn from private sources, a share that is growing.[193] This helps explain the fact that the most and least socioeconomically advantaged districts have performance gaps equivalent to multiple grade levels between them.[194]

Even if we could equalize funding (and have in some cases) between districts, that would not suffice to create genuine equality of educational opportunity. Affluent families residing in affluent districts can raise supplemental funding while poor families in poor districts have much greater needs. The case of *Missouri v. Jenkins* illustrates the chasm between the capacity of poor districts and the needs of their students, and therefore the inadequacy of simply equalizing funding.

In *Missouri v. Jenkins*, parents of minority children sued the state, the Kansas City School district, and the surrounding school districts on the theory that they "caused and perpetuated a system of racial segregation in the schools of the Kansas City metropolitan area."[195] White flight rendered the district over 70% Black, making desegregation practically infeasible, and following *Millikin*, the court declined to draw suburban jurisdictions into a regional, inter-district desegregation plan. Instead, the federal district court ordered the state of Missouri to pour more than $220 million of additional resources into the school district in order to equalize educational opportunity.[196] These funds were used to increase the salaries of instructional and non-instructional staff, fund a "full-day kindergarten; expand summer school; before- and after-school tutoring; and an early childhood development program."[197]

The court's order went beyond the typical notion of equalizing per-pupil expenditures, but was based on an assessment of what was needed to provide equal educational opportunity to extremely disadvantaged students. The extraordinary resource inequities, public and private, between districts, and the much greater needs of the students in the large urban district led to a rough calculation that as much as *six or even seven* times as many dollars per pupil would be needed to achieve that goal.[198] The plan also included a student reassignment policy, and capital improvements to school buildings to make them comparable to suburban facilities, and special programming intended to attract white students. The rehabilitation and renovation of facilities cost an additional $187 million. The magnet school programs, for example, were created so that they would draw "non-minority students from the private schools who have abandoned or avoided KCMSD, and draw in additional non-minority students from the suburbs."[199] Including transportation costs, these programs cost an additional $448 million.

Unfortunately, this bold relief was short-lived. In 1995, a deeply divided U.S. Supreme Court halted the plan. The Court's majority wryly noted the plan was the "most ambitious and expensive remedial program in the history of school desegregation."[200] The Court held the goal of creating an attractive district for students outside of the district was beyond the remedial authority of the district court.[201] In its initial hearing of the case, the Supreme Court halted the lower court's attempt to raise municipal tax revenue.[202] In the second hearing, the Court held that the state legislature's appropriations made under court order went far beyond its constitutional liability, and shut down the program entirely, despite promising initial results.[203]

As the case of *Missouri v. Jenkins* illustrates, truly equalizing educational opportunity in a racially and economically segregation major metropolitan area may require investments that go far beyond "equalization." Additional analysis of states that have pursued compensatory formulas shows the importance of directing funds to the most disadvantaged districts, not simply equalizing expenditures.[204] Other countries, like Germany, spend more per pupil in schools with more socioeconomically disadvantaged students than in affluent schools. American schools are not even equally funded, let alone adequately so.[205]

Recognizing the inequity of private fundraising capacity, some districts have sought to pool parent contributions for the benefit of all schools in the district.[206] The Santa Monica-Malibu school board briefly pursued this approach, but ran into fierce community opposition.[207] Although limited evidence suggests that contribution pooling does not result in a decline in donations (as the opponents argued), we should not prohibit such contributions (even if we could) in the name of equity. Rather, a better approach would be to require states (or districts) to match them or to develop compensatory formulas that account for such inequities, even if that means spending several times as much on the most disadvantaged students as the most advantaged.

There are limits to the capacity of schools to compensate for structural inequities in society or differences in environment that exist before children enter kindergarten. One way to tackle this problem, therefore, is to bring more children into the educational system at an earlier age, by expanding access to high-quality public pre-K instruction. This should be a top policy priority.

In the United States, only 32% of four-year-olds and 5% of three-year-olds attended state funded pre-schools in 2015–2016.[208] Only a handful of states, including, Florida, Oklahoma, Wisconsin, and Vermont, serve more than

70% of four-year-olds with such programs as of the 2019–20 school year.[209] Even when accounting for enrollment in private programs, the United States ranks 26th among OECD countries for enrollment in preschool for four-year-olds and 24th for three-year-olds.[210] The OECD average enrollment for three-year olds in private or public pre-school programs is 70% compared to 38% of American children.

Approximately 25% of American children do not attend preschool programs, but 90% of children born into the top two income quintiles do.[211] In most parts of the United States, pre-K is a private service, paid for by parents who can afford it or are enrolled in subsidized or special programs. Instead, low-income families rely more on family members than professionals.[212] In survey polls, parents say it is difficult to find high-quality pre-K programs in the United States.[213] Not surprisingly, policy experts and strong majorities of Americans across the political spectrum support more public investments in pre-K.[214]

Critics of universal pre-K claim that the positive effects of such programs "fade out" over time, doubt whether successful programs can be scaled up, and express skepticism about whether new initiatives can replicate proven successes.[215] Some studies of pre-K programs found the positive effects were not detectable by 3rd grade.[216] Such "fade out" is a predictable effect of attendance in disadvantaged school systems, and may suggest the need for greater investment, not less. Education is not a one-shot investment, like a vaccination with lifetime coverage. Like the flu shot, you need the annual update or periodic booster.

Moreover, even where cognitive skills developed in programs such as Head Start were harder to detect years later, some researchers found positive social and behavioral outcomes, such as improved etiquette, self-control, and conscientiousness.[217] The behaviors and non-cognitive skills cultivated in preschool programming may be difficult to measure on standardized tests, but they can have profound influences over time.

The quality of the program appears to be critical, and longer-running programs with more stable funding and experienced teachers perform better.[218] The most successful pre-K programs are those like the HighScope Perry Preschool program in Ypsilanti, Michigan, and the Chicago Child-Parent center program.[219] These programs are more expensive, but they are also more comprehensive, involving parent education and additional supports beyond those offered in programs like Head Start. In particular, such programs not only offer families wrap-around supports, but they enshrine the non-academic skills that are vital to future success.[220] Non-cognitive skills such as managing stress and developing impulse control are part of the curriculum.

More recent research shows that longer-term effects of universal pre-K programs are not only detectable, but positive. A study of a preschool lottery in Boston provided a natural experiment to evaluate causal effects of pre-K programs because demand outstripped available slots and assignment was random.[221] Researchers found that although there was no detectable increase in state proficiency test scores, preschool enrollment boosted college attendance, SAT test-taking, and reduced the chance of disciplinary punishments, especially for boys. Another study described as the longest follow-up of an experimentally evaluated early childhood intervention from the 1960s found intergenerationally beneficial effects, especially for low-income Black families.[222]

Finally, we must expand access to education at the other end of the educational ladder, post-secondary education and vocational training. The capacities and skills needed to traverse, let alone apprehend, the pathways of opportunity in contemporary societies with technologically advanced economies require many years of formal education and training. This is why virtually all modern human societies devote tremendous public resources and many years of every citizen's life to such training.

As with K-12, the United States was once the world's leader in higher education. Once reserved for elites, the GI Bill allowed hundreds of thousands of veterans to attend college, which, in turn, led to greater investment and expansion of higher education to accommodate surging enrollment. In-state and public education was well funded, and some public systems were tuition free, including the University of California system.[223] Consequently, the Baby Boom generation far surpassed their international counterparts in educational attainment. In the post-war period, the United States had the highest college completion rate in the world. Today, we are tenth or below.[224] Enrollment in these institutions has slowed and plateaued.

Between 1963 and 2017, the share of American workers with either a college or post-college degree (including two-year programs) grew from 12% to 39% of the labor force.[225] And another 28% of the labor force has at least some college education. Just a third are merely high school graduates or dropouts. Although there is widespread recognition of the importance of post-secondary education, less than 40% of Americans 25 or older hold a bachelor's degree (see Table 2.6).

The technical skills gained through higher educational instruction is not only important to the economy, research also demonstrates the powerful role that higher education plays in promoting economic mobility. As discussed in previous chapters, college graduates have much greater earnings than non-graduates, and much lower rates of unemployment.[226] Accordingly, institutions of higher education are among the strongest engines for social mobility—with the most pronounced effect on improving earnings potential for the greatest number of students from lower-income families.

A study led by Raj Chetty found that the secondary institutions with the greatest buoying effect on lower-income students weren't Ivy League universities or other selective institutions, but rather a tranche of less selective or non-selective colleges like City College of Manhattan, Cal State, and Stony Brook.[227] For example, 76% of the students who enrolled at the City College of Manhattan from families earning in the bottom income quintile in the late 1990s leaped to the top as adults. While that may be partly a consequence of the fact that elite universities enroll relatively few low-income students, public colleges and universities serve far more students, underscoring the importance of these to upward mobility generally.[228]

Despite these facts, there are several factors that explain why the growth in rates of college enrollment and graduation has slowed. First and foremost is the cost of tuition. From 1993 to 2015, average tuition rose 234%, far above the 63% overall inflation rate.[229] Another estimate found a 180% increase in tuition, above inflation.[230] This is not because faculty wages are much more expensive than they were a generation ago (in fact, adjusted for inflation, they may be lower).[231]

The American education public university system has been impacted by state budget cuts during and after the Great Recession, preceded by a longer period of gradual disinvestment.[232] On average, per pupil spending was 20% lower in 2014–2015 than in 2007–2008.[233] Although funding has rebounded somewhat since the depths of the Great Recession, very few states have returned close to pre-recession levels of support, leaving many of these institutions in precarious positions with structural deficits.[234] As of 2016, state support for public higher education was roughly $10 billion below the pre-recession norm.[235]

To compensate for cuts, administrators raise tuition or prefer out-of-state applicants.[236] Tuition rises make higher education less and less affordable, and many students kept pace by borrowing more and more debt.[237] It is estimated that Americans owe more than $1.6 trillion in student debt, which is more than double the amount of debt a decade earlier.[238] The burden of student debt has a knock-on effect, where graduates saddled with student debt (even though they earn higher incomes) have fewer resources to buy a home, build a business, or to invest in children.[239] The growth in student debt has also been connected to a slowdown of household formation and decline in early homeownership.[240]

The national student debt crisis has a clear racial dimension. Black college graduates owe $9,600 more on average than their white peers.[241] Black students not only take on more debt, but they are more likely to drop out without having received their degree, borrow more than other students for the same degree, and are much more likely to default on their loan.[242] In some respects, the debt load difference understates the effect: Four years after graduation, Black graduates have nearly $25,000 more student loan debt than white graduates, and this fact cannot be explained simply by levels of debt taken on as undergraduates. It also has to do with repayment ability, interest rates, and the growth of the for-profit sector of higher education, whose students are disproportionately Black.[243] Estimates vary, but researchers have found that student debt contributes to the racial wealth gap as well.[244]

The end result of budget cuts and rising tuition is that more students are taking on greater student debt, fewer students can afford higher education, especially students from low- or middle-income families. Even for applicants able to hurdle the admissions process, sticker shock dissuades students from enrolling.[245] Qualified applicants from low-income families are more likely to attend two- or four-year colleges located near where they live, which are more likely to be less- or non-selective institutions.[246] Family pressures on young adults to live closer to home to support or otherwise help the family may reinforce these decisions. Many of these decisions are made often without information on the differences in school quality, chances of being accepted into alternative programs or even an understanding of financial aid options, let alone the basic mechanics of how to apply for financial aid.

State disinvestment, tuition hikes, debt burden, and local social networks tend to dissuade lower-income students from college matriculation. But another factor is inequality in the quality and quantity of counselors staffed in high schools, experts who might help or offer guidance navigating the admissions process and identifying programs or schools that students should consider. The ratio of counselors to students in high schools is nearly 500 to 1, on average, making it almost impossible for counselors to provide individualized guidance to all students. In some states, the situation is even worse, where that ratio is close to 1,000 to 1.[247] Our public secondary schools need more guidance counselors to serve these students, encouraging them to apply and matriculate to schools that will propel them further in life.

Consequently, low-income students are more likely to be "undermatched" than affluent students.[248] Undermatching is exacerbating by the climate and environment encountered on elite campuses, where many members of minority groups express a feeling of not belonging or racial isolation. For example, a surprising number of Black students admitted to UC Berkeley enroll at a lower ranked UC institution instead, partly because of the campus climate.[249]

Expanding access to education requires greater investments in non-selective institutions that serve more students so that students are more inclined to enroll and graduate with less debt and can perceive the strong benefits and quality of instruction, but it must also mean more investments in vocational and training programs that can lead to good-paying jobs. We need more post-secondary alternatives to a university education. Many of the advanced skills needed to participate in the economy can be acquired through apprenticeship and vocational training.[250]

In general, however, the U.S. secondary system places far less emphasis on vocational education (now generally known as career and technical education (CTE)) than comparable educational systems in Europe and other OECD nations.[251] Between 40% and 70% of young people in northern and central Europe enroll in coursework after grades 9 and 10 that combines workplace learning. Even Japan and Korea enroll at least 25% of secondary students in programs with a vocational emphasis or concentration.[252] In contrast, just 6% of students in the United States are placed in similar programs. It is not just that we steer fewer students toward CTE than other nations, we channel far fewer students into these programs than a generation ago. Eighteen percent of U.S. secondary students received instruction from qualified vocational programs in the early 1980s.[253]

Some experts claim that a properly supported and expanded apprenticeship initiative would be the most cost-effective way to train young adults for middle-class wages.[254] Apprenticeships, trainings program, trial-period employment, and other vocational training programs not only provide opportunities to develop relevant skills, but they also have the potential to help young people see the relevance of their training to employment prospects.

Unfortunately federal support for CTE has remained flat for a generation. The Perkins Act, enacted by Congress in 1984 and reauthorized several times since, channels more than a $1 billion to the states, who enjoy wide latitude on use, for technical and vocational education.[255] A few states are experimenting with greater investments and emphasis on CTE programming to bridge the "skills gap."[256] More investment and experimentation are needed.

7) End Mass Incarceration and the War on Drugs

The problem of mass incarceration is perhaps the most glaring instance of the intersection of race and the impediments within (and warped and corroded circuits of) the contemporary opportunity structure. Ending mass incarceration is a necessary and critical step toward dismantling structural racism and regenerating opportunity in America.

Incarceration is ruinous to opportunity. By definition it prevents mobility, and in practice inhibits the development of, and is destructive to, human capital, as described in Chapter 2. Mass incarceration not only destroys opportunity and depletes individual human capital, but it drains families and communities of resources. Breadwinners are removed from homes, single parent households multiply, and communities lose social capital, workers, and taxpayers.[*] At the same time, the costs of mass incarceration have engulfed public budgets, crowding out other spending priorities. Although the direct costs of maintaining our carceral system are estimated at around $80 billion a year,[257] one study estimated that the ultimate social cost was more than 10 times that amount.[258]

With rates of incarceration that exceed that but all of a handful of other countries (as described in Chapter 2)," either America has by far the world's largest criminal population, or our laws are criminalizing too much conduct. Recall that nearly 60% of America's incarcerated population is Black and Latino (see Table 2.8), and that nearly a million Black children have a father in jail or prison. It may be the most conspicuous feature of contemporary structural racism.

---

[*] This is not to deny that the enforcement of criminal laws has salutary effects on human health, well-being, and community safety, aspects of life that also contribute to opportunity. But policies narrowly focused and aimed at maximizing opportunity—rather than, say, public order—would be better calibrated and optimized to that goal than our criminal justice system and its product of mass incarceration.

Although ending mass incarceration must be a policy priority, accomplishing this goal is neither simple nor easy. Mass incarceration rests upon several foundations, including overly lengthy and punitive criminal sentences, the deeply misguided War on Drugs, overly zealous and aggressive criminal law enforcement and prosecution, and the revolving prison door due to the collateral sanctions of having a criminal record and failures of re-entry. Each of these must be addressed.

The most obvious step toward unwinding the system of mass incarceration is sentencing reform. As the conservative billionaire Koch brothers explained, "Too many people go to prison—often for far too long—for low-level, nonviolent crimes. People who break the law should be held accountable, but the punishment should fit the crime."[259] Sentencing reform must include abbreviating long sentences (especially for nonviolent offenses), rolling back mandatory minimums and three-strike laws, and reducing or eliminating sentencing disparities.

Public safety and order should be a policy priority for any community, but research shows that the most punitive and draconian sentences not only fail to deter crime, but actually increases the chances of criminal activity. One study showed that each additional year of incarceration increases the likelihood of re-offending by 4–7% after release.[260] Long sentences reduce the chances that former inmates can productively rebuild their lives. Since the chances of re-offending also go down with age, long sentences make little sense with respect to the actual risk to public safety for many criminal offenses.

Mandatory minimums, in particular, epitomize an out-of-control criminal justice system. California, where three strikes laws took early root, has led the way in rolling them back. After confronting prison over-crowding, California reduced sentences on a variety of non-violent crimes.[261] In 2012, Californians adopted an amendment to the three strikes law, requiring that the third strike be a serious or violent crime.[262] Two years later, another successful ballot initiative reduced the sentences on a host of crimes from felonies to misdemeanors.[263] And, in 2016, another approved ballot initiative instituted more lenient parole rules for non-violent offenders.[264]

Confronted with over-crowding and rising costs, Texas also reduced sentences for non-violent drug offenses, eased probation and parole rules, and provided alternatives to incarceration.[265] The results have saved taxpayers millions while crime rates continued to drop.[266] Similarly, in 2017 Louisiana pushed through an impressive package of reform projected to reduce its prison population by 10% and save a quarter-billion dollars.[267] Although the heart of the reform is reducing mandatory minimums and trimming other penalties, it also includes medical furlough, diversion programs, and lifted many collateral sanctions.

Federal efforts have been slower going. President Obama successfully persuaded Congress to more equitably adjust the punishment for possession of crack and powder cocaine, a 100-to-1 sentencing disparity that was undeniably racialized.[268] In December 2018, President Trump signed a federal prison reform bill with wide bipartisan support known as the Formerly Incarcerated Reenter Society Transformed Safely Transitioning Every Person Act (FIRST STEP Act).[269] This law relaxes mandatory-minimum sentences for non-violent drug offenders with no prior criminal record, expands early release programs for good behavior, and offered more training and work opportunities to prisoners. While the FIRST STEP Act encompasses the most significant changes to the federal criminal justice system in decades, in the first year, fewer than 10,000 inmates were expected to have their sentences reduced.[270] And it applies only to federal prisoners, who make up approximately 181,000 of the 2.1 million persons imprisoned in the United States.[271]

At the end of the day, sentencing reform is insufficient to unwind mass incarceration. To return to the 1972 rate of incarceration, America would have to release 80% of her incarcerated population.[272] The War on Drugs needs thorough reconsideration. As a system of punitive laws relating to the sale, distribution, or possession of intoxicating or psychoactive chemicals, the War on Drugs has been not only a failure, but a disaster. It ensnares far too many people, especially for non-violent offenses. In 2009, 1.66 million Americans were arrested on drug charges, and four of five were arrested for possession alone. People of color and communities of color are disproportionately surveilled, arrested, and charged for such offenses.

The War on Drugs has not prevented nor abated the public health problems related to drug use. In recent years, a devastating opioid and heroin epidemic broke out in predominantly white suburban and rural communities.[273] More than 90% of the users are white and more than 75% live outside cities.[274] In fact, some health experts say that being Black is statistically protective of risk for overdose amid this crisis.[275] Yet, in contrast to the addiction crisis of earlier decades, such as the crack epidemic in the 1980s, the response has been much different. Rather than treating the crisis as a public health problem, the victims of the crack epidemic were portrayed as criminals, violent predators, and much worse.[276]

In contrast to the traditional "get tough" rhetoric, politicians and legislators speak about the opioid crisis in more empathetic terms.[277] Although Indiana had prohibited needle exchanges out of a fear that it might encourage drug use, the conservative Governor Mike Pence reluctantly reversed policy in the face of an HIV outbreak among users.[278] In a Republican Presidential debate, New Jersey Governor Chris Christie said that "This is not a moral failing. This is a disease."[279] Governors and mayors across the country pled with Congress to provide funds to address this festering problem. In 2016, Congress passed a comprehensive bill that expanded access to anti-opioid drugs and treatment programs.[280]

Future historians will likely view the War on Drugs in a similar light to Prohibition, regarding both as misguided policy experiments animated as much by social control impulses as concerns over the public health and safety. Just as the temperance movement was motivated, in part, by legitimate concerns over domestic violence and familial abuse as well as nativist anti-immigrant sentiment,[281] the War on Drugs will be viewed as part of a legacy of America's ongoing racial struggles, and each will leave a devastating record of unintended consequences, not only for its targets, but for those victimized by the organized criminal cartels that emerged and flourished under these legal regimes.[282]

Just as criminal violence and urban gang warfare erupted under Prohibition in cities like New York and Chicago, so has public safety been undermined by the War on Drugs by international drug cartels, narco-terrorism, and public corruption. At the 2012 Summit of the Americas, 31 national leaders agreed that the U.S.-led War on Drugs has been a failure. Leaders across Latin American spoke out vigorously for the first time against the failed policy.[283] The Summit concluded that, "the problem with the current war-on-drugs policy is that it is unwinnable—and leads to weakened states, staggering levels of violence and continued drug consumption in Canada and the U.S."[284]

Partly in recognition of this, as of 2025 24 U.S. states have decriminalized marijuana for recreational use, and 38 have legalized it for medicinal purposes.[285] A number of cities and jurisdictions have legalized other federally prohibited drugs, such as psilocybin "Magic" mushrooms.[286] There is broad support for decriminalization from medical organizations as well as human rights groups.[287] Although not without hiccups, states that have legalized recreational marijuana appear to have managed the transition well. If anything, problems associated with de-criminalization have less to do with public health than fiscal and administrative implementation, setting the appropriate tax rate, managing licensing, and avoiding market concentration.[288] Decriminalization also needs to occur at the federal level, and it should be a policy priority.

Ending the federal War on Drugs, however, will not end mass incarceration. Only 50% of federal prisoners are incarcerated because of the War on Drugs, and only about one in ten incarcerated persons are held in federal prisons. The other 90% are held in state facilities, with nearly three-quarters of a million held in city and county jails.[289] The best scholarship suggests that, even absent the federal drug war, there would still have been a nearly fourfold increase in state prison growth between 1980 and 2009.[290]

Decriminalization of non-violent drug offenses, especially possession of small amounts of drugs, is an important first step, but truly reversing mass incarceration is going to require much more extensive efforts.[291] A serious de-incarceration agenda would include, in addition to decriminalization of drugs, reducing the sentences for minor non-drug crimes and even more serious crime, eliminating mandatory minimums, and providing more diversion and alternatives to incarceration, such as treatment. The challenge is immense. A growing perception of disorder, only partly related to drug use, has soured the public mood and dampened enthusiasm and support for these policy ideas, leading to rollbacks where de-criminalization has been attempted.[292]

Nor will ending the War on Drugs repair the damage it has inflicted, which has left a deeper and more painful scar than Prohibition. After just 13 years, Americans corrected the error of Prohibition. But the War on Drugs has pressed on for more than a generation, and the effects are much farther reaching. Redressing these effects requires a concerted set of remedial efforts, including dispensation of marijuana sales and grow licenses in communities most impacted by the war, clearing records of drug-based criminal convictions, more extensive investments in public health and treatment services, education and jobs, and comprehensive efforts to help formerly incarcerated people re-integrate into the community.

As many as 700,000 people with felony convictions are released from state and federal prison each year in the United States, and another nine million cycle through local jails.[293] All told, an estimated 20 million people live in the United States, outside of the carceral system, with a felony record.[294] Another 50 million have some lesser criminal blemish on their record.[295] Re-entry, which refers to the return and re-integration of formerly incarcerated persons into their communities, is one of the single most daunting immediate challenges.[296] Upon re-entry, released individuals encounter many barriers to opportunity, with legally permissible discrimination in housing, employment, and education.

Housing, in particular, is the foundation for healthy re-integration into the community. Ensuring that people released from prison or jails have safe and affordable housing is a critical to securing stable employment, and reducing homelessness and recidivism. Research shows that individuals who cannot find stable housing are more likely to engage in criminal activity.[297] In communities already struggling with inadequate and unaffordable housing, limited resources, and unemployment, the successful re-integration of these individuals is an even greater challenge.

Many formerly incarcerated persons face limited employment prospects on account of low levels of education, limited job skills, and inadequate training or formal work experience. Furthermore, many inmates suffer from mental illness, disabilities, or have substance abuse disorders, compounding the challenge of re-entry.

Above all, however, formerly incarcerated persons and other parolees face legal discrimination in the employment process. A 2012 survey found that 87% of managers perform background checks, up from 51% in 1996.[298] Many employment applications ask prospective candidates if they have ever been convicted of a crime. These forms are often used to screen applicants, even if the prior conviction is unrelated to the job duties. Applicants who check the box are in some cases automatically rejected.[299] For these reasons, criminal records hamper employment options for as many as 70 million Americans and more than one in three working adults.[300] One study found that one year after release, up to 60% of formerly incarcerated persons remained unemployed.[301] Another study found that a conviction reduces hourly wages by approximately 11%, and annual employment by approximately nine weeks.[302]

Some employers use criminal records as a lazy screening mechanism to winnow large applicant pools. "Ban the Box" campaigns seek to remove those questions from employment applications so that hiring managers first get an opportunity to learn about the candidate's experience, skills, and qualifications as they relate to the position to be filled.[303] They do, however, allow employers, in most cases, to conduct background checks later in the process. At least 37 states and over 150 cities and counties have adopted some form of "ban the box" policy in government hiring, and 8 states extend it to private employers as well.[304]

In 2012, the federal Equal Employment Opportunity Commission issued guidance prohibiting the use of the "box" in a broad and unrestricted way.[305] The guidance also makes clear that if an applicant does have a criminal conviction, an employer must look at the seriousness of the offense, the time that has lapsed since it was committed, and the relevance of the crime to the specific job opening. According to the guidance, computerized job applications that automatically reject anyone who answers "yes" to the question "Have you ever been convicted of a crime?" could be violating federal law.

Nonetheless, challenging such rejections is not only difficult, but costly. Few unemployed applicants have the capacity or resources to file a claim against businesses that serially engage in such behavior. The better approach is to enact state and municipal laws that proactively prohibit and monitor such practices by conducting tests, much like those used by fair housing audits.

Such policies should extend beyond the employment context. In addition to legal discrimination and stigma of a criminal record, formerly incarcerated people may be excluded from receiving social security, food stamps, or other assistance. Given the difficulties that a criminal record imposes in obtaining jobs, professional licenses, public housing and other benefits and opportunities, some state legislators are calling for additional ways to help with re-entry. A number of cities, such as Newark, Seattle, and San Francisco have already passed these so-called "fair chance" ordinances prohibiting housing discrimination against formerly incarcerated persons.[306] Colorado and New Jersey are the first states to impose such a ban, although the latter is the most sweeping, with penalties up to $10,000.[307]

Other promising efforts include certificate programs, eliminating or reducing collateral sanctions, sealing or expunging certain records, and tax incentives for hiring former inmates. In Ohio, legislators passed a measure reducing as many as 800 collateral sanctions.[308] The bill recognized that offenders were denied certain state licensures or certificates, and reduced the number of grounds for having a driver's license suspended. As a Republican lawmaker explained, "By doing a better job on offender reentry, we can prevent crimes, we can help strengthen our communities, and we can save taxpayer money."[309] In other states legislators have sponsored a certificate program that would help provide potential employers with increased confidence in the reliability of a potential ex-offender, and give that person a meaningful second chance.[310] Such a certificate would certify good conduct, and signify that the individual has met certain criteria.

An even bolder approach is to make former incarceration a protected status, and presumptively ban discrimination on that basis generally.[311] Although this status is not an inherited or immutable characteristic, that does not mean it is undeserving of protection against discrimination. Local governments already prohibit discrimination on a range of grounds unrelated to inherited or immutable traits, such as political ideology or veteran status. A simple municipal ordinance to that effect could help formerly incarcerated persons re-integrate into society and pursue a wider range of opportunities.

High recidivism rates suggest that our society does not do enough to open pathways of opportunity for formerly incarcerated persons. Providing educational opportunities to prisoners may not be politically popular, but it is wise, and ultimately, pays for itself in terms of future tax revenue from productive citizens and reduced costs of incarceration.[312] A large review of such programs by the RAND Corporation found that correctional education programs reduce both rates of recidivism (at very little expense) by roughly 43%, and increase post-incarceration employment.[313] One program reduced recidivism to 2%.[314] In general, a single dollar spent on prison education may save four or five dollars in future costs of incarceration. Online education has the potential to scale up and reduce the costs of such efforts.

Ninety percent of prisoners will someday be released, but only 22% of people incarcerated in state prisons have some postsecondary education.[315] Many prisoners have the time and appetite to learn skills and acquire knowledge. Unfortunately, the infamous 1994 federal crime bill quashed many of the educational programs that were once offered in prisons, including degree courses.[316] State politicians have proposed educational offerings, but, like Governor Cuomo in 2014, backed down under political pressure.[317] There is limited appetite to use tax money to invest in prisoners' education or job skills, despite the obvious returns to both safety and expense of feeding and housing repeat offenders. Aside from a few boutique programs, this has left mostly private donors and foundations to fill the gap or leave such programs dismantled or defunct.[318]

The costs of incarceration also crowd out investments and other spending priorities that could expand opportunity. The Federal Bureau of Prisons budget grew 1,700% from 1980 to 2010.[319] State correctional costs quadrupled from 1990 to 2010 alone.[320] The United States is estimated to spend a staggering $80 billion a year on incarceration, with state taxpayers paying at least $40 billion.[321] As of 2016, 18 states spent more on incarceration than education.[322]

The full costs of incarceration go beyond governmental outlays and taxpayer expenses. The collateral and social costs are much greater. One particularly ambitious attempt to factor in all of these costs pegs the true cost of incarceration annually at more than $1.2 trillion.[323] The study's authors estimate that every dollar of direct costs of incarceration generate another ten dollars of indirect social costs.

Ultimately the politics of mass incarceration generate a set of dynamics that resist reform. Prisoners and formerly incarcerated people are not a favored constituency. Unions, private prison companies, and many other interest groups benefit from prison building and mass incarceration. Struggling rural areas, in particular, benefit from the employment opportunities afforded by new prison facilities. In the 1990s, more than two-thirds of new prisons were built in rural areas—a de facto jobs program for these communities.[324] These entrenched political interests predictably fight reform.

Mass incarceration distorts our politics in a more fundamental way. Inmates count for census and congressional apportionment purposes as residents of the place of incarceration. Since 1.5 million people incarcerated in state and local facilities count as local residents, this practice enhances the political power of rural communities while diluting the political power of cities and non-white communities. One assessment concludes that "prison gerrymandering" is responsible for changing district boundaries of every political district in the state of New York.[325]

This is compounded by felon disenfranchisement. Several states permanently bar or restrict felons from voting in elections, and many more prohibit felons from voting while on probation or parole.[326] As many as four million Americans are barred from voting because of felon disenfranchisement laws.[327] As a result, an estimated 1 in 22 Black Americans of voting age is barred from voting. Only Maine and Vermont, two of the whitest states in the country, permit prisoners to vote while incarcerated.[328]

A society guided by the goal of promoting and expanding opportunity would do much more to reinvest resources used to contain and control people so that they might become contributing members of society. An opportunity agenda would find ways to promote public safety by investing in the futures of at-risk youth, and prioritize rehabilitation and education of the currently incarcerated, in order to ease re-entry into society. Such an agenda is not squishy, soft-headed thinking. It is based on hard facts and doubts whether the immense costs of mass incarceration to public budgets and society justify the benefits. This is why many conservatives and libertarians support of criminal justice reform.[329] As Texas Governor Rick Perry explained, "You want to talk about real conservative governance? Shut prisons down. Save that money."[330]

8) Reform the Criminal Justice System

The criminal justice system has received withering scrutiny in recent years due to patent injustices evident in its ordinary machinations and the pervasive racial inequality observable in almost every facet of the system, from policing to sentencing. Areas most urgently in need of reform include police misconduct, prosecutorial misconduct, the criminalization of poverty, the underfunding of public defenders' offices, the financing of municipal justice and administration through user fees and fines, and the abuse of cash bail.

Systemic criminal justice policy change needs to start with policing, an area has stubbornly resisted reform. Recall from Chapter 4 that violent police encounters sparked or were the "precipitating incident" for many of the major race-related uprisings of the last 100 years, with the murder of George Floyd as merely one of the more recent and searing instances. Further recall that police practices, including harassment, verbal discourtesy, physical abuse, and impunity were listed as the number one deeply held grievance listed among 12 total grievances ranked across three tiers of intensity by the Kerner Commission.

Ordinary verbal abuse, disrespect, and violation of rights factored high among the criticisms heard by the Kerner Commission, and by investigations since. A survey of Cincinnati residents decades later found that nearly half of all Black respondents reported being personally "hassled" by the police, compared with only 9.6% of whites.[331] They defined "hassled" as being stopped or watched closely when they had done nothing wrong.[332] A study of police encounters in Oakland found that police were more respectful when interacting with white pedestrians and drivers than non-whites.[333] And a large national survey found that 50% of Black Americans felt that they were personally discriminated against when interacting with the police, and 60% felt that they or a family member were stopped or treated unfairly because of their race.[334] Another survey found that Black adults were five times as likely as white adults to say that they have been unfairly stopped by the police (44% to 9%).[335]

There is a pervasive sense that police "serve" white communities and "patrol" Black ones. Many police neither reside in nor grew up in the communities they serve. As the Kerner Report keenly observed, "[t]he patrolman comes to see the city through a windshield and hear about it over a police radio. To him, the area increasingly comes to consist only of law breakers. To the ghetto resident, the policeman comes increasingly to be only an enforcer."[336] Even where cities have enacted residency requirements so that officers are more intimately familiar with the communities they serve, some states have stepped in to overturn them.[337]

The Kerner Commission devoted an entire chapter to "Policing and the Community" and advanced at least 23 specific recommendations for policing reforms under five broad headers pertaining to the use of force, patrol practices, and grievance procedures, among other things.[338] A review of these recommendations reveals that few of these recommendations had ever been implemented, and many of the problems festered in the intervening decades.[339] Many other commissions and task forces advanced similar recommendations, including the Obama-era Department of Justice sponsored Task Force on Twenty-First Century Policing.[340] The Task Force offered dozens of recommendations and action items in six broad areas similar to those of the Kerner Commission, with the same relative inaction. The more urgently framed "Eight that can't wait" grassroots campaign focused on many of the same problems.[341]

One of the overarching concerns around policing is the general sense of impunity among officers. As noted in Chapter 4, the Kerner Commission reported that "Negroes firmly believe that police brutality and harassment occur repeatedly in Negro neighborhoods."[342] This was echoed by the Black Lives Matter Movement, that police violence is disproportionately inflicted on Black people and that police disproportionately target Black neighborhoods and abuse their residents.[343] An analysis of FBI data found that Black Americans accounted for 31% of killings by police in 2012, despite accounting for just 13% of the population at the time.[344] A more recent analysis by the Mapping Police Violence project found that Black victims accounted for about 26% of police killings in 2019.[345] Studies have found that Black Americans are between two and three times as likely to be shot by the police as white people.[346]

Efforts to rein in police use of force have faltered partly because these standards are established by state and federal law. In 1989, the U.S. Supreme Court ruled that the constitutional standard for the use of force is "reasonableness" from the perspective of the officer in light of the totality of the circumstances, and not with the benefit of hindsight.[347] Under this standard, police can claim reasonableness even if they are the aggressor or initiator of violence.

Some state legislatures have contemplated efforts to raise standards on the use of force, especially lethal force, above the federal minimum, although such efforts face intense opposition from police unions and their associations, which have either stymied such efforts or diluted them into less effective compromises.[348] California lawmakers considered a bill that would prohibit the use of deadly force except "where it is necessary to prevent imminent and serious bodily injury or death to the officer or another person."[349] Seattle adopted a similar standard, restricting the use of deadly force to situations in which an "officer fears an imminent threat of injury or death." Since implementing this standard, the Seattle Police Department has had fewer incidents of civilians killed by police officers.[350]

A related problem is the lack of accountability, the cordon of the "thin blue line" where officers protect other officers from being held accountable, even bad apples.[351] There are almost no instances of complaints of police abuse or violations being handled by independent, specialized agencies as recommended by the Kerner Commission. Instead, most complaints are handled by "internal affairs" offices, whose processes are too often as opaque as they are vague. Occasionally, civilian review boards work alongside police departments, but they rarely have independent investigatory powers. It was widely noted that officer Derek Chauvin, the ex-officer who pinned George Floyd to the ground, killing him, had 18 complaints on record against him, and only two noted instances of disciplinary action, formal reprimands.[352]

A lack of accountability was one of the main issues raised in the Department of Justice's investigation into the Ferguson Police Department. As the report observed, "Ferguson's internal affairs system fails to respond meaningfully to complaints of officer misconduct. It does not serve as a mechanism to restore community members' trust in law enforcement, or correct officer behavior."[353] On the contrary, the investigation found that the system repeatedly failed to investigate allegations of misconduct, dissuaded citizens from lodging complaints, and retaliated against those who did.

It is not just that police departments too often fail to hold their rank-and-file officers accountable for abuse and misconduct; so does the criminal justice system. Because of the deference given police and the Supreme Court's prevailing legal standards on the use of force and search,[354] as well as the general faith and reliance on them, prosecutors and Grand Juries are reticent to bring charges, as they decided against doing in the cases involving the deaths of Tamir Rice and Breanna Taylor.[355] Not only do the police appear to act with impunity, but even when charges are brought against police officers, justice is frustratingly elusive.

Perhaps one of the most shocking instances was the brutal killing of Daniel Shaver in an Arizona hotel in 2016, as an officer barked commands to the intoxicated 26-year-old, whose failure (inability) to comply was met with a barrage of lethal bullets from an automatic rifle.[356] The officer responsible for the shooting was acquitted of all charges. Recall, as well, the acquittal in the death of Freddie Gray and the failed prosecutions in the deaths of Eric Garner and Michael Brown. Although there have been exceptions to this trend, especially since the conviction of Derek Chauvin in the murder of George Floyd, these cases collectively illustrate why protestors (and many non-protestors) were so angry.[357]

In addition to these challenges, federal law accords police another layer of protection, known as "qualified immunity."[358] This legal doctrine shields police from civil suits when performing official duties. Even if the jury finds the officer liable for unlawful conduct, federal law does not require the police department to pay a reward to the victim. And even if departments were liable, indemnification would cover most losses.

Although policing requires cultural and systematic reform, prosecutorial discretion and misconduct is another major problem that receives far less attention. Local prosecutors handle about 95% of the criminal docket and enjoy broad discretion in the administration of justice, in selecting cases they wish to pursue or prioritize, decisions about how to handle cases, whom to charge, and the punishments they seek.[359] Of the more than 2,300 chief prosecutors in the country, many are elected rather than appointed, and campaign on "law and order" platforms. This system tends to yield the most zealous prosecutors, which researchers have pinpointed as a major cause of mass incarceration since the 1980s.[360]

Whether conscious or unconscious, prosecutorial discretion in charging decisions may reproduce or exacerbate racial disparities in the criminal justice system. Some research shows that prosecutors are more likely to charge Black people, and more punitively, than white people.[361] A 2017 study found, for example, that white defendants in Wisconsin were 25% more likely than their Black counterparts to have criminal charges dropped or reduced to less serious crimes.[362]

Prosecutorial misconduct takes many forms: selective prosecution, racial or racially coded appeals to juries, discriminatory peremptory strikes in jury selection, and abuse of discovery. Defense attorneys and public defenders rely on information in police files possessed by the prosecuting attorney's office. Prosecutor offices enjoy investigatory powers and resources that defense attorneys and public defender offices generally lack. The most serious form of discovery abuse is the failure to turn over or provide exculpatory evidence. Until 1963, when the US Supreme Court held that this was a violation of constitutional rights, many states did not require local prosecutors or district attorneys to turn over exculpatory evidence.[363] Between 2004 and 2022, there have been at least 386 cases in which a court ruled that a state or federal prosecutor committed a so-called "Brady violation."[364] It is unknown how many actual violations exist, but another study found that courts tend to make such determinations in only about 10% of cases where one is seriously alleged.[365]

Another problem is racial discrimination in the jury selection process. It has long been deemed unconstitutional for prosecutors to strike jurors from a jury pool because of their race, but discovering whether a preemptory challenge is based on race or a racial pretext is difficult.[366] This constitutional protection is easily subverted by fabricating some plausible alternative reason, such as personal idiosyncrasies or attire. Courts have struggled to determine whether such decisions are motivated by race, as several recent Supreme Court decisions grappling with this issue illustrate.[367]

No matter how egregious their misconduct, prosecutors are rarely punished, and convictions based upon them are hard to overturn. A study of over 3,000 cases of prosecutorial misconduct from 1963 to 2013 found that prosecutors were sanctioned in just 63 instances.[368] Even in cases involving Brady violations, prosecutors are rarely referred to or disciplined by state or local bar association, let alone held criminally responsible.[369] Federal prosecutors are not even subject to the same oversight as lawyers working in most federal agencies, the inspector general.[370] At the state level, bar associations and state legislatures should push for clear standards of professional conduct and greater judicial oversight, so that in addition to criminal penalties, prosecutors are held to the same ethical professional standards as private attorneys. State and county governments should collect and publish statistics on race and prosecution, at a minimum.

Our justice system needs to have a larger view of the public good. Several "reform" prosecutors, promising more fairness in the prosecution of justice and expressing commitments to reversing mass incarceration, have won office across the country.[371] Notable electoral victories for this movement include Larry Kramer in Philadelphia and Chesa Boudin in San Francisco, both former public defenders, George Gascón in Los Angeles, and Maryland state's attorney Marilyn Mosby.[372]

Unfortunately these officials have run into considerably headwinds. They have been repeatedly chastised by judges for being too lenient, state legislatures have cut their budgets, governors have ordered state attorney generals to take over some of their cases, and career staff in local offices have subtly undermined reform.[373] In 2022, Marilyn Mosby was defeated in a Democratic primary (although she also faced pending legal charges).[374] The Pennsylvania Republican-led House sought to impeach Philadelphia District Attorney Larry Kramer.[375] In "liberal" San Francisco, opponents forced a recall election for Chesa Boudin, who was ousted amidst a backlash to quality-of-life concerns.[376] Although a similar effort fell short in Los Angeles despite gathering more than half a million signatures, George Gascón lost his re-election bid in 2024.[377]

Prosecutor offices are funded by counties or municipalities, while most public defenders are paid out of state coffers. The result is too often grossly disproportionate support and funding for public defenders.[378] Almost 80% of all criminal defendants rely on public defenders.[379] This fundamental right, however, has been systematically undermined by defunding and overburdening caseloads. In some extreme instances, public defenders are required to have more than 120 cases at a time, which hardly provides enough time for preliminary motions or cross-examination preparation. In Minnesota, one public defender estimated that he only had about 12 minutes to devote to each client.[380]

The vast majority of criminal defendants are indigent.[381] Some defendants waive their constitutional rights to a public defender to avoid having to pay fees, resulting in inadequate defense.[382] Fees and costs are imposed or applied throughout criminal proceedings, in many cases burdening those with the least ability to pay. Some people spend more time in jail for failure to pay a fine than for an original sentence.[383] The consequences are potentially enormous, not just on defendants, but their families and society. Individuals who cannot afford the $60 parole fee in Pennsylvania must be housed at a cost of between $80 and $110 per day by taxpayers.[384] And ongoing economic sanctions make it even more difficult for released individuals to re-enter society.

In 2019, the U.S. Supreme Court ruled unanimously that Eighth Amendment's ban on "excessive fines" applied to the states, reviving a somewhat dormant provision that may be used to challenges these municipal and state practices.[385] And in 2016, the Department of Justice issued guidance on this issue to state and local courts, instructing them, among other things, that courts should not incarcerate for failure to pay a fee or a fine without first determining ability to pay, and that courts should not issue warrants for arrest as a means of coercing payment, and not require bail or bond for indigent defendants.[386] The guidance noted the profound harms attended by such practices, including "los[ing] their jobs; and becom[ing] trapped in cycles of poverty that can be nearly impossible to escape." Moreover, the guidance warned that "to the extent that these practices are geared not toward addressing public safety, but rather toward raising revenue, they can cast doubt on the impartiality of the tribunal and erode trust between local governments and their constituents." Unfortunately, in 2017, the Department retracted the guidance, and removed the letter from its website.[387]

Pre-trial detention is another contributor to mass incarceration. According to some estimates as many as 450,000 people are in pretrial detention in the United States.[388] Although some of these defendants were considered dangerous or flight risks, too many are simply there because they can't afford bail. According to the National Institute of Corrections, as many as half a million people in America are incarcerated on any given day for that reason.[389] In 1990, only 24% of people released from jail before trial were required to pay bail as a condition of release.[390] That number rose to 50% by 2009, and is higher in many jurisdictions.[391]

Nationally only one in ten defendants can afford bail at the time of arraignment. This is not simply because bail is expensive. Only 15% of defendants are able to come up with $500 for bail.[392] Unlike larger bail amounts, commercial bail bondmen are generally unwilling to offer their services because it is not worth their time. Perhaps the most harrowing symbol of this was Sandra Bland, who was found dead in her Texas jail cell after being unable to provide $500 for her immediate release.[393] In New York City alone, roughly 45,000 people a year are jailed because they can't afford bail.[394]

Even when bail is set very low, it may either prove unaffordable or damaging to low-income families, who have to choose between bailing out a breadwinner or parent and paying bills. The threat of bail is used to coerce criminal defendants into plea agreements, especially where the penalty is modest or small. Even brief pre-trial detention can result in lost wages and income, housing, and custody of children. Economically vulnerable people in service or caretaker jobs may be dismissed for even a single unexcused absence. Extended stays in pre-trial detention have serious consequences, such as losing income needed to pay rent under a lease or a mortgage, triggering foreclosure. For the homeless, such detention can mean losing a bed at a shelter. And for parents or other caretakers, the consequences extend to those in their care. Rather than risk lost income or custody, many criminal defendants reluctantly agree to a plea deal that includes misdemeanors, even if they are innocent, simply to avoid the hassle or greater harm.

The abuse of bail is a gut-wrenching but widespread instance of the criminalization of poverty. Although as many as 45% of all misdemeanors and 30% of all felony cases are ultimately dismissed, individuals unable to afford bail—primarily from low-income backgrounds—may be incarcerated for months in pre-trial detention. In one particularly egregious example, a 19-year old from Baltimore was held for 247 days in an adult jail before he was shown to have been nowhere near the scene of the crime.[395] A DUI for a nurse's aide in Baltimore triggered a kafka-esque 18-month odyssey of the criminal justice system that resulted in a month imprisonment for inability to afford $2,500 in bail.[396] A Bronx teenager, Kalief Browder, was arrested on suspicion for stealing a backpack and spent *three years* incarcerated on Rikers Island because his family could not raise $3,000 to pay bail.[397] In the end, the robbery charge was dropped for lack of evidence, and Browder was released. But the trauma of incarceration (which included two years of solitary confinement) haunted him so intensely that he took his own life a few years later.[398]

Pretrial detention on account of bail unaffordability inverts the presumption of innocence, punishing low-income criminal defendants before they have had their day in court. The American Bar Association recommends using bail as only a last resort.[399] Judges and leaders in many states have called for abolishing or curbing abusive bail tactics. Although a handful of states, including Alaska, New York, and California, have implemented bail reform, most have not, or have done so in problematic ways.[400] States like California and New Jersey considered replacing cash bail with algorithmic or computerized risk assessments that may produce similar racialized effects.[401] In 2019, New York eliminated cash bail for many misdemeanors and nonviolent crimes, but a fierce backlash led by police and prosecutors led to a rollback.[402]

The criminal justice system is twisted, not simply with procedural unfairness, but by a set of perverse incentives. Some reform opponents are less concerned with justice and fairness than procedural efficiency, that bail reform would reduce plea deals and further clog up the system as more cases are taken to trial.[403] Moreover, bail is a $2 billion annual industry.[404] In New York City, bail bond companies collected tens of millions of dollars a year.[405] This industry opposes reforms that would undermine such lucrative business.

Although bail is supposed to be tailored to objective criteria, the most revealing fact of all is the relationship between conviction rates and making bail.[406] Pretrial detention is correlated with a significant increase in convictions, primarily due to a greater likelihood of pleading guilty. In one study, 92% of defendants locked up until their cases were resolved were convicted compared to just half of those who made bail.[407] The race of the defendant also shapes bail determinations, independent of the judge's race.[408] In general, Black defendants are deemed higher risk and less likely to be granted pre-trial release. A study of the New York City court system finds that pretrial detention may explain as much as 40% of the Black-white incarceration gap and 28% of the Hispanic-white gap.[409]

In *McCleskey v. Kemp*, the Supreme Court wrote that that if the disparities evident throughout the criminal justice system were constitutionally cognizable, then they would "throw into serious question [our] entire criminal justice system."[410] Although the Court refused to accept that premise, the conclusion is sound. Virtually every major institution within the criminal justice system merits examination for reform or transformation.

9) Limit Occupational Licensing, Non-Compete Clauses, and Other Employment Barriers

Recall the metaphorical conceptualization of opportunity as a set of pathways trod over the life course. Some paths have artificial barriers or obstacles placed on them, which make passage more difficult, if not impossible. As a policy matter, barriers to opportunity should be reduced or removed wherever possible and reasonable.

Norms or laws that enable or permit discrimination inhibit the pursuit of opportunity. The United States has many laws on the books laws that prohibit broad forms of discrimination on the basis of numerous protected categories, such as race, national origin, sex, age, disability, and familial status. Although there is ample room for strengthening or expanding those protections, there will always be groups that slip through the cracks and limits to the capacity to challenge and dislodge such barriers on a case-by-case basis.

As a complement to anti-discrimination provisions, policymakers should consider proactive measures that limit, restrict or curb artificial barriers to opportunity. Foremost among those that merit greater scrutiny are unfair and unnecessary employment screening barriers, such as criminal background inquiries, non-compete clauses, and credit checks, as well as occupational licensing requirements.[411] In addition to expanding personal freedom to pursue opportunity, curbing or more carefully limiting these devices may remove pretexts for identity-based discrimination.

It has become a fact of bureaucratic life that virtually every job classification now has some minimal set of formal requirements, experience or skills. In cases where workers lack the skills to perform a job, investments in education or training can help overcome these barriers and open pathways of opportunity. Unfortunately, too many job cards include qualifications that are not strictly necessary for effective job performance.

One particular expression of this problem is known as "degree inflation." Too many jobs within government but also in the private sector require four-year college degrees or other specialized credentials without a well-founded basis in the job function or responsibilities. Many institutions have job cards on file have not been updated in years, if not decades. When job cards are eventually updated, they are often revised through bureaucratic procedures rather than a careful analysis of the skills required to perform the job.[412] Not only do unnecessary credential requirements reduce opportunity, but they harm people of color, who are less likely to have a college degree.[413] Unnecessary degree requirements by employers reinforce a cultural presumption that college degrees are the only path to a good job. Some state leaders are trying to reverse this trend. In March 2022, Maryland removed four-year degree requirements from tens of thousands of state jobs. Governor Larry Hogan announced that the state would become the first state to remove the requirements from tens of thousands of job positions, and at least 16 states have followed suit so far.[414]

Broadly speaking, any employment qualification, especially those for entry level positions, should be scrutinized and validated or thrown out. Diplomas too often stand-in for the presence of actual skills and relevant experience, and arbitrary requirements such as "X number of years of experience" should correlate to minimally required performance and not used to filter out weaker candidates. Job cards for public or government positions should be systematically and periodically reviewed to ensure that job qualifications and requirements are strictly necessary rather than lazy winnowing tools. Instead, critical job skills can be assessed through tests, interviews, work samples, and reference checks rather than through generic certifications, specific credentials, or arbitrary years of experience.

One particular practice that has been subject to withering scrutiny are inquiries on employment applications that ask about past criminal history, discussed earlier. Beyond the "box," other forms of employment screening that filter out applicants may similarly require attention and regulation. Credit checks were designed for lending purposes, but are increasingly used by employers on dubious grounds.[415] As many as six in ten employers consult credit reports now that such reports are more readily accessible.[416] Certainly, ensuring that someone has decent credit may be a qualification for handling sensitive information, but using it to screen out job applicants where there is no obvious connection or predictive validity to job performance is more problematic. Several states have enacted laws that limit or circumscribe the use of credit checks in employment decisions, and the House of Representatives approved a ban in 2020, although the Senate did not take up the bill.[417] Because of disparities in wealth, curbing this practice should disproportionately help Black job applicants.

A similar set of concerns arises with the use of employment status as another employment qualification. Some employers refuse to consider applicants who are currently unemployed.[418] To appreciate the absurdity, imagine if potential romantic partners screened out single people. The long-term unemployed often have the most difficulty finding jobs, and subsidies and tax policies that subsidize hiring are least likely to benefit them. After all, employment instills experience and develops skills that generate more opportunities. As a result, New Jersey became the first state, in 2011, to bar employers from advertising job openings that refuse to consider unemployed candidates.[419] Several other states have banned unemployment discrimination, but many more should follow suit.[420]

Perhaps even worse than unfair employer-based employment screenings or superfluous job qualifications and requirements are governmental regulations that have the same effect, such as excessive occupational licensing requirements. Occupational licensing generally refers to state or local regulations that mandate certification or special credentials to perform a service or a job. Occupational licensing has become a wildly prolific cottage industry for lobbyists and state legislatures in recent decades, regulating access to more than a thousand occupations.[421]

Stringent occupational requirements harm the least well-off and the least educated, who are prevented, as a result, from gaining experience in a field or occupation. For example, a license to braid hair (a cosmetology license) can require up to 2,100 hours of study in some states such as South Dakota or a year of study in California.[422] New York requires formal instruction and a license in hair braiding. Classes can cost as much as $15,000. In one field after another, unreasonable licensing requirements impede the career path of moderate and low-skilled workers.[423] According to one study, on average the requirements for low- to moderate-income occupations in the United States cost around $200 in fees and require nine months of training.[424]

The percentage of jobs that are subject to occupational licensure has risen from 10% in 1970 to 30% of the national workforce in 2008.[425] Occupational licensing not only diminishes opportunities for employment, but it also limits entrants into new fields or sectors, and restricts upward mobility.[426] Occupational licensing requirements often also screen out individuals who have, by misfortune or bad decisions, tangled with the criminal justice system.

State legislatures may legitimately exercise their police powers to protect the public health, safety, and welfare by enacting such regulations. However, there is evidence occupational licensing or credential requirements are no longer a legislator's good faith estimation of requisite skill and experience needed to prevent harm. A recent study found that many of these licenses effect no improvement on consumer safety.[427] Rather, they are a product of lobbying by special interests, such as trade groups and professional associations.[428] Such licenses create "economic rents for licensed practitioners at the expense of excluded workers and consumers."[429]

The excessive use of occupational licensing has drawn pointed policy attention in recent years, and is an area of possible bipartisan consensus.[430] In 2016, the Obama administration called on states to reduce the prevalence of unnecessary and overly broad occupational licenses, and some states have taken steps to ease licensure requirements or enable license portability.[431] In 2016, Iowa ended a cosmetology license requirement for hair braiders, replacing them with state exams on health and sanitation.[432] In Louisiana, a 2017 law eased some of these onerous requirements, and adopted a policy to proactively and periodically review licensing requirements.[433] Although there has been some progress, overall reforms have been limited and modest.[434]

Another related employment impediment that forms a barrier to opportunity and mobility is the non-compete clause. A non-compete clause is a provision included in an employment contract that bars employees from working for a competitor for a specified period of time. Ostensibly, such measures are used to protect intellectual property, trade secrets or proprietary systems and to prevent other firms from luring talent for the purpose of gaining an unfair advantage. The most notorious examples arise out of Silicon Valley, including an agreement between Apple and Google, and another between Lucasfilm and Pixar, not to poach employees.[435]

While the use of non-compete clauses may be justified in some instances involving specialized employees or highly skilled experts, these clauses are routinely included in employment contracts for fast-food workers, janitors and custodial staff, and other low-wage workers.[436] One survey found that 30% of hair salon workers sign non-compete agreements.[437] According to another study, as many as one in five workers are now subject to non-compete clauses.[438] These practices are so abusive that the economist Alan Krueger has called them part of a "rigged market."[439]

A U.S. Department of Treasury analysis found that such clauses depress wages and reduce labor mobility.[440] The fundamental problem is that such provisions close off opportunities where workers have job-relevant skills. From an opportunity perspective, such clauses should be severely limited, especially for low-income workers.

Ideologically diverse states outright prohibit enforcement of such provisions, including California, Oregon, North Dakota, and Oklahoma.[441] A study evaluating Oregon's 2008 law found significant improvements for workers, in terms of pay and how often they changed jobs.[442] Other states have proposed legislation that would restrict enforcement or prohibit such agreements for certain kinds of workers, such as workers who earn $13 and hour or less, less than $900 a week, or special contractors or temporary workers.[443] However, such legislation predictably engenders stiff opposition from business interests.

At the federal level, efforts to curb such practices have been unsuccessful so far. In 2019, Republican Senator Marco Rubio introduced a bill, the Freedom to Compete Act, which would have prohibited non-compete clauses for low-income workers.[444] Although this bill has been reintroduced, it has not yet passed. In the interim, the Federal Trade Commission in 2023 proposed a rule that severely curtailed the practice, but it was successfully challenged in court.[445] Even where such clauses are prohibited or unenforceable, they too often go unchallenged by employees who are unaware of the law.

Occupational licenses, job skill or credential requirements, credit checks, non-compete, and criminal background checks are among many examples of potentially unnecessary barriers to opportunity that have proliferated beyond rational justification. An opportunity promoting society would carefully scrutinize any artificial barrier to opportunity to validate its existence, and even then, balance the benefits against the societal costs. These policies would not end racial economic inequality, but would ameliorate it while expanding access to opportunity for all.

10) Subsidize Core Capabilities and Critical Access Points

If opportunity requires the freedom to select and set upon a life path, there is not only a powerful affirmative role for government in clearing obstacles upon those pathways, but also for enhancing human capabilities to pursue those opportunities and easing or facilitating advancement along them.

Whereas the previous section dealt with the former (the clearing of obstacles), this final recommendation serves as a catch-all that encompasses the latter.

This book has documented the extent and origins of the racial wealth gap in the United States, which contributes to the unequal distribution of credit and access to credit. A growing international literature on experiments with microfinance broadly illustrates the importance of access to credit.[446] Too many individuals, regardless of talent, industriousness or ambition, are unable to start new businesses and pursue economic opportunity. The National Urban League co-produced a report that surveyed Black entrepreneurs, and found that they were often shut out of traditional financing opportunities and starved of venture capital.[447] Therefore, race-conscious policies that can survive legal challenge should be pursued to address this disparity.

Many businesses take years to turn a profit, and credit is needed to build and sustain these businesses before they become profitable. Microloans have a proven track record globally, and expanding such programs (with loans up to $50,000 or $100,000) for Black and Latino borrowers could provide a significant boost to long-term wealth creation and reducing the racial wealth gap. This is why banks in places like St. Louis, Philadelphia, and Iowa have announced microlending programs for Black borrowers.[448] Such loans allow entrepreneurs and small business owners to invest in equipment, supplies, and facilities. In addition, lower-cost loans could help disadvantaged communities or members of disadvantaged groups, especially if they have been locked out of traditional credit markets.[449] The problem is that many of these programs have been shut down by legislatures or successfully challenged in court in recent years.[450] They will need to be redesigned to survive legal challenge.

In addition to subsidizing borrowing or expanding access to capital, more should be done to invest in community banks, especially Black-owned banks. Only 18 of the more than 4,400 banks in the United States are owned by African-Americans, and they only have $4.4 billion in assets.[451] If these institutions had more capital, they could provide more credit to the communities they serve.[452] A related proposal, postal banking, would help many Americans gain a foothold in the financial system who may be reliant on the predatory institutions described earlier.[453]

One proposal aimed at reducing wealth inequality that has garnered considerable attention are "baby bonds," which would give every American a government-backed savings account at birth.[454] Although this idea could be implemented in a number of ways, the gist is that these accounts would grow with compounding interest after an initial investment, and allow beneficiaries—at some point in life—to draw from them to go to college, afford a home down payment, or start a business. For example, a Washington DC councilmember introduced a proposed that would create a trust account of up to $25,000 for babies born in the district into a household whose income does not exceed 500% of the federal poverty level. Enrollment would be automatic and upon turning 18, the child may withdraw the funds for specified purposes including education, business ownership, business investment, property ownership, and retirement investment.[455]

In addition to broadening access to credit and capital, an opportunity-enhancing policy agenda would subsidize other core capacities beyond public education, including expanding public transportation, childcare, and high-speed internet. Lack of high-quality, affordable, and convenient day care is massive barrier for many Americans to pursuing career ambitions or just trying to hold a job.[456] The United States is a notable outlier in not providing childcare to most parents as a public good.[457]

The U.S. government says that childcare should cost no more than 7% of a family's income, but it is far more expensive in most states.[458] The average cost of child care is more than $16,000 per year.[459] In 33 states and the District of Columbia, infant care costs exceed the average cost of in-state tuition at public four-year institutions.[460] For politicians who emphasize the importance of work, American child card and family leave policies form structural barriers to employment. The evidence suggests that more women participate in the labor force in countries that subsidize childcare and offer more generous leave policies.[461]

Researchers at the right-leaning American Enterprise Institute and left-leaning Brookings Institute have explained how the lack of paid family leave for new parents and affordable childcare impacts young parents' labor market participation rates, especially for young mothers.[462] This not only drags economic growth, but it impedes career development, as parents who cannot afford childcare are forced to stay at home.

But perhaps the most important conduit to opportunity is public infrastructure and transportation. Transit is the most flexible conduit to opportunity, and for connecting residents to more and better job prospects. Recall from Chapter 2 the analysis of the "spatial mismatch" problem, and the additional finding that reducing commute times is one of the most powerful tools for connecting lower-income people to opportunity.[463] A critical case can be made to provide more investments and subsidies for public transportation.

The number of commuters who travel 90 or more minutes to work (super or extreme commuters) is growing. One estimate found that the number of super-commuters rose by almost 50% from 2010 to 2019.[464] Overall, more than 3% or workers nationwide in 2019 were estimated to commute more than 90 minutes to work every day.[465] And in some regions, like the San Francisco Bay Area, that figure is above 5%.[466] Long commutes have many deleterious effects, including higher blood pressure and less sleep and time with family.[467]

Minimizing commute times should be a policy objective at every level of government. While part of the solution must be to construct more housing closer to jobs, for a large portion of super-commuters, distance is not the problem. It is the patchwork of transit options. We need public transit systems, high-speed rail, bus networks, and other infrastructure projects that can carry people from their homes to more jobs more efficiently in terms of

Realizing the American Dream 305

both time and cost. In Baltimore, fewer than one in three residents can get to work in under 90 minutes on public transportation.[468]

When commute times reach unbearable length, workers lose access to job opportunities. When parents must change bus lines multiple times on a one-way commute, it equates to less time at home with children. When bus networks that reach outer-ring suburbs require long waits in cold weather, delayed or inconsistent stops, job seekers are dissuaded from applying, let alone pursuing better job opportunities. Even if families would prefer to move to safer neighborhoods with better schools, low-income families who rely on public transit may be constrained not only by work commutes, but the challenges of getting children or teenagers to school.

There are transit solutions that do not require massive investments in expensive new infrastructure projects. Redeploying bus fleets strategically to reduce commute times can achieve the same objective while relying largely on existing infrastructure.[469] For example, designing bus routes that use dedicated bus lanes in areas with transit bottlenecks can help connect farther flung neighborhoods to business districts and commercial centers more efficiently regardless of existing traffic patterns.

Transportation is a critical element connecting workers to opportunities that would otherwise lie beyond their reach. When public transit does not extend to job opportunities in the regional outer-ring, workers must rely on automobiles. Beyond the expense of owning and maintaining a car, researchers found that two-thirds of young Black men in Milwaukee's poorest neighborhoods lack valid driver's licenses.[470] Across the U.S., too many low-income individuals who cannot afford to pay even a minor traffic ticket have had their license suspended or end up in an escalating cycle of fines and fees. The average license suspension duration in Wisconsin ended up being far longer for "failure to pay" than moving violations (24 months, compared to 6 for reckless driving and 12 for a hit-and-run).

Documents such as birth certificates, social security cards, identification cards, public university applications, and driver's licenses should be provided in a manner and basis that is as accessible and inexpensive as possible. Key conduits to opportunity, like driver's licenses, should not be made inaccessible as punishment for a general or unrelated offense, and then only as a last resort or for public safety reasons, such as driving unsafely or under the influence. Some employers require entry-level applicants to present a valid and current driver's license, even where driving is not a job qualification, to demonstrate a minimal level of responsibility.[471] Driver's licenses and other forms of identification are also commonly used to prove identity and therefore to access or apply for other important goods and services, such as bank accounts, home loans, to register to vote, or other vital documents, like passports and social security card and birth certificate replacements.

Another conduit to opportunity amenable to subsidy is broadband access and reliable high-speed internet. The so-called "digital divide" once described the gap between families or schools with computer technology and internet access and those without.[472] Most families are now connected to the internet, but for those without such access or without high-speed and reliable access, they are left further behind. Basic homework assignments, let alone tests, quizzes and research term papers, often require access to the internet.[473] Beyond educational purposes, the internet is a source of information about job opportunities, news, a way to pay bills, and much more.

In 2017, 30% of rural Americans lacked broadband access.[474] A more recent study pegs the overall figure at about 42 million Americans without such access.[475] The expansion of remote working arrangements in the wake of the Covid-19 pandemic make broadband access even more important as a conduit of opportunity, and a constraint on the capacity of businesses or industries to recruit new workers.[476] Flexible working corporate policies dramatically expand access to opportunity, potentially severing the link between residential proximity and job access, but only for job seekers with a quality internet connection and provider.[477]

Programs that subsidize broadband for low-income families or extend them to rural areas may be as essential this century as electrification was in the previous. Some federal initiatives help, but nothing on the scale that is currently needed.[478] Even ordinarily fiscally conservative business groups, such as the U.S. Chamber of Commerce and the Business Roundtable have called for federal support for the expansion of broadband.[479] A number of cities, nonprofits and private corporations are stepping into this breach. New York City, for example, supported a program called LinkNYC to provide free Wi-Fi in public spaces.[480] These initiatives should be expanded and scaled up.

***

This chapter offered an abundance of solutions to the problem of structural racial inequality paired with a goal of enlarging and expanding access to opportunity. Each of the broad policies proposed here are aimed at the contemporary opportunity structure and its racial effects, either by removing barriers to opportunities, proactively connecting more people to opportunity, endowing people with greater capacities to pursue opportunity, or spurring the generation of opportunity itself.

Yet, even if we adopt the agenda set out here, we may yet fall short. Accomplishing the goal of expanding the pathways of opportunity requires flexibility and adaptability to future conditions and toward individuality and human aspirations. Universal high school education was once an aspiration but is now an inadequate minimum. An opportunity agenda tailored to an agricultural or industrial society would be ill-suited for the digital information age and a service economy. History has shown that the structures of opportunity continually evolve, and new policy responses will be needed to extend and broaden those opportunities. Additionally, different strategies will be needed to support individuals who navigate those pathways at different speeds and styles.[481]

Therefore, it is not enough to focus on equalizing opportunity within existing institutional arrangements. New pathways and destinations will arise. Existing efforts will be inadequate to the task of helping reveal and navigate those pathways. The deeper need is greater structural perceptiveness, with policy solutions that seek not simply to remove blockages and widen bottlenecks within the control of a particular institution, but which take cognizance of the relationships between systems, institutions, and diverse actors. Armed with such perceptiveness, policymakers can move beyond band aids and stop gap solutions and transform relationships within the opportunity structure or the structure itself.

Notes

1. "Fast Facts," Kaiser Permanente, updated June 30, 2024, https://about.kaiserpermanente.org/who-we-are/fast-facts.
2. "Rosie the Riveter WWII Home Front," National Park Service, accessed December 27, 2021, https://www.nps.gov/rori/planyourvisit/placestogo.htm.
3. "The Guide to San Francisco's Mission District Murals," San Francisco Travel Guide, accessed April 29, 2024, https://www.sftravel.com/article/guide-to-san-franciscos-mission-district-murals.
4. Michael Mandel, *San Francisco and the Tech/Info Boom: Making the Transition to a Balanced and Growing Economy* (South Mountain Economics, 2014), https://data.bloomberglp.com/company/sites/2/2014/04/SouthMountain Economics_SF_TechInfo_Boom.pdf. About a third of those jobs were in the tech industry.
5. Hutson, *Urban Struggle*, 27.
6. "San Francisco's Mission District: The Controversial Gentrification," Smart Cities Dive, accessed December 27, 2021, https://www.smartcitiesdive.com/ex/sustainablecitiescollective/san-francisco-s-mission-district-controversial-gentrification/332586/.
7. "The San Francisco Rent Explosion Part III," *Priceonomics*, August 12, 2015, https://priceonomics.com/the-san-francisco-rent-explosion-part-iii/.
8. Lauren Hepler, "Poll Finds More Than Half of Bay Area Residents Plan to Leave for Good. Why? 'It's Housing, Stupid,'" *San Francisco Chronicle*, October 13, 2021, https://www.sfchronicle.com/bayarea/article/Poll-More-than-half-of-Bay-Area-residents-plan-16527796.php.
9. "Who We Are," Leaving the Bay Area, accessed December 27, 2021, https://www.leavingthebayarea.com/who-we-are/.
10. Kate Cimini, "'Not the Golden State Anymore': Middle- and Low-Income People Fleeing California," *The Californian*, January 7, 2020, https://www.thecalifornian.com/story/news/2020/01/07/california-residents-housing-crisis-rent-gas-taxes-gov-gavin-newsom ("The majority of people leaving the state reported an annual income below $100,000, while the state has seen an influx of those making $100,000 and above").
11. Florida, *New Urban Crisis*, xiv; Richard Florida, *The Rise of the Creative Class* (New York: Basic Books, 2002).
12. Drew Hendricks, "Incubators Help San Francisco Businesses Get Noticed," *Forbes*, March 19, 2014, https://web.archive.org/web/20140322012028/http://www.forbes.com/sites/drewhendricks/2014/03/19/incubators-help-san-francisco-businesses-get-noticed/.

13 Nelson D. Schwartz, "Why Corporate America Is Leaving the Suburbs for the City," *New York Times*, August 1, 2016, https://www.nytimes.com/2016/08/02/business/economy/why-corporate-america-is-leaving-the-suburbs-for-the-city.html.
14 Emily Badger and Darla Cameron, "Americans Are Paying More to Live in the Very Places They Once Abandoned," *Washington Post*, June 27, 2016, https://www.washingtonpost.com/news/wonk/wp/2016/06/27/americans-are-paying-more-to-live-in-the-very-places-they-once-abandoned/?noredirect=on.
15 Jackson, *Crabgrass Frontier*, 284, Table 16-1.
16 Wendell Cox, "Urban Cores, Core Cities, and Principal Cities," *New Geography*, August 1, 2014, https://www.newgeography.com/content/004453-urban-cores-core-cities-and-principal-cities.
17 One leading urbanist described this trend as the "great inversion". See Alan Ehrenhalt, *The Great Inversion and the Future of the American City* (New York: Alfred A. Knopf, 2012).
18 Paul Jargowsky, *The Architecture of Segregation: Civil Unrest, the Concentration of Poverty, and Public Policy* (New York: Century Foundation, 2015), 13–14, https://tcf.org/content/report/architecture-of-segregation/. See also Carr and Kutty, *Segregation*, 126.
19 William Frey, *Diversity Explosion: How New Racial Demographics are Remaking America*, 154, (Washington, DC: Brookings Institution Press, 2014).
20 Latifah Muhammad, "Black Residents Leaving New York, Chicago, Philadelphia, and Detroit in Reverse Migration," *Vibe*, July 24, 2018, https://www.vibe.com/news/national/reverse-migration-chicago-philly-nyc-black-populations-597314/; Chris Sommerfeldt and Dave Goldiner, "Black Population in NYC Down 4.5% over the Last Decade, Census Results Show—Brooklyn Sees Sharp Decline," *New York Daily News*, August 13, 2021, https://www.nydailynews.com/news/politics/new-york-elections-government/ny-census-results-new-york-city-black-new-yorkers-20210813-kqew232yyreddferawlcjvdnni-story.html.
21 *Between the Great Migration and Growing Exodus: The Future of Black Chicago?* (Chicago: Institute for Research on Race and Public Policy, 2020), https://uofi.app.box.com/s/vb27q325rrp2sipd8otjs2zawe7ufrue.
22 Elizabeth Burton, "DC's Population Growth Has Affected the Racial and Ethnic Composition of Wards 6, 7, and 8," *Urban Institute*, October 7, 2022, https://www.urban.org/urban-wire/dcs-population-growth-has-affected-racial-and-ethnic-composition-wards-6-7-and-8.
23 The Black population in Atlanta city decreased from 254,062 in 2000 to 233,018 in 2020, and the non-Hispanic white population grew from 130,222 to 192,148. "P004 Hispanic or Latino, and Not Hispanic or Latino by Race – 2000: DEC Summary File 1 – Atlanta city, Georgia," *United States Census Bureau*, 2000, https://data.census.gov/table/DECENNIALSF12000.P004?q=p004&g=160XX00US1304000; "P2 Hispanic or Latino, and Not Hispanic or Latino by Race – 2010: DEC Redistricting Data (PL 94-171) – Atlanta city, Georgia," *United States Census Bureau*, 2020, https://data.census.gov/table/DECENNIALPL2020.P2?q=p2&g=160XX00US1304000.
24 Thomas Fuller, "The Loneliness of Being Black in San Francisco, *New York Times*, July 20, 2016, https://www.nytimes.com/2016/07/21/us/black-exodus-from-san-francisco.html ("One of seven residents was black in 1970. Today, it is nearly one of 20, with most of the city's 46,000 blacks living in public housing").
25 Mahlia Posey, "A new Great Migration: The Disappearance of the Black Middle Class," *Richmond Confidential*, December 10, 2015, https://richmondconfidential.org/2015/12/10/a-new-great-migration-the-disappearance-of-the-black-middle-class/. See also Tony Roshan Samara, *Race, Inequality, and the Resegregation*

of the Bay Area (Oakland: Urban Habitat: 2016), https://urbanhabitat.org/sites/default/files/UH%20Policy%20Brief2016.pdf, for far more detailed regional changes in the composition of communities by race.
26 See Bruce Mitchell and Juan Franco, *HOLC "Redlining" Maps: The Persistent Structure of Segregation and Economic Inequality* (Washington, DC: National Community Reinvestment Coalition, 2018), 18, https://ncrc.org/wp-content/uploads/dlm_uploads/2018/02/NCRC-Research-HOLC-10.pdf.
27 Schafran, *Road to Resegregation*, 4.
28 Brian Resnick, Stephanie Stamm, and National Journal, "The State of Segregation in the Suburbs," *Atlantic*, January 7, 2015, https://www.theatlantic.com/politics/archive/2015/01/the-state-of-segregation-in-the-suburbs/453987/.
29 See Figure 2 from Logan, *Separate and Unequal*, 3.
30 Orfield, *American Metropolitics*, 7.
31 Elizabeth Kneebone, "Keynote" (speech, AHF Live: Housing Developers Forum, Arlington, VA, May 11, 2016). See also Elizabeth Kneebone and Alan Berube, *Confronting Suburban Poverty in America* (Washington, DC: Brookings Institution Press, 2013).
32 Logan, *Separate and Unequal*, 7. Although the schools in these older, inner-ring suburbs are better than their central city counterparts, they are considerably worse than their predominantly white counterparts in the suburbs. See Table 2.
33 Jargowsky, *Architecture of Segregation*, 2.
34 Ben Casselman, "The Poorest Corner of Town," *FiveThirtyEight*, August 26, 2014, https://fivethirtyeight.com/features/ferguson-missouri/.
35 Logan, *Separate and Unequal*, 8–9.
36 George Packer, "The Other France: Are the Suburbs of Paris Incubators of Terrorism?," *New Yorker*, August 24, 2015, https://www.newyorker.com/magazine/2015/08/31/the-other-france.
37 For such an attempt, see Stephen Menendian et al., *Structural Racism Remedies Repository* (Berkeley, CA: Othering & Belonging Institute, 2022), https://belonging.berkeley.edu/structural-racism-remedies-repository.
38 To "expand access to opportunity," per the discussion Chapter 1, tends to denote efforts to remove obstacles to opportunities or upon opportunity pathways, or to widen or open up those pathways so that more people can traverse them. The result of this is to give more people access to those opportunities, and therefore to move closer to equality of opportunity.
39 Fishkin calls this "opportunity pluralism." Fishkin, *Bottlenecks*, 17, 130. As one reviewer characterized his idea, "he replaces the substantive (but elusive to define) goal of equality of opportunity with a procedural goal to expand and diversify opportunities for everyone." Ann Cudd, review of *Bottlenecks, A New Theory of Equal Opportunity*, by Joseph Fishkin, Notre Dame Philosophical Reviews, June 25, 2014, http://www.anncudd.com/wp-content/uploads/2014/06/Bottlenecks.pdf.
40 See, for example, Oren Cass, "This Is What Elite Failure Looks Like," *New York Times*, July 6, 2024, https://www.nytimes.com/2024/07/06/opinion/populism-power-elites-politics.html (arguing against a mobility policy agenda).
41 As the metaphor of a "safety net" implies, some of these policies are not the same as programs focused on human capital formation. There is an ongoing debate about the relationship between safety net programs, economic security, and social mobility. See, for example, Martha Bailey et al., "Is the Social Safety Net a Long Term Investment? Large-Scale Evidence from the Food Stamps Program" (working paper, National Bureau of Economics, 2020): 37–39, https://www.nber.org/papers/w26942; Ross Douthat, "Two Premises on Poverty and Culture," *New York Times,* May 5, 2015, https://douthat.blogs.nytimes.com/2015/05/05/two-premises-on-poverty-and-culture/ (see premise 2). See also Jason Furman, "Smart Social Programs," *New York Times,* May 11, 2015, https://www.

nytimes.com/2015/05/11/opinion/smart-social-programs.html citing Anna Aizer et al., "The Long Term Impact of Cash Transfers to Poor Families," *American Economic Review* 106, no. 4 (2016): https://www.aeaweb.org/articles?id=10.1257%2Faer.20140529. See also Neil Irwin, "Supply-Side Economics, but for Liberals," *New York Times*, April 15, 2017, https://www.nytimes.com/2017/04/15/upshot/supply-side-economics-but-for-liberals.html (also mentioning the Mother's Pension study).

42 Minn. Stat. §§ 473F.01-.13 (1982). See Steven Dornfeld, "Affluent suburbs challenge Twin Cities' unique tax-base sharing law," *MinnPost*, September 22, 2011, https://www.minnpost.com/cityscape/2011/09/affluent-suburbs-challenge-twin-cities-unique-tax-base-sharing-law/; "Regional Tax Base Sharing," Regional Planning for a Sustainable Economy, archived April 16, 2016, accessed October 13, 2022, https://web.archive.org/web/20160416235830/http://www.regionalplans.org/featured-regional-planning-programs-and-issues/tax-base-sharing/.

43 Karen Baker, Steve Kinze, and Lung-Fai Wong, *Minnesota's Fiscal Disparities Program: Tax Base Sharing in the Twin Cities Metropolitan Area* (St. Paul: Research Department of the Minnesota House of Representatives, 1987).

44 *Study of the Metropolitan Area Fiscal Disparities Program* (St. Paul: Minnesota Department of Revenue, 2012), https://www.revenue.state.mn.us/sites/default/files/2018-11/fiscal-disparities-study-full-report.pdf.

45 Cutler and Glaeser, "Ghettos," 838, table 1.

46 Trounstine, *Segregation by Design*, 37.

47 For a good case study, see Rose, *Metaracism*, 136–141.

48 Brett Pulley and Brentin Mock, "Atlanta's Wealthiest and Whitest District Wants to Secede," *Bloomberg*, October 1, 2021, https://www.bloomberg.com/news/features/2021-10-01/buckhead-cityhood-vote-district-wants-to-secede-from-atlanta?leadSource=uverify%20wall. See also Miles Bryan, "How History Made This Atlanta Neighborhood a Secession Battleground," *Vox*, February 16, 2022, https://www.vox.com/2022/2/16/22937599/buckhead-atlanta-today-explained-noel-king; Thomas Wheatley, "Buckxit Won't Happen in 2022," *Axios*, February 11, 2022, https://www.axios.com/local/atlanta/2022/02/11/buckhead-atlanta-secession-buckxit-2022.

49 Nikole Hannah-Jones, "The Resegregation of Jefferson County," *New York Times*, September 6, 2017, https://www.nytimes.com/2017/09/06/magazine/the-resegregation-of-jefferson-county.html.

50 Despite her finding, she ultimately approved the secession plan and the creation of a separate school district. Fortunately, this decision was reversed on appeal. "Eleventh Circuit Reverses District Court Decision, Preventing Gardendale Secession from Alabama School District," *Legal Defense Fund*, February 13, 2018, https://www.naacpldf.org/press-release/eleventh-circuit-reverses-district-court-decision-preventing-gardendale-secession-from-alabama-school-district/.

51 Alvin Chang, "More affluent neighborhoods are creating their own school districts," *Vox*, April 17, 2019, https://www.vox.com/2019/4/17/18307958/school-district-secession-worsening-data; Rebecca Klein, "School District 'Secession' Is Segregation by Another Name," *HuffPost*, September 4, 2019, https://www.huffpost.com/entry/school-district-secession_n_5d6f03e5e4b0cdfe05774614, citing "Case Study: Jefferson County, AL," *EdBuild*, accessed January 26, 2023, https://edbuild.org/content/fractured#jeffco.

52 Genevieve Siegel-Hawley, Sarah Diem, and Erica Frankenberg, "The Disintegration of Memphis-Shelby County, Tennessee: School District Secession and Local Control in the 21st Century," *American Educational Research Journal* 55, no. 4 (2018): 651–692, https://doi.org/10.3102/0002831217748880.

53 Keith Dowding and Thanos Mergoupis, "Fragmentation, Fiscal Mobility, and Efficiency," *The Journal of Politics* 65, no. 4 (2003): 1204–1205, https://doi.org/10.1111/1468-2508.t01-1-00132.

54 Department of Justice, *Investigation of the Ferguson Police Department.*
55 Or, as Shapiro puts it, police became tax collectors, trolling for and extracting municipal fines. See Joseph Shapiro, "As Court Fees Rise, The Poor Are Paying The Price," *National Public Radio*, May 19, 2014, https://www.npr.org/2014/05/19/312158516/increasing-court-fees-punish-the-poor.
56 S.B. 5, 98th General Assembly (Mo. 2015), https://www.senate.mo.gov/16info/pdf-bill/comm/SB590.pdf. See also Stephen Deere, "'Sweeping' Court Reform Comes as Nixon Signs Bill to Cap Cities' Revenue, End Predatory Habits," *St. Louis Post-Dispatch*, July 10, 2015, https://www.stltoday.com/news/local/crime-and-courts/sweeping-court-reform-comes-as-nixon-signs-bill-to-cap/article_cafffb7e-b24d-5292-b7bb-84ef81c6e81d.html.
57 Jennifer S. Mann, "Municipalities Ticket for Trees and Toys, as Traffic Revenue Declines," *St. Louis Post-Dispatch*, May 24, 2015. The lawsuit: Whitner v. City of Pagedale, 4:15-cv-01655 (E.D. Mo. 2016). See Monica Davey, "Lawsuit Accuses Missouri City of Fining Homeowners to Raise Revenue," *New York Times*, November 4, 2015, https://www.nytimes.com/2015/11/05/us/lawsuit-accuses-missouri-city-of-fining-homeowners-to-raise-revenue.html.
58 *Forward Through Ferguson*, 35–36, cited in New York Times Editorial Board, "Policing for Profit in St. Louis County," *New York Times*, November 14, 2015, https://www.nytimes.com/2015/11/15/opinion/sunday/policing-for-profit-in-st-louis-county.html ("A state commission he convened has recommended consolidating police departments and municipal courts to save money").
59 *Overcoming the Challenges and Creating a Regional Approach to Policing in St. Louis City and County* (Washington, DC: Police Executive Research Forum, 2015), 71. https://www.policeforum.org/assets/stlouis.pdf.
60 Jackson, *Crabgrass Frontier*, 138–156.
61 Jackson, 142; Joseph Berger, "The 20 Years That Made New York City," *New York Times*, October 9, 2017, https://www.nytimes.com/2017/10/09/books/review/greater-gotham-mike-wallace.html. As this review notes, the annexation or consolidation effort was viewed in terms of achieving economic efficiency and avoiding "ruinous competition".
62 Jackson, *Crabgrass Frontier*, 146.
63 Jackson, *Crabgrass Frontier*, 147.
64 Jackson, *Crabgrass Frontier*, 153, citing Jon C. Teaford, *City and Suburb: The Political Fragmentation of Metropolitan America, 1850-1970* (Baltimore: Johns Hopkins University Press, 1979). "[T]he group that most vigorously supports metropolitan government are elite businessmen who live in the suburbs whose companies and livelihoods are associated with the larger city. By contrast, those people most opposed to metropolitan government are blue-collar homeowners in the suburbs who fear racial change and higher taxes."
65 Jackson, *Crabgrass Frontier*, 144.
66 Jackson, *Crabgrass Frontier*, 151.
67 Jackson, *Crabgrass Frontier*, 151.
68 William Fischel attributes the mounting reluctance and greater resistance of suburbs to consolidate with their larger neighbors to the widespread adoption of zoning practices in this period. With the advent of zoning, development could be controlled, and with it local governments could better control or direct their "fiscal destiny," making annexation and consolidation less attractive to suburbs. Fischel, *Zoning Rules*, 181-82. In contrast, the historian Kenneth Jackson emphasizes a different set of factors that explain the decline of annexation: (1) sharper racial, ethnic, and class distinctions, (2) new laws that made incorporation easier and annexation more difficult, and (3) improved suburban services. Although the development and proliferation of home rule laws in state constitutions made it easier to incorporate and harder for larger cities to annex their neighbors,

Jackson claims that it was demographics and evolving cultural perceptions of cities that was the overriding factor. Jackson, *Crabgrass Frontier*, 150–151.
69 Fabrizio Barca, Philip McCann, and Andrés Rodríguez-Pose, "The Case for Regional Development Intervention: Place-Based Versus Place-Neutral Approaches," *Journal of Regional Science* 52, no. 1 (2012): 134–152, https://doi.org/10.1111/j.1467-9787.2011.00756.x. See also Andrés Rodríguez-Pose and Callum Wilkie, "Revamping Local and Regional Development through Place-Based Strategies," *Cityscape: A Journal of Policy Development and Research* 19, no. 1 (2017): 151–170, https://www.jstor.org/stable/26328304.
70 Brett Thedos, *Platforms for Place-Based Development* (Washington, DC: Urban Institute, 2021), https://www.urban.org/sites/default/files/publication/104333/platforms-for-place-based-development.pdf.
71 One example was the New Deal flop of "Arthurdale." See C. J. Maloney, *Back to the Land: Arthurdale, FDR's New Deal, and the Costs of Economic Planning* (Hoboken, NJ: John Wiley & Sons, Inc, 2011).
72 powell and Menendian, "Opportunity Communities," 210.
73 "About Place-Based Initiatives," U.S. Department of Housing and Urban Development, accessed September 4, 2022, https://web.archive.org/web/20221126123529/https://www.hud.gov/program_offices/economic_development/place_based/about.
74 "Opportunity Zones Frequently Asked Questions," Internal Revenue Service, accessed September 4, 2022, https://www.irs.gov/credits-deductions/opportunity-zones-frequently-asked-questions#general.
75 Jennifer A. O'Day and Marshall S. Smith, "Quality and Equality in American Education: Systemic Problems, Systemic Solutions," in *Dynamics of Opportunity*, eds. Kirsch and Braun, 328.
76 Will Dobbie and Roland G Fryer, "Are High-Quality Schools Enough to Increase Achievement among the Poor?: Evidence from the Harlem Children's Zone," *American Economic Journal: Applied Economics* 3, no. 3 (2011): 169–179.
77 Sharkey, *Stuck in Place*, 194.
78 Andrés Rodríguez-Pose and Callum Wilkie, "Revamping Local and Regional Development through Place-Based Strategies," *Cityscape* 19, no. 1 (2017): 160.
79 Sharkey, *Stuck In Place*, 140.
80 Internal Revenue Service, "Opportunity Zones."
81 Jessie Drucker and Eric Lipton, "How a Trump Tax Break to Help Poor Communities Became a Windfall for the Rich," *New York Times*, August 31, 2019, https://www.nytimes.com/2019/08/31/business/tax-opportunity-zones.html.
82 "Transforming Anchor Institutions: A Toolkit for Community Organizers," Othering & Belonging Institute, accessed September 27, 2022, https://belonging.berkeley.edu/transforming-anchor-institutions.
83 See Richard Florida, "What the New Urban Anchors Owe Their Cities," *Citylab*, September 21, 2017, https://web.archive.org/web/20180217223000/https:/www.citylab.com/amp/article/540588/in.
84 "Anchor Strategies: Aligning the Interests of Anchors and Communities" (presentation, Design Access Summit, Oakland, February 19–21, 2014).
85 Richard Florida, *Miami's New Urban Crisis* (Miami: Florida International University, 2018), 20, September 21, 2022, https://digitalcommons.fiu.edu/cgi/viewcontent.cgi?article=1008&context=mufi-reports.
86 See Eli Moore, Nadia Barhoum, and Alexis Alvarez Franco, *Anchor Richmond: Community Opportunity & Anchor Strategies for the Berkeley Global Campus at Richmond Bay* (Berkeley: Othering and Belonging Institute, 2014), https://belonging.berkeley.edu/sites/default/files/HaasInstitute_AnchorStrategies_BerkeleyGlobalCampus_DISTRO_0.pdf.
87 AllTransit (website), *Center for Neighborhood Technology*, accessed January 17, 2023, https://alltransit.cnt.org/.

88 Mary Hui, "What City Bus Systems Can Tell Us about Race, Poverty and Us," *Washington Post*, September 7, 2017, https://www.washingtonpost.com/local/social-issues/what-city-bus-systems-can-tell-us-about-race-poverty-and-who-we-are/2017/09/07/6531d26a-9260-11e7-8754-d478688d23b4_story.html.

89 Joel Rose, "Public Transit Systems Try to Avoid a 'Death Spiral' as Remote Work Hurts Ridership," *NPR*, November 15, 2023, https://www.npr.org/2023/11/15/1212879398/public-transit-ridership-down-covid-pandemic-death-spiral.

90 Jessica Howington, "25 Companies Switching to Permanent Remote Work-From-Home Jobs," *FlexJobs*, https://www.flexjobs.com/blog/post/companies-switching-remote-work-long-term/.

91 Henry Holzer, *The Role of Skills and Jobs in Transforming Communities* (Philadelphia: Penn Institute for Urban Research and Federal Reserve Bank of Philadelphia, 2016), 2, https://www.penniur.upenn.edu/uploads/media/Holzer_PennIUR-Philly_Fed_working_paper_091416_(1).pdf.

92 David Card, Jesse Rothstein, and Moises Yi, *Location, Location, Location* (Washington, DC: United States Census Bureau, Center for Economic Studies, 2021), 37–39, https://www2.census.gov/ces/wp/2021/CES-WP-21-32.pdf. (Finding big productivity gains from moving to higher-wage metros. But housing costs more than offset average gains).

93 Sage Singleton, "Rent Control vs. Rent Stabilization: What's the Difference?," Apartment guide, October 24, 2019, archived November 11, 2020, at the Wayback Machine, https://web.archive.org/web/20201111174128/https://www.apartmentguide.com/blog/rent-control-vs-rent-stabilization/.

94 Arthur Acolin And Susan Wachter, *Opportunity and Housing Access* (Philadelphia: Penn Institute for Urban Research and Federal Reserve Bank of Philadelphia, 2016), https://www.penniur.upenn.edu/uploads/media/Acolin-Wachter_PennIUR-Philly_Fed_working_paper_091816.pdf.

95 Sharkey, *Stuck In Place*, 144, 176–178.

96 *Gautreaux*, 425 U.S. 284 (1976)

97 See James E. Rosenbaum et al., "Pathways into Work: Short- and Long-Term Effects of Personal and Institutional Ties," *American Sociological Association* 72, no. 3 (1999): 179–196, https://doi.org/10.2307/2673228; Sharkey, *Stuck in Place*, 142–143; Alexander Polikoff and Clarence Page, *Waiting for Gautreaux: A Story of Segregation, Housing, and the Black Ghetto* (Evanston, IL: Northwestern University Press, 2006).

98 James E. Rosenbaum, "Changing the Geography of Opportunity by Expanding Residential Choice: Lessons from the Gautreaux Program," *Housing Policy Debate* 6, no. 1 (1995): 242, Table 5, https://doi.org/10.1080/10511482.1995.9521186.

99 Edward Goetz, "Fair Share or Status Quo? The Twin Cities Livable Communities Act," *Journal of Planning Education and Research* 20, no. 1 (2000): 30, https://journals-sagepub-com.libproxy.berkeley.edu/doi/10.1177/07394560012899258; Edward Goetz, *Clearing the Way: Deconcentrating the Poor in Urban America* (Washington, DC: Urban Institute Press, 2003), 55–56; Edward Goetz, "Edward Goetz, SFSU's AHRI Distinguished Speaker 2018," recorded lecture, presented November 8, 2018, San Francisco State University, 21:30–31:00, https://www.youtube.com/watch?v=C76s1FNqa3s.

100 Jens Ludwig et al., *Moving to Opportunity for Fair Housing Demonstration Program: Final Impacts Evaluation* (Washington, DC: National Bureau of Economic Research, 2011), https://www.huduser.gov/publications/pdf/mtofhd_fullreport_v2.pdf; Ludwig, *Effects of Concentrated Poverty on the Poor*. Xavier De Souza Briggs, Susan J. Popkin, and John Goeing, *Moving to Opportunity: The Story of an American Experiment to Fight Ghetto Poverty* (Oxford: Oxford University Press, 2010).

101 Jeffrey Kling, Jeffrey Liebman, and Lawrence Katz, *Bullets Don't Got No Name: Consequences of Fear in the Ghetto* (Chicago: Joint Center for Poverty Research, 2001).
102 Sampson, "Moving to Inequality," 202, 205.
103 Polikoff and Page, *Waiting for Gautreaux*, 274. In contrast, the average control group family was in a census tract that was 88% minority. See also Ludwig, *Moving to Opportunity*, 13.
104 Chetty, Hendren, and Katz, "New Evidence from the Moving to Opportunity Experiment," 857.
105 David Kirk, "A Natural Experiment on Residential Change and Recidivism: Lessons from Hurricane Katrina," *American Sociological Review* 74, no. 3 (2009): 484–505, https://doi.org/10.1177/000312240907400308; Malcolm Gladwell, "Starting Over: Many Katrina Victims Left New Orleans for Good. What Can We Learn from Them?," *New Yorker*, August 17, 2015, https://www.newyorker.com/magazine/2015/08/24/starting-over-dept-of-social-studies-malcolm-gladwell.
106 Eric Chyn, "Moved to Opportunity: The Long-Run Effects of Public Housing Demolition on Children," *American Economic Review* 108, no. 10 (2018): 3028–3056, https://www.aeaweb.org/articles?id=10.1257/aer.20161352. For a description of the qualitative research, see Justin Wolfers, "Growing Up in a Bad Neighborhood Does More Harm Than We Thought," *New York Times*, March 25, 2016, https://www.nytimes.com/2016/03/27/upshot/growing-up-in-a-bad-neighborhood-does-more-harm-than-we-thought.html.
107 Santiago et al., *Opportunity Neighborhoods*, 15.
108 For example, neighborhoods with lower crime rates, less pollution, and higher walkability resulted in better physical and behavioral health outcomes for Latino and Black children. The crime rates, social status, and ethnic composition of neighborhoods could also help predict educational outcomes and labor market outcomes for these populations. Santiago et al., *Opportunity Neighborhoods*, 58, 146, 166.
109 Sharkey, *Stuck in Place*, 172–174, discussing Owen Fiss, "What Should Be Done for Those Who Have Been Left Behind?," *Boston Review* 25, no. 3 (2000): 1–8 and George Galster, "An Economic Efficiency Analysis of Deconcentrating Poverty Populations," *Journal of Housing Economics* 11 (2002): 303–329.
110 "Housing Choice Vouchers Fact Sheet," U.S. Department of Housing and Urban Development, accessed September 28, 2022, https://web.archive.org/web/20221230033509/https://www.hud.gov/topics/housing_choice_voucher_program_section_8.
111 Barbara Sard and Douglas Rice, *Realizing the Housing Voucher Program's Potential to Enable Families to Move to Better Neighborhoods* (Washington, DC: Center on Budget and Policy Priorities, 2016), https://www.cbpp.org/research/housing/realizing-the-housing-voucher-programs-potential-to-enable-families-to-move-to.
112 Kirk McClure, Alex Schwartz, and Lydia Taghavi, "Housing Choice Voucher Location Patterns a Decade Later," *Housing Policy Debate* 25, no. 2 (2014): 228, Table 6 https://doi.org/10.1080/10511482.2014.921223.
113 Alicia Mazzara and Brian Knudsen, "Where Families With Children Use Housing Vouchers: A Comparative Look at the 50 Largest Metropolitan Areas," *Center on Budget and Policy Priorities*, January 3, 2019, https://www.cbpp.org/research/housing/where-families-with-children-use-housing-vouchers.
114 U.S. Department of Housing and Urban Development, *Small Area Fair Market Rents*, accessed September 30, 2022, https://www.huduser.gov/portal/datasets/fmr/smallarea/index.html; Samuel Dastrup et al., *Small Area Fair Market Rent Demonstration Evaluation: Final Report* (Washington, DC: U.S. Department of Housing and Urban Development, 2018), https://www.huduser.gov/portal/sites/default/files/pdf/SAFMR-Evaluation-Final-Report.pdf, finding that "HCV holders in the SAFMR PHAs were more likely to live in higher-rent and

higher- opportunity ZIP Codes than they had prior to the demonstration. Households in comparison PHAs saw no change, so we conclude that the shift was due to the SAFMRs."

115 Richard J. Monocchio, "Notice PIH 2023-32, Area Fair Market Rent Implementation Guidance for FY2024 Designated Metropolitan Areas," *Department of Housing and Urban Development*, November 15, 2023, https://www.hud.gov/sites/dfiles/OCHCO/documents/2023-32pihn.pdf.

116 Jacqueline Rabe Thomas, "How Wealthy Towns Keep People With Housing Vouchers Out," *Propublica*, January 9, 2020, https://www.propublica.org/article/how-wealthy-towns-keep-people-with-housing-vouchers-out.

117 Appendix B: State, Local, and Federal Laws Barring Source-of-Income Discrimination" in *Expanding Choice: Practical Strategies for Building a Successful Housing Mobility Program* (Washington, DC: Poverty and Race Research Action Council, 2022), https://www.prrac.org/pdf/AppendixB.pdf.

118 "Low-Income Housing Tax Credit (LIHTC)," *HUD User*, accessed January 26, 2023, https://www.huduser.gov/portal/datasets/lihtc.html.

119 Kirk McClure, "The LIHTC Program, Racially/Ethnically Concentrated Areas of Poverty, and High-Opportunity Neighborhoods," *Texas A&M Journal of Property Law* 6, no. 2 (2020): 107, table 5, https://doi.org/10.37419/JPL.V6.I2.1.

120 Brief of Housing Scholars as *Amici Curiae* Supporting Respondent, Texas Department of Housing and Community Affairs, et al. v. The Inclusive Communities Project Inc., 576 U.S. 519 (2014), 72, Figure 9, https://belonging.berkeley.edu/sites/default/files/Amicus%20Brief%20EPI%20and%20Haas%20Institute%20Texas%20Housing%20Dec%202014.pdf.

121 Molly Scott et al., *Expanding Choice: Practical Strategies for Building a Successful Housing Mobility Program* (Washington, DC: Poverty and Race Research Action Council, 2013), https://www.prrac.org/pdf/ExpandingChoice.pdf.

122 Peter Bergman et al., "Creating Moves to Opportunity: Experimental Evidence on Barriers to Neighborhood Choice" (working paper, National Bureau of Economics, 2020), https://www.nber.org/papers/w26164.

123 Michelle Burris and Emma Britton Miller, "Bridges Collaborative Member Spotlight: A New Model for Combating Housing Segregation Post-Pandemic," *The Century Foundation*, June 17, 2021, https://tcf.org/content/commentary/bridges-spotlight-new-model-combating-housing-segregation-post-pandemic/?agreed=1. For background and overview of this litigation and families affected by it, see Lawrence Lanahan, *The Lines Between Us: Two Families and a Quest to Cross Baltimore's Racial Divide* (New York: New Press, 2019).

124 Chetty et al., "Opportunity Atlas," 6.

125 Maria Krysan and Kyle Crowder, *Cycle of Segregation: Social Processes and Residential Stratification* (New York: Russell Sage Foundation), 45.

126 Krysan and Crowder, *Cycle of Segregation*, 108–111.

127 Bergman et al., *Creating Moves to Opportunity*, 36–37.

128 Michael Strain, "A Jobs Agenda for the Right," *National Affairs* no. 18 (2014): https://www.nationalaffairs.com/publications/detail/a-jobs-agenda-for-the-right; Eli Lehrer and Lori Sanders, "Moving to Work," *National Affairs* no. 18 (2014): https://www.nationalaffairs.com/publications/detail/moving-to-work.

129 "Americans Need More Neighbors," *New York Times*, June 15, 2019, https://www.nytimes.com/2019/06/15/opinion/sunday/minneapolis-ends-single-family-zoning.html; "The Cities We Need," *New York Times*, May 11, 2020, https://www.nytimes.com/2020/05/11/opinion/sunday/coronavirus-us-cities-inequality.html; "Editorial: L.A. Can Begin to Solve Its Affordable Housing Crisis in 2021," *Los Angeles Times*, February 28, 2021, https://www.latimes.com/opinion/story/2021-02-28/los-angeles-housing-element; "Turns Out Los Angeles Voters Do Want Denser Housing in Single Family Neighborhoods," *Los Angeles Times*,

December 15, 2021, https://www.latimes.com/opinion/story/2021-12-05/editorial-turns-out-los-angeles-voters-do-want-denser-housing-in-single-family-neighborhoods; Stephen Menendian, "The $1-million home is becoming the norm in L.A. This is an outrage we could have prevented," *Los Angeles Times*, August 14, 2023, https://www.latimes.com/opinion/story/2023-08-14/los-angeles-la-california-median-home-price-1-million-housing-single-family-zoning-density.

130 Ilya Somin, "The Emerging Cross-Ideological Consensus on Zoning," *Washington Post*, December 5, 2021, https://www.washingtonpost.com/news/volokh-conspiracy/wp/2015/12/05/the-emerging-cross-ideological-consensus-on-zoning/; Vanessa Brown Calder, "Zoning Reform Is For Conservatives, Too," Cato Institute, February 29, 2019, https://www.cato.org/blog/zoning-reform-conservatives-too; Howard Husock, *Soho Forum: Government Caused Housing Segregation. Do We Need More Government to Fix the Problem?*, featuring Howard Husock and Richard Rothstein (2019; New York: Manhattan Institute), video, https://www.manhattan-institute.org/video/soho-forum-public-housing-government.

131 For more information on this, see Sanford Ikeda and Emily Hamilton, "How Land-Use Regulation Undermines Affordable Housing," *Mercatus Center*, November 4, 2015, https://www.mercatus.org/publications/regulation/how-land-use-regulation-undermines-affordable-housing. See also Sara Bronin, "Zoning by a Thousand Cuts," *Pepperdine Law Review* 50, no. 719 (2021): https://papers.ssrn.com/sol3/papers.cfm?abstract_id=3792544# (enumerating different restrictions).

132 Menendian, "Uneven March of Progress," 78–83; Gregg Colburn, *Homelessness is a Housing Problem: How Structural Factors Explain U.S. Patterns* (Oakland: University of California Press, 2022).

133 Sarah Mervosh, "Minneapolis, Tackling Housing Crisis and Inequity, Votes to End Single-Family Zoning," *New York Times*, December 13, 2018, https://www.nytimes.com/2018/12/13/us/minneapolis-single-family-zoning.html.

134 Emily Badger and Quoctrung Bui, "Cities Start to Question an American Ideal: A House With a Yard on Every Lot," *New York Times*, June 18, 2019, https://www.nytimes.com/interactive/2019/06/18/upshot/cities-across-america-question-single-family-zoning.html?module=inline.

135 Henry Grabar, "Minneapolis Confronts Its History of Housing Segregation," *Slate*, December 7, 2018, https://slate.com/business/2018/12/minneapolis-single-family-zoning-housing-racism.html.

136 Joshua Cantong, Stephen Menendian, and Samir Gambhir, "Zoning Reform Tracker," *Othering and Belonging Institute*, March 15, 2023, last updated April 18, 2025, https://belonging.berkeley.edu/zoning-reform-tracker. See also Karina French, "Decoding Zoning: Regulation and Reform in California," *Othering and Belonging Institute*, May 13, 2021, https://belonging.berkeley.edu/decoding-zoning.

137 Stephen Menendian, Samir Gambhir, and Chih-Wei Hsu, "Single-Family Zoning in Greater Los Angeles," *Othering and Belonging Institute*, March 2, 2022, https://belonging.berkeley.edu/single-family-zoning-greater-los-angeles (finding that 72% of the LA region's residential land is restricted to single-family homes only, with a median of about 78%, and that only 11.80% of such land is available for multi-family developments).

138 Laurel Wamsley, "Oregon Legislature Votes to Essentially Ban Single-Family Zoning," *NPR*, July 1, 2019, https://www.npr.org/2019/07/01/737798440/oregon-legislature-votes-to-essentially-ban-single-family-zoning.

139 Menendian, "Uneven March of Progress," 102–103.

140 Menendian, "Uneven March of Progress," 105–106.

141 Laura Bliss, "The Political Battle Over California's Suburban Dream," *Bloomberg CityLab*, April 5, 2019, https://www.bloomberg.com/news/articles/2019-04-05/the-suburbs-that-fear-california-s-housing-bill.
142 Jessica Chuidian-Ingersoll, "No on Wiener's 'Gentrification Bomb' SB 50," *Tenants Together Action Fund*, April 19, 2019, https://web.archive.org/web/20210614141352/https://www.tenantaction.org/no_sb50. Their main concern is that zoning liberalization will increase the value of the land and increase the incentives for landowners to sell or redevelop properties, likely at market rates.
143 "Housing development: approvals," S.B. 9, 2021-2022 S., Reg. Sess. (Cal. 2021), https://leginfo.legislature.ca.gov/faces/billNavClient.xhtml?bill_id=202120220SB9. See also Manuela Tobias, "Duplex Housing Law Met with Fierce Resistance by California Cities," *CalMatters*, April 11, 2022, https://calmatters.org/housing/2022/04/duplex-housing-resistance/.
144 Ben Metcalf et al., *Will Allowing Duplexes and Lot Splits of Parcels Zoned for Single-Family Create New Homes?: Assessing the Viability of New Housing Supply Under California's Senate Bill 9* (Berkeley, CA: Terner Center for Housing Innovation, 2021), 9, https://ternercenter.berkeley.edu/wp-content/uploads/2021/07/SB-9-Brief-July-2021-Final.pdf. See also Aldo Toledo, "Lot-Split Law Hasn't Made a Ripple in Bay Area's Single-Family Neighborhoods," *East Bay Times*, April 3, 2022, https://www.eastbaytimes.com/2022/04/03/lot-split-law-hasnt-made-a-ripple-in-bay-areas-single-family-neighborhoods/.
145 Christopher Robert Berry, "Land Use Regulation and Residential Segregation: Does Zoning Matter?," *American Law and Economics Review* 3, no. 2 (2001): 251–274, https://academic.oup.com/aler/article-abstract/3/2/251/115515?redirectedFrom=fulltext.
146 *The Cost of Building Housing Series* (Berkeley, CA: Terner Center for Housing Innovation, 2020), https://ternercenter.berkeley.edu/research-and-policy/the-cost-of-building-housing-series/; David Garcia and Ben Metcalf, "Making It Pencil: Can We Get Housing for Middle-Income Households to Work?," *Terner Center for Housing Innovation*, May 16, 2024, https://ternercenter.berkeley.edu/research-and-policy/middle-income-development-math/.
147 Mitchell Crispell, Karolina Gorska, and Somaya Abdelgany, *Inclusionary Zoning Policy Brief* (Berkeley, CA: University of California, Berkeley – Urban Displacement Project, 2016), https://www.urbandisplacement.org/sites/default/files/images/urbandisplacementproject_inclusionaryhousingbrief_feb2016.pdf.
148 See Robert Hickey, Lisa Sturtevant, and Emily Thaden, *Achieving Lasting Affordability Through Inclusionary Housing* (Cambridge, MA: Lincoln Institute of Land Policy, 2014), https://www.lincolninst.edu/publications/working-papers/achieving-lasting-affordability-through-inclusionary-housing. See also Inclusionary Housing, accessed October 7, 2022, https://inclusionaryhousing.org/; Emily Thaden and Ruoniu Wang, "Inclusionary Housing in the United States: Prevalence, Impact, and Practices" (working paper, Lincoln Institute of Land Policy, 2017), 26, https://www.lincolninst.edu/sites/default/files/pubfiles/thaden_wp17et1_0.pdf.
149 Hickey, Sturtevant, and Thaden, "Inclusionary Housing," 18–19.
150 For an analysis of inclusionary zoning ordinances in San Francisco, Ayse Pamuk and Jeremy Hill, "Inclusionary Housing in San Francisco: Mapping Racial Integration, Neighborhood Change, and Affordability" (working paper, San Francisco State University Center for Applied Housing Research, 2019), 11, https://pace.sfsu.edu/sites/default/files/documents/cahr-working-papers-2019-a-pamuk-j-hill.pdf.
151 Heather Schwartz, *Housing Policy Is School Policy: Economically Integrative Housing Promotes Academic Success in Montgomery County, Maryland* (New York: The Century Foundation, 2010), 4, https://production-tcf.imgix.net/assets/downloads/tcf-Schwartz.pdf.

152 Schwartz, *Housing Policy is School Policy*, 7; Constantine E. Kontokosta, "Mixed-Income Housing and Neighborhood Integration: Evidence from Inclusionary Zoning Programs," *Journal of Urban Affairs* 36, no. 4. https://doi.org/10.1111/juaf.12068.

153 Kriti Ramakrishnan, Mark Treskon, and Solomon Greene, *Inclusionary Zoning: What Does the Research Tell Us about the Effectiveness of Local Action?* (Washington, DC: Urban Institute, 2019), https://www.urban.org/sites/default/files/publication/99647/inclusionary_zoning._what_does_the_research_tell_us_about_the_effectiveness_of_local_action_2.pdf. Fischel also argues that inclusionary zoning ordinances are a "tax on homebuilders" which results in fewer homes in total, and "so maintains the higher prices of existing homes. Fischel, *Zoning Rules*, 280–281, citing Jenny Schuetz, Rachel Meltzer, and Vicki Been, "Silver bullet or trojan horse? The effects of inclusionary zoning on local housing markets in the United States," *Urban Studies* 48, no. 2 (2011): 297–329, https://doi.org/10.1177/0042098009360683.

154 *Mount Laurel*, 336 A.2d. 724 (1975).

155 "Mount Laurel Doctrine," Fair Share Housing Center, https://web.archive.org/web/20220614055300/https://www.fairsharehousing.org/mount-laurel-doctrine/. See also Douglas S. Massey et al., *Climbing Mount Laurel: The Struggle for Affordable Housing and Social Mobility in an American Suburb* (Princeton, NJ: Princeton University Press, 2013), for a comprehensive account or David D. Troutt, *The Price of Paradise: The Costs of Inequality and a Vision for a More Equitable America* (New York: New York University Press, 2013), 67–70, for a concise narrative of the Mount Laurel saga.

156 "New Jersey Fair Housing Act," N.J. Stat. § 52:27D-301, https://ahpnj.org/pdfs/fha.pdf.

157 See Troutt, *The Price of Paradise*, 69 for a full description of Regional Contribution Agreements (RCAs) ("Over many years, cities like Newark became 'destination hubs' for spokes of sending activity from all over North and Central New Jersey").

158 Brent Johnson, "N.J. Supreme Court Rebukes Christie Administration, Puts Courts in Charge of Affordable Housing," *NJ.com*, March 10, 2015, https://www.nj.com/politics/2015/03/nj_supreme_court_rebukes_christie_administration_puts_courts_in_charge_of_affordable_housing.html.

159 Laura Denker, "N.J. Supreme Court Affirms 'Gap Period' Needs, Rejects Towns' Attempts to Exclude Thousands," *Fair Share Housing Center*, January 18, 2017, https://web.archive.org/web/20210507034808/https://fairsharehousing.org/blog/entry/n.j.-supreme-court-affirms-gap-period-needs-rejects-towns-attempts-to-exclu/.

160 Carolina K. Reid, Carol Galante, and Ashley F. Weinstein-Carnes, "Borrowing Innovation, Achieving Affordability: What We Can Learn from Massachusetts Chapter 40B" (working paper, Terner Center for Housing Innovation, 2016), https://ternercenter.berkeley.edu/wp-content/uploads/pdfs/California_40B_Working_Paper.pdf, citing Mass. Gen. Laws. ch. 40B, § 20–23 (1969).

161 Fischel, *Zoning Rules*, 150.

162 Conn. Gen. Stat. § 8-30g (1991).

163 Matt A.V. Chaban, "In Wealthy Pocket of Connecticut, an Innovative Approach to Affordable Housing," *New York Times*, April 25, 2016, https://www.nytimes.com/2016/04/26/nyregion/in-wealthy-pocket-of-connecticut-an-innovative-approach-to-affordable-housing.html.

164 "Housing: Regional Housing Needs Assessment," Southern California Association of Governments, https://scag.ca.gov/housing; "Housing Elements," California Department of Housing and Community Development, https://www.hcd.ca.gov/housing-elements-hcd.

165 Nikie Johnson, "Report card: How we graded every city, county in California on meeting RHNA housing permit goals," *Mercury News*, February 1, 2021,

https://www.mercurynews.com/2021/02/01/report-card-how-we-graded-every-city-county-in-california-on-meeting-rhna-housing-permit-goals/. Or work to undermine the process of setting targets. See Heather Bromfield and Eli Moore, *Unfair Shares: Racial Disparities and the Regional Housing Needs Allocation Process in the Bay Area* (Berkeley: Othering and Belonging Institute, 2017), https://haasinstitute.berkeley.edu/sites/default/files/haasinstitute_unfairshares_rhnabayarea_publish.pdf.

166 "Land use: housing element," S.B. 828, 2017-2018 S., Reg. Sess. (Cal. 2018), https://leginfo.legislature.ca.gov/faces/billNavClient.xhtml?bill_id=201720180SB828; Irwin Dawid, "Regional Housing Needs Allocation Reform Bill on Gov. Brown's Desk,' *Planetizen*, September 25, 2018, https://www.planetizen.com/news/2018/09/100755-regional-housing-needs-allocation-reform-bill-gov-browns-desk.

167 john a. powell, "Injecting a Race Component into Mount-Laurel Style Litigation," *Seton Hall Law Review* 27, no. 4 (1997): 1380.

168 John Charles Boger, "Toward Ending Residential Segregation: A Fair Share Proposal for the Next Reconstruction," *North Carolina Law Review* 71, no. 5 (1993): 1598–1599.

169 Troutt, *The Price of Paradise*, 79.

170 "Mrs. Murphy" being a proverbial Irish live-in landlord with ethnic prejudices. See James D. Walsh, "Reaching Mrs. Murphy: A Call for Repeal of the Mrs. Murphy Exemption to the Fair Housing Act," *Harvard Civil Rights-Civil Liberties Law Review* 34 (1999): 605–634, https://harvardcrcl.org/wp-content/uploads/sites/10/2015/07/Reaching-Mrs.-Murphy-A-Call-for-Repeal-of-the-Mrs.-Murphy-Exemption-to-the-Fair-Housing-Act.pdf.

171 Fair Housing Amendments Act of 1988, Pub. L. No. 100–430, 102 Stat. 1619 (amending 42 U.S.C. §§ 3601–3619); Ware, "New Weapons," 87–96.

172 Sander, Kucheva, and Zasloff, *Moving Toward Integration*, 146–147.

173 See, for example, Sander, Kucheva, and Zasloff, *Moving Toward Integration*, 7–8 (summarizing the literature).

174 The theory behind disparate impact liability was covered in Chapter 4, but the Fair Housing Act's textual basis is the phrase "or otherwise make unavailable or deny" housing on the basis of a protected category. Fair Housing Act, 42 U.S.C. § 3604 (1968).

175 Texas Dept. of Housing and Community Affairs v. Inclusive Communities Project, Inc., 576 U.S. 519 (2015).

176 "Implementation of the Fair Housing Act's Discriminatory Effects Standard," HUD, 24 C.F.R. § 100 (2013), https://www.federalregister.gov/d/2013-03375; "Discriminatory effect prohibited," 24 C.F.R. § 100.500 (2014), https://www.ecfr.gov/current/title-24/section-100.500. The 2013 rule defined "discriminatory effects" as "A practice [that] actually or predictably results in a disparate impact on a group of persons or creates, increases, reinforces, or perpetuates segregated housing patterns because of race." 24 C.F.R. § 100.500a. Although the intervening Trump administration diluted the rule, the Biden administration subsequently revived it. HUD, "Reinstatement of HUD's Discriminatory Effects Standard"; Richard J. Andreano Jr., "HUD reinstates 2013 Fair Housing Act disparate impact rule," *Ballard Spahr LLP Consumer Finance Monitor*, March 20, 2023, https://www.consumerfinancemonitor.com/2023/03/20/hud-reinstates-2013-fair-housing-act-disparate-impact-rule/.

177 Fair Housing Act, 42 U.S.C. § 3608(e)(5), 3608(d) (1968). This requirement has also been held to apply to state and local grantees. Otero v. New York City Housing Authority, 484 F. 2d 1122 (1973).

178 Housing and Community Development (HCD) Act of 1974, 43 U.S.C. § 5301 (1974), https://files.hudexchange.info/resources/documents/Housing-and-Community-

Development-Act-1974.pdf; "Explore CDBG Programs," HUD Exchange, https://www.hudexchange.info/programs/cdbg/.
179 New York Times Editorial Board, "Ben Carson vs. the Fair Housing Act," *New York Times*, May 13, 2018, https://www.nytimes.com/2018/05/13/opinion/ben-carson-hud-fair-housing-act.html.
180 Roisman, "Affirmatively Furthering Fair Housing."
181 24 C.F.R. § 5.152. See also *Affirmatively Furthering Fair Housing Rule Guidebook* (Washington, DC: U.S. Department of Housing and Urban Development, 2015), https://www.nhlp.org/wp-content/uploads/HUD-AFFH-Rule-Guidebook-Dec.-2015.pdf.
182 "Affirmatively Furthering Fair Housing," *Federal Register* 80, no. 136 (2015): 42309, https://www.federalregister.gov/documents/2015/07/16/2015-17032/affirmatively-furthering-fair-housing.
183 "Community Development Block Grant," HUD Exchange, accessed September 3, 2024, https://www.hudexchange.info/programs/cdbg/.
184 Hannah-Jones, "Living Apart."
185 Matt Taibbi, *Griftopia: Bubble Machines, Vampire Squids, and the Long Con that is Breaking America* (New York: Spiegel & Grau, 2010), 37 (describing organizing to oppose enforcement); "Westchester's Tortured Road," *New York Times*, June 12, 2015, https://www.nytimes.com/2015/06/13/opinion/westchesters-tortured-road.html. See also "Report on Zoning of Westchester Municipalities and the Perpetuation of Segregation and Creation of Disparate Impact," United States of America *ex rel.* Anti-Discrimination Center of Metro New York v. Westchester County, 96-CV-2860 (S.D.N.Y. 2016), https://www.antibiaslaw.com/sites/default/files/592-1%20-%20Expert%20Report%202016%20%2005%2011.pdf.
186 Stanley Kurtz, "How Obama Stole Dubuque," *National Review*, January 13, 2016, https://www.nationalreview.com/corner/affh-preview-obamas-hud-takes-over-dubuque-iowa/; Barone, "HUD's 'disparate impact' war."
187 Local Zoning Decisions Protection Act of 2017, H.R. 482, 115th Cong. (2017); Preserving Community and Neighborhood Choice, 24 C.F.R. § 5.150 (2020).
188 Affirmatively Furthering Fair Housing, 24 C.F.R. § 5 (2023), https://www.ecfr.gov/current/title-24/part-5/subject-group-ECFRb064b8192adda7c; Stephen Menendian, "Affirmatively Furthering Fair Housing in 2023," *Othering and Belonging Institute* (blog), April 21, 2023, https://belonging.berkeley.edu/affirmatively-furthering-fair-housing-2023.
189 Ashleigh Fields, "HUD secretary announcing elimination of rule Trump warned would 'destroy the value of houses'," *The Hill*, February 26, 2025, https://thehill.com/homenews/administration/5165960-hud-trump-zoning-rule-termination/.
190 Claudia Dale Goldin and Lawrence Katz, *The Race between Education and Technology: How America Once Led and Can Win the Race for Tomorrow* (Cambridge, MA: Harvard University Press, 2010). See also David Leonhardt, "The Roots of Obama's Ambitious College Plan," *New York Times*, January 8, 2015, https://www.nytimes.com/2015/01/09/upshot/the-roots-of-obamas-ambitious-college-plan.html.
191 Eduardo Porter, "Government Must Play a Role Again in Job Creation," *New York Times*, May 10, 2016, https://www.nytimes.com/2016/05/11/business/economy/as-jobs-vanish-forgetting-what-government-is-for.html.
192 "U.S. Education Spending Tops Global List, Study Shows," *CBS News*, June 25, 2013, https://www.cbsnews.com/news/us-education-spending-tops-global-list-study-shows/.
193 "U.S. Education Spending," *CBS*. Due to the state cutbacks in public education in the wake of the Great Recession, the desire to raise private funds has intensified. Daniel Farrie and David Sciarra, *$600 Billion Lost: State Disinvestment in*

Education Following the Great Recession (Newark, NJ: Education Law Center, 2020), https://edlawcenter.org/research/$600-billion-lost.html.
194 Jonathan Rabinovitz, "Local education Inequities Across U.S. Revealed in New Stanford Data Set," *Stanford News*, April 19, 2016, https://news.stanford.edu/2016/04/29/local-education-inequities-across-u-s-revealed-new-stanford-data-set/.
195 Missouri v. Jenkins, 515 U.S. 70 (1995).
196 *Missouri*, 515 U.S. 70 at 76.
197 *Missouri*, 515 U.S. 70 at 75.
198 *Missouri*, 515 U.S. 70 at 79. ("The annual cost per pupil at the KCMSD far exceeds that of the neighboring SSD's [surrounding school districts] or of any school district in Missouri"); *Missouri*, 515 U.S. 70 at 99 ("Per-pupil costs within the SSD, excluding capital costs, range from 2854 to 5956, compared to 7665.18 for KCMSD"). See Cashin, *Place Not Race*, 30.
199 *Missouri*, 515 U.S. 70 at 159n.
200 *Missouri*, 515 U.S. 70 at 78, citing Jenkins v. Missouri, 19 F.3d 393 at 397 (W.D.Mo. 1985).
201 The Court approvingly noted a dissenting opinion from the appellate court stating that "the KSCD students have in place a system that offers more educational opportunity than anywhere in America," but that the case "involves an exercise in pedagogical sociology, not constitutional adjudication." *Missouri*, 515 U.S. 70 at 83, citing Jenkins v. Missouri, 11 F.3d 755 (8th Cir. 1994).
202 Missouri v. Jenkins, 495 U.S. 33 (1990).
203 *Missouri*, 515 U.S. 70 at 86–103.
204 Lafortune, Rothstein, and Schanzenbach, "School Finance Reform."
205 EdBuild, *$23 Billion*.
206 Brown, Sargrad, and Brenner, *Hidden Money*.
207 Goldstein, "PTA Gift for Someone Else's Child?" (Not surprisingly, there has also been a secession effort in this district as well.)
208 W. Stephen Barnett et al., *The State of Preschool 2016* (New Brunswick, NJ: National Institute for Early Education Research, 2017), 12, https://nieer.org/wp-content/uploads/2017/09/Full_State_of_Preschool_2016_9.15.17_compressed.pdf.
209 Libby Stanford, "Which States Offer Universal Pre-K? It's More Complicated Than You Might Think," *EdWeek*, January 25, 2023, https://www.edweek.org/teaching-learning/which-states-offer-universal-pre-k-its-more-complicated-than-you-might-think/2023/01; Monica Potts, "Why More States Don't Have Universal Pre-K," *FiveThirtyEight*, February 3, 2023, https://fivethirtyeight.com/features/everyone-agrees-that-universal-pre-k-is-important-so-why-dont-more-states-have-it/.
210 *Education at a Glance 2014* (Paris, France: Organization for Economic Cooperation and Development, 2015), 6, https://www.oecd.org/en/publications/2014/09/education-at-a-glance-2014_g1g44022.html; Juliana Herman, Sasha Post, and Scott O'Halloran, *The United States Is Far Behind Other Countries on Pre-K* (Washington, DC: Center for American Progress, 2013), https://www.americanprogress.org/article/the-united-states-is-far-behind-other-countries-on-pre-k/ (describing 50% preschool enrollment in the United States compared to at least 90% in France and Italy).
211 Greg J. Duncan and Katherine Magnuson, "Investing in Preschool Programs," *Journal of Economic Perspectives* 27, no. 2 (2013): 109, https://pubs.aeaweb.org/doi/pdf/10.1257/jep.27.2.109.
212 Ajay Chaudry et al., *Child Care Choices of Low Income Working Families* (Washington, DC: Urban Institute, 2011), 26–27, https://www.urban.org/sites/default/files/publication/27331/412343-Child-Care-Choices-of-Low-Income-Working-Families.PDF.

213 Pew Research Center, "Child care and education: quality, availability and parental involvement," in *Parenting in America: Outlook, worries, aspirations are strongly linked to financial situation* (Pew Research Center, 2015), https://www.pewresearch.org/social-trends/2015/12/17/4-child-care-and-education-quality-availability-and-parental-involvement/.

214 Claire Cain Miller, "Which of These 4 Family Policies Deserves Top Priority?," New York Times, October 13, 2021, https://www.nytimes.com/2021/10/13/upshot/of-four-family-policies-in-democrats-bill-which-is-most-important.html; Jeffrey M. Jones, "In U.S., 70% Favor Federal Funds to Expand Pre-K Education," *Gallup*, September 8, 2014, https://news.gallup.com/poll/175646/favor-federal-funds-expand-pre-education.aspx.

215 David J. Armor and Sonia Sousa, "The Dubious Promise of Head Start," *National Affairs*, Winter 2014, https://www.nationalaffairs.com/publications/detail/the-dubious-promise-of-universal-preschool.

216 Grover J. "Rust" Whitehurst, "New Evidence Raises Doubts on Obama's Preschool for All," *Brookings*, November 20, 2013, https://www.brookings.edu/research/new-evidence-raises-doubts-on-obamas-preschool-for-all/; Michael Puma et al., *Head Start Impact Study: Final report, Executive Summary*, (Washington, DC: Administration for Children and Families, 2010), https://www.acf.hhs.gov/sites/default/files/documents/opre/executive_summary_final_508.pdf and Michael Puma et al., *Third Grade Follow-up to the Head Start Program Impact Study: Final Report*, (Washington, DC: Administration for Children and Families, 2012), https://www.acf.hhs.gov/sites/default/files/documents/opre/head_start_report_0.pdf. Although there are studies that found longer-term positive effects of Head Start for children and families. See Duncan and Magnuson, "Investing," 118; Terri J. Sabol and Lindsay Chase-Lansdale, "The Influence of Low Income Children's Participation in Head Start on their Parents' Education and Employment," *Journal of Policy Analysis and Management* 34, no. 1 (2014): https://onlinelibrary.wiley.com/doi/abs/10.1002/pam.21799.

217 James J. Heckman and Tim Kautz, "Hard Evidence on Soft Skills," *Labour Economics* 19, no. 4 (2012): 462, https://doi.org/10.1016/j.labeco.2012.05.014; James J. Heckman and Tim Kautz, "Fostering and Measuring Skills: Interventions that Improve Character and Cognition" in *The Myth of Achievement Tests: The GED and the Role of Character in American Life* (Chicago: University of Chicago Press, 2014), 341–430.

218 Timothy J. Bartik and Brad J. Hershbein, "Pre-K Effectiveness at a Large Scale," *W.E. Upjohn Institute for Employment Research* (2018): https://doi.org/10.17848/pb2018-2 and Kathy Hirsh-Pasek et al., "Making Pre-K Work: Lessons from the Tennessee Study," *Brookings*, February 28, 2022, https://www.brookings.edu/blog/education-plus-development/2022/02/28/making-pre-k-work-lessons-from-the-tennessee-study/.

219 Armor and Sousa, "Dubious Promise of Head Start."

220 Sarah Trumble and Janae Erickson Hatalsky, *Making Pre-K Matter: Instilling a Mobility Mentality* (Washington, DC: Third Way, 2014), 1, https://www.thirdway.org/report/making-pre-k-matter-instilling-a-mobility-mentality.

221 Guthrie Gray-Lobe, Parag A. Pathak, and Christopher R. Walters, "The Long-Term Effects of Universal Preschool in Boston," *Quarterly Journal of Economics* 138, no. 1 (2022): 363–411, https://doi.org/10.1093/qje/qjac036.

222 Jorge Luis García et al., "The Dynastic Benefits of Early Childhood Education" (working paper, National Bureau of Economics, 2021): 3, Table 1, https://www.nber.org/papers/w29004.

223 Lilia Vega, "The History of UC Tuition since 1868," *Daily Cal*, December 22, 2014, https://www.dailycal.org/archives/the-history-of-uc-tuition-since-1868/article_12b00b4e-5074-5830-8d89-99fd3bbc148c.html.

224 Gordon, *Rise and Fall of American Growth*, 606.
225 David H. Autor, "Work of the Past, Work of the Future" (lecture, Richard E. Ely Lecture, American Economic Association Annual Meeting, Atlanta, GA, January 4, 2019), 3:26, https://www.aeaweb.org/webcasts/2019/aea-distinguished-lecture-work-of-the-past-work-of-the-future.
226 U.S. Bureau of Labor Statistics, "Employment Status of the Civilian Population 25 Years and Over by Educational Attainment," modified October 7, 2022, https://www.bls.gov/news.release/empsit.t04.htm.
227 David Leonhardt, "America's Great Working-Class Colleges," *New York Times*, January 18, 2017, https://www.nytimes.com/2017/01/18/opinion/sunday/americasgreat-working-class-colleges.html, citing Chetty et al., "Mobility Report Cards" (The new data shows, for example, that the City University of New York system propelled almost six times as many low-income students into the middle class and beyond as all eight Ivy League campuses, plus Duke, M.I.T., Stanford and Chicago, combined). There is also an interactive look-up feature: "Economic Diversity and Student Outcomes at America's Colleges and Universities: Find Your College," *New York Times: The Upshot*, https://www.nytimes.com/interactive/projects/college-mobility/.
228 Chetty et al., "Mobility Report Cards," 67, Table IV, showing how state schools are excellent at moving students from bottom 20% to top 20%, while elite institutions are great at moving a smaller number of students from bottom 20% to top 1%.
229 Steven Rattner, "We're Making Life Too Hard for Millennials," *New York Times*, July 31, 2015, https://www.nytimes.com/2015/08/02/opinion/sunday/were-making-life-too-hard-for-millennials.html. And that's not counting tuition increases during the 1980s, which had the highest average rate of increase. Melanie Hanson, "College Tuition Inflation Rate," *Education Data Initiative*, last modified September 9, 2024, https://educationdata.org/college-tuition-inflation-rate.
230 Melissa Brock, "How Much Has College Tuition Outpaced Inflation?," *Sofi*, March 17, 2024, https://www.sofi.com/learn/content/college-tuition-inflation/.
231 Ryan Quinn, "Full-time Faculty Raises Finally Beat Inflation … Just Barely," *Inside Higher Ed*, April 11, 2024, https://www.insidehighered.com/news/faculty-issues/2024/04/11/full-time-faculty-raises-finally-beat-inflation-just-barely.
232 *Trends in College Pricing: 2013* (New York: College Board, 2013), 3, https://research.collegeboard.org/media/pdf/trends-college-pricing-2013-full-report.pdf
233 Michael Mitchell and Michael Leachman, *Years of Cuts Threaten to Put College Out of Reach for More Students* (Washington, DC: Center on Budget and Policy Priorities, 2015), https://www.cbpp.org/research/state-budget-and-tax/years-of-cuts-threaten-to-put-college-out-of-reach-for-more-students. See the "Declining Support" figure in Leonhardt, "America's Great Working-Class Colleges."
234 Michael Mitchell, Michael Leachman, and Kathleen Masterson, "Funding Down, Tuition Up," *Center on Budget and Policy Priorities*, August 15, 2016, https://www.cbpp.org/research/state-budget-and-tax/funding-down-tuition-up.
235 Sarah Brown, "Bottom Line: How State Budget Cuts Affect Your Education," *New York Times*, November 3, 2016, https://www.nytimes.com/2016/11/06/education/edlife/college-budgets-affect-your-education-but-its-not-all-bad-news.html.
236 Larry Gordon, "UC says higher tuition for out-of-staters will help Californians," *EdSource*, March 6, 2019, https://edsource.org/2019/uc-says-higher-tuition-for-out-of-staters-will-help-californians/609586; Abigail Johnson Hess, "It can cost over $66,000 to go to UC Berkeley—here's how much students actually pay," *CNBC*, July 27, 2019, https://www.cnbc.com/2019/07/26/uc-berkeley-can-cost-over-66000but-heres-how-much-students-pay.html.
237 It is true, however, that student debt accumulation greatly outpaces the rise in tuition costs. Melanie Hanson, "Student Loan Debt Crisis,"

Education Data Initiative, updated July 14, 2024, https://educationdata.org/student-loan-debt-crisis.

238 *Quarterly Report on Household Debt and Credit* (New York: Federal Reserve Bank of New York Center for Microeconomic Data, 2024), https://www.newyorkfed.org/microeconomics/hhdc.html; Abigail Johnson Hess, "U.S. Student Debt Has Increased by More Than 100% over the Past 10 Years," *CNBC*, December 22, 2020, https://www.cnbc.com/2020/12/22/us-student-debt-has-increased-by-more-than-100percent-over-past-10-years.html.

239 Hanson, "Student Loan Debt Crisis."; *Student Loan Debt and Housing Report 2017: When Debt Holds You Back* (Washington, DC: National Association of Realtors Research Department and American Student Assistance, 2017), https://www.nar.realtor/sites/default/files/documents/2017-student-loan-debt-and-housing-09-26-2017.pdf.

240 Zachary Bleemer et al., *Tuition, Jobs, or Housing: What's Keeping Millennials at Home?* (New York: Federal Reserve Bank of New York Staff Reports, revised July 2017), https://www.newyorkfed.org/medialibrary/media/research/staff_reports/sr700.pdf.

241 Marisa Wright, "How Student Loan Forgiveness Can Help Close the Racial Wealth Gap and Advance Economic Justice," *NAACP Legal Defense Fund*, April 17, 2023, https://www.naacpldf.org/student-loans-racial-wealth-gap/;

242 Judith Scott-Clayton and Jing Li, *Black-White Disparity in Student Loan Debt More Than Triples after Graduation* (Washington, DC: Brookings Institution, 2016), https://www.brookings.edu/research/black-white-disparity-in-student-loan-debt-more-than-triples-after-graduation/.

243 Jen Mishory, Mark Huelsman, and Suzanne Kahn, *How Student Debt and the Racial Wealth Gap Reinforce Each Other* (Century Foundation, 2019) https://tcf.org/content/report/bridging-progressive-policy-debates-student-debt-racial-wealth-gap-reinforce/; Ayelet Sheffey, "For-profit schools target minority communities that typically owe more student debt, report says," *Business Insider*, August 24, 2021, https://www.businessinsider.com/for-profit-schools-target-minority-communities-student-borrower-protection-center-2021-8.

244 Charlie Eaton et al., "Student Debt Cancellation IS Progressive: Correcting Empirical and Conceptual Errors," *Roosevelt Institute*, June 8, 2021, https://rooseveltinstitute.org/publications/student-debt-cancellation-is-progressive/.

245 Caroline Ratcliffe and Signe-Mary McKernan, *Forever in Your Debt: Who Has Student Loan Debt, and Who's Worried?* (Washington, DC: Urban Institute, 2013), 4 Figure 3, https://www.urban.org/sites/default/files/publication/23736/412849-Forever-in-Your-Debt-Who-Has-Student-Loan-Debt-and-Who-s-Worried-.PDF.

246 David Leonhardt, "Better Colleges Failing to Lure Talented Poor, *New York Times*, March 16, 2013, https://www.nytimes.com/2013/03/17/education/scholarly-poor-often-overlook-better-colleges.html, citing Hoxby and Avery, "The Missing "Missing 'One-Offs."

247 Rosenberg, "Guiding a First Generation to College."

248 Matthew M. Chingos, "Can We Fix Undermatching in Higher Ed? Would It Matter if We Did?," *Brookings*, January 15, 2014, https://www.brookings.edu/articles/can-we-fix-undermatching-in-higher-ed-would-it-matter-if-we-did/.

249 J. Douglas Allen-Taylor, "Why Black Students Are Avoiding UC Berkeley," *East Bay Express*, November 6, 2013, https://eastbayexpress.com/why-black-students-are-avoiding-uc-berkeley-1/.

250 Laura Coletti and Andrew Simonelli, "Building the Future of Work Requires Skills Training, Flexibility," *Prudential*, October 11, 2021, https://news.prudential.com/building-future-work-requires-skills-training-flexibility.htm.

251 See exhibit ES-3 in Arne Duncan, Denise Forte, and Thomas Weko, *National Assessment of Career and Technical Education: Interim Report* (Washington, DC: U.S. Department of Education, Office of Planning, Evaluation, and Policy Development), xxiv, https://www2.ed.gov/rschstat/eval/sectech/nacte/career-technical-education/interim-report.pdf.
252 Duncan, Forte, and Weko, *National Assessment of Career and Technical Education*, xxiv.
253 Duncan, Forte, and Weko, *National Assessment of Career and Technical Education*, xii.
254 See Robert Lerman, "Restoring Opportunity by Expanding Apprenticeship," in *Dynamics of Opportunity*, eds. Kirsch and Braun, 382.
255 H.R.4164—Carl D. Perkins Vocational Education Act, 98th Cong (1984).
256 Dana Goldstein, "Seeing Hope for Flagging Economy, West Virginia Revamps Vocational Track," *New York Times*, August 10, 2017, https://www.nytimes.com/2017/08/10/us/west-virginia-vocational-education.html.
257 Beatrix Lockwood and Nicole Lewis, "The Hidden Cost of Incarceration," *The Marshall Project*, December 17, 2019, https://www.themarshallproject.org/2019/12/17/the-hidden-cost-of-incarceration.
258 Neil Schoenherr, "Cost of incarceration in the U.S. more than $1 trillion," *WashU Source*, September 7, 2016, https://source.washu.edu/2016/09/cost-incarceration-u-s-1-trillion/.
259 "Criminal Justice," *Stand Together Trust*, https://standtogethertrust.org/issue-areas/criminal-justice/.
260 Don Stemen, *The Prison Paradox: More Incarceration Will Not Make Us Safer* (Brooklyn, NY: Vera Institute of Justice, 2017), 5, https://www.vera.org/downloads/publications/for-the-record-prison-paradox_02.pdf.
261 Brown v. Plata, 563 U.S. 493 (2011).
262 Steven Greenhut, "How California Softened Its 'Tough on Crime' Approach," *R Street Policy* 102 (2017): 4, https://www.rstreet.org/wp-content/uploads/2017/07/102.pdf; Proposition 36, "Three Strikes Law. Sentencing for Repeat Felony Offenders. Initiative Statute," 2012, https://repository.uchastings.edu/cgi/viewcontent.cgi?article=2732&context=ca_ballot_inits, codified at Cal. Penal Code § 667.
263 Proposition 47, "Criminal Sentences. Misdemeanor Penalties. Initiative Statute," 2014, https://repository.uchastings.edu/ca_ballot_inits/1854/.
264 Proposition 57, "Criminal Sentences. Parole. Juvenile Criminal Proceedings and Sentencing. Initiative Constitutional Amendment and Statute," 2016, https://repository.uchastings.edu/cgi/viewcontent.cgi?article=2349&context=ca_ballot_props, codified at Cal. Penal Code § 667.5. However, some of these reforms have been rolled back based upon passage of Proposition 36 in 2024. Proposition 36, Homelessness, Drug Addiction, and Theft Reduction Act (passed November 5, 2024).
265 Greg Glod, *Texas Adult Corrections: A Model for the Rest of the Nation* (Austin, TX: Texas Public Policy Foundation, Center for Effective Justice, 2015), 1–5, https://web.archive.org/web/20160412103553/https://www.texaspolicy.com/library/doclib/PP-Texas-Adult-Corrections-A-Model-for-the-Rest-of-the-Nation.pdf.
266 Donna F. Edwards, "What Ever Happened to Mass Incarceration Reform?" *The Hill*, August 9, 2017, https://thehill.com/blogs/pundits-blog/civil-rights/345909-what-ever-happened-to-mass-incarceration-reform. See also Gerald Malloy et al., *State Expenditures Savings Report* (Columbia, SC: The South Carolina Sentencing Reform Oversight Committee, 2013), 5, https://www.scstatehouse.gov/citizensinterestpage/SentencingReformOversightCommittee/Reports/2013SCSROCStateExpendituresSavingsReport.pdf.

267 Rebekah Allen, "Gov. Edwards Signs Criminal Justice Overhaul into Law, in What Some Laud as a Historic Achievement," *The Advocate*, June 15, 2017, https://www.theadvocate.com/baton_rouge/news/politics/legislature/article_168c6d6e-5089-11e7-a0d6-7f67135f59a4.html.
268 Fair Sentencing Act of 2010, Pub. L. No. 111–220, 124 Stat. 2372 (2010).
269 The First Step Act of 2018, Pub. L. No. 115–391, 132 Stat. 5194 (2018).
270 Justin George, "Okay, What's the Second Step?" *The Marshall Project*, December 19, 2018, https://www.themarshallproject.org/2018/12/19/okay-whats-the-second-step.
271 German Lopez, "The First Step Act, Explained," *Vox*, February 9, 2019, https://www.vox.com/future-perfect/2018/12/18/18140973/first-step-act-criminal-justice-reform-senate-congress.
272 Coates, "Black Family," 83.
273 Rose A. Rudd et al., "Increases in Drug and Opioid Overdose Deaths—United States 2000-2014," *Morbidity and Mortality Weekly Report* 64, no. 50 (2016): 1378–1382, https://www.cdc.gov/mmwr/preview/mmwrhtml/mm6450a3.htm.
274 Theodore J. Cicero et al., "The Changing Face of Heroin Use in the United States: A Retrospective Analysis of the Past 50 Years," *JAMA Psychiatry* 71, no. 7 (2014): 822, https://archpsyc.jamanetwork.com/article.aspx?articleid=1874575.
275 Jake Kara, "Who Is Dying in Connecticut's Opioid Overdose Crisis?," *Trend CT*, https://web.archive.org/web/20210518052741/https://overdose.trendct.org/story/who.
276 Hernandez D. Stroud, "Our Opioid Crisis Reveals Deep Racial Bias In Addiction Treatment," *Time Magazine*, July 15, 2016, https://time.com/4385588/crack-babies-heroin-crisis/.
277 Ekow N. Yankah, "When Addiction Has a White Face," *New York Times*, February 9, 2016, https://www.nytimes.com/2016/02/09/opinion/when-addiction-has-a-white-face.html. See also Julie Netherland and Helena Hansen, "White Opioids: Pharmaceutical Race and the War on Drugs That Wasn't," *Biosocieties* 12 (2017): 217–238, https://www.ncbi.nlm.nih.gov/pmc/articles/PMC5501419/.
278 Megan Twohey, "Mike Pence's Response to H.I.V. Outbreak: Prayer, Then a Change of Heart," *New York Times*, August 8, 2016, https://www.nytimes.com/2016/08/08/us/politics/mike-pence-needle-exchanges-indiana.html.
279 "Republican Candidates Debate in Manchester, New Hampshire," *American Presidency Project*, February 6, 2016, https://www.presidency.ucsb.edu/documents/republican-candidates-debate-manchester-new-hampshire-0.
280 Karoun Demirjian, "Congress Set to Pass Bill to Combat Opioid Abuse," *Washington Post*, July 10, 2016, https://www.washingtonpost.com/politics/congress-set-to-pass-bill-to-combat-opioid-abuse/2016/07/10/a5c6b52a-46cb-11e6-bdb9-701687974517_story.html.
281 Ken Burns, *Prohibition* (PBS, 2011), https://www.pbs.org/kenburns/prohibition/; Lisa McGirr, "How Prohibition Fueled the Klan," *New York Times,* January 16, 2019, https://www.nytimes.com/2019/01/16/opinion/prohibition-immigration-klan.html.
282 Earl Anthony Wayne, "The War on Drugs: The Narco States of North America," *National Interest*, October 30, 2017, https://nationalinterest.org/feature/the-war-drugs-the-narco-states-north-america-22967.
283 Jamie Doward, "'War on Drugs' Has Failed, Say Latin American Leaders," *Guardian*, April 7, 2012, https://www.theguardian.com/world/2012/apr/07/war-drugs-latin-american-leaders.
284 "Summit of the Americas agree war on drugs a failure," *Globe and Mail*, April 16, 2012, https://www.theglobeandmail.com/opinion/editorials/summit-of-the-americas-agree-war-on-drugs-a-failure/article4100610/.

285 "Marijuana Legality by State," *DISA*, updated April 1, 2025, https://disa.com/marijuana-legality-by-state; "State Medical Cannabis Laws," National Conference of State Legislatures, updated June 22, 2023, https://www.ncsl.org/research/health/state-medical-marijuana-laws.aspx.
286 Will Feuer, "Oregon Becomes First State to Legalize Magic Mushrooms as More States Ease Drug Laws in 'Psychedelic Renaissance,'" *CNBC,* November 4, 2020, https://www.cnbc.com/2020/11/04/oregon-becomes-first-state-to-legalize-magic-mushrooms-as-more-states-ease-drug-laws.html.
287 *It's Time for the U.S. to Decriminalize Drug Use and Possession* (New York: Drug Policy Alliance, 2017), 27–30, https://drugpolicy.org/sites/default/files/documents/Drug_Policy_Alliance_Time_to_Decriminalize_Report_July_2017.pdf.
288 Molly Forster, "Oakland May Cut Weed Tax," *East Bay Express*, February 6, 2019, https://eastbayexpress.com/oakland-may-cut-weed-tax-1/.
289 Wendy Sawyer and Peter Wagner, *Mass Incarceration: The Whole Pie 2020* (Northampton, MA: Prison Policy Initiative, 2020), https://www.prisonpolicy.org/reports/pie2020.html. And, as scholars such as John Pfaff have pointed out, drug offenders comprise only 17% of state prison populations and have contributed only about 20% of overall prison population growth since 1980. John F. Pfaff, "The War on Drugs and Prison Growth: Limited Importance, Limited Legislative Options," *Harvard Journal on Legislation* 52, no. 1 (2015): 176.
290 Pfaff, "War on Drugs and Prison Growth," 182.
291 Forman, *Locking Up Our Own*, 449–450 (describing the limitations of centering nonviolent drug offenders in criminal justice reform efforts).
292 Mike Baker, "Oregon Is Recriminalizing Drugs. Here's What Portland Learned," *New York Times*, April 1, 2024, https://www.nytimes.com/2024/04/01/us/oregon-drug-law-portland-mayor.html; Stephen Menendian, "The Problem of California's Prop 36, Criminal Justice Reform, and the Social Justice Blind Spot," *Othering & Belonging Institute*, October 23, 2024, https://belonging.berkeley.edu/the-problem-with-prop-36.
293 "Prisoners and Prisoner Re-Entry," U.S. Department of Justice Office of Justice Programs, https://www.justice.gov/archive/fbci/progmenu_reentry.html; "Incarceration & Reentry," U.S. Department of Health and Human Services, Office of the Assistant Secretary for Planning and Evaluation, https://aspe.hhs.gov/topics/human-services/incarceration-reentry-0.
294 James Elwell et al., *New Estimates of Populations Affected by Criminal Justice by State, Race, and Year* (Washington, DC: White House Council of Economic Advisers, 2016).
295 Rebecca Vallas and Sharon Dietrich, *One Strike and You're Out: How We Can Eliminate Barriers to Economic Security and Mobility for People with Criminal Records* (Washington, DC: Center for American Progress, 2014), 8, https://www.americanprogress.org/wp-content/uploads/2014/12/VallasCriminalRecords Report.pdf.
296 See *Roadmap to Reentry: Reducing Recidivism through Reentry Reforms at the Federal Bureau of Prisons: Reforms at the Federal Bureau of Prisons* (Washington, DC: U.S. Department of Justice, 2016), 2, https://www.justice.gov/archives/reentry/file/844356/download.
297 Kimberly Burrowes, "Can Housing Interventions Reduce Incarceration and Recidivism?" *Urban Institute*, February 27, 2019, https://housingmatters.urban.org/articles/can-housing-interventions-reduce-incarceration-and-recidivism.
298 See *SHRM Survey Findings: Background-Checking-The Use of Criminal Background Checks in Hiring Decisions* (Alexandria, VA: Society for Human

299 Devah Pager, "The Mark of a Criminal Record," *American Journal of Sociology* 108, no. 5 (2003): 937, https://faculty.washington.edu/matsueda/courses/587/readings/Pager%202003%20Mark.pdf.
300 Matthew Friedman, "Just Facts: As Many Americans Have Criminal Records as College Diplomas," *Brennan Center for Justice*, November 17, 2015, https://www.brennancenter.org/blog/just-facts-many-americans-have-criminal-records-college-diplomas; *Americans with Criminal Records* (Washington, DC: The Sentencing Project, 2015), https://www.sentencingproject.org/wp-content/uploads/2015/11/Americans-with-Criminal-Records-Poverty-and-Opportunity-Profile.pdf.
301 Bruce Western, Becky Pettit, and Josh Guetzkow, "Black Economic Progress in the Era of Mass Imprisonment," in *Invisible Punishment: The Collateral Consequences of Mass Imprisonment*, eds. Marc Mauer and Meda Chesney-Lind (New York: The New Press, 2002), 175–176.
302 Western and Pettit, *Collateral Costs*, 4.
303 Tammy La Gorce, "As 'Ban the Box' Spreads, Private Employers Still Have Questions," *New York Times*, November 22, 2017, https://www.nytimes.com/2017/11/22/business/small-business-criminal-record.html.
304 Beth Avery and Han Lu, *Ban The Box: U.S. Cities, Counties, and States Adopt Fair-Chance Policies to Advance Employment Opportunities for People with Past Convictions* (New York: National Employment Law Project, 2021), 2, https://www.nelp.org/publication/ban-the-box-fair-chance-hiring-state-and-local-guide/; Rosenberg, "Have You Ever Been Arrested?"
305 U.S. Equal Employment Opportunity Commission (EEOC), "Enforcement Guidance on the Consideration of Arrest and Conviction Records in Employment Decisions under Title VII of the Civil Rights Act," *EEOC*, April 25, 2012, https://www.eeoc.gov/laws/guidance/enforcement-guidance-consideration-arrest-and-conviction-records-employment-decisions; Robb Mandelbaum, "U.S. Push on Illegal Bias Against Hiring Those With Criminal Records," *New York Times*, June 20, 2012, https://www.nytimes.com/2012/06/21/business/smallbusiness/us-presses-on-illegal-bias-against-hiring-those-with-criminal-records.html.
306 "Article 49: The Fair Chance Ordinance," San Francisco Human Rights Commission, accessed March 12, 2022, https://sf-hrc.org/fair-chance-ordinance; "Fair Chance Housing," Seattle Office for Civil Rights, August 2017, accessed March 12, 2022, https://www.seattle.gov/civilrights/civil-rights/fair-housing/fair-chance-housing.
307 Fair Chance in Housing Act, N.J.S.A. 46:8–52 (2021).
308 Ohio Rev. Code. Ann. § 2953.32, described in Lauren-Brooke Eisen, "Ohio Takes Step to Roll Back Collateral Consequences," Vera Institute for Justice, August 20, 2012, https://www.vera.org/news/ohio-takes-step-to-roll-back-collateral-consequences.
309 *Confronting Recidivism: Prisoner Reentry Programs and a Just Future for All Americans: Hearing Before the Comm. on Government Reform*, 109 Cong. 10 (2005) (statement of Rob Portman, Congressman from Ohio), https://www.govinfo.gov/content/pkg/CHRG-109hhrg20377/html/CHRG-109hhrg20377.htm.
310 S. 2490, 2012 Gen. Assemb. Jan. Sess. (R. I. 2012), https://webserver.rilegislature.gov/BillText12/SenateText12/S2490.pdf.
311 Kimberly G. White et al., *Ending Legal Bias Against Formerly Incarcerated People* (Berkeley, CA: Othering & Belonging Institute, 2019), https://belonging.berkeley.edu/ending-legal-bias-against-formerly-incarcerated-people.

312 "Bard Prison Initiative," Bard College, accessed January 3, 2022, https://bpi.bard.edu/.
313 Lois M. Davis et al., *Evaluating the Effectiveness of Correctional Education: A Meta-Analysis of Programs That Provide Education to Incarcerated Adults* (Santa Monica, CA: RAND Corporation, 2013), xvi, https://www.rand.org/pubs/research_reports/RR266. See also the intriguing op-ed: Elizabeth Hinton, "Turn Prisons into Colleges," *New York Times*, March 6, 2018, https://www.nytimes.com/2018/03/06/opinion/prisons-colleges-education.html.
314 "Correctional Facility Partners," Hudson Link for Higher Education in Prison, accessed January 3, 2022, https://web.archive.org/web/20210122171231/https://hudsonlink.org/partners/correctional-facilities/.
315 Margaret diZerega and Raphael Ginsberg, "Common sense: Remove barriers to education in prison," *Salisbury Post*, April 8, 2018, https://www.salisburypost.com/2018/04/08/common-sense-remove-barriers-to-education-in-prison/.
316 Gerard Robinson and Elizabeth English, *The Second Chance Pell Pilot Program: A Historical Overview* (Washington, DC: American Enterprise Institute, 2017), 2, https://www.aei.org/wp-content/uploads/2017/09/The-Second-Chance-Pell-Pilot-Program.pdf#page=2 ("the 1994 crime bill cut off Pell funding to educational programs in prison almost overnight. In the absence of Pell dollars, a number of college-in-prison programs withdrew their participation…By 1997, it is estimated that only eight college-in-prison programs existed in the United States").
317 Ken Lovett, "Plan for State to Fund Prison College Education Courses Dies in Budget Talks, Cuomo Administration Source Says," *New York Daily News*, March 31, 2014, https://www.nydailynews.com/blogs/dailypolitics/plan-state-fund-prison-college-education-courses-dies-budget-talks-cuomo-administration-source-blog-entry-1.1740865. See also Jesse McKinley, "Cuomo to Give Colleges $7 Million for Courses in Prisons," *New York Times*, August 6, 2017, https://www.nytimes.com/2017/08/06/nyregion/cuomo-to-give-colleges-7-million-for-courses-in-prisons.html.
318 See, for example, Amy Chozick, "The Rikers Coffee Academy," *New York Times*, updated December 30, 2019, https://www.nytimes.com/2019/12/27/business/rikers-island-baristas.html.
319 Jason Furman and Douglas Holtz-Eakin, "Why Mass Incarceration Doesn't Pay," *New York Times*, April 21, 2016, https://www.nytimes.com/2016/04/21/opinion/why-mass-incarceration-doesnt-pay.html.
320 Western and Pettit, *Collateral Costs*, 2.
321 Furman and Holtz-Eakin, "Why Mass Incarceration Doesn't Pay."
322 Christopher Ingraham, "The states that spend more money on prisoners than college students," *Washington Post*, August 7, 2016, https://www.washingtonpost.com/news/wonk/wp/2016/07/07/the-states-that-spend-more-money-on-prisoners-than-college-students/.
323 McLaughlin et al., "Economic Burden of Incarceration."
324 Alex Mayyasi, "How Does Prison Gerrymandering Work?," *Priceonomics*, October 20, 2015, https://priceonomics.com/how-does-prison-gerrymandering-work/. For examples, see "Prison Gerrymandering Project," Prison Policy Initiative, accessed January 3, 2022, https://www.prisonersofthecensus.org/.
325 Mayyasi, "Prison Gerrymandering."
326 "Felony Disenfranchisement Laws (Map)," *American Civil Liberties Union*, Accessed September 24, 2024, https://www.aclu.org/issues/voting-rights/voter-restoration/felony-disenfranchisement-laws-map.
327 Christopher Uggen et al., "Locked Out 2024: Four Million Denied Voting Rights Due to a Felony Conviction," *Sentencing Project*, October 10, 2024,

330 *Structural Racism*

   https://www.sentencingproject.org/reports/locked-out-2024-four-million-denied-voting-rights-due-to-a-felony-conviction/.
328 ACLU, "Felony Disenfranchisement Laws."
329 Molly Ball, "Do the Koch Brothers Really Care About Criminal Justice Reform?" *Atlantic*, March 3, 2015, https://www.theatlantic.com/politics/archive/2015/03/do-the-koch-brothers-really-care-about-criminal-justice-reform/386615/.
330 George Zornick, "Rick Perry at CPAC Panel on Criminal Justice: 'Shut Prisons Down. Save That Money,'" *The Nation*, March 7, 2014, https://www.thenation.com/article/rick-perry-cpac-panel-criminal-justice-shut-prisons-down-save-money/.
331 Sandra Lee Browning et al., "Race and Getting Hassled by the Police: A Research Note," *Police Studies* 17, no. 1 (1994): 1–11.
332 Christine Hauser, "Black Man Is Arrested While Walking, and Minnesota City Starts a 'Conversation'," *New York Times*, October 19, 2016, https://www.nytimes.com/2016/10/20/us/minnesota-video-walking.html.
333 Rob Voigt et al. "Language from Police Body Camera Footage Shows Racial Disparities in Officer Respect," *Proceedings of the National Academy of Sciences* 114, no. 25 (2017): 6522, https://www.pnas.org/content/pnas/114/25/6521.full.pdf.
334 *Discrimination in America*, 6–7.
335 Drew DeSilver, Michael Lipka, and Dalia Fahmy, "10 things we know about race and policing in the U.S.," *Pew Research Center*, June 3, 2020, https://www.pewresearch.org/short-reads/2020/06/03/10-things-we-know-about-race-and-policing-in-the-u-s/.
336 *Kerner Report*, 160.
337 John Eligon and Kay Nolan, "When Police Don't Live in the City They Serve," *New York Times*, August 18, 2016, https://www.nytimes.com/2016/08/19/us/when-police-dont-live-in-the-city-they-serve.html.
338 *Key Kerner Commission Recommendations*.
339 Menendian, Rothstein, and Beri, *The Road Not Taken*.
340 The President's Task Force on 21st Century Policing, *Implementation Guide: Moving from Recommendations to Action* (Washington, DC: Office of Community Oriented Policing Services, U.S. Department of Justice, 2015), https://cops.usdoj.gov/RIC/Publications/cops-p341-pub.pdf.
341 "#8CantWait," Campaign Zero, accessed January 4, 2022, https://8cantwait.org/.
342 *Kerner Report*, 158.
343 "End the War on Black People," Movement 4 Black Lives, accessed April 23, 2025, https://m4bl.org/end-the-war-on-black-people/; Phillip Atiba Goff et al., *The Science of Justice: Race, Arrests, and Police Use of Force* (New York: Center for Policing Equity, 2016), https://policingequity.org/images/pdfs-doc/CPE_SoJ_Race-Arrests-UoF_2016-07-08-1130.pdf.
344 Jenée Desmond-Harris, "If You Don't Understand Black Lives Matter after Terence Crutcher's Death, You Never Will," *Vox*, September 21, 2016, https://www.vox.com/identities/2016/9/21/12993866/terence-crutcher-unarmed-killed-black-lives-matter, citing Dara Lind, "The FBI Is Trying to Get Better Data on Police Killings. Here's What We Know Now," *Vox*, April 10, 2015, https://www.vox.com/2014/8/21/6051043/how-many-people-killed-police-statistics-homicide-official-black.
345 "Mapping Police Violence," accessed February 22, 2023, https://mappingpoliceviolence.org/ (See filter view to access data from each year, state, and demographic).
346 Carl Bialik, "Why Are So Many Black Americans Killed By Police?," *FiveThirtyEight*, July 21, 2016, https://fivethirtyeight.com/features/why-are-so-many-black-americans-killed-by-police/, citing "The Counted: People Killed

by Police in the US," *Guardian*, 2016, https://www.theguardian.com/us-news/ng-interactive/2015/jun/01/the-counted-police-killings-us-database; *Mapping Police Violence*, last updated April 1, 2025, https://mappingpoliceviolence.org/ (finding 90 Black deaths for 32 white deaths per 1 million people in the U.S., 2013–2025).
347 Graham v. Connor, 490 U.S. 386 (1989). For critical commentary, see David D. Kirkpatrick, "Split-Second Decisions: How a Supreme Court Ruling Shaped Modern Policing," *New York Times,* April 25, 2021, https://www.nytimes.com/2021/04/25/us/police-use-of-force.html.
348 Matt Taibbi, "Why Policing Is Broken," *Rolling Stone*, June 17, 2020, https://www.rollingstone.com/politics/politics-features/why-policing-is-broken-taibbi-1014652/
349 Rebecca Worby, "California Could Become the First State to Dramatically Restrict Police Use of Deadly Force," *Pacific Standard*, June 22, 2018, https://psmag.com/news/one-california-bill-could-make-a-big-change-in-polices-use-of-deadly-force.
350 Merrick Bobb, *Ninth Systemic Assessment: Use of Force* (Seattle: Seattle Police Department Federal Consent Decree Monitor, 2017), 76, https://www.documentcloud.org/documents/3538083-Assessment-Use-of-Force.html.
351 See, for example, Justin Fenton, *We Own This City: A True Story of Crime, Cops, and Corruption* (New York: Random House, 2021).
352 Dakin Andoe, Hollie Silverman, and Melissa Alonso, "The Minneapolis Police Officer Who Knelt on George Floyd's Neck Had 18 Previous Complaints against Him, Police Department Says," CNN, May 29, 2020, https://www.cnn.com/2020/05/28/us/minneapolis-officer-complaints-george-floyd/index.html.
353 *Investigation of the Ferguson Police Department*, 82.
354 Terry v. Ohio, 392 U.S. 1 (1968).
355 German Lopez, "Police Officers Are Prosecuted for Murder in Less Than 2 Percent of Fatal Shootings," *Vox*, last modified April 2, 2021, https://www.vox.com/21497089/derek-chauvin-george-floyd-trial-police-prosecutions-black-lives-matter.
356 "Body-Cam Video of Daniel Shaver Shooting | Los Angeles Times," YouTube video, 5:02, posted by "Los Angeles Times," December 8, 2017, https://www.youtube.com/watch?v=VBUUx0jUKxc/; Erik Ortiz, "Daniel Shaver shooting: Ex-Arizona police officer acquitted of murder," *NBC News*, updated December 8, 2017, https://www.nbcnews.com/news/us-news/daniel-shaver-shooting-ex-arizona-police-officer-not-guilty-murder-n827641.
357 Audra D. S. Burch and Kelley Manley, "Police Officers Are Charged with Crimes, but Are Juries Convicting?," *New York Times*, January 1, 2024, https://www.nytimes.com/2024/01/01/us/george-floyd-elijah-mcclain-police-brutality-black-lives-matter-trials-civil-rights.html.
358 42 U.S.C. § 1983 (1871); Pierson v. Ray, 386 U.S. 547 (1967).
359 Samuel Walker, Cassia Spohn, and Miriam DeLone, *The Color of Justice: Race, Ethnicity, and Crime in America* (Belmont, CA: Wadsworth Thomson Learning, 1996), 218.
360 Pfaff, "War on Drugs and Prison Growth," 198.
361 Alana Rosenberg, Allison K. Groves, and Kim M. Blankenship, "Comparing Black and White Drug Offenders: Implications for Racial Disparities in Criminal Justice and Reentry Policy and Programming," *Journal of Drug Issues* 47, no. 1 (2017): 132–142. https://www.ncbi.nlm.nih.gov/pmc/articles/PMC5614457/
362 Carlos Berdejó, "Criminalizing Race: Racial Disparities in Plea Bargaining," *Boston College Law Review* 59, no. 4 (2018): 1191. https://papers.ssrn.com/sol3/papers.cfm?abstract_id=3036726
363 Brady v. Maryland, 373 U.S. 83 (1963).

364 Jennifer Mason McAward, "Understanding Brady Violations," *Vanderbilt Law Review* (forthcoming April 2025), https://dx.doi.org/10.2139/ssrn.4940469.
365 Brandon L. Garrett, Adam M. Gershowitz, Jennifer Teitcher, "The Brady Database," *Journal of Criminal Law and Criminology* 114, no. 2 (2024): 1–66, https://www.jstor.org/stable/48785845.
366 Batson v. Kentucky, 476 U.S. 79 (1985); Richard Gabriel, "Understanding Bias: Preserving Peremptory Challenges, Preventing their Discriminatory Use, and Providing Fairer and More Impartial Juries," *Civil Jury Project at NYU School of Law*, 2022, https://civiljuryproject.law.nyu.edu/understanding-bias-preserving-peremptory-challenges-preventing-their-discriminatory-use-and-providing-fairer-and-more-impartial-juries/.
367 See Flowers v. Mississippi, 588 U.S. 284 (2019); Foster v. Chatman, 578 U.S. 488 (2016).
368 Center for Prosecutor Integrity, *An Epidemic of Prosecutor Misconduct* (Rockville, MD: Center for Prosecutor Integrity), 8, https://www.prosecutorintegrity.org/wp-content/uploads/EpidemicofProsecutorMisconduct.pdf
369 The 2023 study found only cases where prosecutors were charged and only two convictions. McAward, "Understanding Brady Violations," 20.
370 New York Times Editorial Board, "Federal Prosecutors Need a Watchdog, Too," *New York Times*, December 25, 2018, https://www.nytimes.com/2018/12/25/opinion/editorials/prosecutors-justice-inspector-general.html.
371 Emily Bazelon and Miriam Krinsky, "There's a Wave of New Prosecutors. And They Mean Justice," *New York Times*, December 11, 2018, https://www.nytimes.com/2018/12/11/opinion/how-local-prosecutors-can-reform-their-justice-systems.html.
372 Lucy Lang, "SF Election Advances Progressive Prosecution Movement," *San Francisco Chronicle*, November 16, 2019, https://www.sfchronicle.com/opinion/article/S-F-election-advances-progressive-prosecution-14836775.php.
373 Ben Austen, "In Philadelphia, a Progressive D.A. Tests the Power—and Learns the Limits—of His Office," *New York Times*, October 30, 2018, https://www.nytimes.com/2018/10/30/magazine/larry-krasner-philadelphia-district-attorney-progressive.html; Richard A. Oppel Jr., "These Prosecutors Promised Change. Their Power Is Being Stripped Away," *New York Times*, December 2, 2019, https://www.nytimes.com/2019/11/25/us/prosecutors-criminal-justice.html; Rashad Robinson, "The People Who Undermine Progressive Prosecutors," *New York Times*, June 11, 2020, https://www.nytimes.com/2020/06/11/opinion/george-floyd-prosecutors.html; Tim Prudence, "Baltimore State's Attorney Mosby Stands with Progressive Prosecutors, Also Airs Dispute with Gov. Hogan at St. Louis Rally," *Baltimore Sun*, January 15, 2020, https://www.baltimoresun.com/politics/bs-md-ci-20200115-r6j3hfsllbh3vcdpxjoaq36gqu-story.html.
374 Eliza Fawcett, "Baltimore Prosecutor Defeated in Democratic Primary Amid Legal Woes," *New York Times*, July 22, 2022, https://www.nytimes.com/2022/07/22/us/marilyn-mosby-baltimore-primary-ivan-bates.html.
375 Campbell Robertson, "Pennsylvania House Moves to Impeach Philadelphia's Progressive D.A.," *New York Times*, October 26, 2022, https://www.nytimes.com/2022/10/26/us/larry-krasner-philadelphia-impeachment.html; Sam Dunklau, "GOP impeachment managers look to revive Philly DA Krasner's Senate trial," *90.5 WESA*, January 27, 2023, https://www.wesa.fm/politics-government/2023-01-27/gop-impeachment-managers-look-to-revive-philly-da-krasners-senate-trial.
376 Bigad Shaban and Robert Campos, "SF District Attorney Chesa Boudin Officially Forced into Recall Election Next June," *NBC Bay Area*, November 10, 2021, https://www.nbcbayarea.com/news/local/exclusive-sf-district-attorney-chesa-boudin-officially-forced-into-recall-election-next-june/2725737/.

377 Emily Bazelon and Jennifer Medina, "He's Remaking Criminal Justice in L.A. But How Far is Too Far?" *New York Times*, November 17, 2021, https://www.nytimes.com/2021/11/17/magazine/george-gascon-los-angeles.html; Daniel Arkin, "L.A. County district attorney, one of the most progressive in the country, loses re-election," *NBC News*, November 6, 2024, https://www.nbcnews.com/politics/2024-election/la-district-attorney-progressive-loses-re-election-gascon-rcna175906.
378 Campbell Robertson, "In Louisiana, the Poor Lack Legal Defense," *New York Times*, March 19, 2016, https://www.nytimes.com/2016/03/20/us/in-louisiana-the-poor-lack-legal-defense.html.
379 Lincoln Caplan, "The Right to Counsel: Badly Battered at 50," *New York Times*, March 9, 2013, https://www.nytimes.com/2013/03/10/opinion/sunday/the-right-to-counsel-badly-battered-at-50.html.
380 John Pfaff, "A Mockery of Justice for the Poor," *New York Times*, April 29, 2016, https://www.nytimes.com/2016/04/30/opinion/a-mockery-of-justice-for-the-poor.html.
381 One source cites as a statistic that 83% of felony defendants are indigent. Indigent Defense Systems, Bureau of Justice Statistics, accessed February 1, 2022, https://www.bjs.gov/index.cfm/content/data/index.cfm?ty=tp&tid=28.
382 Shapiro, "As Court Fees Rise."
383 Jody Lawrence-Turner, "Debt to Society: Unpaid Court Fees Can Land Released Convicts Back in Jail," *Spokesman-Review*, May 24, 2009, https://www.spokesman.com/stories/2009/may/24/debt-to-society.
384 Paul Pierce and Adam Brandolph, "Pa. Corrections Chief: Closings of Older Prisons to Save $23M in First Year," *Tribune-Review*, January 18, 2013, https://triblive.com/news/allegheny/3313969-74/wetzel-prison-state#axzz2JCoXvJHJz.
385 Komala Ramachandra, "US Supreme Court Rules Unanimously Against Excessive Fines," *Human Rights Watch*, February 22, 2019, https://www.hrw.org/news/2019/02/22/us-supreme-court-rules-unanimously-against-excessive-fines; Menendian, "Shadow Constitution," 376–78.
386 Vanita Gupta and Lisa Foster, "Dear Colleague Letter Regarding Fees and Fines" (official memorandum, Washington, DC: U.S. Department of Justice Civil Rights Division, Office for Access to Justice, 2016), https://web.archive.org/web/20160714124827/https:/www.justice.gov/crt/file/832461/download; Matt Apuzzo, "Justice Dept. Condemns Profit-Minded Court Policies Targeting the Poor," *New York Times*, March 14, 2016, https://www.nytimes.com/2016/03/15/us/politics/justice-dept-condemns-profit-minded-court-policies-targeting-the-poor.html.
387 Charlie Savage, "Justice Dept. Revokes 25 Legal Guidance Documents Dating to 1975," *New York Times*, December 21, 2017, https://www.nytimes.com/2017/12/21/us/politics/justice-dept-guidance-documents.html.
388 Nick Pinto, "The Bail Trap," *New York Times Magazine*, August 13, 2015, https://www.nytimes.com/2015/08/16/magazine/the-bail-trap.html?_r=0.
389 Timothy R. Schnacke, *Fundamentals of Bail: A Resource Guide for Pretrial Practitioners and a Framework for American Pretrial Reform* (Washington, DC: National Institute of Corrections, 2014), 17, https://nicic.gov/fundamentals-bail-resource-guide-pretrial-practitioners-and-framework-american-pretrial-reform.
390 Allie Preston and Racheal Eisenberg, *Profit Over People: Inside the Commercial Bail Bond Industry Fueling America's Cash Bail System* (Washington, DC: Center for American Progress, 2022), https://www.americanprogress.org/article/profit-over-people/.
391 Mathilde Laisne, Jon Wool, and Christian Henrichson, *Past Due: Examining the Costs and Consequences of Charging for Justice in New Orleans* (New York: Vera Institute of Justice, 2017), 5, https://www.vera.org/downloads/publications/past-due-costs-consequences-charging-for-justice-new-orleans.pdf.

392 Pinto, "Bail Trap."
393 David Montgomery, "The Death of Sandra Bland: Is There Anything Left to Investigate?," *New York Times*, May 8, 2019, https://www.nytimes.com/2019/05/08/us/sandra-bland-texas-death.html.
394 Pinto, "Bail Trap."
395 Zina Makar, "How the Right to Speedy Trial Can Reduce Mass Pretrial Incarceration," *American Criminal Law Review Online*, November 5, 2015, https://scholarworks.law.ubalt.edu/cgi/viewcontent.cgi?article=1968&context=all_fac.
396 Shaila Dewan, "Probation May Sound Light, but Punishments Can Land Hard," *New York Times*, August 2, 2015, https://www.nytimes.com/2015/08/03/us/probation-sounding-light-can-land-hard.html.
397 Jesse McKinley and Ashley Southall, "Kalief Browder's Suicide Inspired a Push to End Cash Bail. Now Lawmakers Have a Deal," *New York Times*, March 29, 2019, https://www.nytimes.com/2019/03/29/nyregion/kalief-browder-cash-bail-reform.html.
398 Jennifer Browder, "Kalief Browder, 1993-2015," *New Yorker*, June 7, 2015, https://www.newyorker.com/news/news-desk/kalief-browder-1993-2015.
399 Shaila Dewan, "When Bail Is Out of Defendant's Reach, Other Costs Mount," *New York Times*, June 10, 2015, https://www.nytimes.com/2015/06/11/us/when-bail-is-out-of-defendants-reach-other-costs-mount.html.
400 Louis Casiano, "These States Recently Enacted Bail Reform Laws," *Fox News*, February 22, 2020, https://www.foxnews.com/politics/these-states-recently-enacted-bail-reform-laws.
401 Tom Simonite, "Algorithms Were Supposed to Fix the Bail System. They Haven't," *Wired*, February 19, 2020, https://www.wired.com/story/algorithms-supposed-fix-bail-system-they-havent/; Glenn A. Grant, *Criminal Justice Reform Report to the Governor and the Legislature* (Trenton, NJ: New Jersey Courts, 2017), 11.
402 Jamiles Lartey, "New York Tried to Get Rid of Bail. Then the Backlash Came," *Politico*, April 23, 2020, https://www.politico.com/news/magazine/2020/04/23/bail-reform-coronavirus-new-york-backlash-148299.
403 Samuel R. Wiseman, "Bail and Mass Incarceration," *Georgia Law Review* 52 (2018): 255, https://www.georgialawreview.org/article/7512-bail-and-mass-incarceration.
404 Jessica Silver-Greenberg and Shaila Dewan, "When Bail Feels Less Like Freedom, More Like Extortion," *New York Times*, March 31, 2018, https://www.nytimes.com/2018/03/31/us/bail-bonds-extortion.html.
405 *The Public Cost of Private Bail: A Proposal to Ban Bail Bonds in NYC* (New York: Office of the New York City Comptroller Scott M. Stringer, 2018), https://comptroller.nyc.gov/wp-content/uploads/documents/The_Public_Cost_of_Private_Bail.pdf.
406 Arpit Gupta, Christopher Hansman, and Ethan Frenchman, "The Heavy Costs of High Bail: Evidence from Judge Randomization," *Journal of Legal Studies* 25, no. 2 (2018): 471, https://chicagounbound.uchicago.edu/jls/vol45/iss2/8/ (finding that "the assignment of money bail leads to a 12% increase in the likelihood of conviction and a 6–9% increase in recidivism"). This is even true of the federal court system. See Stephanie Holmes Didwania, "The Immediate Consequences of Federal Pretrial Detention," *American Law and Economics Review* 22, no. 1 (2020): 24–74, https://academic.oup.com/aler/article-abstract/22/1/24/5709919.
407 Mary T. Phillips, *A Decade of Bail Research in New York City* (New York: New York City Criminal Justice Agency, 2012), 116, 158, https://www.prisonpolicy.org/scans/DecadeBailResearch12.pdf.
408 David Arnold, Will Dobbie, and Crystal S. Yang, "Racial Bias in Bail Decisions," *Quarterly Journal of Economics* 133, no. 4 (2018): 1885, https://academic.oup.com/qje/article-abstract/133/4/1885/5025665.

409 Emily Leslie and Nolan G, Pope, "The Unintended Impact of Pretrial Detention on Case Outcomes: Evidence from New York City Arraignments," *Journal of Law and Economics* 60, no. 3 (2017): 529, https://www.journals.uchicago.edu/doi/abs/10.1086/695285.
410 McCleskey v. Kemp, 481 U.S. 279, 314 (1987).
411 Fishkin, *Bottlenecks*, 21, 161 (observing that a legal system could affirmatively require all employer practices that create bottlenecks to be supported by a business justification).
412 See Randall Collins, *The Credential Society: An Historical Sociology of Education and Stratification* (New York: Columbia University Press, 2019); Kathryn Tyler, "Job Worth Doing: Update Descriptions," *Society for Human Resource Management: HR Magazine*, January 1, 2013, https://www.shrm.org/hr-today/news/hr-magazine/pages/0113-job-descriptions.aspx ("Despite the importance of job descriptions, very few HR professionals have a regular policy for updating them"… "Unfortunately, job descriptions often aren't viewed as living documents. Once completed, they may be relegated to dusty three-ring binders or long-unopened text documents").
413 Fred L. Pincus, "From Individual to Structural Discrimination," in *Race and Ethnic Conflict: Contending Views on Prejudice, Discrimination, and Ethnoviolence*, eds. Fred L. Pincus and Howard J. Ehrlich (New York: Routledge, 1994), 122.
414 Andrew Smalley, "States Consider Elimination of Degree Requirements," *NCSL*, updated October 04, 2023, https://www.ncsl.org/education/states-consider-elimination-of-degree-requirements.
415 This is another example of a mechanism that constrains opportunity which was designed for a different purpose, illustrating the complexity and contingency in much of the organization of the contemporary opportunity structure.
416 *SHRM Survey Findings: Background Checking—The Use of Credit Background Checks in Hiring Decisions* (Alexandria, VA: Society for Human Resource Management, 2012), https://www.shrm.org/hr-today/trends-and-forecasting/research-and-surveys/pages/creditbackgroundchecks.aspx.
417 Michael Klazema, "A Guide to the States that Ban Credit Checks for Employment," *Background Checks*, June 12, 2024, https://www.backgroundchecks.com/compliance-and-legislation/a-guide-to-the-states-that-ban-credit-checks-for-employment; Roy Maurer, "House Approves Ban on Most Employment Credit Checks," *SHRM*, January 30, 2020, https://www.shrm.org/topics-tools/news/talent-acquisition/house-approves-ban-employment-credit-checks.
418 Max Freedman, "Looking for a Job? Don't Tell Them You're Unemployed," *Business News Daily*, last modified October 23, 2023, https://www.businessnewsdaily.com/2919-unemployment-bias.html.
419 Fishkin, *Bottlenecks*, 231, citing 2011 N.J. Session Law c. 40, § 1, codified at N.J.S.A. 34: 8B-1.
420 Andrew Lu, "Where Is Unemployment Discrimination Illegal?," *FindLaw*, updated March 21, 2019, https://www.findlaw.com/legalblogs/law-and-life/where-is-unemployment-discrimination-illegal/.
421 Adam B. Summers, *Occupational Licensing: Ranking the States and Exploring Alternatives* (Reason Foundation, 2007), https://reason.org/wp-content/uploads/files/762c8fe96431b6fa5e27ca64eaa1818b.pdf; Lisa Knepper et al., *License to Work: A National Study of Burdens from Occupational Licensing* (Institute for Justice, 2022), https://ij.org/report/license-to-work-3/.
422 Patricia Cohen, "Moving to Arizona Soon? You Might Need a License," *New York Times*, June 17, 2016, https://www.nytimes.com/2016/06/18/business/economy/job-licenses.html.
423 Brittany Hunter, "Ten Most Ridiculous Occupational Licensing Laws," *Generation Opportunity*, August 10, 2016, https://web.archive.org/web/20170504124009/

https://blog.generationopportunity.org/articles/2016/08/10/ten-most-ridiculous-occupational-licensing-laws/.
424 "Occupational Licensing," Institute for Justice, accessed January 20, 2021, https://ij.org/issues/economic-liberty/occupational-licensing/.
425 Morris M. Kleiner, "Occupational Licensing: Protecting the Public Interest or Protectionism?," *W.E. Upjohn Institute for Employment Research* (2011): 1, https://research.upjohn.org/cgi/viewcontent.cgi?article=1008&context=up_policypapers.
426 Steven J. Davis and John Haltiwanger, "Labor Market Fluidity and Economic Performance," *Research Briefs in Economic Policy* 14 (2014): 1–2, https://www.cato.org/sites/cato.org/files/pubs/pdf/research-brief-14.pdf.
427 Matthew P. West, *Clean Cut: How Clipping Unnecessary Licensing Can Grow Opportunities for Barbers and Manicurists and Keep Consumers Safe* (Institute for Justice, 2025), https://ij.org/press-release/new-study-shows-that-heavier-licensing-burdens-do-not-improve-health-and-safety/.
428 Morris M. Kleiner, *Guild-Ridden Labor Markets: The Curious Case of Occupational Licensing* (Kalamazoo, MI: Upjohn Press, 2015), 83, https://research.upjohn.org/cgi/viewcontent.cgi?article=1254&context=up_press.
429 Jason Furman, "Beyond Antitrust: The Role of Competition Policy in Promoting Inclusive Growth" (speech, Chicago, 2016), Obama White House Archives, https://obamawhitehouse.archives.gov/sites/default/files/page/files/20160916_searle_conference_competition_furman_cea.pdf.
430 House Budget Committee Majority Staff, *The War on Poverty: 50 Years Later* (Washington, DC: House Budget Committee, 2014).
431 White House Office of the Press Secretary, "FACT SHEET: New Steps to Reduce Unnecessary Occupation Licenses that are Limiting Worker Mobility and Reducing Wages," *White House, President Barack Obama*, June 17, 2016, https://obamawhitehouse.archives.gov/the-press-office/2016/06/17/fact-sheet-new-steps-reduce-unnecessary-occupation-licenses-are-limiting.
432 Jeannette Richard, "Under New Law, Iowans No Longer Need a License to Braid Hair," *CNS News*, July 7, 2016, https://cnsnews.com/news/article/jeannette-richard/new-iowa-law-doesnt-require-state-license-braid-hair.
433 Rev. Stat. § 42:1701 (2017), https://law.justia.com/codes/louisiana/revised-statutes/title-42/rs-42-1701/.
434 Knepper et al., *License to Work*, 14 ("Since 2017, states have eliminated 26 licenses while adding 16 across our sample of 102 occupations, for a net decrease of 10").
435 Conor Dougherty, "How Noncompete Clauses Keep Workers Locked In," *New York Times*, May 13, 2017, https://www.nytimes.com/2017/05/13/business/noncompete-clauses.html; Eduardo Porter, "Where Are the Start-Ups? Loss of Dynamism is Impeding Growth," *New York Times*, February 6, 2018, https://www.nytimes.com/2018/02/06/business/economy/start-ups-growth.html.
436 Sophie Quinton, "Why Janitors Get Noncompete Agreements, Too," *HuffPost*, May 17, 2017, https://www.huffpost.com/entry/why-janitors-get-noncompete-agreements-too_b_591c5609e4b021dd5a829057; Peter Coy, "Why Are Fast Food Workers Signing Noncompete Agreements?," *New York Times*, September 29, 2021, https://www.nytimes.com/2021/09/29/opinion/noncompete-agreement-workers.html.
437 Matthew S. Johnson and Michael Lipsitz, "Why Are Low-Wage Workers Signing Noncompete Agreements?," *Journal of Human Resources* 57, no. 3 (2022): 689–724, https://jhr.uwpress.org/content/early/2020/05/04/jhr.57.3.0619-10274R2.full.pdf+html.
438 Evan Starr, J.J. Prescott, and Norman Bishara, "Noncompete Agreement in the U.S. Labor Force," *Journal of Law and Economics* 64, no. 1 (2021): 53, https://dx.doi.org/10.2139/ssrn.2625714.

439 Alan B. Krueger, "The Rigged Labor Market," *Milken Institute Review*, April 28, 2017, https://www.milkenreview.org/articles/the-rigged-labor-market.
440 Office of Economic Policy, *Non-compete Contracts: Economic Effects and Policy Implications* (Washington, DC: U.S. Department of the Treasury, 2016), 3, 10, https://www.treasury.gov/resource-center/economic-policy/Documents/UST%20Non-competes%20Report.pdf.
441 Coy, "Noncompete Agreements."
442 Michael Lipsitz and Evan Starr, "Low-Wage Workers and the Enforceability of Non-Compete Agreements," *Management Science* (2020, Revised 2022): https://dx.doi.org/10.2139/ssrn.3452240.
443 The Illinois attorney general brought suit against a check-cashing company with minimum wage workers that requires such clauses. Conor Dougherty, "Illinois Wields New Power to Challenge Noncompete Agreements," *New York Times*, October 25, 2017, https://www.nytimes.com/2017/10/25/business/economy/illinois-noncompete.html.
444 "Rubio Introduces Bill to Protect Low-Wage Workers from Non-Compete Agreements," *Marco Rubio: US Senator for Florida*, January 15, 2019, https://web.archive.org/web/20240625222542/https://www.rubio.senate.gov/rubio-introduces-privacy-bill-to-protect-consumers-while-promoting-innovation/.
445 Noam Scheiber, "U.S. Moves to Bar Noncompete Agreements in Labor Contracts," *New York Times*, January 5, 2023, https://www.nytimes.com/2023/01/05/business/economy/ftc-noncompete.html; Benjamin R. Dryden and David S. Sanders, "Federal Court Enjoins Effect of FTC Noncompete Rule — But Only for Named Plaintiffs," *Foley*, July 5, 2024, https://www.foley.com/insights/publications/2024/07/federal-court-enjoins-effect-of-ftc-noncompete-rule-but-only-for-named-plaintiffs/.
446 See, for example, Kausar Hamdani et al., *Unequal Access to Credit: The Hidden Impacts of Credit Restraints* (New York: Federal Reserve Bank of New York, 2019), https://www.newyorkfed.org/medialibrary/media/outreach-and-education/community-development/constraints-on-access-to-credit.pdf.
447 Rachel Evans, Imani Augustus, and Gabe Horwitz, *The State of Black Business* (Washington, DC: Alliance for Entrepreneurial Equity, 2024), https://www.aeequity.org/product/the-state-of-black-business.
448 Erin Arvedlund, "New $100 million PHL GRIT fund launching to back Philly's Black & Brown-owned businesses," *Philadelphia Inquirer*, January 11, 2022, https://www.inquirer.com/business/bipoc-capital-business-investment-pandemic-20220111.html; Nathan Rubbelke, "St. Louis-Based WEPOWER Teams Up with Nonprofit Lending Platform to Create Interest-Free Loans for Minority Entrepreneurs," *St. Louis Business Journal*, December 18, 2020, https://www.bizjournals.com/stlouis/news/2020/12/18/wepower-partners-to-provide-loans-to-minority.html.
449 See Stephen Hayes, *Special Purpose Credit Programs: How a Powerful Tool for Addressing Lending Disparities Fits Within the Antidiscrimination Law Ecosystem* (Washington, DC: National Fair Housing Alliance, 2020), https://nationalfairhousing.org/wp-content/uploads/2020/11/NFHA_Relman_SPCP_Article.pdf.
450 National Urban League, "Black-Owned Businesses Face Significant Obstacles. Anti-Racial Justice Efforts Are Making Them Worse," *National Urban League*, October 15, 2024, https://nul.org/news/black-owned-businesses-face-significant-obstacles-anti-racial-justice-efforts-are-making-them.
451 Robert F. Smith, "Persuade Companies to Embrace a 2 Percent Solution," *New York Times*, 2020, https://www.nytimes.com/live/2020/fix-america-economy-climate-health#robert-smith-companies-2-percent-solution.

452 Mehrsa Baradaran, *The Color of Money: Black Banks and the Racial Wealth Gap* (Cambridge, MA: Belknap Press, 2017) (arguing that Black-focused lenders are undercapitalized, depriving these communities of economic opportunities).
453 "Professor Darrick Hamilton's 10-Point Plan for a New Social Contract," *Partners for Dignity & Rights*, March 10, 2017, https://dignityandrights.org/2017/03/professor-darrick-hamiltons-10-point-plan-for-a-new-social-contract/.
454 Darrick Hamilton and William Darity Jr., "Can 'Baby Bonds' Eliminate the Racial Wealth Gap in Putative Post-Racial America?," *Review of Black Political Economy* 37, no. 3–4 (2010): 215, https://socialequity.duke.edu/wp-content/uploads/2019/10/Can-Baby-Bonds-Eliminate-the-Racial-Wealth-Gap.pdf; William A. Darity Jr., "The Big Idea - Baby Bonds: A Leg Up for Everyone," *Duke University Sanford School of Public Policy*, accessed February 16, 2022, https://web.archive.org/web/20190410180538/https://dukesanford.atavist.com/the-big-idea-baby-bonds.
455 "Press Release: McDuffie and DC Council One Step Closer to Becoming Second in Nation to Pass Baby Bonds," *DC Line*, July 19, 2021, https://thedcline.org/2021/07/19/press-release-mcduffie-and-dc-council-one-step-closer-to-becoming-second-in-nation-to-pass-baby-bonds/.
456 Michael Madowitz, Alex Rowell, and Katie Hamm, *Calculating the Hidden Cost of Interrupting a Career for Child Care* (Washington, DC: Center for American Progress, 2016), 2, https://americanprogress.org/wp-content/uploads/2016/06/ChildCareCalculator-methodology.pdf, citing Danielle Paquette and Peyton M. Craighill, "The Surprising Number of Parents Scaling Back at Work to Care for Kids," *Washington Post*, August 6, 2015, https://www.washingtonpost.com/business/economy/the-surprising-number-of-moms-and-dads-scaling-back-at-work-to-care-for-their-kids/2015/08/06/c7134c50-3ab7-11e5-b3ac-8a79bc44e5e2_story.html ("A 2015 poll commissioned by The Washington Post found that 62 percent of working mothers and 36 percent of working fathers switched to a less demanding job or stopped working altogether in order to care for children").
457 Claire Cain Miller, "How Other Nations Pay for Child Care. The U.S. Is an Outlier," *New York Times*, October 6, 2021, https://www.nytimes.com/2021/10/06/upshot/child-care-biden.html.
458 Claire Cain Miller, "How Child Care Enriches Mothers, and Especially the Sons They Raise," *New York Times*, April 20, 2017, https://www.nytimes.com/2017/04/20/upshot/how-child-care-enriches-mothers-and-especially-the-sons-they-raise.html; Katha Pollitt, "Day Care for All," *New York Times*, February 9, 2019, https://www.nytimes.com/2019/02/09/opinion/sunday/child-care-daycare-democrats-progressive.html.
459 *The Care Report* (Washington, DC: New America Foundation, 2016), https://www.newamerica.org/in-depth/care-report/.
460 Elise Gould and Tanyell Cooke, *High Quality Child Care Is Out of Reach for Working Families* (Washington, DC: Economic Policy Institute, 2015), 8, Figure D, https://files.epi.org/2015/child-care-is-out-of-reach.pdf.
461 Neil Irwin, "A Big Safety Net and Strong Job Market Can Coexist. Just Ask Scandinavia." *New York Times*, December 17, 2014, https://www.nytimes.com/2014/12/18/upshot/nordic-nations-show-that-big-safety-net-can-allow-for-leap-in-employment-rate-.html. (All things equal—see "Gaps between women and men in labour force participation around the world," Close the Gap, accessed February 23, 2022, https://web.archive.org/web/20230907175819/https://closethegap.studiometric.co/). See also Caitlyn Collins, "The Real Mommy War Is Against the State," *New York Times*, February 9, 2019, https://www.nytimes.com/2019/02/09/opinion/sunday/the-real-mommy-war-is-against-the-state.html.
462 Aparna Mathur et al., *Paid Family and Medical Leave: An Issue Whose Time Has Come* (Washington, DC: AEI-Brookings Working Group on Paid Family

Leave, 2017), 4–5, https://www.brookings.edu/wp-content/uploads/2017/06/es_20170606_paidfamilyleave.pdf. See also Bryce Covert, "The Best Era for Working Women Was 20 Years Ago," *New York Times*, September 2, 2017, https://www.nytimes.com/2017/09/02/opinion/sunday/working-women-decline-1990s.html.

463 Mikayla Bouchard, "Transportation Emerges as Crucial to Escaping Poverty," *New York Times*, May 7, 2015, https://www.nytimes.com/2015/05/07/upshot/transportation-emerges-as-crucial-to-escaping-poverty.html ("In a large, continuing study of upward mobility based at Harvard, commuting time has emerged as the single strongest factor in the odds of escaping poverty. The longer an average commute in a given county, the worse the chances of low-income families there moving up the ladder."); Chetty and Hendren, "Impacts of Neighborhoods on Intergenerational Mobility," 71.

464 Chris Salviati and Rob Warnock, "Explosion of Super Commuters Offers Lessons for Sustainable Growth," *Apartment List*, August 16, 2021, https://www.apartmentlist.com/research/explosion-of-super-commuters-offers-lessons-for-sustainable-growth.

465 Michael Kolomatsky, "Where Are Workers Making the Longest Commutes," *New York Times*, August 26, 2021, https://www.nytimes.com/2021/08/26/realestate/supercommuter-longest-commutes.html.

466 Dougherty and Burton, "2:15 Alarm, 2 Trains and a Bus."

467 Hoehner et al., "Commuting Distance, Cardiorespiratory Fitness, and Metabolic Risk," 571–578.

468 Cashin, *White Space, Black Hood*, 23.

469 Michael R. Strain, *Getting Back to Work* (Washington, DC: Conservative Reform Network, 2014), 21, https://web.archive.org/web/20181124201938/http://conservativereform.com/wp-content/uploads/2016/07/CRN_Employment_FINAL.pdf; Michael R. Strain, "How the government can spend billions of dollars on a new policy and still win conservative support," *Washington Post*, August 22, 2014, https://www.washingtonpost.com/posteverything/wp/2014/08/22/how-the-government-can-spend-billions-of-dollars-on-a-new-policy-and-still-win-conservative-support/.

470 John Pawasarat and Lois M. Quinn, *Issues Related to Wisconsin "Failure to Pay Forfeitures" Drivers License Suspensions* (Milwaukee: Employment and Training Institute at the School of Continuing Education, University of Wisconsin-Milwaukee, 2014), 9, https://web.archive.org/web/20190204143742/https://uwm.edu/eti/2014/FPFSuspensionsReport.pdf.

471 Or it may simply be necessary to reach a job beyond the bus line. Joseph Shapiro, "How Driver's License Suspensions Unfairly Target the Poor," *NPR*, January 5, 2015, https://www.npr.org/2015/01/05/372691918/how-drivers-license-suspensions-unfairly-target-the-poor.

472 Massimo Ragnedda and Glenn W. Muschert, eds., *The Digital Divide: The Internet and Social Inequality in International Perspective* (London: Routledge, 2013).

473 Cecilia Kang, "Bridging a Digital Divide That Leaves Schoolchildren Behind," *New York Times*, February 22, 2016, https://www.nytimes.com/2016/02/23/technology/fcc-internet-access-school.html; Anthony W. Marx, "Too Poor to Afford the Internet," *New York Times*, August 12, 2016, https://www.nytimes.com/2016/08/12/opinion/too-poor-to-afford-the-internet.html.

474 Christopher Ali, "We Need a National Rural Broadband Plan," *New York Times*, February 6, 2019, https://www.nytimes.com/2019/02/06/opinion/rural-broadband-fcc.html.

475 John Busby, Julia Tanberk, and BroadbandNow Team, "FCC Reports Broadband Unavailable to 21.3 Million Americans, BroadbandNow Study Indicates 42 Million

Do Not Have Access," *BroadbandNow Research*, October 21, 2021, https://broadbandnow.com/research/fcc-underestimates-unserved-by-50-percent.
476 Ben Casselman, "Rural Areas Are Looking for Workers. They Need Broadband to Get Them.," *New York Times*, May 18, 2021, https://www.nytimes.com/2021/05/17/business/infrastructure-rural-broadband.html.
477 Cevat Giray Aksoy et al., "Working from Home Around the World," *University of Chicago Becker Friedman Institute for Economics*, September 13, 2022, https://bfi.uchicago.edu/insight/research-summary/working-from-home-around-the-world/.
478 "FACT SHEET: ConnectHome: Coming Together to Ensure Digital Opportunity for All Americans," White House Office of the Press Secretary, July 15, 2015, https://obamawhitehouse.archives.gov/the-press-office/2015/07/15/fact-sheet-connecthome-coming-together-ensure-digital-opportunity-all.
479 "U.S. Chamber Releases Recommendations for Closing the Digital Divide in Rural America," U.S. Chamber of Commerce Technology Engagement Center, June 23, 2020, https://www.uschamber.com/technology/us-chamber-releases-recommendations-closing-the-digital-divide-rural-america; "Business Roundtable Releases Broadband Policy Recommendations," Business Roundtable, September 18, 2020, accessed February 17, 2022, https://www.businessroundtable.org/business-roundtable-releases-broadband-policy-recommendations.
480 LinkNYC, accessed February 17, 2022, https://www.link.nyc/.
481 See, for example, Jeffrey J. Selingo, "Will You Sprint, Stroll, or Stumble Into a Career?," *New York Times*, April 5, 2016, https://www.nytimes.com/2016/04/10/education/edlife/will-you-sprint-stroll-or-stumble-into-a-career.html; Marie Tae McDermott, "Will You Sprint, Stroll, or Stumble Into a Career?: Readers Respond," *New York Times*, April 7, 2016, https://www.nytimes.com/2016/04/07/insider/will-you-sprint-stroll-or-stumble-into-a-career-readers-respond.html.

Conclusion

A 2016 study found that there were a handful of large counties in the United States where Black families earned more than white families, even though the overall Black-white income gap widened in the wake of the 2007–2008 economic recession.[1] In a nation where Black income and wealth disparities are large and persistent, this headline seemed like a hopeful sign of progress. Upon closer examination, a more disturbing explanation emerged.

Each of the counties where Black families earned more than their white neighbors were exurban counties ringing large metropolitan regions flush with well-paying corporate or government jobs. Many high-income Black employees worked in these sectors, but they were commuting much further to work than their white colleagues. Because these families had less wealth to draw from, these families had a more difficult time purchasing homes in higher opportunity neighborhoods closer to their jobs. Longer commute times are associated with a host of health hazards, including stress, higher risk of heart attack, stroke, and hypertension, as well as social impacts, such as less time with family and friends.[2] Rather than a sign of progress, the apparent Black income advantage in these counties was a byproduct of structural disadvantage. To see this, one had to look beneath the rosy surface and examine the underlying structural dynamics, such as the spatial mismatch between residence by race and jobs.

Contemporary racial inequality in the United States is primarily a product of structural forces and dynamics. Even if we could curb racial discrimination and drive out racist ideas, racial inequality would persist on a massive scale. Structural racism is a highly adaptive perpetual motion machine that operates in the absence of racist actors based upon a set of mechanisms, forces, and incentives that require, at most, self-interested actors and indifferent policymakers who are either insensitive to or unaware of the effects of their collective actions and decisions. More precisely, structural inequality is the result of complex set of interactions, most of which are not obviously motivated by racial animus or may even be well-intended. Thus, patterns of persistent racial inequality require no racist actors or racist individuals to maintain themselves over time and across space. Structural racism describes the callous indifference, ongoing neglect, and inattention to the reality of structural racial inequality.

DOI: 10.4324/9781003562764-7

Despite the ubiquity of race in American society, the endless scholarship and commentary, and despite the intimate and traumatic experiences of race and racism for so many, our collective understanding of the production of racial inequality remains surprisingly incomplete and shallow. Our prevailing ways of understanding and talking about race are too often mistaken or only partly accurate, and critical misunderstandings persist.

This book has presented and developed a framework for understanding the production of contemporary racial inequality in structural terms that is hopefully clearer and more comprehensible than has been done before, contrasting it with related ideas and frameworks. It has attempted to demystify this concept by specifying the key mechanisms and processes that undergird and constitute it. In the process, it has attempted to address, if not resolve, many perennial debates, including, but not limited to:

- The relative influence of intentional discrimination, inter-personal racism, racial antipathy, prejudice and animus versus structural, systemic, and institutional conditions and dynamics, and the indifference, neglect, and self-interest that drives or accompanies them, in explaining the extent and persistence of contemporary racial inequality.
- The question of race versus class in understanding the sources and nature of racial inequality.
- The relative influence of the past versus present-day or more recent policies and actions in the production and maintenance of contemporary racial inequality.
- How to think about disparities, whether they are closing or widening in relative versus absolute terms, and in relation to the goal of racial justice, and how to make sense of the possibilities and paradoxical reality of simultaneous progress, stasis, and regress on various indicators of well-being under conditions of contemporary structural racism.
- The optimal design of policies and other programmatic interventions to remedy or dismantle structural racism, including whether they need to be race-specific or targeted or should be more universalistic or broad-based, and whether they should target people and help them work through or around prevailing structural conditions or seek to change structural arrangements.

This book has offered clear, albeit nuanced, positions on each of these issues. For too long, racism has been framed in either interpersonal or institutional terms. The terms "systemic racism," or less frequently, "structural racism," are increasingly used, but there remains a lack of analytic clarity, specificity, or consensus on their definition. Even when invoked, they are frequently erected on premises or assumptions that deny their structural import. Perhaps worse, the definitions are so convoluted as to elude easy understanding. These terms signify something, but they mystify as much as clarify. This book presented a structural model of contemporary racial inequality to demystify this important concept and explain how it operates in clear and comprehensible terms.

This book weaves together two often disparate perspectives: research on upward mobility and the much larger body of scholarship on race and racial inequality. The first chapter opened by deconstructing the concept of opportunity. When opportunity is viewed as the complete range of pathways available to a person over their life course, then both the decisions they make and the options they enjoy are structurally conjoined.

Without falling into hagiography, this book examined the American Dream—the pursuit of opportunity, of social and economic advancement. The foundation of this book is an investigation of opportunity America, where it exists, how it is created, extended and pursued. It examined the components of the contemporary opportunity structure, and the forces that shape it. The United States has fallen behind as a place of social and economic mobility, but there is also significant variation within the United States. This geographic variability helped us identify the forces that facilitate upward mobility, and their respective geographic scales. Opportunity coalesces most powerfully in places where resources are more abundant. The most high-opportunity environments are great neighborhoods nested within flourishing jurisdictions in robust regions with strong economies.

Chapter 2 then mapped race to the opportunity structure, illustrating how the configuration of opportunity in American society produces persistently racialized outcomes. We saw that racial inequity is structured both because of the inequitable distribution of public resources, but also because of the hoarding of private and intangible resources, such as social capital and network relationships. This chapter emphasized the interconnected problems of municipal fragmentation and fiscal inequality and suggested the limits of an agenda that focuses primarily on equalizing public resources. It is unlikely that racial equality can ever be achieved in a racially segregated society.

Chapter 3 provided a historical perspective that traced the origins of the policies and decisions that built the racialized opportunity structure we live under today. We discovered that structural racism is both a product of historical legacies and discrimination as well as developments of recent origin, such as mass incarceration and the War on Drugs, finance and credit practices associated with subprime mortgage lending and the housing crisis, gradual disinvestment in public goods and municipal fiscal distress. Vivid expressions of structural racism can be found in places like Flint, Michigan and Ferguson, Missouri.

Chapter 4 then reexamined familiar debates over race in light of the structural racism model rather than the traditional inter-personal racism model. Within a structural paradigm, there is a greater emphasis on outcomes and analysis than intent and motivation. We should judge people on whether they support or oppose effective policies that ameliorate racial inequality rather than on their personal prejudices or beliefs. The goal of racial justice is not to eliminate bigotry or drive out racist ideas, but to construct a society that affords broad and equitable access to a range of opportunities, and therefore in which race no longer shapes life chances. The remainder of the chapter examined the contours of a structural racism change agenda in light of these objectives, and how a structural perspective changes our assessment of longstanding policy debates, such as affirmative action, disparate impact liability, and reparations.

Chapter 5 advanced a set of ten broad policy recommendations and general principles that would expand access to opportunity and reduce racial disparities. The policies discussed in Chapter 5 were not exhaustive, but they are well-tailored to those twin objectives. Derived from an analysis of structural racism, it called for an expansion and revitalization of the pathways of opportunity, investment in resources that enhance skills and open pathways, and to address the stubborn fact of racial inequality of opportunity.

Building on social science research, this book attempts to sharpen the way we understand opportunity, with a new or clarified model for thinking and acting. It also seeks to strengthen our structural perceptiveness. Consider the fact that 65% of American Olympic gold medals were won by American women in the 2024 Paris Olympics.[3] Why, too, is the US women's soccer team the best or near best in the world, when the men's team, is not even in the top ten? The answer, in part, is institutions and investments.

America not only created institutions that train and reward female athletes in sport and Olympic competitions, but laws such as Title IX ensure that women's athletics at the secondary and collegiate level receive equal funding as men's athletics. Title IX has meant that the United States developed a tremendous pool of skilled athletes and nurtured female talent at all ages relative to most other countries. In many ways, this is the idea of the opportunity structure in miniature. We created institutions and adopted laws that channel individuals through that structure to compete at the highest levels and to achieve their full potential.

When the structures of opportunity impede the achievements of members of particular social groups, such as when women were denied equal resources or opportunities prior to Title IX, then those structures render gender itself a bottleneck in the opportunity structure.[4] In that case, a person's sex becomes a defining constraint or barrier to advancement and success. When this is tolerated and ignored, we might call this structural sexism.

But structural bottlenecks do more than impair individual life chances; they also generate meanings that attach to the identities of individuals and groups impeded. When women are denied equal opportunities to succeed in athletic competition and the resources to nurture their athletic talents, doubts about female athletic ability or interest in sports take root, stereotypes form, and confirmation bias takes over.

Such categorical bottlenecks are the foundation for many social meanings and group-based associations, including those of race. The negative and harmful effects of structural racism on members of racially marginalized groups shape the perception of those groups. Denial of opportunity is the seedbed for negative stereotypes about ability. Exclusion from high-paying jobs and certain sectors or industries is fertilizer for harmful stereotypes about industriousness or diligence. When such meanings become prominent, race is more than merely a negative credential that impairs other opportunities. It becomes a stigmatic harm, prompting members of other races to avoid schools or neighborhoods or even associate with members of the stigmatized group. In this way, structural conditions are the basis for socially significant meanings. Rather than combat those meanings, we should remedy the structures that sustain them.

We have broadened access to opportunity in the past, and we can do so again.⁵ We can and must do better than circumscribe people's life chances based upon circumstances of birth, especially when those circumstances are based on class or race. In this regard, the rise and fall of Detroit is a cautionary tale. In his landmark study, the historian Thomas Sugrue concluded that "the fate of the city is a consequence of the unequal distributions of power and resources."⁶ Referring to the racial strife and prejudice that thoroughly shaped labor competition and housing segregation and pulled the region apart, the seeds of Detroit's fiscal reckoning preceded the global competition and management blunders of later decades.⁷

If we view this observation as more than a historical postmortem, but also as a warning, one can faintly see the outlines of how regions like the San Francisco Bay Area, riven by "unequal distribution of power and resources" might ultimately suffer as well. The suburban communities ringing Detroit initially benefited from white flight and urban decline, but ultimately the consequences could not be cabined to the city limits, and the entire region felt the pain of the city's distress.

We must challenge, resist, and dismantle structural racism. Not only to finally and fully solve racial inequality, but also to help our nation reach its full potential.⁸

Notes

1 Tim Henderson, "The (Very) Few Places with No Black-White Income Gap," *Stateline*, November 10, 2016, https://stateline.org/2016/11/10/the-very-few-places-with-no-black-white-income-gap/.
2 Hoehner et al., "Commuting Distance, Cardiorespiratory Fitness, and Metabolic Risk"; Christian, "Trade-offs between commuting time and health-related activities"; Steve Crabtree, "Well-being Lower Among Workers with Long Commutes," *Gallup*, August 13, 2010, https://news.gallup.com/poll/142142/wellbeing-lower-among-workers-long-commutes.aspx.
3 Kari Anderson, "Women Earned the Majority of Gold Medals for Team USA in Paris — Here's a List of Every American Woman Who Won Gold," *Yahoo Sports*, August 12, 2024, https://sports.yahoo.com/women-earned-the-majority-of-gold-medals-for-team-usa-in-paris--heres-a-list-of-every-american-woman-who-won-gold-171156767.html.
4 Fishkin, *Bottlenecks*, 158.
5 Jacob Hacker and Paul Pierson, "The Great Divide" in *American Amnesia: How the War on Government Led Us to Forget What Made America Prosper*, (New York: Simon and Schuster, 2016); Robert D. Putnam, The Upswing: How America Came Together a Century Ago and How We Can Do It Again (New York: Simon & Schuster, 2020).
6 Sugrue, *Urban Crisis*, 14.
7 Specifically, he argues that "the coincidence and mutual reinforcement of race, economics, and politics in a particular historical moment, the period from the 1940s to the 1960s, set the stage for the fiscal, social, and economic crises that confront urban America today." Sugrue, *Urban Crisis*, 5. It is not difficult to imagine a future historian formulating a similar claim about the Bay Area today.
8 Daron Acemoglu and James A. Robinson, *Why Nations Fail: The Origins of Power, Prosperity, and Poverty* (New York: Crown Business, 2012).

Acknowledgments

Projects of this size and scope take many years, and this is no exception. I staked a commitment to this project sometime around 2010 and had a clear vision and structure by 2011. Despite tremendous and continuous effort, it wasn't until about 2019 that I had a completed rough draft. From there, it took the next five years to complete the citations and endnotes and trim and tame the text into a digestible form. At one point, the manuscript was nearly double the current length, with an overwhelming number of statistics and studies, and the publisher wisely insisted on brevity for your benefit. The work is undoubtedly stronger as a result.

Despite the long gestation, time and intervening events have sharpened, rather than changed, my vision and analysis. I am immensely grateful to the publisher and editors for taking this project on, and bringing my vision to life.

Foremost, I owe a debt of gratitude to john a. powell, a brilliant mentor and friend who has profoundly shaped my life and thinking in ways I cannot fully express or perhaps even fully understand. My work for him, with him, and with his support led me to many of the insights presented in these pages.

I would also like to thank Richard Rothstein, Michael Omi, and Michelle Alexander, colleagues who have spurred me on. All three have written awesome or important books on related subjects while I was working with them, and have inspired me to emulate their work ethic. More importantly, all three have been immensely kind and supportive.

I also owe a debt of gratitude to many research assistants who helped with the manuscript and colleagues and friends who provided more general feedback on the manuscript. For the former, I particularly wish to acknowledge Tatum Hurley, Sanjana Manjeshwar, Skyler Pemberton, Rhea Vermani, Mel Gonzalez, and Ruqayah Ghaus. For the latter, I wish to acknowledge Samir Gambhir, who has long been a close thought partner and helped me with data sourcing, and Nancy McCardle, who is so generous with her time and served as a reviewer.

I would like to thank my colleagues and associates Cecilie Surasky, Eli Moore, Shadrick Small, Olivia Araiza, Maile Munro, Hossein Ayazi,

Nicole Montojo, and Alex Schafran for their feedback, help, or support for this project. If I have forgotten anyone, please forgive me.

I would also like to acknowledge the people who shared their stories with me, and whose lives are represented on these pages. I have used pseudonyms to protect their privacy, but I owe them appreciation and thanks nonetheless.

I also owe thanks to my partners, past and present, who have sacrificed countless date nights and quality time so that I might toil on this manuscript. Without their love and support, this could never have been completed.

Above all, this book is dedicated to my parents, Charlaine and Walter Menendian, who gave me every opportunity they could afford. My love and gratitude to all.

Index

Note: Page references in *italics* denote figures, in **bold** tables and with "n" endnotes.

"the accountability debate" 245n121
affirmative action 6, 222–223, 225–230; and American institutions 226; in contracting 226; in employment 226; formulated in 226; in higher education 226–228; in India 226; race-based 226–230
affirmatively furthering fair housing (AFFH) 276
African Americans *see* Black Americans
Alexander, Michelle 166, 194n303
Allen, Danielle 244n120
All in the Family 204
American Apartheid: Segregation and the Making of the Underclass (Massey and Denton) 109n76
American Bar Association 95, 298
American Dream 13, 15, 45n32, 60, 61, 343; geographic mobility 38–41; homeownership data 88, 145, 149–150, 172–173
American Enterprise Institute 304
American slavery 131, 222, 228; *see also* reparations
American Society of Civil Engineers 98, 176
anchor institutions 262
Anti-Drug Abuse Act 165
antiracism 6, 235
Association of American Colleges and Universities 138
Association of American Law Schools 138
assortative mating 38

bail 292, 297–298; bail bonds 298; bail reform 218, 298; pre-trial 297–298
"baby bonds" 303–304
Baltimore 18, 136, 151, 171, 209, 298, 305
Baltimore Regional Housing Partnership 269
"Ban the Box" 289, 300
Bell, Derrick 223
bipartisan consensus 301
Black Americans 60–64, 79, 303; concentrated poverty 68–70; and Covid-19 pandemic 98–99; educational attainment 83–84; environmental racism 97; health 97; homeownership 172, **172**; population growth 135; racial isolation 79; in racially segregated neighborhoods 185n133; racial networks 91; racial wealth gap 85–86, 89; reported killings of 1; segregation 79, 81–82; spatial mismatch 89–91; upward mobility rate 81
Black children: blood lead levels 177; childhood poverty 65; concentrated poverty 72; durable poverty 74; economic mobility 61–64; educational attainment 85; health 98; incarceration 96–98; integrated neighborhoods 81; racial segregation 81; racial wealth gap 87–88
Black entrepreneurs 303
Black life expectancy 219
Black Lives Matter Movement 208–209, 293, 330n344
Black neighborhoods 70, 79, 90, 97–98, 130, 140–142, 144, 146, 150–151, 163, 170, 172–173
Black youth: educational attainment 83; financial assistance 88; poverty rates

65; racially segregated neighborhoods 85; in segregated schools 84; unemployment 89
Blanton, Thomas Edwin, Jr. 205
Boudin, Chesa 296
Bowling Alone (Putnam) 28
Brookings Institution 61, 304
Browder, Kalief 298
Brown, Michael 208, 294
Brown v. Board of Education 82, 157–158, 160
Buchanan v. Warley 137
Bush, George W. 205, 207
Business Roundtable 306

Coates, Ta-Nahesi 121n234, 122n249
Cabrini-Green complex 267
California's Regional Housing Needs Allocation (RHNA) policy 274
capabilities approach 43n15
capitalism 244n112
career and technical education (CTE) 283–284
Carmichael, Stokely 206
Carter, Prudence 76
Cashin, Sheryll 108n59, 120n222, 145, 184n112, 228, 247n154
census: American community survey (ACS) 107n44, 107n45, 108n47; Census of Governments 127n316, 128n339; decennial census 129
Centers for Disease Control and Prevention (CDC) 97, 176
Chambers, Martin 211
Chauvin, Derek 209, 294
Chetty, Raj 16, 42n7, 46n35, 46n39, 46n41, 46n44, 47n46, 47n47, 48n62, 48n63, 49n77, 51n110, 52n127, 53n128, 54n153, 56n176, 56n188; 63, 89, 91, 106n124, 106n28, 113n115, 118n190, 231, 281, 323n228
Chicago Child-Parent center program 280
Chicago Housing Authority 265
childhood poverty 75; Black and White 66; Black youth poverty rates 65; structural racism inequality 64–67, 66
Christie, Chris 274, 286
Civil Rights Act of 1964 206, 237n13
Civil Rights Movement 210, 234
CMTO (Creating Moves to Opportunity) 269

Clark, Kenneth 232
class: advantages of upward mobility 14–15; dynamics and racial inequality 76; geographic sorting of Americans by 29; middle (*see* middle class); *vs.* race 75–76
"classic social dilemma" 242n89
collaborative regional planning 259
Collateralized Debt Obligations (CDOs) 167
Commodity Futures Modernization Act of 2000 196n337
community benefits agreements 262
community workforce agreements 262
commuting 341 super 304–305; time 32, 89, 339n463; zones 21, 50n99
Comprehensive Crime Control Act 164
Comprehensive Drug Abuse Prevention and Control Act 165
concentrated disadvantage 72, 109n69
concentrated poverty 67–72, **68–69, 70, 71**; Black Americans 68–71; and concentrated disadvantage 72; defined 67
Connor, Bull 132
core capabilities 302–306
Covid-19 pandemic 263, 306; and Black Americans 98–99; communities of color 99
Cowan, Tyler 40
credit checks 299, 300, 302
criminal justice system 291–298
critical access points 302–306
"culture of poverty" 242n94
cumulative effects 73, 179n13
"curb-cut effect" 223

Dalits 226
degree inflation 299
deindustrialization 5, 161–164, 174
Denton, Nancy A. 109n76, 110n84
Department of Housing and Urban Development (HUD) 27, 145, 153, 268–269, 275–277, 315n114
Department of Justice 189n208, 208–209, 233, 275, 293–296; Baltimore Report of 2016 233; Ferguson reports 294
desegregation 5, 130–131, 157–161
Detroit, Michigan 19–21, 129
DiAngelo, Robin 205
digital divide 305–306

discrimination: invidious 236n7; racial 2, 89–90, 205–206, 214, 218, 236n8, 268, 275, 295, 341
disparate impact 224–225
disparate treatment 236n7
displacement 260–264
Dissimilarity Index 78, 80, 133, **134**; dissimilarity score 78–79
Divergence Index 80–81
Diversity, Equity, and Inclusion (DEI): initiatives 1; trainings or workshops 216
downzoning 154
DuBois, W.E.B. 222
durable poverty 72–75

economically disadvantaged 73, 279
economic development 3, 151, 259, 260, 262
economic inequality 105n10; decline in marriage rates 38; and education 84; inequality of opportunity 13; racial 90, 303; in United States 13; upward 7, 37–38
economic justice 244n119
economic mobility 3–4, 13–15, 17, 29, 37–38; inter-generational 83; and race 61–64; relative 45; and social networks 31; upward 60; *see also* mobility
economic segregation 29–30, 77, 81
education: career and technical education (CTE) 283–284; and economic inequality 84; higher (*see* higher education); public 12, 23, 257, 277–284
educational attainment: Black youth 83–85; and mass incarceration 94; racial disparities in 83; structural components of opportunity 84; structural racism inequality 83–85, **84**
emergent properties 217
Emerson, Ralph Waldo 11
employment barriers 299–303
Empowerment Zones 261
Enos, Ryan 241n89
Enterprise Communities 261
environmental racism 97
equal developmental opportunity 44n18
equal educational opportunity 44n18
Equal Employment Opportunity Commission (EEOC) 95, 289
equal opportunity 14, 16, 18, 44n18
exclusionary land use policies 270–275

exclusionary localism 99–103
exclusionary zoning 25, 155–156, 272–273

fair housing 153–156, 276–277
Fair Housing Act 153–157, 207, 275–277
fair housing laws 275–277
Fair Share Act of 1985 273–274
"fair share" policies 273
family: educational attainment of parents 35; and opportunity structure 34–38; parenting 35–36; single-parent household 38; wealth 37–38
Federal Bureau of Prisons 290
Federal Housing Administration (FHA) 145–148, 186n152
Federal Trade Commission 302
Ferguson Commission of 2015 233
Ferguson Police Department 294
Financial Services Modernization Act of 1999 196n337
Finch, Atticus 234
fiscal destiny 311n68
fiscal regionalism 257–260
fiscal zoning 154
Fischel, William 311n68
Fishkin, Joseph 47n52, 245n125, 245n126, 246n145, 247n149, 309n39
Flint, Michigan 173–175, 177
Florida, Richard 48n74, 52n123, 52n127, 58n213, 253, 312n83, 312n85
Floyd, George 209, 217, 294
Ford, Henry 31
Forman, James, Jr. 167
Formerly Incarcerated Reenter Society Transformed Safely Transitioning Every Person Act (FIRST STEP Act) 286
fragmentation: defined 100; jurisdictional 99–103
fraternal twins 76
"freedom of choice" plans 157
Freedom to Compete Act 302
Friedman, Milton 244n113

Gautreaux case 265–267
Galster, George 17
Garcia, Mercedes 252–253, 264
"The Gardner's Tale" 214
Garner, Eric 208, 294
Gascón, George 296
Gates, Bill 11

Gautreaux, Dorothy 265
Geoffrey Canada's Harlem Children's Zone (HCZ) program 261
geographic mobility: labor mobilization 39; opportunity structure 39–41; trends **39**, 39–40; wage gains 41
GI Bill 148, 281; *see also* Servicemen's Readjustment Act of 1944
Gladwell, Malcolm 11–12, 234, 247n151
Glee 31
global financial crisis of 2007–2008 167, 176
globalization 5, 162
Goldin, Claudia 278
Go Set a Watchman 235
Gotham, Kevin Fox 183n92
Gray, Freddie 209, 294
Great Depression 143
Great Migration 134, 140, 255
Great Recession 88, 167, 171, 252, 263, 282
The Green Book 204, 216
Griggs case 245n125

Hamilton, Charles V. 206
Hanna-Attisha, Mona 173
Hannah-Jones, Nikole 221
Harlan, John 219
Head Start 65, 280
health: Black Americans 97; Black children 98; and environment 97–99; structural racism inequality 97–99
hierarchical positioning 204
higher education: access to 277; affirmative action in 225–227; costs of 85; critical institutions of 220; and family wealth and income 37; and GI Bill 281; public 282; public institutions of 129, 176
high-poverty neighborhoods 35, 67–70, 74, 92, 174–175, 262
HighScope Perry Preschool program, Ypsilanti, Michigan 280
Hills v. Gautreaux 265–267
Hinton, Elizabeth 213
Hogan, Larry 300
Home Mortgage Disclosure Act 169
Homeowners Associations 138, 140
Home Owners Loan Corporation (HOLC) 143–145, 148
HOPE VI 261
Housing and Community Development Act of 1974 276

Housing Choice Voucher program (Section 8) 267–268
Houston, Charles Hamilton 157
Hurricane Katrina 203, 207, 219

Ickes, Harold 151–152
identity-blindness 241n92
individual racism model 204–208
industrialization 136, 255
institutional racism 205–206, 214, 224
insular networks 33
"interest-convergence" dilemma 223
intergenerational mobility 231
intergenerational neighborhood poverty 74
intergenerational poverty 64, 73
Internet 263; LinkNYC 306; nationwide broadband 263, 306
Interstate Highway Act 148
"invidious" discrimination 236n7
IZ ordinances 272–273

Jackson, Kenneth 311n68
Jackson, Mississippi 177
James v. Valtierra 155
JFK 183n79, 225
Jim Crow 104, 131–132, 178, 210; segregation 132–134
Jobs, Steve 11
Johnson, Matthew "Peanut" 192n268, 210, 211
jurisdictional fragmentation 99–103

Kain, John 90
Kaiser, Henry 252
Kaiser Company 135
Kaiser Permanente 252
Kansas City School district 278
Kasich, John 59–60
Katz, Lawrence 278
KCMSD 279
Kendi, Ibram X. 205, 219, 236n8, 236n9, 241n91
Kennedy, Anthony 207
Kenwood and Hyde Park Property Association 139
Kerner, Otto 210
Kerner Commission 210, 212–213, 233–234, 240n50, 292–293
Kerner Report 213, 232–234, 292
King, Martin Luther, Jr. 213
Koch brothers 285

Kramer, Larry 296
Krueger, Alan 302
Ku Klux Klan 205

Latino Americans 67, 93
Lee, Harper 234
Lewis, Oscar 242n94
Lincoln, Abraham 11–12
Lindsey, John 210
LinkNYC 306
Livonia 129
Low Income Housing Tax Credit (LIHTC) 268
low-income neighborhoods 69, 72, 103, 163
low-income workers 90, 302
low-opportunity: amusement park 26; areas 265, 268; communities 26, 40, 262; environments 47n51, 92, 96, 264; neighborhoods 270; places 261

market-based economics 243n112
Marshall, Thurgood 132, 157
"Massachusetts Comprehensive Permit Act" (40B) 274
Massey, Douglas 109n76, 110n84
mass incarceration 284–291; Black men 93–96; defined 93; and educational attainment 94; racial composition 94; structural racism inequality 93–96; and War on Drugs 164–167
Mays, Willie 254
McCleskey v. Kemp 298
"metaeffects" 217
microloans 303
middle class 10, 15, 29–30, 35–36, 63, 67–68, 76–77, 79, 81, 92, 103, 129, 135, 149; Black neighborhoods 150; income 163; neighborhoods 175, 272–273; wages 284
Milliken v. Bradley 159–160, 278
Missouri v. Jenkins 278–279
mobility: absolute 45n32; absolute income 15; geographic 38–41; metaphors 43n8; relative 45n32; upward 13–16, 61; *see also* economic mobility
mobility strategies: pursuing 264–270; supporting 264–270
Mosby, Marilyn 296
Mount Laurel case 273–274
Moving To Opportunity (MTO) experiment 27, 29, 266–267

municipal fiscal distress 173–177
municipal inequality 21–26; affluent communities 23; communal resources 23; tax base capacity 22; wealth disparities 23
municipal zoning ordinances 25
Myers, Mike 203

NAACP 138, 273
NAACP Legal Defense Fund 157
National Advisory Commission on Civil Disorders 210; *see also* Kerner Commission
National Assessment of Educational Progress (NAEP) 73
National Association of Real Estate Brokers (NAREB) 139
National Association of Realtors 138
National Industrial Recovery Act 151
National Institute of Corrections 297
National Urban League 303
neighborhood 50n99; Black 70, 79, 90, 97–98, 130, 140–142, 144, 146, 150–151, 163, 170, 172–173; high-poverty 35, 67–70, 74, 92, 174–175, 262; low-income 69; poverty rates 71
neighborhood associations 28, 140; super- 156
neighborhood effects 3, 26–29
neighborhood racial predominance 68, 69, 70, 107n46
New Deal 142–143, 145
New Great Migration 253–256
New Jersey Constitution 273
New Yorker magazine 234
Nicklaus, Jack 10
Nixon, Jay 259
Nixon, Richard 213
Noah, Trevor 17
non-compete clauses 299–302
nonprofit organizations 28
non-violent drug offenses 287
"Not In My Back Yard" (NIMBY) 152

Obama, Barack 167, 172–174, 208–209, 261, 285, 301
occupational licensing 299–303
OECD countries 278, 280, 283
opportunity 3–5, 43n10; creation of pathways 12–13; inequality of 7; metaphors related to 11
opportunity agenda 256–306
Opportunity Atlas 29
opportunity bargains 269

opportunity gap 13–14
opportunity hoarding 100
opportunity pluralism 309n39
opportunity structure 3–4, 10–42; economic segregation 29–30; family matters 34–38; geographic mobility 38–41; municipal inequality 21–26; neighborhood effects 26–29; overview 16–18; place matters 18–19; regional conditions 19–21; social networks 31–34; upward mobility in America 13–16
Opportunity Zone initiative 261
Opportunity Zones program 262
Outliers (Gladwell) 11–12
overprotective parenting 35

Pace, John 140
Pager, Devah 89
parenting 35–36; bulldozer 35; overprotective 35; snowplow 35; styles 36
pathways of opportunity 12–13, 64, 83, 281, 290; opportunity structure 60; social networks 31; upward mobility 16
Pence, Mike 286
Perkins Act 284
Perry, Rick 291
Pew Charitable Trusts 62
Pfaff, John F. 327n289
place-based strategies 260–264
Plessy v. Ferguson 132
police killings 208, 293
Porter, Eduardo 245n121
poverty: childhood 64–67, 66; concentrated 67–72, **68–69**, **70**; durable 72–75; intergenerational 64, 73; intergenerational neighborhood 74; *see also specific types*
predatory lending 167–173
pre-K programs 277, 280
pre-trial detention 297–298
"prison gerrymandering" 291
Prohibition 287–288
Promise Neighborhoods 261
prosecutorial misconduct 295
public education 12, 23, 257, 277–284
public housing 150–153
Public Housing Authority 188n200
public-school funding 22–23
Public Works Administration (PWA) 151–152
Putnam, Robert 28

"qualified immunity" 294

race 2, 7n1; *vs.* class 75–76; economic disparities by 64; economic inequality by 84; and economic mobility 61–64; homeownership by 172, **172**
race-based affirmative action 226–230
The Race between Education and Technology (Goldin and Katz) 278
race riots 140
racial composition 78, **94**
racial discrimination 2, 89–90, 205–206, 214, 218, 236n8, 268, 275, 295, 341
racial disparities 1–2, 5, 7, 60, 64, 75–76, 89, 104, 172, 205, 222; in college graduation rates 88; in educational attainment 83; in employment rates 89; in health 97; in household income and wealth 67; in income and earnings 89; in the poverty rate 65; in well-being and life outcomes 87
racial economic inequality 90, 303
racial inequality 1–2, 4–6, 167; and American society 60; and class dynamics 76; cultural explanations for 242n94; global financial crisis of 2007–2008 167; interpersonal model of 209; structural 77, 170, 174, 178; systemic 77
racialized identities 216
racial justice 244n119; goal of 218–221; structural agenda 218–221
racial justice advocacy 2, 219
racial justice literature 243n112
racially restrictive covenants 137–139
racial residential integration 82
racial residential segregation 5, 77, 98; in the North 133; origins of 134–142; real estate boards 140
racial segregation 76–82; Black families 77; structural racism inequality 76–82; and zoning 136; *see also* segregation
racial sorting 112n111
racial wealth gap: family wealth 87; and homeownership gap 88; structural racism inequality 85–89, **86**; student debt 85, 277, 282; white to Black wealth 86, **86**; between young families 87
racial zoning 136–137, 154
racism: environmental 97; institutional 205–206, 214, 224; interpersonal/individual 215–218, 234; structural

(see structural racism); systemic 1, 213–218; see also structural racism; structural racism inequality
RAND Corporation 290
Red Cross 203
re-entry 285, 288–289, 291
Reeves, Richard 61
regional housing markets 21
Renewal Communities 261
reparations 231–232
residential integration 275–277
residential segregation 132–136
Rice, Tamir 294
"rigged market" 302
"Riot Report" 211; see also Kerner Commission
The Rise of the Creative Class (Florida) 253
Romney, George 153
Roof, Dylan 205
Rothstein, Richard 55n165, 115n139, 181n28, 181n43, 182n64, 182n69, 183n79, 183n96, 184n107, 185n133, 186n148, 316n130
Rothwell, Jonathan 101
Rubio, Marco 302

"safety net" 309n41
Sampson, Robert 28, 63, 109n70
San Antonio v. Rodriguez 159–160
San Francisco Bay Area 20–21
Santelli, Rick 167
SAT scores 33, 37, 84–85, 229–230, 281
school desegregation 157–161
segregation 77–78; institutionalizing 140, 142–147; Jim Crow 132–134; measuring 78; presentations of 110n81; racial (see racial segregation); residential 132–134; types of 110n82
segregation tax 88
Sen, Amartya 43n15
sentencing reform 285–286
Servicemen's Readjustment Act of 1944 148; see also GI Bill
Sharkey, Patrick 63, 74
Shaver, Daniel 294
Shelley v. Kraemer 138
single-parent household 38
Small Area Fair Market Rent Program (SAFMR) 268
smart place-based strategies 260–264
snob zoning 156, 270–275

snowplow parenting 35
Snyder, Rick 173
social capital 28, 91
social groups 225, 344
social justice 218, 244n119
social networks 31–34; of Black and Latino Americans 93; and economic mobility 31; institutional 33; insular networks 33; membership 32, 34; peer networks 28; racial networks 91–93
socioeconomic (SES) mobility 17, 81, 84; absolute income mobility 15; absolute mobility 45n32; downward mobility 60–61, 63, 81; relative mobility 45n32
South Boston High School 130
Sowell, Thomas 105n9, 236n7, 236n8
"spatial mismatch" problem 304
sprawl 99–103
Stamped from the Beginning 205
stereotypes/stereotyping 139, 183n92, 205–206, 344
St. Louis massacre 141
"Stop and Frisk" 166
structural agenda 203–235; affirmative action 225–230; Black Lives Matter 208–209; disparate impact 224–225; goal of racial justice 218–221; individual racism model 204–208; Kerner Report revisited 232–234; principles for 221–224; reparations 231–232; systemic vs. structural racism 213–218; Uprisings of the 1960s 209–213
structural racial inequality 77, 170, 174, 178
structural racism 60, 103–104, 213–218, 223–224; defined 1–2; explication of 93; and opportunity 3–5, 7; origins of 129–178; racial wealth gap 85
structural racism inequality: childhood poverty 64–67, 66; concentrated poverty 67–72, 68–69, 70, 71; durable poverty 72–75; educational attainment 83–85; health and environment 97–99; jurisdictional fragmentation 99–103; mass incarceration 93–96; overview 59–60; race and economic mobility 61–64; race vs. class 75–76; racial networks 91–93; racial segregation 76–82; racial wealth gap 85–89, 86; spatial mismatch 89–91; sprawl 99–103

structured inequality 170
Stuck in Place (Sharkey) 63, 74
students of color 71–72, 82, 226–227, 230
subprime loans 167–170
subprime mortgage crisis 167–173
suburbanization 147–150
Sugrue, Thomas 139
Summit of the Americas (2012) 287
Superdome 203
Sustainable Communities Initiative 261
systemic racism 1, 213–218
systems thinking 217

Task Force on Twenty-First Century Policing 292
Taylor, Breonna 294
Texas Ten Percent Plan 227–228
Thomas, Danny 212
Till, Emmitt 204
Title IX 344
To Kill a Mockingbird (Lee) 204, 234
totalitarian regime 224
toxic mortgages 168
Trounstine, Jessica 102, 110n80, 127n325, 128n337
Trump, Donald 37, 261, 277, 285
Tucker, Chris 204
Tulsa massacre 141
Twain, Mark 232

undermatching 283
Underwriting Manual 146
United States (US): Centers for Disease Control and Prevention (CDC) 97, 176; Chamber of Commerce 306; Constitution 206; Department of Treasury 302
University of California system 37, 281
University of Texas (UT) 227–228
Upper Arlington school system 10, 42n4, 130, 158, 176
Uprisings of the 1960s 209–213
upward mobility 61; in America 13–16; based on parental income and wealth 15–16; pathways of opportunity 16
US Supreme Court 138, 155, 166, 279, 293, 295

venture capital 303
Village of Arlington Heights v. Metropolitan Housing Development Corp. 156
Village of Belle Terre v. Boraas 155
Village of Euclid, Ohio v. Ambler Realty Co. 137
Virginia Military Institute 233

Wagner-Steagall Housing Act 151
Walker, Darren 91
Wallace, George 213
The Warmth of Other Suns (Wilkerson) 135
War on Drugs 1, 164–167, 284–291, 343
War on Poverty 64, 213
Warth v. Seldin 156
wealth disparities 23, 220, 341
wealth inequality 13, 22, 25, 88, 303
West, Kanye 203–204
When Work Disappears (Wilson) 162
white flight 5, 130–131, 149–150, 157–161
white supremacy 7n8
Wilkerson, Isabel 135
William Levitt & Sons 141; Levitt, William 149; Levittowns 141, 149
Williams-Bolar, Kelley 59–60, 102, 104
Wilson, Darren 208
Wilson, William Julius 92, 162
Wired 78
woke 6
working-class communities 254
World War I 134
World War II 15, 39, 135, 141, 147–148, 252

Young, Iris Marion 214, 241n92

zoning: fiscal 154; inclusionary 272, 317n147, 318n151; racial 136–137, 154; reform 271–272; regulations 136, 138, 270–272; use 136–137, 154, 156, 182n65
zero-sum 25, 102, 245n130